Collecting Historical Autographs

Collecting Historical Autographs

What to Buy, What to Pay, and How to Spot Fakes

RON KEURAJIAN

McFarland & Company, Inc., Publishers

Jefferson, North Carolina

LIBRARY OF CONGRESS CATALOGUING-IN-PUBLICATION DATA

Names: Keurajian, Ron, 1967– author.
Title: Collecting historical autographs : what to buy, what to pay,
and how to spot fakes / Ron Keurajian.
Description: Jefferson, North Carolina : McFarland & Company, Inc.,
Publishers, 2017 | Includes bibliographical references and index.
Identifiers: LCCN 2016040920 | ISBN 9781476664156
(softcover : alk. paper) ∞
Subjects: LCSH: Autographs—Collectors and collecting. |
Autographs—Collectors and collecting—United States. |
Autographs—United States.
Classification: LCC Z41 .K48 2017 | DDC 929.8/8075—dc23
LC record available at https://lccn.loc.gov/2016040920

BRITISH LIBRARY CATALOGUING DATA ARE AVAILABLE

ISBN (print) 978-1-4766-6415-6
ISBN (ebook) 978-1-4766-2428-0

Front cover: Photograph of Abraham Lincoln (highlighted) at the site
of the Gettysburg Address on November 19, 1863 (Library of Congress);
Lincoln signature, dated 1861 (courtesy of Nate D. Sanders Auctions)

Printed in the United States of America

McFarland & Company, Inc., Publishers
Box 611, Jefferson, North Carolina 28640
www.mcfarlandpub.com

Glossary

The autograph industry has its own lingo. When you peruse auction listings, dealer catalogs and reference guides (such as this one) you will run across many acronyms that you may be unfamiliar with. Here are some of the more commonly used ones; learning these will make for easier reading. Note that the plural of those referenced below are formed with a lowercase "s" such that ALsS denotes Autograph Letters Signed.

ALS: Autograph Letter Signed.

AMQS: Autograph Musical Quotation Signed; this is where a composer pens a bar or two of music then signs it.

AMS: Autograph Manuscript Signed; this is a writing, either handwritten or typed, of a work or study. A manuscript can range from one page to hundreds of pages. Manuscripts are typically not created for the autograph market, hence most are not signed; those not signed are notated as AM.

ANS: Autographed Note Signed; this is a short writing that is penned and signed by the celebrity.

BCS: Business Card Signed.

BES: Bank Endorsement Signed; this is a signature that appears on the back of a bank check.

DS: Document Signed; this refers to documents such as contracts, promissory notes, stock certificates, warehouse receipts that are signed by the celebrity.

ES: Endorsement Signed; these are short writings usually found on the back of government documents, commonly used prior to the 20th century.

LS: Letter Signed.

POA: Power of Attorney; this is where a person will authorize another to execute documents (such as a contract) on his or her behalf.

SSB: Single Signed Baseball.

TLS: Typed Letter Signed.

Preface

I have always been a collector. As a young kid I collected what most young boys collect: fossils. What could be better than digging through an old rock pile and finding a 350,000,000-year-old sea critter forever entombed in limestone? The thought of finding a brachiopod trapped in a rock may not be appealing today, but to a six-year-old it was just about the greatest of finds. And they were free! I also dabbled in old beer cans. I had, at one time, a rather impressive collection of vintage conetop cans. Every time I would go up north with my neighbors to their cottage in Hale, Michigan, I would rummage through dumps. There were piles of rusty gold set deep in the woods of the north country. On one such excursion I extracted three Phoenix Lager cans from a rather steep cliffside dump and damn near killed myself in the process. Even though they were covered in a fair amount of rust they still retained good value.

I think we are either born as collectors or not. It is hard to explain to a non-collector why I cherish a signature of John Adams or Elmer Flick or Jackie Gleason. Elmer Flick? What's an Elmer Flick? I gave up long ago trying to explain the collecting gene to those who don't have it. We who collect are much more interesting people than those who don't. If nothing else, we collectors are anything but boring! "My hobby is jogging." Good Lord!

Collecting autographs puts me in touch with times past. I reflect on memories and life in general. I feel a close connection with history and times I can never return to. It seems a bit selfish, but that is the allure of autographs, at least to me. A signature of Lou Gehrig stirs warm memories of baseball and Little League. An autograph of Ronald Reagan takes me back to my days in high school and the Go-Go 1980s when the United States was roaring along. Sentimental? Yes. Silly? Perhaps. But that's the basis of collecting, like it or not.

Some hobbies are more popular than others. Coins, stamps, trading cards, movie posters are very popular. I have a cousin who collects shipwrecked artifacts. I have a friend who collects antique barbershop equipment; granted, that's fairly weird. Not only do you collect an object, but also the memory that comes with it.

I have been writing articles about autographs and forgeries for years. I have published many signature studies for the *Sports Collectors Digest* and *Autograph* magazine, too numerous to recall the exact number. In the winter of 2012, I published my first book, titled *Baseball Hall of Fame Autographs: A Reference Guide*. Also published by McFarland, it won the 2013 SABR book award for baseball research.

I enjoy research as much as I do collecting, and it's a whole lot cheaper. There is something very addictive about digging through an old archive or a dungeon full of papers. Unearthing something that has never been seen before is exciting. Like a mole, I spend tons of time digging through old writings and I love it! It's a passion, and a passion is something you never tire of.

I love hearing stories from collectors who find a previously unknown treasure trove of autographs. Whether it's one piece or an entire collection of writings, I find it all so fascinating.

I fancy myself rather an expert of the handwriting of the Georgia Peach, Ty Cobb. I have an extensive reference library of Cobb material. As you read this book you will see many examples, both real and fake, of his signature.

Speaking of Cobb, I am generally not one who goes around confronting auction houses and authenticators about all the forgeries that are associated with them, and believe me, there are many. On occasion, I will speak up when it comes to a significant find that attempts, in some way, to alter history. A few years back a diary, dated 1946, purportedly written by Cobb, was prominently displayed at the National Baseball Hall of Fame in Cooperstown. There were detailed entries of Cobb's golfing exploits with such legends as Babe Ruth and Joe DiMaggio. It portrayed Cobb as a crude and petty individual with substandard writing skills. The diary had originated from the now controversial Barry Halper collection. The diary was held out as a historic baseball relic penned by the greatest player in the history of the game.

But in fact, the diary was a forgery and I pronounced it as such. The FBI got involved and my suspicions were confirmed.

This book covers some of the more popular genres within the hobby. It is by no means exhaustive. Signatures of presidents, scientists, composers, and the like are to be found herein. The book could easily have included many other fields from hockey to opera to the signers of the Declaration of Independence. I have tried to provide detailed studies of historical signatures. Well known forgeries and frauds are also examined. All studies, with an exception or two, include illustrations of signatures. Many of the more historically significant names, such as Washington, Beethoven, and Lord Nelson, will have multiple illustrations. Found herein will be detailed discussions of forging techniques and various mediums to collect (bank checks, letters, photographs, etc.). Evolution of inks and papers is also examined and how learning what was used and when can help you to avoid buying a forgery.

Through the decades, many fine reference guides on the subject of autographs have been published, and they are worth adding to your reference library. Hopefully this book will earn a hallowed spot on the bookshelf.

The intent of this book is to advance the autograph hobby and nothing more. Hopefully, this work will be the catalyst that brings ever more collectors into this great endeavor we know as autograph collecting.

Introduction

I used to keep an old beat-up American League baseball in my bedroom. It was covered in decades of grime and dirt. It was rather mangled. It had a deep rusty brown hue and looked like it had been through the battlefields of World War II. It had, to say the least, seen better days. I kept it on my bookshelf in a plastic holder to protect it from the elements. As ugly as the ball was, to me it was nothing short of a gem. Every now and then I would bring it down from its hallowed resting place and show it to an uncle, a friend, or just the plain curious. The initial reaction was one of bewilderment. Many would smile at this tattered relic of the National Pastime. Some were reluctant to touch it for fear of bacterial infection. It was a rather comical sight to behold. But a curious thing happened once they realized just what they held in their hands. Once they realized who had placed his John Hancock upon that hide-covered sphere, things quickly changed. Their look of sarcasm was replaced with an expression of total awe as if the Holy Grail itself were in their grasp. The eyes widened, the jaw dropped, and the hands trembled. Some placed it gently on the table, not wanting to drop it. That ball stirred great emotions in those who touched it. The signature emblazoned across that old and scarred relic belonged to the greatest baseball player in history. It was signed by the Georgia Peach, the legendary Ty Cobb.

Cobb played way back in the dark and mysterious deadball era of baseball, an era far removed in time from today's fan. The men who played back then are almost mythical figures.

Cobb played his last game in 1928. Most people alive today weren't even born when he hung up the spikes. People I showed my treasured relic were holding a baseball that was signed, that was actually touched, by the immortal Cobb. That is a powerful connection of the human condition. It really does send tingles up your spine. That Cobb-signed baseball takes you back to a time in history that we look upon with great wonderment. It's that powerful flood of emotions that is the key to autographs and why they are so treasured by so many. Abraham Lincoln actually held *that* bank check. Napoleon touched *that* letter. The great Mozart placed pen to *that* very paper and drafted a timeless score of music.

Autographs, like many collectables, stir warm memories of times since past. Christmas ornaments remind us when we were five years old waiting for Santa. That can of White House coffee takes many people back to their childhood and the days of the Great Depression. That rusty 1950s Stroh's beer can stirs memories of many a lazy summer's day at the cottage in Northern Michigan. Collectables remind us of a gentler and simpler time in our lives.

I have a baseball signed by the 1978 Detroit Tigers. It was a lackluster team managed by the great Ralph Houk. They really weren't a contending club, but they were still *my* Tigers. That ball reminds me of a summer long since passed. I was ten years old then. I would sit down in front of the TV and watch that Tigers team. With a cold glass of Kool-Aid and a shoebox full of baseball and *Lost in Space* cards, I watched those games for hours on end, day after day. What grand memories they are. Autographs simply take you to another place and time and that is why they are so cherished.

Collecting venerated writings is a time-honored tradition. It has been going on for hundreds, if not thousands, of years, although ancient collectors would not be recognized by today's hobbyist. Many letters and manuscripts were cherished by the learned class. Libraries, even back in the early Middle Ages, were hoarding precious writings. Some of the biggest collectors back then were the many churches of Europe. The churches in Armenia, Greece, Russia, Romania, Rome, and the like all maintained collections of ancient writings of Christian thought. They were treasured as priceless artifacts and many still exist to this very day, some having been stored for well over 1,000 years.

Autograph collecting, as we know it, is a very old and established field of collecting. It has been, and will forever be, the pursuit of the learned man. Certain genres of autographs have been targeted more than others. Royalty is a fine example. Signatures of Oliver Cromwell and Louis XIV of France have been cherished for centuries. Signatures of composers, religious leaders, and authors are also good examples. It is said that Beethoven received numerous requests from collectors who wished a page or two of musical notes penned by the master himself. Other fields caught on only recently, relatively speaking, some through technological progress. Aviation is a fine example. Aviation didn't come into existence until 1903 when the Wright Brothers lofted a plane over the fields of Kitty Hawk. Collecting flyers' autographs couldn't exist until the field was created. Sure, there was a rare exception here and there, like Ferdinand von Zeppelin and Samuel Langley, but for the most part collecting aviation autographs really didn't occur until the 1920s. Other fields existed but at the time they weren't recognized as an area to collect. Take, for example, botany. Back in the 1800s who would think of asking a botanist for his autograph? Really, is a

person who splices seeds someone you would ask for an autograph? Back then? No. But now? Yes!

Autograph collecting gained wide popularity in the 1920s, when many new fields sparked the collector's interest. Sports is a fine example. Baseball, golf, and boxing became the "in" thing to collect. In the 1800s nobody asked Adrian "Cap" Anson or Charles "Kid" McCoy to sign an autograph, but a couple of decades later collectors' habits changed. The above-mentioned aviators and vaudeville also generated much interest at that time. By this time most of the noted figures of the Civil War had passed on. This correlated into increased popularity. Collectors started to hoard signatures of Stonewall Jackson, Robert E. Lee, William Sherman, Jefferson Davis, and the like. The dime-novel glamorized the Old West. Those stories made legends out of lawman and outlaw alike. Judge Roy Bean, John Wesley Hardin, and Al Jennings became popular among collectors and remain that way to this day.

Even in the early days of collecting, forward-thinking collectors understood the value (historically and monetarily) of content manuscripts and letters. Collectors would spend some serious money on letters with powerful text. These are the most sought-after items in the field of autographs.

In the 1920s and through the Great Depression the focus (at least for the collector with deep pockets) was on the long-deceased names such as Ben Franklin and Isaac Newton. William Howard Taft and Orville Wright were not to be found in these early collections. Today, their autographs are much in demand, but several generations ago they were of little value and even looked down upon as crude scrawls. No self-respecting collector would place a signature of President Taft next to John Hancock and Henry Laurens. This gap was filled by that lovable creature we call the "autograph hound." There are essentially two types of collectors. First are the sophisticated collectors with cash. They purchase rare and valuable signatures and letters with historical content. They bypass the more pedestrian material in favor of the true rarities. They rarely engage in the nuts and bolts of collecting. On the other side of the coin, there are the autograph hounds, those who collect signatures more for the pure fun of it. They request signatures through the mail. They hang out in hotel lobbies, backstage, and at the ballparks. They obtain signatures that the advanced collector would not give a second thought to.

Though the autograph hound can be annoying, many of today's collectors owe a lot to them. These were the guys who asked Orville Wright and Amelia Earhart to sign an autograph album. These are the enthusiasts who would have Robert "Fats" Fothergill, Bucky Harris, and Harry Heilmann sign a baseball at the Statler Hotel in downtown Detroit. Many vintage signatures exist in good number thanks to early autograph hounds.

October 28, 1929, was the day the stock market crashed and plunged America into the Great Depression. Many lost everything. It was a decade of despair, unemployment, and hardship. Like anything else, the autograph hobby was hammered, at least when it came to the high-end material. Collectors were still collecting autographs, but the focus was on the living celebrities. Let's face it, it was much easier to send a letter to Charles Lindbergh requesting an autograph for the price of postage as opposed to shelling out $400 for a George Washington letter. Back in the depression that was some serious money, close to $8,000 of today's dollars.

The 1930s saw more and more collectors requesting signatures through the mail. Photographs, as a medium, gained in popularity with the collector set. In the 1940s the government postcard became very popular. What made them especially nice is that they contained a postmark from the signer's home town. The government postcard was widely used by collectors of sports autographs.

World War II put a damper on the hobby. But when the war ended, the world's economic en-

gine ignited. It led to the fabulous 1950s. People were working and savings accounts were flush. The 1950s saw a rebirth of autographs. The hobby became much more organized and once-worthless signatures started to build value. There were more collectors and dealers. In the 1950s, collectors started to get specific items signed to enhance their collections: first-day covers, gum cards, postal relics, and the like. Values of the longer-deceased names and content letters also increased greatly. At this time, many of the really rare signatures were absorbed into collections. To this day, many have yet to resurface.

Over the past couple of decades autographs have exploded in popularity. Many collectors have recently entered the hobby. A marked increase in demand has occurred, pushing prices ever higher. Content letters of Lincoln, Washington, John Adams, and Thomas Jefferson now sell for more than $100,000. Certain historically significant writings of these gentlemen have crossed the $1,000,000 benchmark. I am often asked which is the most popular field of autographs. The answer is easy: baseball. While signatures of presidents, entertainers, rock & roll, and military are popular, they are nothing when compared to baseball autographs. A search of eBay in April 2015 reported over 540,000 baseball autographs for sale. The demand is tremendous. In 1985, Babe Ruth's signature sold for $50; today that same signature is valued at $2,500. A museum-grade baseball signed by Ruth could be purchased for $200 back in the mid–1980s. Today, it would sell for $40,000 to $60,000. Baseball has become the 90-ton brontosaur within the hobby.

When I started collecting autographs back in the late 1970s, the hobby was far different from what it is today. It was a relaxing and easy-going pursuit. No real money, just a lot of fun. Those days are long gone and they will never return. Today, the hobby has become an industry. Values are great. Auctions push prices ever higher. There is lot of money changing hands, and that invites fraud. I have witnessed a transformation of this hobby like no other and it is not pretty. Forgeries are everywhere. Many auction companies now engage in shill bidding. Authentication companies, with numb-minded experts, certify countless forgeries as genuine. Computer-generated signatures are sold as the real thing to unsuspecting collectors. There is a lot more crime in this industry than there used to be. This ain't your father's autograph hobby anymore.

The following book is based on my thirty-five years of actively collecting and studying sig-natures. The information contained herein is my opinion, so take it for what it's worth. Many auctioneers and authenticators tend to disagree with my conclusions. I have never been very popular in this hobby and never will be—don't care. You read, you decide.

With all the pitfalls in today's hobby it is imperative that you, the collector, build a base of knowledge that will allow you to navigate the treacherous waters of autograph collecting. Hopefully this book will assist you in that endeavor.

Building a Collection

In an episode of *Bewitched*, Darrin Stephens, played by Dick York, said: "You don't pick a hobby, it sort of picks you." Some people collect stamps, other collectors focus on coins, or comic books, or oil paintings, and so on. Whatever the reason, a person becomes fascinated by a particular item and desires to possess it. He or she then becomes a collector. It is a powerful bond and can lead to a lifelong quest (or obsession) to build a collection. Like the archaeologist who spends a lifetime searching for the lost city of Atlantis, the person we know of as the autograph collector will spend thousands of hours in the endeavor to secure that coveted scrawl of ink. After thirty-some years, I am still looking for that elusive "Twilight Ed" Killian autograph.

Some collectors will spend handsome sums for desirable autographs. ALsS of Presidents Lincoln, Washington, Adams, and Jefferson regularly sell for over $25,000. Signed baseballs of Cobb, Ruth, and Gehrig have been known to sell for over $50,000. One pristine Ruth ball sold for over $300,000, and I question the authenticity of the signature. Some signatures are out of reach of most collectors' budgets. Let's face it: 99 percent of us collectors will not add a signature of Mary, Queen of Scots or George Handel to our collections. Edgar Allan Poe? Probably not him either. Frank Selee? Nope.

If you don't have deep pockets, a fine collection of autographs can be assembled on a modest budget. Some signatures are surprisingly affordable. Giants in world history such as Orville Wright, Douglas MacArthur, Washington Irving, Connie Mack, and most presidents of the United States sell for under $300. Signatures of British prime ministers have fallen out of favor and can be purchased for only a few dollars. George Canning's signature for only $25, that's a bargain. In 2013, I purchased an Orville Wright signature removed from a bank check for $240. Not bad for one of the founders of flight. Other signatures are even more affordable. Most signatures of Supreme Court justices can be purchased for under $100.

Other collectors are minimalists when it comes to spending. These collectors obtain signatures in person or through the mail. A fabulous collection can be assembled simply by dropping a request in the mail and waiting a week or two. Back in 1959 one collector I know mailed Ty Cobb four Hall of Fame plaque postcards to sign, to which Cobb obliged. Total cost was about 40 cents. Today, those cards have a collective value of about $10,000. Obtaining signatures through the mail is a great way to build a collection with great depth and diversity. A mere postage stamp can send your autograph request to any part of the globe. I have received signatures from all parts of the world. Mother Teresa sent me a nice letter. From Prime Minister Margaret Thatcher I received a wonderful signed 8 × 10 photograph. General Mikhail Kalashnikov gave me a couple of signed business cards.

Autographs come in all different shapes and sizes. There are endless possibilities. Collections can be assembled with a wide variety of material. There are so many fields. Within fields there are various sub-fields. Golf, presidents, science, movies, hockey, baseball, soccer, rock, opera, composers, criminals, and the lists go on and on. Some collectors focus on western film stars like John Wayne and Ward Bond. Others may just collect Chicago Bears autographs. Some collectors concentrate on just one historical figure such as Abraham Lincoln or Benjamin Franklin. I know of a collector who has 30 items signed by Ty Cobb. Then there are the mediums to collect. Some collectors focus on a single medium. Many collect just signed bank checks. Others will focus on letters, photographs, exhibits cards, 1st edition books, golf balls, or hockey pucks. The possibilities are endless.

My favorite field of autographs is vintage baseball. My rule is the older the better. Most people don't know who William "Germany" Schaefer is and even fewer would want to spend money on his autograph. To me, a Schaefer signature would be a truly amazing find! I also like material signed by astronomers who discovered a planet. Clyde Tombaugh, who discovered Pluto, is one of my favorite autographs. I have a nice Tombaugh ALS in my collection discussing the existence of the planet Vulcan, and no, not the one from *Star Trek*.

As a collector, when first starting out, take it slow and easy. Collect what you like. Don't throw around big money, as there are a lot of forgeries out there. Many forgeries are wrongly certified as genuine by major authentication companies, so proceed with caution. Start out with the less expensive material. For example, if you wish to collect signatures of composers you may want to start out with Aaron Copland, Charles Wakefield Cadman, and Rudolf Friml. These signatures are available for under $200. Study the market and the target signature, and then make your purchase. Skilled forgers typically do not concentrate on signatures of modest value. The rate of return is not sufficient to warrant the effort. On the other side of the coin are Beethoven, Mozart, Bach, and Chopin.

These are signatures of great value. Signatures of these men are valued between $25,000 and $50,000, and as for Bach's signature, more than $100,000. Skilled forgers concentrate on the valuable signatures.

There are many mediums and combinations to collect, far too many to discuss herein, but the following are some of the more popular mediums.

Letters

In general, the most desired medium is the content letter. Letters are generally divided into three categories. The first is the Autograph Letter Signed (ALS). This is a letter where the entire body of which is written then signed by the celebrity. Shorter writings are denoted as Autograph Notes Signed (ANS). In the text I may refer to an ALS as a handwritten letter; there is no difference. ALsS are the most desired of all letters. Then there is the Typed Letter Signed (TLS). This is a letter that is accomplished by a typewriter then signed by hand. The Letter Signed (LS) is a letter signed by the celebrity but the body is written by another. Baseball Hall of Fame member Cy Young was known to send out many LsS due to infirmity of hand in old age.

Letters come in all shapes and sizes. As a collector you will need to become versed in the lingo of the hobby. Dealers will often describe the size of a letter or other paper medium using book notations. The most common sizes are: Folio, sizes vary but generally range from 16" × 20" up to 2' × 3'. Quarto, sometimes referred to as 4to, is a rather large sheet measuring between 10" × 12" up to 16". Octavo, also referred to as 8vo, is sized at 5" × 7" up to 8" × 10". Duodecimo, or 12mo, is a sheet sized at approximately 4" × 6". Sexagesimo-quarto, or 64mo, is the smallest at 1.75" × 2.25". This system may seem a bit arcane but it is still widely used.

Of course, the most important aspect of any

letter is the content. The better the content, the more valuable the letter. Content letters are treasured not only by collectors but also researchers and historians. In *Autographs: A Collector's Guide* (Crown Publishers, 1973), author Jerry Patterson writes: "Content is of very great importance in pricing manuscripts and letters." Letters with routine content, such as accepting a dinner invitation or wishing someone a merry Christmas, are of limited value. In way of example, an Abraham Lincoln ALS, with routine content, is valued at $15,000 to $20,000. A letter with military or manumission content would be highly prized and valued around $100,000. A Lincoln letter discussing the Gettysburg Address or the Emancipation Proclamation would be in great demand and easily valued over

$1,000,000, perhaps $5,000,000. Illustrated is a letter by German Admiral Otto Kretschmer. The letter has good content regarding Adolf Hitler and racial doctrine. It therefore commands a premium.

Content letters are out of the reach of most collectors' budgets. If you wish to obtain a letter signed by Theodore Roosevelt you will most likely purchase a letter with routine content. A Roosevelt letter with good content will set you back at least $20,000. Most collectors simply don't have that type of discretionary income. Even content letters of modern figures are expensive. As an example, President Gerald Ford's signature is quite common. His autograph can be purchased for $25. There are countless Ford letters in the market. Most letters date from his time as a congressman or post-presidency. An ALS is valued at $500. A letter from Ford discussing the Kennedy assassination or the pardon of President Nixon is worth many times more. I have a Ford ALS in my collection in which the president writes of his tenure on the Warren Commission. I turned down $5,000 for it. The Kennedy assassination content correlates into great value.

If you cannot afford these types of letters you can still build a significant collection of writings simply by asking for them. Being an autograph collector gives you access to celebrities, historical figures, or those who were eyewitnesses to history. All are important to building a sound library of letters and a way of preserving the historical record. I have seen some impressive letters that collec-

ALS of German Admiral Otto Kretschmer with good content.

ALS Kretschmer page 2.

James Fenimore Cooper 1842 ALS with legal content—choice specimen.

tors received directly from celebrities. One of my favorites is a letter from explorer Sir Edmund Hillary in which he discusses the existence of the abominable snowman. Hillary writes: "I spoke with only one Sherpa who saw it and he admitted he was drunk at the time." Letters with good content written by just your plain, everyday person can have significant value. For example, a letter penned by an eyewitness to the Lincoln assassination or the sinking of the *Titanic* will have good value to collectors. The day after the attack on the World Trade Center in September 2001, I wrote a letter to a friend of mine in Germany. I had known a fellow banker who was at Ground Zero and placed my thoughts in the letter. That letter will have value simply because of the strong content.

Legendary showman P.T. Barnum once stated: "There's a sucker born every minute." Barnum was referring to the gullibility of the masses and how he could profit off it. Shortly after President Lincoln was shot at Ford's Theatre he was taken to the Peterson House, where he eventually died. Upon the president's death, Secretary of War Edwin Stanton stood before Lincoln's body and said those now immortal words: "Now he belongs to the ages." George Gipp, the great halfback for Notre Dame, died at the young age of 25 of strep infection. Upon his deathbed he told his coach, the immortal Knute Rockne, to: "Win one for the Gipper," a quote now seared into the fabric of Americana.

These quotes are some of the most memorable ever spoken. They are widely used by writers to this day and have become an important part of history. These quotes have one thing in common: none of them were ever said. They are fanciful fiction penned, after the fact, by writers who made liberal use of poetic license. They sound good and enhance a story, but all are merely twaddle. You will find that many historical "facts" are exaggerated, half-truths, or just plain lies. President John Adams once said that facts are stubborn things. Try as you might, a fact will not budge. As an autograph collector you will have access to key events in history, and if you can persuade a celebrity to reduce his or her thoughts to writing, you have secured a wonderful item.

Back in the early 1990s I began writing World War II aviators. Flying Tigers, Doolittle Raiders, *Enola Gay*, *Memphis Belle*, and the like were my targets. I asked them to write me a letter discussing their thoughts about serving their country during war. The letters I received were amazing with deep and thoughtful insight. *Enola Gay* weapons officer Morris Jeppson sent me a letter about the bombing of Hiroshima and how he armed the atomic bomb nicknamed "Little Boy." I often find that these letters contradict the history books and popular culture. You, as an autograph collector, can preserve historical fact that would otherwise be perverted, over time, by unsavory scriveners.

Some of the finest writings, in terms of display value, are illustrated letters. On rare occasion a collector will be lucky enough to procure one of these gems. Illustrated letters incorporate drawings within the text of the letters. They make for a handsome and whimsical presentation. Authors Beatrix Potter, William Nolan, and William Thackeray were known to pen them and they command some serious money. Artists and illustrators, such as George Cruikshank, created some stunning letters. Illustrated is a letter by ceramics artist Mitchell Grafton. His specialty is teapots and his work is simply amazing. The Grafton letter has superior display value. Illustrated letters are among the most expensive in the field but are well worth the money. The rate of return can be outstanding.

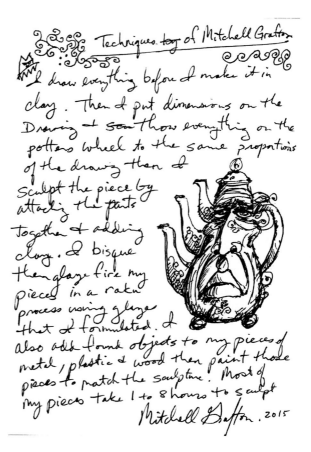

Artist Mitchell Grafton illustrated ALS.

Photographs

Another very popular medium is the photograph. They have excellent display value and look great hanging on the wall. They are many kinds of photographs. Among the earliest were the carte-de-visite (CDV) created by French photographer Andre Disdéri. They were popular in the 1850s and throughout the remainder of the 19th century. The Victorians coveted these cards. Around the same time, cabinet cards became popular. They are similar to the CDV but tend to be larger. In today's language the CDV and the cabinet card are one and the same. I typically refer to both as the cabinet card. Both tend to be on very thick stock. Both are, to this day, commonly counterfeited.

Also popular with collectors is the wire photograph. These became popular in the 1930s. They were used for press reproduction. Wire photographs are on thin stock and contain wonderfully crisp and clear images, necessary for reproduction. They typically have typewritten text along the bottom describing the event. The reverse is stamped by the photograph service (e.g., "Please credit UPI"). Wire photographs are very popular with the collectors of sports autographs.

In general, the more unusual the image, the more demand. A signed 8 × 10 portrait photograph of Harry Truman is valued at $300. However, a signed photograph of President Truman holding up the infamous "Dewey Defeats Truman" *Chicago Daily Tribune* newspaper is valued at $1,500 to $2,000. In the baseball genre, values can be great. The most famous photograph in baseball history is that of Ty Cobb sliding into New York Highlanders 3rd baseman Jimmy Austin. Cobb signed a limited number of these photographs. A nicely signed 8 × 10 photograph of Cobb is valued at $3,500 to $4,000. The

Cobb signed historic image by Charles Conlon.

above-referenced Cobb/Austin photograph signed by Cobb generally sells in the $20,000 range. A substantial premium will be paid for historic images.

There are countless people who take up photography as a hobby. While most of these weekend shutterbugs don't amount to anything, a few of them do. Mathew Brady, Yousuf Karsh, Ansel Adams, and Richard Avedon are just some of the famous photographers. Obtaining signed photographs taken by a famous photographer can greatly enhance value. A signed photograph of Winston Churchill, for example, is valued at $2,500. But an original Karsh photograph signed by Churchill can be worth ten times that amount.

Sports have many well-known photographers. Baseball has a host of famous photographers. Among the most famous are George Brace, George Burke, J.D. McCarthy, and Charles Conlon. Original signed Conlon photographs are quite rare. McCarthy, whom I had known in my younger days, issued thousands upon thousands of picture postcards. Archivists are still cataloguing his images some fifty years later. Signed photographs taken by Alex Morrison are coveted by golf collectors. Frank Certo's photographs of 1950s and 1960s hockey are a hit with hockey fans. Photographs taken by these men command a premium.

In recent years a new type of fraud has hit the market and needs to be discussed. Many times a signed book page will be removed from a book and a photograph will be added over or around the signature. I have seen this done with the above-referenced Harry Truman newspaper photograph. Another common practice is to add Richard Nixon's resignation letter on one of these pages. I have also seen this accomplished with President Bill Clinton, where the photograph of him hugging his mistress Monica Lewinsky is added. These sell for substantially more than just a signature. I consider this to be a fraud. These mock photographs can be identified by a slightly mis-scaled image or a signature that looks a bit out of place.

Bank Checks

This is a highly collected area. Checks are the right size and, in general, a bank check is likely to contain a genuine signature, thus collectors gravitate towards them. Bank checks exist in good quantities. Many presidents, such as Calvin Coolidge, William Howard Taft, Jimmy Carter, and Benjamin Harrison, exist in quantities. Other presidents such as Woodrow Wilson, Ronald Reagan, and Richard Nixon are much scarcer and command a premium. There is a problem with bank checks. The general rule is where there is one there tends to be hundreds, if not thousands, more. This can adversely affect values for years. Orville Wright is a fine example. Wright checks exist in quantities. These were selling for $1,000 in the early 1990s. As time went on it became quite apparent that a large supply existed. The price of Wright checks began to fall. Some twenty years later they can be purchased for a mere $500 and it has been that way for years. Many other expensive signatures have suffered the same fate. Honus Wagner, Douglas Fairbanks, Sr., Jack Haley, Bert Bell, and others have seen a material decrease in value due to a large supply of bank checks. In some cases the decline in value can be extreme. Composer Sigmund Romberg and author Zane Grey are good examples. Both signatures exist in quantities on checks. Romberg checks can be purchased for $50, and as for Grey, I have seen them sell on eBay for a paltry $20. There are so many Haley checks in the market that they sell for $5 to $10!

In other instances, only a check or two will enter the market, then no further examples surface. One check of baseball Hall of Famer Hazen "Ki Ki" Cuyler is known to exist. Cuyler's signature sells for $300. The check, however, being an extreme rarity, is valued at $7,000 to $8,000. Years back I wrote football Hall of Famer Mel Hein. I asked him for a check, which he sent. Some 25 years later I have never seen another specimen. I have many check collectors asking me to sell it. Hein's signature is valued at a mere $10. The highest offer I received on the check is $750, simply because of the unique nature of the piece.

Though checks are an official bank document, there is a caveat. As ironclad as some collectors believe bank checks are, counterfeit checks do exist and in quantities. Checks of George Gershwin, Babe Ruth, Marilyn Monroe, Charles Lindbergh, and the like are common targets. See the chapter on forgeries for further information on bank checks.

lated party, mostly a spouse. Payroll receipts were common in the 19th century and were widely used by sports teams. Payroll receipts are plagued with secretarial signatures. Christy Mathewson and Tony Mullane were known to have their wives sign the receipt for them. I have also run across secretary-signed receipts for boxer John L. Sullivan.

First-Day Covers

Postal covers that are canceled the first day of a stamp's release are popular with collectors. These contain a special first-day commemorative postmark and many have wonderful illustrations which only enhance display value. Many companies issue special covers for stamp collectors. The most popular issuer of these covers is Art-Craft. Another popular postal cover is the victory cover, sometimes referred to as "V" covers. Most of these were issued in 1943 during the height of World War II. V covers are colorful and patriotic-looking. Many collectors get them signed by World War II heroes.

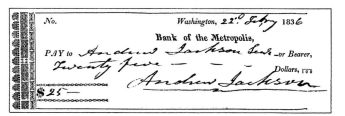

Andrew Jackson, rare double signed check dated one day before the Battle of the Alamo.

Pay receipt, commonly used in the 19th century.

Back in the old days, many businesses used what is known as a payroll receipt. These look similar to bank checks but are not bank issued. They are not negotiable instruments. These receipts evidenced an on-site cash payment. Once the money was handed to the recipient, he signed the receipt as evidence of payment. Unlike checks, which are typically signed by the maker, many times payroll receipts were signed by a re-

Enola Gay crew and Edward Teller signed first day cover.

Crossover Signatures

These are signatures that are collected by two or more genres within the hobby. Many famous figures left their imprint on more than one area of history. Some signatures are so widely collected that values increase at a rapid rate. Ronald Reagan is a good example. He is coveted by collectors of presidential material and well as vintage Hollywood. Being a radio man, he broadcast Chicago Cubs games back in the mid–1930s, thus there is good demand for his autograph in the baseball field. Reagan also played George Gipp in the 1940 film *Knute Rockne, All American*. Because of this, football collectors covet Reagan's autograph. Thus Reagan's signature is in demand in various fields within the hobby. There are many other signatures that fit this category such as Gerald Ford, Jimmy Stewart, Byron White, Eddie Rickenbacker, and Cal Hubbard. Hubbard has the distinction of being a member of the Baseball, Football, and College Football Halls of Fame.

Sports Equipment

Signed equipment is very popular among sports collectors. Golf balls and baseballs (both

Jack Fleck, 1955 U.S. Open champion signed golf ball.

discussed elsewhere) make for fine displays. There are so many different sports to choose from. Hockey pucks and sticks are commonly signed, as are footballs, helmets, soccer balls, bats, basketballs, jerseys, and the list goes on and on. Billiards legend Willie Mosconi signed a limited number of pool balls and sticks. These make for a fine display and command some good money. On occasion, explorer Sir Edmund Hillary signed mountaineering axes. These are rare and sell for over $500. Sports equipment makes for a fine display and can nicely full up a gaming room.

Trade and Exhibit Cards

One of the most popular mediums to collect is signed gum cards. Baseball cards lead the way and are discussed more fully in the baseball chapter. Other sports cards are also popular, such as football, hockey, basketball, and golf. Early Topps issues are highly collected. Pro-Set cards are popular with golf collectors, as they feature many of the greats such as Jack Nicklaus, Arnold Palmer, Payne Stewart, and Hale Irwin. Parkhurst cards are coveted by hockey collectors. Some early edition cards of Gordie Howe, Maurice Richard, Woody Dumart, and Ted Lindsey are quite expensive.

Some signed gum cards are worth their weight

1959 Topps gum card signed by Billy Pierce and Robin Roberts.

in gold. Extreme values are generally limited to early signed baseball cards. A signed tobacco card of Ty Cobb or a 1933 Goudey card of Babe Ruth can sell for $20,000 or more.

Gum cards are not just limited to sports. Many early non–sport cards have been targeted by autograph collectors. *The Beverly Hillbillies, Lost in Space, The Wizard of Oz,* and countless other issues make for fine collectables. Some early aviation cards are highly valued. A 1933 Sport Kings card signed by aviator Jimmy Doolittle is very rare and would likely sell for $500 to $600.

Clayton Moore, the Lone Ranger, signed exhibit card.

1955 Topps All American card signed by Hall of Famer Alex Wojciechowicz.

Another card popular in the autograph world is the exhibit card. These cards are postcard sized and printed on thick stock. They were popular in the 1940s and through the 1950s. They could be purchased out of a vending machine for a penny or two. These cards make for handsome signed display items. These cards were widely used for baseball, football, and boxing. Also many movie stars were featured on these cards. Western figures such as Roy Rogers, the Lone Ranger (Clayton Moore), and Gene Autry were issued on exhibit cards. Today these cards are in high demand.

There are literally tens of thousands of different gum and exhibit cards to choose from. Most signed cards are very affordable at only a couple of dollars each.

Contracts

A contract is a document that evidences an agreement between two or more people, or entities. Many collectors specialize in contracts. Contracts come in all shapes and sizes. Some can be purchased for a few dollars; others are priceless. Sports and entertainment contracts seem to be the most bountiful in the hobby. The most valued are official contracts from the field where a person attained fame. For example, a signed contract of actor Jimmy Cagney with a production studio is in greater demand than say, a contract whereby Cagney agreed to endorse a brand of toothpaste. The former is worth thousands, the latter maybe worth only a couple of hundred dollars. Rock music contracts can sell for significant sums, especially Elvis Presley, Jimi Hendrix, and Jim Morrison. Of course, a contract signed by the Beatles is easily worth over $100,000. I can see a day, in the not so distant future, when Beatles contracts will sell for more than $1,000,000.

Baseball contracts of the early legends of the games are priceless. Ty Cobb, Babe Ruth, and Shoeless Joe Jackson will easily sell for six figures. Jackson's 1919 contract, the year of the World Series fix, would probably be worth at least $1,000,000, if it still exists.

There is a word of caution when collecting contracts. Back in the old days, pre–1930, two or more identical contracts were drafted and signed by the parties involved. Each party retained an original document. Sometimes carbon paper was used. On many occasions, if one party was a business such as a movie studio or a sports team, it would make a duplicate for its files. This third copy would be filled in by hand by a secretary. The secretary would even fill in the signature portion of the document. It should be noted that no attempt is made to replicate the signer's hand. Once completed it is simply filed away in case the original is lost. These are known as "file contracts." Decades later they tend to surface and enter the market. File contracts have little value, but many times are mistaken for the genuine article and sold to an unsuspecting purchaser.

Several years ago a contract surfaced by and between the Dubuque Baseball Club and baseball great Charles "Hoss" Radbourn. The contract was dated 1879. The "signature" on the contract was illustrated many times as a genuine Radbourn signature. Unfortunately, it was merely a file contract writing. The signature was even spelled incorrectly as "Radburn." Because it was published, many mistook this as a genuine Radbourn. The forgers had a field day.

There is one final item to discuss. Famed rock group The Who released the record *Live at Leeds* in 1970. The album contained a fairly high-quality reproduction of The Who's Woodstock contract as an insert. These contracts have been in the market for years and are sold as genuine.

Fantasy Autographs

Perhaps no genre within autographs is more fanatically collected than horror and sci-fi. This genre of collecting has seen a great increase in demand over the past decade and I see no signs of it slowing down. Many former movie and TV stars make a living signing autographs.

Signatures of fantasy/sci-fi authors are also in great demand. Ray Bradbury, J.R.R. Tolkien, Stephen King, and E.B. White are treasured. The area that seems to attract the most interest is Hollywood. Material associated with the 1960s sci-fi TV shows *Lost in Space, The Twilight Zone,* and *Star Trek* have huge followings. The villains generate the greatest demand. Jonathan Harris, who played the nefarious Dr. Zachary Smith on *Lost In Space,* is widely collected. *Star Trek* characters William Shatner (Captain Kirk) and Leonard Nimoy (Spock) are always in demand.

There are seven *Star Wars* movies which provide collectors with countless signatures. Sir Alec Guinness, who played Jedi knight Obi-Wan Kenobi, is highly coveted by collectors. Peter Cushing, who also starred in *Star Wars,* died in 1994 and is a scarce and valued signature. A signed 8 × 10 photograph of Guinness not associated with *Star Wars* is of little value, perhaps $25 to $50. One signed as his character Obi-Wan is worth $500 to $600.

Perhaps the most expensive signatures are the early Hollywood horror actors. Among the most popular are Boris Karloff, Bela Lugosi, Lon Chaney, Sr., and Lon Chaney, Jr. Their signatures are in great demand and if you can find a photograph of any of them in character then the value increases greatly. A signed 8 × 10 photograph of either Karloff or Lugosi is worth around $800 to $1,000. A signed photograph of Karloff as Frankenstein or Lugosi as Count Dracula has far greater value, likely $10,000. A signed photo of Lon Chaney, Sr., as the Phantom of the Opera would be a priceless treasure. There are many other less expensive signatures, such as Vincent Price, that are just as collectable. Glenn Strange, who is best remembered as bartender Sam Noonan on *Gunsmoke*, was Hollywood's other Frankenstein. A signed 8 × 10 photograph of Strange is of marginal value, perhaps $200 to $250. But a signed photograph of Strange as the Frankenstein monster will sell for $3,000 to $5,000. Actress Billie Burke would be a forgotten name in Hollywood history had she not starred in *The Wizard of Oz* as Glinda, the Good Witch of the North. Because of this one movie, her signature is highly prized. Her signature is worth $200 to $250 simply because of the Oz association; otherwise it would be of nominal value. TV shows, movies, comic books, and novels provide collectors with a vast array of material to choose from. Fantasy, sci-fi, and horror will always generate great demand and value.

TV Shows

The 1950s brought forth a boom in television. It was at this time when many memorable television shows hit the airwaves. Who can forget *The Third Man*, *The Rifleman*, *Zorro*, and *Leave It to Beaver*. Since that time there have been hundreds of memorable TV shows. There is a large collector base of this type of material. Collectors try to assemble complete casts. This can lead to high prices for signatures of some of the more obscure cast members or those who died at a relatively young age.

A word of caution: signed items, especially 8 × 10 photographs, of complete casts are rare and seldom surface, if one of the members died before the big autograph boom in the 1990s. Casts of TV shows are commonly forged. For example, Hugh Beaumont, who played Ward Cleaver in *Leave It to Beaver*, died in 1982. He signed very little show-related material. In fact, most Beaumont signatures offered in the market are forgeries. To find an item signed by the entire cast would be an amazing find. I, for one, have never seen one.

The same can be said with John Banner of *Hogan's Heroes*, Guy Williams of *Lost in Space*, and Victor Sen Yung of *Bonanza*. These actors all died before 1990, so finding a signed item with their signature as part of a cast would be a very rare find.

For more information on Hollywood autographs, both vintage and modern, please see *Advanced Autograph Collecting* by Mark Allen Baker (Krause Publications, 2000).

Doodles

Sketches and drawings by celebrities are always in demand. These fall into two categories. The first are professional artists. These are the men and women who make their living off painting or drawing. The artists, illustrators, graphic designers, and comic book artists. There are a surprising number of professional artists who will send a quick sketch for the asking. Theodor Geisel (a.k.a. Dr. Seuss) would, on occasion, draw one of his beloved characters. Charles Schulz, creator of *Peanuts*, would pen Snoopy now and then. Most sketches are quite affordable and can be purchased for under $200. Hank Ketcham is a good example. He created *Dennis the Menace*, and a drawing of one of his characters can generally be purchased for

Ward Kimball, Disney illustrator, signed sketch.

$100. That is a great price for such a prominent artist.

Then there are the painters of great note, such as Salvador Dali, Andrew Wyeth, and Raphael Soyer. Obtaining a drawing from a painter is a much more daunting task. Many don't like to sign autographs, let alone honor a request for a quick drawing. It does, on occasion, happen. Pop artist Roy Lichtenstein was known to sketch something now and then for a lucky collector. In general, sending a request to a painter will be ignored.

Many times an artist's work will enter the market after his death. The estate releases multitudes of material. This happened a few years back with famed illustrator Garth Williams. Williams, who died in 1996, is one of the great illustrators of children's books. *Charlotte's Web*, *Robin Hood*, and *Stuart Little* were just a few of his more famous works. Most of his life's work was auctioned off a few years back. Sketches, proofs, paintings, and the like were all sold. One of his works for the book *Charlotte's Web* sold for $155,000 in 2010 (Heritage Auctions). So much material entered the market that in 2013–2014, Williams sketches were selling for as little as $10 on eBay. Of course, prices have rebounded, but many collectors purchase his work for next to nothing and made a handsome rate of return.

Other drawings were created not for autograph collectors but for industry. Many artists and cartoonists began life as graphics illustrators. They would draw cars, automotive parts, or product labels, do airbrush work, and execute other concept drawings. Years later, usually when a corporation shuts down, this material enters the market. Such was the case of artist Benjamin Kroll, who also worked at Packard Motors as an illustrator. He sketched various concept cars. A few years back many Kroll pieces entered the market and quickly escalated in value. The monetary upside of these pieces can be substantial. They are crossover signature/art pieces and they attract a wide collector's base.

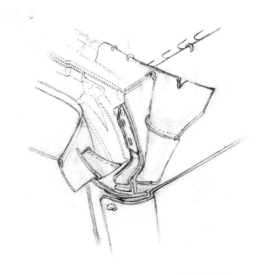

Benjamin Kroll, industrial drawing circa 1955.

The final type of doodle is one penned by celebrities with little artistic skill. They do this to honor autograph requests. These are the athletes, movie stars, and scientists. Their work appears rudimentary at best but it is still highly collectable. Actor Jimmy Stewart would draw "Harvey the Rabbit" from the 1950 movie *Har-*

Garth Williams signed drawing for book illustration.

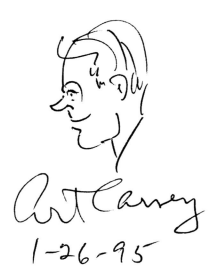

Art Carney signed sketch.

vey. Dr. James Van Allen would sketch the planet Earth with its radiation belts. Sir Edmund Hillary would draw Everest with a stick figure of himself standing on the summit. Many celebrities will honor this type of request and some wonderful material can be added to your collection. Some famous and infamous people have been known to paint, such as actor Tony Curtis and assassin James Earl Ray. Their works now sell for thousands of dollars. These items can have significant value.

Crime

Controversy and violence correlates into strong demand for signed material of criminals. This is a rather controversial genre within the industry but it does have a good following. The passage of time has a way of turning felons and other such miscreants into historical figures. During prohibition, signatures of the gangsters were of little value. No collector would have considered asking Frank Nitti or Harry Fleisher for an autograph. Who would want an autograph from a member of the Purple Gang? Today, however, their signatures are quite valuable and very rare. Some criminals like John Dillinger, John

Wesley Hardin, and Bonnie Parker and Clyde Barrow, have gained legendary status, in a Robin Hood sort of way. Their signatures are extremely rare and valued at over $10,000 each. A few years back an ALS by Fred Barker, of the infamous Barker gang, was auctioned off. It sold for well under $1,000. I decided not to bid on it. That was a big mistake on my part. Other criminals are much more gruesome. Dillinger and Jesse James were local heroes to some. The same cannot be said for the serial killers and mass murderers. Names like John Wayne Gacy, Charles Manson, Edward Gein, and Albert Fish are the stuff of nightmares. Having said that, their signatures are coveted by some. While on death row, Gacy produced many paintings. Today, these paintings are in demand and can sell for $2,000. Personally, I avoid this type of material. It is dubious in nature and, in some cases, simply ghastly. There will always be a market for the crime genre, like it or not.

Return on Investment

Like any other undertaking, one must always be mindful of the money-making aspect of autographs. We invest monies in stocks, bonds, certificates of deposit, and real estate, with the hopes of receiving an acceptable return. It doesn't always work out that way. During the last recession, many retirement nest eggs got clobbered and went down faster than the *Edmund Fitzgerald*. The stability of investments is tied or fettered to macro forces within the marketplace. If the economy is chugging along then the portfolio tends to increase at a pleasant rate, because rising tides lift all boats. If, on the other hand, the economy crashes, well, so does the portfolio.

Discretionary income is the key to a robust autograph market. If times are good, then collectors typically have a lot of coin in their pocket. If times are bad, then the belt-tightening hits. Let's face it: autographs are not a necessity. It is more important to pays bills and put bread on the table than it is to add a Ben Franklin signature to your collection.

In 2009, I was a commercial loan workout officer at Sterling Bank & Trust in Detroit. The bank group I was in handled loans that went into default. That last recession I saw many businesses destroyed and lives ruined. Foreclosure became the norm. Bank failures were happening by the boatload. The once-mighty General Motors filed for bankruptcy. During that time autographs, like other investments, got hit hard. Values plummeted. Very few collectors had money and the ones who did were reluctant to part with it. In some cases a 50 percent decline in value was seen. If you had money and were willing to part with it, the recession was a great time to buy autographs. You could pick up signatures for a song then resell them a few years later for a handsome profit.

What goes up must come down. But what goes down must inevitably go up once again. Like any other investment vehicle, autographs go up and down in value, but in the long run, autographs and manuscripts have proved a truly fine investment.

Let's take a look at a couple of examples. Ty Cobb is a wonderful case study. In the late 1970s Cobb's signature was valued at $10. Yes, you read it correctly, that's not a typo. In the mid–1980s Cobb material reported marginal increases in value. His signature in 1985 was worth $15 to $20. Bank checks could be purchased for $25. In 1990, the baseball market began to heat up and values started to skyrocket. By 1990, Cobb checks were selling for $400 to $500. By the year 2005 the value had increased to $1,000. Early, pre–1930, specimens were selling for close to $2,000. The progression in price continued despite the unending supply of bank checks. Around 2010, during the depths of the economic downturn, Cobb material decreased, but only slightly. Cobb is one of those recession-resistant signatures. Checks, at this time, dropped to the $750 to $800 range. By 2012 checks had rebounded to about $1,000. If you had purchased a Cobb check in 2010 you would have realized a material gain on your investment. The progression of value over a 30-year period is amazing. Cobb's signature went from $15 to $1,000. That is a truly phenomenal rate of return.

With premium Cobb items the increase is even greater. I remember going to a local baseball card show in 1984. A dealer had a stunning Cobb single-signed American League baseball. It was signed in blazing black fountain pen. Cobb had dated the signature in 1946. This ball was a museum-grade specimen. The seller wanted $150 for the ball. Back then that was a lot of money. Potential buyers scoffed at the exorbitant price. Needless to say, the ball did not sell. Today, some thirty years later, that ball has an estimated auction value of $50,000 to $60,000. You do the math. In ten years that ball will easily sell for over $100,000. The same can be said for other Cobb mediums such as 8×10 photographs, baseball cards, and Hall of Fame plaque postcards. In the mid–1980s they were worth just a few dollars. Today, these mediums are worth thousands of dollars.

With other signatures the rate of return has been less pronounced. In 1986 I received a catalog from dealer Robert Batchelder. I remember taking the catalog to school and reading it during one of my breaks. There was one item for sale that really caught my eye. It was a LS by Napoleon I. It was in wonderful condition with Napoleon's typical egotistical signature limited to the letters "Np." I had to have it. The problem was the asking price of $500. That was huge sum of money for a 19-year-old. I purchased it with the blessing of my father, who thought I was nuts.

The annual increase in value of Napoleon material has been positive, but more gradual than that of Cobb material. Today, the Napoleon letter is worth about $2,000. A sound rate of return, to be sure, but not as pronounced as the Cobb example.

Most signatures have seen material increases in value. The more famous the name, the more demand for the signature. George Washington,

John Adams, Paul Revere, and the like will evidence a much better return over the years than signatures of lesser demand. There aren't a lot of collectors lining up for a signature of former Treasury Secretary William McAdoo, Jr.

Some signatures actually have decreased in value. The advent of online auction sites such as eBay has increased the supply of many signatures once thought to be scarce. Take, for example, author Jack London. London is a giant of the literary world and his signature was worth far more 15 years ago than it is today. There is a strong supply of his bank checks in the market. The Internet gave collectors a venue to sell them. The end result was a decline in value. Other signatures have suffered the same fate. Fifteen years ago a signed baseball of Charlie Gehringer was valued at $200. Today, that same ball is worth $100–$125. Gehringer signed countless baseballs and the Internet allowed vast quantities to enter the market. eBay has wreaked havoc with the value of many signatures. This is true for many other collectables as well.

Other signatures have, through the passing of time, simply fallen out of favor with the collector base. Tastes change and demand shifts, leaving some signatures almost worthless. "Times and interests change and he who seeks to speculate in autographs should pick his way warily," writes longtime collector Ray Rawlins in *Four Hundred Years of British Autographs* (Jenkins Publishing, 1970).

In the 1800s, American collectors concentrated on four types of signatures: presidents, Civil War generals, governors, and members of Congress, and that was it. Composers, authors, and scientists were less collected. Nobody bothered to write Stephen Foster for his autograph back in the old days. He was America's greatest composer, but back then he was simply overlooked. He died in 1860 and is a very rare signature. A signature of a congressman who died around that same time period exists in greater quantity. A hundred years ago, a signature of a member of Congress was far more coveted than it is today. In fact they are basically worthless, unless it is one of the more famous members like Daniel Webster or Henry Clay. In general, congressional signatures really have no value. The same can be said for most 19th century governors. A signature of Congressman Joe Knollenberg, who was a powerful member of the House from 1992 to 2008, is worth $10. In one hundred years it will still be worth $10, price adjusted. If you wish to assemble a collection of autographs without spending much money, collect members of Congress.

In short, concentrate on signatures of the truly famous. Spend a little extra money and invest in premium signed material. Purchase the ALS and leave the index card be. In the long run, this should correlate into the best rate of return. Remember, it takes money to make money.

For more information on values and pricing trends, I recommend *The Sanders Autograph Price Guide*, 7th edition, authored by Dr. Richard Saffro (Autograph Media, Inc.).

There are many other mediums to collect, some more fully discussed in other chapters. The combinations are endless. The genres are endless. Books, photographs, government postcards, White House cards, free franks, and the list goes on and on. The diversity of material will lead to endless years of collecting and enjoyment and, perhaps, a lot of cash.

Forgeries

There seems to be a fascination with certain types of crime. Forgery is one such crime. There is a romantic allure with the art of forgery that captivates. Forging an antique manuscript for profit or to alter historical fact is the stuff of movies. You can't say that about carjacking. A skilled forger is a rather sophisticated criminal. Mental defectives need not apply. You need a fair amount of brains to be a successful forger. Not only is the physical skill a must, but so is the understanding of paper, inks, and chemicals. A successful forger must be a student of history. He has to detach himself from the present to understand the past. He must write like Lincoln writes. He must think like Mozart thinks and crawl into the head of Benjamin Franklin. His work must reflect the time which the forgery targets. In *Great Forgers and Famous Fakes* (Crown Publishers, 1980), author Charles Hamilton writes: "The successful faker must disjoint himself from his own age and become part of another time…. He must think the thoughts of another era." A skilled forger can wreak havoc in the world of autographs. His work can fool many and twist historical fact.

A few years ago I was at one the premier museums in the United States. A long-established collection, it had some of the most prized artifacts of American history. Being a certified history nut, I spent hours looking at the rare and valuable relics. All eras of American history were well represented in the collection, from the Revolution to the Civil War to the Kennedy assassination. I took a break for lunch and a cup of joe, then returned to perusing the collection.

Being an autograph collector, I paid particular interest to any writings that were on display. Among the items were a couple of handwritten letters by George Washington and a stunning Benedict Arnold ALS. I turned the corner and reached the Civil War collection.

I find this a particularly fascinating era in history. My neighbor Bill Sinclair knew many Civil War vets from the time of his youth. Back in 1977, Mr. Sinclair was 85 years old or so. I was nine back then. He would always tell me great stories about times since past. Some of his tales were believable and some, well, were not. He could turn a ball of yarn like the greatest of orators and that includes Barnum. He was my "Gus the Fireman." He would tell me stories of the War Between the States. He got his information directly from men who fought on the battlefields of Gettysburg and Shiloh. Though the Civil War ended more than 100 years before I was born, I still had a connection through accounts as told by Mr. Sinclair.

Back to the story. The Civil War display had many rare items; among them were three signatures of President Lincoln. I was drawn to the Lincoln autographs. As I examined the one ALS and two DsS, I was mortified at what I saw. The ALS was a forgery, and a rather ineptly constructed one at that. One of documents also looked fake. I contacted the museum management about the two apocryphal writings. My first two communications were ignored. Eventually, the ALS was removed from display and one of the DsS was relabeled a facsimile. As a collector, you quickly realize just how prevalent forgeries are and just how many experts are really nothing of the sort.

* * *

One who does great things in life will eventually be *discovered* by time. One who does deceitful things in life will eventually by *uncovered* by time. Remember this well, as the autograph hobby is infested with fraud, forgery, and crime. Of all popular collectables, autographs are the easiest to fake. It is this way because no machinery or great technical skill is needed. If you're literate, can hold a pen in your hand, and secure a piece of paper you are in business. Other collectables are much harder to fake. Take, for example, the beer can. Counterfeiting a rare can requires an understanding of metal working, paints, graphics, and a rolling machine to create a convincing fake. Not so with the autograph. Copy a signature of John Kennedy on an old sheet of paper and some gullible collector will likely buy it, and for good money. Little time, no machine, no great technical skill is needed.

As a collector, you will need to accumulate a good deal of knowledge about autographs and the particular nuances of signatures you wish to add to your collection. This is key. If you rely on the expertise of others you will likely get stuck with forged material. No matter what you collect, you will get the following advice: "Buy from a reputable dealer." This is great advice, but…

Autographs are a complex collectable. It takes many years to become well versed in the science of the written word. Just because a dealer is honest and has been in business a long time does not necessarily mean he or she is a competent seller. Far too many times I have found a forgery offered by an established dealer. These are honest people and they intentionally try to deceive no one. They, however, do not possess the requisite knowledge of handwriting analysis, and this allows forgeries to slip by. It's the "white heart, empty head syndrome." The best line of defense is your brain. Knowledge you gain through experience will prove to be your strongest foundation. Study handwriting of the target signer. Learn the idiosyncrasies of the autograph and the way it is formed. Study pen pressure, angles, and strokes. This may seem a daunting task at first but the more you study the easier it becomes. It is like anything else: you gain through exposure to that which you study. Take, for example, Ty Cobb's autograph. I am well versed in his handwriting from all periods of his life, deadball era to deathbed and all points in between. I have seen thousands of signatures, many genuine, many fake. Throughout the years I have owned many Cobb signatures. I still have a couple of choice specimens tucked away in the safety deposit box. When you are exposed to so many signatures you get a feel, or more properly, a deep understanding of Cobb's hand. The knowledge you gain and store in your head allows you to become an expert in a particular signature. It really becomes second nature. After years of exposure you can determine whether a signature is genuine or not in a matter of seconds. It either "clicks" in your head or it does not. I do not need more than a second or two to determine if a Cobb signature is genuine or not.

I cannot say that about William Hogarth's signature because I don't study his hand. I could learn if I so chose. Until I am exposed to Hogarth's handwriting and become familiar with it, I will not purchase his signature.

To many who are new to the hobby this is an intimidating proposition. I hear that a lot. Countless styles of handwriting are accomplished in different time periods of the signer's life. Thousands of collectable signatures, the mediums, the inks, the effects of illness, and on and on. It's true this is an overwhelming thought. Your brain overloads. There are many well-executed forgeries in the market and they fool all but the most trained eye. God knows the authentication companies, with their slab-headed experts, have wrongly certified *hundreds of thousands* of forgeries as genuine.

No matter how good a forgery is, there is some minute defect that will tell a true expert it is a fake signature. Cobb, and only Cobb, can sign a Cobb autograph. No one else in the world can do that. A forger can execute a nice Cobb forgery, but he will not be able to construct it with 100 percent accuracy. The pen pressure will be slightly off, the strokes will not look quite right, a slight hesitation in ink flow will be noted. They may be subtle defects, but defects nevertheless. A signature is as unique as a fingerprint. Just as there are no two fingerprints alike, there are no two writing patterns that are alike. Only you can sign your name and no one else in the world can so do. A forger can try to copy your hand and may come very close, but not close enough.

How can you determine if a signature is genuine or a well-executed forgery? If a skilled forger can produce something that is very close to the target signature, how can it be detected? Good question. You may say to yourself: "I cannot do that." But you, in fact, can. There is one signature that you will always be able to tell if it is real or not. No matter how well-executed a forgery may be, it will not fool you. And this signature is, of course, your own. Your signature has been with you your entire life. You have signed it many thousands of times. It is so second nature to you that you would be able to spot a well-executed forgery in a split second because you have *studied* it for years. So if you can study your own signature, then you can study *any* signature. Exposure, experience, and knowledge are the most important additions to your autograph collection.

For years I have been fascinated with wine sommeliers. You can place ten glasses of wine in front of them. With a mere taste they are able to determine the maker and the vintage. How can they do that? How can they determine the year by a simple sip? The answer: through exposure. Autographs are no different. Knowledge is king.

I have read many books on autographs and interacted with many collectors, dealers, and experts in the field of autographs. Most experts in this field are full of hot air and their hallowed

opinions are tantamount to guesswork. They usually end up as autograph authenticators.

Years ago I was at a baseball card show and watched, in disbelief, a discussion unfold between two dealers. They were in disagreement as to the most accurate method of autograph authentication. One dealer was lecturing the other. He stated that a signature needs to be examined on a letter-by-letter basis. "The letter 'T' is connected to the 'y.' The letter 'T' is always crossed at the top and the 'r' loops under and bisects the letter 's,'" and so on. Others will advise you to look at precise angles and slants. "The letter 'H' will be on a 50 degree angle and spaced precisely five mils from the next letter." Really?

Be warned, this is not the proper way to examine a signature. This analysis works if something is machine made. Signatures are produced in a less precise way. The human hand is not robotic. No one can produce two signatures that look alike. You can sign your signature ten million times if you wish. No two will match. They will all exhibit noticeable differences. All of your signatures are the same, yet different. Line up 100,000 pumpkins: they're all the same type of squash, but since they come in different sizes, colors, and ribbings, they are all different. No two are alike. Letter-by-letter analysis is dangerous and it should be avoided in total. The key is to understand the handwriting of the target signature as a whole, not bits and pieces of it. A forger may be able to replicate a letter or two of the target signature with a great deal of accuracy. One using the letter-by-letter method may be lulled into a false sense of security because a letter or two in the forgery displays itself as genuine.

You may have heard the following: "The only way to know if a signature is 100 percent genuine is to witness it being signed." This statement is utter nonsense and made by those who don't understand the science of handwriting. They should probably find another, more simplistic, hobby. The genuineness of a signature can be determined by examination alone, pure and simple. I don't need to witness President Bush signing an autograph to conclude whether the signature is genuine or a forgery. Examination of handwriting is a science, not an art form. There is no subjectivity in examination of a signature. Those who can't determine the genuineness of a signature do not possess the requisite knowledge and must study the target signature until they become versed at the hand at bar.

Forgeries fall into five categories: poorly executed, traced, freehand, authorized, and well executed.

Poorly executed forgeries are the most common. The vast majority of forgeries fall into this category. The forgery is accomplished by a forger of limited skill. The forgery will exhibit material deviation from the target signature. Hesitation is found in the strokes. A labored appearance is noted. They are rudimentary in nature and are easily exposed upon examination. See illustration of poorly executed Cobb forgeries. Note the unsteadiness of hand. They appear childlike in construction.

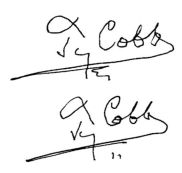

Ty Cobb forgeries—poorly executed.

An offshoot of the poorly executed forgery is the traced forgery. This is produced when a genuine signature is placed usually on a light table and paper is applied over the signature. The light allows the image to replicate itself on the paper. The forger simply traces over the lines of the genuine autograph and produces a duplicate. Unlike poorly executed forgeries, traced forgeries exhibit less unsteadiness due to

the forger following the lines of the genuine signature. The forgery appears methodic with thick and uniform lines. A somewhat labored appearance is noted. Traced forgeries are also rudimentary in construction and are also easily exposed, upon examination, as fake. See illustration of traced Cobb forgeries. Note that the unsteadiness is less pronounced than that which is found in poorly executed forgeries.

Ty Cobb forgeries—traced.

Freehand forgeries are the least used method today. A freehand forgery is created by a forger without knowledge or care of the target signature. These forgeries are usually free-flowing and lack hesitation. The problem is that a freehand forgery looks nothing like the target autograph. This method is usually reserved for the really rare signatures whose exemplars are restricted or, in some cases, nonexistent. Common targets of freehand forgeries are the ultra-rare sports signatures: George Dixon, Sam Thompson, Mungo Park, and the like. Other targets are rare opera singers, composers such as Revered Komitas, and many pre–18th century figures. See illustration of freehand Cobb forgeries. Note the forgeries look nothing like a genuine Cobb autograph.

Authorized forgeries, the so-called ghost signer, are also a problem. These are proxy signatures authorized by the signer and are found in almost all fields of collecting. Typically these

Ty Cobb

Ty Cobb

Ty Cobb forgeries—freehand.

are items signed by the secretary. In the text I will refer to this type of forgery as "secretarially signed" or "ghost signed." Secretarial signatures are most often found in the fields of politics, entertainment, and modern sports.

Many politicians allowed secretaries to sign their names. Early presidential land grants were commonly signed by secretaries, starting with Andrew Jackson's staff. A land grant signed by a president after Jackson is a true rarity. Most secretaries did not attempt to copy the president's signature and hence the autograph looks nothing like the genuine signature. James Buchanan's secretary was an exception. It does have a resemblance to Buchanan's hand. The same can be said for Frank Navin's secretary. Many of the modern presidents delegated signing duties to secretaries. Franklin Roosevelt, Dwight Eisenhower, John Kennedy, and Warren Harding are good examples. Herbert Hoover's secretary, A.G. Shankey, could sign the president's signature with frightening accuracy.

Other politicians, such as congressmen, senators, and governors, make liberal use of secretaries to sign correspondence and even photographs. Fortunately, most autographs of non-presidential politicians are of little value, so these forgeries are harmless.

Hollywood makes liberal use of the secretary's hand. Many signatures obtained through the mail were signed by someone other than the entertainer. Ronald Reagan, Bela Lugosi, Jean Harlow, and Bob Hope are fine examples.

Some, such as baseball legend Shoeless Joe

Jackson, an illiterate, delegated signing duties to his wife. Though Shoeless Joe couldn't read or write, he was able to sign his name, but rarely did so. Secretarial signatures are in the market in great quantities, so caution is warranted. Some secretarial signatures can be worth more than the genuine article. When Honus Wagner was a coach for the Pittsburgh Pirates, he signed autographs for the players. Bulgarian artist Christo would frequently pen signatures on behalf of his wife and fellow artist, Jeanne Claude Denat de Guillebon. These make for interesting collectables. They are coveted simply for the oddity factor.

Then there is the most destructive category: the well-executed forgery. These are the forgers who wreak havoc in the autograph market. Their work product is convincing. Collectors and authenticators usually fall victim to the well-executed forgery. Well-executed forgeries are produced by just a handful of truly skilled forgers. These are forgers who replicate the target signature with good accuracy. The hesitation of hand found in the poorly executed forgery is greatly muted and, in many cases, lacking. Skilled forgers typically target the valuable signatures such as Abraham Lincoln and Thomas Jefferson and generally avoid the less valuable signatures. See illustration of well-executed Cobb forgeries. Note that hesitation

Ty Cobb forgeries—well executed.

is lacking. The forgeries evidence a flowing hand.

The historical significance of a name, coupled with a limited supply of material, will determine who the skilled forger targets. In sports it is Cobb, Babe Ruth, Bobby Jones, Jim Thorpe, Howie Morenz, Marvin Hart, Bob Fitzsimmons, and the like. Common targets of the entertainment genre are Lon Chaney, Sr., Humphrey Bogart, Marilyn Monroe, James Dean, and the like.

Some people produce a signature with strong flow and precise lines. The result is a signature with superior eye appeal. Many skilled forgers will avoid this type of signature simply because replication is too difficult. Chester Arthur is a fine example. There are no well-executed forgeries of Arthur's signature in the market. His signature is simply too complex with superior construction. Arthur is the most difficult of any presidential signature to replicate. John Quincy Adams, on the other hand, signed in a slow and pensive hand. Adams is one of the easiest of all presidential signatures to replicate, hence well-executed forgeries, including ALsS and handwritten poems, exist in quantities. A forger deciding on which presidential signature to target would ultimately pick Adams over Arthur. Simply put, less effort is involved to produce a convincing forgery. The path of least resistance is always best.

The general rule is the better the flow and construction a signature has, the less likely it will be targeted by forgers. The less structured the signature is, the more it will be targeted by forgers. British General John Bagot Glubb's hand is instructive. His signature is illustrated. It is a nonconforming and nonsensical writing. There is not much to the signature, and thus it is easily forged.

Glubb-1, Album page dated 1957.

The signatures of John Kennedy and Judge Kenesaw Landis also exhibit poor structure, thus replication of hand is easy. Take a look at Cy Block's signature when you get a chance! Some signers will alter their hand based on mood or expediency. Illustrated are two signatures of Al Simmons. One is nicely signed with good construction. The other is a hurried scrawl that lacks construction. The latter is much easier to replicate.

Simmons-1, bank check circa 1950s.

Simmons-2, 1942 hurried signature.

A genuine signature is signed in a reckless and carefree hand. It is a physical act that is unique to each of us. We really don't think about signing our name. Place pen to paper and the hand starts scribbling out your autograph. This results in a signature that is free-flowing and careless, and one that does not stay within the lines. We sign our autograph with good speed. No hesitation can be found, just clean-flowing lines. The exception to this rule is one whose hand is affected by illness, infirmity due to advanced age, or injury.

In general, a genuine signature will exhibit racing starts and racing finishes.

A racing start is a stroke that begins as a faint line, then widens as the pen makes greater contact with the paper. The result is a stroke that goes from thin to thick. A racing finish has the opposite effect. As the pen leaves the paper, the width of the stroke decreases. The stroke goes from thick to thin until it disappears. The racing effect gives the signature a clean-flowing appearance.

Racing start, illustrated.

Racing finish, illustrated.

Most signatures will exhibit this effect, though many times it is muted and hardly noticeable. Author Truman Capote signed in a pensive hand. His signature is accomplished in a printed script and rudimentary in construc-tion. Capote's signature still exhibits the racing effect, minimal as it may be. See illustration of Joe Cronin's signature with minimal racing effect.

Joe Cronin signature with muted racing effect.

The racing effect can be diminished by infirmity. Some people will produce a strong signature their entire life with degeneration of hand surfacing only days before death. As we age, the motor skills tend to slow and, in some cases, break down. This will affect the hand, resulting in a signature with impairment. Illness will also affect the signer's hand. Palsy, Parkinson's, benign tremors, and the like will inhibit writing skills and alter the signature. The case of baseball executive Lee MacPhail is instructive. Illustrated are three signatures accomplished at different points of MacPhail's life. MacPhail-1 was signed in the early 1980s. The signature is flowing. No hesitation is evident. The remaining signatures illustrate degeneration of MacPhail's hand. As he aged, his signature became more unstable. The signature is labored, with poor display value. MacPhail-3 was signed a year before his death. It is nothing more than a scribble. As you progress in the hobby you will learn who signed with infirmity and who did not.

Macphail-1 signature circa 1980.

MacPhail-2, signature, circa 2005, evidencing marginal infirmity.

Ty Cobb signature dated 1928.

MacPhail-3, signature dated 2011, evidencing material infirmity.

A forger must not only reproduce a signature that resembles the target signature, but he must do so with proper hand speed. This is a very difficult task and one that cannot be mastered by most forgers. Every person's hand develops a pattern of writing and to deviate from it in order to copy someone else's takes great effort. Forgery is a form of mimicry. A forger changes his hand to copy another person's handwriting. This is laborious and painful. Strong flow is one of the keys to understanding signatures. A signature of President George W. Bush will, as of this writing, exhibit no shakiness of hand. Any Bush signature that evidences unsteadiness, even a *minute* amount, should be considered suspect and avoided. The above-referenced infirmity is the exception. Presidents George H.W. Bush and Herbert Hoover produced materially shaky signatures in old age. Other presidents, like Dwight Eisenhower and Calvin Coolidge, signed in a strong hand their entire lives. The illustrated Cobb signature evidences clean-flowing lines with no hesitation. Even upon magnification the lines appear crisp and clean. Compare this signature to the illustrated Cobb forgery. Upon magnification the forgery evidences subtle hesitation and lacks the crisp flow of the genuine specimen. Arrows highlight areas of hesitation.

Ty Cobb signature dated 1928, in detail.

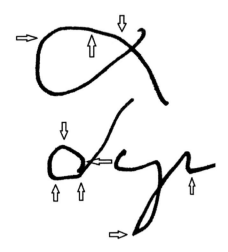

Ty Cobb forgery.

Signatures accomplished on different mediums will display themselves in materially different ways. The signature of artist Zabel Belian, who works in clay, is illustrated. Her signature, I am sure, is effortlessly constructed. However, when the signature is signed in clay it is noticeably labored and methodic in appearance. Such is the nature of the medium. It would be very easy for a forger to replicate Belian's signature in clay in order to produce a counterfeit of one of her works. Signatures on artwork are the same way. New York artist Raphael Soyer, who passed away in 1987, signed his work in a block-like printed script which is illustrated. Soyer's signature is flowing and artistically constructed, but his painted signature is slow, laborious, and easily replicated. This is why it is so easy for a skilled forger to create a counterfeit painting. In short, it is much easier to pass a fake painting off as genuine than it is to pass a forged ALS of Abraham Lincoln.

Belian-1 signature accomplished in clay.

Soyer-1 signature accomplished in paint.

Scale and Point Construction

Learning scale and point construction is very important. Sit down and sign your name ten times. All the signatures look alike. Same stroke, slant, and speed. In addition, they will all be the same size; in other words, they all have the same scale. Signatures accomplished by the signer should all be the same size if signed at roughly the same time frame. Scale can, of course, change over the years. A signature of President Benjamin Harrison signed in 1880 will be the same size as all other signatures accomplished by Harrison at roughly the same time. There is a very large supply of Harrison bank checks in the market. The signatures on these checks, signed at the same time period, will be of the same size. Learning proper scale can help you detect a forgery.

Scale will change depending of the size of the medium. Baseball Hall of Famer Charlie Gehringer signed in a large and striking hand. He would reduce the size of his signature to sign a small medium such as a 1933 Goudey baseball card. Hence all signed Goudey cards should contain a Gehringer signature of the same size.

Point construction is also an important physical trait of a signature. This is where the signer places breaks in the signature. Some signers, such as William Rehnquist, have no breaks in the signature. Other signatures will have many breaks. James Watson's signature is a good example. If you examine a signature with an inconsistent point construction pattern, it may well be a forgery.

Skilled forgers will go to great lengths to make their work product convincing. They will spend many an hour studying the target signature and the minute details of the hand. Johnny Mize once told me that he never dotted his letter "i" but rather finished it off with a dash. It is a trivial detail that would escape the eye of most, but not the alert forger. A skilled forger will learn watermarks, period inks and paper and incorporate this knowledge into his work. A forger of baseball autographs will properly date official league baseballs. Great care will be taken not to forge signatures of the 1926 Detroit Tigers on an E.S. Barnard American League baseball, which wasn't produced until 1928.

Provenance

My dad would always tell me: "It's a cold and cruel world out there." There is a lot of good in this world, but there is also a lot of bad. One of the primary drivers of the human mind is greed. It's greed that leads many a person to perpetrate fraud for financial gain. Whether it's bank robbery, insider trading, price fixing, or counterfeiting, the world is full of minefields. If you're not careful in this hobby, you will get your leg blown off. In the world of collectables and antiques, the criminal element is lurking around every corner. I shake my head in disbelief at the gullibility of some people. They mindlessly drift through life believing every tall tale they hear. In the world of autographs the glass is *always* half empty, not half full. Assume the item is a forgery until you can deem it genuine. Far too many times in history, deceit has been used to perpetrate a fraud or swindle someone out of money.

A couple of years ago a fragment of papyrus, written in Coptic, surfaced that stated Jesus was married. It caused a firestorm. The American media and university "intelligentsia," eager to mock Christianity, splashed headlines across the world about Jesus and his wife. The papyrus contained writing that was in bold black ink that did not exhibit proper age. It looked too clean and neat. This alone should have alerted the scholars it was a forgery. Now think of this: a fragment of ancient papyrus survives through many centuries and it just happened to be the portion of writing about Jesus and his wife. Any alarm bells going off? Yet this scrap of writing was believed by many authorities in the field of antiquities to be genuine. It was later dismissed as a forgery, and a crude one at that, and I am of the same opinion.

It the world of autographs, things that are too good to be true usually are. The Hitler diaries are a fine example. Hitler wrote detailed diaries that just happened to surface many decades later? Really?

What of the Rosetta Stone, one of the ultimate manuscripts in history? A stone suddenly appears in the late 1700s with text of previously undecipherable Egyptian hieroglyphs with corresponding Greek and Egyptian demotic text conveniently situated underneath for translation. Doesn't that seem a bit odd? Is the Rosetta Stone a genuine manuscript or an ingenious hoax? There is something simply too convenient about the Rosetta Stone and its writings. And what of the famed Dare Stones, which supposedly reveal the fate of the lost colony of Roanoke? Are they genuine relics or a hoax? Whether it is for financial gain or to alter history, fraud is everywhere. Writings that are considered ancient antiquities will almost always be a product of forgery.

One the key words in this hobby is "provenance." Everybody seems to use this word without really understanding what it means or the destructive path it can lead collectors down.

Provenance is a word that has grown out of control in the world of autographs. It simply means origin of the item in question. You will hear the term provenance tossed about as the be-all and end-all word in the industry. The question is: should provenance be used to determine the authenticity of a signature? The answer is no! Provenance has really no place in the field of autographs. The genuineness of a signature is based on its physical construction and nothing else. The story behind the autograph is irrelevant. I cannot tell you how many times a collector buys an autograph based, in part, on the story behind it: "It has ironclad provenance!" The signature later turns out to be a forgery. If a forger can create a forgery, does it not make sense that he can fabricate a story to enhance the forgery and allow the item to seamlessly enter the market? Either a signature is genuine or it is not, and the determination is based on the signature itself and nothing more.

In the December 23, 2005, edition of the *Sports Collectors Digest*, autograph dealer Stephen Koschal offers his thoughts on provenance. Koschal, who is generally considered America's leading authority on presidential autographs, states: "Provenance is a major problem today with authenticators because too many authenticators can use the provenance to make their decision for them."

My favorite fraud in the world of autographs occurred back in the late 1800s. A gentleman named George Byron held himself out as kin to the famed poet Lord Byron. George Byron even looked a little like Lord Byron, which only reinforced his claim that he was family. George Byron sold many Lord Byron letters. He seemed to have an endless supply of them. Since they came from a family member, what could be better provenance than that? George Byron also sold letters written to Byron by other notable poets such as John Keats and Percy Shelley. As it turned out, George Byron was not related to Lord Byron. He was a forger and his forgeries made it into the market because of provenance. His work product still causes problems to this day.

Several years ago I was at a sports memorabilia show. An old man, maybe 85 years old, walked in with a 1920s American League baseball signed by Ty Cobb and Babe Ruth. The condition was fairly good; the ball, however, did evidence game wear. He approached me and asked if I was interested in purchasing it. The gentleman told me: "I got it signed at Navin Field in 1924." He had witnessed the two legends sign the ball. He was willing to write a letter supporting his assertions. Great provenance from an eyewitness to the signing, right? Sounded like a pretty good story. The signatures were forgeries and I told him such. He ended up selling the ball to a dealer at the very same show. The dealer swallowed the story hook, line, and sinker and got burned. He used provenance to authenticate something that was not.

In general, forgers will focus their efforts on more modern signatures, post–1900. It is simply easier for the forger not to have to fake the aging process to any measurable degree.

It is easier to forge John Kennedy or Charles Lindbergh on a sheet of book paper using a ballpoint pen. The forger really doesn't have to make these forgeries appear vintage. The same cannot be said about signatures of George Washington or Benjamin Franklin. Signatures of these two are over 200 years old, and to make a forgery look convincing, not only does a forger have to replicate the signature but also replicate the aging process and make the signature appear vintage. Faking the aging process is a very difficult task and, in reality, impossible. Only Father Time can properly age a document. A genuine Kennedy signature, on the other hand, does not give the appearance of an antique because it really wasn't signed that long ago. A forger can skip the task of artificial aging. It simply takes less time to forge Kennedy's signature than it does Washington's.

Time has a way of taking a fresh document and transforming it. The years go by and the decades pass and something magical happens. Mellow shades of earth tones slowly overtake the brightness of the document. What was once clean becomes rich and pleasing to the eye. The white paper turns a gentle golden color. The ink that once shined bright is overtaken by soft shades of grey and ocean blue. It becomes regal in appearance with a vintage take-you-back-in-time look. Like a fine wine, documents age wonderfully with the passage of time. Time and only time has the ability to make this transformation. A forger will attempt to replicate the aging process but he will not be able to match it, though he may come close.

Artificially aging a document is a true art form. It takes years of experience to replicate aging with any degree of accuracy. Some forgers have become very adroit at faking the aging process. There are various levels of aging, from the amateurish to the expert. Rudimentary attempts include brushing paper with tea or coffee, or burning the edges for a rustic look. Some will rub dirt into paper to stain the fibers. This method works well with baseballs. In general, these are unsophisticated attempts to make a document appear that it has been around for centuries. They are easily spotted by the trained eye.

Other methods of aging are much more advanced. They incorporate chemicals, computers, and printing presses.

Several years ago I was offered a 19th-century edition of *Ben-Hur* signed by author Lew Wallace. It had a long and deeply personal inscription. The signature was dated 1891. A signed copy of *Ben-Hur* is rare and would make a welcome addition to any library. The asking price was $1,000, which is fair, considering the wonderful inscription. Wallace signed in a practical hand, resulting in a signature that is fairly easy to replicate. I studied the signature and a flaw presented itself. The writing appeared slightly blurred, somewhat fuzzy if you will. The signature was a forgery.

One of the easiest ways to give a forgery a vintage appearance is to place it on old paper. The paper is brown, a tad brittle, and some foxing is usually evident. Forgeries are often placed on old book paper. This is the most common technique of faking the aging process. The above-referenced Wallace book is a good example and also demonstrates the downfall of this method. Paper is a rather flexible medium. When produced it is durable. It bends and, when bent, retains a high degree of memory. But as time goes by the paper begins to age. The paper's fibers begin to break down. The connectivity begins to fail. The once-flexible paper is now somewhat rigid, with impaired tensile properties. Take a page from an antique book and bend it. You can feel the flexibility is compromised. The paper will tend to crack. This is especially true with cheaper grade paper. When ink is applied to fresh paper it rests upon it until it dries. The ink is held in place, resulting in a smooth and clear image. When wet ink is placed on old paper, the fibers, impaired by time, have become weak and permeable. This allows the ink to seep into the fibers. The result is a writing that appears blurred or fuzzy. It is called the bleeding effect. This is a telltale sign of forgery. If you ever examine a signature that evidences this effect, proceed with caution, as it is likely a forgery. There is one exception to this rule

and it is a rare occurrence but needs to be discussed. Under the right conditions ink applied to new paper will, on occasion, exhibit the bleeding effect. This can occur when the signature is placed in improper storage and exposed to very humid or damp conditions, such as in a basement or cellar. Ink exposed to material dampness for long periods can develop the bleeding effect. The humidity allows the ink to creep into the paper. This rarely occurs but it is worth noting. This problem did surface in some pre–1930 signed bank checks of Honus Wagner.

The bleeding effect can vary in degree depending on the grade of paper. The general rule is the higher the grade of paper, the less the bleeding effect will be noted. United States currency is a fine example. It is a strong linen/cotton blend and holds up well to time. Ink applied to antique currency will evidence little bleeding effect. Furthermore, the bleeding effect is limited to ink and not ball-point or pencil. Anytime a signature appears blurred or fuzzy, you should proceed with extreme caution. Sometimes a forger will apply ammonia hydrochloride to the paper. This alters the pH balance, causing the ink to stay in place while it dries. This method, however, presents its own set of problems. Principally, the ink will crack as it dries, a telltale sign of chemical alteration.

George Washington forgery with pronounced bleeding effect.

George Washington forgery, in detail.

Babe Ruth forgery with pronounced bleeding effect.

Fountain pen ink comes in many colors, but the two most popular are black and blue. Green and red inks come in a distant third and fourth. Fountain ink appears bright, almost glowing. Time, or more properly oxygen, has a way of changing the bright tones of new ink into rich and gentle shades. Black will turn a rustic brown (on newspaper grade paper) or variant gray tones. Blue ink becomes softer, also exhibiting gray tones. Red ink will darken over the years to a deep blood-red color—which is desired for a signature of Bela Lugosi or Max Schreck.

A major hurdle for the forger is to make ink appear as if it was signed decades ago. This is no easy task. The forger must find a way to replace the brightness of new ink in favor of mellow shades. One way to do this is chemical additives.

Several years ago I was offered an album page signed by several members of the Detroit Tigers. It was signed by many old-time Tiger greats, including Hall of Famers Ty Cobb, Hugh Jennings, and Wahoo Sam Crawford. The most expensive signature on the page was, of course, Jennings, which is a rare baseball autograph. As I recall, the asking price was $3,000. I was interested in this baseball gem, so I studied it and studied it. The more I looked the more suspicious I became. Needless to say, I walked away from the offer.

When ink is applied to paper, a smooth and flowing stroke results. Roughness and trunca-tion are lacking. It is a clean line that is pleasing to the eye. This is something that never changes, at least not to the naked eye. Whether the ink was placed on the paper ten years ago or 100 years ago, the smooth flow of the ink will remain essentially unchanged.

Back to the Tigers album page. The signatures on the page did evidence mellow shades of ink, suggesting the ink was applied some time ago. This is a good sign as to the genuineness of the piece, but there was something wrong. The ink appeared slightly off. The above-referenced smooth flow was impaired. Small areas of ink had clumped together. The ink appeared rough, like the skin of a reptile. This is a sure sign that a chemical cocktail has been added to the ink to alter its shade. The right mixture of ammonia and sugars can do some amazing things to ink. It will transform the brightness of new ink and replace it with vintage shades. The transformation is almost instantaneous. But the chemical additive destroys the smooth flow of ink and thus reveals itself. Ink that appears rough, clumped, cracked, or scab-like should be avoided in total. The above-referenced effect does not pertain to ballpoint. Ammonia-based chemicals do alter ballpoint, but in a different way. It gives the ink a faded or washed-out appearance.

In recent years, forgers have become very sophisticated in their craft. Not only have they be-

Babe Ruth forgery with chemically altered ink.

come skilled at forgery but also at creating fake mediums to place their work upon. It is a good idea to learn about ink, papers, postal frankings, and the like. If you run across a signature of Calvin Coolidge signed in ballpoint, alarm bells should go off. You may think this rudimentary, but many collectors are fooled by such errors.

Chemically altered ink.

Ink

There are various types of ink. To learn their properties can help you go a long way in avoiding forgeries. Some inks have been around for centuries, others only a few decades. Some inks are better than others when it comes to particular mediums. The Sharpie pen is a fine example. It is a permanent marker that takes well to high-gloss mediums such as photographs, trading cards, and other items with a hard surface such as a billiard ball or sports helmet. This is a very popular pen among collectors of sports memorabilia. It works on surfaces, such as a baseball bat, where a ballpoint or fountain pen fails. For other mediums, Sharpie is not preferred. A baseball, for example, should always be signed in ballpoint. One signed in Sharpie is worth far less as the ink, over time, bleeds into the hide of the ball. It gives the signature a diseased appearance.

The earliest known ink is carbonaceous based. This is simply carbon ground to a fine texture, then mixed with water or gum arabic. Lampblack and soot were commonly used. The Chinese and Indians used ink for thousands of years. Various plants and graphite were ground, wetted, and applied with a brush. Carbon-based inks can be found on the earliest of documents. It is a stable mixture that does not corrode the paper or vellum it is applied to. It can last for centuries. It is resistant to fading from sunlight, though a document with carbon based ink should be stored in a dark environment. The problem with this type of ink is that it is susceptible to humid environments, even if the ink was applied centuries before.

In the 4th century, iron-gall ink made its debut. It is a mixture of iron salts and gall, primarily of oak. A gall is an abnormal growth found on trees. It forms due to infestation of parasites. Iron-gall was popular for many centuries and produced a bold stroke of ink.

The main problem with iron-gall is its reactive properties. It contains tannic acid, which is corrosive. Once applied it slowly but surely reacts with the host medium. The corrosive ink will break down paper. In extreme cases it will eat completely through it, leaving an outline of where the paper once was. Over the centuries, chemists attempted to make gall ink less reactive. Some added dyes from plants like *Indigofera tinctoria*, though with marginal success. Gall inks tend to fade and there is really no true method to prevent its corrosion of paper. Over time gall inks tend to develop various shades of red. Some say the ink is "rusting." It is best to store this ink in stable environments where fluctuations of temperature and humidity are minimal. Gall ink fell out of favor in the mid to late 1800s, though it was used, in some corners, well into the 20th century.

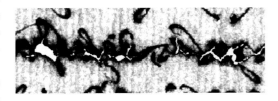

Iron gall ink corrosion.

What we term as modern fountain pen ink is a water-based ink colored with dye rather than pigment. The particulate nature of pigment will tend to clog a fountain pen. Most signatures accomplished in the last part of the 19th and first part of the 20th century are produced with this type of ink. It tends to be permanent but must be kept away from bright light.

In 1937, the ballpoint pen made its debut and received a cold shoulder from the masses. The origins of a ballpoint type instrument dates back to the 1880s. A tanner named John Loud received a patent for it but it failed to produce any commercial success. The ballpoint gained popularity slowly but surely in the post–World War II era, though most people were still using the fountain pen at this time. One of the earliest converts to this technology was Tris Speaker, who used it quite regularly in the mid–1940s to fulfill autograph requests. By the 1950s the world was moving towards the ballpoint and away from the fountain pen. By the 1960s, the fountain pen had all but died off. Today it is used by only a few traditionalists, such as myself, for correspondence. It should be noted that many World War II aviators from Europe used fountain pens well into the 1990s to sign autographs. Most notable were British aces Neville Duke and J.E. "Johnnie" Johnson, as well as many Luftwaffe aces, including Josef Kraft, Walter Krupinski, Hugo Broch, and Walter Schuck.

For further information regarding inks see *Autographs: A Key to Collecting* by Mary Benjamin (R.R. Bowker, 1946).

Paper

Paper is all around us. It is everywhere. But as common as it is, paper has a long and storied history. Paper is essentially fibers of cellulose pulp forced together with the proper amount of moisture. It is unclear just when paper made its appearance and who invented it. The Chinese are typically credited with this invention. Paper first came onto the scene in the 2nd cen-

tury. Some archaeologists have claimed fragments produced as early as the 3rd century BC. exist. The man credited with inventing paper is Cai Lun, though this is tenuous at best. This early paper was produced from various plant materials, most notably morus and hemp. The word paper is derived from the papyrus plant. Papyrus was the first form of "paper," though it is merely a useful part of the plant and not really paper at all.

Modern papers surfaced in the 1300s. Before that time parchment and vellum, both animal by-products, were used almost exclusively for documents and other writings. Collectors will commonly encounter vellum when dealing with early presidential land grants and royal appointments. Vellum and parchment tend to be durable and will last throughout the centuries.

Rag paper is a cotton-based paper. It is much more durable than the modern wood-based papers. It is blended, then laid on wire. Laid paper is easily identified by the horizontal lines running through the paper. Holding laid paper up to the light greatly enhances the striations. Rag paper was also woven. Woven paper tends to be less durable and wire lines, found in laid paper, are lacking.

The invention of wood pulp paper meant paper could be mass produced and available to the general public. Wood pulp is mixed with various chemicals to produce paper cheaply. Pulp-based papers are fragile when compared to their cotton counterparts. Newspapers are printed on very cheap paper, and it begins to oxidize within a matter of months. Wood pulp papers made their debut around 1860.

Learning about paper, and what was popular and when, is useful for autograph collectors. As a collector, you will quickly learn what was the custom of a particular time period. Early writings from the 14th century will typically be found on narrow strips of parchment. A quarto sheet from that time period should send up a warning flag. In the 1800s, octavo sized sheets became very popular. A blue paper, known as Lincoln Blue, became popular in the late 1830s and remained that way until the Civil War. Around 1900 many people would pen letters on hotel stationery. This is especially true with athletes and entertainers, who were constantly traveling from one venue to another.

Towards the end of the Civil War, supplies of raw material in the Confederacy were nearly depleted. Paper produced in the closing year of the war included more and more inferior material, principally cornhusks. This resulted in a poor quality paper. A letter written from that time period on high-quality cotton paper should be considered suspect and examined carefully.

Watermarks are another important factor. A watermark is essentially an area of varying thickness or density in the paper that produces a noticeable pattern in the paper. Watermarks can be seen clearly when held to the light. The watermark was invented in Italy in the 11th century. In the 19th century they became widely used. Machines made creation of a watermark much easier and thus less costly. There are thousands upon thousands of different watermarks. These can be used to help date paper. I can recall a lengthy AMQS purportedly written by Claude Debussy and dated 1911. The forger failed to so his homework, for he placed his work product on paper with a watermark that dated the paper to the 1930s, many years after the great composer died. There are many reference guides available with extensive information about watermarks, their makers, and dates of creation. These have proven an invaluable tool to the autograph collector.

The Evolution of the Forger

Over the past couple of decades forgers have become very sophisticated in their trade. Forgery used to be limited to ripping out an old book page and penning a letter upon it. Today, things are a bit different. The variety of counterfeit mediums forgers create is amazing. It is something to keep in the back of your mind when hunting for signatures.

Several years ago I was sent a small group of government postcards all postmarked from the 1950s. They were signed by some of the great baseball Hall of Famers, Honus Wagner, Bobby Wallace, Harry Heilmann, and the like. One of the cards caught my eye. It contained a bold fountain signature of the immortal Cy Young. The cards were all genuine, at least upon cursory inspection. I studied the Young signature and I became suspicious. The signature looked too clean and bright. The card itself was in near mint condition. There was no wear to the corners. The patina, if you will, was lacking. The card carried a postmark from 1952. I concluded it was a forgery, and a nicely accomplished one at that.

Forged government postcards, complete with spurious postmarks, are in the market. Being a collector of baseball signatures, I have seen many postcards signed with forgeries of the Hall of Fame legends including Grover Cleveland Alexander, Ty Cobb, Amos Rusie, and Babe Ruth. These cards are not limited to baseball signatures. I have inspected a counterfeit card that featured a forgery of Tim Mara. The cards appear too clean and neat. The ink is too flashy and bright. The postmarks are counterfeit and may appear slightly thicker than a genuine postmark. The fake postmarks seem to be limited to the hand-cancel postmarks and not the machine ocean-wave postmark. See illustrations.

Another common practice is to take a genuine signed item and add forgeries to the piece. This technique is fairly tricky, especially when accomplished by a skilled forger. I once examined a multi-signed album page that contained a handful of early Hollywood stars. Anyone remember Conway Tearle? All signatures were of forgotten entertainers. The piece had little value except for a scarce signature of horror actor O.P. Heggie. All signatures were genuine except for the Heggie, which was added many years later by a forger.

This practice in most commonly associated with sports-related items. A team sheet signed

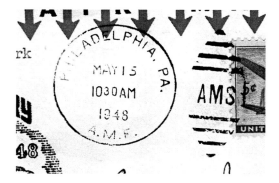

Hand cancel postmark.

Ocean wave postmark.

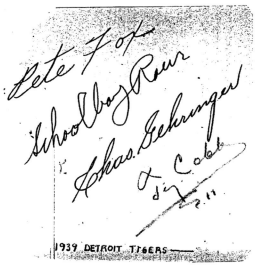

Ty Cobb forgery placed next to genuine Detroit Tiger autographs.

by the New York Yankees with a forgery of Babe Ruth or Lou Gehrig is added to enhance the value. This is also done with multi-signed footballs and baseballs. I cannot tell you how many times I have examined a baseball signed by many old-time players where a forgery of Ty Cobb or Babe Ruth was added. This is a very common practice, so caution is warranted. See the illustrated 1939 album page signed by three Detroit Tigers with a forgery of Ty Cobb added sometime later.

Another practice that has been around for many years is adding a forgery to an item that has nothing to do with the target signature. This practice is most often found in the world of art, where artwork and autographs merge. Forgers will purchase unsigned artwork. The forger will simply add a forgery of a well-known artist on the painting and resell it for a large profit.

Vintage unsigned paintings can be purchased at relatively cheap prices, well under $100. Add a forgery of Garth Williams or Paul Franz Flickel to the painting and the value increases well into the thousands of dollars. Some gullible buyer will snag it.

A few years back the artwork of Benjamin Kroll entered the Detroit art market. Kroll was an illustrator for Packard Motors and Ford Motor Company in the 1950s and 1960s. His paintings were of the WPA school of art. He died in the 1990s. His artwork caught fire and prices went through the roof. Many of his paintings were unsigned. They were purchased at a discounted price. Months later these same paintings reentered the market complete with forged Kroll signatures and no doubt resold for substantial profits.

Another common practice is creating fake letterhead. This is usually accomplished one of two ways. The first method is using a rubber stamp. This gives the letterhead a slightly fuzzy look. The second method is using a computer to generate fake letterhead. Unlike the rubber stamp method, the letterhead is clean and precise, maybe a bit too precise. You will recall in the closing weeks of the 2004 presidential election, military records surfaced regarding President Bush's military service. The records made major headlines. In an apparent effort to aid candidate John Kerry's election bid, CBS aired the story of the records without authenticating them. The records were quickly dismissed as forgeries. The letterhead and typeset appeared too uniform and precise and could not have been produced by typewriters of the day.

While on the subject of letterhead, another common practice is obtain genuine hotel stationary and add a forged ALS or ANS to it. Vintage hotel and business stationary is available in quantities. I have seen this technique used for many famous celebrities: William McKinley, Warren Harding, Francis Ouimet, Charlie Chaplin, Orville Wright, and the like. Some fairly well-executed ALsS of Ty Cobb, accomplished in green ink, exist in quantities. These were produced around 2010.

Along the same lines of genuine ephemera, forgers will obtain a genuine business document, such as a bill of sale or rent receipt, and add a forgery. The forgery is usually accompanied by the words "O.K." or "approved." I saw this technique employed on a rent receipt from the Pennsylvania area. The forger added a signature of Eddie Plank. A genuine Plank signature is a rarity and sells for about $20,000. The forger did some research because Plank lived in Gettysburg and the geographical association enhanced the forgery.

Illustrated Exemplars

I am often asked two questions. First, where can I go to find example signatures for comparison? And second, how do you know if the exemplars are genuine? These are both good questions.

Example signatures of the more famous names have been illustrated for decades in many books written by authorities in the field. This is generally a good way to build a reference library of exemplars. There is a caveat: many books will wrongly illustrate a forgery (or two, or three) as genuine. Some books have illustrated countless forgeries as the genuine article. This, of course, causes confusion. Some signatures have been reproduced so many times that the questionable signature is usually washed out of the mix. If you see a signature of George Washington or James Madison illustrated, chances are very good that it is genuine. There are simply too many specimens in the market. But what of the rare and seldom-seen signatures? Texas patriot William Barret Travis is a fine example. He was killed at the Alamo at the young age of 26. His signature is very rare and highly valued. Elaborate forged Travis documents exist in the market.

Another example would be famed New York Highlanders pitcher Jack Chesbro. He was one of the all-time hurlers of the Cobbian era of ball. He died in 1931 and was elected into the Hall of Fame in 1946. There are fewer than 10 of his signatures in existence. Only two genuine paper signed mediums exist in the market. His signature alone is valued at $20,000 to $25,000.

There are not a lot of published examples of the above-referenced signatures. With Chesbro, previous book illustrations always seem to wrongly illustrate a forgery as the genuine article. So how do you know which signature to trust? How do you know if the illustrated signature is real or fake? In many cases you do not. This is where detective work comes into play. The best way to find confirmed exemplars of the rare signatures is to search for them at various governmental concerns. This is the most foolproof way to find a genuine signature. This does take some effort but it is well worth it.

Register of deeds, courthouses, probates, and military records are excellent sources to find confirmed specimens. Signatures exist on wills, mortgages, marriage licenses, divorce papers, and draft cards. State archives will have documents of famous residents. A signature from one of these sources is very likely genuine. Chesbro's signature exists on a will and a World War I draft card, both of which are the property of public agencies. These are invaluable tools for the autograph collector. This is not to say a secretarial signature will slip by now and then. Presidential land grants are a fine example. You would think that an official grant would be signed by the president, but in many cases the secretary would sign for the commander in chief. Notarized documents will on rare occasion contain a secretarial signature. This practice was known to occur with Negro League sports documents. But for the most part, the above-referenced documents are a wonderful source for signature comparison and confirmation.

Some signatures are so rare that no confirmable example exists, or more properly, has yet been discovered. Negro Leaguer and Baseball Hall of Famer Franklin Grant is a fine example. He died in 1937. Grant's signature is an extreme rarity. There are no known specimens. A few forgeries exist; all vary in construction. Should a genuine specimen surface, I am not sure how it can be confirmed as genuine. I have been unable to locate a confirmed signature from the aforementioned sources. As time goes by, one may surface and solve the mystery.

A good reference library is well worth assembling. It is the best way to broaden your knowledge in the field of autographs.

Facsimile Signatures

"Facsimiles" is derived from Latin which means "make-alike." A facsimile is a copy, reproduction, and/or duplicate of the original writing. With the advancement of computers come high-quality reproductions and some truly amazing facsimiles. A few years back I wrote an article in *Autograph* magazine. It was a study of Ty Cobb's signature. I illustrated a Cobb signed index card from the 1950s. I, to this day, own the original. Years later I was perusing eBay and saw the same signature certified by an authentication company. It was slabbed in one of their holders. How could that be? The watchdog website Haulsofshame.com stated in a March 12, 2012, article: "PSA(DNA) authenticated what appears to be a laser copied piece of paper that features a facsimile of the original." It looks like someone made a copy of the Cobb signature illustrated in my article and

got it certified. This is disturbing because it devalues the signature I own and raises questions as to authenticity. An email sent to the president of PSA for comment was not returned. There is lesson to be learned here. *Never buy a signature that is framed or slabbed so that you cannot examine the item free from obstruction.*

In recent years many high-quality copies of documents, particularly bank checks, have entered the market. Charles Lindbergh, Marilyn Monroe, John Kennedy, Abraham Lincoln, and the like have been produced. These are usually framed and sold as genuine. My guess is there are thousands of facsimiles being sold as genuine in slab holders and/or framed under glass. If you choose to buy material this way, you are asking for trouble.

Facsimiles are not new to the industry. For many decades facsimile letters and notes, typically sending thanks, have been in the market and are often times purchased by an unsuspecting collector. Some facsimiles, such as a known Thomas Jefferson frank and a Robert Louis Stevenson ALS, have been floating around for well over 80 years. Heads of state, particularly presidents of the United States, have made liberal use of facsimile notes. There are facsimiles of handwritten notes from the likes of Herbert Hoover, Charles de Gaulle, Winston Churchill, King George V, Queen Victoria, and the like. Some of these are very convincing, so caution is warranted. In general, be leery of ANsS or short ALsS that are written to "Dear Friend" as opposed to a particular person. Many are simply notes without an opening address. Upon magnification, the strokes will be found to lack the variant pressure of a genuine ink flow.

The Autopen

Robots have greatly enhanced the standard of living for humans. They do many great things. One place the robot is not welcome is in the world of autographs. It is simply a machine that reproduces a signature based on a common template. The convenience of this device is best described in *Presidents of the United States Autopen Guide* by Stephen Koschal and Andreas Wiemer (2009). The authors write: "The Autopen easily and quickly reproduces a signature using almost any type of writing instrument including pencils. Thousands of signatures can be applied to letters, photographs, books, souvenir items and more in a single working day." The autopen first made its appearance in the 1940s. All modern presidents, starting with Dwight Eisenhower, made liberal use of this machine. Politicians in general use this device a lot, as do some sports figures such as Arnold Palmer and Dale Murphy. Autopen signatures are exposed upon examination. The signature appears uniform and methodic. The racing effect is lacking. In general, the thickness of the ink strokes is uniform. When it is placed next to a signature generated by the same autopen template, no variation is noted. Some celebrities have multiple patterns; this is especially true of presidents, who may have dozens of different patterns. Edward Teller also had several different patterns. Autopen signatures are of no value.

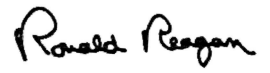

Ronald Reagan, typical auto-pen signature.

Authentication Companies—Authentic but Not Genuine

In recent years the forgers have found themselves a great ally in the form of authentication companies. The authentication company will, for a fee, examine a signature and render an opinion as to the authenticity of the signature. This is fine, at least in theory, but in reality this has turned out to be a disaster. The underlying problem is that an authentication company is only as good as the authenticators it employs. A smart forger will use the certificate of authenticity (COA) issued on a forgery to his advantage. It allows a fake signature to seamlessly enter the market. Unfortunately, most authentication experts in this field aren't really experts at all. Most are about as sharp as a sack of wet mice. This allows many forgeries to be wrongly certified as genuine. In the past couple of years I have seen *tens* of thousands of signatures deemed authentic by the authentication companies that I believe are forgeries. This is especially true in the fields of sports and rock music.

The number of errors, whether intentional or not, likely equals hundreds of millions of dollars. An educated guess is the number of collectors who have been victimized numbers well into the tens of thousands. I often shake my head at collectors who purchase a signature because of a certificate of authenticity. This type of collector does not understand autographs, so he relies on the crutch of the certificate and usually ends up with multiple forgeries in his collection. I have little sympathy for the ignorant.

Countless times a signature which comes with a COA is later deemed a forgery. This complicates matters. Usually the purchaser cannot get a refund from the seller, who hides behind the COA. The certed forgery is usually dumped back into the market and it is sold once again to an unsuspecting collector. Many times an auction company will refuse to give a refund but will gladly take the item back on consignment and auction it off once again. The auctioneer collects yet another commission and yet another collector is stuck with a bogus item. The cycle repeats itself and the fraud continues. The problem has gotten so out of hand that it has drawn the attention of federal law enforcement, which is looking into the authenticators and their dubious business practices. If you have been burned by one of these companies, contact the New York office of the F.B.I. The watchdog website Haulsofshame.com documents the countless number of forgeries certified as genuine by the authentication companies.

Collectors often ask me which authentication service I recommend. I suggest Stephen Koschal Autographs at www.Stephenkoschal.com.

The Black Market

There is a direct correlation between value and crime. The more valuable an item is, the more likely it becomes the target of the criminal element. The bigger the value, the bigger the bull's-eye. Signatures come in all shapes and sizes. Some are treasured, some are not. Vice-presidents of the United States are a fine example. With only a couple of exceptions, signatures of the veeps are of little value and will remain that way for decades. A signature of Vice-President Hubert Humphrey is worth $15. It was worth that 20 years ago and it will be worth that 20 years from now. Humphrey's signature will be of little interest to the forger or the thief.

On the other side of the coin are the rare and valuable signatures. These are the signatures that are always at risk. When purchasing a signature, you must consider its marketability. Title issues are always of concern. Is the item I am about to buy stolen? Are there title issues associated with it? These are questions every collector must ask himself. Far too many times an item comes on the market due to theft. In such a situation the item is not marketable. Many a time a collector will spend good money on an item only to find out some time later the item is stolen. The end result is the item in question is surrendered to law enforcement and the collector it out of luck with no recourse. Before purchasing an item, always consider possible title issues that many arise. Certain mediums should be avoided in total. First and foremost, wills and testaments have caused much controversy. Many court archives have been raided and wills of the famous have been stolen, and

have found their way into collections of unsuspecting collectors. This has been a big problem with the rare sports signatures. Wills of many athletes, such as Jimmy Collins and Tommy McCarthy, have been stolen. These are not allowed in the open market. In general, there should only be one will in existence. Many times a testator will revise his will. In this case, a will that is replaced by an updated will should be destroyed by the drafting attorney. It is improper to have more than one original will in existence at any one time. The only will that should exist, after death, is the one filed with the court. There may be times where this protocol is not followed, but that would be a rare event. I consider wills of any kind, or codicils thereof, to be toxic. Wills should be avoided in total.

Other mediums that should send up warning flags are custom forms. A few years back a customs form signed by astronaut Neil Armstrong entered the market. It was quickly seized by law enforcement. Fingerprint cards are another dangerous minefield. These are the property of the police departments who drafted them. It is apparent that some have been stolen from police libraries. Signatures of the bigger-named criminals, such as Al Capone, Charles "Pretty Boy" Floyd, Alvin Karpis, and Kate "Ma" Barker, are highly collectable and quite valuable. Fingerprint cards have, in recent years, entered the market. As with wills, I consider fingerprint cards to be toxic and thus to be avoided in total.

The value of some signatures and the need to possess them has put institutional collections at risk. It appears the National Baseball Hall of Fame archives were raided several years ago and many priceless writings of the early history of the game were stolen.

August Herrmann was a longtime baseball executive. He was president of the Cincinnati Red Stockings. He served as director of the National Commission from 1902 to 1920. The commission was organized by Major League Baseball to settle disputes. In 1920, the commission was disbanded in favor of one arbitrator; hence, the commissioner's office was born.

The commission dealt with thousands upon thousands of issues. It appears just about all of the writings were saved. They were donated to the Hall of Fame. There are many rare documents in this collection. The archive is simply tremendous.

Today, any letter or document addressed to Herrmann, the National Commission, Tom Lynch, Ban Johnson, Harry Pulliam, Frank Navin, John Heydler, John Tener, John Brush, or Nick Young should be considered suspect and its origins must be investigated carefully, as it may be a stolen.

Moreover, any letter that is addressed to a league executive that involves payment of salary, salary disputes, suspensions, and games that were protested should also be scrutinized as well. These, too, may have been stolen. My advice is to avoid any of the above-referenced items. Hall of Fame officials will not publicly comment on the thefts.

Other thefts include Alexander Cartwright material stolen from the Hawaii state archives. Letters from the Albert Spalding collection housed at the New York Public Library have also been stolen and found their way into the market. The lesson to be learned is don't blindly throw around cash until you are satisfied with the marketability, in terms of title, of the item. For more information regarding stolen documents, see the website Haulsofshame.com.

The Shot Heard Round the World:
The American Revolution and Beyond

By the rude bridge that arched the flood, / Their flag to April's breeze unfurled, / Here once the embattled farmers stood, / And fired the shot heard round the world.—Ralph Waldo Emerson

Perhaps no other writing in our nation's history captures the spirit of America like Emerson's "Concord Hymn." I look back at my years in elementary school with fond memories. Each day would start with a prayer and the Pledge of Allegiance. I learned much about the Declaration of Independence, the Bill of Rights, and the Founding Fathers who had the foresight and vision to create the greatest democracy in the history of mankind. The birth of the United States of America has given us some of the greatest names in world history. It is because of this that signatures from these men are treasured like precious gemstones.

Many figures from the colonial and revolutionary period are household names. Others, having been steamrolled by time, are obscure, known to only a few. Some signatures are extremely expensive while others are downright cheap, relatively speaking.

Signatures of early colonial and protocolonial notables are exceedingly rare. Myles Standish and John Alden fine examples. Signatures of these men rarely, if ever, enter the market, and when they do the asking prices are prohibitive. Documents from the colonial era retain value regardless of signature. Contracts, marriage certificates, slave documents, and deeds are coveted by collectors simply because of the longevity factor. Generic writings, with routine content, will sell for $50 to $250.

Holograph material related to Plymouth, the *Mayflower*, and Jamestown is basically nonexistent. What does survive is typically held by governmental concerns. Searching for signed material of early luminaries will prove a difficult and, in many cases, fruitless pursuit. Rarity abounds from this time period.

Those who wish to collect early American autographs will find much success in the late colonial period and through the Revolution.

Back in the 1600s, well before independence, William Penn, merchant and Quaker, laid the foundation for the city of Philadelphia. He was the founder of Pennsylvania. Penn signed in a choppy and hesitant hand, not uncommon for the day. The signature is generally illegible. Abrupt angles are noted. A paraph completes a rather unappealing signature. Penn's signature is very rare on a per se basis and generally limited to real estate related DsS. Holographic material is exceptionally rare. Many forgeries exist. Secretarial signatures are known to exist. Penn's signature is valued at $2,000. DsS sell in the $4,000 to $5,000 price range. Penn is a very important American autograph.

Penn-1, DS circa 1710 (courtesy Nate D. Sanders Auctions).

The Witch Trial

Around 1692 rumors of black magic spread throughout New England. It led to one of the most bizarre chapters in American history, the Salem Witch Trials. The first to be accused of witchery was Tituba, a slave woman owned by Samuel Parris. When all was said and done, some 20 people were put to death, most of whom were women. Of the magistrates who presided over these trials, none was more famous than Samuel Sewall. Today, he is the face of the witch trials. His signature is in great demand and causes much controversy. Sewall's signature, illustrated below, is of plain and simple construction. It is easily forged and just about all signatures that are purportedly removed from a larger document are forged. There are several variant signatures in the market that are said to be in the hand of Judge Sewall. Below appears one such exemplar. While this may be a Sam Sewall, it is not the witch trial judge. Sewall's brother, Stephen Sewall, was a court clerk and signed many documents. Many were signed as "S. Sewall, cler." These are often sold as Samuel Sewall's autograph. Many of these signatures have been wrongly certified as genuine by the authentication companies, so caution is warranted. A Sewall signed document

will sell for $1,500 to $2,000. DsS by Stephen Sewall can be purchased for $300 to $500.

Another highly collected field is colonial-era documents signed by the early slave traders.

Sewall-2, undated signature.

Sewall-3, ADS circa 1710, apocryphal signature.

Pre-1800 slave documents are rare. Nineteenth-century bills of sale and manumission documents exist in far greater quantities. Signatures of the early European and Colonial slave traders rarely surface. William "Black Bill" Vernon is a fine example. Vernon was an early trader. His signature is very rare and seldom surfaces. Illustrated is what is believed to be Vernon's signature. Vernon also played a key role in the Revolution; thus, demand is quite good for his signature. Signed material of the early African and Barbary slave traders is basically nonexistent. Their names, for the most part, are lost to history.

Vernon-1, DS dated 1767.

Founding of a Nation

The three most important documents in American history are the Articles of Confederation, the Declaration of Independence, and the

Sewall-1, DS circa 1690.

Constitution. The Constitution is probably the most important document in history next to the Bible.

These three documents are signed by a finite number of dignitaries. They are perfect for collectors trying to complete signed sets. Since most, if not all, signers were prominent figures in society, their signatures, for the most part, exist in small but ample quantities. There are exceptions, such as Button Gwinnett. One of the signers of the Declaration of Independence, Gwinnett died in May 1777 and his autograph is an extreme rarity. Many of his papers were lost in a fire. Those who need to complete a set of DOI signers will spend big money for a Gwinnett autograph. While there have been no recent sales, a likely auction price would be somewhere between $500,000 and $1,000,000. This makes his autograph the most expensive in all of autographdom.

Gwinnett-1, signature from the DOI.

Thomas Lynch, Jr., is the second most expensive DOI signer. He died at sea in December of 1779. Some authorities believe Lynch's signature is rarer than Gwinnett's. I do not believe this to be true. Most Gwinnett signatures offered in the market are forged and are likely included in the above-referenced population. In any event, Lynch's signature is worth at least six figures.

Lynch-1, signature from the DOI.

George Taylor's signature is also very rare. His signature is valued between $7,500 and $10,000. His signature is typically found on clips removed from a larger sheet. ALsS are very rare and just about all are forged. A few forged

ALsS, dated 1779 and 1780, are in the market. The writing is a bit too shaky for my taste and the ink is too dark and bold.

Taylor, G-1, signature on the DOI.

For most signers of the DOI and Constitution, however, prices are surprisingly affordable. The sad reality is that interest in these signatures has fallen over the past quarter century. There is far less demand for these signatures in today's market. I find this hard to believe, given that these two documents are the cornerstone of American democracy. Many signatures, such as Thomas Mifflin, William Williams, Robert Treat Paine, Josiah Bartlett, Thomas McKean, and Jared Ingersoll, are available for under $200. DsS are not much more. There are some beautiful manuscripts signed by William Ellery, a Rhode Island signer, which can be purchased for under $500.

The most recognized signature in history belongs to one Mr. John Hancock. His signature on the DOI is the most reproduced autograph of them all. Hancock's hand is bold and striking. The signature is finished off with a complex paraph. A superior display value is noted. His hand started to deteriorate in the early to mid–1780s. Signatures accomplished at this time evidence an unsteady appearance. Signatures accomplished after 1790 evidence a material shakiness of hand.

There is an ample supply of Hancock material in the market, including DsS as governor of Massachusetts. DsS as the president of the Continental Congress are far scarcer and have striking eye appeal. There are many bills of lading in the market that are usually signed in the text, sometimes with the last name only. The signatures that appear on these documents are more written than signed and generate only tepid demand. ALsS are much tougher to locate and should be considered rare on a per se basis. Unfortunately, many are signed with initials only. A nice, full-page ALS is highly treasured and commands a premium.

Hancock's signature is commonly forged. There is one forgery to note. There are many forged signatures in the market that are placed on portions of documents and title pages of books. The paper is irregularly cut and artificially distressed. These forgeries exhibit a paraph that is simple in construction and entirely different from one found under a genuine signature.

There is sound demand for Hancock material. His signature will sell for $3,000 to $4,000, DsS for not much more. A nice, full-page ALS will sell for $15,000 to $20,000. Bills of lading, with the name Hancock penned in the text, are quite affordable at $1,000 to $1,500.

Hancock-1, signature of the DOI.

The Articles of Confederation is a document shrouded in mystery and lore. Many often confuse it with that first great charter, the Magna Carta. Ratified in 1781, the AofC was an agreement among the 13 colonies to form a confederacy. The AofC was the first "constitution" of the United States. It was later scrapped in favor of the Constitution. Nevertheless, the AofC remains an important document. Forty-eight colonial representatives signed the AofC. Many names are familiar, such as John Hancock and Oliver Walcott. Others, such as William Clingan and Nathaniel Scudder, are obscure figures. Some of these signatures are very rare and seldom surface. There is a small but dedicated pool of collectors who collect AofC signers. Prices are very affordable, even cheap. In 2013,

an ADS by Virginia signer John Harvie sold on eBay for a mere $60. I do not believe a detailed study has ever been completed on AofC signers. Hopefully, someone will undertake that endeavor.

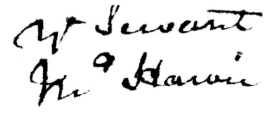

Harvie-1 DS circa 1790.

The Constitution and the Bill of Rights were written by men of great wisdom and foresight. They had the ability to craft doctrine that applied not only to the time for which they were written but also for future generations to be governed by. Some of the greatest minds in history were involved in the founding of the United States of America. It is not surprising that signatures of these men are highly treasured.

Save Washington, Benjamin Franklin is probably the most famous of these men. He was a diplomat, futurist, scientist, author, and visionary. Franklin was a true intellectual giant in world history. His image graces the $100 bill. His signature is highly treasured and quite valuable. His signature is bold and flourishing. It is almost always signed as "B. Franklin" with a complex paraph. Good eye appeal is noted. Franklin's signature is very scarce and is generally limited to DsS as president of the executive council of Pennsylvania. These are a wonderful source of Franklin's signature. ALsS do exist but are considered rare. The aforementioned DsS sell for $12,500 to $15,000. An ALS, with routine content, is valued at $25,000 to $35,000. Content letters are valued in the six-figure range.

The extreme value of Franklin material attracts the truly skilled forgers. There are some sophisticated forgeries in the market including ALsS and DsS complete with paper seal. Noted forger Joseph Cosey created many ADsS and ALsS of Franklin. He would usually add an endorsement of John Nicholson to the document. Many have stated Cosey's Franklin work product is well-executed. I personally don't see that, but to each his own. There are certain DsS, usually land grants, purportedly signed by Franklin as president of the executive council that are worth discussing. They are partly printed documents with a large paper star-seal affixed to the document with wax. They are signed as "B. Franklin" under the seal, as one would expect. Upon examination the signature appears labored and shaky. The line connecting the letters "k" and "l" is typically truncated. This signature lacks flow when compared to other DsS of the same or similar date. The hand almost appears childlike. I do not believe these documents are counterfeit. I do, however, believe that many of these documents were signed by someone other than Franklin, most likely a secretary. Franklin's signature should be studied carefully, as the deviation of hand is material when compared to a genuine specimen. Many of these documents are sold by auction companies, so caution is warranted.

Franklin-1, DS dated 1785 (courtesy Nate D. Sanders Auctions).

Franklin-2, undated signature.

Henry Laurens was a rice farmer turned revolutionary. He became the fifth president of the Continental Congress. Laurens signed in a flamboyant hand. The signature has good display value. The letters "y" and "L" are connected with an elaborate stroke. Signatures accomplished in the last few years of life evidence shakiness of hand. Generally, signatures of continental presidents are of little interest and value. Laurens seems to be an exception to the rule. His signature is very scarce to rare and is limited to ALsS and DsS. There is average demand for Laurens material. Values have actually declined over the years. I think as time goes by the memory of the Continental Congress will continue to fade. Laurens's signature is still valued at $300 to $400. ALsS will sell for around $1,000.

Laurens-1, undated signature.

Daniel Boone remains of one the biggest folk heroes in American history. As an explorer he opened up the Appalachians and "discovered" Kentucky. During the Revolution he was a daring militia officer. Boone signed in a nononsense hand. The signature is legible with average letter construction. Because the signature lacks complexity, replication of hand is easy. Well-executed forgeries exist in quantities. Just about all Boone signatures ever offered for sale are forgeries. Some are elaborate fake ADsS and letters. Genuine Boone material is an extreme rarity. There are forged contracts in the market, some on large, scalloped folios. They contain a forgery of Boone and sometimes a forgery of his wife. The forgery of his wife is signed with an "X," giving the appearance of illiteracy.

Another common forgery is holographic promissory notes on small octavo sheets. "I do promise to pay" or "I promise to pay" begins the text. The forger includes spelling errors in the text to give the semblance of genuineness.

The high demand for Boone's signature, coupled with a minute supply of material, pushes prices ever higher. His signature will sell for $7,500 to $8,000. An ALS or ADS, including land survey documents, will sell for more than $10,000; exceptional specimens are valued at $25,000.

Boone-1. undated signature.

Paul Revere was a noted smith, engraver, merchant, and businessman. He even dabbled in medicine. Revere gained immortality for his midnight ride warning of the advancing British Army. Some 40 years after his death, Revere's ride was set to poem by Henry Longfellow. Revere signed in an elegant and flowing hand. Sound letter construction is noted. A paraph completes the signature. Revere material is very rare on a per se basis. A restricted supply of ADsS and DsS exist. ALsS are extremely rare. Forgery is common with Revere material. Most signatures offered for sale over the past, say, 50 years are forgeries. I would say over 90 percent of market signatures are forged. There are many forged ADsS in the market. They are receipts for the sale of goods. Many are written to the "United State Navy Department" or "United States War Department." A forged signature is added below as "Paul Revere and Son.," or "Revere and Son." The forgery is rudimentary in construction and lacks the flow of a genuine signature. Forged ADsS and ANsS, usually involving payment, are common. Many are dated with just the year and contain a labored signature with an overly accomplished paraph. There are many short handwritten receipts in the market that are actually signed by Paul Revere's son, Paul Jr. His signature is similar to that of his famous father. There are many in the market, typically dated in the late 1700s to early 1800s. Many signatures sold as Revere's are actually

that of his son. The supply of forgeries actually depresses values of the genuine material. Revere's signature is highly treasured. Expect to pay $7,500 to $8,000 for a nice specimen. ALsS will sell for $20,000 to $25,000.

Revere-1, AES circa 1810.

Revere-2, signature of Paul Revere's son.

Ethan Allen was a man of many talents. He is remembered for his role in the capture of Fort Ticonderoga. He is also one of the founders of Vermont. Allen signed in a bold and clean hand. His signature is highly legible and exhibits good display value. Signatures are rare in all forms and are generally found on ADsS and the occasional ALS. His signature should be considered a significant acquisition. Allen's signature is commonly targeted by forgers. There is one forgery to discuss. The forgery contains a capital "E" in the first name with a long underscore that runs the entire length of the signature. The capital "A" in the last name is a large lower case "a." Genuine signatures feature an upper case "A" in the last name. A second forgery is added underneath to give the item a semblance of genuineness. The forger seems to favor "C. Mendenhall" or "Chas. Mendenhall," which is typically placed underneath the Allen forgery. The forgeries are rudimentary in construction and are exposed with little effort. There is strong demand for Allen material. The small supply correlates into good value. Expect to pay $4,000 to $5,000 for a nice specimen.

Allen-1, undated signature.

The Founding Father who was probably number one on George the III's hit list was Samuel Adams. Had America lost the war, Adams would have been the first to find his way to the gallows. Adams, the fourth governor of Massachusetts, signed in a pensive hand. His signature is clean with sound letter construction. It exhibits a certain jaggedness. Overall, a pleasing signature. Due to the slower nature of the signature, replication of hand is very easy. Well-executed forgeries exist, mostly as signatures removed from a document. Adams's signature is rare and almost always found on DsS as governor. Other mediums are very rare. There is strong demand for Adams material. Expect to pay $2,500 to $3,000 for the above-referenced DsS.

Adams, S-1, undated signature.

Corset maker turned journalist Thomas Paine was the most influential pamphleteer in American history. His work *Common Sense* remains one of the greatest writings ever. Paine signed in a legible and clean hand. Letter construction is sound. Signatures penned letter in life will exhibit a slight unsteadiness. Paine material is rare to very rare and in high demand. ALsS, some signed in the third person, are highly treasured. Overall, a signature of very restricted supply. It should be noted that forgeries do exist. Forged ALsS are in the market. In addition, forged bank checks also exist. These are typically signed as "Tho Paine." A thick linear paraph sometimes accompanies the forgery. Caution is warranted, as these checks are very

convincing. Paine material is highly treasured. His signature will likely sell for $7,500 to $10,000; ALsS sell from $15,000 and up.

Paine-1, undated signature.

America's most famous of traitors was General Benedict Arnold. There were essentially two reasons for his defection to the Tories. First, he believed that he had been passed over for promotion and was relegated to mundane jobs within the Army. Second, he thought America was going to lose the war. Arnold signed in a pleasing and legible hand. ALsS retain sound display value. Signatures are typically accomplished as "B. Arnold." The unassuming signature is enhanced by a flourishing paraph. The supply of Arnold material is restricted. Much of his writings, it has been said, were destroyed as a protest to his treachery. His signature is considered rare to very rare on a per se basis. Signatures are typically limited to ALsS and DsS. Due to the strong value, Arnold's signature is commonly targeted by skilled forgers. Forgeries exist in quantities. There is one forgery to note. One forger has produced an unknown number of DsS. These documents are receipts for the purchase or sale of goods (rope, planks, sugar, etc.). The handwriting is typically uneven and with misspaced words. The forgery is typically signed as "Accepted" or "Approved, B. Arnold." The letters are malformed, in particular the "ld" of the last name. The ink will have a faded and washed-out look. They are typically, but not always, inlaid to another sheet. Overall, an amateurish forgery. There is strong demand for Arnold material. Signatures are valued at $1,500. ALsS sell for $4,000 to $5,000. Content letters will likely sell for $15,000 and up. A significant American autograph.

George III ruled England from 1760 until his

Arnold-1, undated signature.

Arnold-2, undated signature (courtesy Mark Allen Baker).

George III-1, DS circa 1790.

George IV-1, DS dated 1812 as PR (courtesy Nate D. Sanders Auctions).

death in 1820. George led England through the revolution. George signed in a regal and legible hand. His signature exhibits good letter construction. The signature is large and bold. Signatures are accomplished as "George R." Earlier signatures, those penned in the 1760s and 1770s, tend to be smaller in scale and more compact. Signatures from the 1790s are fuller with large, sweeping strokes. In the early 1800s, King George's eyesight began to fail. Material signed post–1800 tends to be shaky with misspaced letters, evidencing the lack of sight. This form of signature is less attractive than earlier specimens.

In November 1810, King George's daughter Princess Amelia fell ill and died at the age of 27. Her death led to severe malady, from which the King never fully recovered. From 1811 until his death, King George was unable to discharge his royal duties. Post-1810 documents are secretarially signed for King George by George, Prince of Wales (later George IV). These are signed as "George PR." King George's signature is somewhat scarce but many appointments and documents signed as King are available. George's signature is affordable at $250. DsS can be purchased for around $500. ALsS are rare and are valued at $1,500 to $2,000. DsS by George IV are more affordable at $300 to $350.

British spy John Andre was captured while assisting Benedict Arnold in his attempt to surrender West Point to the British. Andre was tried and convicted of spying against the United States. For his efforts he was giving the rope on October 2, 1780. Andre signed in a neat and angled hand. Sound letter construction is noted. The signature has superior display value. Andre's signature is very rare on a per se basis. A few ALsS exist. Andre's signature is very expensive and one of the key signatures of the Revolution. Expect to pay $10,000 for a nice specimen. ALsS will sell for $20,000 and up.

Andre-1, undated signature.

The other famous British officer was Charles Cornwallis. He was one of the principal generals for the British. He is best remembered for surrendering to the American forces at Yorktown. Cornwallis signed in a slow and pensive hand. His signature is very legible with sound letter construction. Signatures are typically accomplished as "Cornwallis." Because the signature lacks reckless flow and is rudimentary in construction, replication of hand is very easy. Producing a well-executed forgery can be accomplished with minimal effort. Cornwallis's signature is scarce to rare. A restricted supply of DsS and ALsS do exist. As significant a figure Cornwallis is in British history, his signature is quite affordable. Signatures can be purchased for as little as $500. DsS and LsS can be purchased for $800 to $1,200. Many times, full-page ALsS can be purchased for under $1,500. I consider Cornwallis's signature to be undervalued.

Cornwallis-1, undated signature.

Scottish sailor John Paul Jones's heroics during the Revolution earned him the title of "Father of the United States Navy." He died at the young age of 45. Jones signed in a very odd hand. The letters exhibit uniformity. The capital letters are the same size as the lower case letters. The signature is somewhat illegible. If you were not looking for this signature you would pass it by. Jones material is very rare to extremely rare. A few ALsS and signatures removed therefrom exist, but that is about it. His signature has an estimated value of $10,000.

Jones-1, undated signature.

Anthony Wayne was an early militia leader. He was known to take bold, if not reckless, stands to fend off the British. His brashness earned him the nickname of "Mad Anthony." Wayne signed in a bold and powerful hand. Letter construction is fairly sound. The signature exhibits no point construction breaks. The signature is sometimes finished off with a paraph. Overall, a pleasing signature. Wayne's signature is rare on a per se basis. Signatures are typically found on ALsS, ADsS, and DsS. The rather complex nature of hand results in difficult replication. His signature is generally not the target of forgers. Expect to pay $700 to $800 for Wayne's signature. ALsS will sell for $2,000 to $2,500.

Wayne, A-1, undated signature.

The speech concluding "Give me liberty or give me death" immortalized Virginia governor Patrick Henry. He is remembered as one of the most influential of all colonial patriots. Henry signed in a bold hand. His signature is striking and evidences good display value. The signature is almost always accomplished as "P. Henry" with a linear paraph. Henry's signature is scarce but not rare. Due to his tenure as governor he signed many documents. These are the best source for Henry's signature. ALsS are rare. Some DsS as governor contain a secretarial sig-

Henry, P-1, ALS dated 1779 (courtesy Nate D. Sanders Auctions).

nature. See the third example below. Fortunately, secretarial signatures look nothing like a genuine signature. They are easily identified as fake. There is strong demand for Henry material. Signatures range from $900 to $1,100. DsS sell for $1,500 to $2,000. ALsS are highly treasured, so expect to pay $5,000 to $7,500 for a nice specimen.

Henry, P-2, undated signature.

Henry, P-3 common secretarial signature .

General Benjamin Lincoln was the man who accepted the British surrender at Yorktown. Lincoln signed in a heavy hand. His signature exhibits thick strokes of ink. It is an autograph that tends to dominate the medium it is placed upon. Signatures are typically signed as "B. Lincoln." Much controversy centers around Lincoln's autograph. His signature is generally limited to DsS, and that is about it. ALsS are very rare. There are many DsS, dated in the first couple of years of the 19th century. Lincoln signed these documents as collector of the Port of Boston and Charleston. They are typically countersigned by Thomas Melvill. The Lincoln signature on these documents deviates from known signatures on Massachusetts military appointments. The documents signed as collector exhibit a signature with mis-scaled letters. I have always believed that most documents signed as collector are secretarially

signed. I advise collectors to avoid them. Lincoln's signature can be purchased for $250 to $300, making it one of the more affordable Revolutionary War signatures.

Lincoln, B-1, undated signature.

One of the most controversial generals of the Revolution was Horatio Gates. He led the Americans to victory at Saratoga. He was often at odds with George Washington. Gates signed in a very pleasing and refined hand. His signature evidences superior letter construction and legibility. It is one of the nicer colonial era signatures. Gates's signature is surprisingly inexpensive given his stature. His signature is considered scarce but a decent supply of ALsS are in the market. Gates's signature sells for $250 to $300. ALsS are valued at $700 to $1,000.

Gates-1, undated signature.

The Swamp Fox, Francis Marion, was a militia officer during the Revolution. He defended South Carolina and used unconventional military tactics to drive the British Army nuts. Marion signed in a rather odd hand. The capital letters of the first and last name are connected. The signature is typically finished off with a complex paraph. Signatures are penned as "Fran. Marion." Marion's signature is very rare. It occasionally surfaces on DsS and ALsS. Marion signed in a slow and slightly labored hand. The signature lacks flow, thus replication of hand is easy. Well-executed forgeries exist in quantities. A common forgery is receipts for goods signed by Marion as general. A countersignature or two is also added to enhance authenticity. These forgeries are placed on narrow strips of paper that measure 8" to 9" in length and only an inch or two in height. His signature is a true rarity so expect to pay $4,000 to $5,000. ALsS should sell for at least $10,000.

Marion-1, undated signature.

General Nathanael Greene was one of the army's most capable of generals. He defended the Carolinas and forced Cornwallis's retreat. Greene signed in loose hand. Letters tend to blend together which impairs legibility. Replication of hand is fairly easy. Well-executed forgeries do exist as signatures purportedly removed from letters. Greene's signature is rare and in good demand. His signature will sell for $750. DsS are valued at $1,500 to $2,000. ALsS will sell for $4,000 to $5,000.

Greene-1, undated signature.

The French aristocrat Marquis de Lafayette received a commission as a major general from the Continental Congress. He served admirably under George Washington and returned to France a national hero. Lafayette signed in a compact and slightly choppy hand. Legibility is sound. Overall, a signature of average display. Lafayette had a long and distinguished political and military career. This correlates into a good

supply of signed material. His signature is scarce, albeit borderline. ALsS, LsS, DsS, and free franks are available at reasonable prices. Signatures sell for $400 to $500, franks for not much more. ALsS are valued anywhere from $1,500 to $2,500. A significant and undervalued Revolutionary War signature.

Lafayette-1, ALS dated 1834 (courtesy Nate D. Sanders Auctions).

Continental army officer Henry Knox became the first secretary of war under President Washington. Knox signed in a simple hand. Letter construction is sound. A strong display value is noted. Signatures are accomplished as "H. Knox." The capital letters "H" and "K" share a common stroke. Knox material is scarce and generally limited to LsS and free franks. Knox's signature is affordable. LsS and franks sell for $200 to $300. There are some excellent content letters in the market in which Knox begins the letter as "I am directed by the President of the United States." Content letters will sell anywhere from $1,000 to $4,000.

Knox-1, undated signature.

The Duel

Alexander Hamilton was the magazine cover for the Federalists. He is the father of the United States banking system. He served as the first secretary of the treasury. Hamilton signed in a rather plain and unattractive hand. Letter construction is average, as is display value. Most signatures are accomplished as "A. Hamilton." Hamilton's signature is scarce to rare. He was killed in a duel, so never made it to old age. Signatures are generally found on LsS, free franks, and the occasional ALS. Treasury department circulars are also available and make for a handsome display. It should be noted that forged ALsS are in the market. In addition, certain franks are secretarially signed. There is strong demand for Hamilton material. Expect to pay $1,250 to $1,500 for Hamilton's signature. LsS and circulars sell for $2,500 to $3,000. ALsS with good content will sell for more than $10,000.

Hamilton-1, undated signature.

Hamilton's nemesis was Jefferson's vice-president, Aaron Burr. The two men had a long-standing dislike for each other which boiled over in the summer of 1804, when Burr challenged Hamilton to a duel. On July 11 of that year the two met. Hamilton fired first and intentionally missed Burr. Hamilton was hit in the chest. He died the following day. It made Burr one of the skunks of American history. Burr signed in a compact and slightly cramped hand. The signature is plain and unassuming. Most signatures are signed as "A. Burr." A few documents, signed as an attorney, are accomplished as "Aaron Burr." There is a good supply of material in the market, especially bank checks. There is sound demand for his autograph but values are surprisingly low. Bank checks can be purchased for $500 to $600. Many full page ALsS are available for under $1,000.

Burr-1, undated signature.

The War of 1812

After the Revolution, tensions between the United States and Britain remained. British influence slowly started to creep back into American commerce. Border disputes with Canada were common. The British allied themselves with various Indian tribes that proved adversarial to the United States. Probably the biggest reason for the outbreak of war was the British royal navy's systematic impressment (that is, kidnapping) of American sailors. The war lasted a little over two years with America emerging victorious.

The War of 1812 has, in recent years, been relegated to footnote status. It is one of the forgotten wars that barely gets a mention. Unlike other wars, which produced many legendary heroes, the military leaders of the War of 1812 are obscure figures, at best. The most famous of them was neither American nor English, but Indian. Tecumseh, chief of the Shawnee nation, allied himself with the British. Another famous name, Andrew Jackson, hero of the Battle of New Orleans, is discussed in the Presidents chapter.

The leaders of the British are names known only to the hardiest of the war historians. Mention the names George Prevost, Isaac Brock, and Gordon Drummond and the response is typically a blank stare. Their signatures are collected by only a handful of collectors. American naval hero Commodore John Rodgers was a lifelong navy officer. Rodgers fired the first shot of the war. He also gained fame duking it out with pirates during the Barbary Wars. Rodgers's signature is rare and will occasionally surface on LsS. Nonetheless, the demand is muted. A signed letter can be purchased for under $250.

Rodgers-1, ALS dated 1820 (courtesy Navy Department Library).

Francis Scott Key was a lawyer and armchair poet. While aboard the HMS *Tonnant*, Key witnessed the bombing of Fort McHenry in September 1814. At dawn the American flag still flew over the fort. It inspired Key to write what is now the National Anthem. Key signed in an average hand. His signature is pleasing without ostentation. Signatures are scarce but not rare. Material signed during his tenure as an attorney exists in ample numbers. Many handwritten legal briefs will be signed multiple times in the text. Briefs are typically cut down and the signatures sold individually. ALsS are rare. There is one forgery to note. Many forged bank checks are in the market. They are typically dated between 1800 and 1810. The checks are drawn on the Bank of Columbia/Georgetown. The signature appears slightly labored and the paper too clean and bright. These have been floating around for years, so caution is warranted. Legal related signatures keep prices in check. A Key signature will sell for $500 to $600. A full page ALS will sell for $3,000 to $4,000.

Key-1, undated signature.

General Zebulon Pike was killed in action at the Battle of York. He is best remembered as the explorer Pike's Peak is named after. Pike material is rare and valued more as an exploration autograph than a military one. Signatures are typically found on endorsements, LsS, and DsS. ALsS are rare to very rare. His signature is value at $600 to $750. LsS and DsS are valued at $1,250 to $1,750. A highly desirable signature, it should not be confused with that of his father's Zebulon Pike, Sr., also a military officer.

Pike-1, DS dated 1799 (courtesy Nate D. Sanders Auctions).

Birth of a Nation—Texas

The Republic of Texas was founded in 1836. It remained an independent nation until December of 1845 when it was annexed by the United States. Material from the early days of Texas history is quite rare and highly collectable. Any writings associated with the Alamo are worth their weight in platinum. While there are many collectable signatures, the most sought after are the following.

David Burnet was the first president of Texas. His tenure was just a few months. Burnet signed in a nice hand. The signature evidences many fine curved strokes. His signature will sometimes have a paraph. Overall, a signature with good display value. Burnet material is scarce to very scarce. DsS as secretary of state for Texas are a good source for his signature. After his presidency, Burnet returned to the practice of law. There are many signed legal documents in the market, but there is a caveat. Many of these legal documents are secretarially signed. Secretarial signatures deviate greatly from the genuine specimen and are exposed with little effort.

There is good demand for Burnet material when compared against a restricted supply. Burnet's signature can be purchased for $500. DsS will sell for $1,000. ALsS are rare and are valued at $2,000 to $2,500.

Burnet-1 ALS dated 1836 (courtesy Texas State Library and Archives Commission).

Patriot and soldier Sam Houston was the hero of the Battle of San Jacinto. He served as the second and fourth president of Texas. He also served as the seventh governor after Texas became a state, but was removed from office for refusing to take the Confederate oath. He is one of the most significant figures in Texas history. Houston signed in a bombastic and flamboyant hand. It looks more like artwork than signature. His paraph is, perhaps, the most complex of all. It greatly enhances display value. Houston was known to use varying forms of paraph. Overall, a superior signature. Due to the complexity of hand, replication is very difficult. Well-executed forgeries do not exist. There are a certain number of forged signatures in the market. Some contain the word "free" above the signature. The forgeries tend to be on closely clipped and irregularly cut paper. They are signed in fresh black or blue ink that lacks proper toning. There

Houston-1, DS dated 1844 (courtesy Texas State Library and Archives Commission).

is strong demand for Houston material. Signatures will sell for $750 to $1,000. Signatures with striking paraphs can sell for as high as $2,500. Many DsS as governor exist and can be purchased for $1,500 to $2,500. Free franks sell for $1,500. ALsS vary in price from $3,000 to $6,000. Content letters can sell for more than $10,000. An important American autograph.

Mirabeau Lamar was a Texas politician with a deep love of poetry. He was the third president of Texas. His nephew Lucius Lamar served as an associate justice of the Supreme Court. Lamar signed in a legible hand. The signature evidences sound letter construction. Good display value is noted. Lamar's signature is very scarce to rare. LsS and government-issued bonds are a good source for Lamar's autograph. ALsS are rare to very rare. On occasion, Lamar's vice-president, David Burnet, would sign documents on Lamar's behalf. It should be noted that Texas currency is notorious for containing secretarial signatures of Lamar. Lamar's signature is valued at $600 to $800. LsS and bonds sell for $1,250 to $1,500.

Lamar, M-1 LS dated 1839 (courtesy Texas State Library and Archives Commission).

The fifth president of Texas was Anson Jones. Jones was a strong proponent of annexation. Jones signed in an angled hand. The signature evidences sound letter construction. The letter "s" tend to be exaggerated. The signature is finished off with a paraph. Signatures are rare and generally found on DsS (mostly Texas land grants) signed as president. ALsS are rare to very rare. Many are held by institutional concerns. Some secretarially signed documents are known. Because his signature is the rarest of all Texas presidents, signatures command a premium. Expect to pay $1,000 for a nice specimen. Land grants generally sell for $1,750 to $2,250.

Jones, A-1 LS dated 1845 (courtesy Texas State Library and Archives Commission).

William Barret Travis was a colonel in the Texas army. He was killed at the Alamo when he was only 26 years old. Travis material is very rare and limited to a handful of specimens. Like many other treasured American autographs, just about all Travis signatures in the market are forged. Forgeries come in all forms: ALsS, ADsS, and fragments thereof. One forger has created multi-page DsS and ADsS. The conclusion of the documents contain several signatures, including Travis, usually placed at varying points throughout. The appearance of non-uniformity is noted. The forgeries evidence a slightly labored appearance. Spurious ADsS will contain a forgery or forgeries in the text as "W.B. Travis" or "W. Barret Travis," in addition to a forgery at the conclusion of the document. These documents contain moderate and uneven brown toning. There is very strong demand for Travis material. His signature is valued at $10,000. ALsS will sell for $20,000 or more. Values are depressed, as many forged items have been sold as genuine. As such, the supply is wrongly inflated by forged material.

Travis-1, ALS dated 1836 (courtesy Texas State Library and Archives Commission).

Some historical figures gain mythical status. Davy Crockett is one such figure. He was a frontiersman, politician, and explorer. His valiant defense at the Alamo made him a legendary folk hero. Crockett signed in a legible and deliberate hand. The signature exhibits sound letter construction. Reckless flow is lacking. As such, his signature is relatively easy to forge. Well-executed forgeries exist in quantities. Just about 100 percent of all Crocket signatures ever sold are spurious. Crockett's signature should be considered very rare to extremely rare. A handful of DsS and ALsS exist. Many forged signatures purportedly removed from congressional franks are in the market, so caution is warranted. Crockett's signature is a gem of the industry. Expect to pay $15,000 to $20,000 for his autograph. ALsS will likely sell for $40,000 to $50,000.

Crockett-1 undated signature.

Empresario Stephen F. Austin brought the first Anglo settlements to Texas. For that he is known as the Father of Texas. Austin material is rare. His signature is generally found on ADsS, ALsS, and LsS. Many signatures are completed with a paraph. The majority of Austin material in the market is forged. Forged ALsS, ADsS, and receipts are in the market, so caution is warranted. Expect to pay $500 for his signature. ALsS and ADsS will sell for $1,000 to $2,000.

Austin, S-1, LS dated 1836 (courtesy Texas State Library and Archives Commission).

Stephen's father, Moses Austin, was granted land in Spanish Texas by Spain in 1821. He became the first American to receive such a grant. Austin signed in a rather flamboyant hand. A complex paraph enhances display value. Austin material is rare, rarer than that of his son. The occasional ADS and ALS will surface. There is one forgery to note. There are forged legal documents in the market. The content pertains to prisoner transfers, payment of bail, replevin, and the like. At the conclusion is a forgery of Austin next to a holographic seal. There is usually a countersignature or two. The forger prefers the names of John M. Smith, John L. Smith, Moses Bates, and/or John Scott. The forgeries evidence a slight shakiness of hand. Expect to pay $2,500 to $3,000 for an Austin signed document or letter.

Austin, M-1, ALS dated 1809 (courtesy Stephen Koschal Autographs).

Jim Bowie was a frontiersman, soldier, and patriot. He was also a part-time slave trader who played a key role in the founding of Texas. He was killed at the Alamo. Subsequent novels, movies, and other accounts have made him the stuff of legend. Bowie signed in a legible but rudimentary hand. The signature evidences a labored appearance. Substandard display value is noted. The signature is sometimes finished with an elaborate and sloppy paraph. Due to the hesitation of strokes, replication of hand is easy. Well-executed forgeries exist in quantities. Just about 100 percent of Bowie signatures ever transacted are forged. His signature should be considered very rare to extremely rare with only a handful of specimens known to exist. Signatures are typically found on LsS and that is about it. There are many forged signatures removed from documents in the market. In addition, forged holographic checks also exist. I have never seen a genuine bank check. Another common forgery is signed pay receipts or pay orders, which typically read as "Will you please pay Mr. John Doe…" There are probably fewer than ten genuine specimens in the open market.

His signature should sell in excess of $25,000. LsS are valued at $50,000.

Bowie-1, LS dated 1835 (courtesy Texas State Library and Archives Commission).

The 19th century produced some of the greatest statesmen in history, American or otherwise. As a nine-year-old I can remember sitting in the gallery of the U.S. Senate watching North Carolina Senator Jesse Helms railing against President Carter and the pending Panama Canal treaty. Watching democracy in action was, to me, a memorable event.

Congress has produced some truly great and memorable orators. While signatures of most congressmen and senators are of little value, there are exceptions.

Elbridge Gerry served in the house of representatives for two terms. He was vice-president under James Madison. Gerrymandering was named in his honor. He signed both the Declaration of Independence and the Articles of Confederation. Gerry signed in a plain and unassuming hand. What makes the signature stand out is the ridiculously long and complex paraph he sometimes added to the signature. Signatures are scarce. A small supply of DsS as governor of Massachusetts impairs rarity. There is good demand for Gerry material. Signatures will sell for $300 to $500. DsS are valued at $600 to $800. A full-page ALS will likely sell for $2,000.

Gerry-1, signature on DOI.

The Three Giants

One of my favorite Americans is, and will forever remain, Henry Clay. He represented Kentucky in both the House and Senate. He served as Speaker for three separate terms. He is best remembered as the architect of the Compromise of 1850. Clay's signature has always been undervalued for such a significant figure in U.S. history; his autograph can still be purchased for $100 to $125. Free franks are available for not much more. ALsS sell for $300 to $400. Many ALsS tend to be long and drawn-out. Multi-page specimens are highly treasured and will sell for $1,000 to $2,000. An important American autograph.

Clay-1 signature circa 1840.

Daniel Webster was another one of the 19th-century political giants. He and fellow Whig Henry Clay were instrumental in delaying the onset of war. Like Clay, Webster material is undervalued. Signatures can be purchased for as little as $75. Other mediums, including ALsS, sell anywhere from $200 to $250.

Webster, D-1, ALS dated 1851 (courtesy Nate D. Sanders Auctions).

John C. Calhoun had many positions in government. He has the rare distinction of serving as vice-president for two presidents. Due to his long tenure as a public servant, the supply of material is sound. Signatures can be found on many mediums including DsS, LsS, ALsS, and free franks. Calhoun's signature is very affordable. His signature on all mediums, including ALsS, can be purchased for under $200.

Calhoun-1, undated signature.

Powerful New York senator Roscoe Conkling was a kingmaker. He refused a Supreme Court appointment after the Senate had already confirmed him. He was a close ally of President Chester Arthur, a relationship that later soured over civil service reform. Conkling signed in a whimsical and somewhat geometric hand. It is one of the oddest of signatures. Signatures are typically found on album pages and the occasional frank for under $75.

Conkling-1 signature dated 1883.

Brother of General William Sherman, Ohio Senator John Sherman is best remembered for the Sherman Antitrust Act, which he authored. His signature is principally collected for that

Sherman, J-1, undated signature.

reason. His signature can be purchased for $30 to $40. Bank checks are valued at $75.

There are so many other collectable signatures from various eras of American history. Specimens from the 17th century and the centuries that followed will prove wonderful additions to any historical signature library.

The Blue and the Gray:
The Civil War

Wilson's Creek, Pea Ridge, Shiloh, Gettysburg, Vicksburg, Chickamauga, Bull Run, and Antietam. These are names that are forever burned into history. They represent the bloody clashes between the states, the American Civil War. The war officially began on April 12, 1861, when Confederate troops opened fire on Fort Sumter. The war, however, really began on election day 1860 upon the election of Abraham Lincoln as president. The war lasted a little over four years. It ended on June 22, 1865. When all was said and done, an estimated 650,000 Americans were killed. Another 425,000 were wounded in action.

The simple answer as to why the war was fought is "slavery." The real reasons are far more complex. States' rights, cultural sectionalism, and trade policies all pushed America to war.

The Civil War is one of the most important events in world history. It was also a turning point in how war was waged. The more formal line-to-line fighting, favored in earlier wars, was replaced by ambush and guerrilla-style warfare. Though the weaponry was still very much 19th century, the conflict was the first modern war in history. The popularity of the Civil War correlates into a huge pool of dedicated collectors. Civil War–related signatures are probably the most collected from any war, though World War II is gaining fast.

Signatures of the Confederates are in more demand and command higher prices. "Collecting signatures of generals of the Union is a far easier task than their counterparts in the CSA," writes Mark Allen Baker in *Advanced Autograph Collecting* (Krause Publications, 2000). The most valuable signature, on a per se basis, associated with the Civil War is assassin John Wilkes Booth. Other expensive signatures are William Quantrill, Thomas "Stonewall" Jackson, J.E.B. Stuart, Robert E. Lee, and any of the Lincoln conspirators, such as Mary Surratt or Dr. Samuel Mudd. Some of the conspirators' signatures are so rare that they have never been transacted in the open market. A signature of Willie Jett, for example, is a fine example of an extremely rare autograph, if one exists at all. As valuable as these signatures are, most other Civil War autographs are quite affordable. Signatures of many famous generals, other either side, can be purchased for under $100. A signature of Daniel Sickles, for example, a better-known general, can be purchased for as little as $50. Signatures

Sickles-1, ALS dated 1887 (courtesy Todd Mueller Autographs).

of Generals Daniel Butterfield, Joseph Hawley, Fitzhugh Lee, Henry Thomas, George Ruggles, Lorenzo Thomas, Randall Gibson, James Hardie, C.C. Washburn, Alvin Hovey, and the like can be purchased for well under $100, some as low as $20. A nice collection of Civil War generals can be assembled at a surprisingly low price.

Most civil war signatures, whether war-date or not, are of limited value. Marginal value keeps well-executed forgeries to a minimum. It is not worth a skilled forger's time to produce a signature of Sickles only to get $50 for it. Forgeries are typically limited to cabinet style photographs. There are, of course, exceptions: Ambrose Hill, Ulysses Grant, George Custer, Robert E. Lee, and William Sherman have always been the target of skilled forgers. Values of these signatures warrant the effort.

Here are some of the more collectable signatures of the Civil War.

The Gray

Pierre G.T. Beauregard is one of the better-known generals of the war. Born in Louisiana, he was given the nickname Little Creole. He was involved in many battles, including Bull Run and Shiloh. Beauregard signed in a wonderful hand. Just about all signatures omit the first initial of the name. They are signed as "G.T. Beauregard." Given the complex hand, replication is very difficult. Well-executed forgeries do not exist. Beauregard was a fairly big celebrity after the war and was targeted by early autograph collectors. As such, there is an ample supply of material in the market, although signed cabinet photographs are rare, albeit borderline. In addition, there is a large supply of bank checks in the market, which keeps values in check. For being such a big name, Beauregard's autograph is quite affordable. Signatures sell for $125 to $150. ALsS can be purchased for $400 to $500. Banks checks sell in the $250 to $300 range. A nice cabinet photograph is in demand;

therefore expect to pay $1,250 to $1,500. Overall, one of the more desirable Civil War autographs.

Beauregard-1, ALS dated 1864 (courtesy Nate D. Sanders Auctions).

Judah Benjamin was a senator from Louisiana. He served as secretary of war and attorney general for the Confederacy, thus making Benjamin the first Jewish cabinet member in American history. Benjamin signed in a flourishing hand. Large capital letters and a tailing paraph give the signature strong display value. Individual letters tend to blend together, thus impairing legibility. The marginal letter construction correlates into easy replication of hand. Producing a well-executed forgery can be done with ease. The supply of Benjamin material is rather limited. Shortly after the war he fled to England, where he remained until 1883, the year before his death. Once in England he was not a target of autograph collectors like other figures of the war. As such, his signature is scarce on a per se basis and generally limited to ALsS and C.S.A.-related DsS. Expect to pay $500 for Benjamin's signature. DsS sell for $1,000 to $1,500. ALsS are valued at $2,000 to $2,500.

Benjamin-1, undated signature.

Braxton Bragg was one of the top officers in the Confederacy. He was the lead commander in the western theater. He was a West Point man who made a name for himself in the Mexican War. Bragg signed in an aggressive hand. The signature displays itself as truncated. Letter construction is sound. The signature is usually finished off with a paraph, which enhances display value. One of the nicer Civil War signatures. A rather complex letter construction correlates into few well-executed forgeries. The supply of Bragg material is ample. The demand for his autograph is sound. Signatures are usually found on ALsS and small 64mo cards. Prices vary greatly for Bragg material. His signature can be purchased for $200 to $250. ALsS, with routine content, sell for as little as $500. Good content letters will sell for $2,500.

Braxton Bragg.
Genl C. S. A.

Bragg-1, undated signature.

Howell Cobb had a celebrated political career. He served five terms in the House and was Speaker from 1849 to 1851. Later he served as secretary of the treasury under James Buchanan. He was one of the founding fathers of the Confederacy. He briefly served as the first president of the C.S.A. Cobb signed in a straightforward hand. His signature evidences sound legibility and letter construction. Replication of hand would be fairly easy. The supply of Cobb material is ample. There are many free franks in the market, which keep prices reasonable. ALsS are also available. Signed cabinet

Howell Cobb

Cobb, H-1 wardate LS (courtesy Todd Mueller Autographs).

photographs are very scarce. Cobb's signature is very affordable. Free franks sell for $50. A full page ALS is valued at $150 to $200.

Samuel Cooper was one of the longer-serving officers in the military. His career spanned from 1814 until 1865. He served in the Mexican War and the Seminole war. He is the highest-ranking Confederate general. Cooper signed in a flowing and effortless hand. Most signatures are penned simply as "S. Cooper." Cooper is a forgotten name in American history. There is only marginal demand for his signature. Cooper's signature can be purchased for as little as $50 to $75, full-page ALsS for under $150. A nicely signed cabinet photograph is rare and valued at near $1,000. Be warned: there are many facsimile documents in the market. They are titled "General Orders, Washington Mach 15, 1853" and contain a facsimile Cooper signature.

S Cooper

Cooper, S-1, undated signature (courtesy The Sanders Autograph Price Guide).

Jefferson Davis was the first and only elected president of the C.S.A. He served many years in the United States military and gained fame in the Black Hawk War of 1832. Davis signed in a tight and concise hand. The signature evidences sound letter construction. Overall, a signature with good display value. Signatures accomplished in the last few years of his life evidence a slightly labored appearance. Given the rather complex nature of hand, replication is difficult. Well-executed forgeries are few and far between. It should be noted that Davis's wife, Varina, would often answer correspondence for her husband. She became rather good at replicating Jefferson's signature. Her secretarial signature evidences an ever so slight shakiness of hand. The letters are spaced a bit farther apart. The signature displays itself as looser than the genuine specimen. On many occasions she would place a period at the end of the signature. Davis's signature is typically found on ALsS, EsS, LsS, DsS, and the occasional bank check. Photographs of any kind are rare to very rare and most are forged. He served as secretary of war under President Franklin Pierce. Dual-signed documents by both men exist but are considered rare. There is strong demand for Davis's signature. A nice specimen is valued at $500 to $600. A free frank as senator can be purchased for $750. ALsS are valued at $3,500 to $5,000. One with good content is worth more than $10,000. A cabinet card is valued at $6,000 to $7,000. A bank check is valued at $1,250. The aforementioned Pierce/Davis DS is a treasure, so expect to pay $3,000 for a nice specimen.

Davis-1 undated signature (courtesy Nate D. Sanders Auctions).

Davis-2, ALS dated 1855 (courtesy Nate D. Sanders Auctions).

Davis-3, common secretarial by Varina Davis.

Davis-4, Common secretarial by Varina Davis.

Lieutenant General Jubal Early was commander of the Northern Virginia Army. He was a commander at many key battles, including Antietam, Gettysburg, and Chancellorsville. Early signatures are accomplished in an unstructured hand. His signature exhibits mal-

formed letters. It is almost always accomplished as "J.A. Early." In general, his hand is illegible. One of the less appealing Civil War signatures. Replication of hand is easy, so producing a well-executed forgery can be done with ease. Early is one of the tougher Confederate signatures to obtain. There is not much material in the market. Signed photographs are very rare. Expect to pay $500 to $600 for his signature. ALsS will likely sell for $1,500 to $2,000.

Early-1 signature circa 1880s.

Early-1, undated signature (courtesy The Sanders Autograph Price Guide).

Edward Elmore was a colorful character in American history. He served as the first treasurer of the C.S.A. He was also one of the last people to fight a duel in the United States. Elmore's signature is flamboyant and reckless in nature. It appears fast on paper and has superior eye appeal. Replication of hand would be difficult. Well-executed forgeries do not exist. Sig-

Elmore-1 DS dated 1861.

natures are very scarce to rare and generally limited to treasury documents. Other mediums are almost nonexistent. Hand-signed Confederate currency does exist, and higher-grade specimens can sell for many thousands of dollars. Some secretarial signatures do exist on bond receipts. Expect to pay $100 for his autograph. A nice DS will sell for $250 to $300.

Nathan Bedford Forrest is of great interest to collectors. Forrest was a cavalry commander with early successes at Sacramento and Fort Donelson. Forrest is, perhaps, best remembered as the first Grand Dragon of the Ku Klux Klan. Forrest signed in a flowing and uniform hand. Letter construction is poor and individual letters tend to morph into each other. The signature is illegible, but uniformity correlates into good display value. Forrest's signature is scarce. After the war he became president of the Selma, Marion, and Memphis Railroad Company. There is a small supply of corporate documents, mostly bonds, in the market. Were it not for these DsS, Forrest's signature would be quite rare. ALsS seldom surface and are in high demand. I know of no signed Klan-related material. Forrest's signature is valued at $500 to $600. The above-referenced railroad documents generally sell for $1,000 to $1,500. An ALS is a prize and a nice specimen should sell for $5,000 to $7,000. Content letters would easily be worth $10,000 or more.

Forrest-1, DS circa 1870.

Ambrose P. Hill was one of General Lee's most reliable of commanders. He distinguished himself at Bull Run and Cedar Mountain. He was killed at Petersburg at the age of 39. Hill signed in a flowing and pleasing hand. His signature evidences sound letter construction. The effortless strokes correlate into a signature with good display value. Creating a well-executed forgery would take some effort. Signatures are typically accomplished as "A.P. Hill."

Since Hill died at a young age, his signature is rare on a per se basis. Signatures are limited to the occasional endorsement and ALS. A photograph would be an extreme rarity. I have never seen a genuinely signed specimen, though many forgeries do exist. Hill's signature is valued around $2,000. A full-page ALS will sell for $10,000 or more. An exceptional war-date ALS sold for $22,500 (Christie's, 2009).

Hill-1, undated signature.

John Bell Hood is considered one of the top Confederate generals, despite his defeat in the Franklin-Nashville campaign. Hood signed in a nice and effortless hand. The signature evidences wonderful flow with thick bold strokes of hand. Letter construction and legibility are both sound. Bell's signature exhibits superior display value. Most signatures are accomplished as "J.B. Hood." The supply of Hood material is limited. ALsS and EsS do exist but in very limited quantities. Cabinet photographs are rare. The majority of EsS and LsS are secretarially signed. The secretarial signature is signed in a plain hand. It is vertical in nature, with no measurable slant. The strokes are thick and more methodic. Many exist so caution is warranted. They are exposed with little examination. There is sound demand for Hood's signature. It is valued at $500. ALsS sell for $1,500 to $2,000.

Hood-1, undated ALS (courtesy Stephen Koschal Reference Library).

Thomas "Stonewall" Jackson is almost a mythical figure of American history, and certainly one of its biggest names. He was a key commander for the Confederates. He was accidentally shot and killed by his own troops at Chancellorsville. Jackson signed in a practical and plain hand. Letter construction is sound. A good degree of legibility is noted. Signatures are usually accomplished as "T.J. Jackson." To my knowledge there are no signatures in existence signed with his nickname. Jackson's signature lacks complexity, hence replication of hand is very easy. Well-executed forgeries exist in quantities. More than 90 percent of Jackson signatures offered in the market are forgeries. Jackson's signature is rare on a per se basis. The supply of autographs is generally restricted to ALsS, LsS, and EsS. Most writings are military related. Signed photographs are an extreme rarity. I am told genuine specimens do exist, though I have never examined one. There are many forged ALsS and ANsS in the market and usually found on 8vo sheets or smaller. All are written in pencil. These writings have mundane content (e.g., refusing or accepting a dinner invitation). They are all accomplished by the same forger. I have seen quite a few of these forgeries and at least three specimens were addressed to a "Dr. Ross." They are usually dated with a slash mark (i.e., Oct 13/61). The forgeries are rudimentary in construction and are exposed upon cursory examination.

Another forgery that surfaces every now and then is full page ALsS. They are written on lightly lined paper and the text usually includes payment of money, such as "Pay to the order of John Doe the sum of two hundred dollars." Unlike a genuine specimen, this writing evidences a labored and somewhat shaky appearance. To add authenticity to the piece, the forger will draw lines through portions of the text and signature. The ink is either blue or black fountain pen. The ink appears fresh and lacks the subtle tones of vintage ink. I have seen these letters as either single pages or multiple pages. The forgeries are fairly well-executed, so careful examination is needed.

There is strong demand for Jackson material

when compared to a very restricted supply. Expect to pay $6,000 to $7,000 for Jackson's signature. A nice ALsS will sell in the $15,000 to $20,000 range; one with exceptional content is likely worth $40,000 to $50,000. A highly important military autograph.

Jackson, T-1, ALS dated 1855.

Albert Johnston fought in many wars. In addition to the Civil War, he was involved in the Mexican War, The Texas War for Independence, and the little-known Utah War. He was killed in April of 1862 at Shiloh. Johnston signed in a strikingly nice hand. The signature evidences effortless flow and finely constructed letters. Variant thickness in the strokes gives the signature an artistic look. Overall, a superior display signature. Given the complex and flowing structure of hand, replication is very difficult. Well-executed forgeries do not exist. Signatures are almost always found on ALsS or signatures removed therefrom. Photographs must be an extreme rarity. I have never seen a genuine specimen. Many forged cabinet cards exist; most possess a labored and amateurish forgery which is exposed with little effort. There is strong demand for Johnston's signature. Expect to pay $800 to $1,000 for his signature. ALsS sell for $2,500 to $3,000. Johnston is a significant American military autograph.

Johnston-1, undated signature.

Robert E. Lee is considered one the greatest of all American generals. When his home state of Virginia seceded from the Union, Lee followed. To this day he remains one of the biggest names in military history. Lee signed in a brief and choppy hand. The signature has good legibility and letter construction. An average display value is noted. Just about all signatures are penned as "R.E. Lee." Replication of hand is fairly easy. Well-executed forgeries exist in quantities. Signatures are generally found on ALsS, DsS, and bank checks. Other mediums are very rare. Signed cabinet photographs are an extreme rarity. Very few genuine specimens exist. Remember that Lee died in 1870, shortly after the war. He did not have a lot of time to honor autograph requests, especially on the relatively new medium of photographs. You will note there are countless signed cabinet photographs in existence but just about all of them are forgeries. The famous image featuring the floating head of Lee wearing a tie is a common target of one forger. Another commonly forged photograph is an octavo sized oval shaped image. It features Lee in military garb with a sword hanging to his left side. The forgery is usually placed right under the sword on a 45 degree upward angle. The ink is abnormally thick. I have never seen a genuine signed photograph of this image. There is another grouping of forged ALsS that needs to be discussed. Many years ago, forged ALsS entered the market and they appear to have the same M.O. They are written on octavo sized paper, with no letterhead. They are typically addressed to a fellow general and read something to the effect: "Gen'l. John Doe in Smithfield, N.C." The ink appears somewhat faded and slightly blurred. The forger will then artificially impair the paper by adding chip marks to the edges, soiling portions of the paper, and/or adding water stains to the ink. The forger makes a critical error by signing the letter without a closing salutation such as "Yours Truly" or "Truly Your Friend." I have examined many genuine Lee ALsS and all contain a closing line. The above-referenced ALsS do not. There is strong demand for Lee material that pushes prices ever higher. A signature is valued at $1,500 to $1,750. A nice full page ALS will sell for $4,000 to $6,000. One with good content has a value of at least $25,000.

Lee-1, undated signature (courtesy Nate D. Sanders Auctions).

James Longstreet was one of the most skilled generals of the war. He was known as Lee's War Horse. After the war he served as a U.S. marshal, then as U.S. commissioner of railroads. Longstreet signed in an average hand. The signature has marginal letter construction and display value. Longstreet's signature exhibits a certain sloppiness. A lack of precision is noted. Longstreet's signature would be rather easy to forge. Many well-executed forgeries exist in the market. It appears that many period secretarial signatures also exist. These are easily spotted as the signature has a noticeable left-leaning slant. Some authorities in the field have deemed this a variant signature. But I see nothing that resembles Longstreet's hand in this signature. I advise collectors to avoid them in total. Longstreet's signature is valued at $250 to $300. ALsS sell for $600 to $800, with some exceptional specimens crossing $1,000.

James Longstreet

Longstreet-1, undated signature (courtesy Todd Mueller Autographs).

John Mosby was a battalion commander. He earned the nickname the "Gray Ghost" for quick hit-and-run raids. After the war he served in the Grant administration. Mosby signed in an unstructured hand. His signature displays itself as somewhat sloppy. Letter construction is marginal, at best. Most signatures are signed as "Jno. Mosby." Given the lackluster construction, replication of hand is easy. Well-executed forgeries exist in quantities. Mosby's signature is very scarce on a per se basis and generally limited to ALsS or the occasional DS. Photographs are rare. There are forged cabinet photographs in the market. The forger likes using the words "Affectionately" or "Affectionate" in the inscription. There is very good demand for Mosby's signature when compared to a limited supply. Expect to pay $750 to $1,000 for his signature. ALsS, with routine content, can be purchased for $1,500 to $2,000. Content ALsS will sell for more than $5,000.

Mosby-1, undated signature (courtesy Sanders Autograph Price Guide).

Confederate General George Pickett is best remembered for Pickett's Charge at Gettysburg. It was an ill-conceived plan that proved disastrous for the South. Though Pickett was merely following orders, his name is forever associated with that fateful event. Pickett's signature is average in every respect. The letters tend to be slightly unstructured. The display value is marginal. Overall, an unassuming signature. Replication of hand is rather easy. Well-executed forgeries exist in quantities. His signature is rare. Only a restricted supply has survived to the present day. There is strong demand for Pickett's signature. I estimate a value of $1,500 to $2,000 for his signature. An ALS is likely valued at $6,000 to $8,000.

Pickett-1, undated signature.

Leonidas Polk was cousin to President James Polk. Before his military tenure he was a bishop in the Episcopal Church. For this he was known as the "Fighting Bishop." Polk signed in a very hesitant and plain hand. His signature tends to stall at points then picks up once again. There is average letter construction. A degree of legibility is noted. A signature of average display value. Many times he would simply sign his name as "L. Polk." Given the slower nature of his signature, replication of hand is easy. Producing a well-executed forgery can be accomplished with little effort. Polk was killed in action in 1864; hence, his signature is somewhat rare and highly desired. Because of this, most signatures offered in the market are forgeries. Signatures tend to be limited to ALsS. I have never examined a genuinely signed photograph. There is sound demand for Polk material. Expect to pay $500 to $750 for his signature. A full-page ALS is valued at $1,500 to $2,000.

Polk, L-1, document dated 1863 (courtesy Nate D. Sanders Auctions).

Alexander Stephens was vice-president of the C.S.A. He also served in the House before and after the war. Later, he was governor of Georgia from 1882 to 1883, the year of his death. Stephens's signature is average in every respect. Letter construction is sound but not ostentatious. Given the rather plain construction of the signature, replication would be fairly easy. Fortunately, there is not a lot of value associated with this signature; hence, it does not attract skilled forgers. There are no specific forgeries to note. There is average demand for Stephens material. I am surprised at how affordable his signature is. A signature can be purchased for $75. Full page ALsS sell for $200 to $300. Free franks as a congressman are valued at $150 to

$175. Signed cabinet photographs are rare, so expect to pay at least $1,000 for a nice specimen.

Stephens, A-1, free frank as MOC.

J.E.B. Stuart was one of the big three Confederate generals, along with Lee and Jackson. He was a career cavalryman and was a major figure in the capture of radical abolitionist John Brown. He was killed in action at the Battle of Yellow Tavern. Stuart signed in a flowing and rather nice hand. The signature is sound in every aspect. Fine letter construction is noted. It is one of the nicer civil war autographs. Stuart's signature is rare on a per se basis and limited to ALsS, DsS, and EsS. Bank checks are extremely rare. There is a group of forged ALsS in the market. The content is military-related and generally written to another officer. The forger will underline multiple words in the text of the letter. This feature is not dispositive of forgery, as Stuart was known to employ this method while writing. The writing will evidence a slight shakiness of hand, something a genuine Stuart signature will not exhibit. Most signatures offered in the market, over 90 percent, are forgeries, so caution is warranted. There is strong demand for Stuart material when compared to a very restricted supply. Values of Stuart material continue to increase at a steady pace. Expect to pay $3,500 to $4,000 for his signature. ALsS are valued at $10,000 to $15,000. Military content ALsS are valued in excess of $25,000. A significant American autograph.

Stuart-1, ALS circa 1860.

Fightin' Joe Wheeler has the distinction of being the only Confederate general to later serve as a general in the United States army during wartime. After the war he served nine terms as a congressman from Alabama. Wheeler signed in a flowing hand. The signature appears compact. Letter construction is average at best, as some letters appear as mere strokes. Well-executed forgeries are rare simply because values do not warrant the effort. The supply of Wheeler material is sound. He signed many items as a congressman. His signature exists on ALsS, DsS, calling cards, and bank checks. Photographs are scarce, but some were signed in 1890s until his death in 1906. There is good demand for Wheeler material which is balanced with supply. Expect to pay $75 to $100 for a signature. ALsS will sell for $150 to $200. Photographs are valued at $300 to $400.

Wheeler-1, ALS dated 1899 (courtesy Todd Mueller Autographs).

The Blue

Nathaniel Banks was appointed a general by Lincoln but is best remembered as the 25th Speaker of the House of Representatives. Banks signed in a busy and confused hand. The signature displays itself as jagged at times. The signature looks compact. There is not much demand for Banks material. The ample supply keeps prices affordable. Signatures are typically found on ALsS. DsS as governor of Massachusetts are also available. Cabinet photographs are scarce. Given the modest value of Banks material, well-executed forgeries are few and far between. Just about all signed items are available for $250 and under. Cabinet photographs are valued at $400 to $500.

Don Carlos Buell was a major general who

Banks, N-1, signature circa 1860.

fought in the Seminole War, the Mexican War, and the Civil War. Buell signed in a pleasing hand. The signature evidences sound letter construction with excellent display value. Signatures are almost always accomplished as "D.C. Buell." There is a good supply of material in the market, though cabinet cards are very scarce. Given the affordable nature of the signature, it is not the target of skilled forgers. Signatures can be purchased for as little as $50. ALsS sell for a mere $150. A cabinet card will likely sell for $500 to $600. -

Buell-1 signature dated 1885 (courtesy Todd Mueller Autographs).

Ambrose Burnside was a man of many talents. As a general he had many successes on the battlefield. He was the first president of the National Rifle Association. Burnside signed in a vertical hand. The signature is choppy with marginal letter construction. The signature is basically illegible. Display value is substandard. There is an ample supply of Burnside material in the market. Signatures can be found on ALsS, DsS, calling cards, and stock certificates. Cabinet photographs are very scarce. There is marginal demand for Burnside material, which keeps prices in check. A signature can be purchased for $75. ALsS are affordable at $300 to $400. A cabinet card is valued at about $1,000.

Burnside-1 undated signature.

Benjamin Butler was lawyer turned politician turned Civil War general. He was appointed general for political reasons. His lack of military experience made him one of the most feckless generals in American history. Butler signed in a rapid and somewhat sloppy hand. Letter construction is marginal at best. Most signatures are penned as "Benj. F. Butler." Overall, an average Civil War signature. There is a strong supply of material in the market. Mediums include ALsS, DsS, TLsS, and a seemingly unending supply of bank checks. Photographs of any kind are scarce. Butler's signature can be purchased for $50. ALsS, TLsS, and bank checks sell for $100 to $150. His signature can be procured with ease.

Butler-1, TLS dated 1885 (courtesy Nate D. Sanders Auctions).

Joshua Chamberlain performed gallantly at Gettysburg, for which he received the Medal of Honor. He had the distinction of presiding over Lee's surrender at Appomattox. He later served as governor of Maine. He lived until 1914, making him one of the last surviving generals of the war. Chamberlain signed in a flowing and rapid hand. A material right slant is noted. Letter construction is fairly sound, though some letters blend together, albeit slightly. Overall, a pleasing signature with good display value. Replication of hand is fairly difficult, so well-executed forgeries are very limited. Fortunately for collectors, Chamberlain's position as governor gave him the opportunity to sign many documents. These are an excellent source for his signature. Many state-issued pension documents exist. He also signed a handful of stock certificates, which make for a colorful display. There is also a good supply of bank checks in the market. ALsS are scarce and highly desirable. Cabinet photographs are rare to very rare. There is sound demand for Chamberlain material. His signature sells for $400 to $500. Bank checks and DsS are affordable at $600 to $700. A full page ALS will sell for around $2,500.

Chamberlain-1, DS circa 1870 (courtesy Nate D. Sanders Auctions).

Fellow Michigander George Armstrong Custer was a cavalry commander. He was a West Point man who graduated last in his class. He had many successes, but these were overshadowed by the Battle of Little Bighorn, where Custer made his last stand. To this day, Custer remains one of the most famous military officers in American history. Custer signed in a bold and flowing hand. His signature evidences thick lines and it dominates the medium it is placed upon. A sound letter construction is noted. Display value is superior. Overall, one of the nicer Civil War signatures. His signature is scarce and generally limited to ALsS and military-related documents. Front-signed photographs are an extreme rarity. There is a small supply of hand-addressed envelopes in the market written by Custer to his wife, Libby. They are addressed as "Mrs. Gen'l Custer." At $1,000 they make for an affordable alternative to his signature. Custer's signature is difficult to replicate. Producing a well-executed forgery would take some effort. Having said that, skilled forgers have taken up the task due to extreme value. Forgeries can be found on ALsS, cabinet photographs, endorsements purportedly removed from a larger folio, and the like. There are forged bank checks in the market drawn on the Planters National Bank. The demand for Custer material is great and clearly outweighs a restricted supply. Custer's signature will sell for $3,000 to $4,000. A full-page ALS is valued at

$15,000 to $20,000. A letter with historical content would likely be valued at $75,000 to $100,000. Bank checks are very rare, so expect to pay $12,500 to $15,000 for a nice specimen. A very significant and important American autograph.

Custer-1, undated signature.

John Dix was a man of many talents. He was a governor and senator representing New York. He served as secretary of the treasury in the Buchanan administration. He served as a major general in the Union army. Dix signed in a busy and rapid hand. Letter construction is fairly sound. The letter "x" tends to morph into a muted paraph, resulting in a signature with good eye appeal. There is a good supply of material in the market, including ALsS and DsS. Many signatures can be found on documents Dix signed as a commissioner of the New York canal fund. Cabinet photographs are scarce. Dix's signature can be purchased for $50. DsS are available at $150. ALsS are valued at $250 to $300. An undervalued signature.

Dix-1, bank check circa 1870.

Neal Dow was the mayor of Portland, Maine. He is known as the "Father of Prohibition." During the Portland rum riot of 1855, Dow used deadly force to quell the rebellion. When the war broke out, Dow was appointed a colonel in the Maine infantry. Dow signed in a confined hand. His signature is small in scale and average in construction. The signature evidences good legibility. An average display value is noted. Replication of hand would be very easy. Creating a well-executed forgery can be accomplished with little effort. Given the affordable nature of Dow material, his signature is not the target of skilled forgers. Signatures can be found mostly on ALsS and small calling cards. Photographs are rare. Since he has a strong association with the temperance movement, there is decent demand for his autograph. Dow's signature can be purchased for $100. ALsS are valued at $200 to $300.

Dow-1, signed card dated 1892.

David Farragut was an admiral for the Union. During the Battle of Mobile Bay, he uttered those now immortal words: "Damn the torpedoes, full speed ahead!" Farragut signed in a flowing and somewhat sloppy hand. Signatures are usually penned as "D.G. Farragut" and finished off with a paraph. There is good demand for Farragut material. Signatures are found on ALsS, DsS, and cabinet photographs signed on the verso. His signature is modest in value; hence, well-executed forgeries are limited to photographs. Farragut's signature can be purchased for $200 to $250. ALsS are valued at $400 to $500. Front-signed cabinet photographs sell in the $1,500 range.

Farragut-1, undated signature.

Oliver Howard was a Union general and a Medal of Honor recipient. His troops called him the "Christian General" due to his deep religious beliefs. Howard signed in a clean and legible hand. Strong letter construction is noted. Most signatures are accomplished as "O.O. Howard." There is an ample supply of

Howard material in the market. Demand is, at best, average. Given the modest value of his signature, Howard's signature is generally not the target of skilled forgers. Expect to pay $75 to $100 for his autograph. ALsS sell for about $250.

Howard, O-1, signature dated 1871 (courtesy Todd Mueller Autographs).

George McClellan served as general-in-chief of the Union Army. He ran for president in 1864, but lost in a landslide to President Lincoln. McClellan signed in a complex and flowing hand. His signature exhibits large letters. Legibility and construction are marginal. The display value is above average. Forgeries are generally limited to cabinet photographs. A commonly forged image has McClellan in full uniform with his hand behind his back. There are many in the market, so caution is warranted. McClellan's signature can be purchased for $100. ALsS are valued at $300 to $400. Cabinet cards are quite scarce and should sell for $1,250 to $1,500.

McClellan-1, undated signature (courtesy The Sanders Autograph Price Guide).

George Meade was a lifelong military officer. He fought in the Mexican War and the Second Seminole War of 1835. He defeated Lee at Gettysburg. Meade signed in a practical hand. The signature exhibits good flow. Letter construction is sound and lacks ostentation. Overall, an average signature with fair display value. Replication of hand would be fairly easy. Producing a well-executed forgery can be done with little effort. Skilled forgers, for the most part, do not target Meade's signature simply because of limited value. Signatures can be found on ALsS, DsS, and cabinet photographs. Forgeries are generally limited to cabinet photographs. A common forged image shows Meade formally posed in uniform and holding his hat by his waist. There are many in the market, all created by the same forger. Supply and demand for Meade's signature is well-balanced. Meade's signature is affordable at $150 to $200. ALsS sell for $400 to $500. Cabinet photographs are scarce and sell in the $1,000 range.

Meade-1, undated signature (courtesy Todd Mueller Autographs).

David Porter was a longtime naval officer. Porter signed in a rather unassuming and plain hand. There is nothing extraordinary to note about the autograph. Letter construction tends to be slightly impaired, resulting in malformed letters. Porter's signature can be found mostly on ALsS and LsS. DsS also exist, but the supply is limited. Cabinet photographs are scarce. For being such an important figure in American naval history, Porter's signature does not generate much attention. A signature can be purchased for $50 to $75. ALsS and cabinet photographs sell for $200 to $300. One of the more affordable Civil War autographs.

Porter-1 LS circa 1885 (courtesy Todd Mueller Autographs).

Known as "Old Fuss and Feathers," Winfield Scott was the longest-serving general in American history. He served from the War of 1812 to the Civil War. He was the architect of the Anaconda Plan to choke off supplies to the Confederacy. Scott's signature is available on letters and small cards. Signed photographs are scarce and most offered for sale are forged. Scott was targeted by collectors of the day; hence, there is a good inventory of material. Letters can be purchased for $250 to $300. Photographs sell for $600 to $700.

Scott, W-1, DS circa 1840 (courtesy Nate D. Sanders Auctions).

A confidant of Grant, Philip Sheridan, a cavalry general, defeated the Confederates at Shenandoah. Like General Sherman, he was a strong believer in the scorched-earth policy of burning down civilian towns in the South. His siege of Shenandoah is referred to as "The Burning." Sheridan signed in an aggressive and heavy hand. The signature evidences bold strokes. Letter construction is fairly sound as is display value. Most signatures are accomplished as "P.H. Sheridan." On occasion, Sheridan would write in a hurried hand. This form of signature is sloppy and individual letters are reduced to mere bumps. The resulting signature has poor legibility. There is a good supply of Sheridan material in the market. Many ALsS, LsS, and signatures removed therefrom are available. There is also a good supply of bank checks in the market. Signed cabinet photographs are somewhat scarce, but he did sign a limited number in the 1880s. Forgeries are generally limited to cabinet photographs. Sheridan is a rather pedestrian signature. Values have remained relatively constant over the years. A signature is valued at $125 to $150. ALsS and bank checks will sell for $400 to $600. Cabinet photographs can reach $1,000, but many will sell for $500 to $600.

Sheridan-1, undated signature.

William Sherman was an accomplished military strategist and fought in many key battles of the war. He is best remembered for his take-no-prisoners style of warfare against the South. His brutal march through Atlanta is well remembered to this day. Sherman signed in a flowing hand. The signature is dominated by large capital letters. Letter construction is marginal, which results in impaired legibility. Signatures penned in the last few years of life will evidence noticeable shakiness of hand. The hand is relatively unstructured; hence, replication is easy. Many well-executed forgeries exist in the market. Signatures can be found on calling cards, EsS, ALsS, LsS, and war-date DsS. There is a good supply of bank checks in the market. These are an affordable source of Sherman's signature. Signed photographs are rare. There are countless examples in the market, but most, over 90 percent, are forgeries. There are many E. & H.T. Anthony cabinet photographs in the market that bear a forged signature that reads "W.T. Sherman, Lt. Genl." There is strong demand for Sherman material. Fortunately for collectors, there is a good supply of letters, documents, and checks. Sherman's signature is valued at $250 to $300. Checks can be purchased for as little as $350 to $400. ALsS will sell for $800 to $1,200. Signed cabinet photographs will sell for $1,500. Values of photographs are depressed due to all the forged photographs in the market.

Sherman-1, signature circa 1870.

Sherman-2 ALS Dated 1889 (courtesy Todd Mueller Autographs).

Congressman Thaddeus Stevens of Pennsylvania was a member of the radical Republican faction of the House of Representatives. He was a driving force behind the impeachment of President Andrew Johnson. He went to his grave still fighting the war. Stevens signed in a sloppy and unstructured hand. The signature evidences malformed letters and displays itself as a scrawl. Display value is poor. Though scarce, Stevens material is quite affordable. A signature can be purchased for $50 to $75. ALsS sell for under $300. Signed cabinet cards are rare and many forgeries exist. A genuine cabinet photograph is valued at $600 to $700.

Stevens, T-1, undated signature (courtesy Todd Mueller Autographs).

Another Republican congressman was newspaper editor Horace Greeley. He was closely aligned with Stevens. Greeley signed in a loose and sloppy hand. The signature has average display value. His handwriting is sloppy and ALsS take some effort to read. Greeley material is very affordable. ALsS sell for about $100 to $125. Cabinet cards are scarce to rare and will sell for around $400.

Greeley-1, undated signature (courtesy Todd Mueller Autographs).

General John Wool has the distinction of being the oldest general serving during the war. A lifelong military officer, he also served back in the War of 1812. There is nothing extraordinary about Wool's signature. The hand is flowing with a slight choppiness noted. Letter construction and legibility are both average. There is an ample supply of material in the market. His signature can be found on many DsS, ALsS, and EsS. Cabinet photographs are scarce. Signatures of Wool tend to be affordable at $50 to $75. ALsS will sell for $250 to $300.

Wool-1, undated signature.

Lincoln's Cabinet

Lincoln was such a giant in American history that signatures of members of his cabinet are collectable and much more valuable than signatures of cabinet members of other administrations. Cabinet members of, say, Presidents Buchanan or Polk are far less collected. The Lincoln cabinet is a good way to assemble many significant Civil War autographs at an affordable price.

Edwin Stanton is a fine example. After the war, he remained as secretary of war for President Johnson. When Johnson tried to dismiss Stanton, it led to Johnson's impeachment. Stanton's signature is also popular in the Supreme Court genre. He was confirmed as an associate justice but died four days after confirmation. He was also the driving force in the Lincoln conspiracy trial. Eager to obtain convictions, Stanton committed witness tampering to obtain testimony necessary for conviction. His signature is well-constructed and affordable. A nice specimen can be purchased for $100. Nicer war-date DsS will sell for $400 to $500. Signed cabinet photographs are valued between $400 and $500.

Stanton-1, signature circa 1865.

Gideon Welles was secretary of the navy from 1861 to 1869. Like Stanton, he also served two presidents. He bolstered the navy, which enabled effective blockades of the South. Welles signed in a flowing and pleasing script. Letter construction is sound. Overall, one of the nicer Civil War autographs. There is an ample supply of signatures in the market, most notably bank checks. Most letters are LsS. ALsS are very scarce. Signed cabinet photographs are rare and seldom surface. Most mediums can be purchased for under $200. A cabinet photograph is valued at $500 to $600.

Welles-1, undated signature (courtesy Todd Mueller Autographs).

William Seward served as secretary of state for both Presidents Lincoln and Johnson. On the night of April 14, 1865, Lincoln conspirator Lewis Thornton Powell gained entry into Seward's home and stabbed him repeatedly. Seward's signature is average and unassuming. Display value is limited. His signature generates marginal demand. Signatures can be found on ALsS, LsS, and DsS. Cabinet photographs are rare. Signatures are available for $75 to $100.

Seward-1, ALS dated 1846 (courtesy Nate D. Sanders Auctions).

Other mediums are generally under $250. Cabinet photographs rarely surface and sell for close to $1,000.

Hannibal Hamlin was the 15th vice-president of the United States. He also served as congressman and senator from Maine. Hamlin signed in a confined and small hand. It appears almost feminine. Many times he would sign as simply "H. Hamlin." The slower nature of the hand results in easy replication. Producing a well-executed forgery can be done with ease. Fortunately, there is not much value associated with his signature. Signatures and franks sell for $50 to $75. ALsS are valued at $150 to $250. Hamlin was bombarded with requests from collectors asking for a signature of his boss, President Lincoln. There are many ALsS in the market in which Hamlin responds that he has no signatures of Lincoln. These are fine association items.

Hamlin-1, undated signature (courtesy Todd Mueller Autographs).

Simon Cameron served a secretary of war for about a year, then resigned over a corruption scandal. After the war he returned to the United States Senate. Like that of Hamlin, there is marginal demand for Cameron's signature. Signatures can be purchased for $50. ALsS and franks for not much more. It should be noted that some franks are secretarially signed.

Cameron-1, ALS dated 1877 (courtesy Stephen Koschal Reference Library).

Other Notables

One of the great sleeper signatures is that of Reverdy Johnson. He was a diplomat, senator, and attorney general in the Taylor administration. He is also remembered as the attorney of record in *Dred Scott v. Sanford*. He also represented Lincoln conspirator Mary Surratt. Johnson's signature is very affordable. Signatures can be purchased for a mere $25. ALsS at $50 to $75. Given his association with so many famous trials, his signature should command more money. Johnson's signature could be a good investment in the years to come.

Johnson, R ALS circa 1860.

John T. Ford became an accidental footnote in American history. He owned Ford's Theatre, where President Lincoln was assassinated. Ford signed in a hurried hand. Letter construction is marginal. Most signatures are signed as "J.T. Ford." Signatures are rare and generally limited to a restricted supply of ALsS, usually with routine or business content. Expect to pay $800 to $1,000 for an ALS.

Ford, J-1, ALS dated 1883 (courtesy Nate D. Sanders Auctions).

Joseph Holt was a close political ally of president Buchanan and served as his secretary of war. He served as judge advocate general of the army and presided over the Lincoln conspiracy trial. For this, his signature is collectable. Holt signed in a simple hand. There is not really much to the autograph. Most signatures are accomplished as "J. Holt." Signatures signed later in life are penned in a labored and infirmed hand. Holt's signature is affordable at $50. ALsS can be purchased for $100 to $150.

Holt-1 DS dated 1874.

Stephen Douglas was the Democratic nominee for the 1860 presidential election. He is best remembered for the Lincoln-Douglas debates and as the architect of the Kansas-Nebraska Act. He died in 1861 at the young age of 48. Douglas signed in a relatively unstructured hand. Impaired legibility is noted. A signature of average display value. There is good demand for Douglas material primarily because of the Lincoln association. Signatures are considered uncommon but not scarce. ALsS, LsS, and free franks exist in good quantities. Franks are the most affordable at $150 to $200. LsS are valued at $300. ALsS will sell for $400 to $500.

Douglas, S-1, undated signature.

One of the best-known abolitionists was Frederick Douglass. After the war, Douglass opened a newspaper which later failed. He later was appointed the recorder of deeds for the District of Columbia. Douglass signed in a bold and choppy hand. His handwriting is similar to that of Admiral Erich Topp. His signature displays itself as truncated with sharp lines. Letter construction and display value are average. Signatures are typically found on ALsS, album pages, and the occasional TLS. Photographs are

very rare. There are many minefields associated with this signature. Most ALsS in the market are actually written and signed by someone other than Douglass, most likely a family member. The handwriting is less flamboyant than a genuine specimen, almost dainty in appearance. The handwriting looks nothing like Douglass's hand, yet many are still sold as genuine. Many documents are secretarially signed. There is a strong supply of deeds of trust signed by Douglass as recorder in the market. There must have been thousands signed. Be warned, just about all of these documents were filled out and signed by secretaries who did a fairly decent job of copying Douglass's hand. A deed containing a genuine Douglass is a true rarity. Unless one is well versed in Douglass's hand, deeds should be avoided in total. There is sound demand for Douglass material. A signature will sell for $400 to $500. ALsS are valued at $3,000 to $4,000. Exceptional specimens will sell for $7,500 to $10,000.

Douglass, F-1, ALS circa 1880.

Douglass, F-2, common secretarial as recorder.

And then there is John Brown, an ardent abolitionist and terrorist who believed violence was necessary to end slavery. He was known to have killed many slavery supporters. He is best remembered as the man who led an unsuccessful raid on the federal armory at Harpers Ferry. For his efforts he was convicted of high treason against the United States and on December 2, 1859, was hanged. Brown signed in a very plain and deliberate hand. He wrote his name more than he signed it. Letter construction is sound. A high degree of legibility is noted. Unfortunately, replication of hand is very easy. Well-executed forgeries exist in quantities. Brown's signature is rare and generally found on ALsS or signatures removed therefrom. A common forgery is found as a check endorsement. The forgery is either signed in ink or in pencil. The forgery is placed on a clipped portion of a generic period check. These are common. There are also many forged signatures penned as "Your Friend, John Brown," an inscription ill-suited for the mid–19th century. Expect to pay $750 to $1,000 for Brown's autograph. A full-page ALS will likely sell for $5,000 to $7,000.

Lincoln signed in a choppy and rather unattractive hand. Demand for Lincoln's signature exists simply because he is Abraham Lincoln's son. His signature is rather affordable at $100. Bank checks and TLsS will sell for about $200 to $250. There are a certain number of letters in the market with President Lincoln content; these can sell anywhere from $1,000 to $5,000. Signed photographs are rare and are typically signed on the verso. There is an image of Robert Todd, in military uniform, pictured with his family. A few signed images exist. Robert Todd was never photographed in uniform. It is an altered image and was never signed by Lincoln. Overall, a signature of average demand.

Brown, J-1 undated signature.

Robert Todd Lincoln was the only son of President Lincoln to survive into adulthood. He served as a captain for Grant's staff. He became secretary of war under James Garfield.

Lincoln, R-1 undated DS (courtesy Todd Mueller Autographs).

A World at War:
World War I and World War II

The drums of war were, for many decades, banging at a slow and steady pace. By 1910 the die had been cast and war was inevitable. Three principal events led to the outbreak of the war to end all wars. The first can be dated back to the Franco-Prussian War of 1870. Germany annexed the French territories of Alsace and Lorraine. For years following the war, French resentment towards Germany grew. The calls to forcibly take back the provinces grew louder as 1914 approached. Another act of annexation also moved Europe closer to war when Austria-Hungary claimed title over Bosnia and Herzegovina in the Balkan escarpment. Finally, a naval arms race between Germany and Britain at the turn of the 20th century resulted in massive buildup of naval power between the two nations with the U-boats and Admiral John Fisher's dreadnoughts leading the way. The fact that the Turkish government was, at this time, slaughtering Armenian Christians en masse in the name of Islam didn't help the situation, either.

On June 28, 1914, Austrian Archduke Franz Ferdinand and his wife, Sophie, Duchess of Hohenberg, were assassinated in Sarajevo. One month later, on July 28, 1914, Europe was plunged into war.

World War I was a war unlike any other war up to that time. It saw the use of the tank, the airplane, and the modern-day machine gun. The war also gave birth to one of most feared weapons in history—poison gas. On April 22,

1915, at the battle of Ypres, the German army used chlorine gas on the British with frightening results. Less than two years later, the far more lethal mustard gas made its debut. World War I was the first war where technology showed its true power. Machines transformed warfare into a global conflict that had the ability to quickly spread across continents. Battles, for the first time in history, raged in the skies over Europe. The art of mass killing was neatly perfected during that great war. Technological advancement has no greater an ally than warfare.

World War I also made legends of many men. Many great tactical field marshals, on both sides of the conflict, earned a permanent spot in military history. Great acts of heroism from men like Seargent York still resonate to this very day. And, of course, those pioneer flyboys and the dogfights over Europe are the stuff of legend. World War I has proved a treasure trove for the autograph collector. There are hundreds of collectable names, too many to mention here. The following is a list of the more popular figures.

America

Woodrow Wilson was president from 1912 to 1920. He was a two-term president and led the United States through the war. He was a strong proponent of the ill-fated League of Nations. Wilson's signature study can be found in the chapter on presidential autographs.

81

Perhaps no name is more associated with early air combat than Captain Eddie Rickenbacker. His 26 kills are the most recorded by an American ace in World War I. After the war he became president of Eastern Airlines. Rickenbacker signed in a very unique and choppy hand. His signature has good eye appeal. Rickenbacker was a willing and gracious signer his entire life. Today, the supply of material is strong. His signature can be found on commemorative airmail covers, letters on Eastern letterhead, government postcards, photographs of various size, and copies of his autobiography *Rickenbacker*. Bank checks exist in quantities and are an excellent source of Rickenbacker's signature. Rickenbacker's signature is affordable. Signatures can be purchased for as little as $30. Bank checks, airmail covers, photographs, and TLsS are valued at $100 to $150. An ALS is rare, so expect to pay $600 to $700 for a full-page specimen.

years these have become much more difficult to locate. Letters of any kind are rare. There is strong demand for this World War I hero of heroes. His signature is valued at $175. Bank checks sell for $250 to $300.

General John J. Pershing was one of America's greatest generals. Nicknamed "Black Jack," Pershing made a name for himself by defeating Pancho Villa's men in 1916. He was the commander of American forces in Europe during the war. Pershing signed in a bold and powerful hand. Good legibility and display value are noted. Sometimes he would finish his signature off with a paraph. There is a strong supply of Pershing material in the market. TLsS and portrait photographs exist in good numbers. ALsS are rare and highly desirable. His signature is a relatively easy acquisition for collectors. Signatures are affordable at $75 to $100. TLsS sell for $150. Photographs can be purchased for $250 to $300.

Rickenbacker-1, signature dated 1941.

Pershing-1, Album Page dated 1927.

Alvin York, better known as "Seargent York," was one of America's greatest war heroes. A Medal of Honor recipient, York was known to storm German machine gun nests and capture enemy soldiers with great success. York signed in a loose and unstructured hand. His signature has average display value. Replication of hand is fairly easy. York's signature is far less common than that of Rickenbacker. His signature surfaces on album pages and the occasional envelope as a return address signature. A small supply of bank checks are in the market. In recent

Billy Mitchell is considered the father of the United States Air Force. He pushed the idea of air power any chance he could. A man of deep convictions, he was an outspoken critic of military brass. His attitude eventually led to a court-martial. Mitchell signed in a bold hand that evidences rapid flow. Eye appeal is above average. Legibility is slightly impaired. Due to the complex letter structure, well-executed forgeries do not exist. A controversial figure, Mitchell signed material is always in demand. His signature is scarce and generally limited to TLsS. The occasional photograph and ALS surface, but both mediums are considered rare. A signature is valued at $250. TLsS sell for $400 to $500.

York-1, album page circa 1925.

Mitchell, W-1 ALS dated 1926 (courtesy Stephen Koschal Autographs).

American ace George Vaughn scored 13 kills and is noted for shooting down German ace Friedrich Noltenius. He died in 1989 at the age of 92. A responsive signer, Vaughn is one of the easiest of the World War I ace signatures to locate. His signature sells for $40. Signed commemorative prints are handsome displays and can be purchased for $100.

Vaughn-1, undated signature (courtesy Stephen Koschal Reference Library).

Great Britain

George V ruled the United Kingdom from 1910 until his death in 1936. He was cousin to Russian Czar Nicholas II. King George signed in a tempered hand. His signature is legible with good display value. He signed many items, usually as "George R.I." The signature is finished off with a paraph. Replication of hand is easy. Many well-executed forgeries exist. His signature is typically found on formal portrait photographs and official royal appointment documents. Many of these documents are secretarially signed. Letters are a rarity. Any letter with war content is an extreme rarity. DsS are affordable at $300 to $400. Photographs are valued at $500 to $600.

George V-1, ALS dated 1905 (courtesy Nate D. Sanders Auctions).

Herbert H. Asquith served at prime minister from 1908 to 1916. Asquith signed in a sloppy and illegible hand. His signature has poor eye appeal and is easily forged. Given the modest value, his signature is generally not the target of skilled forgers, though a limited number of forgeries exist. Signatures are typically found on album pages and the occasional photograph. Signed letters are rare. Expect to pay $75 for his signature. A TLS will sell for $150 to $200.

Asquith-1, undated signature.

In 1916 Asquith was replaced by David Lloyd George. Lloyd George remains the only Welsh prime minister of United Kingdom. He played a significant role in the Paris peace conference in 1919. George signed in a very odd and truncated hand. Sharp breaks are noted. Due to the truncated nature of the signature, it is easily forged. Like Asquith, signatures are generally limited to album pages and photographs. Letters of any kind are scarce. His signature is valued in the $75 to $100 price range.

George-1 undated signature.

Horatio Kitchener, Irish-born field marshal, was one of England's great war heroes and also one of its most controversial.. He secured the Sudan in the late 1890s and was given the title "Lord Kitchener of Khartoum." He is also the father of the concentration camp that he used effectively during the Boer War. Kitchener signed in a very powerful and heavy hand. His signature has superior display value. Letter construction is slightly impaired. Signatures are sometimes found as "Kitchener of Khartoum." His signature is very hard to forge. No well-executed forgeries exist, primarily because values don't warrant the effort. Signatures are found on ALsS, a medium that seems to be in good supply. Signed formal portrait photographs also exist. His signature is valued at $150. ALsS and photographs sell for $300 to $500.

Kitchener-1, undated signature.

Admiral John Jellicoe was a career naval officer. He fought in the Boxer Rebellion and led the fleet at the Battle of Jutland in 1916. Jellicoe signed in a pensive and confined hand. His signature evidences poor letter construction. It is on the illegible side. Most signatures are signed simply as "Jellicoe." His signature is scarce, albeit borderline. Letters, photographs, and calling cards are available. These days there is not much demand for Jellicoe's signature. A signature will sell for $15 to $20. Signed letters are valued at $40 to $50.

Jellicoe-1, undated signature.

Field Marshal Douglas Haig was a popular commander who led the British at the Somme and Ypres. Haig signed in a plain and no-nonsense hand. Signatures are typically penned a "D. Haig FM." His signature exhibits average display value. He died in 1928 and his signature is rather scarce. It is occasionally found on letters and small cards. There is marginal demand for Haig material. Expect to pay $50 for his autograph.

Haig-1, undated signature.

France

Georges Clemenceau was a two-time prime minister of France. He was one the architects of the Treaty of Versailles. Clemenceau signed in an unassuming hand. His signature exhibits good flow but is not reckless in nature. Most signatures are signed as "G. Clemenceau." Replication of hand would be rather easy. His signature is scarce on a per se basis and generally limited to ALsS. There is average demand for his signature. Expect to pay $150 for an ALS.

Clemenceau-1, undated signature.

Joseph Joffre was marshal of France. He is best remembered for defeating the Germans at the Marne. Joffre signed in a small and confined hand. His signature has average letter construction and moderate display value. There is nothing extraordinary about his signature. It is usually signed as "J. Joffre." Photographs are typically signed near the extreme bottom edge, which impairs display value. His signature is typically found on calling cards and photographs. His signature is considered scarce. There is good demand for his signature, which is valued at $100. A nicely signed photograph will sell for $250 to $300.

Joffre-1, undated signature.

Ferdinand Foch was a career military officer, having seen action in the Franco-Prussian War of 1870–1871. He led forces at the Marne, Ypres, and the Somme. In 1918 he was promoted to marshal of France. Foch signed in a striking hand. His signature evidences bold strokes. The display value is superior. Signatures are typically accomplished as "F Foch" with a bold paraph. His signature is scarce on a per se basis. Typical mediums are calling cards, short ALsS, and formal portrait photographs. There is one forgery to note. There are many 11 × 14 photographs of Foch in uniform leaning against a column and holding a cane. The photographs are tinted in light pastel colors. These are signed "F Foch." The letter F in the last name is malformed and displays itself as slightly labored. These have been in the market for years and are

sold as genuine. Whether these are intentional forgeries or period secretarial signatures I do not know. Whatever the case, these are signed by someone other than Foch. They are easily exposed upon examination. Foch's signature sells for $125 to $150. Photographs are valued at $400 to $500, superior specimens are higher.

Foch-1, photograph dated 1921 (courtesy Nate D. Sanders Auctions).

Philippe Petain gained distinction at Verdun. He was promoted to marshal of France. During the Second World War he was made premier and was a central figure in the Vichy government, which collaborated with the Germans. After the war he was convicted of treason and sentenced to death. His sentence commuted to life in prison, and he died in 1951 at the age of 95. Petain signed in a flowing hand which has good eye appeal. The signature lacks recklessness of hand and thus is one of the easier signatures to replicate. Well-executed forgeries exist. His connection with the Vichy government correlates into strong demand for his signature. Signatures are valued at $150 to $175. TLsS sell in the $250 to $300 range. A nicely signed photograph is valued at $500 to $750.

Petain-1 calling card, circa 1930.

Petain-1, DS dated 1917 (courtesy Markus Brandes Autographs).

Germany

Wilhelm II was the last Kaiser of Germany and King of Prussia. He built an alliance with Austria-Hungary. He is generally considered an ineffective leader and abdicated in October–November of 1918. He lived out the rest of his life in exile in the Netherlands. He died in 1941 at the age of 82. Wilhelm signed in a very bold and artistic hand. His signature is bombastic in nature and has maximum eye appeal. Due to the complex construction of the signature, no well-executed forgeries exist. The Kaiser's signature is in good supply. His signature is found on DsS and many handsome 8 × 10 photographs. Many short ANsS are in the market. ALsS are rare. A sound supply keeps prices depressed. DsS can be purchased for $250 to $300. Signed 8 × 10 portrait photographs sell for $400 to $450. There is one facsimile to note. In 1914 the Red Cross issued a portrait picture postcard featuring Wilhelm in full military uniform. Underneath the image is a printed ANS. The signature is then dated "26 / VIII 1914."

This is a very convincing image and many times the signature is removed from the card and framed and matted under glass, so caution is warranted.

Wilhelm II-2, common facsimile.

Field Marshal Paul von Hindenburg was one of Germany's greatest military heroes. He had retired from the Army in 1911. He was called back to duty when the war began. He soundly defeated the Allies at Tannenberg in 1914. Hindenburg signed in a very heavy and powerful hand. The hand is flowing with complex letter construction. A very hard signature to replicate; there are no well-executed forgeries in the market. Hindenburg's signature is generally found on DsS, ANsS on postcard-sized note cards, and formal portrait photographs. There is a good supply of material in the market. His signature sells for $150. DsS for $250 to $300. A nicely signed photograph is valued at $400 to $500.

Wilhelm II-1, undated signature (courtesy The Sanders Autograph Price Guide).

Hindenburg-1, undated signature.

Victor at Liege, Erich von Ludendorff was a brilliant military strategist who served as chief of staff to Hindenburg. Ludendorff's signature is signed in a powerful hand. Jagged, yet uniform, lines are noted. A signature with good display value. Unlike other prominent leaders of World War I Germany, Ludendorff's signature is rare. Expect to pay $400 to $500 for a nice specimen.

Ludendorff-1, undated signature .

German nobleman Felix von Luckner was a highly successful naval commander during the war. He and his crew saw heavy action at Jutland. His ability to engage in battle with little to no casualties earned him the nickname "Sea Devil." Luckner signed in a flowing and angled hand. The signature has above average eye appeal and would be rather difficult to forge. Luckner was a responsive signer and today many specimens are in the market. Postcard-sized photographs are in good supply, as are calling cards. Letters of any kind are scarce. An affordable signature, so expect to pay $30 to $50 for one. A picture postcard is valued at $75.

Luckner-1, signed card dated 1934 (courtesy Markus Brandes Autographs).

Manfred von Richthofen is almost a mythical name in history. Kids today think he is a character out of a fairy tale. Known forever as the Red Baron of Germany, he is credited with 80 kills, making him the highest-scoring ace of World War I. He was killed in action on April 21, 1918, shot down by Canadian pilot Arthur "Roy" Brown. Richthofen remains the most famous combat flyer in the history of aviation. Richthofen signed in a striking hand. His signature exhibits strong vertical strokes of hand. Though legibility is impaired, the signature still retains strong display value. Replication of hand is rather difficult, but well-executed forgeries do exist. Richthofen has been the target of skilled forgers for decades. Just about all signatures offered in the market are forgeries. In addition, a rubber stamp was employed to fulfill requests for his autograph. A common forgery can be found on small photographs of Richthofen in uniform. He has his arms on his hips and is staring off to his left. These are a bit smaller than a postcard. Along the bottom of the photograph it reads in printed script "Rittmeister Manfred Frhr. Van Richthofen." The forgeries, which are all accomplished by the same forger, are fairly well-executed, so caution is warranted. His signature is of the highest demand. Supply is very restricted. His signature is considered very rare on a per se basis. A signature is valued at $7,500 to $10,000. A nicely signed photograph will sell for $12,500 to $15,000. An ALS, which is an extreme rarity, will easily sell for $25,000.

Richthofen-1, undated signature.

Richthofen-2, common rubber stamp.

Ernst Udet was one of the highest-scoring aces of World War I. His 62 kills puts him second only to his commander, Richthofen, among German aces. During World War II he was a high-ranking officer of the Luftwaffe. He died in a plane crash in 1941. Udet signed in a strong and bold hand. His signature is of traditional German script. It exhibits jaggedness and material choppiness. Eye appeal is sound. Well-executed forgeries do exist, so caution is warranted. Udet's signature is rare, albeit borderline. Signed postcard-sized photographs are available. An authored book surfaces now and then. An ALS is very rare. His signature is valued at $300 to $400. Photographs will sell for $500 to $600.

Udet-1 signature undated.

Otto Roosen was a footnote in World War I history. He was the last surviving German pilot of the war. He lived to over 100 years of age. Roosen had the distinction of being shot down by Canadian ace Billy Bishop. Roosen lived out his life in Canada. He signed very little material. His signature seldom surfaces. I estimate a value of $100, though I know of no recent sales of his signature.

Otto Roosen

Roosen-1, signature circa 1985.

Noted German chemist Fritz Haber won the Nobel Prize in chemistry in 1918. His signature is highly desired because he is known as the "father of chemical warfare," having developed poison gas. Haber signed in a confined and neat

hand. His signature has good eye appeal. Practical construction is noted. Signatures are accomplished as "Fritz Haber" or "F. Haber." Haber died in 1934. Signatures are very rare and just about all are held in institutional collections. A nice handwritten letter, signed with the last name only, sold for €1,400 (Markus Brandes Autographs, 2012).

F. Haber

Haber-1, TLS dated 1907 (courtesy Leo Baeck Institute).

Other Notables

Dutch exotic dancer Margaretha Zelle is best remembered as the spy Mata Hari. She was accused of spying for the Germans. She was tried and convicted of espionage. She died by firing squad on October 15, 1917. Mata Hari signed in a very strong hand. The signature is well-structured with abrupt changes in direction. The signature has good display value. Replication of hand would be rather difficult. Well-executed forgeries are very limited. Her signature is rare on a per se basis. Most signatures are found on ALsS; many are multi pages. Other mediums are just about nonexistent. Expect to pay $2,500 to $3,000 for an ALS with routine content.

Mata Hari-2 ANS undated.

Billy Bishop was the highest-scoring Canadian ace of World War I. He is credited with 72 kills. He remained active in World War II in aviation training. He died in 1956. Bishop's signature is fairly scarce and generally limited to a signed picture page in the book titled *The People's War Book and Atlas*, published in 1920. An autographed edition was issued, and Bishop signed many copies. These books are about the only source for his signature. They are valued at $125 to $150.

Bishop-1 signed book 1930.

Fellow Canadian ace Arthur "Roy" Brown is best known for shooting down the Red Baron of Germany. His signature exhibits nice flow and legibility. He died in 1944 of a heart attack. He was a celebrity of his day and did sign autographs. His signature is considered scarce. Signatures are generally limited to album pages and cards. Other mediums are rare to very rare. His signature sells in the $250 to $350 range.

Brown, R-1 undated signature.

Brown, R-2, signature dated 1918 (courtesy International Autograph Auctions, England).

Willy Coppens was Belgium's leading ace. He is credited with shooting down 35 observation balloons, making him the top balloon buster of World War I. Coppens lived a long life. He died in 1986 at the age of 94. He was a responsive signer and his signature can be found mostly on

postal covers. An affordable signature, it is valued at $40 to $50. Coppens was known as a superb letter writer. He wrote with a cutting pen. He was a staunch anti-communist. His writings often attacked Woodrow Wilson and Franklin Roosevelt as the great "mistakes" of the United States. Other letters praise Ronald Reagan. Such letters are highly prized and command a premium.

Coppens-1 ALS dated 1981.

Nicholas II was the last Czar of Russia. He led his country through most of the war. His mismanagement of the treasury led to economic ruin. He was overthrown in 1917 during the Bolshevik Revolution. He and his family were executed in July 1918. Nicholas II signed in a large and regal hand. His signature dominates the medium it is placed upon. His signature is very scarce on a per se basis and generally limited to DsS and LsS. A certain number of portrait photographs are available, but these should be considered rare. Expect to pay $1,000 to $1,500 for a nice DS. ALsS are rare and will sell for $8,000 to $10,000.

Nicholas II signature 1916.

Grigori Rasputin was a Russian mystic and faith healer who wormed his way into Nicholas's inner circle. He was said to have treated the Czar's son Alexei's hemophilia. He was killed on December 17, 1916, by members of the Russian military. Rasputin signed in a rudimentary and ghastly hand. The writing is a combination of truncated cursive and printed script. The signature is sloppy and evidences much hesitation. Signatures are accomplished as "Grigori." Given the rudimentary construction, replication of hand is very easy. Well-executed forgeries exist, and these include many fake ALsS and LsS. Forged letters have been in the market for decades. Careful study is needed before purchasing Rasputin's signature, as it is one of the easiest of historical signatures to forge. There is a small grouping of forged ALsS in the market. These are typically found on small octavo sheets. These letters have routine content and are typically opened with "My dear sweet." The ink is impaired by brushing or stained with water. A purple or red ink stamp is usually placed somewhere on the page. Overall an amateurish forgery. Rasputin's signature commands much interest. An ALS will sell for $10,000.

Rasputin-1, undated signature (courtesy Stephen Koschal Reference Library).

Communist revolutionary Vladimir Ulyanov (alias Vladimir Lenin), was the first premier of the Soviet Union. Lenin remains one of the most important names of the 20th century, autographically speaking. There are so many variant signatures that are held out as genuine it makes your head spin. In addition, forgeries are prevalent. Just about 100 percent of Lenin signatures offered in the market are forged. Illustrated is what I believe to be the genuine signature. This form of signature is found on period documents and letters that evidence proper aging. There are many ALsS in the market which are written in German and simply signed "Lenin" in a looser, more rounded hand. I have always questioned the authenticity of these letters. There are various telegrams, dated in the 1920s, in the market which purportedly contain ANsS in pencil. These too I question the authenticity. It is unlikely a Soviet premier would employ such a crude method of writing. Lenin's signature is very rare and will likely sell for more than $25,000, if you can find one.

Lenin-1, undated signature.

Victor Emmanuel III was king of Italy from 1900 to 1946. Victor signed in a powerful hand. His signature has above average display value. It is generally limited to signed official documents, of which there are many. A good supply of documents, countersigned by Mussolini, exist. Other mediums should be considered rare. A DS is affordable at $50.

Victor Emmanuel-1, DS dated 1938.

The Polar Bears

The American Expeditionary Force of North Russia was group of American soldiers that intervened in the Russian civil war. They fought the Red Army from the fall of 1918 to the summer of 1919. President Wilson sent troops, mostly Michiganders, to the north country of Russia to protect stockpiles of weapons. Their mission soon turned into combat. When World War I ended, the men, now calling themselves the "Polar Bears," were the last troops to stand down from the war. They were officially disbanded just over a year after the Armistice.

Certain groups gain fame and become collectable. The Doolittle Raiders, Flying Tigers, and Green Berets are good examples. In the past few years the Polar Bears of World War I have gained a lot of attention. This once obscure group of soldiers is finally getting their just recognition. Autograph collectors are starting to take notice. Polar Bear material is becoming popular, and not just signed material, but ephemera as well. Since Polar Bear signatures were not actively collected until recently, the vast majority of signed material is held by family estates. As such any signature is considered rare. As more research is done, the commanders of this famed fighting group will no doubt be coveted by collectors. Illustrated is a signature of Jay Earle Spaulding, a Michigan native and one of the early fighting Polar Bears.

Spaulding-1, World War I draft card (courtesy Record Group 163, Records of the Selective Services Division, National Archives at Atlanta).

* * *

It was often said that World War I was the war to end all wars. During the 1920s, Germany was governed by the provisions of the Versailles Treaty, or as many in Germany called, it the Versailles diktat. The economic depression that hit Germany in the 1920s gave rise to Adolf Hitler. World War II began on September 1, 1939, when German troops crossed the border into Poland. Only days later, France and Britain declared war on Germany. The United States re-

mained an active spectator. The horrors of World War I were still fresh in the minds of Americans. While America did not enter the war, it did assist the Allies in other ways, among them lend/lease and the mid–Atlantic defense zone.

As war raged in Europe, tensions between the United States and Japan began to grow. The Japanese military believed they could deal a death blow to the United States navy by striking Diamond Head. In 1940, the successful British attack of Taranto, Italy, had emboldened the Japanese to engage America in war. On Sunday morning, December 7, 1941, the Japanese navy launched a sneak attack on Pearl Harbor. More than 2,500 servicemen were killed and another 1,300 were wounded. Close to 1,200 sailors perished when the USS *Arizona* was sunk. The next day America declared war on Japan. Pearl Harbor proved the true turning point of the war, for on that day the Axis powers were doomed.

Signatures of World War II notables were of little value for many years. There were the few exceptions, such as Patton and Rommel, but for the most part the market was weak. In the late 1980s, I started collecting signatures from noteworthy figures of World War II: *Enola Gay* crew members, Doolittle Raiders, and the like. I was laughed at by fellow collectors for wasting stamps. Things remained essentially the same throughout the 1990s. In 2000, the World War II market exploded, aided by war documentaries on cable TV. The History Channel is primarily responsible for making the war a popular subject. Today, World War II signatures are highly collectable.

Two men were responsible for defense of military operations in Hawaii during the attack on Pearl Harbor. They were General Walter Short and Admiral Husband Kimmel. Most of the blame for being caught off guard by the Japanese was directed at Kimmel. He lived until 1968 and was a responsive signer through the mail, though his signature should still be considered scarce. Signatures are generally limited to ANsS, index cards, and the occasional first-day cover. Signed photographs are rare. His signature is easily forged, so caution is warranted. There is good demand for Kimmel's signature which is valued at $250 to $300.

Husband E. Kimmel

Kimmel-1, undated signature.

The man who led the raid on Pearl Harbor was Captain Mitsuo Fuchida. After the war he converted to Christianity and took up residence in the United States. This proved a windfall for collectors. Fuchida was responsive to collectors and signed FDCs and index cards. He would usually add a biblical notation underneath the signature. Other mediums are very rare. There is one forgery to discuss. There are many declaration of war typescripts in the market on War Department letterhead. A forgery of Fuchida is placed underneath the declaration in felt-tip pen. Given the ease of forging Fuchida's signature, many exist, so caution is warranted. I have never seen a genuinely signed war declaration signed by Fuchida. Expect to pay $200 to $250 for his signature.

Capt. Mitsuo Fuchida

Fuchida-1, undated signature.

World War II produced the greatest number of collectable signatures of any war. The signatures in the greatest demand are those of United States officers. Naval officers, combat fighters, strategists, and the like offer collectors a wide assortment of signatures. Signatures of the five-star (and one four-star) generals and admirals are the most collected.

Dwight Eisenhower was supreme allied com-

mander of forces in Europe and later the first supreme commander of NATO. His signature is discussed more fully in the presidential signature chapter. Of note, he did employ the use of an autopen during his military career, so caution is warranted. One such pre-presidential autopen is illustrated.

Dwight Eisenhower

Eisenhower-3, war date auto-pen (courtesy Presidents of the United States Autopen Guide, Stephen Koschal & Andreas Wiemer).

Douglas MacArthur is probably the most recognized officer of World War II. In addition to being general of the army, he also held the rank of field marshal of the Philippine army. His name is synonymous with the Pacific Theater. MacArthur signed in a striking hand. His signature exhibits precise lines and crisp angles. It has superior display value. Replication of hand is very difficult; hence, well-executed forgeries are very limited. MacArthur was a willing signer and today there is a good inventory in the market. Signatures are generally found on index cards, government postcards, and many fine portrait photographs. TLsS are uncommon. Full page ALsS are rare. Due to the large supply of material, MacArthur's signature is affordable at $250. A nice 8 × 10 photograph is valued at $500 to $600. ALsS are valued at $2,000 to $2,500.

Douglas MacArthur

MacArthur-1 book signed dated 1956 (courtesy Nate D. Sanders Auctions).

Known as the "G.I.'s general," Omar Bradley was field commander of U.S. forces in Africa and Europe. After the war he served as chairman of the Joint Chiefs of Staff. He was the last surviving five-star general. Bradley's signature is the most common of all five-star generals. He lived a long life and was a willing and gracious signer. Today, his signature can be found on many mediums, including first-day covers, index cards, portrait photographs, and letters. Bank checks also exist in small quantities; these should be considered scarce. His signature is average in construction with moderate display value. Replication of hand is easy. Well-executed forgeries exist in good numbers. Many forged first-day covers have entered the market in the past five or so years. His signature is affordable at $75. A nice photograph will sell for $200. His biography *Bradley: A Soldier's Story* is an excellent book. Many signed copies exist with nice inscriptions. Expect to pay $200 for one.

Bradley-1, undated signature.

Admiral Chester Nimitz was the commander in chief for the Pacific fleet. Later he served as chief of naval operations from the end of the war until 1947. He died in 1966 as the last surviving fleet admiral of the United States. Nimitz signed in a flowing and practical hand. The display value is sound. Most signatures are accomplished as "C.W. Nimitz." Replication of hand is fairly easy; hence, well-executed forgeries do exist. Most forgeries are limited to the historic image of the Japanese delegation signing the instrument of surrender aboard the battleship *Missouri*. The supply of Nimitz material is sound. He was a willing signer. Signatures can be found

on TLsS, ANsS, photographs, and first-day covers. ALsS are scarce to rare. His signature has always been in demand, so expect to pay $200 for a nice specimen. A photograph will sell for $400 to $500. An 8 × 10 photograph of the above referenced Missouri image will sell for $2,500 to $3,000.

Churchill called General George Marshall the "organizer of victory." Marshall served as secretary of state, and the Marshall plan was named in his honor. Marshall signed in a very reckless and flowing hand. His signature has poor letter construction. It is, for the most part, illegible. Due to the artistic nature of hand, his signature has good display value. Replication of hand is difficult, so well-executed forgeries are limited. The supply of Marshall material is somewhat limited. He died in 1959. His signature is considered uncommon to scarce and generally limited to letters and photographs. The occasional first-day cover will surface. His signature is valued at $150 to $200. Premium items, such as 8 × 10 photographs, sell for $500.

Marshall, G-1, undated signature.

William Leahy was the first navy man to receive five stars since Admiral George Dewey. Leahy served in the navy from 1897 to 1939. He was called back into service in 1942 and was the highest-ranking officer in the United States.

Leahy-1, TLS dated 1939 (courtesy Nate D. Sanders Auctions).

Nimitz-1, ALS dated 1964.

Leahy signed in a pleasing hand. The signature is vertical in nature. Sound display value is noted. A signature of average demand and limited supply. Expect to pay $150 for one. TLsS sell for $200 to $250.

Admiral Ernest King is the least remembered of the five-star officers. Mention his name and the reply is usually "Ernest who?" King was a career navy man who served from 1898 to 1956. He even saw action during the Spanish-American War. King signed in a practical hand. His signature lacks flow and evidences a slight choppiness. It is easily forged. King is the toughest of the five-star signatures. It is a scarce signature on a per se basis. Premium items are rare. His signature will sell for $250.

King, E-1 TLS dated 1944 (courtesy Nate D. Sanders Auctions).

Admiral William "Bull" Halsey was a major player in the Pacific Theater. He commanded the Third Fleet. Halsey signed in a legible and no-nonsense hand. His signature has good display value. The practical nature of hand correlates into a fairly easy signature to forge. Halsey's signature is very affordable. He was a responsive signer. Signatures are typically

Halsey-1, DS dated 1943 (courtesy Naval History and Heritage Command).

found on index cards and photographs of various size. Less common are letters. His signature can be purchased for $75 to $100. A nicely signed 8 × 10 will sell in the $300 to $400 range.

Henry "Hap" Arnold is the only man ever to hold two distinct five-star ranks. Arnold was an aviation pioneer and a protégé of Billy Mitchell. He was tagged with the nickname "Happy" during his tenure as a stunt pilot. Arnold signed in a beautiful flowing hand. His signature has superior eye appeal. Signatures are usually accomplished as "H.H. Arnold." The rapid and complex nature of his hand makes replication very difficult. There are no well-executed forgeries in the market. Arnold died in 1950 and was a responsive signer. Many nicely signed photographs exist. Also, signed copies of his book *Global Mission* exist in good supply. His signature will sell for $125 to $150. Signed books and photographs are valued at $350 to $450.

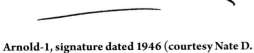

Arnold-1, signature dated 1946 (courtesy Nate D. Sanders Auctions).

General George Patton was a four-star general. He was one of our nation's greatest generals and one of the most famous military men in history, so Patton's signature is in great demand. Outspoken, opinionated, and a brilliant field tactician, Patton is, pound for pound, the most expensive World War II autograph of any American officer. Patton was killed in a car "accident" in December 1945. His signature is somewhat scarce but a decent supply exists. Many military-related letters and documents are in the market. In addition, he was very popular and signed countless autographs for the troops. Album pages are the most common medium. Having said this, most Patton signatures are forgeries. The unstructured nature of his hand lends itself to easy replication. Well-executed forgeries exit in quantities. Forgeries are typically found on genuine military-related postal covers and short TLsS with no letterhead. It should be further noted that many small 4to honorable discharge documents contain a secretarial signature of Patton. Secretarial signatures are very close to the genuine signature but signed in a slightly slower hand. The demand for Patton material is strong. His signature is valued at $800 to $1,000. TLsS sell for $1,500 and ALsS are nearly double that amount. Letters with good content can reach $7,500 to $10,000.

Patton-1, TLS dated 1940 (courtesy Nate D. Sanders Auctions).

A career military officer, General Jonathan Wainwright became commander of the Philippines. Wainwright eventually surrendered to the Japanese. He was the highest-ranking POW of the war. He was a Medal of Honor winner. Wainwright is a surprisingly popular signature among collectors. His signature is penned in a fast and compact hand. It is scarce on a per se basis. A few nicely signed 8 × 10 photographs are in the market. His signature is valued at

Wainwright-1, signed book circa 1950 (courtesy Nate D. Sanders Auctions).

$100 to $125. Signed photographs sell for around $300.

General Matthew Ridgway gained fame in both World War II and the Korean War. In 1952 he replaced Eisenhower as supreme allied commander of Europe. Ridgway lived to the age of 98 and was a responsive signer. Most signatures are found on first-day covers and index cards. Letters are uncommon, and 8 × 10 photographs are scarce. His signature is still very affordable at $40 to $50. Letters sell for $100 to $125.

Ridgway-1 signature circa 1990.

Another four-star general, Anthony C. McAuliffe, was famous for one word. During the Battle of the Bulge he replied "Nuts!" to a German ultimatum to surrender. McAuliffe died in 1975. His signature is uncommon to scarce. Signatures are usually found on index cards, military-related letters, and photographs. He signed in a pensive hand. Replication of hand would be rather easy. His signature is in good demand. Expect to pay $200 for a nice specimen.

McAuliffe-1 GPC dated 1965 (courtesy Nate D. Sanders Auctions).

Known as "31-Knot," Admiral Arleigh Burke made his name in the South Pacific. He commanded a destroyer squadron nicknamed Burke's Little Beavers who fought the Japanese navy with much success. Burke died in 1996 at the age of 94. Burke was a responsive signer through the mail. His signature is mostly found on index cards. Burke would, on occasion, send collectors signed official navy 8 × 10 photographs. These are stunning images and highly coveted by collectors. His signature is affordable at $25 to $35. The above-referenced photograph is valued at $100.

Burke-1 signature circa 1990.

James Forrestal was the last cabinet-level secretary of the navy and the first defense secretary. He died in 1949 from a "fall" out of a window. His death, to this day, is considered a homicide. Forrestal signed in a slower hand. His signature is legible. A sound display value is noted. His signature is uncommon and generally limited to TLsS. The occasional photograph surfaces, but this medium is considered rare. The strange circumstance surrounding his death generates interest in his signature. A TLS can be purchased for $75 to $100.

Forrestal-1 TLS dated 1946.

Raymond Spruance is my choice for America's unsung hero of the war. His name has been buried by the passage of time. He is a five-star admiral with only four stars. Spruance signed in a choppy and compact hand. His signature has marginal eye appeal and is easily forged. The supply of material is small. His signature is considered scarce in any form. He signed very little material for collectors. Expect to pay $250 to $300 for his signature, if you can find one.

Spruance-1, TLS dated 1946 (courtesy Naval History and Heritage Command).

General Mark Clark was the youngest 4-star general of the war. He lived until 1984 and was a responsive signer. He handed out signed 8 × 10 photographs. ALsS are rare. The sound supply of photographs keeps values low. His signature will sell for $40. A nicely signed 8 × 10 photograph can be purchased for $75.

Clark, M-1, TLS dated 1945.

General Carl "Tooey" Spaatz became the first chief of staff of the air force. He died in 1974 and was a responsive signer. Signatures are found on first-day covers, index cards, and TLsS. He also signed an ample supply of 8 × 10 photographs. ALsS are rare. Given the affordable nature of the signature, it is generally not the target of skilled forgers. Some TLsS contain secretarial signatures. Expect to pay $75 to $100 for his signature. A TLS and 8 × 10 photograph will sell for $150 to $175.

Spaatz-1 undated signature.

A few years back, the Navajo code talkers were basically unknown. They were a group of Navajo Indians who passed code through their native tongue. Their names are not well known, but the increased interest in the code talkers has made signatures of this group collectable. Chester Nez was one of the original code talkers and he was a responsive signer. He would even write out code upon re-

Doolittle Raiders—multi signed airmail cover.

quest. The signatures of most code talkers sell for under $50. Handwritten code signed by Nez is rare and generally sells for $200 or more.

Nez-1 signature dated 2000.

American Aviators

By far the most collected signatures are the aviators. Collectable aviation signatures from the First World War are basically limited to the aces like Rickenbacker. In World War II, however, many famed flying groups emerged and are, to this day, popular with collectors. The following is a list of some of the more famous names in aviation.

Doolittle's Raiders: On April 18, 1942, the United States struck back at Japan. In an operation known as the Tokyo Raid, American bombers hit the mainland of Japan. The group consisted of 16 craft with a five-man crew per plane.

The Raiders are the most collected of all flying groups. Many of the Raiders survived the war and attended reunions. As a result, there is a good supply of multi-signed items in the mar-

ket. Illustrated is a nicely signed airmail postal cover. Just about all members were responsive to mail requests. Some, such as Chase Nielson, navigator of plane #6, and Nolan Herndon, navigator of plane #8, wrote many letters discussing the raid. Signed Raider material will always be in demand.

The leader of the raid, Colonel Jimmy Doolittle, emerged from the war a legend. He received his fourth star in 1985 by act of Congress. Doolittle signed in a bold and flashy hand. His signature is usually finished off with a paraph. By the mid–1980s his hand was affected by infirmity. The once complex signature was reduced to a slow and practical hand. This form of signature is easily formed and many well-executed forgeries exist. In the 1920s, Doolittle was a pioneer aviator. He signed period postal covers which make for a fine display. Doolittle was a responsive signer through the mail, which results in a good supply of his signature. He would send signed 8 × 10 photographs and letters regarding the raid. Some nicely signed 8 × 10 photographs exist of Doolittle standing in front of one of his early biplanes; these, too, make for a stunning display. Doolittle material will always be in demand. His signature sells for $50. Signed 8 × 10 photographs are worth $125 to $150. A TLS with raid content is treasured. Expect to pay $400 to $500 for one.

Doolittle-1 signature circa 1980s.

Doolittle-2, signature circa 1990.

In 2001 the movie *Pearl Harbor* was released by Touchstone Pictures. Though it popularized the Raiders to a new generation of Americans, the film's portrayal of the raid was basically fiction. Some of the Raiders, such as William Birch, wrote letters criticizing the film for its distortions. These letters are of great content and coveted by collectors.

Another flying group made popular by Hollywood was the Black Sheep Squadron. The TV series *Baa Baa Black Sheep*, starring Robert Conrad, aired from 1976 to 1978. The Black Sheep provided offensive air support in the Pacific Theater. Its leader was colonel Greg "Pappy" Boyington. Boyington is a high-scoring ace credited with 28 kills. Boyington has always been a popular signature among collectors. He was an erratic signer. Many requests for his autograph went unanswered. His signature is uncommon and generally limited to index cards, small photographs, and a decent supply of bank checks. His autograph is still affordable at $75 to $100. Bank checks sell for $125 to $150. The squadron itself produced some notable fliers, among them aces John Bolt and James J. Hill. Signatures of Black Sheep members are very affordable at $15 to $25 each. Many nice multi-signed items are available for purchase.

Boyington was shot down over Rabaul by

Boyington-1 bank check dated 1986.

Japanese ace Masajiro "Mike" Kawato. In general, signatures of the Japanese aces are difficult to locate. They considered their defeat in war a disgrace and avoided signing. Kawato was one of the exceptions. He was a responsive signer and signed many items, including an authored book. Kawato is of particular interest as he would sign autographs both in English and Japanese. His signature has maximum eye appeal. Expect to pay $50 to $75 for a signature accomplished in both languages.

Kawato-1 Dual signature in English and Japanese, circa 1995.

The American Volunteer Group, better known as the Flying Tigers, is very popular with collectors. Its commander was Lieutenant General Claire Lee Chennault. Chennault signed in a very thoughtful and pleasing hand. His signature has sound display value. The capital "C" in the last name enhances eye appeal. The signature lacks rapid motion; hence, replication of hand is rather easy. Well-executed forgeries do exist. His signature is scarce with premium items bordering on the rare side. Always in de-

Chennault-1, undated signature.

mand, Chennault's signature sells for $200 to $250. A good content letter is valued at approximately $1,000.

The Tigers produced many aces of note. Among them were Dick Rossi, Robert L. Scott, Paul Greene, Chuck Older, Charlie Bond, and Tex Hill. All were gracious signers and many would sign ace playing cards for collectors. Today their signatures sell anywhere from $25 to $35. Letters signed by any Tiger are scarce. One with good Tiger content is valued at $150 to $200. Older became a judge and presided over the murder trial of Charles Manson.

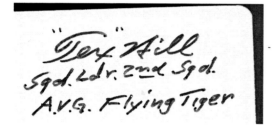

Hill-1 circa 1990 signature.

The *Memphis Belle* was a B-17 Boeing Flying Fortress that completed 25 combat missions. The crew became very popular among collectors when a movie by the same name was released in 1990. For many years the crew was a relatively unknown group and signed very little. In the last 15 to 20 years, crew members became the target of collectors. Captain Robert Morgan and copilot Jim Verinis signed a limited number of items. Crew member Harold Loch was known to write war content letters. Signatures of any crew members are uncommon and generally limited to index cards and photographs. Letters of any kind are scarce. Multi-signed items are in much demand.

On August 6, 1945, the Boeing B-29 bomber named the *Enola Gay* dropped a uranium fission bomb, code named "Little Boy," on Hiroshima, Japan. It is considered the most important event of the 20th century. The crew members of the *Enola Gay* and anything associated with them are highly collectable. There were twelve crew-

men, some of whom died in the 1950s and 1960s. An item signed by the entire crew is an extreme rarity. I have never seen one. Many of the crew lived into the 1990s and were targeted by collectors. Most were responsive signers. The commander, Brigadier General Paul Tibbets, piloted the craft. His signature is available on most mediums. Most common are photographs and postal covers. Letters are uncommon to scarce. A good supply of bank checks are in the market. Navigator Theodore Van Kirk and bombardier Tom Ferebee were also willing signers and their signatures exist in good quantities. A less common signature is that of tailgunner George Caron, who died in 1995. Like Tibbets, a limited number of bank checks have entered the market. Radio operator Richard Nelson was a very tough autograph. He rarely signed for collectors. He died in 2003 and is considered a scarce signature. Weapons officer Morris Jeppson was a gracious signer, and unlike the other crew members, he would write detailed letters regarding the mission. These letters are highly prized by collectors. Most of the above referenced signatures can be purchased for $25 to $50. Bank checks of Tibbets, Van Kirk, Caron, and Ferebee are valued at $75 each. Nelson's signature commands a premium at $100. Letters with mission content are treasured. Content ALsS, by Jeppson, sell anywhere

Tibbets-1, signature, circa 1995.

Van Kirk-1, signature circa 1990.

Richard H. Nelson [signature]

Nelson, R-1 undated signature.

Morris Jeppson [signature]

Jeppson-1, undated signature.

Tom Ferebee [signature]

Ferebee-1 signature circa 1990.

George R. Caron [signature]
TAIL GUNNER

Caron-1 signature circa 1990.

roshima and Nagasaki will always be in great demand.

Charles W. Sweeney [signature]

Sweeney-1, signature circa 1990.

Fred J. Olivi [signature]

Olivi-1, signature circa 1990.

C.D. Albury [signature]

Albury-1 undated signature.

for $400 to $500. The same would be true for other crew members as well.

Three days later, on August 9, another B-29 bomber, named *Bockscar*, commanded by Major General Chuck Sweeney, dropped a plutonium bomb, code named "Fat Man," on Nagasaki. Sweeney was a responsive signer but received far fewer requests than his counterpart Tibbets. His signature is usually found on index cards and photographs. His signature is valued at $50 to $75. A handful of items were signed by both Sweeney and Tibbets, these are scarce and in high demand. Expect to pay $250 to $300 for a dual-signed item. Copilot Fred Olivi signed in a beautiful hand. He was also a willing signer. Ray Gallagher and Charles Albury are also available, mostly on postal covers and index cards. The above-referenced signatures are valued at $30 to $50. Anything associated with Hi-

The United States produced many aces, many of whom died in combat. Many signatures are very rare. Assembling a complete set would be a daunting task. America's ace of aces is Major Richard Bong. He died shortly after the war in a plane crash. His signature is rare in any form and is valued at $1,500 to $2,000. Tommy McGuire is America's second-highest scoring ace with 38 kills. He died in January 1945 in combat. His signature is much rarer than that of Bong. I estimate a value of at least $5,000. The third-highest scoring American ace of the war was Captain David McCampbell. He recorded 34 kills. He died in 1996 and was a responsive signer. Signatures are generally found on first-day covers, index cards, and small-size photographs. McCampbell's signature can be purchased for under $50. Colonel Francis "Gabby" Gabreski was another high-scoring ace in both World War II and Korea. He is credited with 34.5 kills (among both wars). Gabreski was a willing signer. Signatures are generally limited to index cards, 8 × 10 photographs, and first-day covers. Letters of any kind are rare. Expect to pay $50 for his signature.

Bong-1, undated signature.

McCampbell-1, signature circa 1990.

Gabreski-1, signature circa 1990.

Other aces of note are General Chuck Yeager, who later became a test pilot and the first man to break the sound barrier. He was a willing signer for many years but scaled back around 2000. He signed many mediums, among them photographs, books, commemorative plates, airmail covers, and the like. General Joe Foss recorded 26 kills and is popular among collectors. After the war he became the first commissioner of the American Football League. He will eventually be inducted into the Football Hall of Fame. Foss material is a sound investment.

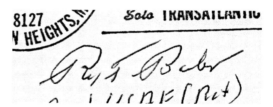

Yeager-1, signature dated 1990.

Foss-1, signature circa 1990.

Colonel Rex T. Barber was the lead pilot in the mission known as Operation Vengeance. The mission was to take out the plane carrying Japanese Admiral Isoroku Yamamoto. Barber and Thomas Lanphier are each credited with shooting down Yamamoto's plane. Barber was a responsive signer throughout the 1990s. There is good demand for his autograph. Lanphier's autograph is scarce. Both signatures are valued at $50 to $75 each.

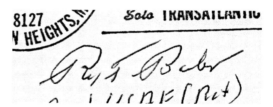

Barber-1, signature circa 1995.

Britain

George VI was never expected to become King of England. He ascended to the throne when his older brother Edward VIII abdicated. George ruled England from 1936 to his death in 1952. King George's signature exhibits good letter construction and legibility. Signatures are typically accomplished as "George R.I." in a slower hand. His signature is easily replicated. Many well-executed forgeries exist. There is an ample supply of signed material in the market, including DsS and Christmas cards, countersigned by his wife Elizabeth. Letters of any kind are rare. Signatures penned as "Albert" are rare and highly desirable. King George's signature is very affordable. His signature is valued at

$100–$125. DsS sell for $200 to $300. Documents countersigned by Prime Minister Clement Atlee are scarce and sell for $350 to $400.

George VI-1 undated signature.

Edward VIII succeeded to the throne upon the death of his father George V in 1936. King Edward ruled for only 326 days before he abdicated. He supported the doctrine of appeasement and proved rather friendly with Hitler. Edward signed in a sharp and jagged hand. Signatures are accomplished as "Edward R.I.," "Edward," "Edward P.," and later as "Edward, Duke of Windsor." Like that of his successor, there is an ample supply of material in the market. Many nicely signed photographs exist. Letters are scarce but a small supply of TLsS exist. Material signed with his wife, Wallis Simpson (Duchess of Windsor), is scarce and highly collectable. Signatures signed as king are rare. It should be noted that there is a large supply of forged postal covers in the market, so caution is warranted. It should be further noted that many MBE (Member of the Order of the British Empire) documents will contain a secretarial signature of Edward. Edward's signature is affordable at $150 to $200. A nicely signed photograph will sell for $400 to $500.

Edward VIII-1 signature as Prince dated 1923 (courtesy Nate D. Sanders Auctions).

Winston Churchill is one of the most significant figures of the 20th century. Churchill signed in a very tight and compact hand. His signature works well on small mediums. Sometimes he signed his name in full, other times as "W S Churchill." Letter construction is substandard where many letters display themselves as indistinguishable strokes. A poor legibility is noted. Churchill material exists in quantities. Many fine content ALsS and TLsS exist. There is a good supply of signed portrait photographs in the market. A few DsS by Churchill and King George V exist, but these should be considered rare. Due to the lack of structure, his signature is easily replicated. Well-executed forgeries exist in quantities. It should also be noted that many convincing facsimile signatures exist in the market, so caution is warranted. Demand for Churchill material is strong and will remain that way. Churchill's signature is valued at $700 to $900. TLsS sell for $1,250 to $1,500. ALsS are valued at $2,500 to $3,000. Content letters will sell for more than $10,000. The above-referenced King George document is valued at $2,000 to $2,500.

Churchill, W-1, signed book dated 1930 (courtesy Nate D. Sanders Auctions).

Generally a forgotten figure, Neville Chamberlain was prime minister from May 1937 to May 1940 and was best known for signing the Munich Agreement of 1938 with Hitler. He was a strong proponent of the doctrine of appeasement. Chamberlain signed in a long, drawn-out hand. His signature exhibits average eye appeal and legibility. The capital "N" in the first name is oddly formed in an otherwise unassuming signature. Replication of hand is fairly easy. Producing a well-executed forgery would not take much effort. His signature is scarce on a per se basis and generally limited to TLsS. ALsS and photographs are rare. There is not much demand for Chamberlain's signature. Expect to pay $150 for a nice specimen. A TLS is valued at $250 to $350.

Chamberlain-1, undated signature.

Clement Attlee was prime minister in the closing months of the war. Attlee signed in a hurried and unstructured hand. His signature has poor legibility and marginal display value. Signatures are almost always accomplished as "C.R. Attlee." The "R" and "A" are typically connected. His signature is marginally scarce on a per se basis. Signatures are generally limited to TLsS and the occasional photograph and album page. Attlee's signature is very affordable at $50 to $75. A nice TLS is valued at $100 to $125.

Clement R. Attlee

Attlee-1, undated signature (courtesy The Sanders Autograph Price Guide).

Always a popular signature with collectors is that of Field Marshal Bernard Law Montgomery of Alamein. A competent field commander, he gained international fame for his leadership during the African campaigns. Montgomery signed in a slower hand that lacks rapid flow. The signature is vertical in nature and exhibits good letter construction. His signature is usually accomplished as "Montgomery of Alamein, F.M." or "B.L. Montgomery." Truncated point construction is noted, and because of this his signature is easy to replicate. Many well-executed forgeries are in the market. Signatures are usually found on index cards, photographs, and books. He also signed many souvenir typescripts. There is good demand for Montgomery's signature. His autograph sells

for $125 to $150. ALsS, with routine content, are valued at $250 to $300. A nicely signed 8 × 10 photograph will command good money at $350 to $400.

Montgomery-1, signed book circa 1945 (courtesy Nate D. Sanders Auctions).

Air Marshal Sholto Douglas was probably the least-liked British officer of World War II. Douglas had a bad habit of rubbing everyone the wrong way, especially his superiors. Douglas signed in an average hand. His signature is fairly legible with sound letter construction. The signature is usually finished off with a small and muted paraph. His signature is rare and seldom surfaces. Expect to pay $200 for a nice specimen.

Douglas, S-1, undated signature.

Neville Duke was the second-highest scoring British ace of World War II. Duke was a willing and gracious signer throughout his life. There is a good supply of material in the market. He was a good letter writer; many with war content are in the market. His signature has average display value and is affordable at $25. ALsS will sell for $100 to $125.

Duke, N-1, ANS dated 2000.

Vice Air Marshal James Edgar "Johnnie" Johnson scored 34 kills, making him the highest-scoring British ace during the war. Like Duke, Johnson was also a gracious signer. His signature is generally found on mediums that could have been signed in the mail; hence, index cards and small photographs are available. Letters of any kind are scarce. He was fond of using the fountain pen to sign autographs. His signature sells for $50 to $75. A nicely signed 8 × 10 photograph is valued at $200.

Johnson, J. E., signed postal cover circa 1990.

Sir Douglas Bader is of particular interest to autograph collectors. He is credited with 20 kills during the war. He is best known as the fighter pilot who had both legs amputated. He lost both legs in a plane crash in the early 1930s. Bader died in 1982; hence, his signature is a lot less common than signatures of Duke or Johnson. Signatures are generally limited to postal covers and index cards. His signature generates good demand and is valued at $75 to $100.

Bader-1, undated signature.

Louis Mountbatten, First Earl Mountbatten of Burma, noted admiral of the fleet, was involved planning the raids on Dieppe and St. Nazaire. Mountbatten signed in a flowing and vertical hand. The signature exhibits good letter construction and legibility. His signature is generally finished off with a linear paraph. He was assassinated in 1979; hence, his signature remained strong his entire life. He was generally an accommodating signer, so there is an ample supply of signatures in the market. Signatures can be found on photographs, letters, postal covers, and the like. His signature is valued at $100. A nice ALS or 8 × 10 sells for $300 to $350.

Mountbatten-1, signature dated 1978 (courtesy Markus Brandes Autographs).

France

Petain's protégé was General Charles de Gaulle. He was leader of the free French forces and an outstanding military strategist who used tank warfare quite effectively. After the war he became prime minister of France. De Gaulle signed in a rapid hand. Letter construction and legibility are both marginal. The signature has limited display value. Most signatures are signed as "C. de Gaulle." Due to the lack of structure, de Gaulle's signature is rather easy to forge. Many well-executed forgeries are in the market. Most de Gaulle signatures are found on photographs, album pages, and calling cards. There is a good supply of TLsS in the market. A handful of ANsS exist, but many are signed with just his initials. A full-page ALS is a rarity. It should be noted that a short facsimile ANS on "Le General De Gaulle" note paper exists. It is only a four-word thank-you message and dated "2. 2. 60." This facsimile is rather convincing, so caution is warranted. Demand for de Gaulle's signature far outweighs supply. His signature is valued at $300 to $400. Signed

de Gaulle-1 signed book dated 1955 (courtesy Nate D. Sanders Auctions).

photographs sell for $750 to $1,000. Exceptional specimens can sell for over $2,000. De Gaulle's signature will always be in demand.

Most French aces are not that well-known. The exception is Marcel Albert, who was the second-highest scoring French ace with 23 kills. Albert signed in an average hand. His signature is practical in nature. After the war he lived in Florida. Albert was responsive to autograph requests. Signatures are found on mediums that could be signed in the mail; hence, index cards, ace playing cards, and small photographs are available. He received relatively few requests for his autograph. He died in 2010 and his signature should be considered uncommon. Premium items such as 8 × 10 photographs and letters are already considered scarce to rare. Albert's signature is affordable at $40 to $50. Small, postcard-sized photographs sell for around $75.

Albert-1, signature circa 2005.

Russia

Georgian Josef Stalin was the most ruthless dictator of 20th century. Because of this, his signature is one of the most coveted of all World War II autographs. Stalin signed in a powerful and flowing hand. No hesitation is noted. The signature is almost always signed with his first initial. The signature has average display value. Stalin was fond of writing in red pencil. Replication of hand would take some effort; however, well-executed forgeries do exist. The extreme value of his signature attracts skilled forgers. Signatures are generally limited to TLsS, DsS, and short ANsS written to his daughter. Signed photographs are an extreme rarity. There are a handful of items signed by the big three (Stalin, Churchill, and Roosevelt). These were likely signed at the Tehran confer-

ence in November of 1943. Stalin's signature was considered a very rare prize before the Soviet Union fell. Since that time, a handful of DsS have entered the market. The increased inventory adversely affected value. Stalin's signature is still considered rare and very valuable. An autograph sells in the $3,000 range. TLsS or DsS are valued at $4,000 to $5,000. A nice content TLS is worth $15,000 to $20,000. An item signed by Stalin, Roosevelt, and Churchill is valued at $20,000 to $30,000. An ALS is an extreme rarity. It should be noted that there are some typed documents that list the names or give orders to execute various political prisoners. A signature of Stalin is added in pencil where he writes his wishes to execute more prisoners, or something to that effect. I have seen three of these documents and all were a product of forgery. Stalin is one of the most valuable of all World War II autographs. His signature is a significant addition to any collection.

Stalin-1, DS circa World War II (courtesy Nate D. Sanders Auctions).

Hovhannes "Ivan" Bagramyan is considered one of the Soviet Union's finest military commanders. He held the title of marshal of the Soviet Union. Signatures of Soviet marshals are, in general, rare. They signed very few items and what was signed was usually held behind the Iron Curtain. Bagramyan is one of the more attainable signatures. He died in 1982 and there is a decent supply of war-date DsS in the market. Bagramyan also authored a couple of books and a signed copy will surface now and then. His signature is somewhat scarce and can be found signed in both Russian and Armenian script. Expect to pay $100 for his autograph. Signed books are closer to $200.

Marshal Georgy Zhukov was the most dec-

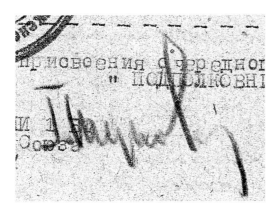

Bagramyan-1 signed book dated 1971 (courtesy Edward & Helen Mardigian Library at St. John's Armenian Church).

orated military officer of the Soviet Union. Zhukov signed in an eclectic and nonconforming hand. His signature has average display value. Given the unstructured nature of his hand his signature is fairly easy to replicate. Zhukov signed material used to be really tough to locate. In recent years an ample supply of signed war-date documents entered the market. It is about the only medium available. Signed photographs and ALsS are very rare. It should be noted that many of the DsS in the market contain a secretarial signature, so caution is warranted. A nice DS is valued at $200 to $250.

Zhukov-1, DS circa 1940.

The Third Reich

Signatures of the Reich, both military officers and Nazis, are highly collected. Germany was in the war longer than America and produced many collectable signatures. There is generally no concern in dealing with signatures of military officers such as aces and U-boat cap-

tains. When it comes to the Nazi leadership, a few Internet sites and auction companies will not handle this type of material. That being said, the demand for German World War II signatures is strong and it continues to push prices ever higher.

Adolf Hitler's signature is the most coveted of all German autographs of World War II. His signature is typically signed as "A. Hitler" in a very odd hand. The signature lacks hesitation and exhibits cutting angles. Towards the end of the war Hitler's hand was affected by tremors brought on by stress. This did affect material signed in the closing months of the war. His hand is complex in nature; hence, replication of hand is very difficult. Well-executed forgeries are very limited. Most forgeries lack flowing lines and a labored appearance is noted. Many documents and cards with printed messages were produced with facsimile signatures. These are high quality. The facsimile signatures are very convincing, so careful study is needed. Hitler did accommodate collectors while in office, but signatures are generally limited to portrait photographs. Letters of any kind are rare. ALsS are an extreme rarity. There is one forger who has, for the most part, mastered Hitler's hand. He produces some very convincing forgeries. His work product can be found on many mediums, including photographs. A common M.O. of this forger is to place forgeries on period postal covers. A nicely executed forgery is placed on a generic postal cover, postmarked in Germany in the 1930s or 1940s. The forgery is written over the postmark. Sometimes a second forgery of Hitler is added below the first. The signature lacks hesitation, but it also lacks flowing lines. The bottom part of the letter "H" is slightly elongated. Common sense should tell any collector that Hitler, then chancellor of Germany, would not autograph such a pedestrian item. These forgeries have been wrongly certified as genuine by the authentication companies, so caution is warranted.

The value of Hitler material has increased markedly over the past five years. Hitler's signature is valued at $1,000 to $1,250. DsS sell in the $1,500 to $2,000 range. A nicely signed 8 × 10 portrait photograph is rare and will sell for $5,000. A full-page ALS has an estimated value of $20,000 to $25,000. A strong content letter will likely sell for over $100,000. In 1925, Hitler published *Mein Kampf*. The book is part autobiography and part political manifesto. A signed copy would be an extreme rarity. Close to 100 percent of signed copies ever offered for sale are forged. A genuine signed edition is valued somewhere between $20,000 and $40,000. Hitler was also a painter, and his favorite medium was watercolor. He painted many landscapes and buildings. His paintings surface every so often and are valued around $50,000. I can only assume that many of these paintings "recently discovered" in an attic are simply counterfeit.

Hitler-1, signed book dated 1925 (courtesy Nate D. Sanders Auctions).

Hitler-2, DS circa 1935.

Signatures of people associated with Hitler are also collectable. Hans Baur was Hitler's personal pilot. He signed many items, including small photograph postcards. Far less common than Baur's signature is that of Traudl Junge. Junge was Hitler's private secretary and was in the bunker when Hitler committed suicide. She was one of the few people who would sign Hitler-related material, including plate blocks with an image of the swastika. Her signature has increased greatly in demand since her death in 2002. Her signature now sells for $100. Otto Gunsche was a Waffen-SS officer who later became Hitler's personal adjutant. He died in 2003 and was generally a responsive signer. The most common medium is picture postcards, which sell for $60 to $80.

Lt. Gen. Hans Baur, Chief Pilot of the Fuhrer

Baur-1 TLS undated.

Junge-1 signature circa 1990.

Gunsche-1, signed photo, circa 1980.

Marshal Hermann Goring's (or Goering) signature is highly collected. Not only was he a high-ranking member of the Nazi party, but he also scored 21 kills during World War I, making him a combat ace. Goring signed in a choppy hand. The signature evidences abrupt turns and poor letter construction. The signature is on the illegible side. Many signatures are accomplished with his last name only. Goring's signature is scarce on a per se basis as he committed suicide in 1946. War date DsS are a good source for his autograph. Signed photographs are rare.

Goering-1, undated signature.

He did sign autographs during the Nuremberg trials. The supply of material is outweighed by demand. Expect to pay $600 to $700 for a nice specimen. A war-date DS is valued at $1,000 to $1,250. Signatures accomplished during his tenure as a pilot should be considered very rare.

Heinrich Himmler was one of the most powerful men in Nazi Germany. He was the Reichsführer of the SS. He committed suicide in May of 1945. Himmler signed in a very bold and heavy hand. His signature evidences thick strokes of ink. Abrupt angles are noted coupled with compact letter formation. The signature evidences a good degree of legibility. Average display value is noted. Just about all signatures are accomplished as "H. Himmler." Replication of hand would take some effort. Well-executed forgeries do exist, given the strong demand for his autograph. His signature is scarce on a per se basis and generally limited to war-date DsS. ALsS and photographs are rare. There is one forgery to note. They are usually found on books and blank album pages. The forgeries are fairly well-executed. The forgeries are angled more to the right and the compactness of the letters, especially the "mm," are spaced farther apart. The forger usually adds a date such as "6.7.39" underneath the forgery. Himmler's signature is one of the most coveted of all World War II figures. It is valued at $600 to $700. DsS sell for $1,000 to $1,250. A full-page ALS is a rarity; therefore expect to pay $3,000 to $4,000 for a nice specimen.

Himmler-1 undated signature.

Paul Joseph Goebbels was the minister of propaganda. He was one of Hitler's most trusted advisers. He and his wife committed suicide on May 1, 1945. Goebbels signed in a confined hand. The signature has substandard letter construction. Poor legibility is noted. Just about all signatures available in the market are signed as "Dr. Goebbels." Rare in any form, signatures are generally limited to DsS. Goebbels's signature is in good demand and rather expensive. His signature is valued at $1,000. DsS are valued at $1,500.

Goebbels-1, LS circa 1940.

Albert Speer was known as "Hitler's architect." He was minister of armaments. He was tried and convicted of war crimes and sentenced to 20 years at Spandau Prison. He was released in 1966. Speer signed in a very compact hand. The letters are tightly aligned. Legibility is not one of Speer's strong points. The signature tends to be signed on a downward

Speer-1, TLS dated 1974 (courtesy Nate D. Sanders Auctions).

plane. Display value is substandard. Speer wrote three books and signed many copies. These are an excellent source for his autograph. TLsS exist in good numbers. ALsS are much more difficult to find. In the 1970s, Speer became the target of autograph collectors. He signed many items through the mail including, first-day covers and picture postcards. His signature is affordable at $50 to $75. Signed books can be purchased for $150 to $200.

Rudolf Hess was Hitler's deputy. He was arrested in Scotland and served a life sentence in Spandau Prison. He died there in 1987. Hess signed in a heavy hand. The signature is dominated with thick strokes and a large capital "R." The signature evidences jaggedness and is somewhat illegible. Many signatures are signed simply as "R. Hess" or "Hess." Hess material is scarce to rare and just about all signatures in the market are of war date. His signature is generally limited to TLsS and picture postcards. ALsS are very rare. There is good demand for this signature of restricted population. A signature is valued at $600 to $700. TLsS and picture postcards sell for $1,000 to $1,500.

Hess-1, DS dated 1938.

Admiral Karl Doenitz (pronounced as "Dare-nitz") was a career navy man who commanded U-boat 68 during World War I. After the death of Hitler, Doenitz became president of the Reich. He was convicted of war crimes and sentenced to prison. He was released in 1956. Doenitz signed in a striking hand. His signature has good display value. Most signatures are signed with his last name only. His hand became labored towards the end of his life. Material signed in the 1970s until death evidence an unsteady hand. Doenitz was a willing signer after his release from prison. His signature can be found on authored books, photographs, first-

day covers, and copies of the German instrument of surrender. Overall, there is an ample supply of material available to collectors. Expect to pay $125 for his autograph. Signed photographs are valued at $200 to $250.

Doenitz-1 TLS dated 1963 (courtesy Markus Brandes Autographs).

Alfred Jodl was the chief of operations for the Wehrmacht. He signed the instrument of surrender for Germany. He was tried and convicted of war crimes. He was hanged on October 16, 1946. Jodl's signature is signed with large blocky letters. The signature is legible with average display value. Most signatures are signed as "A. Jodl" or simply "Jodl." The slower nature of hand makes for easy replication. Well-executed forgeries do exist. His signature is of sound demand and very limited supply. Signatures are scarce and limited to portrait photographs, TLsS, and DsS. He signed autographs during the Nuremberg trial. Expect to pay $300 to $400 for his signature.

Jodl-1 signature, circa 1945.

Alfred Rosenberg was a longtime confidant of Hitler and held the unofficial title of minister of eugenics. He went to the gallows in 1946. Rosenberg signed in a pleasing hand. His signature exhibits excellent letter construction. Display value is sound. Just about all signatures are accomplished as "A. Rosenberg." His signature is fairly difficult to replicate. Well-executed forgeries are few and far between. Rosenberg's signature is scarce and generally found on war-date DsS. Album pages do exist, and these were likely signed at Nuremburg. Photographs of any kind are rare. There is good demand for Rosenberg material. His signature will sell for $600 to $700. DsS are valued at $1,000.

Rosenberg-1, undated signature.

Field Marshal Erich von Manstein was involved in many prominent battles of World War II. He is considered one of the finest field commanders of the war. He died in 1973 at the age of 85, making him one of the last surviving marshals of the war. In the early 1970s, collectors began to write him for autographs. He was a responsive signer. Items are generally limited to index cards, postcard-sized photographs, and ANsS. An 8 × 10 photograph would be very rare. He signed in a very unstructured hand, hence creating a well-executed forgery would be relatively easy. Fortunately, prices do not warrant the effort. Expect to pay $100 for his autograph. A picture postcard will sell for $200 to $250.

von Manstein-1, undated signature.

General Heinz Wilhelm Guderian is generally considered the greatest field commander of the 20th century. He was a brilliant general who incorporated the use of tanks and airplanes into a lightning style of warfare that the world would come to know as "Blitzkreig." Guderian signed in a more muted and rounded hand. His signature has moderate display value. Letter construction is marginal. Guderian's signature is scarce on a per se basis. Signatures are generally limited to album pages, picture postcards, and the occasional TLS. Other mediums, including ALsS, are rare to very rare. There are some signatures in the market that are signed in Armenian script; these, I believe, are forgeries. I know of no genuine signatures signed in Armenian. Guderian's signature generates sound demand. His signature sells for $300 to $350. A signed picture postcard is valued at $500 to $600. Guderian's son, Major General Heinz Gunther Guderian, was a high-ranking officer in postwar Germany. His signature is sometimes sold for that of his more famous father, so caution is warranted. It is of little value or interest.

Guderian-1 undated signature.

Erwin Rommel was Germany's most famous marshal of World War II. Known as the Desert Fox, he gained fame on the battlefields of Africa. Rommel signed in a flowing and fast hand. His signature is illegible but retains good display value. Signatures are typically signed as "Rommel" or on occasion "E. Rommel." A few ALsS written to his wife are in the market. They are simply signed "Love, Erwin." His signature is difficult to replicate; however, skilled forgers have taken up the challenge and produced some well-executed forgeries. Rommel is probably the second-most forged autograph of World War II Germany. There are many war-date DsS in the market, usually signed in pencil. It is said that Rommel preferred to sign military-related documents in pencil, as ink would dry out in arid desert conditions. At least 90 percent of Rommel signed material is forged. The vast majority of the aforementioned DsS are forged. Most forged DsS are on generic paper and lack any sort of letterhead. This makes it easy to counterfeit. Like the genuine documents, the forgeries are signed in pencil. But the forgeries lack the rapid flow of a genuine specimen. The length of the letter R in the last name is sometimes muted and is not as long as found in a genuine signature. If you notice any hesitation in the signature, even a minute amount, it should be considered a forgery and avoided. Many of these forged DsS were produced in the early 1980s. All are signed in pencil, many of which used a blood red or purple pencil. Many begin with "Sehr geehrte (or greehter) Frau (or Herrn) (or Herr)." This forger has also created many forged picture postcards. Rommel was forced to commit suicide in 1944. Therefore his signature is scarce on per se basis. Premium items are rare to very rare. DsS are the most common. ALsS are rare. His signature is valued at $500 to $600. TLsS and DsS sell for $800 to $1,200. A full-page ALS to his wife, signed as "Erwin," sells for $2,500 to $3,000. A good content ALS would likely be valued at $10,000 to $15,000.

Rommel-1, ALS dated 1939 (courtesy Nate D. Sanders Auctions).

The Angel of Death

Dr. Josef Mengele was an SS officer who held the title of physician of Auschwitz. His medical research centered on genetics and race. He put torture under the scientific method and it earned him the title of the Angel of Death. Mengele signed in the typical jagged German script. Abrupt turns and cutting angles are noted. Many signatures are signed with the last name only. Mengele material is rare and generally limited to the war-date period. DsS and ALsS exist,

but in very restricted quantities. Forgeries are common and are found mostly as clipped signatures and medical-related books. Demand is strong for Mengele material. His signature is one of the most expensive autographs of the World War II genre. Expect to pay $4,000 to $5,000 for DsS. ALsS are valued over $5,000.

In 2011, a collection of postwar handwritten, unpublished journals sold for $300,000 (Alexander Historical Auctions, 2011). A very significant 20th century autograph.

Mengele-1, ALS dated 1942.

Wolfram Sievers was managing director of the Ahnenerbe Institute. He was nicknamed the "Nazi Bluebeard." Like Mengele, Sievers also conducted experiments on humans which led to the deaths of hundreds (if not thousands) of victims. He had a fascination with bone collecting. He went to the gallows in 1948. Sievers' signature rarely surfaces and it is much tougher to locate then that of Mengele. The occasional post-war DS will surface and that is about it. One of the rarest of all World War II autographs.

Sievers-1, DS dated 1947.

Luftwaffe

The number of kills recorded by the Luftwaffe is incredible. Most victories were recorded on the eastern front. Many aces scored over 100 kills and a handful reached 200. Luftwaffe aces were some of the most responsive signers. Many aces would hand out signed postcard-sized photographs.

Though there are far too many aces to discuss in total, here are some of the more sought-after names.

First and foremost is Erich Hartmann. He was the ace of aces. His 352 kills make him the highest-scoring ace in aviation history. Known as the Black Devil, Hartmann lived until 1993 and was a responsive signer. His signature is generally limited to index cards and small postcard-sized photographs. There is a good inventory of his signature in the market. It is still affordable at $75.

Hartmann-1 album page circa 1970s.

The same said cannot be said of Gerd Barkhorn, who recorded 301 kills. He is second-highest scoring ace. Barkhorn was killed in a car accident in 1983 and was rarely asked for his autograph. Today, his signature is considered very scarce. Premium items are rare to very rare. I estimate a value of $400 to $500.

Barkhorn-1 ALS dated 1982 (courtesy Stephen Koschal Autographs).

General Gunther Rall recorded 275 kills, good enough for 3rd on the all-time list. Rall was a willing signer. He was targeted by collectors for many years. His signature is common, but generally limited to index cards and small

Rall-1, signature circa 1995.

photographs. He was a good letter writer and there is a decent supply of ALsS in the market. These, however, should be considered uncommon to scarce. His signature sells for $20 to $30. A nice full-page ALS is valued at $100 to $150.

Erich Rudorffer secured 222 kills and was for many years a good signer through the mail. Like Rall's, his signatures are generally limited to index cards and small photographs. He was known to send out short TNsS in German. Value of his signature is comparable to that of Rall.

Rudorffer-1 signature circa 1990.

Frank Neubert is of particular interest to collectors. He is credited with the first aerial victory of World War II. He lived until 2003, but signed relatively few items. His signature is limited to index cards and small photographs. Other mediums are scarce to rare. His signature is tough to locate, so expect to pay $50 to $75 for a nice specimen.

Neubert-1, signature circa 1990.

Hugo Broch scored 81 kills during the war. He was a good signer through the mail and

Broch-1, undated signature.

made liberal use of the fountain pen. His was also a prolific letter writer. Many ALsS are available, though just about all contain routine content. A nice ALS will sell for $50 to $75.

Adolf "Addi" or "Addie" Glunz scored 71 kills. He died in 2002. His signature is uncommon. A small supply of ALsS are in the market, though typically accomplished on index cards. Small postcard-sized photographs are available. His signature is valued at $40 to $50.

Glunz-1, signature circa 1990.

Gerhard Thyben scored 152 victories. He was captured by the British and was released shortly thereafter. He moved to South America and lived out his life in Colombia. The inventory of Thyben material is restricted. Many collectors did not know of his whereabouts; coupled with the unreliable South American mail service, this makes Thyben's signature scarce. The occasional index card or photograph postcard will surface. His autograph generates sound demand. Expect to pay $100 for a nice specimen.

Thyben-1, signature circa 1990.

Adolf Galland was the youngest man ever to attain the rank of general in the Luftwaffe. He scored 104 kills and his signature is one of the most sought-after of the aces. He was a good signer and honored requests for his autograph up to his death in 1996. There is an ample supply of his signatures in the market and the di-

versity of mediums is sound. He is one of the easier ace signatures to obtain on an 8 × 10 photograph. His signature can also be found on index cards, first-day covers, Reich marks, picture postcards, and the occasional TLS. ALsS are rare to very rare. His signature sells for $50 to $75. A nicely signed portrait 8 × 10 photograph is valued at $150 to $175.

Galland-1, undated signature.

Other high-scoring and collectable aces include Dietrich Hrabak, Alfred Grislawski, Peter Düttmann, Heinz Marquardt, Walter Wolfrum, Werner Hoffmann, Walter Schuck, Walter Krupinski, and Fritz Karch. All were good signers and today their signatures can be purchased for $25 to $50. Premium items are valued at close to $100.

Duttmann-1 signature circa 1990.

Marquardt-1, undated signature.

Wolfrum-1, signature circa 2000.

Hoffmann-1 signature dated 1990.

Karch-1, signed photograph 1990.

Krupinski-1 signature dated 1990.

Grislawski-1, undated signature.

Schuck-1 undated signature.

Hrabak-1, signature dated 1993.

Another German aviator of note was Hans-Ulrich Rudel. He was probably the most famous of the Stuka pilots and was the most highly decorated serviceman of the Reich. His signature is signed in a rapid fashion and displays itself as mere up-and-down strokes. There is good demand for Rudel material. His signature is valued at $100.

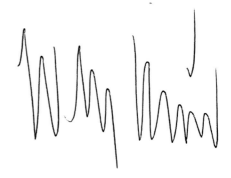

Rudel-1, undated signature (courtesy Stephen Koschal Autographs).

U-Boats

This is a prime example of how that which is of little interest becomes, in time, in much demand. Twenty years ago you could not give autographs of U-boat aces away. There was a small market and little value when it came to the U-boaters. About five years ago, when just about all of the U-boat commanders had passed away, demand exploded. Today, U-boat material is highly collected and continues to increase in value. Many of the aces were willing signers through the mail. However, they were seldom targeted by collectors. Today, many aces who died a mere five to ten years ago are scarce with premium items already considered rare. Signatures of aces who died during the war, such as Gunther Prien, are very rare. Many of their signatures have not been sold in years, so values are hard to determine. Here are a few of the more famous and attainable U-boat aces.

Admiral Otto Kretschmer is the ace of aces. No man sent more tonnage to the bottom of the Atlantic than Kretschmer. He sank 46 ships totaling 273 thousand tons. "Silent Otto" was a willing signer through the mail but signed few items, relatively speaking. He died in 1998. His signature is considered uncommon. Signatures are usually found on index cards and commemorative World War II postal covers. Signed photographs are scarce and limited to postcard-sized images. ALsS are scarce but do exist. Kretschmer was a fine letter writer and many good content letters exist. Kretschmer would write about U-boat patrols, Hitler, and racial doctrines. Kretschmer's signature has increased in value in recent years. His signature is the most coveted of all U-boat aces. Signatures sell for $75 to $100. Signed postcard-sized photographs sell for $150 to $200. A good content ALS now sells in the $400 to $500 price range.

Kretschmer-1, ALS dated 1996.

Admiral Erich Topp is the third-highest scoring ace of the war. He sank 35 ships with a gross tonnage of 197 thousand. After the war he became a consultant for NATO. Topp signed in a very unique and choppy hand. His signature has good display value. Topp also accommodated

Topp-1, ALS dated 1990.

autograph requests through the mail. He died in 2005, and his signature is more common than that of his counterpart Kretschmer. Topp was a prolific letter writer and many letters with military content exist. Topp signed a limited number of 8 × 10 photographs; these are scarce. His signature sells for $50. A full-page ALS will sell for $200.

Other noted U-boat commanders are Alfred Eick, Helmut Witte, and Reinhard Hardegen. Eick would send out signed picture postcards. Witte and Hardegen were known to write letters. Witte would write nice full-page letters, on personal letterhead, which makes for a nice display. Their signatures are valued at $50 to $75.

Witte-1, signature circa 1995.

Hardegen-1 postal cover dated 1993.

Eick-1 postal cover dated 1993.

The Emperor of Japan

Hirohito was the 124th emperor of Japan. In 1931, Hirohito ordered the invasion of Manchuria, and then China in 1937. His actions did not endear him to the West. In 1941, his order to attack the United States would plunge America into World War II. After the war he was spared the hangman's rope. He ruled Japan until his death in 1989, mostly as a figurehead. Hirohito's signature is found exclusively in Japanese script. He rarely honored requests for his signature. As a result, his autograph is considered rare to very rare. Signatures are generally found on official state letters and formal portrait photographs. Given the nature of Japanese script, with its truncated point construction, replication of hand is very easy. Many well-executed forgeries exist, especially on photographs. A common forged photograph features a young Hirohito in formal pose. He is wearing a suit and is holding gloves and a derby. The minute supply of Hirohito material is in great demand. Collectors from Japan will spend big money to obtain his autograph, and as a result, prices are pushed ever higher. Letters will sell for $8,000 to $10,000. A set of signed photographs by Hirohito and Empress Kojun make for handsome displays and will generally sell for $12,500 to $17,500.

Hirohito-1, undated signature.

Then there is the diminutive Iva Toguri, better known as "Tokyo Rose." She was an American who broadcast anti–American propaganda during the war. She was convicted of treason and sentenced to 10 years' imprisonment. In 1977 she was pardoned by President Ford. She died in 2006. Toguri lived a quiet life in Chicago and shunned publicity and autograph collectors. She signed very little. Her signature is considered scarce. ALsS, TLsS, and photographs are basically nonexistent. Given the small supply, her signature is in demand. It is valued at $200 to $250.

Il Duce

Benito Mussolini was the longtime ruler of Italy from 1922 until his death in 1945. He was one of the architects of 20th-century fascism. Mussolini signed in a rapid and powerful hand. The signature evidences poor letter construction. Good uniformity results in above average display value. Due to the complex nature of hand, replication is very difficult. There are no well-executed forgeries in the market. Years ago a flood of documents signed by Mussolini and King Victor Emmanuel III entered the market. The exact count is not known, but it is safe to say several hundred. This trove is the best source of Mussolini signatures, but its sudden appearance impaired the value of Mussolini material. Today, a DS can be purchased for $150 to $200. Signed photographs are also available for $500 to $750. Exceptional signed portraits still retain good value and will sell for $2,000 to $3,000.

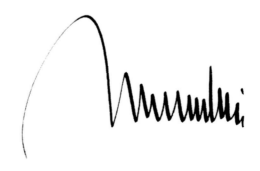

Mussolini-1, DS dated 1938.

The Leader of China

Chiang Kai-shek was a longtime Chinese political leader who held many posts, too many to

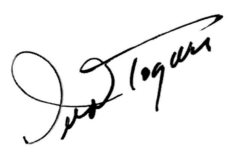

Toguri-1 undated signature.

list here. Chiang signed in the typical vertical Chinese script. His signature, like all Chinese signatures, is very easy to forge. Fortunately, Chiang was a responsive signer, a rarity for a Chinese head of state. There are countless items in the market. Mediums include photographs, DsS, and album pages. Letters of any kind are rare. One of the more affordable

Kai-shek-1, undated signature.

signatures, it is valued at $300 to $350. Photographs sell in the $750 range. Exceptional specimens will sell for over $1,500.

Rank and File Letters

Back in the mid–1980s I went to antique show at the Southfield, Michigan, civic center. Much ephemera was available for purchase. I went looking for baseball material. I happened to run across a dealer selling war-date letters written by soldiers of the Civil War. The asking price was $3 apiece and he had piles of them. I thought to myself, *Who would want that stuff?* Looking back, I dearly wish I had bought some of them. That episode taught me something very important about supply and demand. Something that is of little interest can, in no time, become very popular, and with popularity comes value. Those same Civil War letters are now valued at $150 to $250 each. A letter with Lincoln content can easily sell for more than $1,000. In the past few years, letters written by soldiers of the First World War have gained in popularity and values have started to move. As of this writing, World War II and Korean War letters are of little value. Entire family archives written by a soldier to his family can be purchased for nominal amounts. It you can buy this material, I advise you to do so. Like letters from earlier wars, these too will gain in popularity and should prove a fine investment.

Presidents of the United States

One of the most popular fields of autographs is the presidents of the United States. Only 45 men have secured this position through 2016, if you include David Atchison. Collecting presidents has been a long-established hobby. Presidential signatures were actively sought back before 1850. Relatives of George Washington and Thomas Jefferson received requests from pioneer collectors for a coveted signature. Presidents usually held prominent positions their whole lives; hence, they signed countless items. No presidential signature is considered rare on a per se basis.

The diversity of signatures of all the presidents is strong. Letters, deeds, books, grants, documents, and franks are available. As time went on, more mediums became available, such as photographs, engravings, and White House cards.

Presidents, starting with Richard Nixon, began signing material unrelated to the presidency. Baseballs, golf balls, bumper stickers, buttons, and the like were presented for signature. Ronald Reagan would sign Grover Cleveland Alexander material. Gerald Ford signed footballs and golf scorecards. George H.W. Bush signs World War II–related items. George W. Bush would pen his autograph on Texas Rangers material.

A presidential collection can be assembled with ease if you have the proper budget. Many collectors are unaware at how affordable most presidential signatures can be. Approximately 80 percent of presidential signatures can be purchased for under $500, many under $200.

The "big four" are presidents Washington, Jefferson, John Adams, and Abraham Lincoln. These signatures can be pricey. Signatures of these men start at $2,500. Documents and letters are easily valued at over $10,000. Letters with historical content have been known to exchange hands for more than $1,000,000. John Kennedy is also a treasured autograph and signatures start at $750.

Ronald Reagan is another president in high demand. Values have increased greatly for the Gipper's signature. Premium items such as content letters should be secured when the opportunity presents itself. Reagan's signature will prove the most valued of all 20th century presidents.

As President

Material signed as president is the most coveted by collectors and valued much higher than material signed before or after the presidency. The three most difficult signatures, signed as president, are William Henry Harrison, James Garfield, and Zachary Taylor. All served relatively short tenures in the Oval Office. Harrison was only in office for 30 days when he fell victim to pneumonia and died. Only a scarce few signatures exist of Harrison as president, and values reflect such.

Atchison is a strange footnote in American history. He was president for only one day. Though he is not officially recognized as a president, most collectors require his signature to complete a presidential set. No signatures of Atchison are known signed as president. If one were to surface I would not be surprised if it sold for six figures.

Land Grants

Many a time a soldier who fought for this country received payment not in cash, but with land. It was not uncommon for the taxpayer to compensate a veteran with 100, 200, 500 acres for services rendered during the war in which he fought. Back in the early days of our nation, revenues were tight, but land is something the country had a lot of. Hence, many signed land grants exist. The most common grants are signed by James Monroe, John Quincy Adams, and Andrew Jackson. Less common, but by no means scarce, are grants signed by James Madison. Any grants signed by Madison's predecessors are extremely rare. Any grant signed after Jackson will, in all likelihood, contain a secretarial signature. Many presidents did not sign grants at all. For all practical purposes, the above-referenced presidents are likely the only ones a collector will find on grants.

Free Franks

Franks—mail sent free of charge with an official's signature in lieu of postage—are a specialized medium and very popular among collectors. Many of the early presidents are available on franks, such as Washington, Adams, Jefferson, Quincy Adams, John Tyler, and Madison. Many post–Civil War presidents did not have franking privileges. Franks of Chester Arthur, Grover Cleveland, and the like are an extreme rarity. Just because a president did not have franking privileges did not mean an illegal frank was not signed here and there. A few presidents who served in Congress, such as Lincoln and Garfield, did sign franks. Modern presidents do have franking privileges, among them Truman,

Reagan, Carter, and Ford. Just about all franks of the modern presidents are preprinted signatures and are of no value. A hand-signed frank would be a rarity. Ford did frank a few covers for collectors but they are very rare. Some presidents will not hand-frank material, and this can lead to high prices. By way of example, a Carter signature is worth $25 to $50. A hand-signed frank would be easily worth $1,500.

Certain first ladies, including Lucretia Garfield, Mary Lord Harrison, Edith Roosevelt, and Grace Coolidge, also had franking privileges. A substantial and diverse frank collection can be assembled with the proper budget.

The White House Card

White House cards are extremely popular among collectors. Three distinct cards exist. The first is the "Executive Mansion" card. This card was used by Presidents Grant up to Theodore Roosevelt. Roosevelt found the card too formal and changed it to "White House" cards. Not satisfied, Roosevelt once again changed it to "The White House." It remains that way to this day. Roosevelt-signed Executive Mansion cards are a rarity.

Some cards will have the printing shifted on the card. These variations are generally not considered significant enough to warrant a premium.

For all practical purposes, Rutherford B. Hayes is the first president available to collectors. The earliest known signed card is that of Grant. Being a unique specimen makes it an extreme rarity and unavailable to collectors. Many presidents were partial to these cards and signed many. Other presidents, such as Eisenhower, Ford, Nixon, and Johnson, did not sign these cards as president.

The most important work ever published on this presidential medium is titled *The History of Collecting, Executive Mansion, White House, and The White House Cards* (2006). Authored by Stephen Koschal and Lynne Keyes, it is the most in-depth study ever done on this subject. The book details rarity of specific cards. Variant cards are examined. The book is richly illustrated with cards signed not only by the presidents but also first ladies. No autograph reference library should be without this book.

*   *   *

George Washington

Washington signed in a wonderfully eloquent hand. His signature is marked with fine strokes and effortless flow. Letter construction is fairly sound, but some letters appear malformed to the modern eye. This is more a function of the writing style of the time than a quirk of Washington's hand. Just about all signatures are signed as "G. Washington." Washington's hand remained strong his entire life. A genuine signature will evidence no shakiness of hand and one that does should be considered suspect and avoided. Due to the rather complex nature of his hand, Washington's signature is very hard to forge. Well-executed forgeries are very limited. Washington is probably the third most difficult presidential signature to replicate. Nineteenth-century forger Robert Spring created forgeries of Washington. Short ADsS were his specialty. Many consider his work well-executed, but I do not. His work product is exposed with little effort. Forgeries created by Joseph Cosey have better structure and are harder to detect. In recent years a forger, who I believe resides in Germany, has created some very convincing forgeries of Washington and other early presidents. His also creates some impressive forgeries of baseball pioneer Alexander Cartwright. These forgeries are nicely executed but evidence an *ever so slight* methodic hand. Careful examination is needed to expose this forger's work.

In recent years a forged letter or two has entered the market. No doubt multiple specimens exist. These are multi-page letters with excellent content. The letters discuss Washington's deep need for "peace" or something to that effect. The ink is clean and bright, perhaps too bright for a letter allegedly penned over 200 years ago. The forger's work is sound; however, the handwriting lacks relative speed that would be found in a genuine Washington writing. The giveaway is the "GW" in the forgery. These letters are malformed and evidence a material deviation from Washington's hand.

Washington's signature is somewhat scarce on a per se basis. His signature exists on letters, free franks, lottery tickets, and documents or signatures removed therefrom. A few military appointments and ship papers exist, but these should be considered rare. Ship papers are highly desirable as they are countersigned by then Secretary of State Thomas Jefferson. I have never examined an item signed by Washington and his vice-president John Adams.

Washington is the most desirable of all presidential signatures and the most expensive. Signatures will generally sell for $6000 to $8000. LsS and DsS, with routine content, sell in the $10,000 to $15,000 range. An ALS will sell for $25,000 to $35,000, again with routine content. Any writings of significance can easily sell for more than $1,000,000. In June 2012 a U.S. Constitution-related book owned by Washing-

Washington-1, signature dated 1757. Extremely rare early date.

Washington-2, undated signature.

ton with hand annotations sold for close to $10,000,000.

Washington-3, undated signature.

Washington-4, forgery accomplished by Robert Spring.

John Adams

Adams signed in a very structured and meticulous hand. His signature evidences strong letter construction. Good legibility is noted. Adams's hand lacked speed and produced a signature that appears slightly hesitant. Eye appeal is strong. As Adams aged, his hand was affected by palsy. As a result, material signed late in life is accomplished in a very shaky and unsteady hand. He signed his autograph as "John Adams" and later in life as simply "J. Adams." Due to the slower nature of his hand, Adams's signature is very easy to forge. Many forgeries exist on ALsS, DsS, bank checks, and books purportedly from Adams's library. Well-executed forgeries are everywhere, so caution is warranted.

Adams's signature exists on ALsS, DsS, and LsS. Free franks exist but are considered very scarce. A few signed land grants countersigned by Adams's secretary of state, John Marshall, exist. These documents are rare and highly treasured.

Adams's signature will generally sell in the $2,500 range. Free franks, which typically exhibit an impaired and elderly signature, sell in the same price range. ALsS with routine content sell for $6,000 to $10,000. Adams was probably the finest letter writer of all the presidents. He could write with a cutting pen. A well-crafted Adams letter is a fine addition to any collection. A document countersigned by Marshall will sell in the $8,000 to $10,000 range. An ALS with strong historical content would likely sell for six figures and possibly $1,000,000.

Adams, J-1, undated signature.

Adams-2, undated signature.

Thomas Jefferson

Jefferson signed in a very practical hand. His signature is well structured. Legibility is sound. The display value is of average disposition. He signed his name as "Th. Jefferson." His signature is penned in a slower hand. It is one of the easier signatures to forge. Well-executed forgeries exist in quantities. Jefferson's hand remained strong his entire life. A genuine signature will evidence no shakiness of hand, and one that does should be considered suspect and avoided.

Jefferson material is limited to ALsS, LsS, DsS, free franks, and the occasional bank check. His signature is somewhat scarce on a per se basis. Jefferson is one of the most significant figures in world history. The demand for his writings is great and clearly outweighs supply. ALsS are tricky because Jefferson would write the text of the letter is a small and confined hand. The signature appears large and misscaled next to the body of the letter, giving it the appearance of a LS. Many ALsS, signed in the third person, are in the market, though less desirable than an ALS in full.

Ever a prolific letter writer, Jefferson made copies of many of his correspondence. He used a machine called a polygraph. It would incorporate two quill pens. He would write the letter and the second pen made a duplicate copy for his records. The polygraph letters stand out as the handwriting does not appear smooth. It has an unsteady and scratchy appearance. For more information on this machine and its work product, the 2007 book *Thomas Jefferson's Invisible Hand*, authored by Stephen Koschal and Andreas Wiemer, is instructive.

During the 1930s a bank in Virginia released many facsimile Jefferson ALsS and franked envelopes addressed to Craven Peyton. These were handed out as a promotional. Today these facsimiles are sometimes sold as genuine, so caution is warranted.

Jefferson's signature sells in the $3,000 to $3,500 price range. Franks will sell for slightly more. An ALS with routine content is valued anywhere from $10,000 to $15,000. Bank checks are very rare and sell for about $15,000. There is a small supply of DsS which are countersigned by James Madison as secretary of state. These dual-signed documents sell in the $4,500 to $5,500 price range. There are a few of these dual-signed documents in the market on which the signatures deviate somewhat from genuine specimens. I believe these to be forgeries. Care-

ful study is needed, as these are being sold by auction houses. An ALS with strong historical content would likely sell for more than $1,000,000.

James Madison

Madison signed in a rather confined and neat hand. His signature is small in scale. Letter construction is sound. The signature has a good degree of legibility. His hand evidences strong flow. Hesitation is lacking. Due to the lack of flamboyance, Madison's signature has average display value. Signatures are penned as either "James Madison" or "J. Madison." Replication of hand would take some effort but well-executed forgeries do exist. Madison's hand remained strong his entire life. A genuine signature will evidence only trivial shakiness of hand.

As with most early presidents, mediums are limited to ALsS, DsS, LsS, franks, and the occasional bank check. His signature is somewhat scarce but a good supply of DsS keeps this early president's signature affordable. Signed land grants exist in ample quantities.

Madison's signature can be purchased for $400 to $500. Franks will sell closer to $1,000. DsS sell in the $750 to $1,000 range. ALsS, with routine content, sell for $3,000 to $5,000. Bank checks are rare and sell for $1,500. Documents countersigned by Madison's secretary of state,

Jefferson-1, undated signature.

Madison-1 undated signature.

Jefferson-2, DS dated 1790.

Madison-2, undated signature.

James Monroe, are fine collectables and are surprisingly affordable at $1,000 to $1,500. An ALS with strong historical content would likely sell in the $100,000 price range.

James Monroe

Monroe signed in a very plain and unassuming hand. His signature has strong letter construction with a high degree of legibility. Only a trivial amount of hesitation is noted. He signed his name as "James Monroe" and, on occasion, as "Jas. Monroe." The practical nature of Monroe's signature makes replication of hand easy. Many well-executed forgeries are in the market, so caution is warranted. Monroe's hand remained strong his entire life. A genuine signature will evidence no shakiness of hand, and one that does should be considered suspect and avoided.

In addition to the above-referenced Madison/Monroe documents, Monroe DsS exist countersigned by his secretary of state and future president, John Quincy Adams. Land grants exist in quantities. Documents countersigned by his secretary of war, John Calhoun, are rare and command a premium. It should be noted that many forgeries exist of Madison and Monroe that appear to be clipped from larger documents.

Monroe's signature can be purchased in the $250 to $300 range. Land grants and free franks sell for $400 to $500. ALsS are scarce and sell for about $1,000. Full-page specimens can sell

for nearly $5,000. Documents countersigned by Adams sell for $1,500 to $2,000. A document countersigned by Calhoun is more affordable at $700 to $800.

John Quincy Adams

Son of the second president of the United States, John Quincy Adams signed in a very confined and tiny hand. His handwriting is small and unassuming. The signature appears mis-scaled on folios and 4to documents such as ship papers. His signature is accomplished in a much slower hand. Strong flow is lacking. The result is a signature with a labored appearance. Display value is limited. Due to the slow and hesitant nature of Adams's hand, his signature is very easy to replicate. In fact, it is the easiest of all presidential signatures to forge. As Adams aged, his hand was affected by palsy. Material signed in his later years exhibits a considerable shakiness of hand.

Adams's signature is found on ALsS, DsS, and free franks. Land grants exist in quantities. Bank checks are rare. There are a few DsS countersigned by Adams's secretary of state, Henry Clay. Signed Nathaniel Dearborn engravings do exist but are an extreme rarity. Just about all sold over the past 50 years are forgeries. Forgeries are placed above the image as "John Quincy Adams."

Adams's signature is affordable and can be purchased with little effort. A signature will sell for $200 to $250. Land grants and free franks

Monroe-1, free frank circa 1815.

Adams, J.Q.-1, free frank circa 1820.

Monroe-2, DS dated 1818 (courtesy Nate D. Sanders Auctions).

Adams, J.Q.-2, DS dated 1825 (courtesy Nate D. Sanders Auctions).

are only slightly more. ALsS and bank checks are valued at $1,200 to $1,500. DsS countersigned by Clay are a rarity and sell for $1,000 to $1,500. It should noted that Adams was a poet and once in a while a nice APS will enter the market. These are very rare and will sell in excess of $5,000.

Andrew Jackson

Jackson's signature is bold and aureate, which matched his personality. Jackson's signature evidences sound letter construction. A high degree of legibility is noted. His autograph works well on paper and dominates the medium it is placed upon. The display value is high. Jackson would finish off his signature with a large paraph. Due to the sound letter construction and fluid nature of hand, Jackson's signature is rather difficult to replicate. Well-executed forgeries exist but are very limited. Jackson's hand remained strong his entire life. A genuine signature will evidence no shakiness of hand, and one that does should be considered suspect and avoided.

The demand for Old Hickory's signature is great. He is one of the most popular of all presidents. The most common medium is DsS, specifically land grants. Free franks, LsS, and endorsements are less common. ALsS are scarce and command a premium. Bank checks are rare and seldom surface. There is a small supply of DsS countersigned by Jackson's secretary of state and future president, Martin Van Buren. DsS countersigned by his attorney general Roger Taney are very rare and highly prized by collectors.

Were it not for the good supply of land grants, Jackson's signature would be far more expensive. His signature sells for $500 to $600. Land grants typically can be purchased for $700 to $900. Bank checks are rare and sell for $2,500 to $3,000. The above-referenced Jackson/Van Buren DsS are scarce and are valued at $2,000 to $2,500. The Jackson/Taney

DsS are rare to very rare and should sell for $2,500 to $3,000. ALsS, with routine content, sell for around $2,000. An ALS with good content will easily be worth $25,000. It should be noted that some land grants were secretarially signed during his second term. Fortunately for collectors, the secretarial signature varies greatly from a genuine specimen.

Jackson, A-1, undated signature.

Jackson, A-2, ALS circa 1820.

Martin Van Buren

Old Kinderhook, as he was nicknamed, signed in a sloppy and rather unattractive hand. Letter construction is poor. His signature is somewhat illegible. ALsS are hard to read and need quite a bit of deciphering. Overall, Van Buren's signature has limited display value. Signatures are mostly signed as "M. Van Buren." Van Buren's hand remained strong his entire life. A genuine signature will evidence no shakiness of hand, and one that does should be considered suspect and avoided. There are at least two different secretarial signatures in the market, so caution is warranted.

There is a good supply of Van Buren material in the market. Free franks, ALsS, DsS, LsS, and endorsements exist in sound numbers. Bank checks are rare and are in high demand. Land grants are always signed by Van Buren's secretary and are of little value.

Van Buren's autograph is affordable at $225 to $250. ALsS sell for $400 to $500 with routine content. Van Buren was known to write letters that went on for five or six pages. Expect to pay $2,000 to $3,000 for a lengthy writing. Bank checks are valued at $1,250 to $1,500.

Van Buren-1, ALS dated 1823 (courtesy Nate D. Sanders Auctions).

Van Buren-2, undated signature.

William Henry Harrison

Harrison signed in a very practical and rugged hand. His signature evidences bold and wide strokes. Letter construction is average at best. The signature is fairly legible, but some of the letters display themselves as indistinguishable strokes. The display value is marginal. Most signatures are signed as "W.H. Harrison" or as "Wm. H. Harrison." Signatures penned as "Willm. Henry Harrison" are rare and seldom surface. Harrison's hand remained strong his entire life. A genuine signature will evidence no shakiness of hand, and one that does should be considered suspect and avoided.

There is average demand for Harrison's signature. The supply is limited. His long military career produced an ample supply of signed endorsements and short ADsS, mostly to procure supplies for the army. Bank checks are rare. His presidency only lasted 30 days, the briefest in American history. A signature as president is an extreme rarity. A genuine specimen has not been sold in years. Some signatures accomplished as president, what few there are, have an appearance that differs greatly from a genuine specimen. Many have been sold as genuine; I, however, believe these to be secretarial. I estimate the total market population of Harrison-as-president signatures to be under ten specimens. If you see a Harrison signature signed as president for sale, the chances that it is genuine are slim to none.

A small group of forgeries has surfaced over the past few years and they need to be discussed. These are signatures purportedly removed from presidential appointments. They contain a forgery of Harrison in the upper right signed as "W.H. Harrison." A forgery of Harrison's secretary of state Daniel Webster is added to the lower left next to printed text of "Secretary of State." A shakiness of hand is noted in the signatures. The letter "s" in Harrison is shaky, very elongated with a thick stroke of ink.

There are a couple of small portrait engravings in the market that are signed as "Gen. W.H. Harrison." The signature deviates greatly from a genuine specimen. To my knowledge, no signed images of Harrison exist.

A signature as president will sell for $100,000 to $150,000, but in an auction situation could go much higher. On occasion you will see a signature signed as president that sells for under $50,000. These are typically a signature found on a partial presidential document, such as a land grant or appointment (discussed above). These are almost always forged and the knowledgeable collector will avoid them; hence, the depressed value. As time goes on, the market population of Harrison-as-president signatures will increase as forgeries are certified as genuine by authentication companies. A Harrison signature will sell for $600 to $800. A DS or LS

Harrison, W-1, undated signature.

Harrison, W-2, undated signature.

Harrison, W-3, apocryphal signature.

will sell for $1,000 to $1,250. Bank checks sell for slightly more. An ALS is valued at $1,500 to $2,000.

John Tyler

Like his predecessor, Tyler signed in a plain and practical hand. His signature evidences good letter construction. Sound legibility is noted. Tyler's hand is average, resulting in a signature with limited display value. Most signatures are signed simply as "J. Tyler" and finished with a paraph. Tyler's hand remained strong his entire life. A genuine signature will evidence no shakiness of hand, and one that does should be considered suspect and avoided.

As with other early presidents, signatures are generally limited to letters and documents. Short ALsS are available. DsS as president are scarce and command a premium. Free franks are in good supply and have good display value. It should be noted that one forger has produced signatures and free franks. These signatures evidence a slight shakiness of hand and are exposed upon examination. The forged franks are signed in a tremulous hand as "J. Tyler / U.S.S." and contain a red postmark with the date of "Feb 5." Land grants are secretarially signed and of little value.

Tyler is a signature of limited demand. His autograph and franks sell for $400. LsS are only slightly higher. ALsS are valued around $800 to $900. An exceptional example written to Jefferson Davis sold for $15,000.

James Polk

Polk signed in a nice and neat hand. His signature is confined and works well on small mediums. Letter construction is marginal with malformed letters. His signature can sometimes display itself as illegible. Despite this, his signature has a certain uniformity. The display value of Polk's signature is superior. A complex paraph finishes off the signature, which only enhances display value. Polk signed in a somewhat slower hand; hence, replication is easy. Well-executed forgeries exist. Polk's hand remained strong his entire life. A genuine signature will evidence no shakiness of hand, and one that does should be considered suspect and avoided.

Polk's signature is of sound demand which outweighs supply. Polk's signature is one of the scarcest of all presidents on a per se basis. Signatures can be found on DsS, free franks, and LsS. ALsS are very scarce and command a premium. Many endorsements exist as president

Tyler-1, free frank circa 1840 (courtesy Nate D. Sanders Auctions).

Tyler-2, ALS dated 1860 (courtesy Nate D. Sanders Auctions).

Polk-1, LS dated 1845.

Polk-2, undated signature.

but are typically signed with his initials. DsS countersigned by Polk's secretary of state and future president James Buchanan are rare and highly collected.

Polk's signature is valued at $500 to $600. A routine LS or DS will sell for $700 to $900. A nicely accomplished free frank can sell for $700 to $800. ALsS are tough to locate and will sell for $1,500 to $2,500. The above-referenced Polk/Buchanan DsS are scarce and sell for close to $3,000.

David Rice Atchison

Atchison signed in a flowing and clean hand. His signature evidences smooth strokes. Letter construction is sound. The signature is legible with good display value. Overall, a pleasant signature that works well on paper. Atchison's hand is fairly complex in nature, resulting in a signature that is hard to replicate. There are no well-executed forgeries in the market. It is unclear whether infirmity of hand affected his writing in later years.

There is sound demand for Atchison material. He was president of the United States for only one day, which makes his signature very collectable. He was also involved with the pro-slavery Border Ruffians of Missouri. Signed material is generally limited to his tenure as U.S. senator. ALsS, LsS, and album pages do exist but are scarce.

Atchison-1 album page circa 1850 (courtesy collection of John Keurajian).

Atchison-2, undated signature.

There are very few signed items in the market. His signature generally sells for $400 to $500. ALsS are anywhere from $1,000 to $2,000. A signature accomplished as president has yet, as of this writing, to be discovered.

Zachary Taylor

Taylor signed in a no-nonsense hand. His signature evidences good flow, but a slight choppiness is noted. Letter construction is sound. Legibility is good with big and well defined letters. Taylor signed in a heavy, military-like hand. The display value is average at best. Many signatures signed as an officer are penned as "Zachary Taylor." Material signed as president is typically signed as "Z. Taylor." Because his signature lacks flamboyance, it is a rather easy hand to copy. Well-executed forgeries do exist. Taylor's hand remained strong his entire life. A genuine signature will evidence no shakiness of hand, and one that does should be considered suspect and avoided.

Known as "Old Rough and Ready," Taylor was a career military officer. He had fought in the War of 1812 and the Michigan Hawk War, among others. DsS as a military officer exist and are a good source for Taylor's signature. ALsS and LsS are much scarcer. He served only 16 months in the White House; thus material signed as president is scarce and commands a premium. Free franks signed as president exist, but these should be considered rare, albeit borderline.

Recent auction prices suggest a signature

Taylor-1, DS dated 1849 (courtesy Nate D. Sanders Auctions).

with good demand. Taylor's signature is valued at $1,000 to $1,200. LsS will sell for $2,000 to $3,000. ALsS are typically long, and sell for $4,000. DsS and free franks as president sell for $3,500 to $4,000. An ALsS as president is a rarity. I estimate a value of $15,000 to $20,000. It should be noted that secretarial signed documents do exist.

Taylor-2, DS dated 1849 (courtesy Nate D. Sanders Auctions).

Millard Fillmore

Fillmore signed in a very nice and flowing hand. His signature evidences good speed. Letter construction is sound. The signature is legible. His signature exhibits a degree of complexity and sophistication. Fillmore's signature has superior display value. Most signatures are signed in full. Franks are typically signed "M. Fillmore." Due to the complex nature of his hand, well-executed forgeries do not exist. Fillmore's hand remained strong his entire life. A genuine signature will evidence only slight choppiness of hand in his later years. His hand never produced a truly shaky signature. Overall, one of the nicer presidential autographs.

The diversity of signed mediums increases with Fillmore. His signature is found on ALsS, LsS, free franks, and DsS. Signed photographs are very rare. It appears that Fillmore's personal library, or portions thereof, were released into the market. Books Fillmore signed and dated alongside his name are available for purchase. A few DsS as president exist countersigned by his secretary of state, Daniel Webster. These should be considered very scarce.

A signature of marginal demand results in a very affordable autograph. Fillmore's signature sells in the $200 to $300 range. Franks sell for $250 to $300. ALsS are valued at $500 to $600. Signed photographs are in high demand and a nice specimen is valued at $6,000 to $8,000. The above-referenced Fillmore/Webster documents sell for $1,000. Books from his library are coveted by both autograph and book collectors. Expect to pay $500 for one. A couple of bank checks are in the market; I question the authenticity of these checks.

Fillmore-1, undated signature (courtesy The Sanders Autograph Price Guide).

Fillmore-2, ALS dated 1864.

Franklin Pierce

Pierce signed in a very elegant and complex hand. The signature is marked with large, sweeping strokes. Letter construction is sound. The signature is, for the most part, legible. The large capital letters only enhance display value. Pierce signed his autograph as either "Franklin Pierce," "Fr. Pierce," or "Frank Pierce." Due to the complexity of hand, his signature is fairly difficult to replicate. Well-executed forgeries are limited. It should be noted that Pierce's secretary was well versed at signing the president's signature. Pierce's hand remained strong his entire life. A genuine signature will evidence no shakiness of hand, and one that does should be considered suspect and avoided.

Pierce material is generally limited to ALsS, DsS, and LsS. ALsS have nice eye appeal, but content of these letters is generally dull and routine. Free franks are considered scarce. DsS countersigned by Pierce's secretary of state and future CSA president Jefferson Davis are very scarce and in high demand.

The demand for Pierce's autograph is limited to set completion. Signatures, franks, DsS, and LsS are valued between $300 and $500. Many ALsS exist and can be purchased for $500 to $800. The above-referenced Pierce/Davis DsS sell for $2,500 to $3,000. Land grants are secretarially signed. There are a handful of bank checks in the market. I question the authenticity of these checks.

Pierce-1, ALS dated 1853 (courtesy Nate D. Sanders Auctions).

Pierce-1, free frank circa 1850 (courtesy Nate D. Sanders Auctions).

James Buchanan

Buchanan's signature is one of the finest of all presidential signatures. Buchanan signed in a flowing script. Letter construction is superior. The hand is very legible. Buchanan's signature has maximum eye appeal. Signatures accomplished late in life are signed in a slightly slower hand. Well-executed forgeries do exist but are very limited. Most forgeries are amateurish in appearance. A signature accomplished in a materially unsteady hand should be considered suspect and avoided.

There is a good supply of Buchanan material weighed against average demand. Signatures can be found on ALsS, DsS, LsS, free franks, and endorsements. ALsS have strong eye appeal and are typically written on a slight upward angle. Signed books from Buchanan's personal library are very rare. I am told signed photographs exist, though I have never seen one I would feel comfortable pronouncing as genuine. There is a rather famous image of an elderly Buchanan photographed by Thomas Cummings. There are many CDVs of this image where a forgery is placed along the lower border of the card. The forgery is signed in a plain hand and lacks the flamboyance of a genuine specimen.

Land grants are secretarially signed. It should be noted that one of Buchanan's secretaries was very skilled at signing the president's autograph. The capital letter "J" is very similar in construction, so caution is warranted.

Buchanan material is very affordable. Signatures are valued at $200 to $250. Free franks, LsS, and DsS sell for $400 to $600. ALsS can be purchased for $600 to $800. There are a few canceled bank checks in the market. They are drawn on generic counter checks. I do not believe these are genuine.

Buchanan-1, DS circa 1860.

Buchanan-2, undated signature (courtesy The Sanders Autograph Price Guide).

Abraham Lincoln

Lincoln signed in a rugged and practical hand. There is nothing fancy about his handwriting. The signature is legible with good letter construction. Lincoln signed in a slower hand that lacks precise lines. As such, it is a signature of average display value. Most signatures are signed simply as "A. Lincoln." Documents signed as president, such as appointments, are signed as "Abraham Lincoln."

Material signed as a congressman tends to be signed in a somewhat faster hand. Lincoln wrote many letters. Letters tend to be gracious and will evidence a spelling error here and there. More common is a word or two omitted in total. Due to the slower nature of hand, Lincoln's signature is quite easy to forge. Many well-executed forgeries are in the market. Lincoln is one of the most forged signatures in the field of autographs. Skilled forgers have targeted his signature for decades. The majority of Lincoln signatures in the market are forged. Many are continuously sold by auction companies. Lincoln died of a gunshot wound to the head. His hand remained strong his entire life. A genuine signature will evidence no shakiness of hand, and one that does should be considered suspect and avoided.

There is a good supply of Lincoln material in the market, but not nearly enough to satisfy an insatiable demand. Material signed as a congressman is rare, as he only served one term. A free frank signed as a congressman will surface now and then. Lincoln DsS and LsS as president exist in ample supply. Endorsements are probably the most common. They typically read "Let this man take the oath and be discharged." ALsS from any period are in high demand and are much less common than other mediums. Photographs are a rarity and just about 100 percent are forged. Bank checks are also rare. Many of these checks are counterfeit. These checks are very convincing and careful study is needed. I have come to the conclusion that the majority of Lincoln checks drawn on the Springfield Marine & Fire Insurance Company are counterfeit. Another common forgery is ADsS purportedly signed by Lincoln as an attorney. These are produced by the same forger. They are on strips of paper from 7" to 8" long. The width is usually 2" to 5" and the content is four or five sentences. The text is usually the same. They are receipts from clients or opposing parties. They typically read as "Received from John Doe by (or through) Jim Smith $500 dollars and 50/100 cents." Forger Joseph Cosey was rather skilled at producing Lincoln forgeries, and his work product causes problems to this very day.

Lincoln is the second most valuable presidential autograph on a per se basis. Only Washington's signature has a higher value. Signatures are valued at $3,500 to $4,000. Endorsements and DsS sell for $5,000 to $6,000. ALsS, with routine content, are valued at $15,000 to $20,000. A nice alternative are legal briefs accomplished by Lincoln as an attorney. They are typically signed with his last name only, such as "Peters + Lincoln." These are an excellent source for Lincoln signatures and are affordable. Full page briefs, signed with the last name only, can be purchased for $5,000 to $7,000. Unsigned briefs will sell for under $4,000. ALsS, with historical content, are priceless. In 2008 a one-page ALS with slavery content sold for $3.4 million.

White House Cards

Despite rumors to the contrary, no signed cards exists.

Lincoln-1, signature circa late 1840s as Congressman (courtesy Mark Allen Baker).

Lincoln-2, DS dated 1861 (courtesy Nate D. Sanders Auctions).

Lincoln-3, AES dated 1864.

Lincoln-4, AES dated 1964 (courtesy Nate D. Sanders Auctions).

Lincoln-5, forgery, text is the forged handwriting of John Hay, circa 1930.

Lincoln-6, well executed forgery.

Assassin—John Wilkes Booth

Political assassins can alter history with a single gunshot. Perhaps no assassin in history does this apply to more than John Wilkes Booth, an actor and Southern loyalist whose hatred of president Lincoln came to a boiling point on April 14, 1865. That evening at Ford's Theatre, Booth entered the presidential box and shot Lincoln in the back of the head. After the largest manhunt in American history, Booth was cornered in a barn in Port Royal. Refusing to surrender, he took a bullet to the neck fired from the gun of Sergeant Thomas "Boston" Corbett.

An actor, with the flair for the dramatic, Booth signed in a flourishing and bombastic hand. The signature is large with well-defined letters and sweeping curves. Lines tend to go every which way, resulting in a signature with a very busy appearance. A slight hesitation is noted in the strokes.

Overall, a signature with good display value. Though the signature is complex in nature, it is signed in a slower hand. Because of this, replication is rather easy. Well-executed forgeries exist. Just about 100 percent of all Booth signatures in the market are the product of forgery. Booth's signature is very rare and the total market population is likely around 5 to 10 specimens. A handful of ALsS and DsS do exist, and that is about it. Forgeries exist on all mediums. A common forgery is signed books. These were produced several years ago. The books are of various mundane topics. They are signed as "John Wilkes Booth" and dated beneath the signature. There are a handful of these in the market. I have never seen a genuinely signed book. I have never seen a genuinely signed cabinet photograph. Many photographs are in the market with a forgery placed on the verso. The demand for Booth material is tremendous. He is one of the most treasured of all American autographs, morbid as it may sound. Booth's signature will sell for $25,000 to $30,000. An ALS will likely sell for $50,000 to $75,000. A content ALS should easily cross the $100,000 threshold.

Booth-1 ALS dated 1861.

Andrew Johnson

Johnson is the only tailor ever to become president of the United States. Johnson signed in a very busy hand. His signature appears fast and slightly compacted. Letter construction is marginal, at best. The legibility is impaired. Johnson's signature has average display value. On occasion, signatures would be finished off with a paraph. Due to the rather flowing hand, replication of Johnson's autograph is difficult. Well-executed forgeries are limited. Johnson's hand remained strong his entire life. A genuine signature will evidence no shakiness of hand, and one that does should be considered suspect and avoided.

Most signatures in the market are simply clipped from other mediums. DsS and LsS exist in ample supply. ALsS are very rare. Johnson was not well versed in writing and generally avoided it. Letters contain many spelling errors and the grammar is substandard. That having been said, Johnson expresses strong opinions in his writing. Signed commissions and appointments must be studied carefully because most contain a steel stamp of Johnson's signature. The stamped signature is very convincing. Photographs are extremely rare. There are many forged CDV in the market. There is one CDV to discuss. It is an image of Johnson sitting with his left hand resting on a table. Under the image it reads: "PRESIDENT JOHNSON" in capital letters. The image is taken by M.B. Brady & Co. A comical Johnson forgery is placed on the lower border. The card itself appears to be counterfeit. Many forged brief ALsS and ANsS are in the market. These are typically accomplished in pencil and purportedly written to an autograph collector requesting the president's signature. To my knowledge no bank checks exist.

Signatures are generally valued in the $500 to $600 range. DsS and LsS sell for $600 to $900. The value of a nice ALsS would likely be more than $20,000.

White House Cards

Despite rumors to the contrary, no signed cards exist.

Johnson, A-1, undated signature (courtesy Nate D. Sanders Auctions).

Johnson, A-2, undated signature (courtesy Nate D. Sanders Auctions).

Johnson, A-3 common stamped signature.

Ulysses Grant

Grant signed in a flowing and aggressive hand. His signature is marked with rapid strokes. Hesitation of any kind is lacking. Letter construction is somewhat impaired as individual letters tend to blend together. Legibility is somewhat affected. The signature is dominated by large capital letters. The letter "S" is merely an up-and-down stroke with no closure at the base. The flamboyant nature of the signature correlates into good display value. Grant's signature is rather difficult to replicate, but skilled forgers have taken up the task. Well-executed forgeries exist, so caution is warranted. Secretarial signatures also exist. Grant's hand remained strong his entire life. A genuine signature will evidence no shakiness of hand, and one that does should be considered suspect and avoided.

Grant is one of the top-tier presidents in terms of demand. He is also highly collected by Civil War buffs. Signatures are generally found on LsS, DsS, and bank checks. ALsS are less common but do exist. Content of letters tend to be boring. Letters penned as a general tend to have more authoritative content. Free franks are very rare. Signed CDV photographs are rare to very rare and have nice eye appeal.

Grant material has increased in value over the past few years. Signatures will sell for $600 to $800. DsS and LsS are valued at $1,000 to $1,500. ALsS sell in the $2,000 to $2,500 range.

Signed photographs are valued at $3,000 to $4,000. Nice content letters will sell for well over $10,000. The value of items signed as a general can exceed similar items signed as president.

White House Cards

To my knowledge, only one Executive Mansion card exists. It is signed and dated in purple ink. It is a unique rarity. The value has not been established.

Grant-1 album page 1883.

Grant-2 album page dated 1876.

Grant-3, executive mansion card, likely a unique specimen.

Rutherford Hayes

Hayes signed in a very poignant and demure hand. His signature evidences nice flowing strokes. The signature is rounded and lacks sharp angles. Letter construction is fairly sound; however, the last couple of letters in the last name tend to be poorly formed. His handwriting is inconsistent, giving ALsS a sloppy ap-

pearance. The signature is of average display value. Most signatures are signed as "R.B. Hayes." Replication of hand is fairly easy. It would not take a great deal of effort to produce a well-executed forgery. Hayes's hand remained strong his entire life. A genuine signature will evidence no shakiness of hand, and one that does should be considered suspect and avoided.

There is a good supply of Hayes material in the market. The demand is somewhat muted. His signature exists on DsS, LsS, and ALsS. Free franks are extremely rare. Photographs are rare, with the vast majority being the product of forgery. A restricted supply of bank checks is in the market.

Hayes's signature is valued at $175 to $200. LsS and DsS are not much more. ALsS can be purchased for as little as $400. A genuine signed photograph would sell in excess of $5,000.

White House Cards

Hayes's signature is obtainable on Executive Mansion cards and a decent supply exists, though they should be considered scarce.

There are two variant Executive Mansion cards in existence. The printing of "Executive Mansion, Washington," is typically found in the upper right-hand corner of the card. There are a few cards on which the printing is found in the upper left-hand corner. These are rare but

Hayes-1, ALS dated 1879.

Hayes-2, DS dated 1871 (courtesy Nate D. Sanders Auctions).

do not, in general, correlate into a premium. Hayes signed these cards as "R B Hayes." I have never examined a card signed with his full name. Signed Executive Mansion cards typically sell for $350 to $400.

James Garfield

Garfield signed in a flowing and graceful hand. His signature lacks hesitation and works well on paper. Letter construction is sound. Legibility is also good. Overall Garfield's signature has superior display value. Signatures were accomplished as "J.A. Garfield" and "James A. Garfield." Given the flowing nature of hand, Garfield's signature is difficult to replicate. Well-executed forgeries are very limited.

Garfield was the second president to be assassinated. His presidency lasted a mere 200 days, the second shortest in history. On July 2, 1881, Garfield was struck by an assassin's bullet. Though he did not die immediately, infection caught up with him while he was convalescing. He died on September 19 of that same year. Since he died prematurely, shakiness of hand is not evident. A genuine Garfield signature will evidence no shakiness of hand, and one that does should be considered suspect and avoided.

The supply of Garfield material is ample. Signatures exist on DsS, LsS, free franks, ALsS, and bank checks. Bank checks are usually found on House of Representatives drafts. Signed photographs of any kind are rare. Just about all are forgeries. Material signed as president is very scarce and commands a premium.

Many free franks exist as a member of Congress. Many are secretarially signed. The secretarial signatures are easily spotted as the "G" looks more like a capital "S." On a genuine frank the letters "MC" (for member of congress) are large and bold. The secretarial signatures contain a muted "MC" much smaller in scale.

There are many LsS signed as president in the market that are actually accomplished by his secretary Joseph S. Brown. His secretarial

signature is very close to that of the president. He tried very hard to replicate Garfield's hand. The signature is flowing but signed in a very slightly slower hand. The capital letter "G." is placed much lower in the signature than that found on the genuine specimen. These are well-executed, so careful examination is needed. Many Garfield signatures as president are actually signed by Brown.

Garfield's signature is valued at $300 to $400. LsS, DsS, and franks sell in the $400 to $600 range. Bank checks are slightly more. ALsS are in good supply and sell for $500 to $750. DsS as president are in great demand, so expect to pay $10,000 for one. Exceptional specimens will sell for close to $20,000.

White House Cards

Anything signed by James Garfield as president is rare and in high demand. Signed Executive Mansion cards are no different. It is one of the most difficult cards to locate. They should be considered very rare. A few short ANsS have surfaced on these cards. They are typically signed with his initials. It should noted that many cards contain a stamped signature of Garfield. Value of a genuinely signed card has not been established.

Garfield-1 album page dated 1881.

Garfield-2, undated signature (courtesy Nate D. Sanders Auctions).

Garfield-3, common secretarial as MOC.

Assassin—Charles Guiteau

Guiteau was a lawyer who supported Garfield in the election. He believed that he was entitled to an ambassadorship for his efforts. After many rejections, Guiteau sought revenge. He purchased a pistol and fatally shot the president. Guiteau went to the gallows on June 30, 1882.

Guiteau signed in a large and rapid hand. The signature is dominated by bold strokes. Display value is sound. Guiteau's signature is the most common of any of the presidential assassins, though it is still considered a scarce signature. There is a somewhat ample number of ALsS in the market. Small signed cards are also available. These were likely signed after the assassination. Signed photographs are very rare. Many forged photographs exist, so caution is warranted. Guiteau's signature can be purchased for $400 to $500. ALsS are valued at $800 to $900.

Guiteau-1, undated signature (courtesy The Sanders Autograph Price Guide).

Chester Arthur

Arthur signed in a very rapid and complex hand. His signature evidences no hesitation and dominates the medium it is placed upon. Letter construction is fairly sound. The signature is legible, for the most part. Given the busy nature of the hand, Arthur's signature exhibits good display value. Signatures can be found as "Chester A. Arthur" or "C.A. Arthur." Replication of hand would be very difficult. No well-executed forgeries exist. Arthur's signature is the most difficult of any president to forge. Arthur made it a habit of leaving pen on paper when writing letters. Many of the words are connected with each other. The result is a very sloppy-looking writing. A genuine Arthur signature will evidence no shakiness of hand, and one that does should be considered suspect and avoided.

There is an ample supply of Arthur material in the market. Many LsS and DsS exist from his tenure as the New York port collector. DsS as president exist in good numbers and make for a fine display. ALsS are also available. Letters signed as president on black bordered stationary are rare. There is a decent supply of canceled bank checks in the market. Signed photographs are very rare. Just about all signed photographs are forgeries. Free franks are an extreme rarity.

Arthur's signature can be purchased for $250 to $300. LsS, bank checks, and DsS are affordable at $300 to $500. ALsS are valued at $600 to $700. Photographs are highly treasured and a superior specimen will sell in the $7,000 to $10,000 range.

White House Cards

The supply of Arthur signed cards is sound. They can be secured with little effort. His striking signature works well on this medium and they make for a fine display. A variant form of Executive Mansion card exists; it is black-bordered as a memorial of President Garfield's death. A few specimens signed by Arthur exist

Arthur-2 album page dated 1883.

but are considered very rare. It should be noted that some cards contain a stamped signature of Arthur. A signed card will sell for $350 to $400. The value of a black-bordered card has not been established.

Arthur-2 album page dated 1884.

Grover Cleveland

Cleveland signed in a very choppy hand. The signature evidences many breaks. Letter construction is poor. Cleveland's signature tends to be somewhat illegible. ALsS are hard to read and many words cannot be deciphered. Display value is poor. Overall, a substandard display signature. Cleveland's hand remained relatively constant but signatures accomplished in the last few years of his life evidence a slight unsteadiness. ALsS signed a year or two before his death are written on an uneven plane. Sentences tend to slope downward.

There is not much demand for Cleveland's signature. Cleveland was an accommodating signer throughout his life. Index cards, LsS, DsS, and ALsS exist in good quantities. Signed photographs are rare, albeit borderline. Free franks are very rare.

Cleveland's signature is very affordable at $150 to $175. DsS, LsS and ALsS can all be purchased in the $250 to $500 price range. Photographs sell for $700 to $900 with superior specimens selling for $2,500 to $3,000.

White House Cards

Cleveland's cramped signature works well on this medium. Many signed Executive Mansion cards exist. Cleveland is one of the most available and can be secured for $200 to $250.

Cleveland-1, signature dated 1903 (courtesy Nate D. Sanders Auctions).

Cleveland-2, DS dated 1896.

Benjamin Harrison

Ben Harrison signed in a very rustic and heavy hand. His signature is marked with thick and bold strokes. Letter construction is substandard. The signature has marginal display value. His handwriting is poor and reading one of his ALsS will give you a headache. It goes without saying that legibility is poor. Harrison's signature is rather difficult to forge. Forgeries are generally limited to photographs. Harrison's hand remained strong his entire life. A genuine Harrison signature will evidence no shakiness of hand, and one that does should be considered suspect and avoided.

Harrison material is common among the 19th-century presidents. He was a willing signer throughout his life. ALsS and LsS exist, especially from his tenure as a senator. DsS are generally limited to material signed as president. There is a good supply of material signed as an attorney. Signed photographs of any kind are rare, and most offered for sale are forgeries. Free franks are an extreme rarity. Canceled bank checks exist in good numbers.

Harrison's signature is affordable at $150 to $175. Bank checks can be purchased for $200. DsS as president are valued at $400 to $500.

LsS and ALsS sell for $300 to $500. A nicely signed photograph is valued at $2,000 to $3,000.

White House Cards

Harrison-signed Executive Mansion cards are very rare and one of the most difficult of any president to obtain. No recent sales have occurred. A current value has not been established.

Harrison, B-1 album page 1892.

Harrison, B-2 undated signature (courtesy Nate D. Sanders Auctions).

William McKinley

McKinley was the third president to be assassinated. His signature evolved over the years. Signatures accomplished during his tenure in Congress tend to be smaller and are typically signed as "William McKinley Jr." As president his signature becomes more flamboyant. The scale increases. Letter construction is impaired, with individual letters blending together. He finished off the signature with a long-tailing letter "y." ALsS from this period have impaired legibility. Overall, McKinley's signature is of average display value. Due to the unstructured nature of hand, McKinley's signature is rather easy to forge. Many well-executed forgeries exist, especially on photographs. Due to his

sudden death, infirmity of hand is nonexistent. A genuine McKinley signature will evidence no shakiness of hand, and one that does should be considered suspect and avoided.

The supply of McKinley material is sound. Many letters exist signed as a member of Congress. ALsS, TLsS, and LsS exist in quantities. DsS as president are uncommon, but by no means should they be considered scarce. Canceled bank checks are in good supply. Photographs are rare and most offered for sale are forgeries. Free franks are very rare.

McKinley's signature sells in the $150 to $200 price range. Letters of any kind can be purchased for $350 to $400. Bank checks are valued at $450 to $500. A nicely signed photograph will sell for $1,500 to $2,000.

White House Cards

McKinley-signed Executive Mansion cards are in good supply. Many fine specimens exist. McKinley would center his signature in the middle of the card, which makes for a fine display. On rare occasions he would pen a short quote or note on these cards and would usually sign them as "Wm. McK." These cards command a premium. A card will sell in the $350 to $400 price range.

McKinley-1, ALS circa 1899 (courtesy Nate D. Sanders Auctions).

McKinley-2, undated signature (courtesy The Sanders Autograph Price Guide).

Assassin—Leon Czolgosz

Czolgosz, a native of Alpena, Michigan, was a laborer. He was a loner who drank the Kool-Aid of the anarchist movement. On September 6, 1901, he shot President McKinley in the abdomen. The president died eight days later. Czolgosz was tried for murder and on October 29, 1901, died in the electric chair. Czolgosz signed in a rudimentary and childlike hand. The signature evidences material hesitation and many breaks. Replication of hand can be done with little effort. Czolgosz is a signature of great rarity. There is a signed confession held by an institution. There are a few other signatures in existence that were obtained post-assassination, or so it is said. These signatures deviate somewhat from the signed confession. I cannot be certain of their authenticity. There are a few ALsS in the market signed with his alias of "Nieman." The Nieman hand evidences good flow and lacks the hesitation found in the confession signature. There is a material variance when comparing the handwriting between the confession and the Nieman ALsS. This leads me to believe that the Nieman ALsS are suspect, to say the least. I advise collectors to avoid Nieman letters in total. Autographically, a signature of great rarity.

Theodore Roosevelt

Roosevelt signed in a very no-nonsense and rugged hand. Letter construction is sound with individual letters well defined. A high degree of legibility is noted. Overall, a signature with good display value. Signatures are usually accomplished as "Theodore Roosevelt." Many letters are simply signed as "T. Roosevelt." The one flaw of Roosevelt's hand is the speed. He signed in a slower hand that lacks rapid motion. As a result, replication of hand is easy. Well-executed forgeries exist in quantities. Roosevelt's hand remained strong his entire life; hence, a genuine signature will evidence no shakiness of hand, and one that does should be considered suspect and avoided.

The supply of Roosevelt material is sound. Demand is much greater. Roosevelt is one of the most coveted of all presidential signatures. His signature can be found on most mediums including TLsS, ALsS, DsS, LsS, bank checks, and authored books. A few DsS as president and countersigned by then Secretary of War William Howard Taft exist. These should be considered scarce to rare. Many nice presentation signed photographs are in the market and make for a fine display. Free franks are an extreme rarity. It should be noted that Theodore Roosevelt Jr. signed many autographs and his signature is often mistaken for that of the president.

A signature is valued at $400 to $500. TLsS and LsS sell for $500 to $600. DsS with Taft are a treasure and are valued at $1,000 to $1,250. Signed bank checks can be purchased for $750. A full-page ALS will sell for $1,250 to $1,500. A nicely signed photograph is valued at $2,000 to $3,000. A photograph as a Rough Rider will sell for a substantial premium. Signed books are very popular and sell for $2,000 to $3,000.

White House Cards

Roosevelt exists on three distinct cards. The first is the Executive Mansion card, which was used only briefly. In the book *The History of Collecting Executive Mansion, White House and The White House Cards,* authors Stephen Koschal and Lynne Keyes state that Roosevelt used Executive Mansion cards for only the first month of his presidency. After that point he changed the name to White House. Signed White House cards are available and can be added to your collection with little effort. Roosevelt once again changed the name on the card from White House to The White House. This makes Roosevelt the only president to sign a White House card. Signed White House and The White House cards are in decent supply and can be purchased in the $600 to $800 price range. Executive Mansion cards are very rare, so expect to pay $2,500 to $3,000 for one.

Roosevelt, T-1 album page dated 1901.

Roosevelt, T-2 undated signature (courtesy Nate D. Sanders Auctions).

Roosevelt, T-3, TLS dated 1908, variant signature (courtesy Mark Allen Baker).

Roosevelt, T-4, signature of Teddy Roosevelt Jr.

William Howard Taft

Taft signed in a rapid and heavy hand. His signature is marked with thick, dominant strokes. Letter construction is sound, with bold, pronounced letters. Taft's signature is legible and evidences a strong display value. Signatures are accomplished as "Wm H. Taft." Taft's handwriting exhibits sharp breaks. The result is a hand with choppiness. Due to the rapid and flourishing nature of Taft's signature, replication of hand is very difficult. There are no well-executed forgeries in the market. Taft's hand remained strong his entire life. A genuine signature will evidence no shakiness of hand, and one that does should be considered suspect and avoided.

Taft's signature is of particular interest to collectors. Not only was he president, but after retirement he was appointed Chief Justice of the United States. His signature is widely collected as a judicial autograph. Fortunately, Taft was a willing and gracious signer throughout his life. There is a good supply of material in the market. ALsS, TLsS, DsS, bank checks, and photo-

graphs exist in good quantities. Court-related letters usually contain good content and are worth a premium. Free franks are an extreme rarity.

Taft's signature is valued at $150 to $175. TLsS and bank checks sell for $200 to $250. ALsS have good eye appeal and can be purchased in the $500 to $600 range. A nice presentation photograph is valued at $800 to $1,000.

White House Cards

There is an ample supply of The White House cards signed by President Taft. His bold hand works well on this medium. Many times he would write short notes with his signature. A signed The White House card can be purchased in the $300 to $350 price range.

Taft-1, DS dated 1911 (courtesy Nate D. Sanders Auctions).

Taft-2, TLS dated 1919 (courtesy Nate D. Sanders Auctions).

Woodrow Wilson

Wilson's signature is one that evolved over the years. Early, pre-presidential signatures are signed in a smaller and confined hand. Letter construction is sound. Early signatures will sometimes be finished with a paraph, a feature his later signature disposed of. As Wilson's political star rose, his hand changed greatly. The signature becomes large, bold, and unrestrained.

The signature evidences good flow. The signature is legible and it exhibits sound display value. The signature is usually dominated by a large and trailing letter "n" in the last name. Replication of hand is rather difficult; hence, well-executed forgeries are limited. Wilson fell ill during his presidency but it appears not to have affected his hand. A genuine Wilson signature will evidence no shakiness of hand, and one that does should be considered suspect and avoided. It should be noted that a rubber stamp was sometimes employed to honor autograph requests.

Wilson was an accommodating signer for collectors. There is an ample supply of material in the market, including many signed books and album pages. DsS, TLsS, LsS, exist in good numbers. ALsS are scarce. Many nicely signed portrait photographs exist and they make for a fine display. Bank checks are scarce to rare.

Wilson's signature is valued at $200 to $250. TLsS, DsS can be purchased between $350 and $400. Bank checks sell for $600 to $700. Photographs are also valued in the same price range. A nice ALS will sell for $500 to $700.

White House Cards

Wilson-signed The White Cards are not as plentiful of those of his predecessor. There is still a decent supply in the market. Wilson signed just about all these cards in the upper left-hand corner. Some have speculated that he did this to avoid having anything written above his signature at a later date. Expect to pay $400 to $450 for a nice specimen.

Wilson-1, undated signature.

Wilson-2, signature circa 1900.

Warren Harding

Harding was the first newspaper publisher ever to be elected president. Harding signed in a fluid hand that evidences a slight choppiness. Letter construction is marginal, which affects legibility. As Harding's political career advanced, his hand became sloppy. ALsS are hard to read. The signature has average display value. Due to the unstructured and choppy nature of hand, his signature would be fairly easy to replicate. Secretarial signatures are fairly accurate and fool many collectors. Harding's hand remained strong his entire life. A genuine signature will evidence no shakiness of hand, and one that does should be considered suspect and avoided.

There is an ample inventory of Harding material in the market. The most common medium is publishing receipts signed as editor. These are a wonderful source for Harding's signature. DsS and TLsS are also in good supply, both as senator and president. Signed photographs are somewhat scarce. Many are beautifully inscribed portrait photographs. There is a good supply of bank checks and endorsed checks. ALsS from any period are rare. ALsS as president are very rare. A few DsS countersigned by Harding's secretary of commerce and future president Herbert Hoover are in the market. These should be considered rare to very rare. Free franks are very rare. Anything associated with the Teapot Dome scandal is highly collectable and extremely rare. It is said that many of his writings and correspondence were destroyed by his wife just after his death in 1923. Many forged baseballs are in the market.

Harding's signature is affordable at $150 to $200. Publishing receipts are about the same price. TLsS, bank checks, and DsS as president sell for $300 to $400. A nice portrait photograph is valued at $500 to $700. ALsS will sell for $1,500 to $2,000. The above referenced Harding/Hoover DsS are treasured by collectors and will sell for $2,000 to $2,500.

White House Cards

Harding served less than three years as president. Harding signed The White House cards are limited but do exist. They should not be considered rare by any means. Almost none of them are inscribed. They generally sell in the $400 to $450 price range.

Harding-1, DS dated 1922 (courtesy Nate D. Sanders Auctions).

Harding-2, DS dated 1922 (courtesy Nate D. Sanders Auctions).

Calvin Coolidge

Coolidge signed in a truncated and choppy hand. His signature exhibits substandard letter construction. While early signatures tend to be a bit more structured, those signed as president are illegible. Coolidge's signature has poor display value. It is one of the least attractive of all presidential signatures. Due to the rapid nature of hand, replication is difficult. Creating a well-executed forgery would take some effort. Some presidential appointments are secretarially signed. Coolidge's hand remained strong his entire life. A genuine signature will evidence no shakiness of hand, and one that does should be considered suspect and avoided.

The supply of Coolidge material is sound. His signature is on the common side. It is one of the most affordable of the early 20th-century presidents. His signature can be found on books, DsS, LsS, TLsS, ALsS, bank checks, and album pages. He was the first president to sign commemorative airmail postal covers. Photographs are uncommon but a good number exist. His signature is considered rare on free franks. Many forged baseballs are in the market so caution is warranted.

Coolidge's signature is inexpensive on just about all items. Signatures are valued at $75 to $100. DsS, TLsS, and bank checks sell for $150 to $225. ALsS can be purchased for as little as $250. Photographs are valued at $300 to $400.

White House Cards

Coolidge-signed The White House cards exist in quantities. It is probably the easiest card to obtain of the early 20th century presidents. A nicely signed card can be purchased for $125 to $150.

Coolidge-1, bank check dated 1915 (courtesy collection of John Keurajian).

Coolidge-2, DS dated 1926 (courtesy Nate D. Sanders Auctions).

Herbert Hoover

Hoover was at the wrong place at the wrong time and is usually blamed for the Great Depression—unfairly, I might add. He got T-boned at the intersection of history. Hoover signed in a very bold and powerful hand. His signature evidences wonderful flow. Hesitation of any kind is lacking. Letter construction is sound. His signature is legible. The signature has good uniformity and display value. Replication of hand would be rather difficult; hence, well-executed forgeries are limited to Hoover's private secretary H.G. Shankey, who signed Hoover's name with frightening accuracy. Shankey's work product appears compact and the letters are placed closer together, giving the signature a squished look. Hoover's hand deteriorated as he aged. Signatures accomplished in the 1950s appear slightly labored. In the last few years of his life his hand was affected by material infirmity. Shakiness of hand is noted. Hoover made liberal use of preprinted letters and note cards that contain a facsimile signature. These are often sold as genuine. Any letter or ANS that begins with "My Dear Friend" should be considered suspect.

Hoover was a gracious signer and today the supply of material is sound. His signature is usually found on index cards and TLsS with routine content. Signed photographs are common. A few signed color photographs exist featuring an elderly Hoover smoking a pipe. Signed color photographs are rare. ALsS are rare and are in high demand. Bank checks are very rare. Free franks are an extreme rarity.

There is one forgery to note. Several years ago a small grouping of forged free franks entered the market. There are on White House envelopes that have "The White House, Official Business, penalty for private use to avoid payment of postage $300" printed in the upper left of the cover. A forgery of Hoover is added under the above-referenced penalty. The forgery exhibits poor letter construction and is very choppy. These are exposed with little effort. All of the ones I have seen were signed in black fountain pen. I have never seen a genuine Hoover frank.

Hoover's signature is affordable at $50 to $75. TLsS generally sell for $75 to $100. Signed photographs are valued at $200 to $250. Signed color photographs will sell for $600 to $700. ALsS generally run about $1,500 to $2,000. Many signed books, which the president authored, are affordable at $175 to $225.

White House Cards

Hoover-signed The White House cards are almost as common as those of his former boss Calvin Coolidge. Many nice specimens exist. They can be purchased for $250 to $275.

Hoover-1 DS 1955 (courtesy collection of Dennis Hoffner).

Hoover-2, undated ALS (courtesy Nate D. Sanders Auctions).

Hoover-3, common secretarial.

Franklin Roosevelt

Roosevelt signed in a truncated and choppy hand. The signature exhibits many breaks in the hand, especially in the first name. The signature has marginal letter construction. Legibility is slightly impaired. Roosevelt signed in an aggressive hand, resulting in a signature with good eye appeal. Due to the many breaks in the signature, replication of hand is fairly easy. Well-executed forgeries exist. Many convincing secretarial signatures are also in the market. Many New York Executive Mansion cards are signed with a rubber stamp. Roosevelt's hand remained strong his entire life. A genuine signature, signed late in life, evidences only trivial unsteadiness and may present itself as somewhat sloppy. Roosevelt's hand never produced a truly shaky signature.

Roosevelt had a long career in politics. He was assistant secretary of the navy under Woodrow Wilson and later governor of New York. The result is a good inventory of material. Roosevelt's signature can be found on DsS, TLsS, bank checks, and album pages. Signed photographs are less common but by no means rare. ALsS are scarce and some command a strong price. Free franks are rare but some were signed specifically for collectors. Like many presidents, Roosevelt did not have franking privileges.

Roosevelt is one of our most popular presidents, a fact noticed by the market. His signature is valued at $250 to $275. TLsS and DsS sell in the $400 to $450 price range. A nicely signed photograph is valued between $600 and $750. ALsS are scarce and sell for $1,000 to $1,500.

White House Cards

Roosevelt-signed The White House cards are scarce. They typically have good eye appeal due to a large and dominant signature placed in the dead center of the card. They are in much demand. Expect to pay $500 to $550 for a nice specimen. There are also New York Executive Mansion cards signed as governor. These are more affordable and are valued at $300 to $350.

Roosevelt, F-1, TLS dated 1939 (courtesy Nate D. Sanders Auctions).

Roosevelt, F-2, TLS dated 1939.

Harry Truman

Truman signed in a very rugged and powerful hand. His signature evidences strong lines and thick strokes. Letter construction is marginal as the letters tend to morph into indistinguishable lines. Hesitation of any kind is lacking. The signature has average display value. Due to the rapid nature of hand, replication is difficult. Well-executed forgeries are limited. As Truman entered the final few years of his life, infirmity set in. Elderly signatures exhibit shakiness of hand and have less eye appeal than vintage specimens. These are often erroneously pronounced as secretarial signatures. See illustration.

Truman was a true friend to autograph collectors. He was a willing and gracious signer throughout his life. His signature can be found on most mediums with little effort. TLsS exist in mass quantities. DsS, bank checks, photographs, and engraved greeting cards are available. ALsS are scarce. ALsS as president should be considered rare. There are a handful of dual signed photographs of Truman and President Hoover. These command a premium and should be considered very rare. Free franks are rare and most were signed at the request of collectors. Truman also signed a handful of baseballs.

Truman's signature is highly affordable at $100 to $125. TLsS are about the same price. Photographs sell for $300 to $400. DsS, usually as president, and bank checks sell for $300 to $350. ALsS are valued at $1,000 to $1,500. The above-referenced Truman/Hoover photographs sell for about $1,000. A nice single signed baseball is worth between $5,000 and $7,500.

White House Cards

Truman-signed The White House cards are scarce. Most are inscribed and dated. They have good display value and in recent years have been absorbed into collections. Some cards bearing secretarial signatures exist, so caution is warranted. A nice signed example will sell for $450 to $500.

Truman-1, signed book dated 1955 (courtesy Nate D. Sanders Auctions).

Truman-2, TLS dated 1971.

Dwight Eisenhower

Eisenhower signed in a unique hand. His signature evidences good flow. The letters tend to blend into each other. The result is a signature that has impaired legibility. Letter construction is substandard. The signature exhibits a certain complexity that correlates into above-average display value. Due to the impaired letter construction, replication of hand is fairly easy. Well-executed forgeries exist. Eisenhower's hand remained strong his entire life. A genuine signature will evidence no shakiness of hand, and one that does should be considered suspect and avoided. Eisenhower was the first president to use the autopen. Many variant templates exist. Eisenhower's secretary also signed many items for the president.

His signature is generally found on TLsS, and many are signed with just his initials. Signed photographs are also available. ALsS are rare, and most are signed "Ike" and are of war date. There is a decent supply of military signed franks, many of which are secretarially signed. I have never seen a frank signed after the war. DsS signed as president are very scarce. A handful of single signed baseballs exist. These are very rare. Forged bank checks are in the market, so caution is warranted. A genuine check would be an extreme rarity.

There is strong demand for this general-turned-president. Signatures are valued at $275 to $300. TLsS generally sell for $350 to $450. A nicely signed 8 × 10 photograph will sell for $500 to $600. ALsS sell for $1,500 to $2,000. Signed military franks generally sell for $400 to $450. A DS as president is valued at $600 to $700. A nice single signed baseball is worth $10,000 to $12,500.

White House Cards

An Eisenhower-signed The White House card would be a rarity. I have never seen one I would feel comfortable pronouncing as genuine. Many convincing autopen-signed specimens exist. It should be noted that Eisenhower's secretary would sign these cards on behalf of her boss. In addition, there are The White House cards that contain a printed facsimile signature, so caution is warranted. The value of a signed card has not been established.

Eisenhower-1, DS dated 1960 (courtesy Nate D. Sanders Auctions).

Eisenhower-2, undated signature.

As of this writing, I consider an Eisenhower signed card to be unobtainable.

John Kennedy

Kennedy's signature is one of the most studied and least understood. There are many variations which have been created by secretaries and forgers. A genuine signature is nothing more than a scrawl of ink. Letter construction is nonexistent. Legibility is severely impaired. Among the presidents, Kennedy's signature has the worst eye appeal. Due to the sloppy nature of hand, Kennedy's signature is one of the easiest of all to forge. Well-executed forgeries are everywhere. I estimate over 90 percent of all Kennedy signatures in the market are fake. If you own one, it is probably a forgery. Due to his untimely death, a genuine signature will evidence no shakiness of hand, and one that does should be considered suspect and avoided. Many variant autopen signatures exist.

Signatures of Kennedy are scarce and generally limited to material signed on the campaign trail. Hence, many hurried signatures are found on programs, brochures, and slips of paper. TLsS from any era are rare. Just about 100 percent of TLsS signed as senator are secretarially signed. Signed 8 × 10 photographs are rare; again, most are secretarially signed. ALsS are very rare and usually limited to short writings and signed with the first name only. Forged bank checks, exist so caution is warranted. I have never seen a signed frank of any kind.

Kennedy is one of the most popular of the 20th-century presidents among collectors. The demand for Kennedy signed material is very strong. A signature is valued at $800 to $1,200. TLsS generally sell for $1,500 to $2,000. Signed photographs are highly desirable and are valued at $2,500 to $3,500. Superior images will sell in excess of $10,000. ALsS will sell for $4,000 to $10,000, depending on length. A Kennedy ALS with strong historical content will sell for significant sums, at least six figures, perhaps

$1,000,000. A White House Christmas card, countersigned by Jackie Kennedy, is a treasure. These will sell for $12,500 to $17,500.

White House Cards

Many signed The White House cards bear secretarial signatures. There are many that contain printed facsimile signatures. I have never seen a genuinely signed card, and I doubt one exists. If so, its value is, as of this writing, uncertain.

Kennedy-1, signature circa 1960.

Kennedy-2, signature circa early 1960s.

Kennedy-3, common secretarial during his senate tenure.

Assassin—Lee Harvey Oswald

Oswald was a former U.S. Marine and communist sympathizer who, on November 22, 1963, assassinated President Kennedy. Two days later, he himself was gunned down by Jack Ruby. Oswald's signature is very rare on a per se basis. He died at the age of 24, so only a scarce few signatures survive to this day. Oswald's hand is unstructured and lacks complexity. About the only supply for Oswald material comes from family letters. There are a few ALsS in the market written to his brother, mother, and/or other relative. These are typically signed as "Lee." They also come with the postal cover addressed in Oswald's hand. These are collectable because they incorporate the name "Oswald" in the mailing address. A few DsS also exist, likely released by the family. There is one forgery to note. There are some forgeries signed as "Lee H. Oswald" accomplished in ballpoint pen. They are signatures purportedly removed from a document. These were simply blank documents at one time, and a forgery of Oswald was placed on the signature line, then simply clipped off. I have never seen a genuine signature in this format. I advise collectors to avoid this type of signature in total.

There is strong demand for Oswald material.

The above-referenced ALsS will sell between $10,000 and $20,000 depending on length. The accompanying covers are valued at $3,000 to $4,000. Ruby's signature is available on bank checks, and these sell for $500 to $600.

Oswald-1 ADS dated 1959 (courtesy Nate D. Sanders Auctions).

Lyndon Johnson

Johnson signed in a vertical hand. The signature evidences thick and dominant strokes. The signature evidences choppiness and sharp breaks. It gives the appearance of an EKG line. Letter construction is poor. Letters are blended together, which results in an illegible signature. Display value is marginal at best. Replication of hand would take some effort. There are well-executed forgeries in the market but very limited in supply. Johnson died of a heart attack at a relatively young age. A genuine signature will evidence no shakiness of hand, and one that does should be considered suspect and avoided. Many variant secretarial and autopen signatures exist, so caution is warranted.

The diversity of mediums for Johnson material is limited. TLsS, bookplates, and photographs are the most common. Many TLsS as senator are signed with the first name only. Many are secretarially signed. An ALS of Johnson would be an extreme rarity. Johnson is the rarest of any president in this format. I have never seen a full-page ALS. Most writings are limited to short notes. I have never seen a genuine free frank. There are a couple of bank checks drawn on the Johnson City Bank in the market. The signatures on these checks deviate from a genuine specimen. I consider these checks suspect, to say the least.

Johnson material is of average demand. His signature is valued at $175 to $200. Bookplates are of the same value. A TLS sells in the $250 to $300 price range. A nicely signed 8 × 10 photograph can be purchased for $350 to $400. The value of a nice full-page ALS would likely be in excess of $25,000.

White House Cards

Many signed The White House cards bear secretarial signatures. I have never seen a genuinely signed card. I doubt that one exists.

Johnson, L-1 signed book dated 1969 (courtesy Nate D. Sanders Auctions).

Johnson, L-2, signature circa 1970 (courtesy Nate D. Sanders Auctions).

Richard Nixon

Nixon signed in an average, unassuming hand. As he rose in power, his hand deteriorated. The signature becomes sloppy. Letter construction is pushed aside in favor of expediency. The signature is illegible. The last name is a capital letter "N" followed by a line. The display value is substandard. Nixon's signature is one of the poorest of any president. Due to the unstructured nature of the signature, replication of hand is easy. Well-executed forgeries exist in quantities. Nixon's hand remained strong his entire life. A genuine signature will evidence no shakiness of hand, and one that does should be considered suspect and avoided. Many variant secretarial and autopen signatures exist, so caution is warranted.

Nixon was a generally responsive signer his entire life, especially post-presidency. Signed material includes photographs, books, bookplates, business cards, and TLsS. Less common are ALsS. Once thought to be rare, in recent years a good number have entered the market. Bank checks are rare. Nixon also signed baseballs and a decent supply exists. It should be noted that the vast majority of Nixon-signed baseballs are forgeries. I have never seen a genuine frank of any kind.

There is strong demand for Nixon material. He is considered one of the more important presidents in American history. Also his association with the Watergate scandal creates much interest in the collecting community. His signature is affordable at around $100. Signed books, which exist in mass quantities, can be purchased for $150 to $200. Signed 8 × 10 photographs, usually featuring long inscriptions, are valued at $300 to $350. ALsS will generally sell for $1,250 to $2,000. One with good content would easily be valued at over $10,000. Bank checks sell for $1,500 to $2,000. Signed baseballs are in high demand and now sell for a minimum of $1,000. About two dozen souvenir copies of his resignation letter were signed; hence, they are very rare. Just about all signed resignation letters are counterfeit.

White House Cards

Many signed The White House cards bear secretarial and autopen signatures. There are many that contain printed facsimile signatures. I have never seen a genuinely signed card signed as president. First Lady Pat Nixon did sign The White House cards during her tenure in the White House. Years later a few of these cards were presented to President Nixon for signature. The president did sign a handful after his presidency had ended. These cards are the only official The White House cards you will find signed by the president. Some unofficial or mock cards were created. President Nixon did sign these, but they are of little worth beyond a per se signature value. The value of a card signed as president has not been established.

Nixon-1, signature circa 1980.

Nixon-2, undated signature.

Gerald Ford

Ford signed in a jagged and sharp hand. His signature evidences fast lines with abrupt turns. Letter construction is sound. The signature is legible. Display value is sound. He would take the time to strategically place his signature for maximum eye appeal. Ford was known to write with a cutting pen. Many fine content letters are in the market. ALsS do, on occasion, contain spelling errors. Ford is one of the more difficult hands to replicate. Well-executed forgeries are limited to one forger. Ford's hand generally remained strong his entire life, though signatures accomplished in the last year or so of his life appear smaller and strokes are sometimes truncated. Ford's hand never produced an unsteady signature. Signatures with his birth name, Leslie King Jr., are very rare. Many variant secretarial and autopen signatures exist, so caution is warranted.

Autographically speaking, Ford is the most significant signature of all the presidents. His signature may not be the rarest or most valuable, but he signed material that no other president would sign. The diversity of mediums is amazing. Ford signed index cards, U.S. currency, photographs, books, business cards, campaign bumper stickers, and TLsS. He was a member of the Warren Commission. He would

sign copies of the Warren Commission report. He signed a handful with the inscription; "Oswald Acted Alone." This inscription is considered very rare. To satisfy autograph requests, short TQsS, on personal letterhead, regarding the Kennedy assassination were sent to collectors. Bank checks are very rare. Free franks are very rare. ALsS are scarce. Ford did write a few letters discussing the Kennedy assassination. These letters are considered very rare.

Though he is most remembered for taking a tumble down the steps of *Air Force One*, Ford was the most athletic man ever to sit in the Oval Office. He was noted for his prowess on the gridiron and the links. He also dabbled in boxing. He was even offered a contract to play pro football with the Detroit Lions.

Ford played center and linebacker for the University of Michigan in the early 1930s. He signed many football-related items, including gum cards and footballs. Being an avid golfer, Ford signed golf scorecards, golf clubs, and golf balls. A limited number of signed photographs exist, countersigned by fellow golfer and Hollywood legend Bob Hope. These dual-signed photographs are considered rare. Ford would also sign baseballs and commemorative baseball bats. Ford-signed sports memorabilia is coveted by autograph collectors. It should be noted that the majority of Ford-signed balls of any kind are forged. A countless number have been wrongly certified as genuine by the authentication companies. There are many American League baseballs in the market. A forgery is placed on the sweet spot of the ball with the inscription "Pres. 1974–1977" underneath the signature. I have never examined a genuinely signed baseball with this inscription.

Ford's signature is one of the most difficult of all presidents to forge. There is one forger who produces well-executed forgeries. He forges ALsS and will also write out the presidential oath of office on fake personal letterhead. His work is very convincing. His forgeries are nicely constructed, but unlike a real article, the forger has not quite mastered the proper hand speed. The handwriting appears uniform. It is steady but slow. The racing effect is muted. This forger's work is very good and usually turns up in major auctions.

Ford is the most common of all presidential autographs. The collector had no greater friend than president Ford. Despite this, his signature on certain mediums has increased greatly in value. His signature sells for $25 to $50. TLsS as congressman sell for $150 to $200. TLsS as president are valued at $500 to $750. Signed photographs generally sell for $50 to $75. Football- or golf-related photographs are valued at $200 to $250. Dual-signed photographs with Bob Hope are in high demand and sell for $500. Signed golf balls sell for $300 to $400. Baseballs are valued at $400 to $500. Signed baseball bats are rare and valued at $1,500. Signed footballs are usually signed with his position, jersey number, and the team he played for. They are valued at $1,000. ALsS are scarce and sell for $400 to $600. ALsS with Warren Commission content have an estimated value of $3,000 to $5,000. Signed Warren Commission reports sell for $300 to $400. With the inscription "Oswald acted alone," expect to pay at least $1,000. Bank checks sell for $1,500 to $2,000. Free franks, which were accomplished at the request of collectors, seldom surface and are valued at $1,500. Ford signed a limited number of commemorative copies of the Nixon pardon. Ford did not like to sign these; hence, they are rare and will sell for close to $2,000.

White House Cards

I have never run across a Ford-signed The White House card accomplished as president. During his presidency, cards bearing a facsimile signature were sent to collectors to satisfy autograph requests. In retirement, these cards were sent to President Ford for signature, and he gladly signed. This is about the only way to obtain an official The White House card signed. Many mock cards were created. Unofficial cards

bearing Ford's signature exist in quantities. They are valued at about $75 to $100 simply because they are an attractive display item. An official card bearing a post-presidential signature sells for $250 to $300. The value of one signed as president has not been established.

I recommend the *Gerald R. Ford IACC/DA Concise Autograph Study*, authored by Stephen Koschal. Published in 1998, it is a detailed study of President Ford's hand.

Ford, G-1, ANS dated 1976.

Ford, G-2, signature dated 1994.

Ford, G-3, signature dated March 2004, just before he stopped signing for the public.

Would-be Assassin— Lynette Fromme

Giuseppe Zangara and Richard Lawrence are little-known footnotes in history. Both were would-be assassins who failed in their attempts. In general, would-be assassins are of little interest to autograph collectors; the one exception is Manson follower Lynette Fromme. She spent most of her life in prison. Her signature occasionally surfaces on ALsS and the accompanying signed envelopes. Other mediums are rare to very rare. Shortly after President Ford's death she was paroled. So far Fromme has kept a low profile. Expect to pay $100 for her signature. ALsS will sell for $150 to $250.

Fromme-1, postal cover dated 1982 (courtesy Stephen Koschal Autographs).

Jimmy Carter

Carter signs in a very large and bold hand. His signature is dominated by large capital letters. The signature is legible. Letter construction is sound. It is a signature with good display value. There is one fatal flaw with Carter's signature. It has many breaks. This makes replication of hand easy. Creating a well-executed forgery would be relatively easy. One of his secretaries could sign Carter's name with a high degree of accuracy. Carter signatures are usually penned as "Jimmy Carter." In recent years Carter signs his name as simply "J Carter." At book signings the president employs this form of signature and it is poorly constructed. As of this writing, Carter's hand remains strong. A genuine signature will evidence no shakiness of hand, and one that does should be considered suspect and avoided. Many variant secretarial and autopen signatures exist, so caution is warranted.

Carter has been a responsive signer throughout the years. He does limit the mediums he will sign. Requests to sign first-day covers, U.S. currency, sports items, and engravings are generally declined. As of this writing, Carter typically signs only 8 × 10 photographs and copies of his books. Signed books, and he has authored several, exist in mass quantities. Bank checks from his days in farming are in the market, and they date to the 1950s. Free franks are very rare. He franked very few for collectors he knew personally. ALsS are scarce and many are simply

signed "Jimmy." DsS as president are very scarce. There are a certain number of items signed by Carter and his vice-president, Walter Mondale. Mediums signed by both men are somewhat scarce and command a premium.

Carter's signature is valued at $25. TLsS can be purchased for $125 to $150. Photographs are available at $25 to $50. Signed photographs of the historic Camp David peace accords generally sell for $150 to $200. ALsS are tough to locate and sell for $500 to $1,000. DsS as president are in demand and are valued around $500. Bank checks can be purchased for $175 to $225. Many early bank checks are secretarially signed, so caution is warranted. Signed books are affordable at $25 to $50. The vast number of signed books depresses value of Carter material.

White House Cards

I have never examined a The White House card signed as president. Some unofficial cards were signed by Carter after retirement. The Carter White House was the first to issue a variant White House card. It reads the "White House, Washington" in the upper left-hand corner and features an attractive green vignette of the White House in the center. I have never

Carter-1, program circa 1990.

Carter-2 variant signature dated 2013.

seen one of these cards signed as president. President Carter did sign many after he left office. The value of a The White House card signed as president has not been established. A signed vignette card sells for $275 to $300. Carter no longer will sign these cards.

Ronald Reagan

Reagan signed in a vertical and thoughtful hand. Many signatures will exhibit a slight back slant. Letter construction is sound. Individual letters are well defined, resulting in a high degree of legibility. The signature has average display value. Many letters are simply signed as "R.R.," "Ron," or with his nickname "Dutch." Reagan-signed material spans across many decades. He was signing autographs in the 1930s as a broadcast and movie personality. Vintage signatures are signed in a faster and more rounded hand. Modern signatures are signed in a slower, more pensive hand. They lack rapid motion, and because of this, replication of hand is easy. Well-executed forgeries exist in quantities. In 1994 Reagan announced he had Alzheimer's disease. Despite this, he continued to sign autographs. The illness had little effect on his hand. Signatures signed in the late 1990s evidenced no noticeable change. Reagan signed into 2000, then stopped shortly thereafter. Material from this time frame evidences slight unsteadiness. Reagan's hand never produced a truly shaky signature, at least for autograph purposes. Many variant secretarial and autopen signatures exist, so caution is warranted.

Reagan material dates back to the 1930s. This results in many signed album pages, programs, and studio issued photographs. Many correspondences, at this time, were actually signed by Reagan's mother. Her hand is often confused with that of her famous son. She would sign autographs and pen short notes for fans. Many are found on Warner Brothers studio-issued postcards and postmarked in the

1940s. His being a longtime politician results in a good supply of TLsS, DsS, and ALsS. Reagan is by far the easiest to obtain on ALsS of the modern presidents. He wrote out many draft letters which secretaries would then type. These letters were kept and are a wonderful source of Reagan-signed material. Many of these drafts are signed with initials or the first name only. Photographs are common. Bank checks are scarce. I have never seen a genuine free frank. Reagan portrayed baseball Hall of Famer Grover Cleveland Alexander in the 1952 movie *The Winning Team*. Reagan signed a limited number of Alexander-related items. These should be considered rare to very rare. Signed baseballs are rare and command good money. It should be noted that many forged handwritten presidential oaths of office are in the market, so caution is warranted.

Reagan is the most popular president of the 20th century. The demand for his signature is tremendous. Since his death, a marked increase in values is noted. Signatures are valued at $400 to $450. Photographs sell for $500 to $600. Exceptional examples can sell for $2,000 to $4,000. TLsS are valued at $400 to $500. A nice full-page ALS signed in full will sell for $2,000 to $3,000. Draft ALsS generally sell for $400 and up, depending on length. A good content ALS, even a draft, can sell for over $10,000. Bank checks sell for about $1,250 to $1,500. Signed baseballs are worth $1,500 to $2,000. Signed Alexander-related material is worth over $1,000. Reagan material will increase nicely in value over the years to come. Since he is in the same league as Lincoln, Washington, and Jefferson, one could realistically see a significant content ALS sell for over $100,000 in the coming years and $1,000,000 within the coming decades.

White House Cards

Ronald Reagan did sign The White House cards as president, though they are considered rare. Signed White House vignette cards are available, but they are few and far between. I have never seen a signed vignette card that was dated during his presidency. Signed cards of president Reagan are extremely popular. Either of the above-referenced cards would sell for around $1,250 to $1,500.

Reagan-1, bank check dated 1948.

Reagan-2, signed book dated 1965 (courtesy Nate D. Sanders Auctions).

Reagan-3, signature dated 1985 (courtesy Nate D. Sanders Auctions).

George H.W. Bush

George Bush signed in a very unstructured hand. Letter construction is poor, and individual letters are morphed into indistinguishable strokes. The signature is illegible. Handwritten letters are sloppy in appearance and somewhat difficult to read. Display value is below average. Due to the unstructured nature of hand, Bush's signature is easy to forge. Many well-executed forgeries are in the market. In recent years Bush's hand has been affected with infirmity. Signatures accomplished in the last few years evidence a material unsteadiness. A cramped appearance is noted. Many variant secretarial and autopen signatures exist, so caution is warranted.

Bush was generally a responsive signer throughout his political career. Many TLsS, photographs, and bookplates are available. ALsS also exist in good numbers, but most are short writings penned on personalized note cards. A full-page ALS is scarce. DsS as president are rare. Bank checks are rare to very rare. I have never examined a genuine free frank. Bush was a member of the Yale baseball team, so he likes to sign baseball-related items. Among them are Perez Steele Art postcards and baseballs. There is also a famous photograph of a young George Bush in uniform standing alongside Babe Ruth. Bush signed a limited number of these photographs. They are highly treasured by collectors of baseball autographs. President Bush signed a handful of commemorative Yale baseball jerseys; these are considered rare. It should be noted that in recent years a large quantity of forged photographs have entered the market. They are 8 × 10 photographs featuring President Bush shaking hands with Soviet Premier Mikhail Gorbachev. They are signed across a large white border that runs across the bottom. Both forgeries are typically signed in blue or black Sharpie. The Bush forgery is amateurish, evidencing material hesitation. The forgery appears blocky in nature. The Gorbachev forgery is also malformed and is exposed as a forgery with little effort. These first surfaced in the early to mid–2000s. A genuine signed photograph of Bush and Gorbachev would be very rare.

Bush is an affordable signature which can be purchased for $50. TLsS are valued at $150 to $200. A nice full-page ALS would sell for $1,000 to $1,500. Photographs are common and sell for $125 to $150. Signed baseballs are valued at $300 to $400. Signed Perez Steele cards and Babe Ruth photographs sell in the $300 to $400 price range. Bush signed a limited number of commemorative baseball bats. These are valued at $1,250 to $1,500. Bush signed a limited number of vice-presidential cards during his tenure as veep. These are scarce and are valued at $400. Bank checks are highly treasured and are valued around $1,000 to $1,250.

White House Cards

I have never examined a genuine signed The White House card as president or otherwise. Signed White House vignette cards are available as president but are rare. Bush signed a handful of unofficial The White House cards. A White House vignette card is valued in the $400 to $500 price range. The value of a signed The White House card has not been established.

Bush, G H-1 bookplate dated 1994.

Bush, G H-2 undated signature.

Bush, G H-3, signed photograph dated 2012 (courtesy President George H.W. Bush).

Bill Clinton

Clinton signs in a vertical and compact hand. His signature exhibits strong strokes. The signature is signed without hesitation. Letter construction is slightly impaired. The signature is generally legible. The signature has average display value. Material signed in person is penned in a hurry and appears as nothing more than a scrawl. Clinton's signature is moderately hard to replicate, but a few forgers have produced some convincing examples. As of this writing, Clinton's hand remains strong. A genuine signature will evidence no shakiness of hand, and one that does should be considered suspect and avoided. Many variant secretarial and autopen signatures exist, so caution is warranted.

There is sound demand for Clinton material. It is weighed against a limited supply. Clinton is only one of two presidents to be impeached. The controversy surrounding his presidency generates interest among collectors. Clinton is generally an unresponsive signer, at least through the mail. He signs in person at campaign events and then mostly copies of his book. Books are the most common medium. TLsS are uncommon and just about all signed as president were accomplished by an autopen. ALsS are rare. A few exist signed as governor. Signed baseballs are rare and most offered for sale are forgeries. It should be noted that a few White House envelopes were signed by Clinton in the center of the cover, likely at the request of an autograph collector. A counterfeit Washington, D.C., postmark was added later. They were wrongfully marketed as franks. To my knowledge, no genuine franks are known to exist. Some collectors will take an item signed by Clinton and present it to Clinton's former mistress Monica Lewinsky for signature. Dual-signed items of Clinton and Lewinsky are rare and highly collectable.

Due to the limited supply, Clinton is a rather pricey autograph at $200 to $250. Signed copies of his book, *My Life*, sell for $250 to $300. TLsS are valued at $300 to $400. Signed 8 × 10 photographs can be purchased for $300 to $350.

ALsS are tough to locate and are valued at $1,000 to $1,500. Some content specimens will sell for over $2,000. A signed baseball will sell for $400 to $500.

White House Cards

I have never examined a genuine signed The White House card or a White House vignette card. Many exist with facsimile signatures. It should be noted that some forged The White House cards exist signed in bright blue ink. The cards themselves are likely counterfeit. The value of a genuine signed card has not been established.

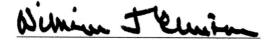

Clinton-1, DS dated 2010 (courtesy Nate D. Sanders Auctions).

Clinton-2, undated signature.

George W. Bush

George W. Bush continues the tradition among modern presidents of having a sloppy and illegible signature. Letter construction is poor. The signature has poor display value. Overall, it is a mere scrawl. Due to the discombobulated nature of hand, Bush's signature is easy to replicate. Well-executed forgeries exist in quantities, mostly limited to baseballs and Texas Ranger team cards. As of this writing, Bush's hand remains strong. A genuine signature will evidence no shakiness of hand, and one that does should be considered suspect and avoided. Many variant secretarial and autopen signatures exist, so caution is warranted.

Bush's signature is available on a limited number of mediums. He is a responsive signer in person. He will sign sports memorabilia and first-day covers. Mail requests are generally answered with an autopen. About the only item he will sign in the mail are bookplates for his book *Decision Points*. Signed photographs exist, but many are machine signed. TLsS are uncommon. ALsS are rare. Signed books are your best source for a genuine autograph.

There is good demand for Bush signed material. Signed books are valued at $100 to $125. A TLS will sell for $275 to $300. A full-page ALS is rarity and is valued at $3,000. A signed baseball can be purchased for $350 to $500. Signed baseball items are in good demand. Bush owned the Texas Rangers. He is likely to be inducted into the National Baseball Hall of Fame someday, which will only increase demand.

White House Cards

I have never examined a genuine signed The White House card or a White House vignette card. As of this writing, the values of these cards have not been established.

Bush, G W-1, TLS dated 2001 (courtesy Nate D. Sanders Auctions).

Bush, G W-2, bookplate dated 2012.

Barack Obama

Obama signs in a fast and sloppy hand. His signature is illegible, and most letters have been pushed aside in favor of scrawls. No hesitation is evident. The signature displays itself as essentially two large letters, a "B" and an "O." He draws a line through the letter "O." Due to the unstructured nature of hand, Obama's signature is easy to forge. Well-executed forgeries exist in quantities. As of this writing, Obama's hand remains strong. A genuine signature will evidence no shakiness of hand, and one that does should be considered suspect and avoided. Many variant autopen and secretarial signatures exist, so caution is warranted.

Signatures are limited to a few mediums, mostly items signed on the campaign trail. Most TLsS are secretarially signed. Signed photographs are uncommon. ALsS are very rare. Many signed copies of his book exist.

As he is the sitting president, there is much demand for Obama's autograph. His signature is valued at $500 to $600. Signed books are essentially the same price. A TLsS can sell for over $1,000. An ALS is valued at $3,000 to $4,000. Once Obama leaves office, values will decrease.

White House Cards

I have never examined a genuine signed The White House card or a White House vignette card. As of this writing, the values of these cards have not been established.

Obama-1, signature circa 2010.

Dick Cheney

Dick Cheney, vice-president under president George W. Bush, became the only non-president to serve as acting president of the United States. This occurred twice, once in June 2002 and then again in July 2007. He served as acting president for a total of four hours while president Bush underwent surgery. While most autographs of vice-presidents are of marginal value, not so with Cheney. This unique designation correlates into greater demand for his signature. If you are trying to assemble a presidential set, you will need to add Cheney's signature to complete it. This will become more evident as the years go by. Cheney's signature sells for a premium.

The Supreme Court
of the United States

The federal judicial system was established by Article III of the United States Constitution. The article requires one Supreme Court and any other such inferior courts as Congress so chooses. Thus the Constitution mandates one, and only one federal court. All other courts are by the grace of the people. The president nominates and the Senate is charged with consenting to or rejecting the appointment. Surprisingly, the Constitution does not specify the number of justices. Currently there are nine justices, but that number can change. President Franklin Roosevelt's failed "court packing" scheme was the last such attempt. Justices can serve for their entire lives if they so choose. Only death has the ability to retire a justice unwilling to do so.

The spectacle of a court trial has always fascinated me, especially criminal proceedings. I worked for many years at Huntington National Bank in Mount Clemens, Michigan. Across the street was the Macomb County Circuit Court. During lunch my co-workers and I used to walk over and watch the murder trials. I got hooked on law and ended becoming an attorney.

The courts have shaped the United States in such profound ways. Many rulings have literally transformed America overnight. Probably the most important opinion ever handed down by the high court is *Marbury v. Madison*, which established the doctrine of judicial review. Other opinions are equally well known. The most important opinion handed down in the last 100 years is very likely *Bush v. Gore*, which determined the outcome of the 2000 presidential election.

As of this writing, there have been 113 justices. This number includes Edwin Stanton, whose nomination was confirmed by the Senate. Unfortunately, Stanton died shortly thereafter and was not able to take the oath of office.

Signatures of justices are widely collected. It is an obtainable set, unlike baseball Hall of Fame members or British Open champions. Many justices held other public offices and as attorneys drafted and signed many documents and letters. The supply of material is sound. Only a few signatures are considered rare. For the signature study of William Howard Taft, please see the chapter on presidential autographs.

There have been countless judges throughout history, both state and federal. Most of their signatures are not collectable. A signature, of say, Arthur Sempliner, a rather well-known Michigan judge, is of little value. There are, of course, exceptions. Robert Bork and Learned Hand, who wrote some of the finest legal opinions in history, come to mind, but for the most part, most judicial signatures have no collector value. Signatures of judges who presided over famous trials are considered collectable, though values are hard to establish. Most are rare to very rare signatures. John Caverly, who was the judge in the murder trial of Leopold and Loeb, would be a collectable signature. Signatures of

Hugo Friend, Charles Older, and James Herbert Wilkerson are also coveted by collectors. Lance Ito, who presided over the O.J. Simpson and Charles Keating trials, is also a collectable signature.

The most treasured judicial signatures are the legendary western judges like Roy Bean and the hangin' judge, Isaac Parker. Signatures of those who hanged the witches of Salem, such as Samuel Sewall and John Hathorne, are very rare and worth their weight in gold.

Supreme Court Chamber card signed by Justice Blackmun.

* * *

John Jay was the first chief justice of the United States. He was appointed to the court by President Washington. He is also known for signing the Treaty of Paris. Jay's signature has sound display value. There is an ample supply of material in the market, mostly LsS and DsS as governor of New York. ALsS are very rare. Given the slower nature of hand, his signature is rather easy to forge. There are many forgeries in the market, most notably franks, with the forgery placed either in the upper left or lower left corner. Many are addressed to "His Excellency." It should be noted that Jay's grandson, John Jay, Jr. (1818 to 1894) signed many letters as "John Jay." His signature is somewhat similar to that of his famous grandfather. Given his stature in American history, one would think Jay's signature would carry strong value, but surprisingly

it is very affordable. His autograph will sell for $400 to $500. LsS and DsS start at $700. Documents with good eye appeal sell for close to $2,000. An extremely undervalued American signature.

Jay-1, undated signature.

Among the original six justices appointed by President Washington was James Wilson. Twice a member of the Continental Congress, he was a signer of the Declaration of Independence. Wilson's signature is legible and practical. It is easily forged. Fortunately his signature is of modest value. Signatures can be purchased for a mere $200 to $250. DsS will sell for slightly more. ALsS are considered rare. Throughout history there have been many famous James Wilsons. Caution is warranted, as you may end up purchasing James Wilson, the fourth secretary of agriculture. Like that of Jay, an undervalued court autograph.

Wilson, J-1, from the DOI.

Of the original justices, William Cushing served the longest at 21 years. Cushing is a rare court autograph that seldom surfaces. His signature, which is typically penned as "Wm. Cushing," is rather easy to forge. There are forged bank checks in the market. They are made payable to "myself" or "AB.," so caution

Cushing-1, undated signature.

is warranted. I know of no recent sales of Cushing's autograph. I estimate a value of $1,500 to $2,000 for a signature.

John Blair served six years on the high court. Blair signed in a confined and legible hand. His signature is pensive in nature and is easily forged. Well-executed forgeries exist. Like that of Cushing, Blair's autograph is rare. His signature is generally limited to Virginia pound currency issued in the 1770s. The notes are countersigned by Peyton Randolph, the first president of the Continental Congress. A rare and highly desirable combination of signatures. Expect to pay $1,500 to $1,750 for a note specimen in acceptable grade.

Blair-1, signature on the USC.

Blair-2, undated signature (courtesy Supreme Court of the United States).

John Rutledge served as an associate justice from 1789 to 1791. He served briefly as the 2nd Chief Justice of the United States, via a recess appointment by President Washington. He is also a signer of the United States Constitution. His signature is rare and generally limited to endorsements and ALsS. There is good demand for Rutledge's autograph. Expect to pay $1,000 for a nice specimen.

Rutledge-1, undated signature.

North Carolinian James Iredell was another charter member of the court. He served nine years, from 1790 until his death in 1799. Iredell is a rare court autograph. Material rarely surfaces and when it does, just about all are forgeries. A few letters are in the market and sell for more than $2,000.

Iredell-1, undated signature (courtesy Supreme Court of the United States).

Another Washington nominee was Thomas Johnson. He was the first governor of Maryland. He served only briefly, and then resigned citing health reasons. Johnson's signature is rapid and exhibits material variance of height. It is rather a hard signature to replicate. His signature is scarce in any form and is typically found on the occasional ALS or ADS. For the level of scarcity, his signature is rather affordable at $200. Letters will sell for around $400.

Johnson, T-1, undated signature.

One of the longer-serving justices appointed by President Washington was William Paterson. He served as the 2nd governor of New Jersey and is a signer of the United States Constitution. Like that of Johnson, Paterson signed in a flowing hand. Signatures are usually penned as

Paterson-1, signature on the USC.

"Wm. Paterson" and would be rather difficult to replicate. There is sound demand for Paterson material, principally because of his association with the Constitution. His signature is scarce in any form, so expect to pay $400. An ALS or ADS will sell for $600 to $700.

Samuel Chase served for fifteen years on the Supreme Court. He was also a signer of the Declaration of Independence. He has the distinction of being the only justice ever to be impeached. He was later acquitted of all charges by the Senate. Chase's signature is average in construction, though dominated by a large letter "C" in the last name. The signature is sometimes finished off with a paraph. Replication of hand is rather easy. Chase's signature is scarce in all forms, but a small supply of ALsS and ADsS do exist. There is a small group of books purportedly from Chase's personal library signed as "S. Chase Jr." Whether these are forgeries or a case of mistaken identity, I do not know. These signatures deviate greatly from a genuine Chase autograph. Expect to pay $750 to $1,000 for a nice signature. Values are elevated due to his association with the Declaration of Independence.

Chase, Sam-1, undated signature.

The last of the Washington appointments was that of Oliver Ellsworth. He was one of the drafters of the Constitution and served as a senator for Connecticut. He served as the third chief justice of the United States. Ellsworth's signature is flowing and retains good display value. His signature is scarce and generally limited to pay order documents. There seems to be a strong supply of these documents in the market, but there is a caveat. I have examined literally hundreds of these pay receipts. The Ellsworth signatures seem to vary in construction; hence, most are secretarially drafted and signed. ALsS are a rarity. The sale of many secretarial DsS depresses value. If an Ellsworth signature doesn't match the illustrated specimens, assume it is a secretarial signature and avoid it. I estimate $500 to $600 for a genuine DS.

Ellsworth-1, undated signature.

Ellsworth-2, undated signature (courtesy Supreme Court of the United States).

Bushrod Washington was one of three justices appointed by President Adams. Washington was the nephew of President Washington. During his long tenure he proved a staunch ally of John Marshall. Washington's signature is average in every aspect of construction. A slight choppiness is noted. Washington's signature is rare, albeit borderline. There is a small supply of ALsS and holograph checks in the market. Replication of hand is rather easy. There is a small supply of forged ALsS in the market, so caution is warranted. His signature generally sells for $250. ALsS and checks are valued at $500 to $600.

Washington, B-1, undated signature.

Alfred Moore was appointed to the high court upon the sudden death of Justice Iredell. Moore himself battled illness, which resulted in a brief tenure of five years on the bench. He wrote only one opinion, *Bas v. Tingy*. He is one of the least known of the justices and his autograph the rarest. Close to 100 percent of all signatures in the market are forgeries. No recent sales. I suspect a value of at least $10,000. His signature *is* the Holy Grail of court autographs.

Moore, A-1 undated signature.

The most significant chief justice of the 19th century was Federalist John Marshall. He was a close confidant of President Adams. He skillfully led the first court through those incipient years when many questioned the court's authority, if not its very existence. With great skill, Marshall slowly but surely established the court's prestige and power. Marshall's signature is the most desired of any court autograph. Marshall signed in a choppy hand. Letter construction is somewhat impaired, resulting in a generally illegible signature. Replication of hand is fairly easy. Well-executed forgeries exist in quantities. Ninety percent of Marshall signatures in the market are forged. Marshall's signature is rare and generally limited to ALsS, DsS, and folio-sized four-language ship papers countersigned by President Adams. One forger has created many forged ALsS, ANsS, and ADsS. They usually contain routine content such as paying a debt or accepting a dinner invitation. The forger has the same M.O by distressing the paper to give the appearance of agedness. The paper is creased. Edges will be foxed or slightly torn. Damp staining and water damage are added, causing portions of the ink to run. The letters are usually addressed "Dear Sir." Many times the date is placed directly under the signature. The grammar is terrible, as if written by an ignorant person. These forgeries are exposed with little effort. There is another small group of forged ALsS in the market purportedly writ-

ten circa 1795 to 1810. They are written in a small and pensive hand. The letters are usually signed as "J. Marshall." The signature is small and has no resemblance to a genuine Marshall signature. The letters are typically penned to government officials such as James McHenry, Thomas Fitzsimons, Benjamin Stoddert, and the like. These letters are nonsensical in construction and exposed with little effort.

There is very strong demand for Marshall material. His signature is valued at $1,000 to $1,500. DsS and LsS sell for $2,000 to $2,500. ALsS are valued at $3,500 to $4,000. ALsS with good content will easily cross the $10,000 threshold. The above-referenced ship papers have exploded in value over the last few years. Once selling for $2,500, they are now approaching $15,000, due to the much increased demand for President Adams's signature.

Marshall-1, undated signature.

William Johnson was the first of three appointments by President Jefferson. He was the first justice of the court who was not a member of the Federalist Party. Johnson's signature is rather attractive in construction. Johnson's signature is rare to very rare in all forms. A restricted supply of DsS exist. No recent sales.

Johnson, Wm-1, undated signature.

Henry Brockholst Livingston was a New York judge who received a recess appointment to the court by President Jefferson. He was later confirmed by the Senate. He was an ally of John Marshall. Livingston's signature is plain in construction. It contains many breaks; thus replication of hand is rather easy. Signatures are usually accomplished as "Brockholst Livingston." The supply of material is restricted. His signature should be considered very scarce and generally limited to ALsS. Expect to pay $250 for his autograph. ALsS sell for $500 to $750.

Livingston, H-1, undated signature.

Thomas Todd was the last of the Jefferson appointments. He served 29 years on the high court and was considered the court's expert of real property law. Todd signed in a neat and precise hand. Todd's signature is flamboyant. The unusual construction gives the signature a uniform and architectural-like appearance. Superior display value is noted. Todd's signature is rare on a per se basis. The occasional ALS will surface. The small supply is clearly outweighed by demand. An ALS is valued around $750 to $1,000.

Todd-1, undated signature.

Gabriel Duvall was appointed by President Madison. He served 23 years on the court. He wrote a mere 15 majority opinions. Signatures are accomplished as "G. Duvall." The signature evidences rounded strokes and is finished off with a muted paraph. Good display value is noted. Duvall's signature is somewhat scarce, but he franked countless postal covers as comptroller of the Treasury. These are a wonderful source for his autograph. Were it not for franks his signature would be quite rare. Duvall's sig-

nature is one that has fallen in value over the years. In the 1980s, franks had a market value of $300 to $400. Today, that same frank can be purchased for $75.

Duvall, circa 1810 free frank.

Joseph Story is best remembered for his opinion in the *Amistad* case. His opinions protecting property rights are considered some of the most important writings ever handed down by the court. Story signed in a rather complex hand. The signature evidences good letter construction with sound eye appeal. The signature is penned in a slower hand, so replication would be rather easy. Story's signature is somewhat scarce and generally limited to ALsS. There is sound demand for Story material. His signature is quite affordable at $100 to $125. ALsS are not much more, starting at $200.

Story-1, undated signature.

Smith Thompson served as secretary of the navy before accepting President Monroe's appointment. Thompson's signature evidences good flow and fine letter construction. A superior display value is noted. Thompson's signature is scarce and generally limited to ALsS and

Thompson, S-1 ADS dated 1811.

DsS. Like that of Story, Thompson's signature is also available at an affordable price. ALsS are valued at $250 to $300.

President John Quincy Adams's only appointment to the high court was that of Robert Trimble. He served only two years before a sudden death due to fever. His signature is rare in all forms and only seldom surfaces. No recent sales.

Trimble-1, undated signature.

Andrew Jackson appointee John McLean served on the high court for 31 years. He was one of two dissenting justices in *Dred Scott v. Sandford*. McLean's signature is rather unassuming with marginal letter construction. The signature has substandard display value. There seems to be a good supply of material in the market, most notably ALsS. There is average demand for McLean material. His signature is valued at $50 to $75. ALsS sell for $150 to $175.

McLean-1, undated signature.

Henry Baldwin served on the court for 14 years. He was the sole dissenter in the *Amistad* case. Baldwin signed in a choppy hand. The signature appears compact. It is typically finished off with a paraph. Very scarce in any form, Baldwin's autograph seldom surfaces. His autograph is tough to locate, so expect to pay $400 to $500 for a nice specimen.

Baldwin-1, undated signature.

James Wayne was the fourth appointee by President Jackson. Wayne served for 32 to years until his death in 1864. Wayne signed in pensive and ordinary hand. Nothing about the signature stands out. A signature of average demand is weighed against an ample supply. Signatures are mostly found on ALsS and small cards. Wayne's signature can be purchased for $150. ALsS sell in the $300 to $400 range.

Wayne, J M-1, undated ALS (courtesy Dr. John Davis, Jr. Autograph Collection of U.S. Supreme Court Justices, Washburn University School of Law Library, Topeka, Kansas).

Roger Taney was appointed by President Jackson. He became the fifth chief justice of the United States. He is best remembered for writing the majority opinion in *Dred Scott v. Sandford*. Taney's signature is available and in much demand. The association with slavery and the Civil War results in a widely collected signature. There is an ample supply of Taney material in the market, including many ALsS, ADsS, and DsS. Cabinet photographs are very rare. There is a small supply of ADsS in the form of legal briefs that Taney wrote while an attorney. These likely date from the 1820s. Some are multiple pages and are signed by Taney at the conclusion of the brief. These are wonderful items and are considered rare. There are a handful of presidential documents signed by President Jackson and countersigned by Taney as attorney general. These are very rare and highly treasured. Taney's signature sells for $125 to $150. ALsS are valued at $400 to $600. Signed legal briefs sell in the $600 to $800 price range. I consider Taney a fine investment signature. A significant American autograph.

Taney-1, ADS undated.

Philip Barbour, a congressman from Virginia, was nominated to the high court by President Jackson. He served five years, and his tenure on the court is of little interest to today's historians. Barbour's signature is of average construction and typically signed "P.P. Barbour." In recent years many Barbour forgeries have entered the market, most being in 18th- and 19th-century leather-bound books. The books are of various subject matter and signed on the inside end page as "P.P. Barbour." The forgery is placed in the center of the end page. It is small in scale and evidences a slightly labored appearance. I have never seen a genuinely signed book of any kind. Barbour is one of the rarer high court signatures and seldom transacted. No recent sales.

Barbour-1, undated signature.

Andrew Jackson appointee John Catron served 28 years on the court. Catron was a slave owner and voted with the majority in *Dred Scott v. Sandford*. Catron is one of the rarest of all court autographs and it hardly comes up for sale. A few of his signatures are held by the Ten-

nessee state archives. Just about 100 percent of all Catron signatures offered for sale are forgeries. No recent sales.

John McKinley was appointed to the high court by President Van Buren. He served 14 years on the bench. McKinley is another lesser-known justice to today's collector. Like that of Catron, McKinley's signature is rare. Signatures, what few there are, are typically accomplished as "J. McKinley." Just about 100 percent of all McKinley signatures offered for sale are forgeries. No recent sales.

McKinley, J-1, undated signature.

Peter Vivian Daniel was a confidant of Andrew Jackson. He was appointed to the court by President Van Buren. He authored few opinions. *West River Bridge Co. v. Dix* is the one of his more important opinions. Daniel signed in a practical hand. He wrote his signature more than he signed it. Replication of hand is simple. Producing a well-executed forgery can be done with little effort. Due to rarity, his signature is a target of forgers. Most Daniel signatures in the market are forged. Daniel's signature is very scarce to rare in all forms. Expect to pay $500 for a nice specimen.

Daniel-1, Album page circa 1860.

Samuel Nelson was appointed to the Supreme Court by President John Tyler. Four previous attempts by Tyler to appoint a justice were shot down by the Whig-controlled Senate. Nelson signed is an unremarkable hand. This signature has substandard letter construction. Display value is poor. Most signatures are

Catron-1, ADS dated 1863 (courtesy Tennessee State Library and Archives).

accomplished as "S. Nelson." There seems to be an ample supply of ALsS in the market. Other mediums, including cabinet cards, are rare and seldom enter the market. There is marginal demand for Nelson material, which keeps prices in check. Nelson's signature sells for $75. ALsS can be purchased for $150 to $200.

Nelson, S-1 ALS dated 1870.

Appointed by President Polk, Levi Woodbury served just under six years on the high court. He had a long career in government, serving as a senator, governor, cabinet member, and secretary of the navy. His tenure on the bench was rather lackluster. Woodbury signed in a plain and unassuming hand. A signature of average display value. There is an ample supply of Woodbury material in the market, mostly found on DsS and ALsS. His signature is affordable at $50. DsS sell for $100. ALsS are valued at $125 to $150.

Woodbury-1, undated signature (courtesy The Oklahoma City University School of Law, Bob Burke Supreme Court Signature Collection).

Robert Grier was another Polk appointee. He was an ally of Chief Justice Taney. Grier was accused of bribery but was ultimately exonerated of the charge. Grier signed in a flowing hand. His signature is typically accomplished as "R.C. Grier." Grier's signature is scarce in all forms and surfaces only occasionally. ALsS or album pages are noted mediums. There is ample demand for Grier material. His signature will sell for $150 to $175. ALsS are valued at $350 to $500. While not rare, it is still one of the tougher court autographs.

Grier-1, album page circa 1860.

Benjamin Curtis was the first and only justice affiliated with the Whig party. He remains the only justice to resign over a matter of principle—that being the Dred Scott case. Curtis signed in an average and somewhat lazy hand. Letter construction is muted. Most signatures are signed as "B.R. Curtis." There is an ample supply of ALsS in the market, some multiple pages. There is only marginal demand for his autograph. His signature can be purchased for $50 to $75. A full page ALS can be purchased for $100 to $150.

Curtis-1, ALS dated 1867.

John Archibald Campbell was appointed to the Supreme Court by President Pierce. He resigned his seat upon outbreak of the Civil War. He served the Confederacy in various positions. Campbell's signature is sloppy and unappealing. Display value is substandard. Campbell's signature is rare in all forms. EsS and the occasional ALS will surface. Expect to pay $600 to $700 for his autograph. A full-page ALS will sell for $1,500 to $2,000.

Campbell-1, undated signature.

Nathan Clifford was appointed to the court by President Buchanan. He was a strong advocate of states' rights and slavery. Clifford signed in a simple and hesitant hand. His signature evidences a slightly labored appearance. Display value is substandard. There is an ample supply of signatures in the market, though mostly limited to album pages and small cards. Other mediums, such as ALsS, are scarce to rare. Marginal demand keeps values depressed. His signature can be purchased for $50. ALsS are valued at $175 to $200.

Clifford-1, undated signature.

Noah Swayne has the distinction of being the first Republican ever appointed to the court. He strongly supported President Lincoln's policies and a powerful federal government. Swayne signed in a flowing and large script. Many strokes and sweeps correlate into a signature with strong display value. One of the nicer court autographs. The supply of Swayne material is sufficient. Signatures can be found on ALsS, album pages, and 16mo cards. An affordable signature that can be added to your collection for $50. ALsS will sell for $125 to $150.

Swayne-1, signature dated 1872 (courtesy The Oklahoma City University School of Law, Bob Burke Supreme Court Signature Collection).

Samuel Miller was another Lincoln appointee, who, like Swayne, favored a strong central government. Miller signed in a flowing hand. The signature has fair letter construction and average display value. Signatures are typically accomplished as "Sam. F. Miller." Miller's signature can be found on album pages, 16mo cards, ALsS, and bank checks. Supply is balanced with demand. Signatures will sell for $35 to $50. ALsS and bank checks are valued at $100 to $125.

David Davis was a Lincoln confidant. He served as Lincoln's campaign manager during the 1860 presidential election. His legal philosophy followed that of Messrs. Miller and Swayne. His signature is of average construction and display value. Signatures are generally found on ALsS, album pages, and 16mo cards. Davis's signature will sell for $50. ALsS are valued at $125 to $150.

Davis-1, signature dated 1880 (courtesy The Oklahoma City University School of Law, Bob Burke Supreme Court Signature Collection).

Stephen Field was a pro–Union Democrat. Field was an unlikely Lincoln appointment. He was an early advocate of substantive due process. His votes generally favored a segregationist platform. Field signed in an aggressive and heavy hand. The signature exhibits thick strokes of ink. The signature appears a bit compact with average display value. His signature is generally limited to small cards and album pages. ALsS are rare. It should be noted that there are many cabinet photographs in the market with realistic facsimile signatures, so caution is warranted. Expect to pay $100 for a nice signature. ALsS are valued at $250 to $300.

Miller-1 bank check dated 1871.

Field-1 undated signature.

Salmon P. Chase's image can be found on the $10,000 bill. He was a close friend of President Lincoln. He became the sixth chief justice of the United States. Chase signed in a rather busy and unappealing hand. Most signatures are signed as "S.P. Chase." There is a sound supply of Chase material. His signature can be found on ALsS, treasury DsS, endorsements, and appointments signed as governor of Ohio. Cabinet photographs are rare. There is one forgery to note. There are many forged cabinet photographs in the market. The image features Chase standing in pose with his right hand tucked into his coat. The forgery is placed at the bottom of the card. These were produced by the same forger. There is solid demand for Chase material. The sound inventory keeps values in check. Signatures can be purchased for $75. DsS are valued at $100. ALsS are a steal at $150. Cabinet photographs are valued at $600 to $800.

Chase, S-1, undated signature.

William Strong was appointed to the high court by President Grant. Grant had initially chosen Edwin Stanton, who died just after Senate confirmation. Strong served ten years. Strong signed in a slightly labored hand. Letters tend to be uniform in size. Most signatures are penned as "W. Strong." Signatures are generally

Strong-1, undated signature (courtesy The Oklahoma City University School of Law, Bob Burke Supreme Court Signature Collection.

limited to ALsS, DsS, and calling cards. Overall, a somewhat scarce signature with muted demand. Expect to pay $75 for his autograph. An ALS will sell for $150 to $175.

Another Grant appointee was litigator Joseph Bradley. Bradley signed in a nice flowing hand. His signature has above average display value. His signature is somewhat scarce but ALsS, calling cards, and album pages do exist. There is not much demand for Bradley material. His signature can be purchased for $50. ALsS are valued at $125 to $150.

Bradley-1 Album page dated 1882.

Ward Hunt was nominated by President Grant, likely as a political favor for New York Senator Roscoe Conkling. He is best remembered for finding Susan B. Anthony guilty of illegally voting in the presidential election on 1872. Hunt signed in a rapid and pleasing hand. The signature evidences good display value. One of the scarcer court autographs. His signature is generally found on album pages. ALsS are rare. In the late 1870s, Ward suffered a severe stroke. There are signatures in the market that are said to have been signed post-stroke. These signatures evidence a very shaky hand with mis-spaced letter construction. Whether these are genuine or not, I do not know. There are many variant post-stroke specimens in the market. I advise collectors to avoid post-illness signatures. Expect to pay $200 to $250 for Hunt's signature.

Hunt-1 undated signature.

Morrison Waite was the 7th chief justice of the United States. The Waite Court was a staunch supporter of many Reconstruction laws. Waite signed in a large and practical hand. His signature is average in every respect. Signatures are typically accomplished as "M.R. Waite." There is an ample supply of Waite material in the market. Signatures are typically found on ALsS, album pages, and small calling cards. Many ALsS are multiple pages. Waite's signature is quite affordable at $50. ALsS can be purchased for $150 to $200. Cabinet photographs are rare, so expect to pay $750.

Waite-1, undated signature (courtesy The Oklahoma City University School of Law, Bob Burke Supreme Court Signature Collection).

John Marshal Harlan was nominated by President Hayes. He was known as the "Great Dissenter." Harlan signed in a flowing hand. His signature has moderate display value and is typically finished off with a paraph. One of the more scarce court autographs. Signatures are found on ALsS and signatures removed therefrom. Cabinet photographs are rare. Expect to pay $200 to $250 for his autograph.

Harlan, J-1, undated signature (courtesy The Oklahoma City University School of Law, Bob Burke Supreme Court Signature Collection).

William Woods served in the Civil War with the 76th Ohio Volunteer Infantry. He rose to the rank of major general, in brevet. He was appointed to the court by President Hayes. Woods signed in a vertical hand. His writing is similar to that of the man who appointed him, President Hayes. Woods is another tough court autograph. Woods's signature should be consid-

ered very scarce to rare. Signatures turn up on ALsS and ANsS, and that is about it. Expect to pay $500 for a nice specimen.

Woods-1, undated signature.

President Garfield's only appointment was fellow Ohioan Stanley Matthews. Matthews wrote the majority opinion in *Yick Wo v. Hopkins*. Otherwise, Matthews had an unassuming tenure on the court. Matthews signed in a flowing hand. His signature is of average construction and display value. Signatures are uncommon to scarce but an ample supply of ALsS and album pages do exist. There is average demand for Matthews material. Signatures can be purchased for $40 to $50. ALsS at $100 to $125.

Matthews-1, undated signature.

Horace Gray was nominated by President Arthur. He served 24 years on the court. He wrote many opinions and sided with the majority in *Plessy v. Ferguson*. Gray signed in a sloppy and unstructured hand. Letters tend to be malformed, resulting in a signature with substandard display value. A good deal of decipher-

Gray-1, undated signature.

ing is needed to read one of his ALsS. His signature is considered uncommon to scarce. A restricted supply of ALsS is in the market. Expect to pay $75 for his autograph. ALS will sell for $250 to $300.

Another Arthur appointee was Sam Blatchford. He was probably the wealthiest man to serve on the high court. His estimated personal net worth was three to four million dollars. That's about $125,000,000 in today's money. Blatchford's signature is flowing. It has a certain artistic flair. Overall, one of the nicer high court signatures. Signatures are scarce on a per se basis. Signatures are typically found on ALsS and album pages. Some ALsS have good content regarding race: he usually writes about blacks in a less than flattering fashion. Signatures are valued at $100. ALsS sell for $150 to $200. ALsS with racial content will sell for $500 or more.

Blatchford-1, signature dated 1892 (courtesy The Oklahoma City University School of Law, Bob Burke Supreme Court Signature Collection).

Appointed by President Cleveland, Lucius Lamar served only five years. He died in office. Lamar signed in a rather practical hand. Strong letter construction is noted. A signature with average display value. Signatures are usually accomplished at "L.Q.C. Lamar." There is an ample supply of Lamar material in the market. His signature is typically found on ALsS, album pages, and small 16mo cards. His signature is affordable at $40 to $50. Expect to pay $100 to $125 for an ALS.

Lamar, L-1 undated signature.

Melville Fuller, a Cleveland appointee, had a striking resemblance to author Mark Twain. Fuller was the eighth chief justice of the United States. Fuller's signature is average in just about every respect. Signatures penned late in life evidence an unsteady and labored hand. There is a decent supply of Fuller material in the market. ALsS, calling cards, and album pages are the most common. Cabinet photographs are rare. Fuller's signature is valued at $50. ALsS will sell for $150 to $175.

Fuller-1, undated signature.

David Brewer was appointed to the court by President Benjamin Harrison. Brewer signed in a flowing and pleasing hand. The signature evidences no breaks in the hand. Signatures penned later in life will evidence a slight unsteadiness. Signatures are typically found on ALsS and album pages. Photographs are considered rare. A signature of average demand, so expect to pay $50 for his autograph. An ALS will sell for $125 to $150.

Brewer-1, undated TLS (courtesy The Oklahoma City University School of Law, Bob Burke Supreme Court Signature Collection).

Henry Brown was a federal district court judge in Detroit. He was elevated to the high court by President Harrison. Brown wrote the opinion for *Plessy v. Ferguson*. Brown signed in a slow and methodic hand. His signature evi-

Brown, H-1, album page circa 1890.

dences uniformity throughout. Letter construction is superior. A sound display value is noted. Signatures tend to be found on album pages and 16mo cards. Other mediums are considered scarce to rare. His signature can be purchased for $100. ALsS are tough to locate, so expect to pay $300 to $350 for a nice specimen.

George Shiras, Jr., served 10 years on the court. He was the pivotal vote in *Pollock v. Farmers' Loan & Trust Co.*, which struck down federal income tax as unconstitutional. Shiras signed in an odd and eclectic hand. It has good display value in a weird sort of way. His signature is uncommon to scarce and generally limited to album pages and 16mo cards. ALsS are scarce. A signature of average demand, it can be purchased for $50. ALsS will sell for $150 to $200.

Shiras-1, undated signature.

Howell Jackson was appointed by President Harrison to the high court. He served just two years, then died of consumption. Despite his brief tenure, there is a small but decent supply of material in the market. He had a long career in public service; hence, signatures will surface on ALsS and album pages. His signature should be considered scarce on a per se basis. Expect to pay $250 for his autograph.

Jackson, H-1 undated signature.

Edward White was the ninth chief justice of the United States. He was appointed by William Howard Taft, who oddly enough succeeded White on the court. White signed in an unattractive and heavy hand. Thick strokes of ink are noted. A slight hesitation is noted. Though White is generally not the target of forgers, many TLsS are secretarially signed. The secretarial signature looks similar to the genuine specimen, but hesitation is even more so. The secretary adds a small downstroke at the based on the "E" in the first name, something a genuine signature should not exhibit. ALsS are notoriously rare. White's signature is affordable at $75. A TLS will sell for $150 to $175.

White, E-1 signature undated.

Rufus Peckham was nominated by President Cleveland. He was a staunch advocate of states' rights and reined in the powers of the federal government. Peckham signed in a choppy hand. The signature is average in every way. Sometimes it is finished off with a paraph. Peckham's signature is somewhat scarce. As with most justices of this era, ALsS and album pages seem to be the available mediums. A signature of average demand. Expect to pay $75 for his autograph. ALsS will sell for $150 to $175. It should be noted that Peckham's father, with the same name, was a congressman from New York. The signatures of the two are strikingly similar and

Peckham-1, signature dated 1896 (courtesy The Oklahoma City University School of Law, Bob Burke Supreme Court Signature Collection).

are often confused. Many times the father's signature is sold as his more famous son's autograph. Peckham Sr.'s autograph is illustrated.

Peckham, Sr.-2, signature of Congressman.

Longtime public servant Joseph McKenna was appointed to the high court by President McKinley. McKenna signed in a pleasing hand. The signature tends to be rather lengthy. Letter construction is sound. One of the nicer court autographs. The supply of McKenna material is sound. His signature can be found on ALsS, TLsS, album pages, and presidential appointments countersigned by McKinley. McKenna's signature is affordable at $50. ALsS sell for $100 to $125. The above-referenced presidential appointments make for a fine display and sell for $400 to $500.

McKenna-1, undated signature (courtesy The Oklahoma City University School of Law, Bob Burke Supreme Court Signature Collection).

Oliver Wendell Holmes, Jr., is the most famous justice, behind William Howard Taft. He was noted for writing opinions with a cutting pen. *Buck v. Bell* was one of his most famous. Holmes signed in an aggressive hand. Strokes tend to be heavy. The signature dominates the medium it is placed upon. The supply of Holmes material is sound. He lived to 93 and was a responsive signer. He was one of the first justices widely targeted by autograph collectors. There are many ALsS in the market, though most tend to be short with mundane content, usually a thank-you letter. Album pages are also available. He was one of the first justices to sign formal

8 × 10 and 11 × 14 portrait photographs. Holmes material has actually fallen in value in recent years. His signature was more expensive 15 years ago. Signatures can be purchased for $150 to $175. Short ALsS are valued at $250 to $300. Content letters will sell for over $1,000. Photographs are somewhat scarce, so expect to pay $600 to $800.

Holmes, O W Jr-1 ALS dated 1904.

William Day was a lifelong civil servant and a close friend of Theodore Roosevelt. Day served 19 years on the bench. Day signed is very plain and unassuming hand. His signature blends well into a crowd. It would be very easy to replicate. Day used to be a rather scarce signature; however, several years back a strong supply of canceled bank checks entered the market. Values plummeted. Today, his signature is of little value. Bank checks can be purchased on eBay for as little as $20.

Day-1 bank check dated 1874 (courtesy collection of Dennis Hoffner).

William Moody was another Theodore Roosevelt appointee. His opinions favored a powerful central government and the expansion of the interstate commerce clause. He was also one of the prosecuting attorneys in the murder trial of Lizzie Borden. Moody signed in a very choppy hand. Abrupt angles are noted. His signature is cubic in appearance. Moody's signature is generally found on TLsS and 16mo cards. ALsS and photographs are scarce to rare. A signature can be purchased for $50. A TLS will sell for $100 and an ALS is valued at $250 to $300. A letter with Borden content would be an extreme rarity.

Moody-2, undated signature (courtesy The Oklahoma City University School of Law, Bob Burke Supreme Court Signature Collection).

Horace Lurton is a name mostly forgotten by history. He was appointed by President Taft, which is odd considering Taft was a Republican and Lurton a Democrat. He served only briefly. Lurton's signature is one of the rarest of all court autographs. His signature only rarely surfaces. No recent sales. The illustrated specimen is from the Supreme Court archives.

Lurton-1, undated signature (courtesy Supreme Court of the United States).

Charles Evans Hughes narrowly lost the 1916 presidential election to Woodrow Wilson. He was appointed to the high court by President Hoover as the 11th chief justice of the United States. Hughes signed in a large and aggressive hand. His signature appears rapid in nature. Hughes lived until 1948 and was a willing and gracious signer. His signature is on the common side and can be found on most mediums, including handsome 8 × 10 portrait photographs. Signatures can be purchased for $40 to $50. ALsS and 8 × 10 photographs sell for around $175 to $200. An inexpensive signature for such a notable figure in American history.

Hughes, C-1, TLS dated 1910 (courtesy Nate D. Sanders Auctions).

Willis Van Devanter, another Taft appointee, spent almost 27 years on the high court. Van Devanter was one of the conservative "four horsemen" of the court. He was a champion of limited government and opposed most of Franklin Roosevelt's New Deal legislation. Van Devanter signed in an odd, almost medieval script. Thick strokes deliberately written enhance display value. Signatures are generally found on engraved calling cards and album pages. Letters of any kind are scarce. Photographs are also scarce. His signature sells for $50 to $75.

Van Devanter-1 signature circa 1930.

Joseph Lamar was another Taft appointment. Lamar, who was related to fellow Justice Lucius Lamar, served only five years on the high court. Lamar signed in a rather lazy hand where individual letters tend to blend together into indistinguishable bumps. Lamar's signature is rare in all forms and easily forged. His papers are held at the University of Georgia. Just about all signatures offered for sale are forgeries. No recent sales.

Lamar, J-1 TLS dated 1912 (courtesy Hargrett Rare Book and Manuscript Library, University of Georgia Libraries).

Mahlon Pitney was a Taft appointee. He served on the court for 10 years. He retired from the bench in 1922 after suffering a stroke. Pitney signed in a bold and flamboyant hand. His signature has good display value. Material signed by Pitney is scarce, but I would not consider it a rare signature. Signatures can be found on ALsS, TLsS, and album pages. Expect to pay $100 for his autograph. A full-page ALS will sell for $300.

Pitney-1, undated signature (courtesy Dr. John Davis, Jr. Autograph Collection of U.S. Supreme Court Justices, Washburn University School of Law Library, Topeka, Kansas).

James C. McReynolds was appointed to the court by President Wilson. He was a constructionist and opposed much of the New Deal legislation. Signatures are penned in a slightly hesitant hand. Most are signed as "J.C. McReynolds." McReynolds's signature is considered uncommon but not scarce. He signed many items. He would hand out countless signatures on slips of Supreme Court memorandum paper. ALsS are scarce and have good display value. Signed photographs are rare. Some handsome 8 × 10 photographs do exist. McReynolds's signature can be purchased for $50. ALsS at $150 to $200.

McReynolds-1 signature dated 1935 (courtesy collection of Dennis Hoffner).

Louis Brandeis was another Wilson appointment. He was the first true liberal activist on the court. Brandeis signed in a very flowing hand. The signature evidences wonderful construction and superior eye appeal. It is one of the nicer court signatures. Due to the complex nature of hand, well-executed forgeries do not exist. Brandeis's signature exists in ample supply. He signed many items, including album pages and government postcards. ALsS exist in good supply. There is sound demand for Brandeis material. It is a signature that has, in recent years, declined in value. Online auction sites, such as eBay, have allowed much material to enter the market. Brandeis's signature can be purchased for $250 to $300. ALsS sell for $600 to $800.

Brandeis-1, undated signature (courtesy The Sanders Autograph Price Guide).

John Hessin Clarke is the least known of the Wilson appointments. He served only six years on the court, retiring in 1922. He was a champion of a dominant federal government. Clarke is one of the more scarce court signatures. A restricted supply of ALsS and TLsS exist, but that is about it. His signature is valued simply to complete a set. Expect to pay $250-$300 for his autograph.

Clarke, J-1, TLS undated.

George Sutherland was appointed by President Harding in 1922. He served until 1938. He was one of the "four horsemen" of the court who knocked down much of the New Deal legislation. Sutherland's signature is uncommon. He lived until 1942 and was a responsive signer throughout. He would hand out signed 8 × 10 photographs and sometimes include an ALS, on court letterhead, as a transmittal. Signatures can be found on album pages and chamber cards. Sutherland's signature is affordable at $70. ALsS and 8 × 10 photographs are valued at $175 to $200.

Sutherland-1 ALS dated 1934 (courtesy Nate D. Sanders Auctions).

The final member of the court's "four horsemen" was Harding appointee Pierce Butler. Butler signed in a rapid hand. Letter construction is marginal as individual letters tend to morph together. Butler died in 1939 and was a responsive signer throughout his life. There is a good inventory of material in the market. Signatures can be found on ALsS, 8 × 10 photographs, chamber cards, and the like. An affordable signature; expect to pay $50 for a nice specimen. Chamber cards and ALsS sell for about $100 to $125.

Butler-1, SCCC dated 1934 (courtesy The Oklahoma City University School of Law, Bob Burke Supreme Court Signature Collection).

Edward Sanford wrote the opinion in *Gitlow v. New York*, which is an important 14th amendment case. He is otherwise a forgotten justice. Sanford signed in a flowing and artistic hand. The signature evidences good letter construction and superior display value. One of the nicer high court autographs. Sanford material should be considered very scarce. There is a restricted supply of signatures. Chamber cards are rare. A signature is valued at $300 to $350. A chamber card and ALS will sell closer to $600.

Sanford-1, album page dated 1929.

Harlan Stone was appointed by President Coolidge. He was later elevated by President Roosevelt to chief justice. Stone signed in a rather jagged hand. The signature features cutting and muted letter construction. Overall, an average signature. Stone material is rather common. The inventory is sound and includes many TLsS. ALsS and photographs are scarce. It should be noted that Stone served as attorney general under President Coolidge. During his tenure, many typed memorandums on "Office

of the Attorney General" letterhead exist. Just about all of these were secretarially signed. The secretarial signatures look nothing like a genuine specimen. Stone's signature can be purchased for $40 to $50. A TLS will sell for $100 to $125.

Stone-1 undated signature.

Owen Roberts was appointed by President Hoover. In *Korematsu v. United States* he voted against the internment of Japanese-Americans during World War II. Roberts's signature is of average letter construction and display value. The supply of Roberts material is sound. Signatures can be found on ALsS, chamber cards, TLsS, and 8 × 10 photographs. A signature is valued at $50. An ALS and 8 × 10 photograph will sell for $150 to $175.

Roberts, O-1, undated signature (courtesy Nate D. Sanders Auctions).

Palsgraf v. Long Island R.R. Co. is one of the most famous cases in tort law. Benjamin Cardozo wrote the opinion that established the doctrine of proximate cause. Cardozo was the second Jewish Justice (the first being Brandeis) to sit on the high court. Cardozo, one of the more famous members of the court, signed in a flowing and sloppy hand. The signature is generally illegible. There is a decent supply of material in the market including ALsS, 8 × 10 photographs, and ANsS. Most letters are short with mundane content. The value of Cardozo material has fallen in the last decade. His signature used to sell for $300 to $400; now it can be purchased for $150 to $200. ALsS are a bargain at

$300 to $400. I consider Cardozo material to be undervalued.

Cardozo-1, undated signature (courtesy The Oklahoma City University School of Law, Bob Burke Supreme Court Signature Collection).

Hugo Black was appointed to the high court by President Franklin Roosevelt. He was an ardent supporter of the New Deal. He was also a member of the Ku Klux Klan. Black signed in a slightly choppy hand. The signature evidences sound letter construction and is generally legible. Black was a willing and gracious signer throughout his long life. There is a good supply of Black material in the market. ALsS should be considered very scarce. Black's signature sells for $30 to $40. TLsS can be purchased for $75 to $100.

Black-1, TLS dated 1939.

Stanley Reed was appointed to the high court by President Roosevelt. He served for 19 years, retiring in 1957. Reed was associated with accused spy Alger Hiss. Reed signed in a bold and flowing hand. His signature dominates the medium it is placed upon. Reed was a responsive signer, resulting in a good supply of material in the market. Chamber cards exist in quantities. ALsS are scarce. A signature of marginal demand so expect to pay $30 to $40 it. Chamber cards sell for about $75.

Felix Frankfurter was another important member of the high court. He was appointed by President Roosevelt. Though Frankfurter was a liberal, he was a strong advocate of judicial restraint and federalism. Frankfurter signed in a flowing and pleasing hand. The signature tends to be on the illegible side. Frankfurter material is rather common. He was a willing signer. His signature can be found on ALsS, TLsS, photographs, and chamber cards. Like that of Cardozo and Brandeis, the value of Frankfurter material has fallen over the past ten years. His signature can be purchased for a mere $100. Chamber cards will sell for $250.

Frankfurter-1 ALS undated (courtesy Stephen Koschal Autographs).

William Douglas was the longest-serving justice in history. He was also one of the most liberal members of the court. In his dissent in *Sierra Club v. Morton*, Douglas argued that inanimate objects, such as weeds, have judicial standing. Plagued by scandal, Douglas was the target of two impeachment proceedings, one spearheaded by then congressman and future president Gerald Ford. Douglas signed in a pensive and confined hand. The signature tends to be small and unassuming. Signatures produced late in life tend to be cramped and evidence a slightly labored appearance. Douglas was a responsive signer throughout his life. The supply of material is sound. Signatures can be found on most mediums. ALsS are considered scarce. Douglas's signature can be purchased for $30 to $40. A chamber card is valued for not much more.

Reed-1 TLS dated 1965.

Douglas-1 signature dated 1940 (courtesy Nate D. Sanders Auctions).

Frank Murphy was a local legend in Michigan. He held several offices, including governor and mayor of Detroit. He was appointed to the court by President Roosevelt. He served only nine years, then died. Murphy signed in a malformed and sloppy hand. The signature is illegible. Individual letters appear as mere strokes. It should be noted that many TLsS are secretarially signed. Signatures on most mediums sell for $50. There is not much demand for Murphy material.

Murphy-1 USSC Chamber card, undated.

James Byrnes was appointed to the court by President Roosevelt. He served 15 months before resigning to head another department of the government. Byrnes signed in a rapid and flowing hand. Display value and letter construction are average. Byrnes was a willing signer throughout his life. He signed many items, mostly limited index cards and first-day covers. TLsS are uncommon; ALsS are rare. Byrnes's signature is affordable at $40 to $50.

Byrnes-1, undated signature.

Robert Jackson was the last justice to serve without having a law degree. He was also the chief prosecutor for the United States at the

Nuremberg trials. Jackson's most famous opinion was that of *West Virginia Board of Education v. Barnette*. In *Barnette*, the court declared it unconstitutional to require school kids to salute the American flag. Jackson signed in an average and plain hand. The signature tends to be legible. There is an ample supply of material in the market, including a surprising inventory of chamber cards. TLsS and photographs also exist. ALsS are considered rare. There is marginal demand for Jackson material, which seems odd to me, given his association with the World War II war crime trials. Signatures can be purchased for $50. Chamber cards sell for $100.

Jackson, R-1 undated signature (courtesy The Oklahoma City University School of Law, Bob Burke Supreme Court Signature Collection).

Wiley Rutledge was appointed by President Roosevelt. He served just six years, then died of a stroke at age 55. Rutledge signed in a flowing and beautiful script. Superb letter construction is noted. ALsS have stunning display value. The supply of Rutledge material is not as prevalent as that of some of his contemporaries. His signature can be found on ALsS and chamber cards. Photographs are scarce to very scarce. A chamber card, which is usually inscribed, will sell for $100 to $125. ALsS will sell for $250 to $300.

Rutledge, W-1, signature circa 1945.

Harold Burton was appointed to the court by President Truman. Before his tenure on the bench, Burton served as mayor of Cleveland and United States senator from Ohio. Burton signed in a muted hand. His signature lacks height. The supply of Burton material is ample. Signatures can be found on most mediums, including nicely signed 8 × 10 portrait photographs, chamber cards, TLsS, and ALsS. Burton's signature is affordable at $30 to $40. ALsS sell for $125 to $150. Chamber cards can be purchased for $75.

Burton, H-1 signature dated 1941.

Frederick Vinson was a lifelong public servant and close friend of President Truman. He became the 13th chief justice of the United States. He died suddenly at age 63, a victim of a heart attack. Vinson signed in an eclectic hand. The signature evidences good flow and sound letter construction. It is a signature with sound display value. There is a good supply of Vinson material in the market. His signature used to be on the scarce side, then, a while back, a sizeable cache of canceled bank checks entered the market. These are an excellent source of Vinson's signature. Bank checks can be purchased for $50 to $75.

Vinson-1, bank check dated 1951 (courtesy The Written Word Autographs).

Tom Clark was President Truman's attorney general. Truman appointed him to the court in 1949. He served until 1967. He was a liberal member of the court and allied himself with Vinson and, later, Earl Warren. Clark signed in a lazy hand. The signature evidences impaired construction, resulting in substandard display value. Signatures can be found on TLsS, photographs, and chamber cards. ALsS are uncommon. A signature of marginal demand. Just about all mediums can be purchased for under $100. Signatures sell for as little as $15.

Clark-1 signed photograph dated 1973 (courtesy Nate D. Sanders Auctions).

Sherman Minton was a senator for Indiana. He was one of the President Roosevelt's most staunch supporters in Congress. Minton signed in a pleasing and flowing hand. Effortless strokes create a signature with superior display value. There is an ample supply of Minton material in the market. TLsS, photographs, and chamber cards exist. ALsS are scarce. Minton's signature can be purchased for $30 to $40. Chamber cards and TLsS sell for $75 to $100.

Minton-1, signature circa 1950.

President Eisenhower called his appointment of Earl Warren to the high court the biggest mistake of his presidency. Warren was chief justice from 1953 to 1969. Warren signed in a precise hand. His signature is rather pleasing to the eye. Warren was a responsive signer, resulting in a good supply of material in the market. Signatures can be found on TLsS, photographs, and first day covers. Signed chamber cards seem to be lacking in the market. It should be noted that many letters signed as governor and attorney general of California were secretarially signed. Due to the large supply of material, prices are quite reasonable. Signatures can be purchased for $40 to $50. TLsS and 8 × 10 photographs sell for $75 to $100.

Warren, E-1 TLS dated 1938.

John Marshall Harlan II was the grandson of John Marshall Harlan. He was appointed to the high court by President Eisenhower. Harlan signed in a choppy and illegible hand. Letter construction is marginal at best. Signatures are limited in supply when compared to other justices of his era. TLsS, ALsS, and ANsS are available. Other mediums are rare. Harlan's signature can be purchased for $50 to $75. A TLS will sell for $100 to $125.

Harlan-J M II-1, signature circa 1965.

William Brennan, though appointed by Dwight Eisenhower, turned out to be one of the most liberal of justices. Brennan signed in a nice flowing hand. Legibility is impaired. Signatures are typically accomplished as "Wm. J. Brennan." Brennan was a willing and gracious signer

Brennan-1, undated signature (courtesy The Sanders Autograph Price Guide).

throughout his tenure on the court. He would usually send a short TLS with a signed chamber card. Photographs are also available. ALsS should be considered rare. His signature can be purchased on a chamber card or TLS for $40 to $50.

Charles Whittaker served only five years on the court. He was considered a swing vote on the court. Whittaker signed in an odd and flowing hand. His signature has sound display value. One of the nicer court autographs. Signatures are uncommon and generally limited to chamber cards and government postcards. ALsS are very scarce to rare. Whittaker's signature can be purchased for $75. Chamber cards are valued at $125 to $150.

Whittaker-1 USSC chamber card undated.

Potter Stewart was appointed by president Eisenhower. He was considered a centrist vote on the court. Stewart signed in a slower more thoughtful hand. The signature exhibits poor letter construction. Stewart's signature is generally illegible. There is a good supply of Stewart material in the market. He was a willing signer. Signatures are typically found on chamber cards and first day covers. Photographs are uncommon. ALsS are rare. Supply is balanced with demand. Stewart's signature is affordable at $30 to $40 on a chamber card.

Stewart, P-1 USSC chamber card dated 1978.

Byron White was appointed by President Kennedy. He was a liberal justice who, as time went on, moved to the right. He often found himself allied with Chief Justice William Rehnquist. White is of particular interest as he was a great football player. He played for the Detroit Lions in the early 1940s and was inducted into the College Football Hall of Fame. White signed in an average and somewhat lazy hand. The signature is of average construction. Material signed in the last couple of years of life evidence moderate shakiness of hand. White was a responsive signer and would even autograph football-related material. He was not particularly fond of his nickname "Whizzer" and would not sign autographs using such. He would sign items with football inscriptions, such as his jersey number or position. Signatures can be found on TLsS, chamber cards, and photographs; all can be purchased for under $75. Signed 8 × 10 photographs in football attire are valued at $100 to $125. A signed football is rare and will likely sell for $600 to $750. There are many forged Topps 1955 All American football cards in the market, so caution is warranted. A genuine specimen will sell for $400 to $500.

White, B-1 TLS dated 1990.

Another Kennedy appointee was Arthur Goldberg. He served a little under three years, then resigned. With the exception of *Griswold v. Connecticut*, his tenure was of little consequence. Goldberg signed in a slightly choppy hand. His signature is of average construction. Goldberg material is available. His signature is typically found on TLsS, first-day covers, and photographs. ALsS are rare. A signature of marginal demand; expect to pay $25 to $50 for his autograph. TLsS sell for $50 to $75.

Goldberg-1, undated signature (courtesy The Oklahoma City University School of Law, Bob Burke Supreme Court Signature Collection).

Abe Fortas was a crony of President Johnson. It is said that Johnson pressured Goldberg to resign in order to place friend Fortas on the court as a sure pocket vote. Fortas served only three and a half years on the court. He resigned under an ethics cloud and threat of impeachment. Fortas signed in a compact and rapid hand. The signature appears cramped and illegible. There is an ample supply of material in the market. TLsS are the most common. Photographs and first-day covers are also available. ALsS are rare. I have only seen a couple of signed chamber cards, so they must be rare. There is marginal demand for Fortas material. Signatures can be purchased for $50 or under on most mediums.

Fortas-1, TLS dated 1965.

Thurgood Marshall was appointed by President Johnson. He was the first black appointed to the court. He became one of the court's great dissenters on the Rehnquist court. Marshall signed in a jagged and unattractive hand. The signature evidences substandard letter construction. Overall, a signature of marginal display value. Being the first black justice correlates into good demand for his signature. Replication of hand is rather easy. Well-executed forgeries have entered the market. Marshall was a willing signer. Signatures exist on TLsS, photographs, chamber cards, and first-day covers. ALsS are rare. Signatures are valued at $50 to $75. Chamber cards and TLsS sell for $100 to $125. I consider Marshall's signature a good investment, though limited to premium items.

Marshall, T-1, undated chamber card.

Chief Justice Warren Burger was appointed to the court by President Nixon. Burger was a centrist, and his court failed to overturn many rulings of the Warren Court, as was first expected. Burger signed in a loose and nonconforming hand. The signature is of average construction and display value. Burger was a responsive signer and there is a good supply of material in the market. Signatures exist on photographs, first-day covers, and TLsS. ALsS are scarce to very scarce. A signed chamber card is a rarity. Most mediums are available for under $75. A full-page ALS will sell for $250 to $300.

Burger-1 postal cover dated 1985.

Harry Blackmun was appointed to the court by President Nixon. He started off on the right and ended up as one of the more liberal members of the court. His most famous opinion was *Roe v. Wade*. Blackmun signed in a methodic and confined hand. His signature exhibits good display value. Blackmun was fond of using a fountain pen and many chamber cards were signed with such. A signature of marginal demand. Most mediums are available for $50 to $75.

Blackmun-1, signature circa 1990.

Lewis Powell, Jr., was another Nixon appointment. He quickly drifted to the center of the court and stayed there for his fifteen-year run. Powell signed in a slow and deliberate hand. He wrote his name more than signed it. Powell was a responsive signer for most of his life. Signatures can be found on TLsS, chamber cards, photographs, and first-day covers. Chamber cards are typically inscribed. Powell material is quite common and most mediums can be purchased for under $50.

Powell, L-1, chamber card circa 1985.

While the Burger court exercised something likened to judicial detente, the court led by William Rehnquist did not. It was one of the most conservative courts and reversed and/or limited much of the Warren and Burger courts' rulings. Rehnquist signed in a rapid and busy hand. The signature is of average construction and display value. Rehnquist was a willing and gracious signer throughout most of his life. Sig-

Rehnquist-1 undated signature.

natures can be found on TLsS, first-day covers, BEP engravings, chamber cards, and photographs. ALsS are rare. Two autopen templates are noted. There is good demand for Rehnquist material. A signature is valued at $50. Chamber cards sell for $100.

Rehnquist-2, common autopen.

Rehnquist-3, common autopen.

President Ford's only appointment was that of John Paul Stevens. Stevens signs in a vertical and illegible hand. Letter construction is poor. Overall, an unsightly autograph. There is a good population of Stevens material in the market. He has been a willing signer, though in recent years he has cut back substantially. Signatures can be found mostly on chamber cards and photographs. ALsS are rare. He signed a limited number of the *Bush v. Gore* opinions; he no longer signs them. One autopen template is known. Stevens's signature can be purchased for $25. A signed *Bush v. Gore* opinion will sell for $175 to $200.

Stevens-1 USSC chamber card circa 2010.

Sandra Day O'Connor was appointed by President Reagan. She was the first woman on the court. Her voting record was center-right. O'Connor signed in a strong hand. The signa-

ture evidences sound letter construction and display value. O'Connor is generally a responsive signer and there is a good supply of material in the market. ALsS should be considered rare. Two autopen templates are known, and most chamber cards signed since 2005 feature an autopen signature. She typically does not sign the *Bush v. Gore* opinion. O'Connor's signature is available on most mediums for $25 to $35.

O'Connor-1 signature circa 2005.

O'Connor-2, auto-pen signature.

Antonin Scalia was appointed to the court by President Reagan. He was considered one of the more conservative justices on the court. Scalia signed in a bold and flamboyant hand. His signature is somewhat illegible but still retains good display value. The supply of Scalia material is limited. Prior to his death early in 2016, requests for his autograph were generally ignored. He would, on occasion, sign books which he authored. A TLS will surface now and then. ALsS and chamber cards should be considered rare, I have seen only one signed chamber card. Signed books sell for about $100.

Scalia-1, TLS dated 1988.

Anthony Kennedy was President Reagan's alternate choice after Robert Bork's nomination was rejected by the Senate. Justice Kennedy signs in a ghastly hand. Letter construction is nonexistent. His signature is perhaps the ugliest of all court autographs. It looks like a spider that has been stepped on. Replication of hand is very easy. Just about all Kennedy signatures in the market are forged. Like Scalia, Kennedy generally does not honor autograph requests. He will, on occasion, sign items that have already been signed by other justices. Chamber cards almost always contain an autopen signature, of which one template is noted. Expect to pay $75 for his autograph.

Kennedy, A-1, signature circa 1990.

Kennedy, A-2, auto-pen.

David Souter was appointed to the court by President George H.W. Bush. He was a bit of an unknown and aligned himself with the liberal wing of the court. Souter's signature is of average construction and typically completed with a linear paraph. Generally he is a responsive signer, so signatures can be found on photographs, chamber cards, and first day covers. ALsS are rare. Signed copies of the *Bush v. Gore* opinion are scarce. Souter's signature can be purchased for $25 to $30 on most mediums. A signed copy *Bush v. Gore* will sell for $175 to $200.

Souter-1 Chamber card circa 2005.

Clarence Thomas was the other appointment by President Bush. Thomas was the second black on the court and is solidly conservative. Thomas signs in a bold and flowing hand. The signature tends to be large. Thomas is a willing and gracious signer, so his market inventory is sound. Signatures can be found on chamber cards, first-day covers, photographs, and the like. ALsS are rare. He will sign copies of the *Bush v. Gore* opinion. Signed copies of his book *My Grandfather's Son* usually contain wonderful inscriptions. Thomas's signature is affordable at $25 to $30. A signed copy of *Bush v. Gore* will sell for $175 to $200.

Thomas-1 Chamber card 2005.

Ruth Ginsburg was the first of two appointees by President Clinton. Ginsburg is one of the more liberal members of the court. Ginsburg signs in the most rudimentary of hands. The signature is basically a printed script. Display value is substandard. Ginsburg used to be a responsive signer, but profiteers changed her habits. Tired of seeing her signature sold on sites like eBay, Ginsburg stopped honoring requests for her autograph. As a result, the supply of material is not nearly as great as Justices Thomas, Souter, or O'Connor. Chamber cards and photographs sell for $50. A signed copy of *Bush v. Gore* will sell for $175 to $200.

Ginsberg-1 USSC chamber card circa 2010.

Stephen Breyer was appointed to the court by President Clinton. He tends to side with the liberal wing of the court. Breyer's signature is a crude scrawl. It is a line looped over itself. Letter construction, legibility, and display value are nonexistent. Breyer typically does not honor autograph requests. He will sign copies of his book *Active Liberty* and that is about it. I have never seen a signed chamber card. Expect to pay $50 for Breyer's autograph.

Breyer-1, signed book dated 2014.

John Roberts's signature is proving to be a modern rarity. Justices who typically don't sign autographs will do so when presented with material signed by other justices, but not so with Roberts. He rarely signs autographs, resulting in a very limited supply. Like other modern justices, Roberts signs in an illegible and unstructured hand. Substandard display value is noted. Replication of hand is fairly easy; well-executed forgeries exist, so caution is warranted. There are many forged 8 × 10 photographs in the market. These are typically signed in gold or silver Sharpie. His signature is in high demand simply because of the minute supply.

Roberts, J-1 signature dated 2014 (courtesy Supreme Court of the United States).

Samuel Alito was appointed to the court by President George W. Bush. He regularly votes with the conservative wing of the court. His signature tends to be sloppy and unstructured. Substandard eye appeal is noted. Alito is generally a responsive signer. He will sign chamber cards. Almost all signatures are inscribed. Two different variations of signatures are noted with material variation of hand. I suspect one is secretarial. I contacted Alito's office twice for confirmation but received no response. See illustrations. Alito's signature is available for under $50.

Alito-1 USSC chamber card dated 2012.

Alito-2, USSC chamber card dated 2010.

Sonia Sotomayor was appointed by President Obama. She is the first Hispanic on the court. She is a reliable vote for the liberal wing. Sotomayor's signature is hurried and illegible. Letter construction is limited to two capital letters and that is about it. A substandard display value is noted. Sotomayor is a responsive signer and tends to sign court-issued photographs. She will sign copies of her book *My Beloved World*. Autopen and/or secretarial signatures can be found on court-issued photographs. Her signature is available on most mediums for $25 to $30.

Sotomayor-1 signed photograph dated 2014.

Justice number 113 is Elena Kagan, who was appointed to the high court by President Obama. Kagan signs in a sloppy and illegible hand. Letter construction is sacrificed in favor of expediency. Overall, a substandard signature. Kagan has proved to be a willing and gracious signer. She usually sends a transmittal TLS with a signed chamber card. Photographs are also available. ALsS are rare. Signatures can be purchased for $25 to $30 on most mediums.

Kagan-1, USSC chamber card dated 2014.

Pax Americana:
An American Timeline

The diversity of American autographs is as big as the American melting pot. Over two centuries later, the American experience still roars forward. The diversity of culture has left its imprint on the history that is the United States. Immigrants from all parts of the globe flocked to the New World for opportunity and a better way of life. They came from Europe, Asia, South America, India, and all points in between. The result is a microcosm of regions and cities influenced by customs and traditions from all parts of the world. Detroit, in its long history, has been home to various ethnic groups. They brought their music, cuisine, literature, and acumen that built Detroit into the motor capital of the world. Henry Ford and the other auto magnates transformed Detroit into a world-class city. Perhaps no other nation in the world has produced more collectable autographs than the United States. Starting from colonial times through the Industrial Revolution to the opening act of the 21st century, the expansive inventory of American autographs is mind-boggling.

Most autograph collectors, myself included, have a deep and incurable passion for history, a passion that, perhaps, borders on obsession. I have spent countless hours with my nose buried in history books. My personal favorite subjects are the Revolutionary War, the Roaring Twenties, Prohibition, and old-time baseball, the Cobbian era to be exact. It is this understanding of history that helps fuel the desire to possess a signature from times since past.

In Dearborn, Michigan, we have the world-famous Henry Ford Museum and Greenfield Village. For those of you who have never visited the Ford, I suggest you put it on your bucket list. Mr. Ford had many historic homes and buildings dismantled and reassembled on the grounds of the village: the Noah Webster house, the Wright Brothers Cycle shop, Ford's first manufacturing facility, and on and on. Stepping into Thomas Edison's Menlo Park lab is truly a life-changing experience. This is where Edison himself worked and created many of the greatest inventions in the history of mankind. Every time I visit the museum I get the urge to buy another historic autograph.

The mid– to late 1800s is one era that many Americans can relate to thanks, in part, to Hollywood. For years television shows like *Little House on the Prairie, Gunsmoke, Have Gun Will Travel*, and *Bonanza* brought 19th-century life into the family room every night. For collectors, the Old West is of particular interest. The dime store novels made legends out of many cowboys, outlaws, and shootists. Signatures of Roy Bean, Wild Bill Hickok, Billy the Kid, Al Jennings, and Bat Masterson are treasured like precious gemstones. They are some of the most expensive of all autographs, American or otherwise.

Among the most famous of western legends is Wyatt Earp. A professional gambler, Earp was the marshal of Tombstone, Arizona. He secured a hallowed place in American history for his part in the gunfight at the O.K. Corral. Earp signed in a rugged and practical hand. The signature exhibits a certain hesitation. Earp's autograph has average display value. The slower nature of the hand makes replication easy. Earp's signature is very easy to forge. Just about 100 percent of all Earp signatures in the market are forged. Earp's signature is very rare, which is surprising given the fact that he lived until the late 1920s. Signatures are generally limited to DsS as a lawman. Sometimes he would pen a short endorsement to the documents. Forged endorsements do exist. There are books in the market that are said to have come from Earp's personal library. A forgery of "Wyatt Earp" is placed on the inside title page. The forgery is amateurish in construction and almost childlike. These forgeries are exposed with little effort. They have all been produced by the same forger. I know of no books from Earp's library in the market. Demand is very strong for this legend of the Old West. A DsS will sell for $25,000 to $35,000.

Earp-1, AES dated 1870 (courtesy Stephen Koschal Reference Library).

Christopher "Kit" Carson was a trapper, fur trader, and Indian fighter. He is best remembered as a guide for John C. Fremont's expeditions to the West Coast. His exploits were put into print by Charles Averill. It made Carson a western legend. Carson signed in a very modest and practical hand. A simple, yet sound, letter construction is noted. There is not much to his signature. Most signatures are accomplished as "C. Carson." Given the signature's unpretentious structure, replication of hand is very easy. Well-executed forgeries exist in quantities. Close to 100 percent of all Carson autographs in the market are forgeries. Carson material is very rare. It is generally limited to a few signa-

tures removed from LsS. I have never seen an ALS. There are many cabinet cards in the market. I have only seen one I would feel comfortable pronouncing as genuine. It was signed as "C. Carson." There are many signatures in the market signed as "Kit Carson." Several years back many cabinet cards signed as "Kit" entered the market. I do not believe these to be genuine. I have never examined a genuine signature signed with his nickname. I doubt that one exists. The strong demand far outweighs an almost nonexistent supply of material. Expect to pay $10,000 to $12,500 for his signature.

Carson-1, DS dated 1863 (courtesy Stephen Koschal Reference Library).

Buffalo Bill and Pawnee Bill are two names forever intertwined in Old West lore. Bill Cody was a scout and buffalo hunter, hence his nickname. In 1883 he started *Buffalo Bill's Wild West Show*. He was the consummate showman and one of the most colorful characters to tumble out of the pages of American history. Cody signed in a choppy and hesitant hand. The signature is usually accomplished as "W.F. Cody." He would add "Buffalo Bill" underneath the signature. The signature lacks flow, hence replication of hand is relatively easy. Well-executed forgeries exist in quantities. Cody's signature is one of the most forged of all 19th-century autographs. Forgeries exist on cabinet cards, calling cards, photographs, ALsS, and the like. There are counterfeit bank checks in the market. There is a good supply of genuine material in the market, including many business related ALsS. Cody ALsS have excellent display value simply because of the gaudy and colorful letterhead. There is very strong demand for Cody material. His signature will sell for $750 to $1,000. Photographs are valued at $2,000 to $2,500. Exceptional specimens will sell for close to $5,000. ALsS are valued at $1,500 to $2,000.

Cody-1, TLS dated 1903 (courtesy Nate D. Sanders Auctions).

Indian agent and frontiersman Gordon W. Lillie, better known as "Pawnee Bill," partnered with Cody in the wild-west shows. Lillie signed in a nice and flowing hand. Lillie lived until 1942 but was not really targeted by collectors. His signature is a bit tougher to locate than that of his more famous business associate. Signatures can be found on ALsS (many accomplished in pencil), album pages, and photographs. Bank checks are very scarce. Due to the modest value of Lillie's signature it is generally not the target of skilled forgers. Demand is average at best. Pawnee Bill's signature can be purchased for $150 to $200. ALsS are valued at $400 to $500.

Lillie-1, ALS dated 1905 (courtesy Nate D. Sanders Auctions).

Judge Isaac Parker was appointed to the federal bench by President Grant. He served in the western district of Arkansas. Today he is best remembered as the "Hanging Judge." Parker signed in a rapid and somewhat unstructured hand. The signature displays itself as sloppy. A substandard display value is noted. Signatures are typically accomplished as "I.C. Parker." Well-executed forgeries do exist, and they are typically found as clipped signatures and in books. Parker's signature is somewhat rare. Signatures exist on ADsS, ALsS, and DsS (typically law-related). Parker material has actually declined in recent years. Today his autograph can be purchased for $400 to $600. ADsS and ALsS are valued at $750 to $1,000.

Parker, I-1, Legal document dated 1865 (courtesy Stephen Koschal Autographs).

Another famous lawman from that era is Pat Garrett, sheriff of Lincoln County, New Mexico. Best known as the man who shot and killed William Bonney (a.k.a. Billy the Kid), Garrett was assassinated in 1908. Garrett signed in a rather loose hand. Decent legibility is noted, but letters tend to be slightly ajar. The signature has average display value and is usually signed as "P.F. Garrett." Replication of hand is rather easy. Well-executed forgeries exist in good numbers, mostly as clipped signatures. Forged ALsS are also in the market. Garrett's signature is very scarce to rare. Signatures are typically found on ALsS, TLsS, and endorsements. The occasional Alabama Gold and Copper Mining Company stock certificate will surface, signed by Garrett as company secretary. I have never seen a genuinely signed photograph of any kind. There is good demand for Garrett material. Expect to pay $1,000 for his autograph. TLsS sell for $1,250 to $1,500. ALsS are valued at $2,000 to $2,500.

Garrett-1, stock certificate circa 1900.

"Little Sure Shot," Annie Oakley was the star of *Buffalo Bill Cody's Wild West Show.* She was one of the greatest, if not the greatest, exhibition shooters ever. Oakley signed in a slow, labored, and rudimentary hand. The signature is legible. Sound letter construction is noted. Signatures are sometimes accomplished as "Annie Oakley Butler" and sometimes as "Annie Butler." Due to the pensive nature of the signature, replication is very easy. Well-executed forgeries exist in quantities. Close to 100 percent of all Oakley signatures offered in the market are forged. Signatures are very rare on a per se basis. A restricted supply of ALsS are in the market. A couple of handsome portrait photographs of a middle-aged Oakley are also in the market. There is one forgery to note. Forgeries signed "Compliments. of Annie. Oakley" (note the periods) are in the market. These are typically found on album pages and on the reverse of cabinet cards. They are signed on a 45° angle, give or take a few degrees. A genuine signature is of high demand. Expect to pay $3,000 to $4,000 for her signature. ALsS and photographs sell for $7,500 to $10,000.

Oakley-1, undated signature.

Emmett Dalton was part of the infamous Dalton gang. During a botched robbery he was shot over five times but survived. After his bank-robbing days were over, he became an author and actor. Dime store novels made him and his brothers western legends. Dalton signed in a practical and no-nonsense hand. The signature is legible. An average display value is noted. Dalton would be a very rare signature if it were not for signed copies of his book *When the Daltons Rode*. There are many nicely inscribed books in the market. TLsS are rare. ALsS and photographs are very rare. Forgeries do exist and in quantities. Forged books and photographs are common. There is sound demand for this outlaw turned author. Signatures will sell for $1,250 to $1,500. A signed copy of *When the Daltons Rode* will cost you about $2,500.

Dalton-1, undated signature.

Brigham Young founded Salt Lake City and became the first governor of the territory of Utah. He was president of the Church of Jesus Christ of Latter-day Saints for thirty years. He is probably the most remembered of the Mormon leaders. Young signed in a very nice hand. The signature evidences sound letter construction and good legibility. A sound display value is noted. Some signatures are accomplished simply as "B. Young" and many times overlooked. Producing a well-executed forgery would take some effort, though they do exist. Young's signature is scarce on a per se basis. His signature is typically found on small cards, LsS, and DsS. ALsS are very rare. DsS with Mormon association are highly collected. Young's signature is valued at $500 to $700. LsS and DsS will sell for $2,500 to $3,000. A letter with strong religious content would easily sell for more than $25,000.

Young, B-1, undated signature (courtesy The Sanders Autograph Price Guide).

Never let sanity get in the way of your goals in life. Joshua Abraham Norton is known to the world as Norton I, Emperor of the United States of America, or at least San Francisco. After losing his family fortune, Emperor Norton went a bit off the deep end. He declared himself absolute ruler of the USA and, in the process, gave autograph collectors one of the most peculiar signatures in American history. Norton's signature is widely collected just because he was such

Norton I-1, ALS dated 1870 (courtesy Stephen Koschal Reference Library).

an eccentric fellow. He even had bank scripts printed that read the "Imperial Government— Norton I" which he would sign. ALsS do exist with strange, often cryptic, content. His signature is very scarce. Expect to pay $300 to $400 for the above-referenced mediums.

Phineas T. Barnum was the world's greatest showman. He was the founder of the *Barnum & Bailey Circus*. Mr. Barnum signed in a hurried and unstructured hand. The letters in the last name typically display themselves as indistinguishable bumps. Barnum loved to sign autographs and today there is a more than ample supply of signatures in the market. Mediums include album pages, checks, ALsS, and cabinet cards. Due to the modest value of his autograph, Barnum is generally not the target of skilled forgers. The one exception is cabinet cards and photographs. Forged Barnum photographs exist in quantities. One forger has produced many. A small forgery is placed at the bottom of the card. It is signed as "P.T. Barnum, Bridgeport, Ct." and dated. The forgery evidences a slight shakiness. Overall, these forgeries should not be considered well-executed.

In order to satisfy requests for autographs, Barnum had cabinet cards made with a facsimile signature placed below the image that reads: "P.T. Barnum. 1885." and "1886." If you see a cabinet card with either of these dates, it most likely a facsimile signature. Be warned: the major authentication companies have been known to wrongly certify this facsimile as genuine. For being such a giant in history, Barnum's signature is a bargain at $175 to $200. ALsS sell for $400 to $500. Cabinet cards are treasured and valued at $1,500 to $2,000.

William "Boss" Tweed was a one-term congressman from New York's 5th District. He became the ring leader of Tammany Hall, a corrupt Democratic political machine. He was eventually convicted on 200+ criminal counts. He remains one of the most colorful criminals in American history. Tweed signed in a sloppy and loose hand. The signature exhibits poor letter construction. Legibility is impaired. Signatures are typically accomplished as "W.M. Tweed." As a New York City government official, Tweed signed countless documents, including contracts that were a couple of feet in length. These are an excellent source for Tweed's signature. The supply is quite sound and keeps prices in check. Other mediums are rare to very rare. A New York City DS can be purchased for about $125 to $150, which I consider a steal. Signatures of other members of the Tweed ring are also available, and most of these can be purchased for under $25. Boss Tweed's signature is a wonderful addition to any collection.

Tweed-1, DS dated 1868.

Tweed's nemesis was editorial cartoonist Thomas Nast. Nast is best remembered as the creator of the modern-day Santa Claus, as well as the Democratic donkey and the Republican elephant. His cartoons are wonderfully caricaturistic. Nast signed in a simple hand. Several breaks are noted in the hand. The signature is rather unappealing and signed usually as "Th. Nast." There is average demand for Nast material. His signature is quite affordable. Forgeries are limited to 87 Union Square cabinet photographs, sketches, and drawings. Nast's signature can be purchased for about $100. Bank checks are not much more. Political drawings are avail-

Barnum-1, signature dated 1874 (courtesy Nate D. Sanders Auctions).

Barnum-2, common facsimile dated 1885 and 1886.

able for $2,000 to $3,000, but remember, most offered for sale are forged.

Nast-1, ALS dated 1894 (courtesy Stephen Koschal Reference Library).

Lizzie Borden took an axe and gave her mother forty whacks, and when she saw what she had done, she gave her father forty-one. Borden is the most famous axe murderess in history. She ruined my image of actress Elizabeth Montgomery, who portrayed her in a 1975 TV movie. Borden signed in a very feminine and clean hand. The signature is well constructed with good flow. Signatures are typically signed as "L.A. Borden." Signatures penned as "Lizzie" are a rarity. Replication of hand is rather difficult. Well-executed forgeries are few and far between. Borden's signature is very rare and limited to the occasional ALS with boring business or property content. She was not a person collectors of the day would ask for an autograph. I have never seen a genuinely signed photograph, though a few forged specimens do exist. Borden's signature is in high demand. ALsS will sell for $5,000 to $10,000, depending on length.

Borden-1, DS dated 1891.

Susan B. Anthony was an abolitionist and an early suffrage supporter. She is perhaps best remembered as the woman whose image is on the most unpopular coin ever issued by the U.S. Mint. Anthony signed in a clean and well-structured hand. Her signature evidences a sound degree of legibility. Due to the affordable nature of the signature, Anthony's signature is generally not the target of skilled forgers. For-

geries are generally limited to cabinet cards. Though the Anthony coin, to this day, remains a numismatic abomination, it gave Anthony a huge boost in publicity. Her signature can be purchased for $250 to $300. ALsS will sell for $400 to $600. A cabinet card is valued around $1,500.

Over the past few years, boxing autographs

Anthony-1, undated signature (courtesy Nate D. Sanders Auctions).

have fallen out of favor. Unless it is a rare signature like that of Harry Greb or Marvin Hart, values have plummeted. This will, of course, reverse itself someday and demand will once again rise. John L. Sullivan is one of the exceptions to the rule. His signature is one of the most popular of all boxing autographs. Sullivan's signature is unstructured and haphazard. It has an average display value. Signatures penned in the 1880s and 1890s tend to be less flamboyant and smaller in scale. Overall, it is just an average signature. Sullivan's signature is scarce to very scarce, but a small supply of ALsS and album pages are in the market. Cabinet cards and photographs of any kind are very rare. There are many fairly well-executed forgeries in the market, mostly clipped signatures or album pages. Sullivan's signature is valued at $900 to $1,200. ALsS tend to be short with routine content and are valued at $1,500. A full-page ALS will sell for $2,500 to $3,000.

Sullivan-1, undated signature (courtesy The Sanders Autograph Price Guide).

Sullivan's most famous opponent was Gentleman Jim Corbett. He beat Sullivan to become heavyweight champion of the world. Corbett signed in a nicer, more structured hand than that of Sullivan. The signature tends to be legible with good construction. The signature is typically accomplished as "Jas. J. Corbett." The supply of Corbett material is far greater than that of Sullivan. Corbett lived until 1933 and signed many items, including some handsome 8 × 10 photographs. As a result, the value of his autograph is affordable. A signature can be purchased for as little as $200. ALsS are a bargain at $400 to $500. I consider Corbett to be an undervalued sleeper signature.

James J. Corbett

Corbett-1, undated signature (courtesy The Sanders Autograph Price Guide).

When you think of giants of American industry, the name John D. Rockefeller Sr., comes to mind. Rockefeller was one of the most powerful men in America. He was co-founder of Standard Oil Company. Rockefeller signed in a most unusual hand. Most signatures in the market are signed in an elderly and shaky hand. Signatures tend to be large in scale. The signature is legible with pronounced capital letters. Early signatures, circa 1880s, are also signed in a slower hand. These, too, will evidence a somewhat shaky appearance. There is an ample supply of signatures. Many post–1900 TLsS, with routine content, are in the market. There is also a good supply of Standard Oil Company stock certificates in the market. These are especially nice, as they are countersigned by Henry Flagler. Given the labored hand, replication is very easy. Well-executed forgeries do exist and can be found on books, album pages, and photographs. There are many photographs featuring an elderly Rockefeller sitting at a desk and writing a letter. A forgery is placed at the bottom. A genuine signed photograph is rare to very rare. There is sound demand for this most famous

of industrialists. Rockefeller's signature will sell for $400 to $500. TLsS are valued at $600 to $900. The aforementioned certificate, countersigned by Flagler, is highly prized. These sell for $2,000 to $2,500.

Rockefeller-1, TLS dated 1915 (courtesy Nate D. Sanders Auctions).

Scottish industrialist Andrew Carnegie was one of the most wealthy and powerful men in the world. In 1901, he sold Carnegie Steel to J.P. Morgan for $480 million. Carnegie's signature is scarce, albeit borderline. Signatures are typically found on ALsS, TLsS, books, and small cards. Portrait photographs do exist, but they are considered rare. Carnegie's signature is generally not the target of skilled forgers. It should, however, be noted that many TLsS are secretarially signed. There is average demand for Carnegie's signature, which can be purchased for $200 to $225. ALsS are valued at $600 to $800. A photograph makes for fine display, so expect to pay $1,500 to $2,000 for a nice specimen.

Andrew Carnegie

Carnegie-1, undated signature (courtesy The Sanders Autograph Price Guide).

John Pierpont Morgan, Sr., was the most famous banker in American history. A powerful financier, Morgan was a key player in the creation of General Electric. Morgan signed in an illegible and sloppy hand. Signatures are signed as "J. Pierpont Morgan." Morgan's signature is not as common as signatures of Carnegie and Rockefeller. Signatures are found on DsS and the occasional letter or check endorsement.

ALsS are very scarce. Photographs of any kind are rare. There is a small supply of signed bonds for the Jersey Junction Railroad in the market. These make for a handsome display. Morgan's signature is generally not the target of skilled forgers. Values are such as to not warrant the effort. Morgan's signature is valued at $175 to $200. DsS and letters can be purchased for $300 to $500. A nicely signed 8 × 10 photograph would likely fetch close to $2,000. Signatures of his son, with the same name, are in the market. Fortunately, Morgan Jr.'s signature looks nothing like that of his father's signature.

Morgan, J-1, undated signature.

Jim Thorpe is generally considered the greatest athlete of all time: football Hall of Famer, Olympic gold medalist, and outfielder for John McGraw's New York Giants. Thorpe signed in a rudimentary hand. The signature evidences a certain hesitation. The letters tend to be blocky in construction, which impairs legibility and eye appeal. Early signatures, those signed in the 1930s and before, are slightly more flowing in nature. Due to the hesitant nature of the signature, replication of hand is easy. Well-executed forgeries exist in quantities. Thorpe's signature is a minefield. There are many variant signatures in the market that are sold as genuine. This, of course, cannot be the case. Like Joe Jackson, Thorpe delegated signings duties to his wife. Many signatures obtained through the mail were signed by Mrs. Thorpe. Her signature is more flowing and legible. Her signature lacks the rugged blockiness of a genuine signature. In addition, she wrote much of her husband's correspondence. Some ALsS are written and signed by Mrs. Thorpe. A genuine Thorpe ALS is a true rarity; seldom do they enter the market. If you run across an ALS, it is most likely secretarial.

Ninety percent of Thorpe signatures in the market are forged. There are many forged baseballs in the market. I have never examined a genuine single-signed baseball. There are many forged single-signed baseballs on Hatch brand professional model baseballs. They typically feature a forgery on the side panel or the sweet spot and are dated with the year. There are many forged New York Giants team baseballs from Thorpe's playing days in the market. Purportedly signed during the World War I era, they contain signatures of Christy Mathewson, Fred Merkle, John McGraw, Jeff Tesreau, Rube Marquard, and the like. They come complete with multiple certificates of authenticity from the major authenticators. I have never seen a signed Giants team ball from this era. It is very doubtful a genuine specimen exists. These team balls should be avoided in total. There are also many signed footballs in the market. The balls are of various manufacturing dates. I have never seen a genuine specimen.

There is another medium that puzzles me and it is worth discussing. There are a certain number of promissory notes drawn on the First National Bank of Prague, Prague, Oklahoma. The notes are dated in the late teens and early 1920s. They are signed by Thorpe and his wife. Thorpe's signature is incorrectly signed as "James Thorp" and countersigned by his wife, Iva. She also signed the last name as "Thorp." I did some research trying to locate this alternate spelling. Period sports cards, newspaper articles, photographs, and documents make no reference to an alternate spelling of the last name. An incorrectly signed bank note raises warning flags. From a legal perspective, it would be hard for the issuing bank to enforce upon default, especially since the body of these notes do not list the debtors' names, in this case Jim and Iva *Thorpe*. This alone makes me believe the bank would not accept the signatures as presented. The Thorpe signatures which appear on these notes evidence a material variation from a genuine signature. I advise collectors to avoid these notes, as I believe them to be the product of forgery.

There is sound demand for Thorpe material. His signature is valued at about $1,000. DsS sell for closer to $2,000. A nicely signed 8 × 10 photograph is valued at $2,500 to $3,000. Thorpe is a very significant American autograph.

Thorpe-1 signature dated 1952.

Early auto racers are remembered by only the most die-hard of racing bugs. Lou Meyer and Wilbur Shaw are names that few have heard of. Barney Oldfield tends to be the exception to the rule. An early pioneer of racing, he appeared in the 1914 and 1915 Indy 500. He was one of the first inductees into the Racing Hall of Fame. Oldfield signed in a flowing hand. The signature has good letter construction and is legible. Like Ty Cobb and Francis Ouimet, Oldfield liked to sign autographs in green ink. His signature is uncommon to scarce. His signature is generally found on ALsS, government postcards, and photographs that show him either sitting in a race car or chomping on a cigar. The supply is well balanced with demand. Given the marginal value of his signature, Oldfield is generally not the target of skilled forgers. Oldfield's signature can be purchased for $100. ALsS and photographs will sell for $200 to $300.

Oldfield-1, World War I draft card (courtesy Record Group 163, Records of the Selective Services Division, National Archives at Atlanta).

William Jennings Bryan was one of the most important figures in the Democratic Party. He ran three times for president. He was counsel in the famed Scopes Monkey Trial of 1925. Bryan signed in a nice and flowing hand. The signature exhibits sound display value. Signatures are typically accomplished as "W.J. Bryan." There is marginal demand for Jennings material, which I find hard to believe. There is an ample supply of letters and cards. Bryan also served as secretary of state under President Wilson, but resigned upon America's entrance into World War I. Appointments signed by Wilson and Bryan are in the market. They are considered very scarce. Bryan's signature is valued at $50 to $75. ALsS will sell for $150 to $200.

Bryan-1, TLS dated 1913 (courtesy Nate D. Sanders Auctions).

The opposing counsel in the Monkey Trial was famed attorney Clarence Darrow. Darrow was involved in many noted criminal trials, including those of Leopold and Loeb and Ossian Sweet. Demand for Darrow's signature is average. Unfortunately many TLsS, books, and signatures obtained through the mail were secretarially signed. Secretarial signatures are signed in a slower, more methodic hand. Genuine signatures are typically signed as "C.S. Darrow" while the secretarial signatures are usually signed as "Clarence." Some ALsS are actually written and signed by his secretary. Darrow's signature is much scarcer than Bryan's signature. The demand for Darrow material has declined in recent years and values have followed. As time goes by, Darrow becomes more and

Darrow-1, undated signature (courtesy Stephen Koschal Autographs).

more of a minor footnote in history. Signatures can be purchased for $200. TLsS are valued at $400 to $500. Twenty years ago his signature was worth far more.

Bill Tilden is generally considered the greatest tennis player in history. He won countless tournaments. He was a controversial figure who had many run-ins with the law on morals charges. Tilden signed in a vertical and bold hand. The signature evidences a pronounced racing effect. His signature has nice display value. Tilden's signature is scarce. For years his signature was found on album pages and that was about it. A few years back a large cache of letters, written from prison, entered the market. They are accomplished in pencil and typically signed "Bill." Many come with the mailing envelope. A full Tilden signature is found in the return address portion of the postal cover. Demand appears to be average for Tilden's signature, which can be purchased for $150. The above-referenced letters sell for $200 to $250.

Tilden-1, undated signature (courtesy The Sanders Autograph Price Guide).

Secure knots secure not Houdini. Another legendary name of the 20th century, Harry Houdini is one of the most famous men in history. He was a noted escape artist and magician extraordinaire. Houdini's signature is as flashy as his performances must have been. The signature offers sound letter construction. A good degree of legibility is noted. On occasion, the signature will contain a paraph. Overall, a signature with superior display value. Many signatures are signed with his last name only. Early signatures, those generally accomplished before 1920, tend to be signed in a slower and somewhat plain hand. Houdini was such a famous person that he was targeted by collectors. As a result, there is a good supply of material in the market. In addition, many correspondences, in the form of TLsS, are available for purchase. As a performer and media hound, Houdini loved to sign pictures of himself. There is a somewhat ample supply of photographs in the market. Having said this, the majority of Houdini autographs are forgeries. Replication of hand is rather simple; hence, well-executed forgeries exist in quantities. Houdini is one of the most forged of all American autographs. Forgeries exist on all mediums from letters to photographs to album pages. It should be noted that there are some forged TLsS in the market, typically signed in pencil. The forger copied Houdini's letterhead that reads "H O U D I N I, 278 West 113th Street, New York, N.Y." The forgery evidences a slightly labored appearance and lacks the strong flow of a genuine signature. Careful examination is needed, since these are pretty convincing fakes.

Another forger has created many fake signatures. His work can be found on photographs, album pages, and especially books. The forgery is signed in a slower and more rudimentary hand. It lacks the effortless flow of a genuine specimen. Many of these forgeries use a huge letter "H" and incorporate the rest of the signature using the "H." These forgeries are typically signed as "Harry Handcuff Houdini." The demand for Houdini material is very strong and prices are pushed ever upward. Houdini's signature will sell for $750 to $1,000. TLsS are valued at $1,250 to $1,500. A full-page ALS is a rarity. I estimate a value of $5,000 to $6,000. Photographs, which tend to be postcard-sized, are handsome display items, so expect to pay $3,000 to $4,000. A nicely signed 8 × 10 photograph is very rare and will likely sell for more

Houdini-1, undated signature (courtesy The Sanders Autograph Price Guide).

than $7,500. Books, such as *Houdini's Paper Magic*, contain fine inscriptions, and can be purchased for $1,500 to $2,000.

Houdini-2 common forgery.

In his youth, Al Capone was a member of the Five Points Gang in Brooklyn. In the early 1920s, he moved to Chicago to avoid prosecution and became a bodyguard for mobster John Torrio. When Torrio retired, Capone became the boss of the Chicago outfit. Capone is the most well-known organized crime figure in American history. Capone signed in a powerful and rapid hand. His signature evidences a man of power. Capone material is very rare. He wasn't a person collectors targeted. Today, Capone is a historical figure, but back in the day he was merely a thug. That doesn't mean a handful of collectors didn't seek out his signature. Capone loved baseball and frequented the Chicago ballparks. It gave a forward-thinking collector access to Capone. Having said that, there are probably fewer than ten genuine signatures in the market. Close to 100 percent of all Capone signatures offered for sale are forgeries. Capone forgeries exist on many mediums, including album pages, letters, baseballs, and baseball scorecards. There are many forged baseballs in the market. Some contain a Babe Ruth forgery. They purportedly originated from the estates of former MLB players. I have never seen a genuinely signed baseball and I seriously doubt one exists. I have never seen a genuinely signed photograph; again, I doubt one exists. There are a few ALsS in the market of various dates, which were written after his release from prison in November of 1939. I find these letters interesting, as Capone was paroled because of mental impairment brought on by neurosyphilis. In the final year of his life his mental capacity was reduced to feeblemindedness. Letters dated in the 1940s tend to be written in a flowing hand. The text is rather lucid, evidencing a man who could still write coherent sentences, albeit with spelling errors. This is in direct conflict to the reason behind his parole (i.e., dementia). I am not so convinced these letters are genuine.

One final thought: one of Capone's fingerprint cards is in the market. It is from the Philadelphia P.D. files and dated 1929. It is signed by Capone. Why this is in the market I am not certain. The most common explanation is that it was probably stolen from the police department. Capone's signature is valued at $10,000 to $12,500.

Capone-1, World War I draft card from 1917 (courtesy Record Group 163, Records of the Selective Services Division, National Archives at Atlanta).

A very important sports autograph is that of the Galveston Giant, Jack Johnson. In 1908 he became the first black heavyweight champion. He retained his title until 1915, when he was defeated by Jess Willard. He was killed in a car accident in 1946. Johnson's signature is average in every respect. It is generally legible though loosely constructed. A certain jerkiness to the signature is noted. This characteristic makes replication of hand easy. Well-executed forgeries exist in quantities. Ninety percent of the Johnson signatures in the market are forgeries. Johnson's signature is rare on a per se basis. Signatures are generally limited to album pages, small photographs, and TLsS. ALsS and 8 × 10 photographs are very rare. There is one forgery to note. There are a handful of forged 8 × 10 photographs in the market. These feature Johnson in a boxing pose. He is shirtless and wearing tight pants. A forged inscription and signature are placed to the left of the right leg. The forgeries are average in construction but should be exposed upon cursory examination. Many have wrongly been certified as genuine by the authentication companies, so caution is warranted. There is strong demand for Johnson material. His signature is valued at $1,000. TLsS sell for $2,000. A nicely signed picture postcard is valued at $2,500 to $3,000. A desirable boxing autograph.

Johnson, J-1, undated signature (courtesy The Sanders Autograph Price Guide).

Though there have been many great matchups in boxing history, the most famous was the Dempsey vs. Tunney fight of 1926. It was one of the most publicized sporting events in history. This fight made these two men giants of American sports. Dempsey lived a long life and signed countless items. He was very responsive to collectors. For many years he owned a restaurant in New York City. He signed many restaurant-related items. There are many 8 × 10 photographs to choose from, many dating back to the 1920s. Signed boxing gloves are extremely rare. The supply of Dempsey material is so great that his signature can still be purchased for $25. That is a very low price, considering he was probably the greatest fighter ever. Signed restaurant-issued postcards featuring the Dempsey vs. Jess Willard fight sell for a mere $25. Signed 8 × 10 photographs sell for $75 to $100. Vintage specimens have excellent eye appeal and are valued at $200. An ALS would be a rarity; I estimate a value of $500. A boxing glove would easily sell for more than $1,000. I have never seen a genuine specimen, though many forged gloves do exist.

Dempsey's opponent was Gene Tunney. Like Dempsey, Tunney also was an accommodating signer. Tunney's signature has marginal

Dempsey-1, signature circa 1970.

letter construction. It tends to dominate the medium it is placed upon. The supply of Tunney material is less than that of Dempsey. Signatures can be found mostly on index cards signed in the 1960s and 1970s. Signed 8 × 10 photographs are uncommon. ALsS are rare. Boxing gloves are an extreme rarity. I have never examined a genuinely signed glove. Though generally not the target of forgers, there is a caveat. Tunney loved to send out letters, in the form of TLsS. There are several in the market, most of which date from the late 1930s to the mid–1960s. Be warned: the majority of these are secretarially signed. The secretarial signature deviates in that the letters in the last name lack definition but appear as indistinguishable strokes. There is good demand for Tunney's signature. Expect to pay $40 to $60 for an index card. A nicely signed 8 × 10 will sell for $250 to $300. TLsS are valued at $100.

Tunney-1, undated signature.

Tunney-2, common secretarial.

Harold "Red" Grange was one of the giants of 1920s American sports. Known as the Galloping Ghost, Grange is a charter member of the Football Hall of Fame. Grange signed in a rapid and aggressive hand. The signature tends to be large in scale. Infirmity of hand existed in old age. Signatures accomplished in the last 10 years of his life are signed in a slower and somewhat labored hand. Grange was a willing and gracious signer throughout his life. The supply of material is quite sound. Signatures can be found on index cards, government postcards, gum cards, photographs, and books. Goal Line Arts cards are somewhat scarce. ALsS and footballs are rare. Due to the large supply of material, Grange's signature is generally not the target of skilled forgers. Forgeries are limited to essentially two mediums: Goal Line Art cards and footballs. Forgers use the elderly, infirmed signature as a template. Grange's signature is valued at $40 to $50. Signed 8 × 10 photographs and commemorative football cards (such as the Swell Football Greats issue) sell for $75 to $100. Goal Line Art cards are highly desired and will sell for $250 to $275. A nicely signed football is valued at $750.

Grange-1, signature circa 1980.

Another immortal of 1920s football was Notre Dame coach Knute Rockne. He led the Irish to four national championships and is generally considered the greatest coach in college football history. Rockne signed in a legible and plain hand. The signature has good letter construction. There is nothing flamboyant about the signature. Rockne's signature is scarce to rare. His signature can be found on TLsS, programs, and album pages. Signed 8 × 10 photographs and ALsS are very rare. Given the slower nature of the signature, replication of hand is very easy. Well-executed forgeries exist in quantities. At least 90 percent of all Rockne signatures offered in the market are forged. Forgeries include album pages, index cards, photographs, books, etc. Rockne is one of the most forged of all sports autographs. In addition, many TLsS, on Notre Dame letterhead, are secretarially signed. The secretarial signature does bear a resemblance to a genuine signature. There is a small grouping of forged 7 × 9 and 8 × 10 photographs in the market that were produced by the same forger. They feature a smiling Rockne in a suit and spotted tie. The forger always begins the inscription with "To my friend, John Doe." The handwriting appears labored. Caution is warranted, as these are being certified as genuine by the authentication companies. There is very strong demand for Coach Rockne's signature. His signature is valued at $1,000. TLsS will sell for $1,500 to $2,000.

Rockne-1, album page circa 1930.

Though there have been many great comedy duos, none are so great as Stan Laurel and Oliver Hardy. I used to love watching their shorts as a kid and still love 'em today. Ever popular, signed material of these two greats is always in high demand. Signatures are typically found on album pages and picture postcards. There is also a decent supply of Laurel bank checks and TLsS in the market. Most Laurel letters are signed with the first name only. Hardy's signature is scarcer than Laurel's. His signature is rare on letters or documents. I have never examined a genuine Hardy ALS. Both signatures are relatively easy to forge. Forgeries exist in quantities. Most dual-signed items are forgeries. After Hardy's death, Laurel continued to sign photographs picturing both men. A forgery of Hardy is sometimes added to these postcards. Careful study is needed because a genuine signature of Laurel is alongside a forgery of Hardy. In 1937, Hardy was involved in a bitter divorce. There are copies of the *Hardy vs. Hardy* legal opinion issued by the Supreme Court of California in the market. A forgery of Hardy is placed at top. The forgeries are fairly well-executed, but deviation from a genuine Hardy specimen is noted. It is nonsensical to think Hardy would sign copies of his divorce petition for collectors. These should be avoided in total. It should also be noted that rubber-stamped signatures of Hardy are in the market. Laurel's signature is valued at $250. Bank checks can be purchased for $350 to $400. A nicely signed 8 × 10 photograph will sell for $1,000. TLsS, signed in full, are valued at $450 to $500. Hardy's signature is more pricey at $350 to $400. An 8 × 10 photograph is a rarity so expect to pay $2,000. A dual-signed index card or album page will sell for $700 to $900. A nicely signed 8 × 10 photo of both men is a gem and will likely cost $2,500 to $3,000.

Laurel-1, album page undated.

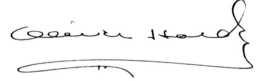

Hardy, O-1, album paged undated.

Another great comedic duo was William "Bud" Abbott and Lou Costello. Their movies were a staple of the Sunday morning matinee. Abbott signed in a nice flowing hand. Costello's signature is more abrupt in construction. Both signatures are in high demand and commonly forged together. Abbot's signature is much more difficult to replicate than that of Costello. Well-executed forgeries of Costello exist. Abbott forgeries, on the other hand, tend to be labored in appearance. There is an ample supply of material in the market. Mediums include TLsS, photographs, bank checks, and government postcards. Costello checks exist in a far greater quantity than Abbott checks. ALsS are rare to very rare. There are dual-signed *Abbott & Costello Radio Show* bank checks. They are highly prized and make for a handsome display. Signed photographs of both are scarce and most offered for sale are forgeries. A rather common forgery is found on *Who's On First?* records. Forgeries of one or both are placed on the yellow record label. There are many of these forgeries in the market. I have never examined a genuine signed record and it is doubtful that one exists. Recently, many $1 silver certificates with forgeries of both have entered the market. They have surfaced on internet sites such as eBay, so caution is warranted. Abbott and Costello have always had a huge following and always will. Their signatures are of comparable value. Expect to pay $225 to $250 for their autographs. Signed 8 × 10 photographs will sell for $400 to $500; exceptional specimens are valued at over $1,000. An 8 × 10 photograph signed by both is valued at $1,500. Costello bank checks can be purchased for $250 to $300. Abbott checks are much tougher to find and will sell for $500 to $600. The above-referenced dual-signed checks will sell for $1,250 to $1,500. Two very significant autographs of the Hollywood genre.

[Abbott signature]

Abbott-1, undated signature (courtesy Sanders Autograph Price Guide).

[Costello signature]

Costello-1 undated album page.

Then there are the immortal Three Stooges. These guys are my personal favorites. They brought slapstick to an entirely new level. There were six men who made up the Stooges at one point or another. The original trio was Moe Howard, Samuel "Shemp" Howard, and Larry Fine. Jerome "Curly" Howard, Joe Besser, and Curly Joe DeRita round out the team. Shemp and Curly, who died at young age, are the scarcest of the signatures. Larry exists in far greater quantities. The supply of Moe signatures is more than ample. Signatures of Moe,

signed with his nickname, "Bugs," are very rare. A large cache of checks were released by the family to raise money for medical research. The initial selling price was a mere $10 per check. Curly Joe is the easiest of the Stooges to obtain. Many bank checks are in the market. Other actors and producers are collectable simply because of their association with the Stooges, among them Jules White, Emil Sitka, and Ted Healy.

Shemp's signature is very easy to replicate. Well-executed forgeries exist in quantities. His signature is generally found on album pages and a scarce few bank checks. Letters and photographs are rare. A Shemp ALS would be an extreme rarity. Photographs are highly desirable because Shemp would typically write odd and funny inscriptions to the recipient. Shemp's signature is valued at $500 to $600. Bank checks will sell for not much more. A nicely signed 8 × 10 is valued at $2,000.

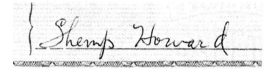

Howard, S-1 bank check dated 1954.

Curly is the Stooge whose signature is in the highest demand. Supply is limited as he died in 1952, victim of a stroke. Curly's signature is scarce to rare. Market supply is grossly inflated due to the quantity of forgeries transacted. Signatures are typically signed with his first name only. Album pages tend to be the most common medium. TLsS and photographs are very rare. ALsS are an extreme rarity. I have never examined a genuine specimen. Curly's signature is one of the most forged of all Hollywood autographs. More than 90 percent of all Curly signatures offered for sale are forged. His signature is of simple construction; thus replication of hand is rather easy. A full signature is valued at $1,000. A nicely signed 8 × 10 photograph, signed in full, is valued at $3,000.

Howard, C-1, undated signature.

Howard, C-2 album page circa 1940s (courtesy Nate D. Sanders Auctions).

The supply of Moe signatures is sound due to a nice supply of bank checks. In his later years he wrote many letters to fans. Many ALsS are in the market, though usually signed with his first name only. Signed 8 × 10 photographs are rare and highly sought after. Moe's signature is affordable at $150. Checks sell for $250 to $300. ALsS signed with the first name only can be purchased for under $200. An ALS signed in full is valued at $600 to $800. Forgeries are generally limited to album pages and photographs featuring the entire team.

Howard, M-1, bank check dated 1971 (courtesy Nate D. Sanders Auctions).

Larry died in 1975 and is a tougher signature to locate than that of Moe. There is an ample supply of material in the market. Much of it was signed in the 1940s. Album pages are a good source for his autograph. Photographs are somewhat scarce. There is a good supply of bank checks in the market. In 1970, Fine was hit with a rather severe stroke. It left him par-

tially paralyzed and confined to a wheelchair. There are many ALsS in the market accomplished after his illness. The letters are neatly written and tend to be long. Many mention his illness. Many of these letters were written and signed by a secretary or relative. If you have a post–1970 letter it is probably one written and signed by the secretary. Fine's signature can be purchased for $250 to $300. Bank checks will sell for $400 to $500. A nicely signed 8 × 10 photo is valued at just over $1,000.

Fine-1, bank check dated 1969 (courtesy Nate D. Sanders Auctions).

Walt Disney was a cartoonist and filmmaker. Disney has given the world some of the most beloved cartoon characters of all time, among them Mickey Mouse and Donald Duck. Today, the Disney empire is worldwide. Walt Disney is one of the biggest names of the 20th century. I really love signatures of animators. Their signatures are gaudy and bold. A high degree of artistic flair is noted. Disney's signature is no exception. The bold strokes of ink and the pronounced sweeps give the signature an almost fairytale look. The signature is typically finished off with a complex paraph. The display value is very high. Given the complex nature of the signature, replication of hand is very difficult. Well-executed forgeries exist, but are very limited. The extreme value of certain mediums attracts skilled forgers. In addition, there are many secretarial signatures in the market. Many signatures obtained through the mail were ghost-signed. Typically, a signature that is accomplished in printed script should be avoided as a secretarial. Disney was generally a responsive signer. There is an ample supply of material in the market, though demand is far greater. Signatures are found on most mediums, including

TLsS, album pages, and photographs. ALsS are very rare. Bank checks are also in the market. Checks were once advertised as very rare but it is apparent there is a good supply of them in the market. Disney was a staunch anti-communist. There are letters in the market with strong patriotic content. Letters such as these are highly prized by collectors. Sketches and hurried doodles of his characters also exist. These are gems and even quick sketches can fetch over $20,000. Genuine sketches are very rare. Most obtained through the mail were accomplished by a staff animator. Forgers produce drawings by the boatload. Just about all Disney's sketches, close to 100 percent, in the market are either forged or secretarially accomplished. There are many quick pencil sketches of Mickey Mouse and Donald Duck in the market. They contain a forged signature in printed script at the bottom. The letters in the forgery are mis-spaced and the characters don't have that charming cute look of a genuine Disney sketch. They look almost alien-like with mis-scaled eyes and ears. In general, this is a common trait of forged drawings. Many of these forged sketches are placed in the front end page of Disney-related

Disney-1, bank check circa 1950.

Disney-1, common secretarial.

books. Disney's signature sells for $1,000 to $1,250. Bank checks and DsS are valued at $1,500 to $2,000. TLsS generally sell for $1,500 to $2,000. Political content letters will sell for much more. A nicely signed 8 × 10 photograph is valued at $4,000 to $5,000. Unusual images, featuring Disney with one of his characters or an animal, will sell closer to $10,000. Sketches will sell for $15,000 to $25,000.

It is safe to say the most powerful lawman in the history of the United States was J. Edgar Hoover. He served as director of the F.B.I. and its predecessor agency from 1924 until his death in 1972. He proved a key figure in the Cold War. Hoover signed in a confined and thoughtful hand. The signature works well in small places. Overall, an average signature. The supply of Hoover material is great. There are thousands of TLsS, on F.B.I. letterhead, in the market. Many fine 8 × 10 portrait photographs exist. ALsS are very rare. It is apparent that Hoover loved to sign his name because secretarial signatures seldom surface. Just about all TLsS are signed by Hoover. Due to the vast supply of TLsS, values are kept in check. His signature, on most mediums, can be purchased for under $100. Letters with strong political or legal content will sell for $250 to $500. A very affordable American autograph.

Hoover, J-1 TLS dated 1943 (courtesy Nate D. Sanders Auctions).

Melvin Purvis was one of the most famous of the gangster-busting G-Men. He led the manhunts against John Dillinger and Charles "Pretty Boy" Floyd. In 1960, he accidentally shot himself to death while cleaning out a pistol. Purvis signed in a confined hand. The signature is average in most respects. Given the affordable nature of the signature, it is generally not the target of skilled forgers. Signatures are generally limited to just three mediums: ALsS, TLsS, and bank checks. Any one of the three can be purchased for about $150 to $200. I consider Purvis's signature undervalued.

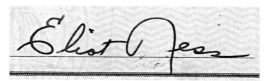

Purvis-1, TLS dated 1934 (courtesy Nate D. Sanders Auctions).

Perhaps the most famous of G-Men was Eliot Ness. Ness was a Treasury agent assigned to the Chicago office during Prohibition. His group of agents became known as the Untouchables. Ness's signature has odd formation. The large letter "N" dominates an otherwise plain signature. It is of average display value. Ness's signature used to be rare. There was very little material in the market. A few years back a cache of canceled bank checks entered the market and made this once-rare signature available to collectors. It is about the only medium you will find Ness's signature on. I have never seen an ALS or 8 × 10 photo. TLsS are rare to very rare. Expect to pay $500 to $600 for a bank check.

Ness-1, signed bank check dated 1945 (courtesy Nate D. Sanders Auctions).

There were many great fighters from the depression era of boxing. Many names are collectable such as Lou Ambers, Jimmy "Baby Face" McLarnin, Henry Armstrong, Barney Ross, and the like. Perhaps the greatest fighter of the 1930s was the Brown Bomber, Joe Louis. He became a household name due to the two fights with former heavyweight champion Max Schmeling. Schmeling, Hitler's superman, won the first fight. In the rematch Louis knocked out

Schmeling in the first round. Louis signed in a rather loose hand. The signature tends to be sloppy and lacks uniformity. As such, it is easily forged. Many forgeries exist in the market. Louis died in 1981, well before the era of mass signings. He signed very little. He was generally not a responsive signer. Mail requests for his signature generally went unanswered. His signature is typically found on album pages and photographs; many images are of an elderly Louis. The vast majority of all 8 × 10 photographs are forged, so caution is warranted. Letters of any kind are rare. I have never examined a genuine ALS or boxing glove. There is strong demand for Louis material. There is one grouping of forgeries to note. There are many forged TLsS in the market. They are usually dated in the 1930s and placed on fake letterhead that reads "Joe Louis, 381 Edgecombe Avenue, New York, New York." While the forgery is fairly well-executed, the rest of the letter is almost comical. The type is generated either by an electric typewriter or computer. The type-script is perfect, evidencing no deviation from letter to letter, something that would be found in a typewriter from the 1930s. These letters are clean and evidence no age. They were likely produced within the past 5 years. Louis's signature sells for $250 to $300. A nicely signed 8 × 10 photograph is valued around $500 to $750. Exceptional specimens will sell for over $1,000.

Louis-1, undated signature (courtesy The Sanders Autograph Price Guide).

Schmeling, on the other hand, lived until the age of 99, and signed for most of his life. He was one of the best signers of all. He was signing autographs until they shut the coffin lid. He was known to sign 10 to 20 items at a time in the mail for collectors. Schmeling's signature is common and can generally be purchased for under $25. Signed boxing gloves are rare and sell for $450 to $500. In 1973 *Sports Illustrated* issued a limited edition print of the Schmeling v. Louis fight. These prints were signed by both in pencil. They are in high demand and sell for close to $1,000. Schmeling-signed gloves should prove a fine investment.

Schmeling-1, signature dated 1990.

Many consider Rocky Marciano the greatest fighter of them all. Known as the Brockton Blockbuster, Marciano is the only heavyweight champion in history to go undefeated. He was killed in a plane crash in 1969. He remains one of the biggest names in sports history. Marciano signed in a bold and flowing hand. The signature is rapid in nature. Letter construction is fairly sound, though some hurried specimens evidence impaired legibility. The supply of Marciano material is good. He was a willing signer. There are many album pages and other in-person signatures in the market. There is also a good supply of photographs in the market. Checks and TLsS are uncommon to scarce. ALsS are very rare; in fact, I have only examined a couple in my lifetime. Given the rapid nature of his hand, well-executed forgeries are few and far between. There is one group of forgeries to note and they were created by the same forger. There are several forged TLsS in the market on Marciano letterhead. These letters were the subject of a June 20, 2013, article on Haulsof

shame.com written by Peter Nash. The letters exhibit excellent boxing content. From Hauls ofshame.com: "All of the questioned letters are dated between 1961 and 1969 and are all addressed to an alleged writer named William H. Reinmuth Jr. from a magazine called 'Sports Quest.'" A detailed handwriting analysis is given by Travis Roste, an authority on boxing autographs. Many of these letters have been certified by the authentication companies, so caution is warranted. Any letter addressed to Reinmuth must be examined carefully, as it may very well be a forgery. There is strong demand for Marciano material. Expect to pay $400 to $500 for a nice signature. Checks will sell in the $750 range. Signed 8 × 10 photographs will sell for $750 to $1,000 but exceptional images will sell for over $2,000. An important 20th-century sports autograph.

Marciano-1, document dated 1968 (courtesy Haulsofshame.com).

Glenn Miller's signature is one of my favorites. His signature has wonderful flowing lines. Display value is nice despite marginal letter construction. Miller was one of the most famous of band leaders. He was flying to France to entertain troops when his plane crashed in the English Channel in December of 1944. Miller was a superstar of his day. He was targeted by autograph collectors. The supply of material is sound. There are countless album pages, menus, and photographs of various size. Letters of any kind are rare. Demand for Miller material has declined in recent years. Prices have fallen slightly. Miller's signature is generally not the target of skilled forgers. Miller's signature can be purchased for $100 to $150. Signed 8 × 10 photographs are valued at $250 to $300.

Miller, G-1, undated signature.

Alger Hiss is a name that people have heard of, even if they are not really sure who he was or what he did. Hiss was an aide to President Truman and a suspected spy for the Soviets. Fingered by Whittaker Chambers, Hiss was convicted of perjury. Hiss signed in a very plain and unattractive hand. The signature has impaired letter construction and could easily be forged. After his conviction, Hiss withdrew from public life, and was not really accessible to collectors. Though he died in 1996, his signature is considered scarce and generally limited to ALsS. Other mediums are tough to find. An 8 × 10 photograph would be rare. There is average demand for Hiss material. Expect to pay $250 for one of the above-mentioned ALsS.

Hiss-1, ALS dated 1989.

Lucile Ball is the most famous woman in Hollywood history. *I Love Lucy* was one of the most successful sitcoms of all time. Ball's signature is of good letter construction and legibility. Signatures are sometimes accomplished as "Lucille Ball Arnaz." Many signatures are simply signed "Love, Lucy." In recent years a large supply of bank checks has entered the market and

adversely affected values. Ball's signature is generally not the target of skilled forgers. A signed check will sell for $200. An 8 × 10 photograph signed with the first name only is valued at $250 to $300. A photograph signed in full is not much more at $400. A dual-signed photograph with husband Desi Arnaz is valued at $750. An item signed by the cast of *I Love Lucy* would be an extreme rarity and its value is indeterminate, with William Frawley's signature being the toughest of the group. Desi Arnaz checks are on the cheap side and can be purchased for as little as $50.

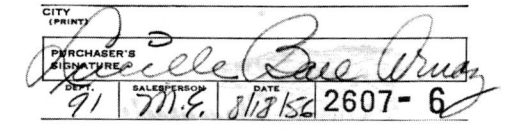

Ball-1, Receipt dated 1956 (courtesy Nate D. Sanders Auctions).

In my opinion the greatest movie star of all time is John Wayne. No man shaped the world's image of the American west more than the Duke. Wayne's signature is dominated by a large capital letter "J." It is of average construction. Display value is acceptable. There is a sound inventory of Wayne material in the market. Mediums include album pages, TLsS, DsS, books, and photographs. Photographs are almost always inscribed, sometimes with cryptic inscriptions. There is very strong demand for Wayne material and it pushes prices ever higher. Wayne's signature is commonly targeted by skilled forgers. There are many forged photographs, album pages, and index cards in the market. Before the movie *The Shootist* was released, the producer issued many John Wayne business cards to promote the movie. On one side was Wayne's name. On the reverse was a facsimile signature that reads: "Good Luck, John Wayne." Often times these are framed as sold as genuine. What makes some of the cards tricky is that part of the facsimile runs off the edge of the card, giving the appearance of being hand-signed. There are variant examples of these facsimiles, so caution is warranted. Wayne's signature sells for $600 to $700. TLsS are valued at $1,000. An 8 × 10 photograph will sell for $1,000 to $1,500. Photographs of characters from movies such as *True Grit*, *The Shootist*, and *Rio Bravo* are in great demand. Choice specimens have been known to sell for over $5,000.

Wayne, J-1, TNS dated 1976 (courtesy Nate D. Sanders Auctions).

Humphrey Bogart was Hollywood's premier tough guy. Well, except for maybe Jimmy Cagney. Bogart is one of the all-time Hollywood legends. As such, his signature is in strong demand. Bogart signed in a rather unstructured and vertical hand. Impaired legibility is noted. There is a large supply of Bogart material in the market, mostly on album pages. TLsS and photographs are also available. ALsS are rare. Some secretarial signatures are noted. Bogart's signature is valued at $600 to $800. TLsS and 8 × 10 photographs will sell for $1,000 to $1,500. Exceptional 8 × 10 photographs can sell in excess of $5,000. Material signed with his wife, Lauren Bacall, is rare and worth a premium.

Bogart-1, DS dated 1949.

Hockey is a real niche field within the autograph industry. The collector base is a relatively small group of dedicated fans. Despite this fact, some rare hockey signatures, such as Howie

Morenz and Harry "Hap" Holmes, are very expensive. Gordie Howe and Wayne Gretzky are considered the greatest hockey players of all time. Howe, known as Mr. Hockey, was a willing and gracious signer throughout his life. He also engaged in many mass signings. The supply of Howe material is almost limitless. Photographs seem to be the most common mediums. There are also many pucks and commemorative jerseys. Despite this abundance, his signature retains good value. Auction results on eBay are surprisingly strong. Pucks sell for $125. Hockey sticks are valued at $300. Early hockey cards will sell for $100 to $500, depending on the issue. A 1954 Topps signed card sold for $700 (eBay, July 2012). Photographs signed by all three members of Detroit's famed Production Line (Howe, Sid Abel, Ted Lindsey) sell for $300 and pucks at $400 to $500.

Howe-1, GPC dated 1995.

Two of the biggest mysteries of the 20th century are the disappearances of New York judge Joe Crater and Teamster boss Jimmy Hoffa. Hoffa ran afoul of the Detroit mob and disappeared on July 30, 1975. He is buried somewhere in northern Oakland County in Michigan, or so I have been told. Hoffa's signature is somewhat scarce, but he did sign for collectors. Signatures are typically found on album pages, union-related programs, and TLsS. Many letters are secretarially signed. Hoffa's signature is very easy to forge. One autopen template is known. Well-executed forgeries are produced with little effort. There are many forged 8 × 10 portrait photographs in the market. Hoffa's signature is a good association piece with 1970s Americana. There is average demand for his signature, which sells for $300. TLsS are valued at $400 to $500.

Hoffa-1, signature dated 1965 (courtesy Stephen Koschal Reference Library).

Martin Luther King is the most famous civil rights leader ever. He is a key figure of 1960s American history. King signed in an average hand. The signature has good letter construction with average display value. Though he was assassinated at a young age, there is an ample supply of material in the market. TLsS are the most common medium. Signed copies of his book *Stride Toward Freedom* are also available. ALsS are very rare. King's signature lacks recklessness; hence, replication of hand can be accomplished with relative ease. Well-executed forgeries exist in the market. There are many forged index cards in the market, all produced by the same forger. These are signed as "Best Wishes, Martin Luther King," and they are all accomplished in a bluish-gray fountain pen ink. Demand for King material has increased greatly in recent years. In the 1990s, his signature was very affordable with only marginal demand. Today, King's signature will sell for about $1,500. TLsS will sell for $3,000 to $4,000. Signed books are valued about the same. A nicely signed 8 × 10 photo is a rarity and will sell for $7,500 to $10,000. A letter with strong civil rights content would be a treasure and could possibly sell for over $100,000.

King-1, undated signature (courtesy Nate D. Sanders Auctions).

King's assassin, James Earl Ray, is also of interest to collectors. Ray wrote amazing content letters discussing the assassination and who framed him. In the letters he even names federal agents who he claimed set him up. Ray also wrote a book titled *Who Killed Martin Luther King?* Signed first editions will sell for $400 to $500. While Ray's signature is only worth about $100, the above-referenced content letters are highly prized by historians. They rarely if ever come onto the market. These letters have an estimated value of $1,500 to $2,000. While in stir, Ray dabbled in painting. He used to sell paintings for $75. His artwork rarely comes onto the market. Value is indeterminate. I estimate a value of $3,000 to $5,000.

Ray-1, signed book dated 1995.

Four-star General William Westmoreland commanded U.S. military operations from 1964 to 1968. He later served as army Chief of Staff. Westmoreland signed in a bold hand. His signature tends to be long and drawn-out. Since his passing in 2005, demand for his signature has increased. His signature exists in ample supply, though mostly found on index cards. Signed 8 × 10 photographs and TLsS are less common. ALsS are very scarce. Expect to pay $30 to $40 for his autograph. TLsS and 8 × 10 photographs will sell for $100. I consider Westmoreland's signature to be a good investment.

Westmoreland-1, undated signature.

The pool of collectors for basketball auto-graphs is much smaller than that of football or baseball. Having said that, there is still sound demand for basketball material. James Naismith invented the game. His signature is in much de-mand. Naismith signed in a pleasing hand with superior letter construction. Given the complex nature of hand, replication would be difficult. There are no well-executed forgeries in the mar-ket. There is one group of forgeries to discuss. There are many forged album pages and index cards in the market signed "James Naismith, Lawrence Kansas, Originated basketball in 1891." It is then dated is the upper right of the paper. The forgery is slightly labored and ex-posed as a forgery with little examination. This was once a rare signature, but the supply of ma-terial has increased greatly in recent years. Many letters, documents, and postal covers have en-tered the market, making his signature available to collectors. Naismith's signature can be pur-chased for $600 to $750. There is a good supply of ALsS in the market, though most signed with his first name only. These can be purchased for under $1,000.

Naismith-1 signature circa 1920.

There are many collectable signatures from the world of hoops. George Mikan, Wilt Cham-berlain, Bob Cousy, Oscar Robertson, Michael Jordan, Norm Hankins, and on and on. College basketball has given sports some of the greatest coaches ever. My personal favorite is Jerry Tarkanian. Perhaps the biggest name is John Wooden. Wooden was a willing and gracious signer for most of his life. He would sign bas-ketballs, photographs, commemorative cards, and the like. He was known to pen poignant let-ters. He would even draw basketball plays. Pedestrian material is quite affordable at $50 or under. Basketballs are valued at $150 to $200. ALsS at $100 to $125. Handwritten plays are rare and are worth about $400 to $500. Pre-mium Wooden items will prove a sound invest-ment in years to come.

Wooden-1, undated signature.

This chapter could go on and on forever. There are so many collectable American auto-graphs that it boggles the mind: Bob Hope, Jimmy Stewart, Robert Kennedy, Helen Keller, Stanley Ketchel, William McGuffey, Clare Boothe Luce, Willie Mosconi, Bill Shoemaker, and countless more. American autographs pro-vide the most diverse pool of signatures for col-lectors and a great way to immerse yourself in the American Experience.

From the Fields of Kitty Hawk
to the Rings of Saturn:
Space and Aviation

Since long before recorded history, man has been fascinated with the heavens. For centuries we humans have looked to the skies and watched birds soar high into the air. Flight has forever captured the imagination of man. For hundreds of years, long before Leonardo, humans have endeavored to build a flying machine. The first practical invention was the balloon. China was well versed in the use of these contraptions and used them to gain military advantage over their enemies, who thought them divine gods. The kongming lantern was probably the earliest of these proto-balloons. The kongming was nothing more than a paper bag with an oil lamp attached underneath. The hot air collected in the bag and caused it to lift.

Another early invention of flight was the wood bird, also a product of the Chinese. It was a form of kite not much different from the kites you can buy today. From 300 BC to AD 1000, flight was pretty much limited to these devices. Fanciful, to be sure, but nothing that could yet lift a human into the skies.

Right around 1000, an English monk named Eilmer of Malmesbury strapped on a pair of wings and jumped from a tower at the Malmesbury Abbey. Eilmer is said to have glided nearly 660 feet before crash-landing in tall grass. For his historic efforts he was rewarded with two broken legs. It was his first and last flight.

The Renaissance brought renewed interest in flight and many learned men of the day worked to build the first true flying machine. Leonardo da Vinci put forth his aerial screw, which had the rough constructions of the modern helicopter.

In 1783 came a great year for the advancement of aviation, or at least the balloon. Many great ballooning firsts took place that year, and all in France. It was in this year that the first hydrogen-filled airship took flight.

In 1852, French inventor Henri Giffard flew close to 20 miles in his airship. It was the first time a powered and controlled machine took flight. As great as these crafts were, they proved too weak for sustainable flight, and most died an early death.

The birth of modern flight would not occur until the invention of the internal combustion engine. In 1896 retired astronomer Samuel Langley built a heavier-than-air craft. He called it the aerodrome. Launched from a catapult, the aerodrome was the first successful engine-driven flight of a heavier-than-air craft. He later built a scaled-up model with the hopes of manned flight. In the end the aerodrome was too fragile and never did carry a pilot. Though Langley never did realize his dream, history still honors him as a pioneer of flight. His signature is somewhat rare and mostly limited to TLsS and ALsS, either of which can be purchased for $250 to $300.

Langley-1, undated signature (courtesy The Sanders Autograph Price Guide).

* * *

Kitty Hawk

Just after the close of the Civil War, two brothers were born in Dayton, Ohio. Their names were Orville and Wilbur Wright. In the 1890s they owned and operated the Wright Cycle Company. They used profits from the business to feed their growing interest in building a flying machine. After many failed attempts, success finally came on December 17, 1903, when Orville took to the skies at Kitty Hawk, North Carolina. His flight lasted a mere 12 seconds. That flight flew the Wright brothers right into the pages of history. They had done what no one else had ever done: the Wright brothers made the first successful powered, controlled, human flight in a heavier-than-air craft.

The Wrights are the two most significant names in aviation history. This correlates into great demand for their autographs. The difference in rarity between the two signatures is demonstrable. Wilbur died in 1912 at the age of 45. He was a victim of typhoid fever. Orville, on the other hand, lived until 1948. For many years he was targeted by autograph collectors and signed many items. His signature is available and generally found on commemorative airmail covers and typed letters signed. In addition, there are several hundred bank checks in the market. They have been available for years and make for an attractive display. Checks have actually proved a poor investment. In the mid–1990s a check signed by Orville was valued as $1,000. Checks can now been purchased for $400 to $500, a marked decline in value.

Orville signed many early pilot licenses and more than a handful exist to this day. Other mediums should be considered rare to very rare. ALsS are extremely rare. Signed photographs are few and far between. Close to 100 percent of all signed Orville Wright photographs in the market are forgeries. TLsS are valued at $800 to $1,200. A signed photograph of the Wright plane in flight will sell for $2,000 to $2,500.

Wright, O-1 postal cover dated 1928.

Wright, O-2, well executed forgery.

Wilbur's autograph is very rare. He did not live long enough to sign items for autograph collectors. Today, very few specimens exist. A few bank checks and documents have been bought and sold, and that is about it. Just about all autographs of Wilbur in the market are forgeries. Forged bank checks exist, so caution is warranted. There are many signed photographs in the market and just about 100 percent are forged. There are many postcard-sized and 4 × 6 photographs in the market featuring the Wright airplane in flight. A forgery of Wilbur is placed in the lower right of the image and typically dated. Many TLsS, on Wright Cycle Company letterhead, are secretarially signed. TLsS will sell in the $10,000 range. ALsS will sell for $15,000 to $20,000. Content letters can easily sell for $25,000 or more.

Wright, W-1, undated signature.

By 1910 these crazy flying machines were everywhere. Soon entrepreneurs realized there was money to be made with the airplane. Investors started to take interest in the business aspect of flight. It became apparent that the airplane would be a useful tool for the United States Postal Service. It led to the birth of airmail. Earle Ovington, a one-time lab assistant to Thomas Edison, was fascinated with this new technology. In 1911, Ovington made the first official airmail flight in the history of the United States. He flew a sack of mail from Garden City, New York, to Mineola. He signed many commemorative airmail covers and today they make for a fine addition to any signature library. Ovington's signature can be purchased for $50 to $100 on most mediums.

Ovington-1, flight cover circa 1930.

By the 1920s airmail exploded in popularity. There were hundreds of pilots flying mail to all parts of the country. It was common practice for the pilot to sign his name on the mail he was flying. Though these pilots were not famous, the covers, signed by forgotten fliers, make for a colorful and affordable collectable. Most signed flight covers can be purchased for under $15. Many of them were also signed by the local postmaster as well.

As with any new invention, there is a need to be the first to do something with it. First to cross the ocean, the longest flight, the highest, and so forth. To do something that no one has done before gains the aviator a certain amount of fame. In 1909, French inventor Louie Bleriot became the first man to cross the English Channel in an airplane. Even though the channel is not particularly wide, it was nevertheless a huge accomplishment. Bleriot died in 1936. His sig-

nature is in good demand. Generally found on album pages and letters, Bleriot's signature should be considered scarce. Given the affordable nature of his signature, he is generally not the target of skilled forgers. Expect to pay $200 to $500 for one, depending on the medium.

Bleriot-1, album page circa 1920.

Naval pilot Walter Hinton became the first man to fly from North America (New York) to South America (Brazil). Hinton's signature can be found on commemorative airmail postal covers, which seem to be in good supply. Letters and photographs are also available but less common. Hinton's signature is affordable at under $100.

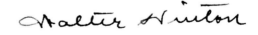

Hinton, flight cover dated 1931.

Englishman Thomas O.M. Sopwith was an accomplished man. His signature is of interest not only to aviation collectors, but also those interested in hockey and yachting. Sopwith was an early aviation manufacturer. His company, the Sopwith Aviation Company, produced close to 20,000 combat aircraft for deployment in World War I. Sopwith died in 1989 at the age of 101. He was a willing signer his entire life. Collectors began targeting him in the 1970s for his autograph. Most signatures offered in the market are signed in an elderly and infirmed hand. His signature is considered uncommon but affordable. Index cards and postal covers will sell for $50.

Sopwith-1, signed cover circa 1980.

The Lone Eagle

Born in Detroit in 1902, Charles Augustus Lindbergh seemed like the most unlikely of heroes. He was a reserved fellow who led a very private life. Tall and lanky, his nickname as a youth was "Slim." Lindy was an unassuming airmail pilot who became the first man to fly solo across the Atlantic Ocean. He left Roosevelt Field in New York on May 20, 1927, and landed the next day in Paris to a worldwide celebration. Anything signed by Lindbergh is in very high demand. Lindbergh signed in a very strong and powerful hand. The resulting signature appears fast on paper and dominates the medium it is placed upon. Early Lindbergh signatures have excellent display value. He would sign his name as "Charles A. Lindbergh" and many times as simply "C.A. Lindbergh." Early signatures have complex letter construction and are rather difficult to forge. Well-executed forgeries are very limited. Fortunately for collectors, Lindbergh signed many items, including photographs, letters, and commemorative airmail covers that he personally flew in 1928. ALsS from any time period are very scarce.

In the evening of March 1, 1932, Lindbergh's son, Charles Jr., was kidnapped. The toddler's body was found a little more than two months later near the Lindbergh home. It was an event that changed Lindbergh forever. He retreated to Europe for a period of time and rarely signed autographs. Material signed after 1932 is very scarce and generally limited to letters.

As the years progressed, Lindbergh's hand went through a noticeable change. The once flamboyant signature of the 1920s had changed to a much more reversed hand. More modern signatures are signed in a smaller and tighter hand. The overall scale of the signature de-

creases. Speed decreases. This form of signature is much easier to forge. Many well-executed forgeries exist and can be found on Lindbergh-authored books and TLsS on blank stationary. The vast majority of post–1930 signatures offered for sale are forged. Lindbergh passed away in 1974 and his signature is in great demand. TLsS and books, which are almost always inscribed, can be purchased for $600 to $1,000. Bank checks are scarce and sell for $1,250 to $1,500. Signed 8 × 10 photographs are valued at $1,500 to $2,000, with exceptional specimens worth close to $5,000.

Lindbergh-1, signed program circa 1930.

Lindbergh-2, signature circa 1970.

Barnstormers

The interest in airplanes exploded in the 1920s. The aviators were the rock stars of the day. Americans were enthralled with flight and attended air shows by the millions. Jimmy Doolittle (discussed in the World War chapter) gained fame as an air racer, winning the Schneider Cup in 1925. Roscoe Turner was also an early star of 1920s aviation and won many races. He was best known as a spokesman for Gilmore Oil Company. Frank Hawks was an early stunt pilot and is best remembered for being the first pilot to refuel while in flight. His signature is uncommon to scarce, as he was killed in 1938 while flying an experimental Gwinn Aircar. There is a limited supply of signed airmail covers signed by Hawks in the market. Hawks did have a rubber stamp made of his signature, so caution is warranted. Signatures of either Hawks or Turner can be purchased for $75 to $100.

Turner-1, undated signature (courtesy The Sanders Autograph Price Guide).

Hawks-1, signature circa 1930.

Then there is a gentleman named Douglas Corrigan, an early stunt pilot who gained immortality for trying to fly from New York to California and somehow ending up in Ireland. Citing heavy cloud cover for his error, Corrigan was given the nickname "Wrong Way." Corrigan lived until 1995 but proved an elusive signer. His signature is in great demand, partly because of his catchy nickname. He would sometimes add odd inscriptions such as "South to North Dakota!" His signature generally sells in the $150 to $200 range.

Corrigan-1 postal cover 1972.

In 1930, Frenchmen Maurice Bellonte and Dieudonne Costes completed the first Atlantic crossing from Europe to America. Costes was also a noted ace of World War I. Both were responsive signers but received relatively few requests. Both signatures are considered uncommon to scarce. Signatures are generally limited to index cards and first-day covers. Costes was known to sign early airmail covers. Other mediums are scarce to rare. A few dual-signed photographs exist; they feature both men sitting in an airplane. Signed photographs of any kind are scarce. Their signatures are affordable at $50 each. A dual-signed photograph is valued at $150 to $200.

Bellonte-1, signature dated 1931 (courtesy Stephen Koschal Autographs).

Coste-1 flight cover circa 1930.

Those Giant Sausages

As flight progressed, aviation made a slight, if not strange, detour. It would give birth to the most beloved and whimsical era of flight.

Back during the American Civil War, long before the days of the Wright Brothers, a dreamer, not unlike Jules Verne, got the idea to combine the grace of a balloon and the power of the engine to create a new machine, a grand machine that would gently carry passengers from one end of the globe to the other. He envisioned giant floating crafts larger than life. His name was Ferdinand von Zeppelin and his craft: the dirigible.

On July 2, 1900, on the shores of Lake Constance near the city of Friedrichshafen, the first German zeppelin (as they were now being called) was unveiled. Labeled LZ1, it was nearly 420 feet in length and resembled, as one author put it, "a long sausage." The flight lasted only a short time before the craft contorted and crashed. Zeppelin continued his work on his giant airships. He died in 1917 at the age of 79.

Zeppelin's signature is in high demand. Complex in nature, it has good eye appeal. Zeppelin signed in a fast and illegible hand. Though the signature is difficult to read, it has uniform letter construction and is thus difficult to forge. Well-executed forgeries are limited. Zeppelin's signature is generally found on letters. Signed photographs, usually formal portraits, are very rare and command a premium. Zeppelin's signature generally sells for $500 to $600. ALsS will sell in the $2,000 price range. Demand will always be great for Count von Zeppelin's signature.

eBay. The forgeries are signed in full, but some are signed simply as "Dr. Eckener."

Eckener-1, undated signature.

The *Graf Zeppelin* proved a worthy ship and flew for years without incident. The same could not be said for her sister ship, LZ129, the *Hindenburg*. The *Hindenburg* incorporated the latest in airship design and used the finest of materials. Zeppelin 129 was only in operation for about a year. On May 6, 1937, the great ship burst into flames over Lakehurst, New Jersey. Thirty-six souls were lost that fateful day. The *Hindenburg* had no fewer than five pilots aboard. The most famous was Ernst Lehmann. Lehmann was badly burned and died the day after. Being somewhat of a celebrity of the day, Lehmann signed many items. His signature is mostly found on album pages and thick stock index cards. On any other medium his signature is considered rare to very rare. His signature is difficult to find and sells in the $150 to $200 range.

von Zeppelin-1, undated signature (courtesy The Sanders Autograph Price Guide).

After Zeppelin's death, Dr. Hugo Eckener took center stage in zeppelin development. Eckener piloted LZ127, the *Graf Zeppelin*, during the 1920s. He signed many items, mostly zeppelin-flown postal covers. His signature is affordable and generally can be purchased for under $100. Premium items can sell for $500. In recent years a large supply of forged postal covers has entered the market, mostly through

Lehmann-1, undated signature (courtesy Stephen Koschal Reference Library).

The whereabouts of *Hindenburg* crew members were generally unknown. This explains the lack of signed material in the market. Signatures of any crew member are scarce to rare. They simply were not asked to sign autographs. For many years the aviators of the *Graf* and *Hinden-*

burg would meet regularly in Friedrichshafen. In the early 1990s they signed a limited number of items for aviation collectors. Among them were Eugen Bentele, Alfred Grozinger, Helmut Lau, Theodore Ritter, Walter Muller, Albert Stoffler, and Werner Franz. The chief electrical officer of the *Graf Zeppelin*, Georg Holl, also signed a limited number of items. A few zeppelin-flown covers were signed at these gatherings, but they should be considered very rare and in high demand.

Bentele-1, signature dated 1990.

Franz-1 signature dated 2004.

Grozinger-1, signature circa 1995.

Holl-1, signature dated 1990.

Muller-1, signature circa 1990.

Ritter-1, signature circa 1990 .

WLS radio broadcaster Herb Morrison was on hand that tragic day to report on the landing of the *Hindenburg*. He watched the ship crash and broadcast the disaster live as it happened. He uttered the now famous phrase, "Oh, the humanity!" Morrison died in 1989 and his signature is of much interest to collectors. Expect to pay $100 for it.

Morrison-1, undated signature (courtesy The Sanders Autograph Price Guide).

German airships were not the only giants to capture the imagination. The United States navy had in its arsenal four rigid airships, the *Akron*, the *Macon*, the *Los Angeles*, and the *Shenandoah*. Their tenure in the skies lasted from the mid–1920s through the 1930s. Three of the four ships crashed, killing many seamen. Only the *Los Angeles* survived to live out a peaceful retirement. Anything signed by crew members of these ships is a rarity. A few survivors began signing autographs in the 1990s.

Schellberg-1, ALS dated 1994.

Lust-1 signature circa 1990.

John Lust of the *Akron* and Gene Schellberg of the *Macon* come to mind. Their autographs are very scarce.

Much more common is the signature of Vice-Admiral Charles Rosendahl. He was a career navy man who was the biggest advocate for the airships. Rosendahl signed many items and was actively sought out by autograph collectors. His signature is generally found on index cards, photographs, and airmail covers. Expect to pay $50 to $75 for a nice specimen.

Rosendahl-1, 1934 postal cover.

British aeronautical engineer H. Roxbee Cox (1902–1997) was another significant figure in airship design. He worked on the design of the British airship R101. At the time it was built in 1929, it was the largest flying machine in the world. It crashed in France in 1930. In 1965 Cox received peerage from Queen Elizabeth II and was known thereafter as Lord Kings Norton. He was a responsive signer and signed many items related to the House of Lords. Expect to pay $50 for his signature.

Norton-1, TLS dated 1995.

Wiley Post and Amelia Earhart

In 1931, Wiley Post, along with aviator Harold Gatty, were the first to fly around the world in a heavier-than-air craft. Just two years later, Post would accomplish this feat again, this time by himself. He became the first man to fly solo around the world. Post befriended humorist Will Rogers, also an enthusiast of flight. On Au-gust 15, 1935, Post and Rogers took off from a remote airfield in Alaska. The plane crashed in a shallow lagoon. Both men were killed instantly.

Post signed in a nice and flowing hand. The signature has good display value. Sound letter construction is noted, but complexity is lacking. It is easily forged. Many well-executed forgeries exist, so caution is warranted. Many period airmail covers with Post forgeries have entered the market, mostly through eBay, so caution is warranted. Post's signature is considered scarce. Premium items are rare to very rare. His signature is generally found on album pages and commemorative airmail covers. Some covers are countersigned by Gatty, which make for a fine display. Post's signature can generally be acquired for $500. The above referenced Post/Gatty dual-signed postal covers sell for $750 to $1,000.

Post-1, 1931 flight cover (courtesy Nate D. Sanders Auctions).

Gatty-1, flight cover dated 1931 (courtesy Nate D. Sanders Auctions).

Aviatrix Amelia Earhart was the first woman to fly solo over the Atlantic and was the first aviatrix to be awarded the Distinguished Flying Cross. She was fascinated with long-distance flight. She attempted a circumnavigational flight of the Earth. On July 2, 1937, Earhart and navigator Fred Noonan departed from Lae. Their destination was Howland Island in the Pacific. They never made it. They disappeared somewhere over the ocean. Earhart was officially declared dead in January 1939.

Earhart's signature is of great interest to collectors. A per se scarce signature, it is generally limited to album pages and airmail covers. Earhart's signature lacks structure and uniformity. Because of this, her signature is easily forged. Many well-executed forgeries are in the market. Many forgeries have been wrongly certified as genuine by the authentication companies. Given the high demand, her signature sells for around $500. Signed 8 × 10 photographs and autographed letters signed are very rare and sell in the $1,500 to $2,500 range. Exceptional signed specimens are worth closer to $4,000.

Earhart-1 undated album page (courtesy Stephen Koschal Autographs).

Earhart-2, well executed forgery.

Bradford Washburn, a noted man of science, was an early aviator. He was also well versed in cartography. Because of this, Earhart asked him to accompany her on the ill-fated flight. Washburn, citing safety concerns, refused. Years later Washburn penned a few letters regarding Earhart and her death. In these letters Washburn tells of the advice he gave Earhart and why she died. The content is stunning and highly sought out by collectors. Washburn, who died in 2007, was responsive to autograph requests. His signature is valued at $25. The above-referenced Earhart letters carry a substantial premium.

Washburn-1, ALS dated 1993.

Other aviatrix include German pilot Elly Beinhorn. She was one of the earliest long-distance pilots in aviation history. She died in 2007 at the age of 100 and was a responsive signer. Signatures are generally limited to index cards and postal covers. Beinhorn's signature is affordable at $50. French aviatrix Jacqueline Auriol was a stunt and test pilot. She was generally a responsive signer, and like that of Beinhorn, her signature is generally limited to index cards and postal covers. Her signature can be purchased for $25 to $35.

Beinhorn-1, undated signature.

Auriol-1 postal cover dated 1977.

* * *

Many collectable signatures are of people who really never took to the skies. Inventors who advanced the technology of flight are equally as collectable. Willy Messerschmitt, famed German designer, whose fighter plane during World War II was a staple of the Luftwaffe, is a highly desired signature. Anton Fokker designed fighter planes for use in World

Fokker-1, undated signature (courtesy The Sanders Autograph Price Guide).

War I. Fokker died in 1939. His signature is a scarce to rare. Sir Geoffrey de Havilland, an early British aviation pioneer, is noted for designing the "Mosquito." It is considered the most successful combat plane in history. Modern aviation was greatly aided by the flight simulator invented by Luther Simjian. Simjian also invented the automatic teller machine.

Sir Geoffrey De Havilland

de Havilland-1, undated signature (courtesy The Sanders Autograph Price Guide).

Inventors from the eastern European countries, such as the Soviet Union, were not nearly as accessible to collectors, and today their signatures are hard to come by. Armenian jet designer Artem Mikoyan, known as the "father of the MiG fighter jet," died in 1970, and today his signature is considered rare to very rare.

Howard Hughes

Howard Hughes was an influential aviator and an enigma of his day. Hughes was a business magnate, real estate investor, film producer, and one of the richest men in the world. Hughes was an outgoing eccentric who loved the spotlight. He set many speed records and designed the famous 319-foot-long wooden airplane known as the *Spruce Goose*.

Hughes signed in a rather plain and unassuming hand. His signature has limited display value. The lack of structure results in a signature that is easily forged. Over 90 percent of all Hughes signatures offered for sale are forgeries. The supply of Hughes's signature is very limited. Documents, letters, and the occasional air-

mail cover will surface. Signed 8 × 10 photographs are very rare. Hughes did honor autograph requests in the early part of his life. As the years progressed, Hughes became more distant and wound up a recluse. Material signed after the 1940s is near nonexistent. Many signatures and TLsS penned after 1940 are secretarially signed. His signature will sell for $1,000 to $1,250. TLsS are valued at $2,500 to $3,000. A full-page ALS is likely worth at least $10,000.

Hughes-1, signed menu, circa 1935 (courtesy Nate D. Sanders Auctions).

In 1943 Hughes was flying a Sikorsky-S43 amphibian aircraft. While he was attempting a touch-and-go landing on Lake Mead, the plane crashed, killing two passengers. Hughes almost died. The Sikorsky was manufactured by the Sikorsky Aircraft Corporation. It was founded by Russian designer Igor Sikorsky. Sikorsky is credited with creating the first workable helicopter

Sikorsky signed in a rapid hand whose letters tend to blend with each other. The signature is basically illegible. Most signatures are signed as "I. Sikorsky." Sikorsky lived a long life and was a responsive signer. Many nicely signed photographs exist and just about all were inscribed to the recipient. TLsS exist, but these should be considered scarce. There is good demand for Sikorsky's autograph. His signature is generally not the target of skilled forgers. Sikorsky's signature can be purchased for under $200 on most mediums.

Sikorsky-1, signature dated 1971.

The "X" Pilots

General Chuck Yeager is best known as the first man to fly through the sound barrier. Flying an X-1 experimental jet, Yeager reached Mach I on October 14, 1947. Yeager's signature study can be found in the World War chapter.

Yeager was one of the most famous of the early "X" pilots, but many others are collectable. Astronaut William "Pete" Knight is of particular interest. In 1967, he reached 4,520 miles per hour in an X-15, the fastest manned flight to date. His signature is in good demand. Knight signed in a very busy hand. His signature is sloppy and on the illegible side. He was a responsive signer up to his death in 2004. Scott Crossfield was the first man to reach Mach 2, twice the speed of sound. He flew more rocket plane missions than any other aviator. He was a responsive signer and his signature is in good demand. There are many X-pilots to choose from and their signatures make for fine collectables. Signatures of pilots who were killed during a test flight, such as Mike Adams, are rare to very rare.

Crossfield-1, undated signature.

Knight-1, undated signature.

Space Exploration

I have always considered humans landing on the moon to be the greatest achievement of mankind. It still boggles my mind that 12 Amer-icans walked on the surface of another world. The race to understand the outer heavens is due mostly to man's insatiable curiosity. The need to top the Soviets in the Cold War certainly didn't hurt either.

Space autographs are widely collected and prices continue to increase at a marked rate. Astronauts of the 1960s through the 1970s are the most collected. Signatures of space shuttle astronauts are in much less demand.

On April 12, 1961, Russian cosmonaut Yuri Gagarin became the first human in outer space. Gagarin's signature is much sought after and the vast majority of autographs in the market are forgeries. His signature is not terribly complex; hence, replication of hand is rather easy. Well-executed forgeries exist in quantities. In March 1968, Gagarin was killed in a plane crash. His signature is considered scarce on a per se basis and premium items are rare to very rare. Gagarin's signature is valued at $600 to $800.

Gagarin-1 undated signature (courtesy Stephen Koschal Autographs).

The first woman in space was Soviet cosmonaut Valentina Tereshkova. In June of 1963 she piloted *Vostok 6*. Tereshkova signs in the typical Russian script with good uniformity but poor legibility. There is an ample supply of material in the market, but it is generally limited to Soviet-era picture postcards and 8 × 10 photographs. Letters of any kind are rare. Mail requests for her autograph typically go unanswered. In recent years forged photographs and postcards have entered the market. They appear to be originating from Bulgaria. There is good demand for Tereshkova's signature. Expect to pay $100 to $125 for her autograph. A photograph is valued at $250 to $300.

Tereshkova-1 undated signature.

Project Mercury was the first space flight program of the United States. It consisted of seven military pilots: John Glenn, Alan Shepard, Gordon Cooper, Deke Slayton, Wally Schirra, Scott Carpenter, and Gus Grissom. The demand for these signatures is strong and weighted against a limited supply. The rarest is that of Grissom. Grissom was killed in 1967 during a pre-launch test of *Apollo 1*. His signature was, for many years, considered rare. In recent years a good supply of canceled bank checks have entered the market and made his autograph accessible to collectors. Premium items such as 8 × 10 photographs and ALsS are very rare. More than 90 percent of Grissom signatures in the market are forgeries, so proceed with caution. Many have been wrongly certified as genuine by the authentication companies. Grissom bank checks sell for $600 to $800.

The most common signature is that of John Glenn. He served as a senator from Ohio and was a willing signer, though sometimes he would go through phases of personalizing anything he signed. His signature can be found on most mediums, though ALsS are rare. Some signed photographs obtained through the mail, as senator, were signed by an autopen. Slayton, Cooper, and Schirra were also good signers and many nicely signed items can be purchased at an affordable price. TLsS of any of these men are scarce. ALsS are rare to very rare. It should be noted that there is a good supply of Schirra bank checks in the market. Shepard is a more difficult signature. Most signatures obtained through the mail were secretarially signed. He did engage in some book signings.

Many signed copies of his book *Moon Shot* are available.

In 1962, *We Seven* was published and gave firsthand accounts of the astronauts' training and preparation for space flight. Various signed copies exist. To find a copy signed by all seven is a rarity. Grissom, of course, is the key signature. A complete signed book will sell for over $5,000. In later years, many copies were signed by Glenn, Cooper, Schirra, etc. They make for a fine addition to any library. They will sell for a minimum of $200.

Carpenter-1, undated signature.

Shepard-1 undated album page.

Shepard-2, common secretarial.

Schirra-1, signature circa 1990.

Grissom-1 signed bank check dated 1965 (courtesy Nate D. Sanders Auctions).

Slayton-1, undated signature.

Glenn-1, signature circa 2000.

Cooper, G-1, signature circa 1995.

One Small Step for a Man

On July 20, 1969, man landed on another world. *Apollo 11* carried three men to the moon: Neil Armstrong, Buzz Aldrin, and Michael Collins. With only 30 seconds of fuel left, the lunar module touched down on the surface of the moon. At 2:56 UTC, Neil Armstrong stepped onto the surface and said those now immortal words: "That's one small step for a man, one giant leap for mankind."

Armstrong proved an erratic signer for many years. Sometimes he would sign and sometimes he would not. Back in the early 1990s he sent me two signed 8 × 10 photographs. It is often said that Armstrong never engaged in signing autographs, but this is simply an incorrect statement. Over the last 15 or so years, he rarely signed anything through the mail. Obtaining a signature from him over the last few years would have been a great accomplishment. The profiteers turned Armstrong into a non-signer.

Armstrong signed in a very unstructured and unappealing hand. The signature is generally illegible and the many truncated lines make for a signature of limited display value. His signature is very easy to forge. Many well-executed forgeries exist. Just about all Armstrong signatures offered for sale are forgeries. In addition, Armstrong autopen signatures are in the market, so caution is warranted. In a letter dated June 2011, Armstrong stated: "Many, if not most, of the items that were offered for sale at exorbitant prices, we believe to be forgeries."

Armstrong's signature is generally found on 8 × 10 photographs. They are usually signed and inscribed. Many non-inscribed photographs do, however, exist. Signed business cards are scarce but do surface every now and then. First-day covers are also available but scarce. Signed letters are very scarce and typically limited to typed letters signed. An autographed letter signed would be very rare. Armstrong favored blue ink when signing official NASA-issued photographs. Photographs signed in black ink should be considered per se suspect and examined very carefully as they are very likely forgeries.

His signature sells in the $400 to $500 range. Signed 8 × 10 photographs and letters can sell for over $1,500. Exceptional images will sell for more than $5,000. ALsS are typically signed with his first name only, and are valued at $6,000 to $8,000. I have often wondered what a signature penned with his famous quote would sell for. I have never

Armstrong-1, undated signature (courtesy Nate D. Sanders Auctions).

seen a genuine quote signed. I think it would easily sell for $25,000.

Armstrong-2, undated signature (courtesy Nate D. Sanders Auctions).

Aldrin's signature is far easier to obtain. He engages in mass signings and the supply is much greater than that of crewmate Armstrong. Aldrin's signature can be found on letters, photographs, and index cards. A few canceled bank checks are in the market. Many signed copies of his books *Encounter with Tiber* and *Men from Earth* are in the market and are a good source for Aldrin's signature. Aldrin-signed books can be secured for $50 to $75. Signed photographs sell in the $100 range with exceptional specimens valued at $400 to $500. Signed bank checks should sell for $200.

Aldrin-1, undated signature.

Michael Collins's signature is less common than that of Aldrin. By all accounts he seems to be a very private man. As with Armstrong, obtaining a signature in the mail would be un-

likely. His signature is generally found on 8 × 10 photographs and the occasional first-day postal cover. They are many forged 8 × 10 and 16 × 20 photographs in the market. They are signed as "Michael Collins, Apollo XI Command Module Pilot, June 20, 1969." These forgeries are fairly well-executed, so caution is warranted. His signature sells for $150 to $200. Signed 8 × 10 photographs are valued at $500 to $600.

Collins, M-1 signed book (courtesy Nate D. Sanders Auctions).

To find all three signed on one item is a treasure. Signed 8 × 10 photographs and the occasional first-day cover do surface. Anything signed by all three is very scarce and commands a premium. More than 90 percent of *Apollo 11* crew-signed material is forged, so caution is warranted. Genuine signed items are typically valued in the $4,000 to $6,000 range. There is one forgery to discuss. These are 8 × 10 photographs featuring the lunar landscape with the Earth floating in the backdrop. Forgeries of Armstrong, Aldrin, and Collins are placed on the surface of the moon. An inscription, purportedly in Armstrong's hand, is typically written in the center of the moon's surface just under the image of the Earth. Some are inscribed to members of the NASA team as "Thanks for your years of effort" or something to that effect. The forgery of Aldrin typically lacks the paraph that is found on a genuine signature. The forgeries are well-executed, so caution is warranted.

Other Moonwalkers

In addition to Armstrong and Aldrin, 10 other men have walked on the lunar surface. They are Pete Conrad, Alan Bean, Alan Shepard, Edgar Mitchell, David Scott, Jim Irwin, John Young, Charles Duke, Gene Cernan, and Harrison Schmitt.

Signatures of the above referenced men are in high demand and greatly coveted by collectors. Three have since passed on: Irwin, Shepard, and Conrad. Their signatures are typically found on photographs, postal covers, and business cards.

Shepard hit two golf balls on the lunar surface. He is the only human ever to play golf on another world. Signed golf-related material is in much demand and rarely surfaces. Signed golf balls are in the market and close to 100 percent are forgeries. A genuine signed golf ball is likely valued over $5,000. Signed 8 × 10 photographs sell anywhere from $300 to $500. Exceptional signed images will sell for $1,000 to $1,500.

Conrad was a fairly responsive signer and his signature is found on photographs and postal covers. There is also a small supply of bank checks in the market. Checks are uncommon and sell for $75 to $100.

Irwin's signature has superior eye appeal and on occasion he would draw a crescent moon after his name. Replication of Irwin's hand would be rather difficult. Well-executed forgeries are limited.

Bean signs in a very unusual hand. The signature is vertical in nature and accomplished in a somewhat printed script. His signature has good display value. Bean is also an artist who paints moonscapes. The paintings are unique in that he applies a small amount of moon dust to the paintings. Paintings sell for a minimum of $25,000. Some of his works sell for over $200,000.

Bean-1, undated signature (courtesy Nate D. Sanders Auctions).

Cernan-1, undated signature.

Conrad-1, bank check dated 1989.

Duke-1, undated signature.

Irwin-1, undated signature with sketch (courtesy collection of Dennis Hoffner).

Mitchell, E-1, undated signature.

Schmitt-1, undated signature.

Scott-1, undated signature.

Young, J-1 undated signature.

Young, J-2, autopen.

Apollo I

The first manned mission of the Apollo program was to occur on February 21, 1967. During a preflight test on January 27, 1967, the command module caught fire, killing crewmembers Grissom, Edward H. White, and Roger Chaffee. White signed in a complex and flowing hand. Letter construction is sound. A superior eye appeal is noted. White's signature is somewhat scarce but a decent supply of material exists. He was targeted by collectors in the 1960s. Signa-

tures can be found on NASA-issued 8 × 10 photographs, TLsS, and FDCs. His signature is complex in nature, so well-executed forgeries are limited but do exist. Forgeries can be found on TLsS. In addition there is a large supply of forged photographs featuring White's spacewalk. His signature is in much demand, so expect to pay $500 to $600. TLsS sell for $1,250 to $1,500. A nicely signed 8 × 10 photograph will sell closer to $2,000.

White, E H-1, signature circa 1965 (courtesy collection of Richard Saffro).

A far less common signature is that of fellow crew member Roger Chaffee. His signature is legible and simple in construction. The signature is accomplished in a slower hand. Replication of hand is fairly easy. Well-executed forgeries exist in quantities. Many forged photographs exist in the market. Signatures are generally found on postal covers and NASA issued 8 × 10 photographs. Letters of any kind are scarce to rare. Demand and value are comparable to those of Edward White.

Chaffee-1, signature circa 1965 (courtesy collection of Richard Saffro).

There are many astronauts to choose from and all make fine additions to any signature library: Jack Lousma, Jim Bagian, Joe Kerwin, Bill Anders, Vance Brand, and the list goes on. Signatures of the early astronauts will continue to increase in value and will prove to be one of the finest investments you can make.

*   *   *

In 2012, forgeries of early aviation legends entered the market. Given the sound execution of the forgeries, they need to be discussed. They have appeared on the Internet, including the auction site eBay. The main target of this forger appears to be vintage aviation autographs, but given his skill I am sure other non-aviation forgeries exist. Forgeries include Orville Wright, Charles Lindbergh, Amelia Earhart, Ferdinand von Zeppelin, Italo Balbo, Hugo Eckener (signed as "Dr. Eckener"), Jimmy Doolittle, and Wiley Post and Harold Gatty. Forgeries of the less expensive signatures, such as Richard Byrd, C.E. Rosendahl, and Canadian ace Billy Bishop also exist.

The forgeries are placed mostly on early commemorative airmail postal covers and vintage picture postcards. Many of the Lindbergh forgeries are placed on Lindbergh-flown airmail covers which are postmarked in 1927 or 1928. Given the complex nature of Doolittle and Zeppelin signatures, the forgeries of these two are exposed with little effort. The Earhart, Lindbergh, Post, and Wright forgeries are very nice. Under careful examination it becomes clear that the forger does not quite have the right hand speed. An *extremely* slight hesitation can be seen in the forgeries. Magnification enhances this ever so slight hesitation. The forgeries tend to be slightly mis-scaled. The Earhart forgeries have slightly more height than a genuine specimen. The Lindbergh tends to be a bit smaller than his flamboyant signature of the 1920s.

Nonetheless, this forger's work product is very good.

These forgeries are being offered for sale at low prices, which should raise a warning flag. Wright, Earhart, and Lindbergh-signed covers are being offered for well under $500. These are very tricky, so careful examination is needed.

Project Excelsior

Joe Kittinger was a test pilot who made the first solo crossing of the Atlantic in a hot air balloon. On August 16, 1960, Kittinger made the highest parachute dive in history, known as Project Excelsior. He jumped 102,000 feet (19 miles) and reached record speeds of over 600 miles per hour. His record stood until 2012. Kittinger has for many years been a willing signer. His signature is still considered uncommon and generally limited to postal covers.

Kittinger-1, signature circa 2005.

Mechanics, Medicine
and Molecules: Science

I have always been fascinated by science. It was the one area of study I excelled at in an otherwise average scholastic career. Science, simply put, is the study of the natural world based upon facts learned through observation and/or experimentation with an occasional assumption tossed in. There are many fields of study to choose from: astronomy, paleontology, chemistry, biology, geology (my personal favorite), and on and on. Some of the most famous names in history arise from the sciences. Thomas Edison, Albert Einstein, and Isaac Newton are almost mythical figures in history.

Science can trace its birth to the nebulous world of mysticism. After the fall of the Roman Empire, Europe entered a period known as the Dark Ages. At that time, the primary goal in life was survival. There was no time for the pursuit of abstract thought. As the centuries progressed, a certain uniformity settled across Europe and Asia, allowing time for more intellectual activities. During the height of the Middle Ages man was engaged in experimenting with the world around them. The scientists of the day were more like snake-oil salesmen. To answer why was less important than the outcome. It led to fantastic claims of spinning common metals into gold, love potions, and the fabled homunculus conjured up from incense and spices.

The mid– to late Renaissance brought forth many great minds. At this time science advanced greatly. Though the period of intellec-

tual rebirth ended in the late 1600s, many great men of this era remain household names. The greatest among them were Leonardo da Vinci, Nikolaus Copernicus, Tycho Brahe, Galileo Galilei, and Rene Descartes.

Today, the progress of science and technology is so great that mankind can peer into the nether regions of the atom, cast a gaze upon the outer heavens, send probes to the ice worlds of the Kuiper Belt, and turn lead into gold (no longer is alchemy a nonsensical pursuit of the mad man).

Autographs, manuscripts, and other scientific writings have been actively pursued for hundreds of years. Some of the early science-related signatures are extremely rare and basically unobtainable. Most of the very rare signatures are held by governmental concerns. Some do not exist at all. Collectors will focus on the more attainable signatures. Some fields are more popular than others. Astronomy and medicine seem to garner the most attention, though other fields are collectable.

Astronomy

Astronomy is an utterly fascinating field of study. The universe and its hidden mysteries are truly mind-boggling, and can lead to heated debates. While attending Lawrence Tech, I questioned one of my astronomy professors as to the validity of the Big Bang, which I personally consider nonsense. To my esteemed professor's statement: "It was the beginning and that all matter that exists today originated from the singularity," I replied, "Who or what created the matter and placed it in the singularity to begin with?" My question was met with silence. When all was said and done, I think it cost me a full grade. Such is life.

Here are a few of the more collectable names associated with the study of the outer heavens.

Frederick William Herschel was a man of many talents. He was an astronomer, a man of letters, and a composer. He is most famous for discovering the planet Uranus and two of its moons. He died in 1822. Herschel's signature is rare and seldom enters the market. When is does, it is typically found on ALsS or signatures removed therefrom. Signatures are signed as "Wm. Herschel." His signature is a target of forgers. Many period letters have variant signatures with inconsistencies among the signatures. Some are likely written and signed by someone other than Herschel. Herschel's signature is quite affordable and letters can be purchased for under $1,000. His signature should not be confused with that of his son Sir John Frederick William Herschel (d. 1871), also a man of science.

Herschel-1, undated signature.

Clyde Tombaugh is only one of four men in the history of mankind, outside of the ancients, to discover a planet within the Solar System. In 1930 he discovered the planet Pluto. Tombaugh signed in a rather plain but legible hand. His signature has sound letter construction and average display value. Tombaugh lived until 1997 and was a responsive signer. There is an ample supply of science-related material in the marketplace, including signed images of Pluto. Index cards exist in quantities. Many ALsS, with stunning astronomy content, exist and are

highly prized by collectors. Letters discussing the possibility of life on Europa or the destruction of the inter-Mercurial planet Vulcan can be found. Content letters are being removed from the market, likely by institutional collections, and are becoming harder to find.

In recent years the demand for Tombaugh material has increased dramatically due to much interest in Pluto and its status as a planet. In 2006 some European astronomy club downgraded Pluto to dwarf-planet status. Though generally not accepted in the United States, the designation generated much press and interest in Tombaugh. The July 2015 flyby performed by the probe *New Horizons* kept Pluto in the headlines. Demand outweighs supply for Tombaugh's signature. His signature is a real sleeper name in the world of autographs. As time goes by, Tombaugh's signature will be in great demand. Secure all you can. Index cards are the most affordable at $25 to $30. ALsS with routine content sell for $100 to $150. An ALS with planetary content is valued at $500 to $750. Items countersigned by fellow astronomer James Christy, who discovered Pluto's moon, Charon, are scarce and make for a fine collectable.

Tombaugh-1, signature dated 1989.

John Couch Adams was a British astronomer and mathematician who discovered the planet Neptune via mathematical formula. The discovery is also claimed, in part, by French mathematician Urbain Le Verrier. Adams signed in a precise and flowing hand. His signature is rare, even rarer than that of Herschel. The occasional ALS, sometimes in the third person, enters the market. Portions of his diary from the mid–1840s, with scientific content, have survived. These are generally held by an institutional concern. There have been no recent sales of Adams's signature. His signature is a true 19th-century rarity. Le Verrier is much more common, at least when compared to Adams. A decent supply of ALsS are in the market. Expect to pay $200 to $300 for a nice Le Verrier specimen.

Adams, J. C.-1 undated ALS.

Le Verrier-1, ALS dated 1868.

American physicist James Van Allen is best remembered as the man who discovered Earth's radiation belts, named the "Van Allen Belts" in his honor. He was also deeply involved with military rocketry during World War II. Van Allen signed in a pensive hand. His signature is average in all aspects. Van Allen was a willing and gracious signer throughout his life. Today, there is an ample supply of material in the market, mostly limited to index cards and first-day covers. Signed 8 × 10 photographs are uncommon and many images have Van Allen posing with a rocket. These are highly collectable. ALsS are scarce and a few will have scientific formulas incorporated within the text of the letter. Like Tombaugh, I consider Van Allen to be another sleeper name. Index cards can be purchased for $10 to $20. Signed 8 × 10 photographs are valued at $50 to $75. A full-page ALS

is worth $150 to $200. An ALS with the aforementioned formulas imbedded in the text is highly prized by collectors, so expect to pay $300 to $400 for a nice specimen. Van Allen should prove a fine investment signature in the years to come.

Van Allen-1 signature dated 2003.

American physicist Arno Penzias received the Nobel Prize for his discovery of cosmic background radiation. Penzias signed in a rapid and unstructured hand. His signature has poor display value. Letter construction is substandard, and individual letters are replaced by straight lines. There is a limited supply of Penzias signatures in the market, generally limited to index cards. Other mediums are scarce. Signed books do exist and some are penned with full-page ALsS which make for a treasured item. His signature is valued at $35 to $40. Signed books are valued at $100.

Penzias-1, signature dated 1990.

Isaac Newton is perhaps the greatest name in the history of science. Though a mathematician by trade, he is best remembered for "discovering" gravity. His book *Philosophiae Naturalis Principia Mathematica*, published in 1687, is considered one of the most important writings ever. Newton signed in the typical labored hand of the 17th century. The hand is slow and pensive. The display value is average. There is nothing remarkable about the construction of the signature. Most signatures are accomplished as "Is. Newton." Given the rudimentary nature of hand, replication is very easy. Producing a well-executed forgery can be created with ease. Forgeries exist in quantities, and just about 100 percent of all Newton signatures ever offered for sale are the product of forgery. Forgeries exist on letters, documents, signatures purportedly removed from ledger pages, and the like. Many forged AMs are also in the market. Newton is one of the most desired autographs. The cost of his signature is prohibitive. Back in the 1980s Newton's signature was valued at $4,000 to $5,000. Today, expect to pay $12,500 to $15,000. ALsS are very rare and will likely sell for $75,000 to $100,000. Short fragments of AMs are valued at $10,000 to $15,000. A full-page AM will sell for $50,000 to $75,000. Significant content writings will likely sell for many hundreds of thousands of dollars.

Newton-1, undated signature.

American Edwin Hubble is considered one of the greatest astronomers in history. He was an early pioneer of intergalactic studies. Hubble signed in a clean and crisp hand. The signature has good letter construction and legibility. An average display value is noted. Hubble died in 1953 and his signature is rare on a per se basis. The occasional ALS will surface but that is about it. Other mediums are very rare. Given the extreme value of his signature, he is commonly targeted by forgers. Just about all signatures in the market are forgeries. His signature is valued at $1,500 to $2,000. A full-page ALS will sell for at least $5,000.

Hubble-1, signature circa 1930.

Sir Fred Hoyle is one of my favorite scientists. He was a nuts-and-bolts astronomer who dealt with the science of astronomy and not the fanciful theories best left to Captain Kirk and Dr. Smith. He coined the term "Big Bang," a theory he dismissed as folly. Needless to say, he is not a favorite of the "bangerhead" crowd. Hoyle signed in a carefree and rather unstructured hand. The signature displays itself as sloppy. Though he died in 2001, his signature is rather uncommon. He authored many books on astronomy and science fiction. These are a wonderful source of Hoyle's signature. TLsS are also available. Other mediums are scarce. His signature sells for about $50. Signed books are available at $100.

Hoyle-1, undated signature.

Medicine

I have always admired the medical profession and the doctors who endeavor to heal the sick. Surgeons are of particular interest to me. The knowledge, confidence, and steady hand needed to operate on the human body are skills out of reach for most of us lay persons. Decades ago, Dr. Ralph Magnell was a rather famous stomach surgeon in Detroit. Whenever a police officer took a bullet to the gut, it was Magnell who would spend 10 to 15 hours in the operating room undertaking a very delicate and life-saving surgery. Men and women of medicine are very much admired and because of this, their signatures are widely collected.

Edward Jenner was an English physician who developed the smallpox vaccine. He is considered the father of immunology. Jenner signed in a choppy but legible hand. His signature evidences sound letter construction. His signature is consider rare and is generally limited to ALsS or signatures removed therefrom. The occasional signed book from Jenner's library will surface. In the 1980s his signature was of little interest and value. Today, there is good demand for Jenner material. Expect to pay $1,000 for his autograph. An ALS will sell for $3,000 to $3,500.

Jenner-1, signed book (courtesy Nate D. Sanders Auctions).

Canadian doctor Frederick Banting was the doctor who, along with Charles Best, discovered insulin. Banting's signature is average in all respects. There is nothing extraordinary about it. Given the practical nature of the signature, replication of hand is easy. Well-executed forgeries do exist. Banting died in 1941 from injuries sustained in a plane crash. Due to an early death, Banting's signature is rare on a per se basis. His signature is usually found on album pages where he adds "University of Toronto" under the signature. ALsS do exist, and most are signed with just his first name. Photographs, usually portraits, are rare and highly desired. There is strong demand for Banting's signature, which is valued at $400 to $500. An ALS signed in full is valued at $1,500.

Banting-1, album page dated 1937.

Best lived until 1978 but signed relatively few items. For a man who died so relatively recently, his signature is scarce on a per se basis. He was a willing signer, but time, for autograph purposes, passed Dr. Best by. Collectors rarely sought him out for an autograph. Today, his sig-

nature is in good demand simply because of the restricted supply of material. His signature surfaces on the occasional index card or TLS. Photographs are rare. Expect to pay $75 to $100 for his signature. Premium items are valued at $200 to $250.

Best-1, undated signature.

South African surgeon Christiaan Barnard performed the first heart transplant on December 3, 1967. Barnard signed in a very flowing and unstructured hand. The signature evidences good flow but is generally illegible. Letters tend to blend together. Display value is average. Barnard was generally not a responsive signer in the mail. There is a less than ample supply of his signatures in the market. Signatures are generally found on index cards. Letters and photographs are uncommon. An ALS is very scarce. Barnard's signature is still relatively affordable. Index cards can be purchased for under $50. TLsS and photographs are more expensive and generally sell for $100 to $150. A full-page ALS would likely sell for $500.

Barnard, C-1, undated signature (courtesy The Sanders Autograph Price Guide).

American surgeon Denton Cooley was the first surgeon to implant an artificial heart. Cooley signs in a confined and flowing hand. The signature evidences good letter construction and legibility. Average display value is noted. Cooley has been a responsive signer for years. His signature is typically found on index cards, first-day covers, photographs, and ANsS. Signed business cards do exist but are scarce. Due to the sound market inventory, Cooley's signature is quite affordable. Most mediums can generally be purchased for under $50. A full page ALS is rare and will likely sell for $200 to $250.

Cooley-1, signature dated 2011.

An American surgeon of Lebanese descent, Michael DeBakey was one the first surgeons to perform heart bypass surgery. He developed the roller pump, which made open heart surgery a reality. DeBakey signed in a rapid and flowing hand. The signature appears fast on paper. Signatures are usually accomplished in fountain pen, which makes for a handsome display. DeBakey lived to the age of 99. He was a willing signer for most of those years. Today, there is a sound supply of material in the market. Signatures can be found on most mediums, though index cards and first-day covers are most common. ALsS are scarce and usually limited to short writings. TLsS are much more common. As of this writing, there seems to be marginal demand for DeBakey material. His signature can be purchased for $25. TLsS and 8 × 10 photographs are valued at $75. A full-page ALS is in demand, so expect to pay $250 to $300.

Debakey-1 signature, circa 1990.

Alexander Fleming was a Scottish biologist who won the Nobel Prize in 1945 for the discovery of the antibiotic penicillin. Fleming signed in a flowing hand. Legibility and letter construction are sound. The letter "F" in the last name enhances display value. The signature is sometimes finished with a paraph. Overall, an average, yet pleasing signature. Signatures

penned in the 1950s will evidence a slight unsteadiness of hand. The supply of Fleming material is ample, as many letters, both TLsS and ALsS, are in the market. Some of these have excellent medical content. After winning the Nobel Prize, he became a target of autograph collectors; hence, there are many album pages, index cards, and calling cards in the market. Signed photographs are somewhat scarce. There is good demand for this giant of 20th-century medicine. His signature sells for $200 to $250. TLsS are valued at $400 to $500. A full-page ALS will easily sell for $1,000, one with medical content closer to $2,500. Signed photographs are desirable and are valued at $750 to $900.

Fleming, A-1, undated signature (courtesy The Sanders Autograph Price Guide).

Sigmund Freud was an Austrian neurologist. He is considered the father of psychoanalysis, a pseudoscience that attempts to explain why we do what we do. Freud signed in a bold and slightly choppy hand. The signature is marked with heavy strokes and jutting lines. Signatures are typically signed as "Sigm. Freud." Many times he signed letters with his last name only. Given the slower nature of the hand, replication is rather easy. Well-executed forgeries exist in quantities. Signatures are generally found on TLsS, ALsS, and ANsS. There is a small supply of ALsS, written to fellow doctors, that have very good, somewhat rambling medical content. These are treasured by collectors. Photographs are rare to very rare, and most offered in the market are forged. There is very strong demand for Freud material. A signature is valued at $1,000 to $1,250. TLsS sell for $2,500 to $3,000. ALsS are valued at $4,000 to $5,000. Full-page ALsS with content will easily sell for more than $10,000. Photographs are also highly valued. A nice portrait specimen will sell for $10,000 to $15,000.

Freud-1, ALS dated 1938.

Noted Swiss psychiatrist Carl Jung founded what is known as analytical psychology. It is a school of thought that develops the inner self with societal needs. Jung signed in a neat hand. His signature is compact. Display value and letter construction are on the average side. Signatures are usually signed as "C.G. Jung." Hand speed is muted; hence, replication is easy. Producing a well-executed forgery can be done with ease. Forged photographs are in the market. The forgery appears unsteady. Many of these are accomplished in bluish-green fountain pen. The forgery is usually, but not always, placed at the bottom of the image. Jung's signature is scarce. He lived until the 1960s but was a reluctant signer. Signatures are found on TLsS or signatures removed therefrom. Full-page ALsS are very rare. There is good demand for Jung material. His signature is valued in the $500 to $600 range. A TLS will sell for $1,250 to $1,500. A nice ALS is valued in the $4,000 to $5,000 price range.

Jung-1, undated signature (courtesy The Sanders Autograph Price Guide).

French physician Joseph Ignace Guillotin advocated the use of Antoine Louis's beheading machine to carry out executions in a humane fashion. The machine now bears his name and is synonymous with Robespierre and the French Revolution. Guillotin signed in a bold and flamboyant hand. Display value is sound as the large capital letter "G" enhances eye appeal. Signatures are accomplished with his last name only. Given the slower nature of hand, replication is easy. Well-executed forgeries exist in quantities. Chances are if you see a signature for sale it is a forgery. Signatures are rare to very rare on a per se basis. There is a restricted supply of DsS and LsS in the market. There is a small cache of forged LsS in the market. They are typically addressed to fellow doctors or university officials. The letters are typically dated on the left side of the paper, towards the bottom of the page. The forgeries evidence a slight unsteadiness. Overall, these forgeries are rather convincing. Signatures of another French doctor, J.M. Guillotin, and a French government official with the same last name are in the market. Their signatures should not be confused with the famous Dr. Guillotin, but often are. His signature is valued at $1,000. LsS are closer to $2,000.

Guillotin-1, undated signature.

Guillotin-2, a Guillotin but not THE Guillotin.

Michigander Jack Kevorkian is known as the Angel of Death. He openly advocated for medically assisted suicide. I had the opportunity to speak with Jack on several occasions as he did his after-dinner constitutionals walking the streets of downtown Royal Oak, Michigan. Kevorkian signed in a practical hand. Letter construction and legibility are sound. The display value is average. Most signatures were inscribed and he would add the letters "M.D." after his signature. The supply of material is limited. He did not honor mail requests for his signature. He would generally not sign for the public on advice of counsel. Signatures tend to surface on books that he authored, such as *glimmerIQs.* Other mediums, such as photographs and letters, are rare. Kevorkian was a rather skilled painter of the macabre and he signed a limited number of prints. There is good demand for Kevorkian material. Though he died in 2011, his signature is valued at $100. Signed books are closer to $200. The asking price for prints is $500. Actual paintings are rare and have an estimated value of $15,000 to $30,000. Kevorkian's signature should prove a fine investment in the years to come.

Kevorkian-1, signature dated 1995.

American biochemist Arthur Kornberg won the 1959 Nobel Prize for his pioneer work of the DNA structure. Kornberg signed in a very muted hand. The signature tends to be small with malformed letters. Both legibility and letter construction are poor. The signature has poor display value. Signatures are typically signed as "A. Kornberg." There is a good inventory of signatures in the market as Kornberg was a willing and gracious signer through the mail. Most signatures are found on index cards and first-day covers. Letters, business cards, and photographs are uncommon to scarce. A full ALS is rare and highly desired. Demand for Kornberg material is balanced with supply. His signature is affordable at $25. A nice ALS will sell for $225 to $250.

Kornberg-1 signature circa 1990.

British surgeon Joseph Lister made great advances in surgery by introducing sterilization of surgical instruments. He was the strong advocate of using carbolic acid to clean wounds. His recommendations led to a reduction in post-operative death due to infection. Lister signed in a pleasing hand. The signature lacks hesitation. Average display value is noted. Signatures are sometimes accomplished with just his last name. Due to average letter construction, replication of hand is relatively easy. Well-executed forgeries do exist. Lister's signature is typically found on ALsS or signatures removed therefrom. Other mediums are very rare. Lister lived until 1912; hence, he did sign a limited number of cabinet cards. These are usually inscribed to fellow doctors. Signed photographs of any kind should be considered rare. Demand seems to have waned for Lister material over the past decade. Values have declined slightly. Lister's signature can be purchased for $200 to $250. A signature with his last name only is valued at $100 to $125. ALsS sell for $600 to $700. A letter signed with his last name is affordable at $300 to $350.

Lister-1, undated signature (courtesy The Sanders Autograph Price Guide).

William J. Mayo and Charles H. Mayo were two of the founders of the Mayo Clinic. The signatures are of average letter construction. Both tend to have a degree of choppiness, more so with Charles. Average display value is noted.

The supply of material is ample. Both signed many autographs for collectors. Given the limited value of the signatures they are typically not the target of skilled forgers. Album pages and index cards are the most common. Photographs are scarce, albeit borderline. TLsS are uncommon but available. An ALS of either is rare. Charles Mayo's son, Charles W. Mayo, was a noted surgeon; his signature is sometimes confused with his father's signature. Signatures of the Mayo brothers have been, and will likely remain, affordable. There has not been much movement in price over the past decade. Signatures are valued at $50 each. Signed portrait photographs can be purchased for $150 to $200, which seems like a bargain considering the significance of the Mayo name in the field of medicine.

Mayo, C-1, signed card (courtesy Nate D. Sanders Auctions).

Mayo, C-2, signature of Charles Mayo, Jr.

Mayo, W-1, signed card (courtesy Nate D. Sanders Auctions).

English surgeon James Paget is best remembered for the bone disease that bears his name.

Paget signed in a very angled and precise hand. The tight letter formation results in a signature with above average display value. It is one of the nicer medical autographs. Though he was generally not targeted by autograph collectors of the day, there seems to be a good supply of ALsS and ANsS in the market, which makes Paget's signature rather affordable. ALsS, usually penned on small 8vo or 16mo sheets, are available at $75 to $125. One of the more attainable 19th-century medical autographs.

Paget-1 ALS dated 1891.

Albert Sabin developed the first oral polio vaccine. He was the first to determine the virus resided in the intestines and his vaccine prevented the bug from entering the bloodstream. Sabin signed in a smaller, more confined hand. Tight letter construction is noted. His signature works well on small mediums. The supply of Sabin material is ample. Signatures are found on index cards and first-day covers. ALsS are scarce and have superior eye appeal. Sabin wrote gracious, well-thought-out letters. Signed 8 × 10 photographs are uncommon. Sabin's signature is valued at $75. An 8 × 10 photograph is valued at $250 to $300. A full-page ALS is prized, so expect to pay $450 to $500.

Sabin-1, undated signature.

Jonas Salk was the man who first developed the polio vaccine. Salk signed in a very pensive hand. His signature lacks rapid motion and is easily forged. Many well-executed forgeries exist in the market. Given the ease of replication, I estimate that 90 percent of all Salk signatures in the market are forged. Salk proved an erratic signer at best. Most mail requests for his signature were ignored. Signatures are usually found on index cards and first-day covers. Signed 8 × 10 photographs are uncommon to scarce, though Salk handed out portrait photographs on occasion. Letters of any kind are rare. Salk is a giant of 20th-century medicine, which correlates into sound demand. His signature is valued at $50. Signed 8 × 10 photographs are valued at $200 to $250. Signed books sell for $175 to $225. A full-page ALS is valued at $500 to $600. Certain medical content letters are highly valued. One superior TLS, regarding AIDS research, sold for $2,600 (RR Auctions, 2010). First-day covers countersigned by fellow polio researcher Sabin are in high demand and are valued at $250 to $300.

Salk-1, undated signature.

James Watson and Francis Crick won the 1962 Nobel Prize, along with Maurice Wilkins, for their discovery of the DNA structure. This is a very popular group of autographs. Watson's signature is small and of rudimentary structure. For one so brilliant, his signature is so simple. It is easily forged. Well-executed forgeries exist in quantities. Crick also signed in an average hand as well. His signature can be replicated with relative ease. Well-executed forgeries exist in quantities. Chances are if you run across an item signed by both, it is just about guaranteed to be a forgery. Watson was a generally responsive signer in the mail, but cut back substantially in 2012. Crick was much tougher. The supply of Crick material is restricted. The demand for these two signatures is quite sound. Value continues to increase at a sound pace. Watson authored *The Double Helix* and signed first editions are valued at over $1,000. Later editions sell for $400 to $500. *The Double Helix* is one of the most forged books published in the last 50 years. A book signed by both men will sell for $1,500 to $2,500. Another common forgery is the famous photo of Watson and Crick standing near a model of a DNA structure. This is one of the most forged pictures of all time. Many times this photograph contains a genuine Watson signature and a Crick forgery is added. A genuinely signed photograph of both men is a rarity. Wilkins is a scarce signature on a per se basis. An item signed by all three is very rare. Wilkins's signature is valued at $200 to $250. A Wilkins ALS will sell for $1,000 to $1,250.

Wilkins, M-1, AMS circa 1950 (courtesy Nate D. Sanders Auctions).

Watson-1 BCS 2005.

Crick-1, undated signature.

Chemistry

Marie Curie was a Polish chemist who pioneered research in the field of radioactivity. She, along with her husband Pierre Curie, discovered the "miracle" element of radium in 1898. She is considered one of the most important chemists ever. In 1934 she died of cancer, likely caused by exposure to radioactive elements. Curie signed in a pleasing flowing and legible hand. Recklessness of hand is lacking. The signature has sound letter construction with well-formed letters. Most signatures are accomplished as simply "M. Curie." Her signature is rare on a per se basis. Signatures are found mostly on letters or signatures removed therefrom. Photographs are very rare and just about all ever offered for sale are forgeries. I estimate that more than 90 percent of Curie signatures in the market are forgeries. There is one common forgery to discuss. Several years ago a small grouping of forgeries entered the market. They are signed 5"x4" (approximately) note cards. The letterhead reads "Faculté Des Sciences De Paris." A forgery of Curie is placed on the bottom edge of the card signed as either "M. Curie" or "Marie Curie." The rest of the card is left blank. The forgeries are fairly well-executed but exposed upon examination. There is strong demand for Curie's signature, which is valued at

$1,000 to $1,250. ALsS with routine content are valued at $5,000 to $6,000. Letters with good scientific content are valued at $15,000 to $20,000. Pierre's signature is even rarer with comparable value.

Humphry Davy was an English chemist who discovered many elements, among them calcium and magnesium. Davy signed in a rather unassuming hand. The signature is pensive in nature. The signature evidences good letter construction and legibility. Most signatures are accomplished as "H. Davy." The signature lacks complexity; hence, replication of hand is easy. Well-executed forgeries are in the market. Many forgeries are found on engravings of Davy. Davy's signature is scarce to rare on a per se basis. Signatures are found almost exclusively on ALsS. Many signatures are found in the text of the letter as a third-person signature. There is average demand for Davy material, which to me seems surprising. Given the restricted supply of material, prices for his signature are surprisingly affordable. ALsS can be purchased for $750 to $1,000.

Davy-1, undated signature (courtesy The Sanders Autograph Price Guide).

Curie, M-1, signed book dated 1923.

Curie, P-1 undated signature.

Michael Faraday was an English chemist. He discovered benzene. He also did much to advance the study of electromagnetism. Faraday signed in a very odd hand. He signed his name beginning with the last name and incorporating the letter "M" of the first name. Signatures are almost always found as "M. Faraday." It is a signature of average construction and display value. The many breaks in the hand result in easy replication. Well-executed forgeries do exist in the market. There is a restricted supply of material in the market and basically limited to ALsS or portions thereof. His signature is in good demand and outweighs supply. Faraday's autograph will sell for $300 to $400. ALsS range from $500 to $1,500 depending on length.

Faraday-1, undated signature (courtesy The Sanders Autograph Price Guide).

French chemist Louis Pasteur was one of the first scientists to understand the link between microbes and disease. He is known for creating vaccines against rabies and anthrax. Pasteur is one of the most important figures in the history of science. Pasteur signed in a flowing hand. His signature is average is just about every respect. Signatures are accomplished as "L. Pasteur." There are many variations of Pasteur's hand in the market. Some authorities attribute this to moodiness on the part of Pasteur. I attribute these variations to the work product of forgers. Well-executed forgeries exist in quantities. Forgeries are found on ALsS, ANsS, and cabinet cards. Forged letters of Pasteur have been in the market for decades. They have attained a nice vintage appearance due to age. Pasteur letters must be examined carefully as many forgeries exist. Pasteur is always in demand, so expect to pay $500 to $750 for a nice signature. ALsS will

Pasteur-1, undated signature.

sell for $4,000 to $5,000. An ALS, with scientific content, is valued at $10,000 or more. Autographically, an important signature.

American Glenn Seaborg was a chemist who discovered 10 elements including plutonium and element 106, now called seaborgium in his honor. Seaborg signed in a fairly rapid yet unstructured hand. Letter construction is marginal, as many letters display themselves as indistinguishable strokes. An average display value is noted. Given the loose construction of his signature, replication of hand would be rather easy. Producing a well-executed forgery would take little effort. Seaborg was a willing and gracious signer through the mail. There is a good supply of material in the market, though mostly limited to index cards and first-day covers. Other mediums, such as letters and photographs, are uncommon. A restricted supply of ALsS exist, many with scientific content. Seaborg would, on occasion, hand out multi-page AMsS to collectors. These have wonderful chemistry content and are worth a premium. The demand for Seaborg material is sound. His autograph should prove a sound investment. Seaborg's autograph is affordable at $40 to $50. TLsS and 8 × 10 photographs are valued at $100 to $125. A full-page ALS should sell for $300 to $350. The above-referenced manuscripts are in much demand, so expect to pay $500-$750 for a nice two- or three-page writing.

Seaborg-1, signature circa 1990.

Linus Pauling was a chemist and peace activist. He did much study on chemical bonding. He was awarded the 1954 Nobel Prize. Pauling signed in a large and legible hand. Superior letter construction is noted. Pauling was generally a responsive signer and today there is a good supply of material available for purchase. Signatures can be found on TLsS, books, first-day covers, small photographs, and index cards. His signature can be purchased for $50 on most mediums; hence, he is not the target of skilled forgers. ALsS are rare and will likely sell for $300 to $400.

Pauling-1, undated signature.

Physics

Danish physicist Niels Bohr dedicated his life to the world of quantum theory. He was awarded the Nobel Prize in 1922. Bohr signed in an average hand. His signature evidences good flow but lacks complexity. Replication of hand is rather easy. Well-executed forgeries exist in quantities. There is an ample supply of material in the market. Early signatures are generally limited to letters. In the late 1950s, Bohr became popular with the autograph set and signed many items for collectors, including index cards and small postcard-sized photographs. There is a small group of forged ALsS in the market. They are placed on 16mo or 8vo sheets. These letters, which are written in English, contain routine content such as responding to an invitation or Christmas greetings. The letters are typically addressed to fellow doctors. There is good demand for Bohr's signature,

Bohr-1, undated signature (courtesy The Sanders Autograph Price Guide).

which will cost around $250 to $300. Photographs and ALsS are in the $1,500 to $2,000 range.

Perhaps the greatest mind of the 20th century is that of the German theoretical physicist Albert Einstein. He developed the theory of relativity. It is the most famous of all equations. He won the 1921 Nobel Prize. Einstein signed in a neat and compact hand. The signature lacks hesitation though recklessness is lacking. The signature is thoughtful and somewhat pensive. A sound letter construction is noted. The signature is legible. An average display value is noted. Einstein's hand remained strong for his entire life. Material signed only months before his death evidence only the slightest hesitation of hand. The pensive nature of hand results in a signature that is easily forged. Well-executed forgeries exist in great quantities. The vast majority of Einstein signatures offered in the market are forged. Unfortunately, many enter the market via established auction houses. Due to extreme value, Einstein is one of the most forged signatures in the field of autographs, science or otherwise. Skilled forgers have gone to great lengths to produce convincing forgeries. Embossed letterhead, bank checks, and postmarked covers have been counterfeited to enhance the forgeries. One forger has produced an exceptional quantity of forgeries. This forger usually takes genuine letterhead (not related to Einstein), such as hotel stationery, and places a forgery on the blank sheet. He then will add collector's notations as to where the signature was purportedly signed, to further the illusion of authenticity. This forger has also produces TLsS and photographs. The photographs are typically inscribed to fellow doctors. The forgeries are typically dated from the mid to late 1940s. The forgeries evidence a moderate amount of shakiness of hand, something a genuine signature would not exhibit. To the trained eye these forgeries are easily exposed. I am surprised at how many of these fakes are sold by long-established dealers and auction companies. Many are wrongly certified as genuine by the authentication companies. Another group of forgeries that surfaced years ago consist of handwritten scientific formulas signed by Einstein at the bottom of the page. These forgeries are fairly well-executed, but a slight unsteadiness of hand is noted. Many were accomplished in bright blue and aqua-blue fountain pen ink. Genuine Einstein written formulas are very rare and just about all ever offered for sale are forgeries. Many forged AQsS are in the market. They are typically written in German and limited to two to three sentences in length. They are accomplished in an overly fine fountain pen nib, which makes the strokes appear dainty and feminine. A favorite quote of this forger is, "One must tolerate the small follies of mankind in order to prevent the large ones." The sad truth is if you see an Einstein signature for sale, it is likely the product of a skilled forger. In addition, many TLsS on Emergency Committee of Atomic Scientists letterhead are secretarially signed. Secretarial signatures appear choppy and the individual letters appear compacted.

Demand for Einstein material is great and vastly outweighs supply. Values increase at a stunning rate. Signatures will now sell for $2,000 to $3,000. TLsS are valued at $4,000 to $5,000. ANsS, usually found on postcards, sell for $4,000 to $5,000. ALsS are highly treasured and regularly sell for $8,000 to $10,000. Good scientific content letters are actively sought by major institutions and can sell for $25,000 and up. Letters with historic content will easily sell for $100,000. A letter drafted to President Roosevelt, but never sent, with atomic bomb content sold for $2 million (Christies, 2002).

Einstein-1, undated signature.

Irish physicist Lord Kelvin (William Thomson) is best remembered for pinpointing the correct temperature of absolute zero at -459.68 F or 0 K. The Kelvin scale of temperature was named in his honor. Kelvin signed in a plain hand. His signature exhibits large letters with strong legibility. The hand is pensive and lacks reckless flow. Replication of hand would be rather easy. Producing a well-executed forgery can be done with ease. Kelvin's signature can be found signed before and after peerage. His signature is scarce on a per se basis but not rare. Most signatures are found on LsS. Signed cabinet cards are rare and most offered for sale are forged. There is average demand for Lord Kelvin's signature. It is quite affordable. LsS can be purchased for $150. A signature is valued around $100.

Kelvin-1, signature circa 1900.

Kelvin-2, signature before peerage.

Max Planck was a theoretical physicist who first put forth the quantum theory, a science dealing with the diminutive world of energy waves. Planck is not what you would call a household name, but to collectors his signature is in good demand. Planck signed in a choppy and abrupt hand. The signature evidences many starts and stops. An average letter construction is noted. Due to the many breaks in the hand, the signature is easily replicated. Producing a well-executed forgery can be done with relative ease. Planck was not targeted by collectors of the day. His signature is very scarce and generally limited to ALsS and ANsS. Photographs are very rare. Demand clearly outweighs a restricted supply. Planck's signature will sell for $400 to $500. A full-page ALS in valued at $1,250 to $1,500. As the science of quantum mechanics is further explored, Planck's signature will increase in value in the years to come.

Planck-1, ALS dated 1943.

Planck-1, undated signature.

Wilhelm Röntgen was a German physicist who is best remembered for the discovery of X-rays. For this he won the Nobel Prize in 1901. Röntgen signed in an aggressive and choppy hand. The signature is marked with abrupt strokes. Legibility is fairly sound, though letters are sometimes muted. The signature is usually finished off with a paraph. It is an average, unassuming signature. Replication of hand is fairly easy. Creating a well-executed forgery can be done with little effort. Röntgen's signature is very scarce and usually limited to ALsS and ANsS. Röntgen is a significant figure of early 20th-century science, and there is sound demand for his autograph. The restricted supply of material pushes values ever higher. An ALS is valued at $1,500 to $2,000. One with strong scientific content is closer to $5,000.

Röntgen-1, ALS circa 1900.

Hungarian theoretical physicist Edward Teller was a truly brilliant scientist and is remembered as the "father of the hydrogen bomb." He was also a member of the Manhattan Project. Teller signed in a sharp and rapid hand. The signature has impaired letter construction and legibility. The signature appears fast on paper. Due to the sloppy nature of hand, the signature has below average display value. Signatures signed in the last couple of years of his life evidence misplaced letters and moderate unsteadiness. It should be noted that Teller used an autopen to honor mail requests. Several template patterns for the last name exist. The first name has, to my knowledge, only one template. See illustration. There is an ample supply of Teller material in the market. Signatures are generally limited to index cards, first-day covers, and 8vo signed photographs. Letters of any kind are scarce. A full-page ALS is a rarity. Limited edition *Easton Press* books are also in the market but contain an infirmed and less attractive signature. There is good demand for Teller signed material. His signature is valued at $50. TLsS are valued at $125 to $150. A nice ALS should sell for $400 to $500.

Teller-1, signature dated 1990.

Teller-2, common auto-pen.

Peter Higgs is a British theoretical physicist of little notoriety outside of the academic world. His work led to the discovery of the Higgs boson. In 2013, he was awarded the Nobel Prize. In recent years his popularity among collectors has increased greatly. Higgs's signature is scarce on a per se basis. There is very little material in the market. He was never the target of autograph collectors. The occasional index card and photograph will surface. Letters of any kind are rare. Expect to pay $75 to $100 for Higgs's signature, which will prove a fine investment in years to come.

Higgs-1, signed photo dated 2015.

Exploration

Exploration is probably the most fascinating field of science and a favorite among collectors. It is actually one of the few fields of study the average person can undertake. You can't say that about quantum mechanics. All you need is a pair of hiking boots and a good deal of curiosity. Admittedly, that may be an oversimplification of the matter, but many people become casual explorers, usually on the weekends. Many explorers have secured a place in history by going somewhere where no man, or woman, has gone before. The following are a few of the bigger names in the world of exploration.

The great Norwegian explorer Roald Amundsen was polar explorer who became the second man to reach the North Pole after Admiral Byrd. Amundsen signed in a very complex and aggressive hand. The signature is dominated by large capital letters. Letter construction is marginal, and many letters tend to morph into indistinguishable strokes. Amundsen's signature displays itself in a unique way. Eye appeal is sound. There is a very restricted supply of material in the market. In June of 1928, Amundsen was killed in a plane crash in the Arctic. Signatures will occasionally surface on album pages and banquet programs. DsS and letters of any kind are very scarce to rare. There is average demand for Amundsen material, though time seems to be passing him by. Fewer and fewer

people know his name and values have stagnated in recent years. Expect to pay $200 to $250 for his signature.

American explorer Admiral Richard Byrd was the first man to fly over both the North and South Poles. For this he has gained a permanent spot in exploration history. Byrd signed in a very odd hand. His signature has angles that abruptly stop. The signature has a certain arithmetic appearance. It is a signature of average display value. Just about all signatures are signed as "R E Byrd."

Byrd was a superstar of his day. He was targeted by autograph collectors. Today, there is a good supply of material in the market. His signature can be found on books, photographs, commemorative airmail covers, government postcards, plate blocks, and TLsS. ALsS are rare. A few years back, a decent supply of personal bank checks entered the market. It should be noted that some TLsS are secretarially signed.

In recent years there has been much press as to whether Byrd actually flew over the North Pole. A few armchair historians from Europe claim it was Amundsen, and not Byrd, who first accomplished this feat. Some have tried, unsuccessfully, to discredit Byrd's legacy in favor of Amundsen. In any event, demand is sound for Byrd material. Values are depressed due to the large supply of material in the market. Most mediums can be purchased for under $100. Books and checks sell for $30 to $40. A full-page ALS has a likely value of $500 to $600.

Byrd-1, signed book dated 1930.

William Clark and Meriwether Lewis are the biggest names in exploration. They led the first expedition to the western United States. The trek began in May of 1804 and ended in September of 1806. Clark signed in a rather average

Amundsen-1, ALS dated 1907 (courtesy Nate D. Sanders Auctions).

hand. Letter construction is sound. Good legibility is noted. A complex paraph increases display value. Most signatures are signed as "Wm Clark." It should be noted that there are many forged ADsS and DsS in the market, so caution is warranted. The forgeries appear sloppy in construction. The content usually deals with payment of salaries or purchase of supplies. The paper is typically irregularly cut.

Lewis signed in a more structured hand. The signature is short on height with good length. Letter construction is sound. The signature has good display value. Both signatures are rare on a per se basis. Clark is basically limited to DsS. ALsS are very rare. A Clark DsS will typically sell for $1,750 to $2,250. A full-page ALS will likely sell for more than $10,000. Lewis's signature is rarer than that of Clark, as he was murdered in 1809. Signatures are typically limited to DsS. A DsS will sell for $7,500 to $8,000. A full-page ALS is likely valued at $20,000. An ADS by Lewis relating to the expedition sold for $30,700 (Nate D. Sanders Auctions, 2012). Accompanying the expedition was the Shoshone Indian, Sacagawea, who acted as interpreter. She died in 1812; I know of no signatures in existence.

Clark, W-1, ALS dated 1831.

Lewis-1, undated signature.

American General Adolphus Greely was a polar explorer, Civil War officer, and Medal of Honor recipient. Greely signed in a flowing and carefree hand. The signature has loose letter construction. An above average display value is noted. Most signatures are accomplished as "A.W. Greely." Greely's signature is fairly scarce. Most signatures are found on ALsS, ANsS, and album pages. Signed cabinet cards exist but should be considered rare. There is good demand for Greely material. He is collected not only for his exploration accomplishments but also for his Civil War association. His signature is quite affordable. Album pages can be purchased for $50 to $75. Full-page ALsS and cabinet photographs are valued at $200 to $300.

Greely-1, undated signature.

New Zealand mountaineer Edmund Hillary is the most famous of the 20th-century explorers. He and Tenzing Norgay were the first to reach the summit of the great Mount Everest, the tallest mountain in the world. Hillary signed in a fairly aggressive hand. The signature has loose letter construction and lacks hesitation. Signatures accomplished in the last few years of life are signed in a slower, more methodic hand. A moderate unsteadiness is noted. Hillary was a very good signer his entire life. Signatures can be found on first-day covers, photographs, books, and TLsS. ALsS are far less common. Some letters have amazing content, including one TLS in which he discusses the existence of the Abominable Snowman. At the request of collectors, he would also sketch a comical image of himself atop Mount Everest holding a pickax. Many forgeries do exist, though almost exclusively limited to the elderly, infirmed signature.

The supply of Hillary material is very good. It is balanced with a sound demand. Hillary's signature is affordable at $30 to $40. Signed 8 × 10 photographs, books, and TLsS are valued at $75 to $100. ALsS are tough to locate, so expect to pay $400 to $500 for a nice specimen. Sketches are scarce and will sell for $250 to $350. Hillary will prove a fine investment signature in the years to come.

Hillary-1, signed book dated 1979.

Hillary-2, signature dated 2006.

English Army officer John Hunt (later Baron Hunt) was the leader of the 1953 Mount Everest expedition. Hunt signed in a very hesitant and jagged hand. The signature evidences abrupt angles and turns. It is very choppy, which limits display value. The signature is typically finished off with a paraph. Hunt was not generally targeted by collectors, though he was a willing signer. The supply of material is much less abundant when compared to that of Fuchs or Hillary. Signatures are generally limited to index cards. Other mediums are uncommon to scarce. ALsS are tough to locate. Signed copies of the book *The Ascent of Everest* are available and

Hunt-1 postal cover circa 1990.

make for a fine addition to any library. As of this writing there is tepid demand for Hunt material. Signatures can be purchased for as little as $25. Signed books are a bargain at $50 to $75. A nice full-page ALS will likely sell for $150 to $200. I consider Hunt's signature to be undervalued.

Tenzing Norgay was a Nepalese Sherpa mountaineer. He, along with Hillary, was the first to reach the summit of Mount Everest. Norgay signed in a jagged script. The signature evidences poor letter construction. A substandard display value is noted. Replication of hand is fairly easy. Well-executed forgeries do exist. Forgeries are typically placed next to a genuine signature of Hillary or Lord Hunt. There is an ample supply of material in the market, mostly limited to index cards and first-day covers. An 8 × 10 photograph or letter of any kind is rare. An ALS would be considered very rare. There is sound demand for Norgay material. His signature is valued at $250 to $300. A dual-signed first-day cover with Hillary will sell for $500 to $600.

Norgay-1, undated signature (courtesy Stephen Koschal Reference Library).

English explorer Vivian Fuchs led the expeditionary team that completed the first overland crossing of Antarctica in 1958. Fuchs signed in a rather plain and rudimentary hand. Letter construction is sound but hesitation is noted. The signature is of average display value. Given the simple construction of the signature, replication of hand would be easy. Creating a well-executed forgery would be an easy undertaking. Fuchs was a willing signer throughout his life. There is an ample supply of material in the market, though generally limited to index cards and first-day covers. Signed 8 × 10 photographs are scarce. There is a decent supply of ALsS in the market, as Fuchs loved to correspond with those interested in exploration. Sometimes he would pen letters on original 1950s Antarctic Expedition letterhead, which makes for a great association item. There is average demand for Fuchs material. Signatures are affordable at $25 to $30; 8 × 10 photographs are valued at $100 to $125. A nice ALS, on original expedition stationary, should sell for $250 to $300.

Fuchs-1 postal cover circa 1990.

Dr. David Livingstone was a Scottish missionary and explorer of Africa who has become a fabled figure in history. Livingstone became fascinated with the Nile River and spent much of his life studying it. Livingstone signed in a very practical hand. The signature is legible with good letter construction. There is a certain pensiveness to the signature. As a result, replication of hand is easy. Well-executed forgeries do exist. His signature is scarce on a per se basis and generally limited to ALsS and LsS, typically with routine content. Other mediums are basically nonexistent. There is good demand for Livingstone material. Signatures sell for $400 to $500. ALsS are valued at $1,250 to $1,500. Multi-paged specimens can sell for over $2,000. Overall, a desirable autograph.

British explorer Henry M. Stanley set out to

Livingstone-1, signature dated 1857 (courtesy Nate D. Sanders Auctions).

locate Livingstone, who had disappeared in Africa. In November 1871, Stanley found his man and spoke those now legendary words, "Dr. Livingstone, I presume?" Stanley did much exploration in the Congo. Stanley signed in a very flowing and rapid hand. His signature has marginal letter construction. The complex nature of hand correlates into a high display value. The signature is finished off with a paraph. Overall, a pleasing signature. There is good demand for Stanley's signature. Unlike Livingstone, there is an ample supply of Stanley material in the market, including a decent supply of ALsS. Signatures can also be found on AQsS, check endorsements, and cabinet photographs. His signature is far more affordable than that of Livingstone. Signatures can be purchased for $125 to $150. ALsS are a good buy at $300 to $400.

Stanley-1, ALS dated 1878 (courtesy Nate D. Sanders Auctions).

Oceanographers Jacques Piccard and U.S. navy Lieutenant Donald Walsh made, perhaps, the most dangerous ocean dive ever. On January 23, 1960, both descended into the Mariana Trench in a bathyscaphe named *Trieste*. They reached an incredible 35,815 feet below the surface of the ocean. These are two wonderful signatures to obtain. More men have walked on the face of the moon than have visited Challenger Deep. Piccard died in 2008 and signed only a limited number of items. There is a less than ample supply simply because collectors did not target him for autographs. Signatures are generally limited to index cards and first-day covers. Photographs and letters are scarce. Walsh is a willing signer and in recent years his popularity among collectors has grown. There is an ample supply of material in the market; as with Piccard, most signatures are found on index cards and first-day covers. Photographs are also available. Letters of any kind are scarce. Items signed by both are rare. I consider these two signatures to be great investments in the years to come. Either signature can be purchased for under $50 on an index card or first-day cover.

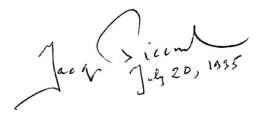

Walsh-1, signature dated 2012.

Piccard-1, signature dated 1995.

In 1909, American admiral Robert Peary was the first man to reach the geographical North Pole. Peary signed in a truly odd hand. His signature is accomplished with very heavy strokes of varying thickness. It gives the signature a very geometric look. The display value is above average. Signatures are usually penned on a down-ward angle. Signatures are usually accomplished as "R.E. Peary." Peary was a willing signer and it appears many collectors targeted him for his autograph. Today, there is an ample supply of inventory in the market. Signatures can be found on album pages, calling cards, TLsS, ALsS, and bank checks. Photographs of any kind are rare. His signature is quite affordable at $50 to $75. A nice ALS will sell for $300 to $500. Bank checks are a bargain at $125 to $150.

American John Wesley Powell was best known for his exploration of the American West. In 1869 his expedition made the first crossing of the Grand Canyon. He served as the director of the U.S. geological survey from 1881 to 1894. Powell signed in a rugged and unstructured hand. The signature is choppy and evidences thick bold strokes. Letter construction is poor, resulting in a signature with substandard legibility. Most signatures are accomplished as "J.W. Powell." Powell's signature is rare on a per se basis. It is generally limited to TLsS and LsS or signatures removed therefrom. ALsS are very rare. There are many TLsS in the market on Department of the Interior—United States Geological Survey letterhead. Just about all are secretarially signed. The secretarial signature is signed in a small and very plain-looking hand. These forgeries differ greatly from a genuine signature and are exposed with little effort. There is good demand for Powell material when compared to a restricted supply. Expect to pay $500 to $700 for his signature.

Powell, J.-1, Undated LS.

Peary-1, undated signature (courtesy Nate D. Sanders Auctions).

Irish explorer Ernest Shackleton was another early polar explorer who led three expeditions to the Antarctic. Shackleton signed in a sharp and angular hand. The signature exhibits bold and heavy strokes. A certain choppiness is noted. Legibility is substandard. The signature has average display value. Shackleton died in 1922, a victim of a heart attack. Due to an early death, his signature is scarce on a per se basis. Signatures are typically found on ANsS, TLsS, and ALsS. Many are simply signed as "Shackles." Bank checks are very scarce. Photographs are rare. I have always been amazed at the demand for Shackleton's signature. He did not accomplish any "firsts" in the field of exploration, yet collectors treasure his autograph. A signature will sell for $600 to $750. A full-page ALS is valued at $2,500 to $3,000. Bank checks sell for $1,500 to $2,000. Signed photographs are valued at $2,000 to $2,500.

Shackleton-1, undated signature (courtesy The Sanders Autograph Price Guide).

Vilhjalmur Stefansson was a Canadian explorer and ethnologist. He was noted for the Canadian Arctic Expedition of 1913 and the voyage of the ill-fated *Karluk*. Stefansson signed in a very choppy hand. The signature has cutting angles and is truncated in nature. His hand is similar to that of Riggs Stephenson. The signature appears busy, which impairs legibility. There is an ample supply of material in the market. The most common medium is books. He wrote several books, all pertaining to exploration. Photographs are scarce. TLsS are scarce. ALsS are rare. Most letters are signed with the first name only or his nickname "Stef." Demand for Stefansson's signature is, as of this writing, marginal. Values have declined in recent years. This is a good opportunity to secure his autograph. A signature can be purchased for as little as $25. TLsS, signed in full, and books are valued at $50 to $75. A full page ALS has a value of $400 to $500.

Stefansson-1, signature dated 1959.

Inventors

The inventors, tinkerers, and weekend gearnuts are the cornerstone of technological advancement. Some are formally trained; most, however, are just people with an insatiable curiosity to find out how things works and how to make things better. Some inventions transformed the world and have made their inventors giants in history. The light bulb, telephone, dynamite, cotton gin, Internet, and television are some of the greatest advancements of mankind. Most inventors are not really known by the masses and their signatures are not really collectable even though their contributions are great. Whitcomb Judson is a fine example. He is basically an unknown figure. Yet his invention, the zipper, is used by billions of people every day. There are many signatures of inventors you can purchase for nominal values. A rather sizable collection can be assembled on a modest budget. The following is a list of some of the more famous inventors.

Alexander Graham Bell was the man who brought the world closer together through his invention, the telephone. For this, Bell has gained a significant and permanent place in history. Bell signed in a compact and tight hand. The signature evidences good flow; however, individual letters appear cramped. His signature works well on small mediums. Replication of hand is moderately difficult, though skilled forgers have taken up the task. Well-executed forgeries exist in quantities. There is an ample supply of signatures in the market. He was targeted by autograph collectors and signed many items, mostly ANsS. Signatures are also found on LsS, TLsS, and bank checks. ALsS are rare. Photographs are very rare. There is strong demand for Bell material. Fortunately for collectors, the market inventory keeps prices from exploding. Bell's signature sells for $400 to $500. LsS, TLsS, and bank checks are valued in the $1,250 to $1,750 price range. A full-page ALS is a rarity and should sell for $3,000 to $4,000. Exceptional examples will easily sell for more than $10,000.

Bell, A-2, undated signature (courtesy Nate D. Sanders Auctions).

German physicist Ernst Ruska won the Nobel Prize in physics. He is the "father of the electron microscope." Ruska signed in a plain and legible hand. He died in 1988 but signed few autographs. His signature is considered scarce on a per se basis. His signature is slow and methodic. It is easily replicated. Forgeries have, in recent years, entered the market. Ruska's signature is valued at $75 to $100. His signature should see a nice rate of return in the coming years.

Ruska-1, undated signature.

Intangible, yet real as granite, was the air that carried radio. American Lee de Forest held numerous patents, including one for the vacuum tube, which he invented around 1905. De Forest signed in an angular and slightly choppy hand. The signature has average letter construction and display value. Overall, just a plain and unassuming signature. There is an ample supply of de Forest material in the market. Signatures are generally found on TLsS, index cards, and bank checks. Many TLsS are secretarially signed, especially those found on *Lee de Forest Laboratories* letterhead. In the 1950s, de Forest

was targeted by collectors, which increased the market population greatly. There is decent demand for de Forest material. His signature is affordable at $125 to $150. TLsS sell for $250. A full-page ALS will approach $1,000.

de Forest-1, undated signature (courtesy The Sanders Autograph Price Guide).

American businessman George Eastman was the first to perfect rolled film. He was the founder of Eastman-Kodak. Eastman signed in a flowing script. The signature is large and flamboyant. Letter construction is slightly impaired as individual letters morph into indistinguishable strokes. Overall, a pleasing signature. Signatures accomplished in the last few years of life are signed in a slower, slightly shaky hand. This is likely due to spinal problems which led to increased pain and ultimately suicide in 1932. Some letters signed in the late 1920s until death are secretarially signed. His signature is scarce and generally limited to business-related TLsS. Photographs are rare. ALsS are very rare. Eastman's signature sells for $125 to $150. TLsS are valued at $400 to $500. A nicely signed photograph will likely sell for $1,000.

Eastman-1 signed book (courtesy Stephen Koschal Autographs).

Perhaps no man transformed the world like Thomas Alva Edison. His phonograph, motion picture camera, and, of course, light bulb, brought us into the modern age. If there was ever a man who could be considered a real-life wizard, it is Mr. Edison. Edison signed in a rather plain and slow hand. Letter construction is sound. Good legibility is noted. The display value is superior thanks to the umbrella-like letter "T" in the first name. Given the slow nature of hand his signature is easily forged. Well-executed forgeries exist in quantities. Being such a giant of science, he was targeted by early autograph collectors. Edison signed countless autographs. In addition, there is a strong supply of DsS, corporate minutes, and bank checks in the market. Many ANsS, accomplished in pencil, are also available. These contain short writings and most are simply signed with his initials. Many of these notes are the product of forgery. Signed photographs are scarce, but a restricted supply does exist. Full page ALsS are very rare. A good supply of material keeps prices in check. His signature is rather affordable considering his significant place in history. His signature can be purchased for $500 to $600. Bank checks and corporate minutes are not much more at $750 to $900. Signed 8 × 10 photographs are valued at $2,000 to $2,500. Exceptional examples are valued at $5,000. A nice ALS will sell for around $6,000 to $8,000; should it have scientific content, $10,000 or more should be expected.

Edison-3, variant signature typically found on business notes (courtesy Mark Allen Baker).

American inventor Philo T. Farnsworth is a name that most people have never heard of but his invention, the television, is one of the most important creations in the history of man. Farnsworth signed in a poor, almost child-like hand. His signature has uneven construction, with mis-spaced letters. The signature is pensive and a certain hesitation is noted. Display value is poor. His signature is very easy to forge. Producing a well-executed forgery can be done with ease. For years his signature was considered rare to very rare. Very little material was in the market. About ten years ago, several books from his personal library entered the market. Most books are science-related. They are signed in the upper right on the end paper. When these books were first released they were selling for over $1,000. Over the years prices have steadily dropped, and that same book can now be purchased for $100 to $150. This is about the only medium available to collectors.

Edison-1 undated signature, vintage (courtesy Nate D. Sanders Auctions).

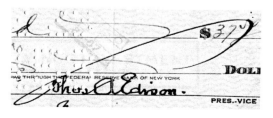

Edison-2, signed bank check dated 1928 (courtesy Nate D. Sanders Auctions).

Farnsworth-1, undated signature.

The name Ford is one of the most recognized on Earth. Henry Ford gave civilization the first affordable, mass-produced automobile and changed the world forever. He is one of the most important figures in world history. Ford signed in a pleasing and practical hand. The signature evidences good letter construction and legibility. There is a good supply of material in the market. Ford was often targeted by collectors of the day. Signatures can be found on album pages, TLsS, and programs. Signed photographs are scarce and most offered for sale are forgeries. Many Detroit-area banquet menus, signed by Ford and other dignitaries of the day, are available. ALsS are an extreme rarity. Because the signature lacks reckless flow, replication of hand is fairly easy. Well-executed forgeries exist in quantities. There are many forged photographs and album pages in pencil. Many TLsS on "Henry Ford Dearborn, Michigan" letterhead are secretarially signed. There is very strong demand for Ford material. His signature sells for $700 to $900. Portrait photographs are valued at $2,000 to $2,500. TLsS sell for $1,000 to $1,500. A full-page ALS would have a likely value of $10,000. Signatures of his son Edsel Ford and grandson Henry Ford II are also collectable and are generally available for $100.

Ford-2, undated signature (courtesy The Sanders Autograph Price Guide).

Automotive development is a highly collected field and signatures can get quite expensive. Walter Chrysler's signature is scarce and commands some good money. Signatures are valued at $250 and TLsS sell for $1,000 to $1,250. John Kelsey, Ransom Olds, Louis Chevrolet, and the like are also in high demand. Signatures of other inventors like Charles Duryea, an early automotive designer, are also collectable. Duryea was, at one time, a rare sig-

Chrysler-1, undated signature.

nature. In recent years a large supply of signatures removed from business checks caused prices to fall. Signatures can now be purchased for $25.

Duryea-1 undated signature.

American engineer Robert Fulton created the steamboat and other nautical craft. Fulton signed in a rather large and bold hand. The signature evidences thick and heavy strokes. Letter construction is fairly sound. Average legibility and display value are noted. Most signatures are penned as "R. Fulton" and are often finished with a paraph. Fulton's signature is rare on a per se basis and limited to letters, DsS, or signatures removed therefrom. Replication of hand is fairly difficult. Skilled forgers have, however, produced many well-executed forgeries. There is one forgery that needs to be discussed. There are many forged ADsS in the market. The content usually pertains to ordering of supplies such as coal or wheat or something similar. The forgeries are placed on irregularly cut sheets of paper. The forgeries are signed in full as "Robert Fulton" in a slightly labored hand. There is strong demand for Fulton material and his signature is highly prized, so expect to pay $750 to $1,000. ALsS are treasured and a full-page specimen is easily worth $10,000.

Fulton-1, undated signature.

American inventor Richard Gatling patented many inventions, most dealing with farming. He is, however, best remembered as the man who created the first machine gun, known as the Gatling gun. Gatling signed in a wonderful flowing script. Variant thickness of strokes gives the signature maximum eye appeal. A complex paraph only enhances the display value. One of the finer signatures in the world of autographs. There is an ample supply of material in the market. His signature is generally limited to ALsS, ANsS, and a few AQsS. There is good demand for Gatling material. His signature is not only collected by science collectors but Civil War and military buffs as well. Signatures tend to sell for $300 to $400. A full-page ALS is valued at $1,000. There are a few multi-page letters in the market and these sell for a marked premium.

Gatling-1, undated signature (courtesy The Sanders Autograph Price Guide).

Infuse sulfur into rubber and it becomes much more durable. This process, known as vulcanization, was the brainchild of American inventor Charles Goodyear. Goodyear signed in a super script. The signature has excellent letter construction and superior eye appeal. Most signatures are accomplished as "Chas. Goodyear." His signature is scarce on a per se basis. Bank checks are the most available medium. ALsS and ANsS are somewhat rare. Other mediums are basically nonexistent. There is decent demand for Goodyear material. Bank checks sell for $300 to $400. A full-page ALS is valued at $1,000.

Goodyear-1, undated ALS (courtesy Nate D. Sanders Auctions).

American physicist and inventor Robert Goddard built and launched the first fueled rocket. This amazing achievement occurred on March 16, 1926. Goddard signed in a pleasing and relaxed hand. His signature exhibits marked laziness. A good degree of legibility is noted. Display value is average. Most signatures are accomplished as "R.H. Goddard." Since his work was rather esoteric in nature and had no practical application to everyday life, he was not a well-known figure. He was seldom approached by collectors of the day. His fame grew after his death in 1945. As a result, his signature is rare on a per se basis and generally limited to TLsS or signatures removed therefrom. Other mediums are basically nonexistent. I have never examined a genuinely signed photograph, though many forgeries do exist. Unfortunately for collectors, Goddard made liberal use of the secretary. Most letters contain secretarial signatures. These are distinguished as they are typically signed as "Robert H. Goddard." Secretarial signatures are signed in a choppy hand and lack the smooth curves of a genuine signature. They are exposed upon cursory examination. Goddard's signature is in much demand simply because the supply is so restricted. Expect to pay $500 to $600 for a nice specimen. A TLS will sell for $1,250 to $1,500.

Goddard-1, undated signature (courtesy Mark Allen Baker).

Russian general Mikhail Kalashnikov was a small-arms designer best remembered for the AK-47 assault rifle. Kalashnikov signed in an almost printed script. The signature appears very truncated. Letters display themselves as hieroglyphic-like. Given the severed point construction, signatures are very easy to forge. Many well-executed forgeries are in the market. Kalashnikov was a very responsive signer through the mail. Most collectors did not know of his whereabouts; hence, he signed very little material. He died in 2013 at the age of 94 and his signature is considered scarce on a per se basis. Signatures are generally limited to index cards, first-day covers, and small photographs. Letters of any kind are rare. He would also send out signed business cards to collectors. There is good demand for Kalashnikov material. He is collected not only in the science genre but also military and World War II fields as well. His signature is valued at $100. A nicely signed 8 × 10 photograph where he is holding the AK-47 is prized by collectors and sells for $400 to $500.

Kalashnikov-1 postal cover circa 1990.

American electrical engineer Jack Kilby invented the integrated circuit, more commonly known as the "microchip." His invention gave birth to the personal computer age. Kilby signed in an average and unattractive hand. Letter construction is loose and lacks precision. Display value is substandard. Given the ununiformed nature of the hand, replication is very easy. Producing a well-executed forgery would take little effort. Kilby won the Nobel Prize in 2000 and died five years later; hence, he did not sign many autographs. Prior to the Nobel award, he was not the target of collectors. The supply of material is somewhat limited. Signatures appear mostly on first-day covers, index cards, and the occasional business card. Letters of any kind are rare. Kilby would, on request, sketch a mi-

Kilby-1 undated signature.

crochip along with his signature. These make for an attractive display. His signature generates average demand. Expect to pay $50 to $75 for a nice specimen. With a drawing, the value increases to $150 to $200.

Simon Lake was an American engineer who was an early pioneer in the design and manufacture of submarines. Lake signed in a muted hand. His signature is average in every respect. Signatures work well on small mediums. Replication of hand would be easy. Creating a well-executed forgery would take little effort. Fortunately, his signature is not the target of skilled forgers. His signature can be purchased for little money. About 20 years ago a large number of canceled bank checks entered the market and drastically cut the value of his autograph. Due to a tepid demand to begin with, prices never really recovered. Bank checks can be purchased for as little as $20. Full-page ALsS sell for a mere $100. The colorful Lake Torpedo Boat Company stock certificates, which Lake founded, make for a fine collectable and are valued at $100 to $150. They contain a nice signature of Lake at the bottom of the document.

Lake-1, undated signature (courtesy The Sanders Autograph Price Guide).

Italian inventor Guglielmo Marconi gave the world the wireless radio. He won the 1909 Nobel Prize for his efforts. Marconi signed in a sharp and cutting hand. The signature evidences thick strokes and abrupt angles. A thick linear paraph completes the signature. Overall, a pleasing autograph. There seems to be a good supply of fairly well-executed forgeries in the market. Forgeries are typically found on album pages, calling cards, and photographs. Loose letter construction is noted, and letters tend to be spaced farther apart. The supply of Marconi material is ample. Signatures can be found on calling cards, ANsS, TLsS, and photographs.

Full-page ALsS are rare. Marconi's signature is very affordable at $350 to $400. TLsS are not much more. Signed portrait photographs make for fine presentation pieces, so expect to pay at least $1,000.

Marconi-1 undated signature (courtesy Stephen Koschal Autographs).

American chemist and inventor Hudson Maxim is best remembered as the man who created smokeless gunpowder. Maxim signed in an aggressive and reckless hand. The signature is very flowing. Letter construction is substandard, and some letters tend to be malformed and illegible. Overall, a signature with average display value. There is good demand for Maxim material. There is an ample supply of material in the market. His signature is found on calling cards, ANsS, LsS, TLsS, and authored books. Less common are ALsS. Photographs of any kind are rare to very rare. Maxim's signature is quite affordable. Nice specimens can be purchased for $100. Letters and DsS are valued at $200 to $250. Signed books are valued at $250 to $300.

Maxim-1 signed card dated 1911.

Samuel F.B. Morse started out as a painter, then turned to inventing. He gave the world the telegraph. Morse code, which he also invented, is still used to this day. Morse signed in a powerful and flowing hand. The signature evidences sound letter construction. Signatures are accomplished with his middle initials and finished with a paraph. Display value is superior. The

supply of Morse material is ample. There seems to be a good supply of ALsS and ANsS with routine content in the market. Many are accepting dinner invitations. Signed cabinet photographs are rare and many forged specimens are in the market, so caution is warranted. Morse's signature is surprisingly affordable at $300 to $400. ALsS sell for $500 to $600. Cabinet cards are in high demand and generally sell for $2,500 to $3,000.

Morse-1, undated signature (courtesy The Sanders Autograph Price Guide).

Swedish chemist Alfred Nobel gave the world one of the most important inventions ever. It allowed for mass extraction of ores and minerals. His invention was dynamite, and it enabled industry to flourish on a grand scale. Nobel signed in a loose and unstructured hand. The signature is basically illegible. The signature has average display value. It is usually signed as "A. Nobel." Due to the lackluster structure, replication of hand is easy. Well-executed forgeries exist, including forged ALsS. His signature is rare on a per se basis and generally limited to ALsS. Expect to pay $2,000 for a nice ALS. Scientific content letters sell for substantially more.

Nobel-1, undated signature.

American physicist William Shockley won the 1956 Nobel Prize for co-inventing the transistor along with John Bardeen and Walter Brattain. Shockley signed in a practical hand. The signature has sound letter construction. Good legibility is noted. Most signatures are signed as "W=Shockley." Shockley's signature is rather plain looking and lacks recklessness. His signature would be easy to replicate. Shockley was a responsive signer through the mail. Most signatures are found on index cards, first-day covers, and photographs. Many times he would sketch a small transistor above his signature. Letters of any kind are scarce to rare. Shockley's signature is affordable at $25 to $50; with a sketch, closer to $100. I consider Shockley to be a sleeper signature in the years to come.

Shockley-1, signature dated 1988.

Serbian-American engineer Nikola Tesla was a dreamer and futurist whose work was not really appreciated until long after he died. He did much experimentation with X-rays, AC current, and direct energy concentrations (aka the death ray). Tesla signed in a simple hand. The signature is flowing with good letter construction. An average display value is noted. During his life, most people had no idea who Tesla was and few really cared. As a result, his signature is rare to very rare on a per se basis and just about all signatures offered in the market a forgeries, easily more than 95 percent. Signatures are generally limited to TLsS. Signed photographs are an extreme rarity. ALsS are very rare but a few do exist. There is a small group of forged TLsS in the market. They have all been accomplished by the same forger. They are on blank sheets of paper and typically dated from the mid to late 1890s to around 1910. Content is routine, such as declining or accepting an invitation. Typed across the top of the sheet are the place, date, and address of "Houston Street." The forgery is signed as "N. Tesla." The signature lacks the flow of a genuine specimen and exhibits an ever-so-slight hesitation. These forgeries are

fairly well-executed, so caution is warranted. There is good demand for Tesla material weighted against a very restricted supply. Expect to pay $1,000 for his signature. A TLsS will sell for $2,000 to $2,500.

Tesla-1, undated signature (courtesy The Sanders Autograph Price Guide).

Wernher von Braun was a leading scientist for the Third Reich. After the war he became a leading figure in American rocketry. Von Braun signed in a heavy and uniformed hand. The signature evidences thick strokes and tight letter construction. The signature has excellent display value. It is one of the nicer signatures for display purposes. Given the complex nature of hand, well-executed forgeries do not exist. Von Braun was well known and signed many autographs for collectors. Today, there is an ample supply of material in the market. Many mediums are available; however, ALsS are very rare. Signed photographs exist in quantities. Most feature von Braun with scaled-down rockets in the background. These make for a fine display. He also signed many photographs in which he is pictured with President Kennedy. There is good demand for von Braun material. His signature remains affordable. Index cards and first-day covers sell for $150. TLsS are valued at $250 to $300. A nicely signed 8 × 10 photograph will sell for $500 to $750.

von Braun-1, undated signature.

Eli Whitney invented the cotton gin and was one of the fathers of the industrial revolution.

Perhaps no other invention transformed the early American economy more than the gin. Whitney signed in a strong and rugged hand. The signature evidences thick strokes of ink and has tight letter construction. An elongated down stroke to the letter "Y" enhances the display value. Many times the signature is finished off with a paraph. Overall, a very pleasing signature. Whitney's signature is rare to very rare and basically limited to ALsS. He is the target of skilled forgers and many well-executed specimens do exist. A common forgery is holograph bank checks. There is strong demand for Whitney material. The restricted supply correlates into high value. Expect to pay $4,000 to $5,000 for a nice ALS. Multi-page specimens will sell for more than $10,000. Autographically, a very important American autograph.

Whitney-1, ALS dated 1818 (courtesy Nate D. Sanders Auctions).

Other Notable Scientists

American Botanist Luther Burbank developed countless varieties of plants, vegetables, and cacti. He was kind of a mad scientist of the plant world. Burbank signed in a flowing and stunning hand. His signature has superior letter construction. Legibility is sound. The sweeping letter "L" only enhances eye appeal. Overall, a superior signature. The supply of Burbank material is ample. His signature can be found on ALsS, cabinet cards, and many, small thick-stock cards. His signature is very affordable at $50. Cabinet cards can be purchased for a mere $200. A signed 12-volume set of *Luther Burbank: His Methods and Discoveries* are highly prized by book collectors. Signed sets can be purchased for $500 to $600, which, in my opinion, is a steal.

Burbank-1, undated signature.

Botanist George Washington Carver is best known for developing uses for the peanut. Carver signed in a compact and choppy hand. The signature is of average construction and display value. Most signatures are signed as "G.W. Carver." There is an ample supply of Carver material in the market. Most signatures are found on TLsS and ALsS. There is a restricted supply of multiple-page ALsS in the market. Photographs are rare. In 1943 the book *George Washington Carver: An American Biography* was released. There are many signed copies in the market. It should be pointed out that Carver died on January 5, 1943, so I am not sure how he signed copies of this book. It has been stated by some that he pre-signed blank sheets of paper in advance of publication. There is no evidence of this and the signature that appears in these books look to be forgeries. In any event, I have never seen a genuinely signed copy of this book. Signed copies of this book should be avoided in total. There is average demand for Carver-signed material. Expect to pay $150 to $200 for his signature. ALsS will sell for $300 to $400, multi-page specimens for more.

Carver-1, undated signature (courtesy The Sanders Autograph Price Guide).

English naturalist Charles Darwin advanced one of the most controversial theories in the history of science. His theory of evolution, which states that we all came from frogs or something to that effect, still stirs great debate. His book *On the Origin of Species* is still widely read today. Darwin signed in a rather rudimentary hand. His signature lacks structure. Letters tend to be malformed and mis-spaced. The signature has average display value. Due to the simple structure of hand, replication is easy. Well-executed forgeries exist in quantities. His signature is very scarce on a per se basis and generally limited to letters. Other mediums are basically nonexistent. There are signed cabinet cards in the market, but just about all of them are forgeries. A genuine signed photograph is a rarity. There are many Elliot & Fry cabinet cards in the market with a forgery placed at the bottom of the card. There are also many of these same cards that feature a facsimile signature. In addition, forgers have created counterfeit letterhead of Darwin's "Down, Beckeham, Kent" stationary. Forged ALsS and LsS exist, so caution is warranted. The sad fact is if you see a Darwin signature in the market it is very likely a forgery. There is very strong demand for Darwin material. His signature sells for close to $3,000. ALsS, with routine content, sell for around $10,000. A genuinely signed cabinet card will sell for $20,000 to $30,000 depending on eye appeal.

Darwin-1, undated signature.

Swiss geologist Louis Agassiz was known for his extensive studies of Earth's natural history. He was the first to forward the theory of repeating ice ages. Agassiz signed in an eclectic and busy hand. The signature evidences average letter construction and eye appeal. It is generally finished off with a paraph. There is an ample supply of material in the market, from letters to checks to calling cards. Photographs are scarce and many are signed and inscribed on the verso. There is only fair demand for Agassiz's signature, which keeps prices in check. Agassiz's signature is affordable at $50 to $75. A full-page

ALS can be purchased for $250. Cabinet photographs are valued at $350 to $400.

Agassiz-1, ALS dated 1869 (courtesy Haverford College).

Howard Carter is the most famous of the 20th-century archaeologists. In November of 1922 he located the tomb of Pharaoh Tutankhamen (aka King Tut). Carter signed in a rapid and flowing hand. The signature is fairly well-structured. The letter "H" is the first name is oddly formed. The rather complex nature of hand makes replication difficult. Well-executed forgeries do not exist. Carter's signature is rare to very rare. His fame continued to grow after his death. Demand is very strong for Carter material. Signatures are generally limited to ALsS and TLsS. Signed copies of his book, *The Tomb of Tutankhamen,* are very rare. TLsS are valued at $3,000. ALsS are valued from $6,000 to $8,000. The above-referenced book will sell for $8,000 to $10,000. A highly desirable autograph.

Carter, H-1, LS dated 1903 (courtesy Nate D. Sanders Auctions).

Charles Steinmetz was a Prussian engineer and mathematician. He was an early pioneer of alternating current and hysteresis. Steinmetz signed in a beautiful and thoughtful script. His signature is scarce on a per se basis. A small supply of bank checks keeps this signature from being considered rare. Letters and photographs are rare. Expect to pay $150 for a check.

Steinmetz-1, bank check dated 1904.

There doesn't seem to be a lot of demand for autographs of ornithologists. The exception is John Audubon. He wrote *The Birds of America*, which is considered the finest ornithological study ever published. Audubon signed in a beautifully flowing hand. The signature evidences sweeping curves and superior letter construction. The signature is finished off with a complex and stunning paraph. Due to the complex hand, replication is very difficult. There are no well-executed forgeries in the market. Audubon's signature is very scarce on a per se basis and limited to ALsS, ANsS, and signatures removed therefrom. There is sound demand for Audubon's signature, which sells for $700 to $900. A nicely accomplished ALS will sell for $2,500 to $3,500. An ALS with strong scientific content will likely sell for over $10,000.

Audubon-1, undated signature (courtesy Stephen Koschal Reference Library).

The Bone Wars

Signatures of paleontologists are collectable but not highly valued. Barnum Brown, Benjamin Franklin Mudge, and Edwin Harris Colbert are unfamiliar to most of today's collectors. As a result, signatures from this field can be picked up for a few dollars. There are two exceptions to this rule: two fanatical fossil hunters whose rivalry led to what has become known as the great bone war of 1877. Paleontologists Edward Drinker Cope and Othniel C. Marsh used their family fortunes to collect dinosaur bones in the badlands of Wyoming. The rivalry between these two was so great it included bribery, theft, hijacking, and violence. Both died relatively penniless in the late 1800s, all in the name of paleo-supremacy. Both signatures are much in demand and both are rare. Signatures are generally limited to a few signed letters. Marsh's signature is a bit more common. Some nice portrait photographs of Marsh exist. Expect to pay $150 to $200 for each of their signatures. A nice full-page ALS has an estimated value of $500 each.

Cope-1, ALS circa 1885 (courtesy Haverford College).

Marsh-1, ALS dated 1871.

Signatures from Cooperstown: Baseball

There is no sport quite like the game of baseball. Uniquely American, it is a game deeply woven into the fabric of America. To understand baseball is to understand America. Baseball's origins can be traced back to Elihu Phinney's farm in Cooperstown, New York. It was here, back in 1839, that the first baseball game in history was played. Over the next two centuries, baseball has evolved into the national pastime of these United States. Almost every child and adult alike has fond memories of the game. I can remember those days long ago when the most important thing in my life was catching a Tigers game on the radio. Listening to Ernie Harwell and Paul Carey broadcast a late-night west coast game was simply great. Recalling the days of Rusty Staub, Mark Fidrych, Mickey Lolich, and other Tigers of my youth stirs wonderful memories.

Because baseball has such a grip on the American experience, it is the most widely collected of all autographs. Values of the early immortals of the game, such as Ty Cobb, Honus Wagner, Babe Ruth, and Christy Mathewson have exploded. Prices of certain signatures on premium mediums have sold for tens of thousands of dollars. The most expensive American signatures are not what you would think. If you guessed George Washington, Abraham Lincoln, Ben Franklin, or Paul Revere you would be wrong. Pound-for-pound the most expensive signatures, American or otherwise, are the long-deceased Baseball Hall of Fame members. William "Buck" Ewing, Sam Thompson, Tim Keefe, and Charles "Hoss" Radbourn are among the most valued. To illustrate the point, signatures of Ben Franklin and George Washington will sell for $5,000 to $7,000. Ewing or Radbourn, on the other hand, are valued between $40,000 and $50,000.

The immense demand for baseball autographs has pushed values ever higher. This invites forgery. The market is literally flooded with fake material. Ninety percent of the Cobb, Ruth, and Lou Gehrig signatures in the market are forgeries. The same can be said for the other early legends, such as Wagner, Cy Young, Harry Heilmann, Mordecai Brown, and the like. Many of these forgeries have been wrongly certified as genuine by the authentication companies. More disturbing is the percentage of forged material of the truly rare Hall of Fame signatures such as Jack Chesbro, George "Rube" Waddell, and Jake Beckley. I estimate that 99.9 percent of what I term ultra-rare signatures are forgeries. Some have never been offered for sale. If you see a signature of Radbourn for sale, it is basically guaranteed to be forged.

Forgeries of the ultra-rare signatures enter the market primarily through the auction houses. They come complete will ill-issued certificates of authenticity. To illustrate the point, let us look at the signature of Jack Chesbro. Many Chesbro signatures have been sold over the years through auctions. Photographs, letters, index cards, DsS, and other mediums have changed hands. To my knowledge, there are only two genuinely signed Chesbro signatures in the market, at least when it comes to paper mediums. Both are bank checks.

The extreme value of museum-grade baseball material has attracted the truly skilled forgers like flies to honey. Their work product is convincing and fool most collectors and authenticators alike. Three signatures most targeted by forgers are Cobb, Ruth, and Gehrig. Back in the early 1980s, signed Cobb and Ruth baseballs, of fair and average disposition, and were selling for $75 to $100. Gehrig was always more expensive, but only slightly so. Today, signed baseballs of these legends sell for $4,000 to $6,000. The value increases exponentially for signed baseballs in high-grade condition. Museum-grade specimens of these three immortals have reached auction prices of $50,000, $75,000, and beyond. Unfortunately, these museum-grade balls surfaced only in the past ten to twenty years and are nothing more than well-executed forgeries. If you see an immaculate signed baseball of Ruth or Gehrig, on a cream-white to white baseball, with a bold dark signature that looks like it was signed yesterday, well, it *was* signed yesterday. Fully 99.9 percent of museum-grade Ruth and Gehrig baseballs are forgeries. In the early 1980s, they could not be found. When values of vintage baseball signatures increased in the 1990s, then they began to surface in quantities. The same can be said for early New York Yankees baseballs with Ruth, Gehrig, and Miller Huggins. If you examine a high-grade example of a 1920s Yankee-signed team baseball, it is very likely forged.

Cobb is a slightly different story. Cobb lived until the early 1960s and was signing autographs up to the last few months of his life. In the 1950s, Cobb was specifically targeted by collectors; hence, the population of museum-grade Cobb balls is greater than the basic nonexistence of Ruth and Gehrig in this medium. In *Heart of a Tiger* (ECW Press, 2013), author Herschel Cobb (Ty's grandson) documents how Cobb would mail out countless

signed baseballs to young collectors to satisfy requests for his autograph. Though the population of Cobb-signed museum-grade baseballs is greater, the vast majority are forgeries.

No field of autographs is more infested with forgery and incompetent authentication than baseball, so careful study is key. If you are not well-versed in baseball autographs, consider another field, such as the safely pedestrian presidents of the United States. I cannot tell you how many collectors, with deep pockets, throw around big money and end up with a collection loaded with forgeries, complete with certificates of authenticity. A few years back I had the chance to view a substantial autograph collection of baseball legends. The collection contained many ultra-rare signatures such as Keefe, Radbourn, Chesbro, and the like. They were purchased from some of the "most respected" dealers in the industry. Just about all of them were forged.

Fraud is not limited to autographs. The percentage of counterfeit "game used" bats and jerseys is quite high. A few years back, a jersey purportedly worn by disgraced Chicago White Sox outfielder Shoeless Joe Jackson was exposed as a counterfeit by the watchdog website Haulsofshame.com. The jersey originated from the collection of Barry Halper and ended up on display in the Baseball Hall of Fame. Exposed as fraud, it now resides in the basement of Cooperstown.

The "game used" trade is the area with the most fraud. For years "gamer" bats of the early legends such as Ross Youngs, Sam Crawford, Joe Tinker, and the like have been sold for serious money. The chances that these bats were used in major league play are slim to none. "Game used" is, at best, a tenuous term. There is no way to tell for sure if any early bat is genuine *and* was used in major league play. A collector must take a leap of faith and convince himself that the bat is game used. Most often, the bat is merely a store-bought bat altered to appear as the genuine article. Many times a forged inscription will be added to the bat to establish use in major league play.

Sports autographs, in general, offer collectors a wide variety of mediums to collect. Most fields are limited to just a few mediums. Composers, scientists, and authors are generally limited to letters, notes, books, photographs and calling cards. Baseball signatures can be found on a wide array of mediums: baseballs, bats, jerseys, helmets, Hall of Fame plaque postcards, gum cards, Perez-Steele cards, government postcards, and so on.

Gum Cards

The most popular medium is the baseball card. There are so many options to choose from. Early Topps issues are the most popular. Many stars can be purchased for just a few dollars. Mickey Mantle for $250 to $300. Stan Musial for $100. Al Kaline, George Kell, Brooks Robinson, and Ernie Banks can be had for anywhere between $25 and $50.

Goudey Gum cards make for a wonderful display; however, most offered in the market are forgeries. Genuine signed Goudey cards of the longer-deceased Hall of Famers are quite expensive. Jimmie Foxx and Mel Ott are valued at $2,000 to $3,000. Babe Ruth and Lou Gehrig will set you back $15,000 to $25,000. Many collectors try to obtain signed T-206 cards. These are early tobacco cards issued around 1910. Just about all signed T-cards are forgeries. Only a few players who lived into the late 1960s, such as Richard "Rube" Marquard and Larry Doyle, were presented with T-cards to sign. Hall of Famer Sam Crawford died in 1968 and a signed T-card is very rare. If you are trying to find signed T-cards of Cy Young, Joe Tinker, Frank Chance, and the other longer-deceased names, your search will be futile. With one exception, I have never seen a genuinely signed T-206 card of any Hall of Famer who died before 1968. The exception is Ty Cobb. Cobb was presented with these cards and a few genuine specimens exist, but are highly treasured. Expect to pay $20,000 to $25,000 for one.

Single-Signed Baseballs

Almost as popular as cards is the signed baseball. Single-signed baseballs are coveted by collectors and can be quite valuable. Travis Jackson, who died in 1987, is already expensive. A signed Jackson baseball is valued at $750 to $900. Hank Greenberg, who died around the same time, is valued at $1,500. Some Hall of Famers, like Goose Goslin, are extremely rare on a single-signed ball. Goslin died in 1971 and a nice signed specimen is easily worth $5,000. Hall of Famers who died after 1990 signed baseball in quantities for collectors. Charlie Gehringer, Walter "Buck" Leonard, Rick Ferrell, Billy Herman, Joe Sewell, and the like are quite affordable at $50 to $150.

This is a medium that the skilled forgers have concentrated their efforts on, and well-executed forgeries exist in mass quantities. If you run across a single-signed baseball of players such as Walter Johnson, Cy Young, Honus Wagner, Tris Speaker, and the like, chances are close to 100 percent they are forged. Not to say these signatures don't exist on this medium; they do, but are rare to very rare. The longer a player has been deceased, the less likely his signature will be found on this format.

The general rule is that a Hall of Famer who died before 1945 does not exist on a single-signed ball. Gehrig and John McGraw are exceptions, of course, but these are the odd anomalies. If you're looking for singles of Amos Rusie, Dan Brouthers, Christy Mathewson, Frank Chance, Willie Keeler, John "Bid" McPhee, Jack Chesbro, Joe McGinnity, Eddie Plank, George "Rube" Waddell, and the like, they simply don't exist. Sorry.

Team Baseballs

Team baseballs are a popular way to obtain many signatures on one ball. Team-signed baseballs have been popular with collectors and many are undervalued. Most team-signed baseballs from the 1970s and 1980s are available for under $200, some under $100. Even older teams are reasonably priced. A 1938 Detroit Tigers ball with hall of famers Earl Averill, Charlie Gehringer, and Hank Greenberg is valued at only $700 to $800. That is a good price for such a vintage team ball.

Team-signed baseballs increase demonstrably when longer-deceased names are present on the ball. As example, a 1936 Tigers team baseball is valued much more than the above-referenced 1938 ball, simply because it features signatures of Al Simmons and Mickey Cochrane. Both are members of the Hall of Fame. Both Simmons and Cochrane died over fifty years ago. Both are desired signatures. A 1936 Tigers team-signed baseball is valued at $1,500 to $1,750.

Team-signed baseballs that include signatures of the immortals of the game push prices into the multiple thousands of dollars. Ty Cobb, Eddie Collins, Tris Speaker, Hack Wilson, and the like are highly treasured on team baseballs. A 1926 Tigers team baseball, with signatures of Cobb, Harry Heilmann, Heinie Manush, and Fats Fothergill, is valued at $6,000 to $7,000. A 1920 Tigers team ball has signatures of Cobb and Heilmann, as well as Hughie Jennings, Bobby Veach, Jack Coombs, and Hubert "Dutch" Leonard. A choice specimen will sell for $10,000 to $15,000. It is all about supply and demand. The older the ball, the less supply. The less supply, the greater the value.

New York Yankees team baseballs are among the most popular. The vast number of stars correlates into good demand. Team balls from the 1920s have Ruth, Gehrig. Tony Lazzeri, Miller Huggins, Urban Shocker, and Herb Pennock. Later Yankees balls contain such hallowed names as Joe DiMaggio, Bill Dickey, Yogi Berra, and Whitey Ford. The combination of Mickey Mantle and Roger Maris on a team baseball is highly treasured.

Among the highest prized baseballs are early All-Star baseballs. The 1933 American League team is the greatest prize. The 1933 National League team, with a scarce John McGraw signature, is also in great demand. All-Star team baseballs from the 1950s through 1970s have a vast array of Hall of Famers and are surprisingly affordable. Some can be purchased for as low as $400. Some are more expensive if they feature desirable signatures. Thurmon Munson, Nellie Fox, and Roberto Clemente come to mind.

I have run across many pre–1920 signed team baseballs, well into the hundreds. Pre-1920 signed team baseballs are an extreme rarity. I have only examined three, maybe four, genuine specimens in my life. Before 1920, collecting baseball autographs was rarely done. Nobody was asking Fred Snodgrass or George Mullin to sign an autograph back then. I have seen many of these early signed team baseballs and just about all are forgeries. I shake my head at collectors who purchase the really early signed team baseballs (circa 1910). These are nothing but a product of forgery.

The most desired team-signed baseball is the 1927 Yankees. This ball is currently valued at $50,000. Other popular team baseballs are the New York Giants teams of the 1920s with signatures of John McGraw, Ross Youngs, Hack Wilson, Billy Southworth, and then coach Hughie Jennings. Team baseballs from the 1927 and 1928 Philadelphia Athletics are very popular. These teams had such an assortment of legends. The rosters included Ty Cobb, Eddie Collins, Zack Wheat, Mickey Cochrane, Al Simmons, Tris Speaker, Eddie Rommel, Connie Mack, Jimmie Foxx, and Lefty Grove.

Unfortunately, the above-referenced baseballs are also the most commonly forged of all team baseballs, and many convincing forgeries exist. Many come with multiple certificates of authenticity, so caution is warranted.

A couple of baseballs need to be discussed. First is the 1919 Chicago White Sox baseball. This is the most valued of all baseballs. The infamous team of Black Sox players threw the World Series in return for substantial bribes. This team contains the eight conspirators,

among them Shoeless Joe Jackson, Eddie Cicotte, Claude "Lefty" Williams, and Arnold
Gandil. A genuine signed 1919 Sox baseball is
priceless. I have seen a few baseballs purportedly signed by this team. All came with multiple
certificates of authenticity. The ones I examined
all had signatures that evidenced a labored appearance. All were clearly forgeries. I have concluded that this team-signed baseball does not
exist.

Babe Ruth's first year in the major leagues
was 1914. He broke in with the Boston Red Sox.
A couple of Bosox team-signed baseballs from
this year are in the market. They feature a
rookie Ruth signature. It is clear to me that the
same forger produced these baseballs as both
were signed in the same hand. The forgeries
were labored and actually rudimentary in construction. This is another team-signed baseball
that very likely does not exist.

Finally, another significant baseball needs to
be examined. The 1901 Pittsburgh Pirates signed
a reunion ball. Members of this team gathered
for a reunion sometime in the mid–1920s at the
Hotel Schenley in Pittsburgh. They signed a
limited number of baseballs. These reunion
baseballs are very rare and highly treasured.
They are valued at near $20,000 because they
include a very rare Jack Chesbro signature.
Other significant signatures include Hall of
Famers Honus Wagner and Fred Clarke.

I estimate a total population of under ten
genuine specimens, most of which are in impaired condition. Several years ago a forger created a handful of forged reunion baseballs. They
differ from the genuine specimens as the forgeries all have uniform ink thickness. They are
easily identified, as the forger placed the signatures in the same order on each baseball. If you
examine one of these baseballs where the signatures of Deacon Phillippe, Honus Wagner,
Jack Chesbro, and Jess Tannehill are under each
other, in that order, it is very likely one of these
forged baseballs.

Chesbro-1, Will dated 1926.

Forged Baseball Inventory

A few years back I had a conversation with
collector Dan Cariseo regarding single-signed
baseballs. He pointed out something very important and it is worth discussing. There seems
to be a good supply of single-signed baseballs
in the market of players who died young.
Roberto Clemente, Roger Maris, Jackie Robinson, Gil Hodges, and Thurman Munson come
to mind. The question is, why do so many
single-signed baseballs of these players exist?
When they were alive, collecting single-signed
baseballs was not really in fashion. It would be
a rare event to have only Hodges sign a baseball.
Back then the goal was to get as many players
as possible to sign one baseball. Yet there seems
to be a good quantity of the expensive single-
signed baseballs in the market. Why?

Cariseo points out that other players of this
era, who lived a long time, are very rare on vintage single-signed baseballs, much more so than
the above-referenced players. Good point.
When was the last time you saw a single-signed
baseball of Duke Snider, Al Kaline, George Kell,
Robin Roberts, or Billy Pierce signed in the
1950s? Never? Why is a vintage single-signed
baseball of Kaline harder to find than that of
Clemente or Hodges? He was just as popular.
The reason why there are more single-signed
baseballs of the tougher signatures, like Clemente, is that forgers produce them in quantities given the high value. It is not worth a
forger's time to create a vintage Kaline single-
signed baseball only to sell it for $100. Had Ka-
line died young, there would be far more single-
signed baseballs in the market, compliments of
the forger.

The case of Nellie Fox is instructive. Fox was
an outstanding second baseman for the Chicago

White Sox from the late 1940s to the 1960s. He died in 1975 at the young age of 47. Before 1997, single-signed baseballs of Fox were nowhere to be found. They had some value, but not much. Single-signed Fox baseballs rarely, if ever, turned up for sale, and then only for a couple of hundred dollars. Then in 1997 something happened. Fox was inducted into the Hall of Fame. Within a year, Fox baseballs surfaced like weeds. They are now available in far greater quantities. Why? Because now a single-signed Fox ball is worth $2,000 to $3,000. It is now worth a forger's time to produce these as the financial return is far greater.

Bart Giamatti is a fine example. Giamatti died in 1989 at a young age. He signed very little material for collectors, relatively speaking. Single-signed baseballs are rare; seldom do they surface. I am convinced that Giamatti will someday find his way into Cooperstown. When he does get elected, single-signed Giamatti baseballs, like those of Fox, will surface in quantities shortly thereafter. The one argument I have heard to the contrary is that people hoard signed material of players before their induction, then release it after they gain entrance into Cooperstown. This seems a silly position as most material of this type enters the market from estates or people who are not collectors. It is brought forth upon discovery, not induction into the Hall of Fame. The reason is clear: Clemente, Robinson, Hodges, and other valuable signatures are continuously created by the forger, hence the greater inventory.

* * *

It all began way back in 1839 when a young military officer named Abner Doubleday laid the foundation for the game we know as baseball. Eyewitness accounts from Abner Graves, a highly respected mining engineer, have Doubleday organizing the first game in a cow pasture in Cooperstown, New York. In honor of Doubleday's innovation, the national Baseball Hall of Fame was built on that very site. Dou-

bleday's signature is in high demand and quite scarce. It would be an extreme rarity but for his career as a military officer. A restricted supply of military-related letters and documents do exist. These are a critical source of Doubleday signatures. Doubleday signed in a slower hand. His signature is very legible. An above average display value is noted. During the Civil War, Doubleday attained the rank of general for the Union. There are writings penned by Doubleday in which he refers to baseball and orders equipment so the troops can play the game.

In recent years there has been much interest in Doubleday and it has increased demand for his signature. In 1905, Major League Baseball formed the Mills Commission, which included three National League presidents. The commission, after conducting extensive research, pronounced Doubleday as the father of the game. Over the past ten or so years a few revisionist baseball historians, with a bit too much time on their hands, have attempted to dethrone Doubleday as the inventor of the game. Their evidence is an early engraving published before 1839 portraying a game similar to baseball but with wooden posts in the middle of the field. I don't ever recall seeing wooden posts on a baseball diamond—must be a National League thing.

Much to the dismay of the revisionists, MLB, in a September 2010 statement released by commissioner Bud Selig's office, reaffirmed General Doubleday as the man who invented the game of baseball. Doubleday's signature can be purchased for $800 to $1,000. ALsS are closer to $2,000.

Doubleday-1, undated signature.

Throughout the 1840s and 1850s, baseball gained in popularity. Town ball became a popular pastime, mostly east of the Mississippi. In 1869 the first professional game was played. The Cincinnati Red Stockings became the dominant team. Their star shortstop was George Wright. Wright's major league career spanned from 1869 to 1882. Wright's signature is fairly rare and in demand. He signed in a flowing hand. Early writings evidence a signature with strong eye appeal. Most signatures are penned as "Geo. Wright." Around 1910 Wright was afflicted with some type of palsy. Signatures accomplished from 1910 until his death in 1937 evidence material unsteadiness. Signatures penned after 1920 are very unsteady. Signatures from this era are very easy to forge and many well-executed forgeries exist. Wright's signature was, for many decades, a rare to very rare signature. In 2013, a collection of Dickson & Wright corporate documents entered the market. Many were sold on eBay. Approximately 60 signatures were released into the market, mostly on corporate minutes. They were quickly absorbed by collectors. This cache likely tripled the total population of Wright signatures. His signature is still valuable. The above referenced DsS are valued at $1,000 to $1,250. This is a good price considering DsS were, at one time, selling in the $5,000 to $7,500 price range. Values will rebound over the next few years.

Wright, G-1 stock proxy dated 1916.

Wright's brother, Harry, was also a key figure of the pioneer days of baseball. He also played for the Red Stockings. Wright's signature is among the finest of the Hall of Fame members. His signature glides effortlessly on paper and exhibits strong letter construction. The sweeping curves create a signature with superior display value. Due to the complex construction of Wright's signature, replication of hand is ex-

tremely difficult. Well-executed forgeries do not exist. His signature is much rarer than that of his brother George. A few DsS and ALsS exist. It should be noted that many Wright signatures were stolen from the New York Public Library. If you find a Wright signature in the market it is very likely stolen. Careful examination is needed with pre–1905 signatures of either Wright, as title issues may exist. Early Wright-signed documents cause much controversy and the matter is actively being investigated by federal law enforcement. Harry's signature is valued at $1,500 to $2,000. A nicely accomplished ALS will sell for about $10,000.

Wright, H-1 ALS dated 1871.

By the 1870s baseball was sweeping across the nation. It was now being referred to as the national pastime. More cities began fielding teams and the game was moving westward. The game started to produce star players. The first superstars were Adrian "Cap" Anson and Mike "King" Kelly.

Anson was the first member of the hallowed 3,000 hit club and the biggest name in 19th-century ball. Anson signed in a choppy and reserved hand. His signature lacks flow. Marginal eye appeal is noted. Most signatures are penned as "A.C. Anson." Anson signatures are rare but not unobtainable. He held the position of clerk for the city of Chicago in early 1900s for a single two-year term. Anson signed many documents and letters and this is about the only way to obtain his signature. The majority of clerk-related documents are, however, signed by a secretary, so caution is warranted. Some handwritten endorsements were penned by Anson on the back of letters sent to the clerk's office. I spoke with a city employee regarding these endorsements.

The city has no record of these being released, so they are likely stolen.

A few theatrical contracts dated in the teens are in the market. Anson did some acting with his daughters. These contracts are signed as "Captain Anson and daughters." These are secretarially signed and not signed by Anson. Theatrical contracts should be avoided in total.

Anson's signature likely does not exist on a baseball, photograph, or gum card. Multisigned forged baseballs are in the market, so caution is warranted. A couple of signed banquet menus exist and the signatures are accomplished in pencil. The best way to obtain Anson's signature is on one the above-referenced city of Chicago documents. Anson's signature is in great demand. Expect to pay $1,500 for a nice specimen. An ALS is valued at $4,500 to $5,500. Content letters will easily sell for more than $10,000.

Anson-1, post 1900 signature (courtesy Jim Stinson Sports).

Anson-2 a common secretarial.

Anson-3, a common secretarial.

King Kelly was another giant of the game, but unlike Anson, a Kelly signature is an extreme rarity. Kelly signed in a flowing hand. Letter construction and eye appeal are both sound. Signatures are signed "M.J. Kelly." Kelly died at a young age of pneumonia; hence, the population of signatures in the market is, to my knowledge, only one. It is a signed contract. The Baseball Hall of Fame holds a few signed financial documents. Many forgeries, on various mediums, have been sold as genuine. Autographically, Kelly's signature is excessively rare. I estimate a market value of the contract at $100,000 to $150,000. A few years back a signed photograph on a program sold at auction for six figures. It was signed as "Yours truly, M.J. Kelly." I have my doubts as to the authenticity of this piece.

Kelly, M-1 Prom. Note dated 1890 (courtesy National Baseball Hall of Fame and Museum).

Another early star of the game was Big Dan Brouthers. He began his major league career in 1879 with the Troy Trojans. He compiled a .342 lifetime average and is considered one of the greatest players of 19th-century ball. Brouthers's signature is extremely rare. Only a couple of specimens are in the open market; both are letters, one of which is illustrated. Brouthers has been targeted by forgers, and one particular forgery needs to be examined. About fifteen years ago, album pages and envelopes surfaced that are purportedly signed by Brouthers. They are typically signed with a return address. Many are signed with the words "Polo Grounds" underneath the forgery. Others are signed with "West 96th Street, New York." An unsteadiness of hand is noted. One of these forgeries is illustrated; note the material deviation from the genuine specimen. I know of no signed baseballs or photographs. Just about all Brouthers signatures ever sold, and there have been many, are forgeries. A genuine signature is likely valued at $30,000 to $40,000.

Brouthers-1 ALS dated 1917.

Brouthers-2 common forgery.

Baseball was looked down upon as a game for gamblers, drunkards, and other such cutthroats. In the 1890s that was beginning to change. Soon baseball gained a measure of respectability. The number of town ball and semipro teams also increased. Suddenly baseball was everywhere. It was the modern-day equivalent of the Cambrian Explosion. Soon players like Rube Waddell, Nap Lajoie, and Honus Wagner entered the stage.

Honus Wagner, the mythical Flying Dutchman, began his major league career in 1897 with the Louisville Colonels. He is considered one of the greatest baseball players in history. Wagner's signature has always been popular with collectors, and fortunately he was a willing signer throughout his life. Wagner signed in a very flowing and artistic hand. His signature has wonderful eye appeal. Signatures accomplished in the last ten or so years of his life evidence shakiness of hand. Signatures can be found on letters, government postcards, and a large supply of bank checks. Single-signed baseballs are rare and highly treasured. Wagner's signature can be purchased for $700 to $800, checks for $1,000 to $1,250. ALsS are very tough to locate and a full-page letter will sell for $3,000 to $4,000. A nice single-signed baseball is worth at least $10,000.

Wagner, H-1 ALS dated 1943.

Wagner-H-2, circa 1950 signature.

Napoleon "Larry" Lajoie was another rock star of turn-of-the-century ball. Like Wagner, he is considered one of the all-time greats. Lajoie began his career in 1896 with the Philadelphia Phillies and played 21 years of major league ball. Lajoie signed in a sophisticated and pleasing hand. His signature exhibits sweeping curves. A high degree of legibility is noted. Material signed in the 1950s tends to evidence shakiness of hand, but not to the extent found in Wagner's signature. His signature is found on most mediums, although single-signed baseballs are rare to very rare. ALsS are also rare and seldom encountered. One signed 1933 Goudey Gum card exists. Lajoie's signature can be purchased for $500 to $600. Other mediums are typically valued over $1,000. A full-page ALS sells for $3,000 to $4,000. A nice single-signed baseball is closer to $10,000. The above-referenced Goudey card is a unique gem and would likely sell in excess of $100,000.

There is one group of Lajoie forgeries to discuss simply because they are so nonsensical. About ten years ago a small group of forged 1939 Hall of Fame induction pieces entered the market. They were first-day covers and 8 × 10 sheets of paper with a blue Abner Doubleday stamp placed in the center of the sheet. Forgeries of most of the 1939 Hall of Fame inductees are added, along with lesser names: Ruth, Cobb, Cy Young, Connie Mack, Charlie Gehringer, Postmaster General James Farley, and/or other signatures. The Lajoie forgery easily stands out as the forger misspells the first name Larry as "Larrry" with an extra letter "r." Sadder yet is that these items usually come complete with certificates of authenticity from the major authentication companies. If you run across one of those "Larrry Lajoie" signatures, take my advice and avoid it.

Lajoie-1 circa 1950 signature.

A teammate of Lajoie was Big Ed Delahanty. Delahanty was one of the all-time greats with a .346 lifetime batting average. Delahanty's signature is extremely rare. Only three specimens are believed in the market and one has title issues. Delahanty-signed material is very expensive and out of the reach of most collectors' budgets. There are a handful of letters in the market that cause great controversy, simply because of poor authentication. These letters are purportedly written by Delahanty. One letter, written to Hillerich & Bradsby and dated 1899, received much press. Unfortunately, the letters in question were written and signed by Delahanty's manager William Shettsline. These forgeries are easily spotted as Shettsline misspells the last name as "Delehanty." Shettsline's secretarial signature deviates greatly from a genuine specimen. These letters should be avoided in total. A signed Delahanty postal cover, postmarked 1903, recently sold for $20,000. It is the only public sale I know of since 1994.

Delahanty-1 ledger circa 1895.

Even rarer is the signature of George Edward "Rube" Waddell. Waddell also played with the Colonels and went on to stardom with Connie Mack's Athletics. Waddell is considered one the fastest pitchers of all time. He died in 1914 at the age of 37, a victim of consumption. To my knowledge only one genuine Waddell signature is in the market. It is a signed banquet menu accomplished in pencil and countersigned by other players, among them fellow Hall of Famer Joe McGinnity. Waddell's divorce file surfaced a few years back. It contained three signatures, one of which is illustrated. These signatures are held by a governmental concern and will never be released into the market. It is highly unlikely a signed baseball of any kind exists. A few years back a few forged baseballs entered the market. They are signed on the side panel of the ball with a forgery accomplished in printed script. Autographically speaking, an extreme rarity. I estimate a value of at least $40,000.

Waddell-1 Legal DS dated 1909.

In 1901 the American League played its first full season as a major league. Its first president was Byron "Ban" Johnson. He was the catalyst behind the fledgling league and remained president until 1927. Johnson died in 1931 at the age of 66. Johnson's signature is scarce, but only mildly so. There is a good supply of league-related letters, documents, and contracts in the market. His signature is probably the easiest of the long-deceased Hall of Famers to obtain.

Johnson, B-1 undated signature.

TLsS can be purchased for a mere $300. Secretarially signed letters are known, though deviation of hand is great.

When Johnson was forced from the league he created, longtime Cleveland general manager E.S. Barnard was elected the league's second president. He served until his unexpected death in 1931. Barnard letters are scarce, but a restricted number of TLsS do exist. Some TLsS came out of the Jacob Ruppert estate. Often mentioned as a possible Hall of Famer, Barnard is a good signature to pick up. Letters are currently valued at $200. Should he be so honored with induction into Cooperstown, those letters will increase in value to $1,000.

Barnard-1, TLS dated 1928.

In 1900 began a new era of baseball. As a student of the game, I have always been fascinated with the dark and mysterious "deadball" era. To the modern-day bug, it is a period of the game as distant as the Ice Age. Its players have attained a revered status of sorts. The number of Hall of Famers and notable journeymen from this era offers collectors a vast assortment of collectable names.

On August 30, 1905, John "Happy Jack" Chesbro was pitching against the Detroit Tigers at old Hilltop Park. He faced a rookie making his first plate appearance in the major leagues. He got a double off Chesbro. His name was Tyrus Raymond Cobb. He would get 4,190 more base hits. He hit an incredible lifetime average of .367, 12 batting crowns, and 1,961 RBIs. When he retired in 1928, he held the record for holding records.

Ty Cobb signed in a flowing and aggressive hand. His signature features bold strokes. Letter construction and legibility are above average. The signature is almost always finished off with a paraph. Cobb's hand remained strong most of his life; only in the closing days of his life did infirmity affect his writing. For collecting purposes, a genuine Cobb signature will evidence no shakiness of hand, and one that does should be considered suspect. Cobb's signature is fairly difficult to copy; hence, replication of hand does take effort. Given the value of Cobb's signature, well-executed forgeries do exist and in mass quantities. Cobb was a willing signer throughout his entire life. In addition, the family released thousands of bank checks to raise money for the Cobb Educational Foundation. His signature is on the common side. Cobb was a prolific man of letters and penned literally thousands of them, most of which survive to this day. Letters are well-written and gracious. Some have excellent baseball and business content. Cobb ALsS are probably the most common of *all* the Baseball Hall of Famers. I have personally owned over a dozen in my lifetime.

Cobb-signed baseballs exist but are generally limited to post–1950 specimens. Single-signed baseballs from his playing days are scarce. Signatures can be found on most mediums including books, Hall of Fame plaque postcards, gum cards, government postcards, photographs, and team-signed baseballs.

Cobb is one of the most forged signatures, baseball or otherwise. Cobb forgeries exist in quantities. I estimate that 90 percent of all Cobb signatures offered in the market are forgeries. Countless forgeries and even facsimiles have been wrongly certified as genuine by the major authentication companies, so caution is warranted. There are two forgeries that need to be discussed.

Cobb's ill-gotten reputation as a madman can be traced to writer Al Stump. Cobb was, and still remains, one of the biggest names in American history. So when an elderly Cobb chose the relatively unknown author Stump to write his biography, you would think Stump would have been appreciative. Instead, once Cobb died, Stumpy stuck a knife in his back and wrote a biography that was basically gibberish fiction and made Cobb out to be a lunatic. Stump used his relationship with Cobb to perpetrate one of the biggest frauds in the field of autographs. After Cobb died, Stump got ahold of countless sheets of Cobb's personal letterhead. Years later, typed Cobb letters, addressed to Stump; with amazing baseball content, entered the marketplace. Letters discussing Shoeless Joe Jackson, Babe Ruth, Mel Ott, Honus Wagner, the Black Sox, and the like surfaced in quantities. Some contained crass comments. A crude Cobb forgery was affixed to the letters, most likely by Stump himself. Dr. William R. Cobb discussed these letters at length in his award-winning article titled "The Georgia Peach: Stumped by the Storyteller." It was published in the 2010 edition of *The National Pastime* by the Society for American Baseball Research. Cobb wrote: "On cursory inspection, they [the letters] appear authentic, since they are typed on apparently genuine Ty Cobb letterhead.... Ultimately these letters were sold into the market and then were discredited as forgeries by numerous authenticators.... They were first offered to Mike Gutierrez, a prominent authenticator, who authenticated them as genuine and then sold them directly and at auction to trusting buyers...." The forged Stump/Cobb letters contain such an amateurish forgery that it is surprising that they were accepted as genuine by *anyone*. Fortunately, the forgeries are so poor they are identified with little examination. These letters still surface every now and then, so caution is warranted.

A relatively new forgery has surfaced in the past few years and it needs to be discussed. Several years ago a photograph of Detroit Tigers 2nd baseman George "Hack" Simmons, taken by photographer Charles Conlon, was reproduced in a sports book. The book incorrectly identified the image as that of Ty Cobb. Future publications reprinted the image and perpetuated the mistaken identity. Over the years Simmons became Cobb. Years later, forgers, believing the Simmons photograph was that of Cobb, used it to produce many forged photographs.

Of course, Cobb would never sign a photograph of Simmons. It was a publishing mistake that tripped up the forgers. The authenticators exacerbated the problem by erroneously pronouncing them as genuine. I have illustrated the Simmons photograph in question. If you see this photograph "signed" by Cobb, and many exist, it should be avoided as a forgery. It should be noted that Cobb had a rubber stamp made of his signature. He rarely, if ever, used it for autograph purposes. It is illustrated.

The value of Cobb's signature has increased greatly since the 1980s. Back then a signed bank check could be purchased for $10 to $20. Today, that same check is worth $1,000. Signed 8 × 10 photographs sell for $3,500 to $4,000. Superior specimens will easily sell for more than $10,000. ALsS with routine content are valued at $1,500 to $2,000. Letters with content will easily cross $10,000. In 2013, a four-page Cobb letter written to fellow Hall of Famer Stan Musial sold for a record-setting price of $71,000 (Heritage Auctions). A single-signed baseball of average grade is valued between $4,000 and $6,000. A museum-grade specimen will sell for $50,000 or more. A major league contract would be an extreme rarity. According to auctioneer Josh Evans of Lelands.com: "There has not been a Cobb contract sold since the Sotheby's auction of the Barry Halper collection in 1999. At that time the price was in the $65,000 range. If a nice specimen were to become available, it would bring $150,000 to $250,000 in today's market."

Cobb-1 very rare ALS dated 1915.

Cobb-2, album page dated 1927.

Cobb-4 common stamp circa late 1950s (courtesy Herschel Cobb).

The deadball era produced many stars and journeymen who are favorites among today's collectors. A few of these players lived into the 1970s and were good signers. Some great signatures, such as Davy Jones, John "Hans" Lobert, and Fred Snodgrass, can be purchased for under $50. Others are so rare that values are not established. William "Germany" Schaefer was one of the oddest characters to tumble out of the Cobbian era. He died in 1919, and his autograph is extremely rare and desired by many. I cannot recall his signature ever being transacted in the open market. Detroit Tigers pitcher Wild Bill Donovan has borderline Hall of Fame numbers. He was killed in a train wreck in 1923. His signature rarely surfaces and is valued at $1,000 to $1,500.

Cobb-3 forged TLS to Al Stump dated 1960.

WITNESS:

Donovan-1, signature, circa 1920.

By 1910 Denton True "Cy" Young was winding down his career. Many consider Young the greatest pitcher in the history of the game. His 511 kills is a record that will never be

Cobb-5, photograph of Hack Simmons wrongly believed to be Cobb.

touched. Young signed in a no-nonsense and pleasing hand. His signature evidences sound letter construction and good legibility. Signatures accomplished in the last few years of life evidence a material shakiness of hand. There is strong demand for Young's signature. It is considered somewhat scarce but an ample supply exists. Most signatures are found on government postcards and index cards. Less common are letters and Hall of Fame plaque postcards. Single-signed baseballs are rare and most are forgeries. There is one stamped signature to note. This stamp was used by Young to identify certain personal belongings, mostly snapshot photographs. They were stamped on the back. Many of these photographs have entered the market, so caution is warranted. Forgeries exist on most mediums, especially the above-referenced plaque postcards. Strong demand pushes prices ever higher. A signature is valued at $700 to $800. ALsS sell for $2,500 to $3,000. A nice single-signed baseball is worth $ $8,000 to $10,000.

Young-1 signature dated 1940.

Another immortal whose career spanned the late Victorian era of ball and the deadball era was the diminutive William "Wee Willie" Keeler. At only 5'4", Keeler was the most unlikely of stars. He was one of the greatest hitters of all time and secured a lifetime average of .343. Keeler signed in a legible and no-nonsense hand. Signatures are unassuming with average letter construction and display value. There is nothing exceptional about his hand. Keeler died on New Year's Day 1923; hence, his signature is very rare and borders on the nonexistent. Just about 100 percent of all Keeler signatures ever offered for sale are forgeries. I estimate a total

market population of fewer than five specimens, all letter or document related. I have never examined a signed baseball or photograph of any kind and they likely do not exist. A genuine signature will likely sell for more than $25,000.

Keeler-1 Will dated 1922.

The Big Six, Christy Mathewson, was one the greatest pitchers of all time. Matty's signature causes much controversy. Not only are many forgeries pronounced as genuine, but many real signatures are wrongly dismissed as fake. Mathewson signed in a pleasing and thoughtful hand. Letter construction is sound. A high degree of legibility is noted. The signature usually exhibits and overly large letter "s" in the last name. On occasion, Mathewson signed with a variant form of signature. It is vertical in nature and more pragmatic in appearance. It is often dismissed as secretarially signed. It is not. Some bank checks will exhibit both variations of hand. Mathewson died at the age of 45, a belated victim of mustard gas. Mathewson's hand remained strong his entire life. A genuine signature will exhibit no shakiness of hand. Due to the pensive nature of his signature, replication of hand is fairly easy. Well-executed forgeries exist in quantities. Just about 100 percent of all Mathewson signatures ever sold are forgeries. Many have been wrongly certified as genuine by the authentication companies, so caution is warranted. After his death, Mrs. Mathewson would send out canceled bank checks to satisfy requests from collectors. Just about all signatures in the market are on these checks. The only other medium you will find are letters, which are very rare. Other mediums are basically nonexistent. I have only seen one genuinely signed photograph and one multi-signed baseball in my life. Many single-signed baseballs have sold at auction for big money, $100,000 or more. These balls feature the variant signature, vertical in nature. I believe them to all be forgeries. I have yet to see a genuine single-signed baseball. I seriously doubt one exists.

Skilled forgers have targeted Mathewson's signature for years. They have produced some convincing fakes. Recently complete bank checks, made payable to Mathewson, have entered the market. A forged Mathewson endorsement signature is added on the reverse. These are very convincing, as forged bank endorsements are stamped on the back. Sometimes a postage stamp or paper stamp, with red lettering, is affixed to the checks. This forger has also produced forged Joe McGinnity checks of the same style.

Mathewson authored a book titled *Won in the Ninth*. It was published in 1910. The publisher released many presentation copies. A bookplate, with the recipient's name typed in, was affixed to the book. The plates contain a signature purportedly signed by Mathewson. The signature is more sharply angled. Material deviation is noted when compared to a genuine specimen. These presentation copies are secretarially signed and not signed by Mathewson. I only know of one genuinely signed Mathewson-authored book. Signed presentation copies of *Won in the Ninth* should be avoided in total.

For more information on Mathewson-signed books, see the June 12, 2005, *New York Daily News* article "Sotheby's Auction Forges Ahead," by Michael O'Keeffe.

Mathewson's signature is valued at $5,000 to $6,000. Bank checks are valued at $12,500 to $15,000. A full-page ALS is a gem and is worth $25,000. Should a *real* single-signed baseball ever be discovered, it would be valued in excess of $100,000.

Mathewson-1 circa 1920s signature.

Mathewson-2 bank check dated 1922 variant form of signature.

Ask the question who was the fastest pitcher of all time and the answer is Walter Johnson. Nicknamed the "Big Train," Johnson racked up 416 kills against 279 losses. Johnson signed in a crisp and clean hand. His signature has nice letter construction and sound eye appeal. A distinctive capital letter "J" is noted. He died of a brain tumor in 1946 and his hand remained strong his entire life. A genuine Johnson signature will exhibit no shakiness of hand. Johnson was a willing signer his entire life. There is an ample supply of index cards, government postcards, and bank checks in the market. Less common are letters, photographs, and single-signed baseballs. Signed Hall of Fame plaque postcards are extremely rare. I have never seen a genuine specimen. The large supply of bank checks in the market depresses value. Johnson's signature can be purchased for $700 to $800. Bank checks sell for $1,000 to $1,250. A full-page ALS is valued at $2,000 to $2,500. A nice single-signed baseball is valued at $6,000 to $7,000.

Johnson, W-1 undated signature.

Obtaining items signed by players linked in history has always been popular and highly collected. Collectors often obtain dual-signed items for addition to their collections. Ralph Branca and Bobby Thomson, Warren Spahn and Johnny Sain, Mickey Owen and Tom Henrich, and the like. Broadcast teams are also popular with collectors such as Ernie Harwell and Paul Carey, George Kell and Al Kaline, and so on. Some combinations are much tougher to find.

In the 1930s the Detroit Tigers had the famed G-men of Charlie Gehringer, Hank Greenberg, and Goose Goslin. All are Hall of Fame members. Finding an item signed by just these three would be a rare treasure. I have never seen one. Their signatures together can only be found on Tigers signed team sheets and baseballs. Gehringer signatures sell for a mere $10 to $15. Greenberg, who died just before the era of mass signing, retains higher value at $75 to $100. Goslin's signature is worth $125 to $150. A single-signed baseball of Goslin is very rare and just about all in the market are forgeries. An item signed by just these three would carry a premium of somewhere between $750 and $1,000.

Gehringer-1 album page dated 1939.

Goslin-1 photograph dated 1934.

Greenberg-1 government postcard circa 1940s.

Connie Mack's $100,000 Infield would be an exceptional find with Stuffy McInnis, Eddie Collins, Jack Barry, and Home Run Baker. Their signatures are each valued in the $150 to $300 range. An item with all four signatures would easily sell for more than $2,000.

The ultimate combination is the famed double play team of the Chicago Cubs back around the turn of the last century: Tinker to Evers to Chance.

The signature of Frank Chance is by far the rarest of the three. He died in 1924 and signed very little material. A few signed letters and maybe one or two other items exist, but that is about it. Chance's signature is flowing with precise strokes. Strong display value is noted. Replication of hand would be difficult; hence, producing a well-executed forgery would take effort. I know of no signed photographs, baseball cards, or baseballs in existence. Forged lower grade T-206 cards exist in quantities, so caution is warranted. There are a few forged baseballs in the market. They are signed "Compliments of Frank L. Chance." Chance-signed baseballs should be avoided in total. Chance's signature is probably worth $10,000 to $15,000. An ALS is closer to $20,000 or perhaps $30,000.

Chance-1 ALS circa 1910.

Joe Tinker was the shortstop in this fabled trio. He lived into the 1940s and the market population is far greater than that of Chance. Tinker signed in a slower hand. Material signed in the late 1930s until his death in 1948 will evidence some shakiness of hand. Due to the pensive nature of his hand, producing a well-executed forgery can be done with little effort. The vast majority of Tinker signatures in the market are forgeries. Signatures are typically limited to index cards, and ANsS on government postcards. Signed 8 × 10 photographs and ALsS are extreme rarities. I have never examined a genuine signed 8 × 10 photograph. Tinker-signed baseballs are extremely rare. I have only seen a couple of multi-signed baseballs. I have never examined a single-signed baseball in my life. Tinker's signature can be purchased for $750 to $900. Government post-cards are valued at $1,250 to $1,500.

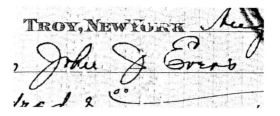

Tinker-1 TLS dated 1913 (courtesy National Baseball Hall of Fame and Museum).

Johnny Evers is the final member of this trio. His signature is the most available of the three, though it should still be considered scarce on a per se basis. Premium items are very rare to nonexistent. Evers signed in a choppy yet flowing hand. His signature evidences cutting angles and crisp lines. Letter construction is fairly sound. Like that of Tinker, Evers's signature is typically found on index cards and government postcards. ALsS are rare but do exist. Evers had more than one business venture; hence, letters with business content can be found. Letters written to young fans are also available. These have charming content and are worth a premium. Signed baseballs of any kind are very rare. I have examined a couple of single-signed baseballs I would pronounce as genuine. Bank checks are also available, but these seldom surface. He is often targeted by forgers, so fake Evers material exists in quantities. There is one forgery to note. Many forged album pages, index cards, and ANsS are in the market. Signatures evidence a slightly labored appearance, something a genuine specimen would not have. The forger usually dates the forgeries in the following style: "11/24/39." Evers was fond of dating signatures, but would spell out the month, such as "Jan. 4. 32" or "Oct. 31. 44." Any Evers signature (not on a document) where the month is not spelled out should be avoided in total. Evers's signature is available for $600 to $700. An ALS or bank check is valued in the $3,000 price range. A single signed baseball would sell between $20,000 and $25,000.

Evers-1 bank check dated 1915.

Items signed by all three are limited to a couple of signed banquet menus, circa 1910, that include many other signatures of Cubs players. These were signed in pencil. One sold in the recession of 2008 for a mere $8,200 (Robert Edward Auctions) which, to me, is a steal. I estimate a current market value of $20,000.

Gilder Jackson, professor of history at Lawrence Technological University, once stated: "Tris Speaker was the finest defensive outfielder in the history of the game." Speaker was one of the all-time greats and a superstar of the Cobbian era of ball. Speaker signed in a very odd and mechanical hand. The signature evidences odd angles and is cubic in appearance. Letter construction is sound. Like most of the old-time greats, Speaker was a willing signer. Signatures are typically found on index cards, government postcards, and team-issued picture postcards. Full-page ALsS and single-signed baseballs are rare but do exist. Speaker is one of the more affordable signatures of the pre–1940 Hall of Fame inductees. His signature will sell for $400 to $500. Picture postcards are valued at $600 to $700. A nice single-signed baseball is valued at $4,000 to $5,000.

Speaker-1 1950 signature.

One of the greatest pitchers of all time was Grover Cleveland Alexander. Alexander began his career in 1911 with the Philadelphia Phillies.

His win/loss record is 373 to 208. Alexander signed in a very rudimentary hand. The signature lacks precision. Letter construction is marginal as some letters are malformed. Replication of hand is rather easy. Many well-executed forgeries are in the marketplace, especially on baseballs. Alexander was a bit reclusive in his retirement years, due to illness and drink. His signature is far less common than other Hall of Famers who lived until the 1950s. Signatures are usually found on index cards and team-signed baseballs from the 1920s. Government postcards, photographs, and ALsS are rare. Single-signed baseballs are very rare. I have only seen three genuine specimens in my life. Over 90 percent of Alexander signatures in the market are forgeries. His signature sells for $1,000. A full-page ALS is valued at $3,500 to $4,000. Values of single-signed baseballs are depressed simply because so many forged ones have been sold. A genuine specimen is valued at $20,000.

Alexander-1, circa 1940s government postcard.

Another of the early immortals is Eddie Collins. Collins's career paralleled that of Cobb, Speaker, and Joe Jackson. He secured a .333 lifetime average and is a member of the 3,000 hit club. Collins signed in a flowing and elegant hand. His signature exhibits wonderful letter construction. Display value is superior. Given the complex nature of hand, well-executed forgeries do not exist. Collins is one of the more affordable of the early Hall of Fame inductees. He held an executive position with the Boston Red Sox for many years. There is a lavish supply of signed letters and documents in the market, which depresses values. Single-signed baseballs are an extreme rarity. I have only seen one genuine specimen in over 30 of searching. Letters, mostly TLsS, can be purchased for under $250. ALsS are much tougher to find and sell for

$1,000 to $1,500. Single-signed baseballs and Hall of Fame plaque postcards are highly treasured.

Collins, E-1 TLS dated 1943.

"Gorgeous George" Sisler was the last surviving member of the of the 1939 induction ceremony. He died in 1973 and is the most available of the pre–1940 inductees. Sisler signed in a choppy and unattractive hand. Display value is marginal at best. Sisler's signature is generally found on index cards and Hall of Fame plaque postcards. Other mediums are uncommon to rare. The occasional letter and 8 × 10 photograph will surface. Single-signed baseballs are rare and most offered in the market are forged. Sisler's autograph sells for $50. Signed plaque postcards are valued at $125. A single-signed baseball is highly treasured, so expect to pay $4,000 for a nice specimen.

Sisler-1 circa 1965 signature.

The 1919 season brought forth baseball's darkest hour. In was in that year that eight members of the Chicago White Sox conspired with New York gamblers, principally Arnold Rothstein, to throw the World Series to the Cincinnati Reds. It was the biggest scandal in the history of sports. These players would go down in history as the Black Sox. Among them was Shoeless Joe Jackson, a player whose skills rivaled those of Ty Cobb and Babe Ruth. Jackson was an illiterate but was able to sign his name. Signatures are tremulous and appear childlike. Display value is very poor. Close to 100 percent of Jackson signatures offered in the market are forgeries. To my knowledge, there are about ten genuine specimens in the market; *all* are document-related. I know of no genuinely signed gum cards, baseballs, album pages or photographs. Jackson rarely signed autographs and then only for legal matters. Mail requests for his signature were signed by his wife.

Let's be clear: Jackson did not sign autographs for collectors. More than one old-time collector has said that when they stopped by Jackson's liquor store and asked for an autograph, he would reach under the counter and give them a pre-signed index card, accomplished by Mrs. Jackson. If they requested a specific item be signed (e.g., a baseball), Jackson would tell them to leave it and pick it up the next day. Again it would be signed by his wife. Her signature looks nothing like a genuine specimen.

A common forged photograph has Jackson in a formal portrait pose wearing a suit and tie. These are signed across the chest in fountain pen. Another common forgery is multi-signed baseballs featuring a Jackson signature with four or five other forgeries. Cy Young's signature, and sometimes Ty Cobb's, are added to the baseballs. These are signed on Tri-State League baseballs. There are a handful of forged Addie Joss benefit game balls in the market, purportedly signed by Jackson and other players attending the game. These baseballs are stained a dark brown. They should be avoided in total.

Another common forgery was created many years ago. There are a certain number of the period envelopes, postmarked in the 1940s, that originated from the Jackson estate. Hence they are addressed to Jackson. A crude forgery or two is placed on back of the envelope. Sometimes a partial signature, such as "Jo" or "Joe Jac," is added to give the forgeries a flavor of genuineness. The forgeries themselves are rudimentary in construction. Common sense tells you that autograph requests are not honored in such an odd fashion. When have you ever seen a signer pen his signature two or three times on the back of an envelope that is not part of a re-turn address? These envelopes should be avoided in total. A genuine specimen is valued somewhere between $25,000 and $50,000.

Jackson, J-1, World War I draft card (courtesy Record Group 163, Records of the Selective Services Division, National Archives at Atlanta).

Jackson, J-2, common secretarial by Mrs. Jackson.

The most attainable Black Sox signature is Eddie Cicotte. Cicotte lived out a quiet retirement in Farmington, Michigan, and was an obliging signer. Signatures are generally limited to government postcards and index cards. The occasional book photograph will surface, but these are rare. Single-signed baseballs are very rare but a few do exist. His signature is the most affordable of all the fixers. Index cards sell for $250 to $300. Government postcards are valued at $500. A single-signed baseball has a likely value of $15,000 to $20,000.

Cicotte-1 signature circa 1960.

The rarest signature is that of Fred McMullin. He was a lackluster player with a forgettable record. I think he hit one home run in his life, no doubt an inside-the-parker. McMullin signed in a legible hand. Letter construction is sound. The only confirmed specimen I have seen is on a World War I draft card. I have never seen a genuine signature offered for sale. Forgeries exist on 1919 team-"signed" baseballs. A few forged multi-signed baseballs are in the market. The forger typically signs them as "F. McMullin." These are signed on Federal League and Western League baseballs. Value of a genuine specimen is indeterminate.

Frederick McMullin

McMullin-1, World War I draft card (courtesy Record Group 163, Records of the Selective Services Division, National Archives at Atlanta).

Oscar "Hap" Felsch died in 1964 and signed a limited number of items. Like Cicotte, he mostly signed index cards and government postcards. Felsch's signature is rather easy to forge and just about all in the market are forgeries. I have never seen a genuinely signed baseball, ALS, gum card, or photograph. His signature is valued at $1,500. A government postcard is valued around $2,500.

Oscar Felsch

Felsch-1, World War I draft card (courtesy Record Group 163, Records of the Selective Services Division, National Archives at Atlanta).

Claude "Lefty" Williams was an outstanding pitcher and, like Cicotte and Jackson, would have likely found his way into Cooperstown. Williams signed in a very rudimentary hand. The signature evidences slight hesitation. It is an unassuming signature with substandard display value. Williams's signature is very easy to replicate. Well-executed forgeries exist in quantities. His signature is very rare on a per se basis,

and generally limited to a few signed documents and check endorsements. Just about 100 percent of all Williams's signatures in the market are forgeries. I estimate a value of $7,500 for his autograph.

Arnold "Chic" Gandil was one of the architects of the fix. He was a fine defensive first baseman. He died in 1970 and, like the other Black Sox, signed relatively little material. The occasional index card will surface. A small grouping of signatures removed from bank checks are in the market. His signature is less common than that of Cicotte. Index cards sell for $350 to $400. Gandil's 1919 MLB contract, countersigned by Charlie Comiskey, sold for $44,000 in 2012 (Robert Edward Auctions). There is a small group of forged single-signed baseballs in the market. They are easily spotted as they are signed in printed script across the sweet spot.

Chic Arnold Gandil

Gandil-1, World War I draft card (courtesy Record Group 163, Records of the Selective Services Division, National Archives at Atlanta).

Charles "Swede" Risberg was the last surviving member the Black Sox. He died in 1975. Risberg signed in an unassuming hand. The signature is of average construction. In later years, post–1955 I estimate, his hand was affected by infirmity. Signatures evidence a material shakiness of hand. Like that of Cicotte and Gandil, signatures are limited to the occasional index card and government postcard. His signature is less common than that of Cicotte. Expect to pay $350 to $400 for his signature.

Charles August Risberg

Williams, L-1, World War I draft card (courtesy Record Group 163, Records of the Selective Services Division, National Archives at Atlanta).

Risberg-1, World War I draft card (courtesy Record Group 163, Records of the Selective Services Division, National Archives at Atlanta).

Then there is the strange case of George "Buck" Weaver. Weaver appears to be the most sympathetic player of the group. He claimed never to have taken any bribe money. Weaver signed in a choppy hand. Signatures are usually penned as "George (Buck) Weaver." He was fond of using a pencil. Rare on a per se basis, signatures are found on index cards, government postcards, and the occasional program from the 1920s or 1930s. There are many forgeries in the market on most mediums. Baseballs are a common target. A few years back, forged baseballs of Weaver and Joe Jackson entered the market. Each forgery occupies its own panel. These are easily identified as fake given the rudimentary nature of the forgeries. Weaver's signature sells for to $1,500 to $2,000. A government postcard is valued at $2,500 to $3,000.

Weaver-1, World War I draft card (courtesy Record Group 163, Records of the Selective Services Division, National Archives at Atlanta).

The 1920 season was a turning point in the game. The strategy-rich deadball era was coming to an end. Its once glorious stars soon began to fade into the backdrop of time. A new, livelier baseball, known as the rabbit ball, would transform the game. The home run would replace the stolen base as king. The era of the slugger had come of age.

The first great slugger was the now forgotten Ken Williams. In 1922, he hit an amazing 39 home runs for the St. Louis Browns, an unheard-of number back in those days. He had a .319 batting average over 14 years. Williams is a legitimate candidate for induction into the Hall of Fame. Williams signed in a plain and deliberate hand. The hand is methodic and lacks reckless flow. Legibility is sound. The capital letter "K" in the first name displays itself as the letter "R." Williams's signature is somewhat scarce on a per se basis. He did sign items in the 1950s,

mostly index cards and government postcards. There is solid demand for his autograph. His signature generally sells for $200 to $250.

Williams, K-1, GPC circa 1950.

The greatest slugger is the history of the game is the immortal Babe Ruth. The Babe is the only player who gives Cobb a serious run at the title of the greatest player of all time. No man could crush the baseball like the Bambino. He was the biggest drawing ticket in the history of the game and the most beloved athlete of them all.

Ruth signed in a strong and powerful hand. His signature is bold with sweeping curves. Letter construction is sound. Superior display value is noted. Ruth's signature dominates the medium it is placed upon. Ruth's signature is one that has evolved. Early signatures, accomplished pre–1925, tend to be smaller in scale and lack the bold strokes of later specimens. Early signatures are a bit choppy in construction. From the late 1920s, Ruth's signature deviated little. Signatures signed just before death tend to be a bit smaller in construction, but no shakiness of hand is noted. Ruth was a willing and gracious signer throughout his life. Baseballs, album pages, photographs, programs, and government postcards exist in good number. Signed Goudey gum cards are available, but these are rare. Full page ALsS are very rare. Signed bats are an extreme rarity, though a few do exist. One genuine signed Hall of Fame plaque postcard is known.

The strong value of Ruth's autograph has attracted forgers of skill. Ruth's signature is one of the most forged signatures in history. Forgeries exist on all mediums, most notably baseballs. Most Ruth-signed baseballs in the market are forgeries. Items with Ruth and Lou Gehrig forgeries are common, as are Ruth and Cobb dual-signed items. Forged bank checks are also in the market. They first surfaced in the early 1990s. They are generic counter checks. It is clear that these were made on a small press because the print quality of the checks is poor, exhibiting slightly blurred lines. The forgery evidences an unsteadiness of hand. Many of these checks are made payable to golf and country clubs.

There is one forger to note. He has Ruth's hand down to the fine points. There is a famous photograph of Ruth swinging a bat looking directly into the camera. A forgery is placed across Ruth's chest as "Sincerely Babe Ruth." Forgeries also exist on multi-signed first-day baseball covers, album pages, government postcards, and even one 8 × 10 photograph signed and inscribed to actor Gary Cooper. Though the forgeries are fairly well-executed, the forger does not quite have the proper hand speed. The forgeries are not shaky by any means, but methodic and precise, too precise. The forgeries look too neat and uniform. They lack the bouncy feel of a genuine Ruth signature. I have illustrated one of these forgeries as Ruth-4. Note the striking differences in speed and recklessness of hand.

Ruth's signature is of the highest demand. When I started collecting back on the late 1970s, Ruth's signature could be purchased for $30 to $40. Today, that same signature is valued at $2,500. Government postcards sell for $3,000 to $3,500. Signed 8 × 10 photographs are valued at $5,000. Museum-grade specimens sell between $15,000 and $20,000. Bank checks exist in quantities and sell in the $4,000 range. A handful of trustee bank checks are in the market and signed as "George Herman Ruth." These are extremely rare and are valued at $20,000 to $25,000. A single-signed baseball of fair and average disposition is valued at $4,000 to $6,000. A museum-grade specimen is valued at a minimum of $50,000. Some stunning forged specimens have sold for more than $100,000. A full-page ALS is a rare find and should sell for $15,000 to $20,000. The only known signed

Hall of Fame plaque postcard sold for $62,000 in 2009 (Philip Weiss Auctions). An MLB contract is valued in the high six figures.

Ruth-1 team sheet dated 1922.

Ruth-2 album page dated 1927.

Ruth-3 government postcard dated 1936.

Ruth-4, well executed forgery.

Ruth's teammate was the Iron Horse, Lou Gehrig, another great slugger of the 1920s. Gehrig signed in a pleasing hand. Sound letter construction is noted. The display value is sound. In the 1930s, Gehrig's signature decreased in scale. The once sound letter construction becomes impaired as individual letters diminish into indistinguishable strokes. Signatures from the 1930s appear more compact in nature. Gehrig's hand remained essentially the same until mid to late 1939. By late

1939, amyotrophia impaired his motor skills. He stopped signing autographs at that time and mail requests for his signature were signed by his wife. Her signature does not resemble a genuine signature and is exposed with little examination.

Early Gehrig signatures are fairly easy to forge and many well-executed forgeries are in the market. The 1930s signature is more difficult to forge. As with Ruth, forgeries exist on all mediums. Lower-grade Goudey gum cards are a common target. Government postcards, complete with counterfeit postmarks, are in the market. By 1940, the disease made quick work of Gehrig's body, and signing autographs became an almost impossible task. Gehrig was hired by the New York City parole commission, a job he essentially held in name only. There are many TLsS, on commission letterhead, in the market. These should be avoided in total, as they were not signed but feature a stamped signature of Gehrig.

There is very strong demand for Gehrig-signed material. His signature is valued at $2,000 to $2,500. Bank checks, which are very rare, are valued at $7,500. A full-page ALS has strong eye appeal and is valued at $10,000 to $15,000. Content letters can sell for $25,000 to $50,000. Signed 8 × 10 photographs sell for $4,000 to $5,000, with superior specimens easily valued at $10,000 to $15,000. Single-signed baseballs are rare, much harder to find than a Ruth or Cobb single. A single-signed baseball is valued at $10,000 to $12,500. A museum-grade specimen is valued at $40,000 to $50,000. A signed MLB contact is worth between $75,000 and $100,000.

Gehrig-2, circa 1930s signature.

Gehrig-3, common secretarial signed by wife.

Gehrig-4, 1940 rubber stamp.

Another great slugger from the Ruthian era of ball was Lewis "Hack" Wilson. Built like a fireplug, Wilson holds the record for most RBIs in a season (190 in 1930). He was a great hitter but excessive drink was his downfall. Wilson signed in a bold and powerful hand. The signature is marked with crisp lines and effortless flow. Display value is superior. Wilson died at the young age of 48. His hand was never affected by infirmity. Well-executed forgeries are difficult to create. Most forgeries evidence unsteady lines. Wilson's signature is scarce on a per se basis. It is generally found on team-signed items and material signed at the ballpark; hence, album pages are a good source. Other mediums are very scarce to very rare. Single-signed baseballs are an extreme rarity. I have only seen three genuine specimens in over thirty years. Signed bank checks are very scarce to rare. Approximately 300 were released into the market in the mid–1980s. Wilson's signature is valued at $750. Other mediums are very expensive. A bank check is valued at $2,000 to $2,250. A nice single-signed baseball is worth over $10,000.

Gehrig-1, album page dated 1927.

Wilson, H-1 Album page dated 1933.

The greatest right-handed hitter of all time was Rogers Hornsby. He batted .358 lifetime, second only to Cobb's .367. Hornsby loved to sign autographs for kids. He loved to talk baseball and was bluntly opinionated. He had the finesse of a hand grenade. Hornsby's signature matched his personality. It is bold with reckless flow. The signature appears fast on paper. A strong racing effect is evident. Hornsby's signature is fairly complex in nature. Creating a well-executed forgery would take a good deal of effort. There is a good supply of Hornsby material in the market. Single-signed baseballs are scarce. But some nice condition specimens do exist. Hornsby remained close to the game, as a manager and coach, in the 1950s and 1960s. This gave fans access to him at the ballpark. Full-page ALsS are rare. Index cards and government postcards exist in good inventory as Hornsby was a willing signer through the mail. There is strong demand for this legend's signature. His signature sells for $300 to $400. Signed 8 × 10 photographs and ALsS are valued between $1,500 and $2,000. Single-signed baseballs are valued at $3,500 to $4,000.

Hornsby-1 1962 Signature.

Another great batsman of the game was Detroit Tigers first baseman Harry "Slug" Heilmann. In a career that lasted 17 years, Heilmann

batted .342 lifetime and won four batting crowns. Heilmann signed in a pleasing and fluid hand. The signature has well-formed capital letters which enhance display value. Heilmann hung up his spikes in 1932. He embarked on a career in broadcasting and became the Tigers' play-by-play man for 17 years with WXYZ. This gave fans access to him. There are many signatures of Heilmann on scorecards, album pages, and multi-signed baseballs. Letters of any kind are rare. A full-page ALS is very rare. Single-signed baseballs are also very rare. I have only seen maybe five genuine examples in over 30 years of searching. All were signed on the side panel. I have never seen a genuine single-signed baseball with the signature on the sweet spot. There is a small supply of bank checks and promissory notes in the market. A few checks are made payable to fellow Hall of Famer Heinie Manush, who endorsed them on the back. This is a fine baseball treasure signed by two early Tiger legends.

There is very good demand for this early immortal of the game. Heilmann's signature will sell for $500. Bank checks are valued at $800 to $1,000. The above-referenced Heilmann/Manush checks command a premium at $1,500. It should be noted that one of these dual-signed checks sold for $2,900 in 2005 (Lelands.com). A TLS is valued at $1,000 to $1,250. The very rare ALS should sell for $3,500 to $4,000. A nice single-signed baseball has an estimated value of $10,000.

Heilmann-1, bank check dated 1949.

By 1933, depression-era baseball was in full swing. It was the one outlet where Americans could escape the harsh realities of life, albeit for a brief moment. This was the year of the first All-Star game. Some of the game's greatest legends played in this inaugural midsummer classic. The manager of the American League was none other than Connie Mack. He was the longest-serving manager in major league history. Mack signed in a very structured and thoughtful hand. The signature is dominated by large letters. Due to the slower nature of hand, replication is quite easy. Well-executed forgeries exist, though generally limited to single-signed baseballs and Hall of Fame plaque postcards. He managed the Philadelphia Athletics from 1901 to 1950. During those years he signed countless letters and documents. The supply of Mack material is sound. He was a willing signer throughout his long life. Signatures exist on album pages, team-signed baseballs, scorecards, photographs, books, and the like. His signature is one of the easier of the long-deceased Hall of Famers to obtain. Mack's signature is quite affordable at $125. TLsS are valued at $175 to $225, ALsS at $300 to $350. A single-signed baseball of average disposition is valued at $1,500. Hall of Fame plaque postcards are rare to very rare; therefore expect to pay $3,000 to $4,000 for a nice specimen.

Mack-1 circa 1940s signature.

Managing the National League team was perhaps the greatest manager of them all, John J. McGraw. Known as "Mugsy," McGraw was a master of small ball. Like Mack, McGraw enjoyed a long career in the big leagues. He was the longtime manager of the New York Giants. McGraw signed in a slower hand. The signature lacks reckless flow. Signatures penned in the late teens until death evidence a slight shakiness of hand. Due to the slower nature of the signature, replication of hand is easy. Well-executed forgeries exist in quantities. The vast majority of McGraw signatures in the market, easily over 90 percent, are forgeries. Unlike Mack, McGraw signatures are very scarce on a per se basis and generally limited to signatures removed

from checks. Mrs. McGraw handed these out to satisfy requests for her husband's autograph after his death in 1934. Signatures can also be found on team-signed baseballs and sheets. Other mediums are very rare. Only a few genuine single-signed baseballs exist. Forged baseballs are in the market which feature forgeries of McGraw and fellow Hall of Famer Hughie Jennings. Each forgery occupies its own panel.

There is strong demand for McGraw's autograph. A signature removed from a check is valued at $750 to $1,000. TLsS should sell for $1,500 to $2,000. ALsS are valued at $5,000. A nice single-signed baseball has an estimated value of $20,000. The value of a single-signed baseball is depressed due to all the forged baseballs that have sold over the years.

McGraw-1 team sheet circa 1920s.

Jimmie Foxx was another great slugger of the 1920s and 1930s. He hit 535 home runs lifetime and 58 in 1932. Foxx is generally considered one of the ten greatest ballplayers of all time. Foxx's signature went through a marked change. Early signatures tend to be signed in a slower, more pensive hand. Legibility and letter construction are sound. As his career progressed, the signature becomes less structured and hand speed increases greatly. It remained that way until his untimely death in 1968. Replication of hand can be done with little effort, at least when it comes to early signatures. Modern signatures are more difficult to forge. The majority of well-executed forgeries use the early signature as a template.

Foxx was a willing signer throughout his life, resulting in an ample supply of material in the market. The most common mediums are those which could be obtained through the mail. Index cards, government postcards, and picture postcards are the most common. Full-page

ALsS are rare. Single-signed baseballs are highly treasured, but a restricted supply does exist. Team-signed baseballs are an excellent source of Foxx's autograph. In recent years, many forged single-signed baseballs have entered the market. They are forged on American League baseballs (Joe Cronin, pres.) and signed in bold purple ink across the sweet spot. There is strong demand for Foxx material and values continue to rise. Foxx's signature is valued at $500. Picture postcards sell for $600 to $700. A full-page ALS is a treasure; therefore expect to pay $2,000. A nice single-signed baseball will sell for $3,500 to $4,000.

Foxx-1 circa 1930s signature.

Foxx-2 1964 signature.

Foxx's teammate Al Simmons was another of the all-time greats. Simmons secured a .334 lifetime average with an incredible 1,827 RBIs. He had six 200-hit seasons and two batting crowns. Simmons signed in a pleasing and flowing hand. The signature has fair legibility, though some letters in the last name blend together. Simmons was an accommodating signer throughout his life. There is an ample supply of material in the market, typically limited to team signed baseballs, scorecards, and album pages. Single-signed baseballs are very rare and just about all ever offered for sale are forgeries. Simmons is a fairly easy signature to forge. Well-executed forgeries exist in quantities. Goudey gum cards and Hall of Fame plaque postcards are a favorite of forgers. Values for Simmons material has stagnated over the past few years due to the

large quantity of canceled bank checks in the market. A check can be purchased for $250 to $300. His signature is about the same value. A single-signed baseball is a rarity, so expect to pay $10,000.

Simmons-1 bank check circa 1950s.

Another superstar from the 1930s was New York Giants outfielder Mel Ott. A member of the 500 home run club, Ott broke into the major leagues in 1926 at the young age of 17. Ott signed in a crisp and clean hand. His signature is highly legible with sound letter construction. Ott was killed in a car accident in 1958. Since he never reached old age, infirmity of hand does not exist. Due to the precise and effortless strokes, replication of hand is difficult. Producing a well-executed forgery would take a great deal of effort. Ott was a willing signer throughout his career. In retirement he broadcast Detroit Tigers baseball in the 1950s with Van Patrick. This gave fans access to him. The supply of signatures is ample, though outweighed by a strong demand. Signatures can be found on material that was signed at the ballpark. Album pages, scorecards, and team-signed baseballs are good sources for his autograph.

Other mediums are scarce to rare; these include ALsS, single-signed baseballs, and Goudey gum cards. In the 1980s, Mrs. Ott would cut off Ott's signature from bank checks and send them to collectors to satisfy autograph requests. She did send out a couple of full checks, but these are an extreme rarity. His membership of the 500 home run club correlates into sound demand for Ott's signature, which is valued at $500. An

Ott-1 undated signature.

ALS is a rarity, so expect to pay $2,500 to $3,000 for a nice specimen. A single-signed baseball is valued at $5,000 to $6,000. Museum-grade specimens will sell for $15,000 to $20,000.

The mid–1930s saw the rise of the Detroit Tigers. In 1934, the Tigers replaced interim manager Del Baker with Mickey Cochrane. In 1934, the Tigers won the American League pennant and a year later, in 1935, they won their first World Series. Cochrane is considered the greatest catcher in the history of baseball. Cochrane signed in an aggressive and angled hand. The signature is compact with a material slant to the right. Letter construction is somewhat impaired as letters sometimes morph together. The signature has average display value. Due to the rapid nature of hand, replication is rather difficult. Well-executed forgeries are limited and generally reserved for premium items such as single-signed baseballs. Cochrane was a willing signer throughout his life. There is a decent supply of material in the market. The family released countless bank checks, which are a wonderful source of Cochrane's signature. Index cards, album pages, scorecards, and government postcards are available. Less common are single-signed baseballs, Hall of Fame plaque postcards, and letters of any kind. Cochrane authored a book titled *Baseball: The Fan's Game*, and signed many copies as "Gordon S. Cochrane." It should be noted that many requests, sent in the 1930s, for his autograph were accomplished with a rubber stamp. Cochrane is a rather affordable signature at $150. Bank checks are valued at $225 to $250. A Hall of Fame plaque postcard is worth $750 to $800. A nice single-signed baseball will sell for about $2,000 to $2,500. The above-referenced book can be secured for $300 to $350.

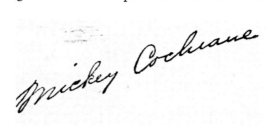

Cochrane-2 rubber stamp, circa 1930s.

One of the most colorful characters in baseball history was Jay Hanna "Dizzy" Dean, the ace of the St. Louis Cardinals' fabled "Gas House Gang." Dean was the last pitcher to win 30 or more games in a season in the National League. Dean signed in a rather unstructured hand. Early signatures are legible, but letters tend to be slightly ajar. Signatures accomplished after retirement are signed in a much more refined hand. The signature develops an artistic look. Letter construction is impaired but the overall display value increases greatly. Dean's signature is rather easy to replicate; well-executed forgeries exist in quantities, mostly on baseballs and 8 × 10 photographs.

In recent years the market has been flooded with forged index cards. The forgeries are fairly well-executed. A slight shakiness is noted. Many of them have been wrongly certified and slabbed as genuine by the authentication companies, so caution is warranted. Many signatures obtained through the mail in the 1960s until his death were signed by Dean's wife. Dean was a spokesman for Falstaff Brewing Company.

Cochrane-1 1961 signature.

Dean-1 1973 Signature.

Many letters, on Falstaff letterhead, are in the market, but just about all are secretarially signed.

Dean was a willing signer throughout his life. Signed index cards are affordable at $75 to $100. Hall of Fame plaque postcards can be purchased for $150 to $175. A single-signed baseball is valued at $1,250 to $1,500. Material signed with his brother and fellow major leaguer, Paul "Daffy" Dean, is scarce and commands a premium.

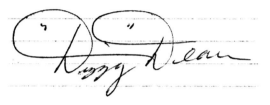

Dean-2 common secretarial.

The 1920s and 1930s offer collectors some of the greatest names in the game. Hall of Famers like Hazen "Ki Ki" Cuyler, Eppa Rixey, Jim Bottomley, Joe Medwick, Chuck Klein, Harold "Pie" Traynor, Leo "Gabby" Hartnett, and Frank Frisch are just some of the collectable names. Non-Hall of Fame stars are equally plentiful, such as John "Pepper" Martin, Floyd "Babe" Herman, Moe Berg, and Lynwood "Schoolboy" Rowe. Some signatures, such as Robert "Fats" Fothergill, are rare and command good money. The rotund Fothergill died in 1938. A student of Cobb, Fothergill batted .326 lifetime and his signature is on most wants lists. Expect to pay $400 for a nice specimen.

Robert Roy Fothergill

Fothergill-1, World War I draft card (courtesy Record Group 163, Records of the Selective Services Division, National Archives at Atlanta).

The biggest name of the 1940s was the Yankee Clipper, Joe DiMaggio. He is one of the most famous players of all time and he was known to generations as "Mr. Coffee." DiMaggio signed in a complex hand. The signature evidences good flow. Letter construction is sound. An above-average display value is noted. For collecting purposes, a genuine signature should exhibit no shakiness of hand, and one that does should be considered suspect. There are a handful of genuine signatures in the market that evidence material shakiness. These were signed in the closing days of DiMaggio's life. The total population of these is minuscule and they cause controversy. There is simply too much DiMaggio inventory in the market to bother with deathbed signatures.

DiMaggio signed countless items and today there is a sound supply in the market. He engaged in many mass signings. He also honored autograph requests through the mail. His signature is common on most mediums. Letters of any kind are scarce. Marilyn Monroe–associated material is very uncommon but he did sign images that featured his wife. Many dealers have advertised signed baseball bats as "rare." While uncommon, many signed bats exist. They are certainly not rare. Over the past decade a substantial cache of canceled bank checks have entered the market and can be purchased for around $200.

DiMaggio's signature is a common target of forgers. Many fairly well-executed forgeries exist, usually limited to premium items. There are many forged photographs of DiMaggio with Ted Williams and/or Mickey Mantle. Many signatures obtained through the mail were signed by DiMaggio's sister. There are two variant secretarial signatures known to exist. Some of the above-referenced bank checks were signed by DiMaggio's sister.

DiMaggio's signature is affordable at $75. Signed 8 × 10 photographs, hall of fame plaque postcards, and baseballs are available in the $200 to $300 price range. Signed baseball bats are valued at $750 to $1,000. Premium items should prove a sound investment in the years to come.

Another great from 1940s baseball was the

DiMaggio-1 government postcard 1986.

Dimaggio-2 common secretarial by his sister.

Splendid Splinter, Ted Williams. Generally considered the third-greatest player of all time, Williams is just behind Cobb and Ruth. He hit .344 lifetime and was the last player to reach the .400 mark. Williams signed in a flowing and angled hand. His signature has sound display value. Good letter construction is noted. Williams's signature works well on baseballs and bats. It is one of the nicer Hall of Fame autographs. The supply of genuine material is basically limitless. He engaged in many mass signings, resulting in a huge inventory of material in the market. Williams's signature can be found on most mediums from photographs to baseballs to bats. Letters of any kind are uncommon to scarce. There is a large supply of canceled bank checks in the market.

Williams has long been targeted by forgers and many well-executed forgeries exist. Forgeries are common on baseballs, bats, and Perez Steele cards. There is a common photograph with Williams, DiMaggio and Mickey Mantle all holding bats. This photograph is a common target of forgers. Most offered in the market are forgeries. Williams rarely honored mail requests for his signature. Many items, including correspondences, were signed by a secretary.

Williams material was pricey during his life. There has not been much increase in value simply because of the large supply. His signature is valued at $75. Photographs, baseballs, and Hall of Fame plaque postcards can be purchased in the $125 to $200 price range. The above-referenced bank checks are common and will sell for $125 to $150. Baseball bats are far more common than DiMaggio bats, so expect to pay $400 to $500.

Williams, T-1 undated signature.

Williams, T-2 common secretarial.

The other giant of 1940s baseball was Stan "the Man" Musial. Like Williams, Musial is also considered one of the greatest ball players of all time. Musial signed in a pleasing hand. His signature evidences bold vertical strokes. No measurable slant is evident. Letter construction is sound. Average legibility is noted. Musial's signature is one of my favorites. Material signed in the last few years of his life evidences an unsteadiness of hand. Musial as of this writing is generally not the target of skilled forgers. There is simply too much material in the market that keeps values in check.

Musial was a willing signer through the mail and also engaged in mass signings. His signature can be found on most mediums. Baseballs, bats, photographs, and the like can be found in quantities. Letters of any kind are uncommon. There is a decent supply of bank checks in the market. Most items are available in the $50 to $100

Musial-1, government postcard dated 1954.

price range. Baseball bats can be purchased for $125 to $150. Bank checks sell for about $75. I consider bats and checks to be good investment pieces; other mediums not so much.

On April 15, 1947, Jackie Robinson broke into the big leagues. He became only the third black man to play major league baseball and the first of the post–World War II era. Robinson signed in a practical and legible hand. There is nothing extraordinary about the signature. An average display value is noted. Early signatures are signed as "Jack R. Robinson." Robinson died at a relatively young age. His hand was not affected by infirmity. A genuine signature will evidence no shakiness of hand.

Robinson was generally a responsive signer in the mail. There is a good supply of material in the market, though the supply is outweighed by a sound demand. In retirement he worked for Chock Full O' Nuts Coffee Co. There is a good number of TLsS in the market. Signatures can be found on material signed during his playing career. Team baseballs, album pages, and scorecards are the most common. Single-signed baseballs are scarce, but a decent number exist. During the 1960 presidential election, Robinson actively campaigned for then Vice-President Richard Nixon. On the campaign trail he signed baseballs with the inscription "Vote for Nixon." These signed baseballs are very rare and command a premium. The family released many canceled bank checks.

Robinson has long been the target of skilled forgers. Forgeries exist in quantities on baseballs, gum cards, and the book *Baseball Has Done It*. Many forged Hall of Fame plaque postcards exist. These are typically signed on the back as "Best Wishes Jackie Robinson." Many are signed in a sea-blue/green felt-tipped pen. Robinson's signature sells for $500 to $600. TLsS and bank checks are valued at $800 to $1,000. A single-signed baseball is valued at $3,000. Exceptional examples will sell for $7,000 to $10,000. The above-referenced Richard Nixon baseballs are highly treasured and are valued at $6,000 to $7,500.

Robinson, J-1, circa 1960s signature.

The 1950s brought forth the biggest drawing ticket of the post–World War II era, his name was Mickey Mantle. Known as the Commerce Comet, Mantle is one of the biggest names in the baseball memorabilia trade. Mantle signed in a very nice hand. His signature is marked with flowing lines and artistic capital letters. Early signatures, those signed in the 1950s, tend to be plain looking. Mantle's hand remained strong his entire life. A genuine signature will evidence no shakiness of hand.

Mantle's signature has been targeted by skilled forgers for years. Even during his life, Mantle forgeries existed in quantities. No sports figure's signature is more forged than Mantle. Forgeries exist on most mediums including baseballs, bats, gum cards, and any other medium you can think of. The supply of Mantle signatures is very strong as he engaged in mass signings for years. Mail requests for his signature were ignored. Mantle showed little interest in baseball fans. His primary goal was turning a profit. The inventory of material is basically limitless. Baseballs, bats, Hall of Fame plaque postcards, Perez Steele cards, and the like are available. Letters of any kind and bank checks are rare. Material signed with fellow Yankee slugger Roger Maris is scarce and in great demand.

No post–World War II signature commands more demand than Mantle. His signature sells for $100 to $125. Signed 8 × 10 photographs and Perez Steele cards are valued at $250 to $300. Single-signed baseballs sell for $300 to $400. Exceptional display specimens will sell for over $1,000. Bank checks are treasured, so expect to pay $1,500 for a nice specimen. Mantle- and Maris-signed 8 × 10 photographs sell for $1,250 to $1,500. Dual-signed baseballs have been known to sell for $5,000 to $7,500. Signed plates from his restaurant are attractive display pieces and are valued at $300 to $400.

Mantle-1 1951 signature.

Mantle-2 circa 1985 signature.

Also in good demand is Mantle's teammate, Roger Maris. He still holds the steroid-free record for most home runs in a single season with 61. Because of this, his signature is one of the most desired names of 1960s baseball. Maris signed in an average hand that transformed through the years. Post-retirement signatures have sound eye appeal. His signature is very flowing with good letter construction. Maris died in 1985, just before the era of mass signings. There is an ample supply of material in the market. Signatures are generally found on index cards and Topps gum cards. Single-signed baseballs, most of which are inscribed, are scarce and most are forged. Letters of any kind are rare. In recent years a flood of forged photographs, cards, and index cards have entered the market. Many have been wrongly certified as genuine by the authentication companies. There is strong demand for Maris's signature, which sells for $200 to $250. Topps

cards are valued between $400 and $600. Signed 8 × 10 photographs sell for $350 to $400. Single-signed baseballs are valued at $750 to $1,000. Superior specimens can sell for over $2,000. Maris's signature should prove an excellent investment.

Maris-1 undated signature.

One of the greatest hitters of the 1960s was Pittsburgh Pirate great Roberto Clemente. He is a member of the 3,000 hit club and batted .317 lifetime. He was killed in a plane crash on New Year's Eve 1972. Clemente's hand went through a major transformation. Early signatures are penned in a labored and hesitant hand. The signature displays itself as methodic, almost childlike. Autographs from the 1960s are signed in a rapid and complex hand. The earlier signature is completely replaced by one with fast sweeping strokes and nonexistent letter construction. Most material offered in the market was signed at the ballpark. Scorecards, album pages, and multi-signed baseballs are the most common. Letters are very rare. A small supply of canceled bank checks is in the market.

Early signatures are rather easy to replicate; later signatures are not. There are some nice forgeries in the market. In addition, many signatures obtained through the mail were secretarially signed. There are many lower-grade 1955 Topps rookie cards that feature a forged signature in ball-point pen. I have never seen a genuinely signed Clemente rookie card. Single-signed baseballs are scarce, and just about all in the market are forgeries. A common forged baseball has the inscription and signature all crammed on the sweet spot. The best way to obtain Clemente's signature on a baseball is to find a nicely signed Pirates team ball.

Clemente's signature sells for $500 to $600. Signed photographs, typically octavo, sell for $750 to $1,000. Teams signed Pirates baseballs are valued at $750 to $1,000. Pre-1960 teams are closer to $1,500. Signed bank checks are valued at $1,250 to $1,500. Single-signed baseballs will sell for $3,000 to $4,000.

Clemente-1 bank check dated 1972.

Clemente-2, common secretarial.

Yankees catcher Thurman Munson was on his way to Cooperstown when his career was tragically ended in a plane crash in 1979. Munson signed in a bold and large hand. The signature is fairly legible. An average display value is noted. Material is generally limited to items signed at the park; hence, album pages and scorecards are good sources for his signature. Other mediums are scarce to rare such as letters and 8 × 10 photographs. Single-signed baseballs are rare and just about all in the market are forgeries. A team signed Yankees baseball is your best bet to obtain a Munson-signed baseball. In general, signed Topps baseball cards are very rare; just about all offered for sale are forgeries. A signed 1979 Topps card is an extreme rarity. In recent years, forged dollar bills have entered the market; they are signed across the federal reserve seal in ball-point pen. The forger adds "N Y Yankees 1976." Other years exist as well. The value of Munson autographs has increased greatly in recent years. A signature will sell for $750 to $1,000. Team-signed Yankee baseballs are valued at $800 to $2,500 depending on the year and condition. The value of a signed 1979 Topps card is uncertain. I have only seen one genuine specimen. Many forgeries of this card exist. I estimate a value of somewhere between $5,000 and $10,000. A signed pilot's license sold for $6,400 (Robert Edward Auctions, 2009).

Munson-1 album page circa 1975.

Baseball memorabilia, both signed and unsigned, is widely covered in the media. In recent years reporting has focused a critical eye on the industry. A growing number of media outlets have put the sports memorabilia trade under an investigative microscope. Bob D'Angelo of the *Tampa Tribune*, Michael O'Keeffe of the *New York Daily News*, Peter Nash of Haulsofshame. com, David Seideman of *Forbes*, and Bill Wagner (who writes a column under the name of Babe Waxpak) of Scripps-Howard News Service are some journalists who often examine the industry's good and bad points. These writers are excellent sources of information that will broaden your knowledge of the memorabilia trade.

Potential Hall of Famers

There are many players who await induction into the Hall of Fame. Speculation on who will get inducted pushes prices ever higher. Collectors will obtain signatures of players, umpires, and league executives with the hopes that they will gain induction into the Hall. Once a player is inducted, the demand for his signature increases demonstrably. A signature that was worth very little now becomes quite valued. Case in point is Boston pitcher Vic Willis. Willis died in 1947 and his signature is quite rare. Before his induction in 1995, a signed index card could be purchased for $150 to $200. After he was elected to the Hall of Fame, the value of Willis's signature spiked. Today, that same index card is worth between $7,500 and $10,000. There are many players worthy of induction, most notably Allie Reynolds, Babe Herman, Jack Morris, Alan Trammell, Bobby Veach, Steve Garvey, Sam Leever, Mel Harder, Tony Mullane, Gil Hodges, Harvey Kuenn, Jim Kaat, Ken Williams, Rusty Staub, Roger "Doc" Cramer, and others.

Veach's signature, for example, is rare. He died in 1945. He played in the same outfield with Ty Cobb and Sam Crawford, so he tends to get overlooked. Veach's signature seldom turns up for sale, and when it does it sells for $700 to $900. Should he be inducted into Cooperstown, the signature will jump in value. It would likely sell in the $5,000 to $7,500 price range. That is a stunning rate of return.

Veach-1, signature circa 1930.

It is also a good idea to obtain signatures of league executives and commissioners. Chub Feeney, John Heydler, Fay Vincent, John Tener, John Fetzer, Gene Budig, Bud Selig, Frank Navin, Bart Giamatti, Leonard Coleman, and the like will very likely be inducted someday. It may not happen overnight. William Hulbert was a National League founder who died in 1882. He was not inducted until 1995, but better late than never, I suppose. Arthur Soden was a longtime baseball exec and owner of the Boston Beaneaters. He is considered the father of baseball's reserve clause. He is often mentioned as a potential Hall of Famer. There is a small supply of signed stock certificates in the market which can be purchased for $300 to $400.

Soden-1 1881 stock certificate.

The Negro Leagues

This is a segment of the hobby that has a small but dedicated collectors' base. Negro League material is not nearly as collected as MLB material, but there is still solid demand for signatures of the old-time players. Negro League signatures became fashionable in the 1980s and popularity increased greatly in the 1990s. Many players would attend card shows and engage in mass signings. Most were responsive signers through the mail. In general, signatures of players who lived into the 1990s are not worth a lot, simply because there is an ample supply of this material in the market. I remember writing Bill Byrd, Cecil Kaiser, and Lou Dials, and they would send six or seven signatures back to me. Kaiser sent me a nicely signed 8 × 10 photograph to boot. These signatures are nice to have, but the values will remain nominal for decades to come.

Signatures of those who died before 1990 are harder to find. Signatures of many players who died before 1980 are just plain rare. Big Bill Drake died in 1977. His signature seldom surfaces and is valued at $250.

Drake-1, signature circa 1970.

If you wish to collect Negro League material, concentrate on players who died before 1990. Inventory of this material is scarce and becomes very rare for players who died before 1970. Very few collectors were requesting signatures from these players and today many don't exist at all. Former Memphis Red Sox Oscar "Heavy" Johnson died in 1966. The occasional index card surfaces, but that is about it. His signature is rare to very rare and is valued at $1,000.

Johnson, O-1, undated signature.

Another rare signature is that of Spotswood Poles. He played in the teen years and was said to be one of the fastest players in the league. He is often mentioned as a possible Hall of Fame inductee. His signature is illustrated from his World War II draft card. I know of no signatures in the open market. Another rare signature is that of Elwood "Bingo" DeMoss. He died in 1965 and, like Poles, may gain entrance into Cooperstown someday. His signature, from a draft card, is illustrated. To my knowledge there are no signatures of DeMoss in the open market. The value of DeMoss and Poles signatures is not known. I estimate a value of around

Poles-1, World War II draft card dated 1942 (courtesy U.S. National Archives—St. Louis).

$2,500 to $3,500. Were they to be inducted into the Hall of Fame, the value of their signatures would increase greatly to, perhaps, $30,000 to $40,000.

DeMoss-1, World War I draft card (courtesy Record Group 163, Records of the Selective Services Division, National Archives at Atlanta).

"Candy Jim" Taylor was a standout manager in the Negro Leagues and just missed induction in 2006. His signature is an extreme rarity. There are only a couple of specimens in the open market. I assume he will be inducted into Cooperstown someday, and when that happens, Taylor's signature will become extremely valuable, at least $30,000.

Taylor, J-1 Negro League document dated 1942.

Negro League signatures can very expensive when it comes to members of the Hall of Fame. Josh Gibson is probably the most desired but certainly not the rarest. His signature is rare but does enter the market now and then. Just about 100 percent of Gibson signatures in the market are forged. His signature is generally limited to a few signed documents and one signed team baseball.

A common forgery is single-signed baseballs. They appeared in the market in the early 1990s. They feature a grayish to black or blue fountain pen signature and are signed on the side panel just under the stitching. The forgery follows the contour of the stitches. I know of no genuine single-signed baseballs in existence.

Another forgery to watch for is period secretarial signatures on pay receipts and contracts. Just because a signature is on a contract or legal document does not guarantee the genuineness of the signature. I know of one Gibson baseball contract that features a secretarial signature of Gibson. The signature is labored in appearance.

It should be noted that forged picture postcards exist. They feature Gibson in a Homestead Grays uniform wearing his catcher's mitt. They are signed "Joshua Gibson" along the bottom of the card or sometimes across the chest. Some contain a second inscribed forgery on the reverse. These forgeries evidence a slightly labored hand but are fairly well-executed. Gibson's signature is valued at $10,000 to $15,000. A signed contract is worth between $35,000 and $45,000.

Gibson, J-1 LS dated 1944 (courtesy Newark Public Library, Newark Eagles Papers).

One of the biggest names of the old Negro Leagues was Leroy "Satchel" Paige. Most of his career was played in the Negro Leagues. At age 42, Paige remains the oldest rookie in MLB history. His signature is choppy and rather unattractive. It is also easily forged. Many well-executed forgeries exist, though generally limited to premium items. A signed limited edition Perez Steele art postcard is a modern rarity. Paige died shortly after the set was released. The same can be said for Hall of Famer Lloyd Waner. I have seen multiple examples of both the Paige and Waner cards certified by the authentication companies. I have yet to see one of either I would feel comfortable pronouncing as genuine. The more I research this issue, the more I doubt either card exists signed.

There are many forged Paige Perez cards, all produced by the same forger. The forgery reads "Best wishes from Satchel Paige" and is signed in either thin black or blue Sharpie. Expect to pay $150 for Paige's signature. Single-signed baseballs are valued at around $1,500.

Paige-1 undated signature.

In 2006, a special committee of Negro League baseball was formed. As a result, 17 players and owners were inducted into the Hall of Fame, including the first woman, Effa Manley. This induction sparked interest in the Negro Leagues, which correlates into increased demand. Signatures of some of these Hall of Fame members are extremely rare to nonexistent. It is generally believed by experts that a signature of Franklin Grant does not exist, or more properly has yet to be discovered. Signatures of Jose Mendez and Cristobal Torriente exist only on World War I–era draft cards held by the National Archives in Atlanta. For years Jud Wilson autographs have been bought and sold as genuine. Unfortunately, they have been the product of forgery. I know of no Wilson signatures in the open market. The two known specimens of Wilson's signature are held by governmental concerns. Kansas City Monarch owner J. Leslie Wilkinson was an innovator of the game. He died in 1964 and his signature is very rare. As of this writing only 11 market signatures are known to exist. An early Negro League document, signed by Wilkinson, privately exchanged hands for $35,000. In 2013, a bank

Wilkinson-1, warranty deed dated 1942.

counter-check sold for $13,000 (Jim Stinson Sports).

Many rare signatures have yet to be confirmed. Grant "Home Run" Johnson is good example. Unfortunately, most signatures of the rare Negro League names are the product of forward-thinking forgers who created the forgeries years ago. These fake signatures had been accepted by many as genuine despite the lack of confirmed exemplars.

Bruce Petway is a fine example. He died in 1941 and his signature is an extremely rarity. For years Petway signatures were in the market and all varied in construction, evidencing the lack of a confirmed example. Recently, Petway's World War I draft card, dated 1917, surfaced. The signature on the card looks nothing like the others sold over the years. To date, this is the only confirmed example of Petway's signature in existence.

Petway-1, World War I draft card (courtesy Record Group 163, Records of the Selective Services Division, National Archives at Atlanta).

Dick "Cannonball" Redding was another important figure of Negro League baseball. He began his career in 1911 with the Lincoln Giants. Here is another example of forgers filling in the gap where a genuine specimen was lacking. Like that of Petway, Redding signatures are in the market and all vary in construction. There are a few Redding ALsS in the market. The problem is Redding was illiterate, as evi-

Redding-1, World War I draft card signed with his mark (courtesy Record Group 163, Records of the Selective Services Division, National Archives at Atlanta).

denced by his World War I draft card, where Redding simply signed with an "X."

Negro League signatures are a good way to build a collection of rare signatures. It is, however, a field where little research has been done. Collectors and researchers have barely scratched the surface on the vintage signatures and much study needs to be done. As more research is completed, many signatures will become confirmed and many signatures once accepted as genuine will be exposed as forgeries. This is an area of the hobby that is fraught with danger.

Disgraced Ball Players

There is also a special place in the autograph hobby for the fallen. These are the players and execs who brought shame upon the national pastime. Signatures of the gamblers, fixers, and felons seem to generate good demand within the hobby. It shouldn't be that way but it is. First and foremost were the Black Sox of 1919. Joe Jackson, whose memory should be erased from baseball, is an extremely valuable signature. Hal Chase, Joe Gedeon, and Phillies owner William Cox are all rare signatures and command good money. Cox, for example, died in 1989, and his signature seldom surfaces. It is valued at $300 to $400 simply because he is the only owner to been banned from baseball for life. Chase was on his way to the Hall of Fame, but gambling ended his career and any chance induction into Cooperstown. His signature is highly sought after. The occasional index card or ALS will surface, almost always penned in purple ink. Expect to pay $1,000 for his autograph. A nice, full-page ALS will sell closer to $3,000.

Chase, H-1, World War I draft card (courtesy Record Group 163, Records of the Selective Services Division, National Archives at Atlanta).

The great William Joseph "Billy" Maharg played two games of major league baseball. He batted a whopping .000. His signature is extremely rare and quite valuable simply because he was one of the conspirators of the 1919 World Series fix. Value is indeterminate. I know of no signatures in the open market.

Maharg-1, World War I draft card (courtesy Record Group 163, Records of the Selective Services Division, National Archives at Atlanta).

Marge Schott received the same punishment as Cox but was reinstated before her death. She remains the only woman ever to be banished by MLB. She was banished for improper speech. Signed baseballs of Schott sell for $100 to $150. These should prove a sound investment item.

Schott-1, undated signature.

Then there is "Charlie Hustle," Pete Rose, who has taken banishment to new heights. He will sign copies of the Dowd Report and inscribe signatures with "I'm Sorry I Bet On Baseball" and other such odd inscriptions for a fee. There is obviously a market for this material. The more controversy, the more demand, plain and simple.

Sic Transit Gloria Mundi

It is said that every person has fifteen minutes of fame. To many, fame is fleeting, but in baseball it can correlate into that desired autograph. Some players only played a brief time but are today well remembered. Former Detroit Tigers pitcher Mark "The Bird" Fidrych burst onto the baseball scene in 1976 with a 19–9 record. An injury shortened his career. He lingered in baseball, without much success, until 1980. He was a one-year wonder. Today, fans still speak of the Bird and his memorabilia is in good demand. Given his untimely death, Fidrych signatures, on premium items, should realize a sound rate of return.

On May 15, 1912, a fat, loud-mouthed New York bug named Claude Lueker became a footnote in baseball history, and a bloody footnote at that. The Detroit Tigers were playing the New York Highlanders at old Hilltop Park. The drunken Lueker began to bombard Ty Cobb with an unending attack of profanity. After enduring five innings of vicious attacks, Cobb bolted into the stands and made a beeline for the vulgar-mouthed fan. For his uncivilized behavior, Mr. Lueker earned himself one bloody nose. League President Ban Johnson suspended Cobb indefinitely. In response, the entire Tiger team went on strike. In order to avoid a hefty league fine for failing to field a team, the Tigers assembled a ragtag group of players. A couple players were retired big leaguers, but most were semi-pro players whose skills were that of grade–C town ball. The man who was recruited (or should I say shanghaied) to replace Cobb was a part-time boxer named William C. Leinhauser. He played just one major league game and went hitless, but for one fleeting moment he became the only man in the history of the game to replace the legendary Georgia Peach. Because of this, his signature is desired by collectors. Signed index cards are affordable at $40 to $50.

Leinhauser-1, signature dated 1973.

Cook County circuit court judge Hugo Friend presided over the trial of the eight

Chicago players accused of throwing the 1919 World Series. Because of his association with Joe Jackson and the Black Sox scandal, Friend's signature is highly desired. It is an extreme rarity; only a couple of letters are known to exist. Value of his signature is indeterminate. Friend's signature is illustrated from a TLS dated 1933 on judicial letterhead.

Friend-1, TLS dated 1933.

Other players are just as collectable. Eddie Gaedel, Fred Merkle, Al Travers (the only priest ever to play in the big leagues), and Archibald "Moonlight" Graham, made famous by the movie *Field of Dreams*, all come to mind. Graham is of particular interest and his signature is quite valuable. Pitchers who gave up famous hits are also desired by collectors. Washington Senators pitcher Tom Zachary gave up Babe Ruth's 60th home run in 1927. In that same year, Detroit Tigers pitcher Sam Gibson gave up Ty Cobb's 4,000th base hit. Both are collectable due to their association with a famous moment in baseball history.

Graham, World War I draft card (courtesy Record Group 163, Records of the Selective Services Division, National Archives at Atlanta).

*   *   *

The following is a population list of the rare to ultra-rare Hall of Fame signatures. This is based on my more than 30 years' experience in the field. Given the number of forged baseballs,

the following table will list total estimated **market population** (autographs for sale) and **baseball population** (autographs in curated collections), single-signed or otherwise. You may have seen these signatures for auction, such as a Frank Chance signed baseball. I have likely seen them as well. I, however, believe the signatures offered for sale are forgeries. The population does not include signatures held by governmental concerns (i.e., wills and draft cards). Signatures that are believed stolen from public institutions, such as the Tommy McCarthy will, are also not included in the table. Stolen documents, though transacted, are not legally marketable. When dealing with a signature that is unconfirmed but has sound credentials, I will use the qualifier "possibly." Not surprisingly, authenticators and auction companies tend to vehemently disagree with my conclusions, as they have authenticated and sold this material in the past.

Players	Market Population	Baseball Population
Anson, Cap	<50	0
Beckley, Jacob	<5	0
Brouthers, Dan	<5	0
Brown, Ray	<10	0
Bulkeley, Morgan	<200	0
Cartwright, Alexander	<50	0
Chadwick, Henry	<25	0
Chance, Frank	<10	0
Charleston, Oscar	<10	0
Chesbro, Jack	<10	<10
Clarkson, John	0	0
Collins, James	<20	0
Connor, Roger	Possibly 1	0
Cooper, Andy	0	0
Cummings, Candy	<5	0
Davis, George	2	0
Delahanty, Ed	2	0
Ewing, Buck	0	0
Foster, Rube	<10	0
Galvin, Pud	<5	0
Gibson, Josh	<20	1
Grant, Franklin	0	0
Hamilton, Billy	<20	0
Hanlon, Ned	<20	0
Hill, Pete	0	0
Hulbert, William	<20	0
Joss, Adrian	Possibly 1	0

Players	Market Population	Baseball Population	Players	Market Population	Baseball Population
Keefe, Tim	0	0	Selee, Frank	<5	0
Keeler, Willie	<5	0	Spalding, Albert	<100	0
Kelley, Joe	<20	0	Suttles, Mule	0	0
Kelly, Mike	1	0	Taylor, Ben	<10	0
Lloyd, John	<20	0	Thompson, Sam	1	0
Mackey, James	<5	0	Torriente, Cristobal	0	0
Mathewson, Christy	<100	1	Waddell, Rube	1	0
McCarthy, Tom	<5	0	Ward, John	<5	0
McGinnity, Joe	<20	1	Welch, Mickey	<5	0
McPhee, Bid	<5	0	White, Deacon	<5	0
Mendez, Jose	0	0	White, Sol	<5	0
O'Day, Hank	<10	0	Wilkinson, J.L.	11	0
O'Rourke, James	<10	0	Williams, Joe	0	0
Plank, Ed	<20	1	Willis, Vic	<20	0
Pompez, Alex	<20	0	Wilson, Jud	0	0
Posey, Cum	<100	0	Wright, George	<100	0
Radbourn, Hoss	0	0	Wright, Harry	<25	0
Rogan, Bullet	0	0	Youngs, Ross	<50	<25
Rusie, Amos	<10	0		< = fewer than	
Santop, Louis	<5	0			

From the Links: Golf

The origins of the game of golf are unclear. Some historians date the game as far back as ancient Rome. The modern game of golf was born in Scotland in the 15th century. It is said that King James II banned the game around 1450 because it distracted noblemen from engaging in more learned pursuits. Winston Churchill once said of the game: "Golf is a game whose aim is to hit a very small ball into an even smaller hole with weapons ill designed for the purpose." For many, golf starts as a recreational sport but it evolves into something more, a tender madness that stays with them the rest of their lives. Thousands upon thousands of men and women have played the game professionally. While there are many golfers to choose from, the only signatures that are truly collectable are from those who have won a major tournament. There are six tournaments that are considered "majors." They are the British Open, United States Open, PGA, and the Masters, plus two amateur majors, one American and one British. The signature of a golfer who hasn't secured a major is of little value. There is, of course, an exception here and there, such a Lighthorse Harry Cooper, but for the most part values remain nominal.

Cooper, H-1 signature circa 1985.

For decades collecting golf autographs was a very limited pursuit. Very few collectors existed before 1980, and then only the active players were targeted. With a few exceptions, the old-time major winners were rarely asked to sign an autograph. There are many who died in the 1980s and their signatures are considered scarce on a per se basis. Signatures obtained in the 1980s and before were generally signed at tournaments. Scorecards, programs, and album pages were the most common mediums to have signed. A golfer signing a golf ball before the 1980s was a rare event. Signed golf balls from most early major winners do not exist.

Most collectors attempt to complete signed sets of the various major tournaments. Collecting Masters champions is the most popular approach with collectors. It is also the easiest set to complete. While many signatures of Masters winners are scarce, all are obtainable. None are considered rare, at least on a per se basis. The hardest set to complete would be the British Open. As of this writing it is not possible to complete a signed set of British Open champions.

The British Open

The oldest of the four professional majors is the British Open. The first Open was played at Prestwick Golf Club in Scotland back in 1860. The first champion was Willie Park Sr. There was no prize money, but at least Park did get to shake the hand of the Earl of Eglinton.

Signatures of the 19th-century Open champions are extremely rare to nonexistent. Just about all of the signatures in the market of the early champions are forgeries. Most vary in construction, evidencing a lack of confirmed specimens for forgers to use as a template.

The earliest signatures that are readily obtainable are J.H. Taylor, Harold Hilton, and the legendary Harry Vardon. Vardon is one of the giants of professional golf. He turned professional at the young age of 20. He would win the British Open an amazing six times. He died in 1937 and today his signature is rare. Premium items are very rare. ALsS are typically written on very colorful letterhead which enhances display value. Some ALsS are secretarially written and signed. Vardon's signature is in high demand. Close to 100 percent of signatures in the market are forged. A small supply of letters exists and will sell in excess of $1,500.

Vardon-1, ALS dated 1924.

Hilton's signature is also rare and limited to the occasional album page or document. Hilton signed in a pleasing hand. His signature rarely surfaces and then typically on an album page or calling card. Letters of any kind are very rare. Hilton's signature will sell for $500 to $700. Taylor lived until 1960; thus, the supply is far greater than that of Vardon and Hilton. Taylor's

Hilton-1, undated signature.

signature is scarce and can generally be purchased for $300. Letters can sell for $500 to $1,000 depending on length and content. Signed picture postcards exist, but these should be considered rare, so expect to pay $700 for a nice specimen.

Taylor, J-1, ALS dated 1924 (courtesy collection of Dustin Raymond).

Another high-demand signature is that of Alex "Sandy" Herd. He was a colorful Scottish golfer who won the Open in 1902. Herd died in 1944 and signed very few items. His signature is rare in any form. A small supply of ALsS exist and generally sell in the $500 price range. Signed photographs are very rare.

Herd-1 TLS dated 1926 (courtesy Mark Emerson Golf).

Between 1901 and 1910, James Braid won the Open five times. The demand for Braid's signature is strong and clearly outweighs a very limited supply. Braid signed in a bold hand. He finished off the autograph with a striking paraph. He died in 1950 at the age of 80. His signature is typically found on album pages and banquet menus. A few ALsS are in the market. They are considered rare. His signature generally sells in the $500 price range. A nice letter will easily sell for $1,000. It should be noted that there is a rather famous surgeon with the same name. Dr. Braid died in 1859. Moreover, there are many forged album pages and calling cards in the market. They are accomplished by the same forger. They are signed as "James Braid, Champion Golfer" and dated in the early 1900s. A labored appearance is noted. These forgeries are rudimentary in construction and are easily exposed.

Braid-1, undated signature (courtesy Dr. Richard Bagdasarian).

The first American to win the Open was Jock Hutchison. He broke the dry spell in 1921. Hutchison's signature is scarce in all forms. The occasional album page surfaces. He died in 1977 but signed very little. Photographs of any kind are rare. Expect to pay $200 to $250 for his signature.

Hutchison-1, signature circa 1920.

From 1921 to 1933 the Americans dominated the Open. Walter Hagen, Bobby Jones, and Gene Sarazen proved supreme. Tommy Armour won the 1931 Open. Armour's signature is in much demand and typically limited to album pages and government postcards. His signature lacks uniform letter construction but still retains good eye appeal. There are forged photographs in the market, so caution is warranted. These photographs feature an image of Armour in follow-through and looking directly at the camera. An inscribed forgery is placed in the lower left portion of the photograph by the right leg. His signature, which sells in the $200 to $300 range, is easily forged.

The 1923 Open at Royal Troon went to Arthur Havers. He beat Walter Hagen by one stroke. Havers's signature is scarce and is generally limited to album pages. Other mediums are rare to very rare. He signed very little in retirement. Autograph collectors seemed to have forgotten him and never bothered to request an autograph. Expect to pay $150 to $200 for his signature.

Havers-1, undated signature (courtesy collection of Dustin Raymond).

The 1934 Open was won by the flamboyant Henry Cotton. Cotton was a very colorful figure in golf history. He won the Open a total of three times. His signature is highly sought after by collectors. Cotton was a willing signer throughout his life. Today, there is a good supply of material, mostly limited to album pages, scorecards, and index cards. Signed 8 × 10 photographs and letters do exist, but both mediums should be considered uncommon to scarce. Cotton signed in a slower hand. The signature tends to have muted letter construction. His signature is easy to forge, so caution is warranted. His autograph is affordable at $100.

Armour-1, undated signature (courtesy The Sanders Autograph Price Guide).

Cotton-1, undated signature (courtesy Dr. Richard Bagdasarian).

The 1930s gave the golfing world many one-time major winners, and not just in the British Open. Alf Perry, 1935 winner, died in 1974. His signature is somewhat rare and generally limited to the occasional album page. Premium items are very rare. Most signatures are accomplished as "A. Perry" in a confined and small hand. His signature is valued at $150 to $200.

Perry, A-1, album page dated 1935.

A year later, at Royal Liverpool, Alfred Padgham won the Open. Padgham died in 1966 of cancer and his signature is more difficult to locate than Perry's signature. Padgham's signature is generally limited to album pages signed during his career. Material signed post-career is basically nonexistent. It is obvious he received few, if any, requests for his autograph in retirement. Padgham signed in a very nice and legible hand. He would finish off the signature with a paraph. His signature has very good display value, but it rarely surfaces. Most offered for sale are forgeries. Expect to pay $300 to $400 for a genuine specimen.

Padgham-1 Album page circa 1935.

The 1938 Open was played at Royal St. George. The winner was Reginald Whitcombe. It was his only major. Signatures are typically accomplished as "R.A. Whitcombe" and finished with a paraph. This signature is scarce and generally limited to album pages and scorecards. Letters and photographs are rare. Expect to pay $200 to $225 for his autograph.

Whitcombe-1 undated signature.

Richard Burton won the 1939 Open at St. Andrews. His signature, like that of Perry and Padgham, is tough to locate. Burton died in 1974 and is generally limited to material signed during his career. Album pages are the most common medium. Premium items are very rare. Burton signed in a nice flowing hand. He typically signed material as "R. Burton." Burton's signature will sell in the $200 range and will prove a significant acquisition for any collection.

Burton-1, undated signature.

The Open was suspended from 1940 to 1945 due to World War II. It resumed in 1946 at St. Andrews. American legend Sam Snead secured the jug. Signatures of the 1940s and 1950s Open winners exist in far greater supply. Their signatures are much easier to locate. Irishman Fred Daly won the Open in 1947. His signature is available on many lesser mediums. Letters are rare. Signed 8 × 10 photographs are also rare, albeit borderline. Some nice examples exist. Daly was a responsive signer. He died in 1990. His signature can be purchased for $50 to $75.

Daly-1, GPC circa 1955.

In 1949 the aureate South African Bobby Locke secured a place in golf history by winning at Royal St. George. Locke was the first really successful golfer to come out of South Africa. Locke would go on to win the Open a total of four times. The demand for Locke's signature is strong and outweighs supply. Locke signed in a nice vertical hand. His signature has good eye appeal. His signature is uncommon but an ample inventory does exist. Premiums items, such as letters and 8 × 10 photographs, are considered very scarce. There is a small supply of signed scorecards personally used by Locke. They make for a nice game-used artifact. These should be considered rare to very rare. In the last 15 or so years, forged golf balls entered the market. They are signed in either Sharpie marker or felt tip. I have never seen a genuinely signed Locke golf ball, so proceed with caution. Locke's signature can be purchased for $150 to $175. Game-used scorecards are a treasure so expect to pay $500 for a nice specimen.

Locke-1, undated album page (courtesy collection of Dustin Raymond).

The 1951 Open fell to boxer turned golfer Max Faulkner. Faulkner was a very reserved man. He was said to have one of the finest collections of putters in the world. Faulkner-signed material is scarce, and this from a man who died in 2005. Material signed in the 1950s is really tough to locate. He was not a target of collectors. In the 1990s, Faulkner signed a limited number of items through the mail. In general, he proved an elusive signer. The majority of mail requests for his autograph went unanswered. Faulkner signed in a stunning hand. He made liberal use of the fountain pen. The nice flowing lines make for a signature with maximum eye appeal. His signature is typically found on index cards and golf scorecards. Signed letters are very scarce. Signed golf balls are already considered rare. Faulkner's signature can be purchased for $50 to $75. Golf balls are valued at $300 to $400.

Faulkner, M-1 signature circa 2000.

Pete Thomson won the Open five times. Thomson has been a responsive signer and there are many nice examples in the market. His signature tends to be illegible with limited display value. His signature is very affordable at $25 to $30. Signed golf balls are valued at $50 to $75. The 1960 Open winner Kel Nagle's signature is also a fairly common. He was a good signer for many years. His signature is priced around $20 to $30. There are some nice golf content letters in the market. These sell for about $100.

Thomson-1, GPC dated 2003.

Nagle-1, undated signature.

Tony Lema, 1964 Open champ, is one of the more scarce signatures of modern major winners. In July 1966, en route to a golf tournament, the plane he was on ran out of fuel. It crashed, killing Lema at the young age of 32. His signature is scarce on all mediums and generally limited to material signed at golf outings.

Album pages and golf tickets are a good source. Premiums items such as 8 × 10 photographs and letters are rare to very rare. A decent supply of Lema's book *Golfers' Gold* is in the market, some with nice inscriptions. A Lema signature will sell in the $150 to $200 range. Signed books sell for $250 to $300.

Lema-1, signature circa 1965.

The United States Open

The U.S. Open is the second oldest of the professional majors. It is considered the most prestigious of all professional golf tournaments. The first Open was played in 1895 at Newport CC in Rhode Island. Horace Rawlins won the inaugural match. Like the British Open, completing a signed set of U.S. Open champions is also very unlikely. Some signatures of the early winners are very rare. Jim Foulis, Joe Lloyd, Willie Smith, and Laurie Auchterlonie signatures are extremely rare.

Scottish golfer Fred McLeod won the 1908 Open at Myopia Hunt in Massachusetts. McLeod died in 1976 at the age of 94. He signed a limited number of items. His signature should be considered scarce to rare. His signature is legible but most were signed during old age; hence, a choppiness of hand is noted. McLeod's

McLeod-1, undated signature (courtesy Mark Emerson Golf).

autograph is generally limited to index cards. Letters and photographs are very rare. His signature is valued at $200 to $225.

Perhaps the most significant year for golf in America was 1913. Before that time golf was a game reserved for the rich. Most Americans were not familiar with the sport, opting instead for baseball and boxing. That changed with a man named Francis Ouimet. Ouimet took up golf as a caddy. He played for many years and qualified for the 1913 Open. Before that time, just about all the major tournaments were won by golfers from the other side of the Pond. Ouimet, a virtual unknown, beat Ray and Vardon in an 18-hole playoff. Ouimet's win captured the imagination of America. Ouimet's signature is in high demand that vastly outweighs supply. His signature exhibits fine strokes and strong letter construction. Like Ty Cobb, Ouimet liked to sign autographs in green fountain pen. His signature has excellent eye appeal. His signature is generally limited to government postcards and index cards. Premiums items such as letters and 8 × 10 photographs do exist but should be considered rare. Ouimet's autograph generally sells for $500. A nicely signed 8 × 10 photograph should cost around $1,500.

Ouimet-1 undated signature (courtesy Dr. Richard Bagdasarian).

Jerome Travers won five majors, the 1915 U.S. Open and four U.S. Amateurs. Travers died in 1951. Travers signed in a clean and legible hand. An average display value is noted. He was, for many years, a rare signature. Recently, a decent supply of canceled bank checks has entered the market. Checks have greatly increased the market inventory of Travers signatures. Checks sell for $250 to $300.

Travers-1, World War I draft card (courtesy Record Group 163, Records of the Selective Services Division, National Archives at Atlanta).

A year later, three-time major winner Chick Evans won the Open. He is another significant major winner. He died in 1979 and was a very responsive signer his entire life. His signature is generally found on index cards and government postcards. Autograph letters signed are scarce and typically are penned on postcards. Evans is a signature that has dropped in value over the past 10 years. Many signatures surfaced on eBay. It is clear the supply of Evans material is sound. In 1995, his signature sold for $150; today it can be had for $60 to $75.

Evans-1, undated signature.

The 1920 Open went to British golfer Edward "Ted" Ray. Ray died in 1943 and his signature is considered very scarce on a per se basis. His signature is typically found on album pages. Premium items are very rare. He would typically sign autographs as simply "E. Ray" in a rudimentary hand. His signature is quite easy to forge and most offered for sale are forgeries. A genuine specimen will sell for $500 to $600.

Ray, E-1 undated signature (courtesy collection of Dustin Raymond).

From 1926 to 1964 the Americans dominated the Open. Johnny Farrell became champion of the United States in 1928. Farrell's signature is uncommon and generally limited to index cards. He died in 1988 and was a responsive signer. He received relatively few requests for his autograph. A few 11 × 14 signed presentation photographs exist, but these should be considered rare. Autograph letters signed are also rare. His signature has excellent letter construction. The display value is superior. Expect to pay $100 for his autograph. The above-referenced photograph will sell for $500 to $600.

Farrell-1 GPC dated 1975.

The stock market crash of 1929 and the depression that followed proved a benefit to the game. Americans more than ever needed distractions from the economic miseries of the time. In the 1930s, golf brought a new generation of golfers who played more for the love of the game than for the prize money, which was drastically reduced due to the economic downturn.

Olin Dutra, who won the PGA just two years before, secured the 1934 Open. Dutra signed in a wonderfully flowing hand. His signature has superior display value. He died in 1983. His signature is considered scarce and typically found on period album pages. He did sign a limited number of index cards. Like so many other golfers of this era, he received relatively few requests for his autograph. Premium items are rare. Expect to pay $150 for his signature.

Dutra-1, TLS circa 1945.

A year later an unknown golfer named Sam Parks Jr. captured the 1935 Open. He lived out a quiet retirement in Florida. He died in 1997. His signature is already considered very scarce. Premium items are rare. I spoke with Parks in the early 1990s and he told me he rarely received mail requests for his signature. His whereabouts were generally unknown to the collectors of the day. His signature is very legible. Most of the time it is finished off with a large paraph. Towards the end of his life health issues affected his hand. The result is a signature that evidences material unsteadiness. Some mail requests signed in the last couple of years of his life were secretarially signed. His signature is generally limited to index cards, which sell for about $100. He signed a very limited number of golf balls. Balls are considered rare and were selling for $500 about ten years ago. I know of no recent sales of Parks-signed balls. Many forgeries exist, so caution is warranted. It should be noted that there are many forged 8 × 10 photographs in the market. The image features Parks holding a golf trophy. The forgery is placed across the trophy. These have been around for years, so caution is warranted.

Parks-1 signature dated 1990.

Parks-2 common secretarial.

The 1936 Open went to Tony Manero. Manero won a total of eight professional tournaments. He was a responsive signer during his years as a player but signed next to nothing in retirement. Today, his signature is scarce and generally limited to period album pages and scorecards. Manero's signature sells for $100 to $125.

Manero-1, signature circa 1940.

Lawson Little won the 1940 Open, one of five majors for Little. His signature is somewhat scarce but many period items exist. Signatures are generally limited to album pages and programs. Letters and photographs are rare. There is marginal demand for Little's signature. Expect to pay $75 for his autograph.

Little-1, album page circa 1940.

The Open was suspended from 1942 to 1945 because of World War II. In 1946 golf roared back. The first postwar Open was played at Canterbury Golf Club in Ohio. The dashing Lloyd Mangrum won by outpointing Vic Ghezzi and Byron Nelson. Mangrum died in 1973 at a relatively young age. He signed in a bold hand. His signature has good display value.

Mangrum-1, undated signature.

It is uncommon to scarce, with premium items bordering on the rare side. Expect to pay $100 for his autograph.

The 1952 Open, which was played at Northwood in Dallas, fell to three-time major winner Julius Boros. Boros died in 1994 at the age of 74. Boros was a responsive signer, though premium items such as golf balls and 8 × 10 photographs are uncommon to scarce. Overall an affordable signature at $25.

Boros-1 signature circa 1985.

Many of the post–1950 Open winners are affordable and their signatures can be purchased for under $25. Jack Fleck, Tommy Bolt, Ed Furgol, and Billy Casper are all welcome additions to any signature library. The quick-tempered Bolt is of particular interest to collectors. Fellow golfer Jimmy Demaret once said, "Bolt's clubs have more air time than Lindbergh." This is a reference to Bolt's propensity of throwing his club after a bad shot. Despite his curt personality, Bolt was a willing and gracious signer through the mail. He was also a prolific letter writer. Many fine golf content letters are in the market and they command a premium.

* * *

The PGA Championship

The third professional major began in 1916. The first PGA was played at Siwanoy CC in New York. Jim Barnes outpointed Jock Hutchison for the win. There is good demand for Barnes material. His signature is scarce and generally limited to index cards, government postcards, and period album pages. Letters and photographs are rare. There are many Barnes forgeries in the market signed in a slow and labored hand, so caution is warranted. Expect to pay $300 for his signature.

Barnes-1, signature circa 1950.

World War I put the championship on ice for a couple of years. Leo Diegel was known to hack a wicked chip shot. He won back-to-back championships in 1928 and 1929. Diegel's signature is of average construction and display value. The signature is legible. Diegel died in 1951 at a young age. His signature is scarce and generally limited to material signed at the course. Album pages and scorecards are the best source for his signature. Premium items are very rare. I have never examined a genuine full-page ALS. Diegel's signature will sell for $150 to $200.

Diegel-1, World War I draft card (courtesy Record Group 163, Records of the Selective Services Division, National Archives at Atlanta).

The 1931 PGA went to a relatively unknown golfer named Tom Creavy. Creavy's career was cut short by illness. He died in 1979. His signature is rare on a per se basis. Creavy's autograph

Creavy-1, signature circa 1965 (courtesy Dr. Richard Bagdasarian).

is one of the toughest of all PGA champions and a modern rarity. The occasional government postcard and index card will be offered for sale, but that is about it. His signature is one of the keys to completing a PGA champions set. His signature is of average display value. A signed government postcard exchanged hands for $500 a few years back.

The 1934 champion, Paul Runyan, was a willing signer for his entire life. In 1938 he won his second PGA by edging out Sam Snead. Runyan signed in a very nice hand. His signature is legible. The display value is superior. Runyan's signature is generally found on index cards. He also wrote many letters. Signed 8 × 10 photographs are scarce. He also signed many golf balls that make for a fine collectable. Runyan signed many copies of his book *Paul Runyan's Book for Senior Golfers*. It was first published in 1962. Runyan's signature is affordable at $40 to $50. Balls and the above-referenced book will cost $125 to $150. Overall, one of the nicer golf signatures.

Runyan-1 signature circa 1995.

In 1935 the championship went to longtime golfer Johnny Revolta. Revolta lived until 1991, but he signed relatively few items. His signature is uncommon and basically limited to the occasional index card. There is moderate demand for his autograph. Expect to pay $75 to $100 for a nice specimen.

Revolta-1, undated signature.

Denny Shute won the 1936 and 1937 championships. He also won the 1933 British Open. Shute signed in a clean hand. The signature is legible with sound letter construction. There is a fairly good inventory of material in the market, the majority of which was signed during his playing days. Album pages are a good source for his signature. His signature sells for $75 to $100.

Shute-1, undated signature.

Vic Ghezzi won the 1941 championship. His signature is considered scarce as he died in 1976 at the age of 65. Material signed during his playing days is more common than signatures accomplished in retirement. His hand is unassuming with marginal letter construction. There are many breaks in the signature, so replication of hand would be very easy. There is average demand for Ghezzi's signature. It will cost about $100.

Ghezzi-1, album page circa 1945.

World War II brought an abrupt halt to the championship. It resumed in 1944. Jim Ferrier won the 1946 championship at Plum Hollow

Ferrier-1, undated signature.

CC in Southfield, Michigan. Ferrier died in 1986, but like other old-time major winners, he signed very little in retirement. Signatures are generally found on government postcards and index cards. There has never been much demand for Ferrier material. A signature can be secured for $50.

Postwar golf saw the entry of many new golfers, and 1950 was a banner year for a tall lanky golfer named Chandler "Old Bones" Harper. He won the championship at Scioto in Ohio. Harper was a willing and gracious signer for collectors. He signed many items, including a good supply of golf balls. He also loved to write letters about the game. Many fine ALsS are in the market. Harper handed out bank checks to collectors. Harper's signature is very affordable at $10 to $20. Letters and bank checks sell in the $75 to $100 price range.

Harper-1 signature circa 1995.

In 1953, Michigan native Walter Burkemo secured the championship at the Birmingham CC in Michigan. Burkemo's signature has excellent display value with sound letter construction. His signature would be difficult to forge. His signature is usually found on golf programs and album pages. Burkemo died in 1986 at the age of 66. His signature is somewhat scarce. Expect to pay $100 to $125 for his autograph.

Burkemo-1, undated signature.

Chick Harbert prevailed in 1954. Harbert, like Burkemo, was a Michigan favorite. He won the Michigan PGA championship several times. He scored his only major by beating out Bur-

kemo. Harbert was a responsive signer through the mail. He signed mostly index cards and first-day covers. The supply of material is ample. His signature should be considered uncommon. Premium items, such as ALsS and golf balls, are rare. Harbert died in 1992. His signature can be picked up for $25 to $50. A golf ball will sell in the $300 range.

Harbert-1 1980 signature.

The 1955 and 1956 championships went to Doug Ford and Jack Burke, respectively. Both would also win the Masters. Both men were, for many years, responsive signers, resulting in a good supply of material. The 1957 championship was won by Lionel Hebert. Hebert died in 2000. His signature is generally found on index cards and is an uncommon autograph. His older brother Jay Hebert won the 1960 PGA. Jay's autograph is tougher to locate. Dow Finsterwald won the 1958 championship. His autograph is common.

Hebert-1, signature dated 1992.

The winner of the 1959 championship was Bob Rosburg. Rosburg died in 2009 and signed many items including balls, photographs, and scorecards. Back in 1939, at the age of 12, Rosburg played then Olympic Club member and baseball immortal Ty Cobb in match play. The 12-year-old Rosburg beat Cobb. Rosburg wrote a limited number of letters regarding his game with Cobb. These letters are in high demand. Expect to pay $100 for one.

Rosburg-1, signature circa 2000.

The Masters

The most popular of all majors is the Masters. Played at the revered Augusta National GC in Georgia, the Masters is biggest name in modern golf. It was founded by golf legend Bobby Jones and Cliff Roberts. It is an invitational event and the winner gets the coveted green jacket. The Masters is the most popular among collectors. It is, by far, the easiest set to complete. There are no rare Masters signatures, at least on a per se basis.

The first Masters was played in 1934. The green jacket went to Horton Smith. Smith would win the Masters two years later in 1936. He retired from the tour and became the golf pro at the Detroit GC. He was also president of the PGA in the early 1950s. Smith is a significant golf signature. The demand for the first Masters champ is strong and weighed against a limited supply. Smith's signature is considered very scarce and generally limited to album pages and golf programs. About ten years ago, the estate of golf instructor Alex Morrison was liquidated. There were many signed letters from various golf personalities. The letters dated from the 1930s to the 1970s. About 20 to 25 letters written by Smith to Morrison were sold. There were also many signed envelopes of the same date. Some letters were typed and some were handwritten. All had golf content and were quickly absorbed into private collections. The letters were selling for $500 to $1,000 for those signed as "Horton." Letters signed in full were selling for $1,500. Signed 8 × 10 photographs are rare to very rare and sell for $2,000. There

are a few forged Royal and Walter Hagen brand golf balls in the market. The forgeries are signed in black or blue fountain pen and accomplished on a bifurcated plane. The last name of "Smith" displays itself as "Smtth." The letter "i" is elongated. These forgeries are childish in construction but they are being transacted, so caution is warranted. I know of no signed golf balls, and it is very doubtful that one exists.

Smith H-1 undated signature (courtesy collection of Dr. Richard Bagdasarian).

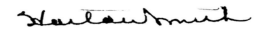

Smith H-2, variant signature dated 1944.

The 1935 Masters went to the legendary Gene Sarazen. Sarazen won an incredible seven majors and is one of only five golfers to win all four professional majors. Sarazen signed in an average hand. His signature is legible. Letter construction is plain, resulting in a signature with average display value. Sarazen was a willing and gracious signer his entire life. His signature exists in quantities on most mediums: golf balls, scorecards, photographs, letters, and the like. Signed bank checks are also available, though uncommon. Sarazen is a significant figure in American golf. His signature is a welcome addition to any library. Sarazen's signature sells for $25 to $50. Checks and 8 × 10 photographs sell for $50 to $60. Golf balls sell in the $225 to $250 price range.

Sarazen-1, ALS dated 1971.

Five-time major winner John Byron Nelson won the 1937 Masters. He would win the tournament a second time in 1942. Nelson, like Sarazen, is considered one of the immortals of the game. Nelson was also a gracious signer. He was always responsive to mail requests for his signature. He was known to sign autographs up to two weeks before his death in 2006. Nelson's signature is legible. It exhibits strong flow. The display value is sound. His signature is found on most mediums, including golf balls, photographs, gum cards, scorecards, and the like. Signed letters of any kind are uncommon to scarce. Nelson published a book titled *Winning Golf*. It was released in 1946. He signed multiple copies and just about all were inscribed. Nelson had an odd habit of adding a paraph to his signature when signing books. It is the only medium I know of where he would add this to his signature. Nelson's signature sells in the $30-$40 price range. Signed copies of the above-referenced book sell for $200 to $300. Golf balls are valued at $225 to $250. Nelson's signature should prove a sound investment in the years to come.

Nelson, B-1 signature dated 1990.

It should be noted that longtime Detroit Tigers broadcaster and baseball Hall of Famer Ernie Harwell broadcast the 1942 Masters. He signed a limited number of Masters items, including photographs featuring Ernie with famed golf writer O.B. Keeler.

The 1938 Masters went to a sharp-dressed New Englander named Henry Picard. Picard is my favorite golfer of all time and was a personal friend. A year after winning the Masters, he won the PGA championship. Picard signed in a bold and striking hand. He typically signed his name as "H.G. Picard." On rare occasions he would pen it as "Henry G. Picard." He was a willing signer but did not receive that many requests

for his autograph. He lived out a quiet retirement in South Carolina. Picard signatures are generally limited to index cards and the occasional first-day cover. Signed 8 × 10 photographs and letters of any kind are scarce. Signed golf balls are rare. Signed bank checks are very rare and seldom surface. About 50 letters and contracts, dating from the 1930s, were released from the above-referenced Morrison papers. They were quickly purchased by collectors. There is sound demand for this early Masters champ. His signature will sell for $75. ALsS were selling in the $500 range in the mid–2000s. Prices have pulled back somewhat. Today, an ALS will sell for $350 to $400. Picard's signature is about the toughest Masters winner you can find on a golf ball. Golf balls are very rare. A superior specimen sold in 2010 for $1,500.

Picard-1 signature dated 1990.

Just about all Picard golf balls in the market are forged. If you're looking for signed balls of Smith, Jimmy Demaret, Claude Harmon, Ralph Guldahl, and Craig Wood, you will be looking for a long time. I have come to the conclusion that these signatures do not exist on golf balls.

Then there is the strange case of one Ralph Guldahl, winner of the 1939 Masters. In the late 1930s Guldahl was probably the most dominant player in the game. In a three-year period he won three majors. He also won the prestigious Western Open three years in a row. Then, in 1940, something went dreadfully wrong. Guldahl's game disappeared like Judge Joe Crater, never to return. Fellow golfer Paul Runyan lamented, "He went from being the absolute best player in the world to one who couldn't play at all."

Guldahl signed in a very pleasing hand. Vintage signatures exhibit wonderful letter construction. A slight jaggedness is noted. The display value is high. Guldahl had an alternate form of signature that he signed at tournaments. This form of signature is hurried and very unattractive. As Guldahl aged, his hand slowed greatly. A slight shakiness of hand is noted.

Guldahl died in 1987. His signature is scarce on a per se basis. Premium items are rare. ALsS usually have routine content and are only a few sentences long. I have never examined a genuinely signed golf ball. Guldahl is one of the "key" signatures to completing a Masters set. Expect to pay $500 for his autograph. Premium items, such as 8 × 10 photographs and letters, will sell for $1,000 to $2,000. Guldahl co-authored a book titled *From Tee to Cup*, published in 1937. There are several copies of this book in the market that contain a Guldahl forgery signed in bold black fountain pen. These were accomplished by one forger.

The total collapse of his career, to this day, remains a mystery. It only enhances the demand for Guldahl memorabilia. Some blamed it on weight gain. Others said he simply lost interest in golf. The real reason appears more ominous and a bit creepy. Back in 1939 Guldahl wrote a book titled *Groove Your Golf*. It was a how-to book to improve the golf swing. He wrote that book and it somehow destroyed his game. The great Guldahl of old was no more. I have had more than one old-time golfer, including Mr. Harwell, tell me that the book is cursed. If you happen to run across a signed copy, you may just want to avoid it.

Guldahl-1, signature dated 1938.

The 1940 Masters went to the colorful and fun-loving Jimmy Demaret. He won the Masters a total of three times in a ten-year span. Demaret signed in a very unstructured hand. Let-

ter construction is poor. The signature has substandard display value. Demaret died in 1983 of a heart attack. His signature is uncommon to scarce. After retiring from the game, he became a golf commentator. This gave collectors access to him. Premium items are rare. Demaret's signature, which is typically found on index cards and album pages, sells for $300 to $400. An exceptional signed 1940 Masters ticket sold for $8,600 (Green Jacket Auctions, 2014).

Demaret-1, undated signature (courtesy collection of Dustin Raymond).

The 1941 tournament gave golf collectors the toughest Masters signature to obtain in one Craig Wood. Not only did he win the Masters that year but also secured the U.S. Open. Wood died in 1968 and is a very scarce to rare signature. Wood signed in a very carefree hand. His signature is large. Rapid strokes are noted. Signatures are few and far between. They are typically limited to album pages. Letters and

Wood-1, undated signature.

photographs are very rare. His signature is commonly forged. There are a handful of forged Royal brand golf balls in the market. Wood very likely does not exist on this medium. At least 90 percent of Wood autographs in the market are forged. Wood's signature sells in the $750 to $1,000 range.

World War II interrupted the Masters. It resumed in 1946 and a recently discharged navy veteran named Herman Keiser won the green jacket. Keiser was reserved man and few knew his name. He bested Ben Hogan for the win. Keiser retired with a total of five PGA wins. I once spoke with Keiser. He told me he was seldom asked for an autograph and rarely received requests through the mail. His signature is scarce on a per se basis. He died in 2003 from complications of Alzheimer's. Keiser signed in a plain and slower hand. Replication of hand is very easy. Many well-executed forgeries exist. He did pen a few letters about the 1946 Masters and the conspiracy to give the tournament to Hogan. These letters are of fine content and are highly cherished by collectors. His signature sells for $100 to $125. Signed golf balls, which are rare, sell for about $500. Just about all signed golf balls in the market are forgeries.

Keiser-1, signature circa 1990.

The 1948 Masters fell to golf instructor Claude Harmon. Harmon signed in a fast and flowing hand. The signature evidences good display value. Harmon died in 1989 and was

Harmon-1, scorecard dated 1970 (courtesy collection of Dustin Raymond).

generally not the target of autograph collectors. His signature is considered very scarce on a per se basis. It is generally limited to material signed during his playing days such as album pages and scorecards. Letters and photographs of any kind are rare. His signature is valued at $600 to $700.

Sam Snead won the 1949 Masters. He won a total of three green jackets and seven majors in his lifetime. Snead holds the record for most tournament wins with 82. He is considered one of the greatest golfers of all time, if not the greatest. Snead was a willing and gracious signer his whole life. He signed many items. His signature can be found on golf balls, photographs, scorecards, gum cards, bank checks, and the like. ALsS are scarce. A few photographs featuring Snead and Hogan exist. They are signed by both legends and make for a fine collectable. Snead material is in great demand and should prove a sound investment. His signature sells for $50. Premium items will range from $100 to $300. Bank checks are valued at $75.

Snead-1 signature dated 1985.

Many people have dreams but few drop everything to pursue them. Dr. Cary Middlecoff was one of those few. "Doc" Middlecoff had a successful dental practice but pushed it aside for a career in golf. He was rewarded with three majors including the 1955 Masters. Middlecoff signed in a very choppy and unsightly hand. His signature has limited display value. It lacks flow and thus is easily forged. Many well-executed forgeries exist. Middlecoff's signature is uncommon. Premium items are scarce. Middlecoff proved an erratic signer through the mail. Many requests were honored but more were ignored. His signature is typically found on index cards. Photographs and golf balls are scarce. An ALS is rare. Many forged golf balls exist, so caution is warranted. Middlecoff's signature has marginal letter construction to begin with. On the dimpled and uneven surface of a golf ball it looks even worse. A genuine signed golf ball will be illegible. The general rule is if you can read the Middlecoff signature on a ball, it is forged and should be avoided. Index cards sell for about $100. Signed 8 × 10 photographs sell for $175 to $200. Golf balls are valued at $400 to $500.

Gary Middlecoff signature

Middlecoff-1 signature, circa 1990.

Arnold Palmer remains one of the most popular figures of American sport. He won the 1958 Masters and went on to win a total of eight major championships. Palmer's signature is in high demand. Luckily for collectors, the supply is also strong. Nicknamed "The King," Palmer had always been a willing and gracious signer in person and through the mail. His signature can be found on most mediums though ALsS are scarce. Beginning in 2010 Palmer curtailed signing through the mail. Many signatures obtained in the last five to ten years of his life are accomplished by an autopen, so caution is warranted. A signature is valued at $20 to $30. Signed 8 × 10 photographs sell for $50 to $60. Golf balls are valued at $100 to $125.

The second member of the "Big Three" golfers of the 1960s is South African Gary Player. Known as the "Black Knight," Player won a total of nine majors, including three Masters. Player is one of the best signers of all the major winners. He has signed countless items for collectors, both in person and through the mail. The supply is very strong. ALsS are scarce. Player's signature can be secured for $20. Golf balls sell for $50 to $75.

Player-1, signature circa 1990.

The Golden Bear, Jack Nicklaus, is considered by many as the greatest golfer of all time. Nicklaus won a record-setting six Masters. He has a total of 20 majors to his credit, the most of any golfer. Nicklaus's signature is in great demand. He has been a good signer throughout the years, both in person and through the mail. His signature is signed in a rapid motion with impaired letter construction. Individual letters tend to be poorly formed. Because of this, his signature is easy to replicate. Many well-executed forgeries are in the market. His signature can

Palmer-1 signature dated 1990.

Nicklaus-1, signature circa 1990.

be found on most mediums. TLsS are scarce. ALsS are rare. A signature will sell for $30 to $40. Signed 8 × 10 photographs are valued at $75. Golf balls are in high demand, so expect to pay $200 for a nice specimen.

Walter Hagen

Walter Hagen was probably the most colorful man ever to play professional golf. He didn't want to be a millionaire; he just wanted to live like one. Hagen is one of the greatest golfers in the history of the game. He won 11 majors, and had he taken the game a bit more seriously, he probably would have won 11 more. He won the PGA championship four years in a row from 1924 to 1927.

Hagen was a product of the golden age of American sports, the 1920s. He was often targeted by collectors. He signed many items during his career. He was also a willing and gracious signer in retirement. His signature is considered uncommon but not scarce. Hagen signed in a large and striking hand. His signature dominates the medium it is placed upon. Hagen's signature has maximum display value. He usually finished it off with a large paraph.

Hagen's signature is difficult to replicate. Well-executed forgeries are limited but do exist. Hagen's signature can be found on index cards, government postcards, scorecards, photographs, and typed letters signed. ALsS are rare. He also loved to sign copies of his book *The Walter Hagen Story*. This book is a great read. Hagen would usually sign it with a fine inscription to the recipient. There are a couple of Walter Hagen (red label) brand golf balls purportedly signed by Hagen in black fountain pen. They have sold for some significant money, but I have my doubts as to the authenticity of these balls. I seriously doubt a genuine signed Hagen golf ball exists. The demand for Hagen material is strong. His signature is valued at $250 to $300. A nicely signed 8 × 10 photograph is valued at $1,250 to $1,500.

Hagen-1, signature circa 1935 (courtesy collection of Dr. Richard Bagdasarian).

One final note: Hagen's son, Walter Jr., also played golf. His signature is similar to that Walter Sr. but differences are material. Sometimes his signature is mistaken for that of his famous father.

Hagen-2, Hagen's son's signature.

Ben Hogan

Ben Hogan is one of the biggest names in sports. He was known as the "Ice Man" for his emotionless constitution. Hogan won nine majors. In February of 1949 Hogan and his wife were involved in a near-fatal car accident. Hogan was badly injured and nearly killed.

Hogan's signature is in great demand. Hogan signed in a flowing hand. His signature exhibits good letter construction. The display value is superior. His signature is rather difficult to replicate. In later years his signature changed. The hand evidences infirmity. Signatures accomplished in the 1980s until death have a labored appearance. The once flowing lines are replaced by jaggedness and thicker strokes of the hand. This signature is much easier to forge. Forgers typically focus on the elderly signature for replication.

Hogan was a willing signer during his career. In his retirement, obtaining a signature through the mail was a daunting task. He rarely honored requests. In the early 1990s, during a two- or three-year window, Hogan did start to honor mail requests. He signed many items for collectors.

Signed 8 × 10 photographs, first-day covers, index cards, and scorecards are all available. TLsS are scarce. Most are signed by his secretary. ALsS are rare. A few years back a good inventory of canceled bank checks entered the market. These are a wonderful source of Hogan's autograph. Checks have declined in value. When they were first marketed, dealers were asking $400 to $500. Today, a Hogan bank check can be purchased for $75 to $125. A nicely signed 8 × 10 photograph sells for $150 to $200. A golf ball is valued at $600 to $700.

About 25 years ago I spoke with Hogan over the phone. During our conversation the topic of signed golf balls came up. Hogan told me that he *never* signed non–Hogan brand golf balls. Forgers commonly make the error of placing a Hogan forgery on a non–Hogan brand ball. If you run across non–Hogan signed equipment of any kind it should be considered a forgery and avoided. Well over 90 percent of Hogan signed golf balls are forgeries. He did not like to sign them.

Hogan-1, signature circa 1970.

Hogan-2, signature circa 1990.

Hogan-3, common secretarial.

Bobby Jones

The most significant figure in the history of the game is Bobby Jones. Jones won 13 majors and is only player in history to win the Grand Slam. In 1931 Jones was at the zenith of his game. He shocked the world of sports by announcing his retirement at the age of 29. He remained close to the game and was the catalyst behind the Masters.

There are two types of Jones signatures that are the subject of study: vintage signatures, those which were signed up to late 1940s; and modern signatures, those which were signed after 1950.

Vintage signatures are signed in a sharp and flowing hand. Sound letter construction is noted. Display value is superior. Vintage signatures are difficult to replicate. Well-executed forgeries do not exist. Just about all vintage signatures are signed as "Robt. T. Jones Jr." Vintage signatures are scarce on a per se basis. They are typically found on album pages, government postcards, and typed letters signed. Signed 8 × 10 photographs exist and are in high demand. Superior specimens have been known to sell for over $5,000. A vintage Jones signature can be purchased for around $700 to $900.

A word of caution: many TLsS, such as those found on American Golf Institute letterhead, are secretarially signed. The secretarial signature looks nothing like a genuine specimen and is exposed with little effort.

In 1948, Jones was diagnosed with spinal rot, a degenerative vertebral disease. It robbed Jones of his mobility. As the disease progressed, it eventually confined him to a wheelchair for the rest of his life.

The illness altered Jones's hand greatly. The

once-flowing signature was replaced with a tremulous and shaky hand. Display value is greatly impaired. There are no similarities between vintage and modern signatures. Modern signatures are easily replicated and most offered for sale are well-executed forgeries. Modern signatures are generally limited to index cards and the occasional 8 × 10 photograph. TLsS are rare. ALsS are near nonexistent, though many forgeries do exist. Modern signatures are in much less demand and can be purchased for $400 to $500. There are many signed golf balls in the market. I have never found one I would feel comfortable pronouncing as genuine.

Jones, B-1 photograph circa 1930 (courtesy collection of Dr. Richard Bagdasarian).

Jones, B-2 signature dated 1932 (courtesy Nate D. Sanders Auctions).

Jones, B-3, signature circa 1965.

The Amateurs

The British Amateur began in 1885. Many who won the British Opens also won the Amateur. Amateur winners are not as widely collected as their professional counterparts. Signatures of the early winners are very rare and seldom, if ever, surface. There are, however, some desirable names to be had. The first American to win was Missouri native Jesse Sweetser. He won it in 1926. Sweetser also won the 1922 U.S. Amateur. His signature is one of my favorites. A superior display value is noted. He died in 1989 but signed material is scarce. Premium items are rare. Expect to pay $150 for his autograph.

Sweetser-1 undated signature .

Cyril Tolley is another popular winner. He won the Amateur in 1920 and then again 1929. His signature is scarce and is generally found on album pages and the occasional bank check. It is valued at $100.

Tolley-1 album page circa 1950 (courtesy Mark Emerson Golf).

Georgia native Charlie Yates, a close friend of Jones, won the 1938 Amateur. He signed a few items, mostly index cards. His signature is considered scarce. Irishman Joe Carr won the Amateur three times. His signature is also scarce. His signature has odd letter construction and makes for a fanciful display. Americans Frank Stranahan and Harvie Ward each won one Amateur. Their signatures are scarce and should prove a fine addition to any golf library. Signatures of the above four gentlemen can be purchased for $50 each.

Yates-1, signature dated 2004.

Carr-1, GPC dated 2000.

Stranahan-1, photograph circa 1965.

Ward, E-1, signature circa 1985.

The United States Amateur first began in 1895 and signatures of many early winners have yet to be confirmed. Some post–World War II winners are of interest, such as Sam Urzetta. Urzetta is a scarce signature and was known to pen letters with fine golf content. These are highly collectable. Urzetta's signature will sell for $40 to $50. Golf balls are valued at $100. Willie Turnesa, of the famous Turnesa brothers, won two Amateurs, one in 1938 and then again in 1948. He also won the 1947 British Amateur.

Turnesa signed in a confined hand. His signature works well on golf balls. Signed balls have good display value and are scarce. Turnesa's signature can be purchased for $25. Golf balls sell in the $100 to $150 price range. Robert "Skee" Riegel won the 1947 Amateur. He died in 2009 and his signature is already considered scarce. He rarely signed autographs for collectors.

Urzetta-1 signature circa 2000.

Turnesa, W-1, signature dated 1985.

Riegel-1, signature circa 1990.

The LPGA

The collectability of the lady golfers has, for many years, been muted. In recent years the interest in the LPGA has increased greatly. Demand for these signatures has started to move. Signatures of the very early major winners are extreme rarities. Many are not known to the collecting community and values have not been established. Probably the best-known female golfer was Babe Didrikson Zaharias. Didrikson is widely considered the greatest female athlete of all time. In a ten-year period, from 1940 to 1950, she won the Western Open four times. She captured the U.S. Open three times. Babe is a member of the World Golf Hall of Fame. Didrikson's signature is scarce, as she died in 1956 at the young age of 45. Her signature is generally found on album pages and golf programs. Premium items are rare. Her signature sells in the $500 price range.

Didrikson-1, undated signature.

Other golf signatures that have sound demand are Joyce Wethered and Glenna Collett Vare. Wethered won the British Amateur four times in the 1920s. She is a highly sought-after signature. It is apparent she signed very little in her lifetime. She died in 1997 and her signature is considered very scarce. Premium items are rare. Her signature sells for $200. Vare is also a desirable autograph. She was the most dominant golfer in the 1920s and perhaps the greatest there ever was. Vare signed in a very artistic and flowing hand. Her signature has superior eye appeal. She died in 1989 in Florida. Like that of Wethered, Vare's signature is also scarce. Her signature will sell in the $200 price range.

Collett-1 album page dated 1930 (courtesy Mark Emerson Golf).

Wethered-1 signed postcard (courtesy Todd Mueller Autographs).

Virginia Van Wie was another well-known golfer from the golden age of sports. She is best known for winning the U.S. Women's Amateur three years in a row (1932 to 1934). Van Wie died in 1997. Her signature is scarce on a per se basis. Index cards are about the only medium available. Her signature has good display value; expect to pay $75 for one.

Van Wie-1, signature dated 1985.

Patty Berg won the Western Open an amazing seven times. She captured the U.S. Open in 1946. Berg was a very responsive signer through the mail. She signed many items, resulting in a strong supply of material, including golf balls. She died in 2006 and today her signature is plentiful. Letters of any kind are scarce. Her signature sells anywhere from $25 to $150, depending on the medium.

Berg-1, signature circa 1990.

Louise Suggs was another popular golfer on the 1940s and 1950s. She won 60 professional tournaments and captured the U.S. Open twice. Suggs material is uncommon and generally limited to index cards and scorecards. Letters of any kind are scarce. Being one of the founders

Suggs-1, signature circa 1990.

of the LPGA makes her signature a welcome addition to any golf library. Suggs's signature is available and can be purchased for $15 to $20.

Elizabeth "Betsy" Rawls is another golfer of note. She won the U.S. Open four times and the LPGA championship twice. Rawls's signature, like that of Suggs, is uncommon and generally limited to index cards and scorecards. Signed 8 × 10 photographs do surface, but not that often. Letters of any kind are scarce. Her signature sells in the $15 to $20 price range.

Rawls-1, signature circa 1990.

The LPGA is one area of autographs that should see a good increase in values over the coming years. Little research has been done on the early lady golfers. Signatures of the early major winners have proven, to this day, elusive.

The Pipes

One of the oddest collectables in the world of golf memorabilia are signed antique clay pipes. Every once in a while I will run across one of these benign little things. They are signed by golfers of old. Some contain multiple signatures. I could never figure out why anyone would want a signed pipe. I began doing some casual research, and the more I dug around the more disturbing the story became. It is, to say the least, a rather ghoulish tale. I was good friends with Henry Picard. I spoke with him often. I asked him about the origins of the pipes. He said he did not want to talk the subject and advised me to "stay well away from them." He did admit that he was guilty of signing a few in his younger days. His answer took me by surprise. I asked Hall of Famer Paul Runyan for

some insight and he replied, "Let sleeping dogs lie." After my unsettling chats with Messrs. Runyan and Picard, the signed pipes took on a rather creepy persona. From what I have been able to piece together, these pipes are cursed and misfortune falls upon anyone who owns them. I did get Picard to tell me that an owner of two of these pipes, who lived in Charleston, was brutally murdered by his estranged wife. To be honest, I would think the story is utter nonsense but for the fact that the golfers of old seem to be genuinely fearful of these artifacts. Several years ago I had a chance to buy one of these pipes signed by Walter Hagen. I missed out on the purchase, and looking back, that was probably a good thing. Signed pipes are very rare and seem to stir unnerving stories of old that usually involve the untimely death of some unfortunate soul. I suppose they are to golf what the Hope Diamond is to gem collectors. If you run across one of these harmless-looking pipes, you may just want to steer clear of it and let Mr. Runyan's sleeping dogs lie.

Mueller Enterprise Golf Cards

Brainchild of longtime autograph dealer Todd Mueller, this is a limited edition set which features 30 cards of legendary golfers. Titled "Golf's Greatest," it is limited to 10,000 sets. The set features the artwork of Bart Forbes. This set is to golf what the Perez Steele cards are to the baseball world. Forbes's artwork is amazing and the cards exhibit wonderful eye appeal. Ben Hogan, Lee Trevino, Ray Floyd, and Gene Sarazen are among the greats featured in this set. Many were signed and have proved to be in great demand. The set also includes cards featuring President Gerald. R. Ford and Bob Hope. In recent years signed cards have become expensive. Ford, who willingly signed them, is valued at $300. Sarazen, Hogan, and Snead are valued at $125 to $150. A Byron Nelson signed card is very rare. He objected to the text on the back of his card and refused to sign them until it was corrected. Perhaps the rarest signed card is that of Joyce Wethered. She died in 1997 and signed very few of these cards. Today they are considered rare. The Mueller Enterprise golf card set makes for a fine display.

The list of collectable golf signatures seems endless. The modern era give collectors names such as Billy Casper, Greg Norman, Tiger Woods, Hale Irwin, and Nick Faldo. Other names, not as well known to fans, are still highly prized: Billy Burke, Johnny Goodman, Alex Kyle, James Bruen, and far too many others to name. Assembling signatures of major winners can be a rewarding lifelong pursuit.

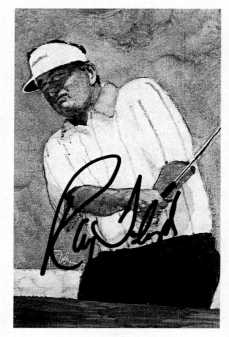

GOOD OL' REBEL

RAY FLOYD

Mueller Enterprises Golf card of Ray Floyd.

From the Pages of
Literature: Authors

One of the most popular fields in autographs is signatures of authors. Signed letters, manuscripts, and, of course, books have been coveted by collectors for hundreds of years. There is sometime magical about possessing a writing by a renowned author from the pages of yesteryear. It also one field where collectable signatures come from every corner of the globe. Many fields are limited to one particular country. Basketball autographs, for example, are generally limited to us Americans. British Prime Ministers are, of course, of interest mainly to the British. But with writers the geographical possibilities are endless: Europe to Asia to South America to these United States. Another attractive feature about this field is that authors have been around for centuries. This correlates into a diverse pool of signatures to add to your library. Many writers of old have been gone for centuries, yet their names and works are ever popular today. Geoffrey Chaucer, who died in 1400, is today still a household name. His most famous of works, the *Canterbury Tales*, is still widely read.

The most important work of early Anglo-Saxon writings is the famed story of *Beowulf.* It is generally believed that this work was created sometime between AD 800 and 1000. It is a story of good triumphing over the evil, skull-wielding Cormoranian beast, Grendel. While the name of the author who created this work is lost to history, his or her story is still read by just about every child. *Beowulf* is required reading.

Signatures of the early authors are extremely rare and costly. What little supply exists has been absorbed by institutional collections. Collectors would love to add signatures of William Shakespeare, Jonathan Swift, Daniel Defoe, and other legendary writers of old to their collections. This is unlikely to happen. Many of these signatures have not been sold for decades and are no longer in the open market. If one these signatures were to come up for sale, the cost would be prohibitive to all but the wealthiest of collectors. Should a Shakespeare signature ever enter the market, it would easily sell for $1,000,000. Others, such as Fyodor Dostoyevsky and Miguel de Cervantes, are extreme rarities. Market specimens are just about nonexistent. The intent of this chapter is not delve into the rarest of signatures but to focus more on the obtainable names such as Tolkien, Dickens, Saroyan, Vonnegut, and the like. While Chaucer is an extremely significant signature, you are likely never to run across one at the local flea market. Mark Twain, on the other hand, will surface now and then in the most unlikely of places.

Manuscripts

The most significant medium in this field is the manuscript. Manuscripts are works of the author that were later published. Some, of course, were not published. The early manuscripts are handwritten with many corrections. The more modern manuscripts are typed but usually contain many handwritten corrections. The value is dependent on the writer. The more famous the writer, the higher the value. In the early 1970s, James Fenimore Cooper's manuscript of *The Pathfinders* sold for an astounding $35,000. Today, it would easily bring $100,000. Back in 1944, Poe's manuscript of *Murders in the Rue Morgue* sold for the amazing price of $34,000. Today, that manuscript would fetch more than $1,000,000. I paid noted crime author Elmore Leonard a visit or two at his home in Bloomfield Village. Whenever I needed a first edition signed, I would drop by for a coffee and a signature. I can remember watching him working on a book and seeing all those handwritten pages for his upcoming work. I was never able to pry a manuscript out of Dutch, but believe me, it wasn't for lack of trying!

Not all manuscripts are valuable. With the lesser-named authors, complete manuscripts can be had for under $1,000. The manuscript for this book, for example, would probably sell for less than $500, and then probably would be purchased by a family member.

There are many barriers to collecting manuscripts. First, the prohibitive cost. You cannot purchase these for $15 to $25 like you can a signed book. The unique nature of manuscripts creates great demand and thus high prices. Secondly, many sellers have chopped up complete manuscripts and sell individual pages. This practice can, in many instances, maximize value for the seller. Of course, it destroys an important literary piece, but the profiteer cares little for preserving history. Once a manuscript is pieced out, it is basically impossible to reassemble.

The final problem is the competition. This is the one medium that major institutions will spend big money on. If you, the collector, are trying to secure a manuscript that is being courted by a trust, you will likely lose it to the institutional collection. Manuscripts are the cornerstone of any collection, but be prepared to spend significant sums to build it.

Books

Signed books present a problem with autograph collectors. Not only are you competing against fellow autograph collectors, but book collectors as well want that cherished book. In other words, you are going up against twice as many people who want the book. Signed books come in all shapes and sizes. Some are rare and valuable while others have little value. You will be pleasantly surprised at how affordable some signed books can be. Others will give you sticker shock. It seems some authors fall out of favor with collectors and the value drops. This is a good time to buy. The time may come when that author becomes popular again and the investment potential can be great. Take, for example, Georgia native Erskine Caldwell. He wrote two memorable books in *God's Little Acre* and *Tobacco Road*. Signed books of Caldwell were, at one time, rather expensive, but as time has proved, some authors tend to be overlooked by modern society. Today, either of the above referenced books can be purchased for as little as $25.

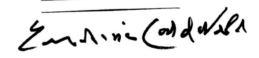

Caldwell-1, signed book 1978.

Noted English poet Edgar Guest, who wrote many years for the *Detroit Free Press,* is also affordable in book form. Signed books by Guest can be purchased for as little as $15 to $20 today. That is not bad, considering he died in 1959.

Guest-1, signed book dated 1920.

The most valuable of the signed books are first editions. Whether signed or not, some legendary titles can sell for large sums of money. Signed first editions of even contemporary authors are highly treasured. First editions from J.K. Rowling's *Harry Potter* series already are valued into the thousands of dollars. A signed first edition of *To Kill a Mockingbird* by reclusive author Harper Lee would easily sell for $20,000. That's a good amount for a book that was published a mere 56 years ago.

Signed first editions of the mythical titles are out of the reach for most collectors. Famed works of Dickens such as *A Christmas Carol* and Lewis Carroll's *Alice in Wonderland* will sell for six figures.

Some of the better titles are reissued in limited leatherbound editions. Made specifically for the collector's market, these are nice additions to any library. Easton Press and Franklin Library make some handsome editions for collectors. These books are topically diverse as they issue works not just of literary authors but books from other fields as well, from Buzz Aldrin to James Watson to Fay Vincent and all points in between. In addition to being a good

HEART *of a* TIGER

GROWING UP WITH MY GRANDFATHER, TY COBB

4-30-2013

HERSCHEL COBB

So Ron Keurajian —

with thanks and Best Wishes,

Herschel Cobb

ECW PRESS

Heart of a Tiger **signed by author Herschel Cobb.**

investment, they also make for a fabulous display on the library wall.

Letters

As one might expect, authors, masters of the written word, pen fabulous content letters. As with other premium pieces, you will be competing against institutional buyers for quality writings. The bigger the name, the more the competition. Letters of the lesser authors can make quite a nice addition to one's collection. The affordable nature of the these authors means you can build a diverse collection on a limited budget. Authors love to write letters; the same can't be said about artists and composers. The result is a good supply of letters from various writers from all genres. One of my favorite letters is written by Robert Bloch. Bloch, a student of H.P. Lovecraft, penned many a horror story, including his most famous work, *Psycho*. A collector wrote Bloch, requesting the author pen a handwritten letter for addition to his collection. An elderly Bloch, near death, denied the request, then proceeded to write a humorous letter on how he was too ill to write a letter. Letters such as these are of great value to collectors. One of the most significant collections you, as the collector, can assemble are letters from famous authors.

*   *   *

Writings of authors date back many centuries. Europe has given us many great names. Many collectable signatures originate from England, Italy, Russia, Germany, France, Poland, and so on. Other areas of the world, such as Asia and South America, have a rich literary history. Writers from these locations are far less known to the world and their autographs can be purchased for surprisingly low prices.

The other great literary powerhouse is the United States. America's rich history and open expanses have given collectors some of the biggest names in the hobby. American authors have told stories that are, well, uniquely American. Writers such as Zane Grey and Glendon Swarthout take you back to the days of the wild west; Mark Twain, to the shores of the Mississippi; Herman Wouk, to the Pacific Theater of World War II; Upton Sinclair, to the urban jungles of America.

Swarthout-1, ANS dated 1966.

America has produced some of the most important writings ever. Its melting pot of humanity results in stories diverse in thought, culture, and ancestry. Noted author William Saroyan gained international fame through his works *The Daring Young Man on the Flying Trapeze* and *My Name Is Aram*. He often wrote stories that centered on his Armenian heritage and his days growing up in farming communities near Fresno. Another important American author was the Russian-born Ayn Rand. Rand's two most important works are *The Fountainhead* and *Atlas Shrugged*. Her works centered on the greatness of capitalism and objective thought. Rand's writings were, no doubt, influenced by her early days in Mother Russia, where the free market

Saroyan-1, ALS dated 1936.

Rand-1, signed book dated 1967 (courtesy Nate D. Sanders Auctions).

was held under lock and key. Unlike Saroyan, whose signature is fairly common, Rand material is much harder to find. Saroyan's signature can be purchased for a mere $75 to $100. Rand is far pricier at $400 to $500. The inventory of Rand material is very limited.

America authors gained legitimacy early in our nation's birth. Most of the early writers were those of political thought who wished to break away from George III and British oppression. Patriotic emotions were stirred by pamphleteers of the day. As America established itself as an independent nation, it settled peacefully into middle age. It was at this time authors focused on novels diverse in genre and thought.

Europe has always been rich in literary history and its origins date back many centuries, far more than America. Signatures of pre–1800 European authors are rare and, for the most part, very expensive. Most collectors focus on the 19th-century writers. Signatures of authors from other parts of the world seldom surface; they simply were not targeted by collectors. Most of the names are unfamiliar outside of their native lands.

James Fenimore Cooper was one of America's great novelists. He wrote about the American Indian culture and the frontier days with a splash of romanticism that created a uniquely American genre. His great work was *The Last of the Mohicans*. Cooper signed in a pleasing hand. His signature is legible and displays well. His signature is somewhat scarce. Values are depressed due to the good supply of canceled bank checks in the market. They date from the 1830s and 1940s. Were it not for these checks, his signature would be much rarer. He died in 1851 and today checks can be purchased in the $225 to $250 range. ALsS are also available, and

Cooper, J-1 undated signature.

ones with routine content are affordable at $500 to $750. Probably the most undervalued American author.

Another American writer who helped define a nation was a tax resister. *Walden,* a story about secluded life in the forest, was written by Henry David Thoreau. It was published in 1854 and became a classic. This is another uniquely American story. Thoreau's signature has excellent flow and superior eye appeal. His signature is rare in all forms with premium items boarding on the nonexistent. Expect to pay $2,000 for his signature. A handful of manuscript pages are in the market and should sell for $7,500 to $10,000 per page. A commonly forged signature; just about all Thoreau signatures offered in the market are spurious.

Thoreau-1, undated signature.

As America began its ascendency in industrial might, *Leaves of Grass* was released in 1855 by poet Walt Whitman. This writing caused quite a stir for its obscene undertones. Whitman signed in a strong and powerful hand. His signature works well on paper. Replication of hand is difficult. Producing a well-executed forgery would take a forger of skill. Whitman material was formerly of little value. For many decades it could be purchased for a few dollars. About fifty years ago there was a revival in his works, causing demand to spike. Today, his signature is valued at $1,000. Bank checks are nearly double that amount. ALsS are a very rare; seldom do they surface in the market. Whitman is one of the few 19th-century authors who can be found in photographic form.

Whitman-1, signature dated 1886 (courtesy Nate D. Sanders Auctions).

He liked to sign pictures of himself. However, most signed photographs in the market are forgeries. Expect to pay $2,500 to $3,000 for a genuine specimen.

One of the early writers of the Romantic movement was Nathaniel Hawthorne. His works centered around New England life. His most famous works are the *House of the Seven Gables* and *The Scarlet Letter.* Hawthorne signed in a powerful script. His signature is bold and a bit choppy. Signatures are usually penned as "N. Hawthorne" or "Nath. Hawthorne." Letters of any kind are rare and highly desirable. Thanks to an appointment by President Franklin Peirce, Hawthorne held the title of American consul in Liverpool. This correlates into many signed documents. This is the best source for Hawthorne's signature. Be advised that many of these documents are secretarially signed and usually as "N. Hawthorne." Another surprisingly affordable signature, it can be purchased for $300 to $400. DsS sell in the $500 to $600 range.

Hawthorne-1 signature circa 1845 (courtesy Stephen Koschal Autographs).

Lew Wallace was born in 1827. He was a lawyer by profession. Later he served as a general in the Civil War. Today, he is best remembered for writing one of the most influential novels of the 19th century, and perhaps all time. *Ben-Hur: A Tale of the Christ* was released in 1880. For writing such an important book, Wallace's signature is inexpensive. Signatures can be purchased for $100. ALsS can be secured for $200. DsS as territorial governor are very rare and almost never surface. Many forged cabinet photographs are in the market. They are usually signed along the bottom border with the year underneath the signature. Genuine signed photographs of Wallace are very rare. Signed copies of *Ben-Hur* are in the market and they make a wonderful addition to any library. Expect to pay $800 to $1,000 for a nice specimen.

[signature: most truly, Lew. Wallace, 2.? '88.]

Wallace-1, book dated 1888.

Another author born around the same time as Wallace was the Frenchman Jules Verne. Verne was a very important pioneer of the fantasy and sci-fi genre. His works include such fabled titles as *Twenty Thousand Leagues Under the Sea* and *Journey to the Center of the Earth*. Verne signed in a very unassuming hand. His signature lacks rapid flow and therefore replication of hand is easy. Many well-executed forgeries exist on photographs and short ALsS. A genuinely signed photograph is very rare and close to 100 percent in the market are forgeries. His signature is in great demand and will sell for $600 to $700. ALsS can be secured for $1,250 to $1,500.

[signature: Jules Verne]

Verne-1, undated signature (courtesy The Sanders Autograph Price Guide).

Norwegian playwright and poet Henrik Ibsen is an important literary autograph. His works are considered by many to have established the modern theater as we know it. Ibsen signed in a very slow and meticulous hand. His signature is very legible. Display value is superior. It has a certain artistic and regal look. The shortfall, of course, as with any signature signed in a slow hand is the ease in producing a well-executed forgery. Most Ibsen signatures offered in the market are forged. Ibsen has good staying power with collectors. His signature will cost $400 to $500. ALsS are much more valuable at $2,000. Signed photographs exist but are very rare and sell in the $3,000 to $4,000 range.

[signature: Henrik Ibsen]

Ibsen-1, undated signature (courtesy The Sanders Autograph Price Guide).

Harriet Beecher Stowe wrote many forgettable novels. Her 1852 work *Uncle Tom's Cabin* is the exception. It depicted the lives of slaves in the United States and is considered one of the most important works of the antislavery movement. Her signature is in much demand. It is valued at $200 to $250. ALsS can be purchased for $300 to $400. Many AQsS exist with Christian references. These also sell in the $300 to $400 price range.

[signature: Harriet Beecher Stowe]

Stowe-1, undated signature.

Another influential writer and abolitionist was Julia Ward Howe. She is best remembered for writing "The Battle Hymn of the Republic." She lived a long life and signed many autographs. Her signature is affordable at $100. ALsS can be purchased for $200 to $250.

[signature: Julia N. Howe]

Howe-1, undated signature (courtesy The Sanders Autograph Price Guide).

Willa Cather wrote many books that brought frontier life into the living room. She won the

Pulitzer in 1922 for *One of Ours*. There is an ample supply of autographs in the market, including many signed books. Her signature can be purchased for $100. Books are valued at $250 to $350.

Cather-1, undated signature.

Louisa May Alcott's works were influenced by her New England upbringing. She is best remembered for the novel *Little Women*. Alcott signed in a pensive hand. The signature evidences sound letter construction. Display value is above average. The signature exhibits a material back slant. Generally she was not the target of skilled forgers, though forged cabinet cards do exist. Alcott's signature is somewhat scarce. Signatures can be found on 16mo cards, ALsS, and ANsS. Cabinet cards are very rare. Expect to pay $400 to $500 for her signature. ALsS will sell for $1,000, with some exceptional specimens at $2,000.

Alcott-1, ALS dated 1883 (courtesy Nate D. Sanders Auctions).

English novelist Thomas Hardy spent many years writing poetry, without much success. His novels, such as *Jude the Obscure*, secured him a place in literary history. Like Dickens, his writings often attacked Victorian society. Hardy's signature is choppy and on the illegible side. The display value is substandard. It is a rather easy signature to forge. His signature is usually found on letters. Photographs are very rare and most offered in the market are forged. There is a group of forged cabinet cards to discuss. They are produced by the same forger. The forgery is fairly well-executed. The forger adds a small linear paraph under the forgery. In recent years demand for Hardy's signature seems to have waned a bit. His signature is affordable at $200 to $300. ALsS, with good content, still retain good value.

Hardy-1, undated signature (courtesy Sanders Autograph Price Guide).

Fellow English author Rudyard Kipling gained fame as a short story writer. His works centered around life in India. His most famous work is *The Jungle Book*. It is a compilation of many delightful stories, including that of a heroic mongoose named Rikki-Tikki-Tavi. Kipling signed in a pensive and practical hand. His signature has marginal display value and is easy to forge. Many forged signed books are in the market, so caution is warranted. There is a good supply of ALsS and signatures on small, thick-stocked cards. An affordable autograph at $125 to $150. ALsS are not much more at $300 to $400.

Kipling-1, undated signature.

Sticking with the jungle theme, American author Edgar Rice Burroughs was an early sci-fi writer. He is the creator of Tarzan. Tarzan was lord of the jungle and Burroughs wrote two dozen books on his favorite creation. His signature exists in quantities. Many letters are in the market. In recent years a large cache of bank

Burroughs-1, check dated 1936.

checks became available for collectors. The price of his signature has declined since release of the checks, which can be purchased for as little as $75.

Irish author Abraham "Bram" Stoker was a relatively undercollected signature until the 1992 movie *Bram Stoker's Dracula* was released. This generated much interest in Stoker and today his signature is still in demand. His signature has poor letter construction. Trying to read his handwriting can give you a headache. Most signatures are found on letters or ANsS. Photographs are extremely rare. Stoker was secretary to British actor Sir Henry Irving and penned many of his letters, which Irving would then sign. Expect to pay $300 to $400 for his autograph. ALsS can sell for $750 to $1,000. The above-referenced Irving letters can be purchased for as little as $150.

Stoker-1, undated signature.

Scottish author Sir James Barrie wrote many books but is most remembered as the creator of Peter Pan. Barrie signed in a sloppy and illegible hand. ALsS appear as scratches of ink on paper. They are very hard to read. His signature lacks structure; thus, replication of hand is easy. Creating a well-executed forgery would be no problem. His signature is almost exclusively found on ALsS and short ANsS. There is a good supply of both. His signature is very af-

fordable at $100. ALsS will sell for $200 to $300.

Speaking of flying characters, Helen Goff, who wrote under the pen name of Pam Travers, told tales of an English nanny named Mary Poppins. Travers signed in a vertical and slower hand. Signatures are typically accomplished as "P.L. Travers." Travers lived until 1996 but signed very little material. Her signature is considered scarce and in much demand. Signed books are the most common medium and generally sell for $300 to $400. Other mediums are rare. Travers's signature should prove a fine investment.

Travers, P-1 signed book 1975.

The writer John Aubrey once wrote that Edmund Waller "did possess a great mastership of the English language." Waller was a noted English poet and his most famous work, "Go, Lovely Rose," is still popular today. What makes Waller such an interesting figure in history was his attempt, in 1643, to overthrow anti–Royal factions, the "Roundheads" in the British Parliament. Waller, a royalist, wanted to restore the power of Charles I. It became known as "Waller's Plot." It failed and he and his conspirators were sentenced to death. Waller, a very wealthy man, bribed his way out of the chopping block. His comrades were not so lucky. Waller is a good example of a signature that is

Barrie-1, ALS circa 1900.

Waller-1 signature circa 1670.

collected by more than one field of interest. His signature, like all literary figures of the 17th century, is very rare. A significant literary signature of great rarity. No recent sales.

English novelist Jane Austen wrote of romance and the gentry. She is one of the most famous of authors. Her signature is an extreme market rarity and of the highest demand. Austen wrote in a very clean and legible hand. The signature exhibits sound letter construction. A sound display value is noted. She died of cancer at the young age of 41; hence, there is very little material in the market. A handful of ALsS and manuscripts exist as fragments. Most material is held by institutional collections. Forgeries do exist, mostly as signatures on slips of paper. There are typically signed as "Jane Austen, -Jany. 1812-." I know of no signatures accomplished in this manner. A signature of great value. An ALS will sell for over $50,000.

Austen-1, undated signature (courtesy Stephen Koschal Reference Library).

Famed Scottish poet Robert Burns is best remembered for the poem "Auld Lang Syne." Burns signed in an aggressive hand. The signature displays itself as fast. Letter construction is sound. Good legibility is noted. Signatures are typically penned as "Robt. Burns." Burns's signature is rare to very rare and seldom enters the market. A few ALsS are available. There are many forged ALsS and poems in the market, accomplished by forger Alexander Smith. He became rather skilled at replicating Burns's hand. These forgeries have been in the market for

Burns-1, undated signature (courtesy Stephen Koschal Reference Library).

many decades and have attained a vintage appearance. There is much demand for Burns's signature, which is valued at $5,000 to $6,000. A nice, full-page ALS will sell for $15,000 to $20,000.

An English poet of the Romantic genre, Percy Shelley was a contemporary of Byron. He is considered one of the most influential poets in history. Shelley signed in a rapid and flowing hand. The signature exhibits good letter construction. An above-average display value is noted. Signatures are typically accomplished as "P.B. Shelley." Shelley drowned at the young age of 29; hence, his signature is rare to very rare. Signatures are generally limited to bank checks and a handful of ALsS, some of which are signed in the third person. There is sound demand for Shelley material. Bank checks sell for $4,000. ALsS are valued at $15,000 to $20,000.

Shelley-1, undated signature (courtesy Stephen Koschal Reference Library).

William Sydney Porter was born in 1862. He was a banker by trade who went to jail in 1898 for embezzlement. While in jail he wrote short stories under the name "O. Henry." He was released after a couple of years. A heavy drinker, he died of cirrhosis in 1910. Porter's signature is rare on a per se basis. The occasional ALS will surface and that is about it. Signed photographs are an extreme rarity. Many forged portrait photographs exist. These are usually signed as "Yours continuously, O. Henry";

Henry-1, signed with his true name.

some are dated. The forgery is signed on a 45-degree angle. An ALS, which is typically written on a 5 × 7 sheet, is valued at $1,000 to $1,500.

Perhaps no one captured the essence of 19th-century rural America better than Laura Ingalls Wilder. Her works of the Little House have been immortalized by the NBC television series *Little House on the Prairie*. Wilder lived a long life. She died in 1957 at the age of 90. Despite this, her signature is rare. The occasional letter will surface. I have never examined a genuinely signed photograph. Wilder's signature is very legible. Good eye appeal noted. The hand lacks reckless flow, and as such is very easy to forge. Just about all signatures in the market are spurious. There are many forged ALsS, sometimes multiple pages, in the market. They usually contain routine to sentimental content. They are usually dated in the 1940s and accomplished with a labored hand, as one would expect a Wilder letter from this time frame would exhibit. Despite this, the writing is slow and methodic, unlike a genuine specimen, where the hand is a bit jerky. The ink is slightly faded, giving it a washed-out look. The text usually contains the words "Ma and Pa" or "Mother and Father." The letters typically begin with "Rocky Ridge Farm, Mansfield, MO." in the upper right corner of the letter. These forgeries are well-executed and careful examination is needed. Wilder's signature is a modern rarity, so expect to pay $500 for her autograph. ALsS will sell for $1,500 to $2,000.

Ingalls-1, ALS dated 1949 (courtesy Nate D. Sanders Auctions).

Russian author Maxim Gorky was a popular figure in the Soviet Union. An early Marxist, he openly embraced communism. Gorky material is very scarce to rare. It is generally limited to ALsS and LsS. Signed photographs are very rare. On occasion, his wife would sign his auto-graph for him. Her signature looks like a genuine signature but evidences shakiness of hand, and so is easily spotted. Expect to pay $300 to $400 for his autograph.

Gorky-1 undated signature.

A native of Indiana, James Whitcomb Riley was known as the Hoosier Poet. His works were targeted at children. He is best remembered for his poem "Little Orphan Annie." Riley signed in a wonderfully constructed hand. His signature is whimsical and artistic in nature. Display value is superior. Signatures accomplished later in life evidence a slight shakiness of hand. His signature is usually found on calling cards, books, ALsS, ANsS, and AQsS. The ample supply of his signature results in an affordable autograph. Signatures can be purchased for $40 to $50. ALsS and signed books sell for $150 to $200. An undervalued literary signature.

Riley-1, undated calling card.

Zane Grey's writings romanticized the American West. His greatest work, *Riders of the Purple Sage*, was released in 1912. Grey signed in a nice hand. A high degree of legibility is noted. The price of Grey signed material has seen a marked decrease in value. This due to the large inventory of canceled bank checks in the market. Checks can be purchased for as little as $25. Signed books and ALsS are selling for $100 to $150. I do not see much movement in Grey's signature in the years to come; the supply is just too great.

Grey, Z-1 bank check dated 1939 (courtesy Nate D. Sanders Auctions).

Robert Frost was a prolific poet who, like Hawthorne, often wrote about life in rural New England. Frost signed in a very confined and slow hand. In later years his hand was affected by infirmity. Frost's signature is one of the easiest of all authors to forge. Many well-executed forgeries are in the market. Frost lived a long life and because of this he signed many books, some limited editions. His association with President Kennedy enhances the desirability of his autograph. Expect to pay $150 to $200 for his autograph. Signed books can be purchased for $350 to $500, depending on the title. ALsS are valued at $600 to $800.

Frost-1, signed book dated 1935.

G.K. Chesterton was an English author whose interests crossed many genres. He wrote poetry, plays, Christian thought, and detective novels. Chesterton signed in a slower, more methodic hand. His signature is vertical in nature and presents itself geometrically. It is a very easy signature to forge. His signature is scarce on a

Chesterton-1, undated signature (courtesy Sanders Autograph Price Guide).

per se basis. His signature will surface on limited edition books. ALsS are rare. Signed photographs are an extreme rarity. I have never examined a genuine one. There is sound interest in Chesterton material, primarily because of the detective/crime genre in which he wrote. Expect to pay $250 to $300 for his autograph.

American detective novelist Dashiell Hammett created famed gumshoe Sam Spade in his most famous work, *The Maltese Falcon*. The book became stuff of legend when Warner Brothers released the 1941 film starring Humphrey Bogart as Spade. Hammett signed in a sharp and precise hand. His signature has good display value. Replication of hand would be rather difficult. Well-executed forgeries are few and far between. Hammett's signature is scarce in all forms and highly desirable. His signature is valued at $600 to $700. Signed books sell for $1,000 to $1,250. ALsS and 8 × 10 photographs are rare to very rare. Either would sell for $3,000 or more.

Hammett-1, TLS dated 1934 (courtesy Stephen Koschal Autographs).

Jack London was one of the first writers to exploit short story fiction for magazines. He also wrote many novels that centered around the wilds of the north country. His most popular works are *White Fang* and *Call of the Wild*. London signed in a somewhat reckless hand. His signature has good flow but letter construction is marginal. It is an unassuming signature with average display value. For many years London material was rare. He died at the young age of 40, overdosing on pain killers. About 15 years ago a large cache of signed bank checks entered the market, making this once-rare signature accessible to collectors. A bank check can be purchased for $100 to $150. ALsS and TLsS are rare and can sell for $1,000 to $3,000 depending on content.

London-1, bank check dated 1907.

American poet Carl Sandburg won three Pulitzers. He was best known for his extensive writings about Abraham Lincoln. Sandburg signed in a slow and heavy hand. It has average display value and is very easy to forge. There is little interest in Sandburg material these days. This correlates into an affordable signature which is valued at $25 to $35. Signed books can regularly be purchased for under $100.

Sandburg-1, signed book dated 1926 (courtesy Nate D. Sanders Auctions).

Czech-born author Franz Kafka was a complex personality. His works reflect darkness, conflict, and torment. He is considered one of the great Jewish writers of the 20th century. Kafka signed very little for collectors of the day. He did not become popular until after his death. He died of consumption at the young age

Kafka-1 circa 1915 signature (courtesy Stephen Koschal Reference Library).

Kafka-1, signature dated 1913 (courtesy Nate D. Sanders Auctions).

of 40. A handful of letters survive to this day, as does the occasional signed postal cover. His signature is very rare and valued at $5,000. An ALS will likely sell for $20,000.

Just because some signatures are rare does not necessarily equal great value. Many fine writers of old can be purchased for just a few dollars. Their signatures make a welcome addition to any collection. Eugene Prussing was a lawyer by trade. He also wrote extensively about George Washington. Prussing signed in a beautiful hand. His signature is rare but of little value. Bank checks can be purchased for $15 to $20. Poet Hrand Nazariantz is also a rare signature. He signed a limited number of portrait picture postcards, few of which have entered the market. Signed postcards, which are almost always signed in Armenian, can be purchased for a mere $40 to $50. Will Durant was an American writer best remembered for his 11-volume set titled *The Story of Civilization*. His name has all but been forgotten by modern society. A large supply of bank checks is in the market. A check can be purchased for $15 to $20. Some of the more famous literary names are surprisingly affordable. Henry Longfellow, James Whitcomb Riley, and Oliver Wendell Holmes Sr. were prolific 19th-century writers. Their signatures can be purchased for nominal sums. The signature of Stephen Duck, an early 18th-century English poet, is very rare but of marginal value simply because of tepid demand. Irvin Cobb and James Russell Lowell were giants of their day, but in recent times have fallen out of favor with collectors. Signatures of these two men were far more pricey 20 years ago. Today, signatures of either can be purchased for under $25. Quaker poet John Greenleaf Whittier was a strong abolitionist. He signed in a lovely hand

Duck-1 undated signature.

resulting in a signature with superior eye appeal. His signature is also on the cheap side at $50 or under. ALsS can be purchased for $125 to $150. Cabinet cards are somewhat rare but affordable at $350 to $400.

Nazariantz-1 photograph dated 1932.

Prussing-1 bank check dated 1921.

Cobb, I-1 undated TLS.

Longfellow-1 undated signature.

Holmes, O. W. Sr-1, undated signature.

Lowell, J R-1 undated signature.

Whittier-1, ALS dated 1871 (courtesy Stephen Koschal Autographs).

World War I had a profound impact on American poet Ezra Pound. One of most controversial figures of 20th century literature, Pound was once arrested for treason. His signature is uncommon to scarce. There is moderate demand for his material. There is one common forgery to note. There are signed photographs in the market that feature a bearded Pound in profile. A forgery of Pound is placed in the lower border, sometimes with a nonsensical inscription. The forgery is slow and labored. It is easily exposed upon exanimation. A signature will cost you $300 to $400.

Pound-1, signature dated 1963.

"Poems are made by fools like me,/But only God can make a tree" wrote noted American poet Joyce Kilmer in his most famous poem, "Trees." Kilmer signed in an average hand. The most dominant feature is the elongated crossbar of the letter "J" in the first name. His signature is generally found on TLsS and the occasional ALS. Other mediums are rare to very rare. He died at the young age of 31, cut down by machine gun fire at the Marne. Given the restricted supply of Kilmer material, his signature is surprisingly affordable. Expect to pay $300 to $350 for a TLS. An ALS is only slightly more. I consider Kilmer's signature a sleeper name among literary autographs.

Kilmer-1, ALS dated 1913 (courtesy Georgetown University).

T.S. Eliot was an American poet who moved to England in 1914. He was an accomplished publisher. His work "The Love Song of J. Alfred Prufrock" gained him international fame. Eliot signed in a very reserved and plain hand. He wrote his name more than signed it. As a result, replication of hand is very easy. Many well-executed forgeries are in the market, mostly on photographs. He died in 1965 and was targeted for many years by autograph collectors. The supply of genuine material is sound, though mostly limited to index cards and TLsS. Always a popular signature, so expect to pay $250 for it. A TLS will run about $400.

Eliot-1, undated signature (courtesy The Sanders Autograph Price Guide).

American Pearl Buck spent a good deal of her life in China immersed in the country's rich culture. Her most famous work is *The Good Earth*. She won the Nobel Prize in 1932. Buck's signature flows nicely. Those penned in the last few years of her life evidence hesitation. Elderly signatures are very easy to forge, though not the target of skilled forgers due to the marginal value of her autograph. Buck is a name that time has all but passed by. Her signature generates little interest among today's collectors. Buck's signature can be purchased for as little as $20. Signed books are also affordable as $30 to $50.

Buck-1, signed book circa 1945.

American educator Kate Douglas Wiggin authored many children's books, the most famous being *Rebecca of Sunnybrook Farm*. Wiggin signed in a rapid and nonconforming hand. The signature tends to be sloppy with impaired legibility. Her signature is uncommon to scarce. Signatures are generally found on many an authored book. Demand, as of this writing, is tepid at best. A nicely signed book can be purchased for $30 to $50.

Wiggin-1 signed book circa 1915.

Another famous author of the time was Agatha Christie, a British crime writer who penned over 60 novels. Her work is very popular to this day. Christie signed in a rapid hand. Letter construction is marginal at best. The hand tends to be on the illegible side. Christie lived until 1976 and was an accommodating signer her entire life. There is a good supply of signatures in the market, mostly on bookplates, index cards, and other mediums that could be signed through the mail. Signed photographs exist but are considered scarce. Many short ANsS are in the market. Christie's signature can be secured for $150 to $200. Signed books and letters are in the $300 to $500 price range.

Christie-1, undated signature.

Lecturer and journalist Christopher Morley wrote many poems and novels. His most famous work was *Kitty Foyle*, published in 1939. It was made into a movie starring Ginger Rogers. Morley is another famous author who has fallen out of favor with the modern-day collector. His signature is of little interest. Signed books can be purchased on eBay for $10, which I find simply amazing.

Morley-1, undated signature (courtesy The Sanders Autograph Price Guide).

H.P. Lovecraft was one of the oddest of authors. His works of horror and ghastly fiction still captivate audiences today. Lovecraft signed in a cramp and confined hand. His signature is tight with good display value. Most ALsS, what few there are, tend to go on for pages and are usually just signed with his initials as "H.P.L." Letters tend to have strong and controversial content. Racial comparisons are common in his writings. Lovecraft died in 1937 at the age of 47.

His signature is rare to very rare and seldom enters the market. A nice ALS is valued at $3,000 to $4,000.

Lovecraft-1, World War I draft card (courtesy Record Group 163, Records of the Selective Services Division, National Archives at Atlanta).

New Englander E.E. Cummings was a poet, painter, and writer. He wrote close to 3,000 poems. His works, which incorporated eroticism and racial overtones, caused much controversy. Controversy correlates into demand. His signature still generates much interest. His signature is typically signed as "E.E. Cummings." Some signatures are well constructed, while others have no letter construction to speak of and are simply a scrawl of ink. Hurried signatures are the easiest of all authors to forge. Expect to pay $200 for his autograph. A signed book sells for $300 to $400.

Cummings-1, undated signature (courtesy Mark Allen Baker).

American William Faulkner won the 1949 Nobel Prize for literature. His 1929 novel *The Sound and the Fury* is considered one of the greatest novels of all time. Faulkner signed in a confined and cramped hand. His signature has poor eye appeal. The many breaks in the signature correlate into a signature that is easily forged. Most Faulkner signatures offered in the

Faulkner-1, signed book 1951 (courtesy Nate D. Sanders Auctions).

market are forged. Faulkner's signature is generally limited to signed books. Signed photographs and letters are rare. Signed books can be purchased for $500 to $800.

Many fine works were produced in the 1930s and 1940s. Walter Gibson, who wrote under the name of Maxwell Grant, is a fine example. He was a pulp fiction writer who developed the mysterious crime fighter, The Shadow. Collectors did not actively target Gibson, and today his signature is scarce. Premium items are rare. Signed books of *The Shadow* can still be purchased for $100 to $150.

Gibson, W-1 signed book.

American playwright Thornton Wilder won three Pulitzers. Wilder signed in a pleasing hand. His signature has good display value. As with many writers, interest in his signature has declined in recent years. Today there is not a lot of demand for his signature and signed books can be purchased for $75 to $125.

Wilder-1 undated postal cover.

English playwright Sir Noel Coward was a man of many talents. A writer, composer, director, and actor, he also was an intelligence officer during World War II. His numerous plays were

written from the 1920s through 1950s. Coward's signature is flamboyant and has a certain artistic and geometric appearance. His signature is still popular today so expect to pay $150 to $200 for a nice specimen.

Coward-1, undated signature (courtesy Nate D. Sanders Auctions).

Poet and writer Robert Penn Warren won the 1947 Pulitzer for his novel *All the King's Men.* Warren died in 1989 and was a responsive signer. Today, his signature is affordable at $10. Signed books can be purchased for as little as $25.

Welsh poet Dylan Thomas signed in a very neat and pensive hand. He is best known for his poem "Do Not Go Gentle into That Good Night." There is extremely strong demand for Thomas material. His signature is rare and treasured by collectors. He blew out his liver in 1953 at the age of 39 due to excessive drink. His signature is easy to forge and many forged ALsS are in the market, many of which are accomplished in red or purple fountain pen. His signature is valued at $400 to $500. A routine ALS will sell for $2,000 to $3,000. A good content letter is worth nearly double that amount. One exceptional letter sold in 2006 for over $10,000.

Thomas, D-1, signed book dated 1934 (courtesy Stephen Koschal Reference Library).

Alex Haley is one of the best-known black authors. He is most remembered for the novel *Roots: The Saga of an American Family.* Haley died in 1992 of a heart attack. He was a responsive signer and many books and photographs are in the market. A large inventory of bank checks were released into the market. His signature is easily acquired. Bank checks can be purchased for $25, signed books for about the same price.

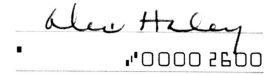

Haley-1, bank check dated 1988.

Then there is Isaac Asimov. A biochemist by trade, Asimov was a prolific sci-fi writer. Asimov wrote hundreds of works, including *I, Robot*. Asimov signed in a very bold and pleasing hand. His signature is difficult to replicate. There are no well-executed forgeries in the market. He was an erratic signer; sometimes he would honor requests and sometimes he would not. He was known to write with a cutting pen, and there are many fine content letters in the market in which Asimov's persecution complex surfaces. Signed books exist in quantity, so expect to pay $75 to $125. He worked in a genre that generates much interest. Value of Asimov material should increase nicely in the years to come.

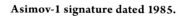

Asimov-1 signature dated 1985.

Noah Webster's house is on display at Greenfield Village in Dearborn, Michigan, compliments of Mr. Henry Ford. It is said to be haunted. Webster is the most famous lexicographer in history. His dictionary has sold more copies than any other book except for the Bible. Webster's signature has been targeted by many collectors and institutions. As such, market

population has gone from scarce to rare. Demand has increased greatly. Signatures are limited to ALsS, DsS, or signatures removed therefrom. The population of forgeries has increased greatly in the last ten years, due to increased values. Expect to pay $400 to $500 for a signature. ALsS will sell for $4,000 to $5,000. Exceptional content letters should sell for $10,000.

Webster, N.-1, undated signature.

Joseph Pulitzer was a writer and a successful newspaper publisher. He was the nemesis of William Randolph Hearst's *New York Journal*. He is best remembered for his endowment of the Pulitzer Prize. His signature is rapid and complex. It is one of my favorites. Replication of hand is very difficult. Well-executed forgeries do not exist. His signature is scarce on a per se basis. A small supply of bank checks exist. ALsS and photographs are rare. A check can be purchased for around $500.

Pulitzer-1, bank check circa 1880.

Arthur Henry Ward is known to the literary world as Sax Rohmer. He is best remembered for creating the Chinese villain Fu Manchu. His works cause much controversy in today's politically correct world. Rohmer signed in a very nonconforming hand. The signature displays itself as mis-spaced. The signature is signed on an uneven plane. The letter "S" is typically accomplished as a "$." Rohmer's signature is scarce and generally limited to letters and album pages. Photographs of any kind are rare. Controversy correlates into good demand.

Rohmer's signature will sell for $200. Signed books and ALsS are valued at $300 to $400.

Rohmer-1, undated signature.

Bengali author Rabindranath Tagore became the first non–European to win the Nobel Prize in literature. He opened up Indian literature to the West. Tagore signed in a pensive and well-structured hand. Good legibility is noted. Signatures are found in both English and Bengali script. Replication of hand is fairly easy. Well-executed forgeries exist in quantities, mostly on photographs. The vast majority of Tagore photographs in the market are forged. There is sound demand for Tagore material. His signature will sell for $700 to $900. A nicely signed photograph is valued at $3,000 to $3,500. A full-page ALS will sell for $3,000 to $4,000. There is no premium for signatures in Bengali script.

Tagore-1, Album page dated 1926 (courtesy Nate D. Sanders Auctions).

Truman Capote and Tennessee Williams were drinking buddies. They would hang out at used-book stores and sign autographs for book enthusiasts. Williams's material used to be quite pricey, but in recent years a seemingly unending supply of bank checks has entered the market. Checks have adversely affected supply. Williams

checks can now be purchased for as little as $75. Capote's signature is, from an analysis standpoint, a nightmare. He signed in a slow and printed script. It is perhaps the easiest of all signatures to forge. Your best bet is to purchase a limited signed edition of one of his works issued directly by the publisher. *Other Voices, Other Rooms* was issued in limited edition by the Franklin Library in 1979. These were hand-signed by Capote. These books are the best source of Capote material in the market. Expect to pay $250 to $300 for one.

Williams, T-1, bank check dated 1945.

Capote-1 undated signature.

Lewis Carroll was the pen name of English writer Charles Dodgson. Dodgson was a mathematician by trade. A part-time deacon and photographer, Carroll wrote in the fantasy genre. His most famous works are *Alice's Adventures in Wonderland* and *Through the Looking Glass*. His works are very strange and fanciful nonsense. Whatever the reason, his works are some of the most widely read to this day. Carroll material is in high demand. He was known to sign with both his real name and his pseudonym. His signature is rare in all forms and generally limited to ALsS and signatures removed therefrom. Some letters ramble on for pages. Most ALsS in the market are forged. Many of these fake letters are accomplished in purple ink on small 8vo sheets. The hand evidences a slightly labored appearance. The grammar seems contrived. A word or two will be underlined. The forged letters are usually closed with "Yours truly." Carroll material will always be in strong demand. His signature is valued at $750 to $1,000. A nice full-page ALS will sell for $3,000 to $4,000.

Carroll-1, undated ALS (courtesy Stephen Koschal Autographs).

Carroll-2, undated ALS (courtesy Stephen Koschal Autographs).

François-Marie Arouet very few have heard of. He was one of the most important writers of all time. Most know him by his nom de plume, Voltaire. He was a writer of great depth. He wrote on a wide array of subjects from religion to science to poetry. He remains one of the most famous writers of all time. Voltaire signed in a neat and legible hand. Signatures are usually accomplished as "Voltaire" or sometimes simply as "V." His signature lacks speed. The pensive nature of the hand makes replication easy. Well-executed forgeries exist in quantities. The vast majority of Voltaire signatures offered in the market are forged. His signature is rare and generally found on LsS. ALsS also exist but seldom surface. Secretarial signatures are noted and are similar to Voltaire's hand. There is very strong demand for Voltaire material. His signa-

ture is still attainable at $2,000. LsS will sell for $6,000 to $10,000. Content letters will likely sell for $25,000 or more.

Charles Dickens signed in a very powerful hand. His signature has good display value. A striking paraph only enhances the eye appeal of the signature. His signature is found mostly on letters, franks, and bank checks. ALsS tend to have routine content, but on occasion Dickens would write with whimsical panache. His handwriting tends to be on the illegible side and deciphering a letter can pose a challenge. Signed photographs are an extreme rarity and just about all ever offered for sale are forgeries. Forged photographs are typically signed in light blue ink. In recent years another forgery has entered the market. There are many forged franked envelopes in the market. These are signed in a bluish-gray ink. The ink evidences light spots, giving the writing a speckled and washed-out look. This is a telltale sign of artificial aging. The handwriting is slightly labored. They all contain a fake "Rochester" postmark, sometimes posted on the verso of the cover as well. They come complete with a CD monogram on the back flap of the cover. These are nicely created, so careful examination is needed, as many counterfeit postal covers are in the market. Author of many classics works including *A Christmas Carol* and *Oliver Twist*, Dickens is one of the greatest writers in history, if not the greatest. Values in recent years have increased nicely. Signatures are now valued at $750 to $1,000. ALsS sell for $2,000 to $2,500 with routine content. Bank checks are becoming tougher to locate. In early 2000 they sold for $400 to $500; today they are valued at $1,250 to $1,500.

Voltaire-1, undated signature.

Dickens-1, undated signature.

William Thackeray was a prominent English author of the 19th century. His works, which were deeply satirical, culminated in the classic *Vanity Fair*. Thackeray wrote in a very tight and compact hand. Good legibility is noted. Like Christy Mathewson, Thackeray had the habit of changing the slant of his writing to vertical. Many letters will exhibit variant forms of writing. His signature is generally limited to ALsS and ADsS. Signed photographs are very rare and most offered in the market are forgeries. There are many forged cabinet cards in the market. They feature an image of Thackeray sitting in a chair with his left leg outstretched. They are signed across the bottom border with ink that evidences the bleeding effect. This is evidence that the forgery was added many decades after the card was produced. His signature is very affordable given his stature in the literary world. ALsS with routine content can still be purchased for $200 to $250. Fragment manuscripts surface every now and then and can be purchased for as little as $500 per page. Thackeray was also quite skilled at drawing and a few unsigned sketches are available for purchase. His artistry is fairly sound.

Thackeray-1 ALS undated.

The mind of Edgar Allan Poe is a study of the macabre. His writings are so bizarre that much interest is generated in his works. His signature is very rare and highly prized by collectors. Poe signed in a practical hand. The signature evidences a slight choppiness. It is finished off with a linear paraph. His signature is relatively easy to forge, and just about all Poe autographs in the market are spurious. Signed material is limited to a few ALsS or signatures

removed therefrom. Most Poe ALsS are forged. Many forged ALsS are signed with the last name only. Many can be found on octavo-sized Lincoln blue stationary. There are forged holographic bank checks in the market. These are signed Edgar A. Poe. The forger crosses out the forged signature to give the appearance of bank cancellation. I have never seen a genuine signed check. Poe's signature is one of the most expensive of all American autographs. His signature has seen a marked increase in value. In 2000 Poe's signature was valued at $8,000 to $10,000. Today it is nearly double that amount. Brief ALsS routinely sell for $25,000 to $40,000. A nice content letter would easily sell for $100,000 or more. Remember, close to 99 percent of Poe signatures offered in the market are forged.

Poe-1, ALS dated 1837 (courtesy Stephen Koschal Reference Library).

Poe-1, ALS dated 1844.

Poe-3, well executed forgery likely by Joseph Cosey.

Alexandre Dumas was one of the greatest of French writers. His works are legendary, among them *The Three Musketeers* and *The Count of Monte Cristo*. Dumas signed in a bold an aggressive hand. His signature has good display value. Like most writers of this time, his signature is typically available on ALsS. Most ALsS are short with routine content and can be purchased for a surprisingly affordable price. Signed photographs do exist but are rare to very rare. Most offered in the market are forged. Dumas's signature sells for $150 to $200. Short ALsS are not much more. Full-page ALsS sell anywhere from $500 to $1,500. I consider Dumas signed material to be a good investment in the years to come. It should be noted that Dumas's son, Alexandre Dumas-fils, became a successful playwright. His signature varies greatly from his more famous father's hand. It is in much less demand and can be purchased for as little as $50.

Dumas A. F.-1, undated ALS (courtesy Nate D. Sanders Auctions).

Dumas A. P.-1 ALS undated (courtesy Nate D. Sanders Auctions).

Herman Melville burst onto the literary scene in the 1840s with his work *Typee*. Though he gained fame, it proved fleeting. By the 1850s, Melville was all but forgotten. He never did regain his stature as a literary force during his life. Melville material was not collected until the 1930s, when there was a revival of his works,

specifically *Moby-Dick*. Since that time Melville has become a widely coveted signature. His signature is rare and is usually limited to ALsS, most of which are short writings. Melville wrote in a sloppy hand and most signatures are accomplished as "H. Melville." Many forgeries exist, usually as signed and dated album pages where Melville purportedly writes a two- or three-word phrase above the signature. Many of these forgeries are penned in dark purple ink. Melville material has become quite valuable. Signatures now sell for over $2,000. Brief ALsS will sell in the $5,000 to $10,000 price range. Content letters are valued at $20,000 to $30,000. A significant literary autograph.

Melville-1, undated signature.

George Gordon Byron was one of the most important English poets of the Romantic movement. He was a larger-than-life figure who traveled abroad from Greece to Armenia to Italy and many other places as well. He died at the young age of 36 of sepsis. Lord Byron's signature is generally limited to franked envelopes and ALsS, neither of which exist in quantity. Byron's signature is considered rare. Content ALsS are an extreme rarity. Byron signed in a sloppy and unstructured hand. Replication of hand is rather easy. Many well-executed forgeries are in the market, so caution is warranted. See the chapter on forgery for further information. Several decades ago, a high-quality facsimile of a letter written by Byron to Monsieur

Byron-1, undated signature.

Galignani, 18 Rue Vivienne, Paris was produced in quantities. They are very convincing. To this day these reproductions cause a lot of confusion, so caution is warranted. Expect to pay $2,000 for a signature or frank. Content ALsS are valued at $5,000 to $7,500.

Byron-2, forgery by George Byron.

Johann Wolfgang von Goethe was a poet, statesman, artist, and man of letters, and is one of the most important German literary figures. Goethe signed in a sharp and angled hand. It is complex in nature and rapid in execution. The signature is typically signed with the last name only. A few signatures signed as "J.W. Goethe" exist. Goethe material is rare to very rare and generally limited to LsS. ALsS are very rare. Fragments of writings exist; though unsigned, they are still highly treasured. Forgeries do exist, mostly as short ALsS. They are fairly well-executed, so caution is warranted. There is strong demand for Goethe material. Goethe's signature is one of the most treasured in all of literature. His signature is valued at $3,000 to $3,500. LsS will sell for $5,000 to $10,000. A nice ALS is valued anywhere from $15,000 to $25,000. A highly important literary autograph.

Goethe-1, undated signature.

L. Frank Baum was the man who gave us Oz. Baum was a writer of many talents who wrote mostly in the fantasy genre. He also wrote many books under various pseudonyms. While most of his works have been passed over by time, one still stands out: *The Wonderful Wizard of Oz*. Baum signed in a rapid and striking hand. His signature is large and exhibits a left slant. Eye appeal is strong. Overall, a pleasing signature. Baum's signature is rare to very rare on a per se basis and generally limited to ALsS and the occasional TLS. Signed Oz books of any kind are very rare and most offered for sale are forgeries. There are quite a few forgeries in the market that are signatures purportedly removed from TLsS. The forger places a Baum forgery underneath a typed closing such as "Sincerely yours" or "Cheerfully yours." A signature in much demand, so expect to pay $1,500 to $2,000 for one. A nice full-page ALS is valued at $4,000 to $5,000. A signed Oz book will sell for $15,000 to $20,000.

Baum-1, ALS dated 1901 (courtesy Nate D. Sanders Auctions).

John Steinbeck wrote many notable works; his most famous was *Of Mice and Men*. In 1962 he was awarded the Nobel Prize for Literature. Steinbeck signed in a confined and choppy hand. Letters tend to morph together into indistinguishable strokes. The compact size of his signature works well on small mediums. Replication of hand is fairly easy. Many well-executed forgeries exist in the market. Steinbeck was a responsive signer in the mail. His signature is found on index cards and ALsS, many of which are written on yellow legal paper. Some letters have strong content that reflect Steinbeck's socialist tendencies. A signature can be purchased for $400 to $500. Letters of any kind are expensive and start at $1,000. A good content ALS will sell for $3,000 to $5,000.

Steinbeck-1, signed book dated 1953 (courtesy Nate D. Sanders Auctions).

J.R.R. Tolkien, who told tales of Middle Earth, is one of the most popular of all 20th-century authors. His work *Lord of the Rings* is one of the true classics of the fantasy genre. Tolkien signed in a very odd and whimsical hand with artistic tones. His signature is marked with strokes of various thickness and algebraic design. His signature looks as if were penned by a medieval scrivener. Eye appeal of an ALS is superior. His hand rivals baseball legend Joe Kelley's stunning writing. His signature is signed in a slower hand with many breaks. It would not be difficult for a forger of skill to produce a well-executed forgery. Signatures are generally limited to letters. Signed books are also available but command large sums. Signed photographs are very rare. In recent years, values have seen a demonstrable increase. Signatures will sell for $1,500 to $2,000. TLsS can be purchased for $3,000 to $4,000. The highly coveted ALS sells for $7,500 to $10,000.

Tolkien-1, TLS dated 1966 (courtesy Nate D. Sanders Auctions).

Famed Scottish writer Sir Walter Scott wrote in the Romantic genre. He was a prolific author and penned many fine works, among them *Rob Roy* and *Ivanhoe*. Scott signed in a tight and choppy hand. His signature has poor letter construction and is hard to read. ALsS are a nightmare to decode as letters tends to morph into indistinguishable strokes. The signature is usually finished off with a paraph. Due to poor let-ter construction, Scott's signature is easy to replicate. His signature is almost exclusively limited to ALsS. The occasional ADS will surface, but these are much harder to find. A signature is valued at $250 to $300. ALsS can be purchased for around $500.

Scott-1, undated signature (courtesy The Sanders Autograph Price Guide).

Mark Twain was perhaps the greatest writer in American history. Twain was born Samuel Langhorne Clemens in 1835. Twain had many a profession, from journalist to river boat captain to a not-so-successful gold miner. His works are a keyhole look back into 19th-century America. Twain signed in a rugged hand, resulting in a signature with good eye appeal. He signed autographs both with his real name and his more famous pen name. Unlike many authors of his day, he was actively sought out by autograph collectors. There is a good supply of signed album pages and calling cards in the market. Signed letters are also available and many are written in pencil. Bank checks should be considered somewhat scarce. The occasional manuscript leaf will surface, but these are quickly purchased. Twain is a fairly easy signa-

Twain-1, undated signature (courtesy Nate D. Sanders Auctions).

Twain-2, check dated 1875 (courtesy Nate D. Sanders Auctions).

ture to forge. His signature is one of the most forged of all American authors. Most signed photographs in the market are forgeries. The demand for Twain material is great. His signature is valued at $500 to $600. Bank checks sell for $1,000 to $1,250. Prices for ALsS vary widely, anywhere from $1,500 to $7,500.

Theodor Seuss Geisel (a.k.a. Dr. Seuss) is one of the most famous men in history. He was a prolific writer of children's stories. *Cat in the Hat, The Lorax, Green Eggs and Ham,* and of course *How the Grinch Stole Christmas!* are just some of his fabled stories. Seuss signed in a rudimentary script as simply "Dr. Seuss." It is usually followed by a nonconforming paraph, sometimes simple, sometimes complex. His signature can be found on a variety of mediums from index cards to government postcards to photographs and books. He would on occasion sketch characters such as the Grinch. The main problem with Seuss's signature is it so easy to forge. Just about all signatures in the market are forged. Many have been wrongly certified as genuine by the authentication companies. I estimate that 90 percent of Seuss material is forged. Books with forged signatures are very common. In recent years many fake drawings have entered the market. Seuss drawings are scarce and close to 100 percent in the market are spurious. Seuss's signature is affordable at $100. Signed books will sell in the $200 to $400 range. Sketches can sell for $1,000. Exceptional specimens can reach $5,000. Seuss material will prove a sound investment in the years to come.

Seuss-1, GPC dated 1988.

Arthur Conan Doyle was born in Edinburgh, Scotland, in 1859. He was a physician who dabbled in writing. He would become the greatest author of the crime genre, principally through Sherlock Holmes. Conan Doyle signed in a very neat and refined hand. His signature tends to be on the diminutive side. The signature is generally legible and lacks reckless flow. As such, his signature is easy to forge. Creating a well-executed forgery would be rather easy. ALsS tend to have good eye appeal despite the choppy nature of his hand. Letters are scarce as most are secretarially signed; this includes ALsS. Photographs are very rare and just about all are forgeries. Signed books are scarce. In recent years the demand for Conan Doyle material has increased greatly. Prices have seen a material increase. His signature sells in the $500 to $600 range. ALsS are becoming harder to find as they find their way into collections. ALsS are valued at $800 to $1,000. Content letters will sell for much more. Conan Doyle should prove a fine investment signature.

Conan Doyle-1, ALS undated (courtesy Stephen Koschal Autographs).

Jerome Salinger is best remembered for one work: *The Catcher in the Rye.* It is a story which was based, in part, on his own boyhood experiences. Though he wrote other novels, none reached the heights of *The Catcher.* Salinger signed in a choppy and unappealing hand. Point construction notes many breaks in the signature, making replication of hand very easy. Well-executed forgeries exist in quantities. Salinger was a recluse and refused public appearances and autograph requests. Hence, his signature is very scarce and in high demand. Signatures are usually found on TLsS and the occasional endorsed bank check. Expect to pay $1,000 for his signature. TLsS, even those signed with initials, sell for $4,000 to $6,000. A letter of content would likely sell for more than $10,000.

Salinger-1, TLS dated 1977 (courtesy Nate D. Sanders Auctions).

Ernest Hemingway's life was itself an adventure. His larger-than-life persona and violent death generate much interest among collectors. Hemingway signed in a vertical and powerful hand. His signature has good display value despite impaired legibility. Many letters are simply signed "Papa." His signature is rather difficult to replicate, but skilled forgers have produced some convincing fakes. Hemingway material is diverse. There is a good supply of ALsS, TLsS, bank checks, photographs, and personal calling cards in the market. Hemingway liked to sign photographs of himself with the rugged outdoors as the backdrop. Superior specimens can sell for $10,000 to $15,000. Signed books are in high demand and later editions typically sell for $3,000. Bank checks seem to be the most affordable at $800 to $1,000. Hemingway's signature is one of the most collected of all authors. It is a sound investment signature.

Hemingway-1, undated ALS (courtesy collection of Dan Cariseo).

Born Eric Blair, George Orwell was an English writer whose works on totalitarianism are widely read. *Animal Farm* and *Nineteen Eighty-Four* are his most famous writings. Orwell's signature is very rare. He died of consumption in 1950. He was only 46 years old. His signature rarely surfaces and is typically found on short ALsS. Material signed with his real name is equally rare, if not rarer. He would finish off his signature with a paraph. A few dual signatures exist signed with both his real name and pen name. Close to 100 percent of Orwell signatures offered in the market are forgeries. Many

forged TLsS are in the market with scientific content. These letters are on blank sheets of paper and lack letterhead. His signature is valued at $3,000 to $4,000. The value of a nice full-page ALS would likely sell for $10,000 to $15,000.

Orwell-1 undated signature—commonly reproduced as a book facsimile.

Noted Danish writer of fairy tales, Hans Christian Andersen is an extremely important European literary signature. His works are known to children across the globe and have been printed in dozens of languages. Andersen signed in a very choppy hand. His signature is penned as "H.C. Andersen." Letter construction is poor. Eye appeal is substandard. Due to the lack of structure, his signature is very easy to forge. Well-executed forgeries exist in quantities. He was a larger-than-life figure and his signature was actively collected in the 1800s. His signature can be found on letters, album pages, and short poems he would specifically pen for collectors. Signed books are rare to very rare. Signed photographs are very rare and most offered for sale are spurious. There are cabinet cards in the market with a forged inscription on the verso. These are typically personalized to an attorney (e.g., "To John Doe, Esq.") and signed in English script. In much demand by collectors, signatures sell for $750 to $1,000. ALsS, photographs, and handwritten poems are valued at $2,000 to $2,500. Manuscripts are valued at $4,000 to $5,000 per page.

Andersen-1 undated signature.

C.S. Lewis, a close confidant of Tolkien, wrote *The Chronicles of Narnia,* which included *The Lion, the Witch, and the Wardrobe.* Lewis signed in a very plain and thoughtful hand. The signature evidences pensive construction and lacks reckless flow. Signatures are generally accomplished as "C.S. Lewis." Replication of hand is easy. Producing a well-executed forgery takes little effort. The vast majority of Lewis signatures offered in the market are forged. His signature is very scarce of a per se basis and typically limited to letters. Lewis was an atheist who, later in life, turned to Christianity. Many of his writings reference religion and old-world Europe. Letters tend to have good content and are highly treasured. Other signed mediums are very rare. I have never examined a genuinely signed 8 × 10 photograph. Signed books are also quite rare, which is surprising, considering he died in 1963. There are many forged copies of *The Last Battle* in the market. The association with the fantasy genre creates strong demand for Lewis material. TLsS will sell for $1,500 to $2,000. A nice full-page ALS is valued at $4,000 to $5,000.

Lewis-1, undated signature.

Beatrix Potter was a British author and illustrator. She was fascinated by fairies, pixies, and other mythical creatures. Her most famous work is *The Tale of Peter Rabbit.* Potter signed in a pleasing and legible hand. Letter construction is sound and exhibits good display value. A few signatures are signed with her married name "Heelis." Like those of other fantasy writers, her signature is in much demand. Signatures are limited to ALsS, greeting cards, and the occasional album page. Signed photographs are an extreme rarity. There is one group of forgeries to note. Several years ago a rather skilled forger created some nicely executed watercolor paintings featuring animals, mostly of Peter the

Rabbit. A short verse from the book is usually placed underneath the illustration and then signed and dated, all purportedly in Potter's hand. The forgeries are nicely executed but evidence a trivial hesitation, which is the tipoff they are fake. Genuine paintings and drawings by Potter are extremely rare. Illustrations of Potter are typically accomplished in ink and found intermixed in ALsS . These letters are of museum quality and will sell for $10,000 to $20,000. Potter's signature is valued at $2,000. An ALS is valued at $3,500 to $4,500.

Potter-1, signature circa 1920.

Famed British writer A.A. Milne is best known for his works about a teddy bear named Winnie-the-Pooh. Milne signed in a very nonconforming hand. His signature is marked with good flow and a slight choppiness. Letter construction is substandard. He usually finished off his signature with a paraph. Milne signed material is limited. He lived until 1956 but signed very little for collectors. The lack of index cards and photographs confirms this. Signatures are generally limited to ALsS, many of which are signed only with his initials, and books. Many books are limited editions. It should be noted that many forgeries exist on books and slips of paper. Many forgeries are placed on stationery with letterhead that reads "13, Mallord Street, Chelsea, S.W.3." The letterhead is printed in black or deep orange ink. Milne ALsS are val-

Milne-1, undated signature.

ued at $750 to $1,000. Signed books can be purchased for $300 to $1,000 depending on the title.

H.G. Wells is one of the fathers of science fiction. His works *The War of the Worlds* and *The Time Machine* are legendary. Wells signed in a confined and odd hand that is weirdly engaging. The display value is sound. Signatures are accomplished as "H.G. Wells." Wells was an accommodating signer, so there is an ample supply of ALsS, ANsS, and signed books in the market. For being such a legend in the world of literature, his signature is surprisingly cheap. Signatures can be purchased for $100 to $125. Books are a bargain at $300 to $350.

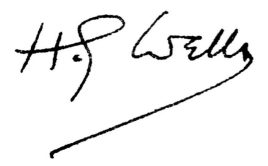

Wells-1 signed book 1931.

F. Scott Fitzgerald was a product of the Jazz Age. Fitzgerald wrote stories of promise and despair. His most famous work, *The Great Gatsby*, remains a classic of 20th-century literature. Like Hemingway, Fitzgerald wrote in a vertical and powerful hand. His signature has wonderful eye appeal which only enhances desirability. His signature exhibits many breaks; as a result, it is a rather easy hand to replicate. Most Fitzgerald signatures offered in the market are forgeries. Fitzgerald is a rare signature on a per se basis. He died in 1940, a victim of consumption. Most signatures are found on very brief ALsS, TLsS, album pages, or signatures removed therefrom. Full-page ALsS are an extreme rarity and generally sell for $15,000. A signature will sell in the $2,000 range. Brief ALsS are valued at $3,000 to $6,000. Signed later edition books

are a minimum of $5,000. A very important American literary signature.

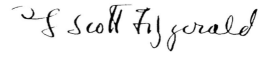

Fitzgerald-1, signature circa 1935.

Washington Irving was one of the great authors of early 19th-century America. Irving was a historian who served as ambassador to Spain in the 1840s. Two short stories, *The Legend of Sleepy Hollow* and *Rip Van Winkle*, gave Irving international fame. Today, he is a somewhat coveted autograph. Irving signed in a nice flowing hand. A decent amount of legibility is noted. His signature has average display value. Irving's autograph is uncommon but a good market inventory exists. Signatures are generally limited to ALsS, which usually are penned on 8vo sheets with routine content. His signature is surprisingly affordable. ALsS can be purchased for as little as $300 with signatures at $150. Manuscript pages will sell for $750 to $1,250 per page. I consider Irving's signature to be one of the most undervalued of all American authors.

Irving, W-1, undated signature.

Scottish writer, composer, and traveler Robert Louis Stevenson remains a very popular author in today's world. He signed in a vertical and pensive hand. The signature has sound display value. Letter construction is slightly impaired. Most signatures are found on bank checks. Fortunately for collectors, there is an ample supply of checks. ALsS are very scarce to rare. Signed photographs are an extreme rarity. Common forgeries are found on ALsS, short endorsements authorizing payment, and photographs. There is one facsimile letter to discuss. It was written to one Mrs. Ehrich. The letter contains the following sentence: "I am in bed and in the least gallant and least grateful frame of mind." A collector made several high-quality facsimiles to give to friends and family. When these facsimiles were created is unknown, at least to me. They were likely produced before 1920. The quality of these facsimiles is amazing. They go so far as to incorporate various shades of ink. If you happen to see the above-referenced sentence you should avoid the letter as a copy. Stevenson stroked out at the young age of 44; thus, overall supply is limited. His works *Treasure Island* and *the Strange Case of Dr. Jekyll and Mr. Hyde* are legendary writings. His signature will always be coveted by collectors. A signature is valued at $400 to $500. A bank check will sell for $600 to $700. A full-page ALS is valued at $2,000 to $2,500.

Stevenson-1, undated signature.

Ralph Waldo Emerson was a lecturer, poet, and champion of the school of self-reliance. His great work "The Concord Hymn," gave us the immortal phrase "the shot heard 'round the world." Emerson's signature has moderate display value and is rather easy to forge. Sloppy letter construction is noted. Emerson penned many letters and today they are a good source of his signature. Much less common are handwritten poems and AQsS. These command substantial premiums. Bank checks are also available, though they should be considered scarce. ALsS, with routine content, are affordable at $300 to $500. Poems and AQsS are much in

Emerson-1, undated signature (courtesy The Sanders Autograph Price Guide).

demand; expect to pay between $2,000 to $5,000 depending on length.

Former British intelligence officer Ian Fleming created one of the greatest characters ever to step out of the pages of literature: 007, James Bond. Just about all his books have been turned into major motion pictures. Fleming signed in a very rapid and sweeping hand. The signature evidences poor letter construction and is generally illegible. His signature is moderately difficult to replicate, but given the extreme value of his signature, skilled forgers have taken up the challenge. He is one of the most forged of all authors. More than 90 percent of Fleming signatures in the market are forgeries. The vast majority of signed Fleming books in the market are forged. If you think you have a genuine signed book in your collection, think again. Forgeries lack the nice sweeping flow of a genuine specimen and are signed in a more practical (and less reckless) manner. Both ALsS and TLsS exist and many are signed with just his first name. His signature is treasured by collectors, so expect to pay $1,000 for one. A nice ALS will sell for $4,000 to $5,000. Letters with Bond content will sell for $10,000 to $15,000.

Fleming-1, signed book circa 1965 (courtesy Nate D. Sanders Auctions).

Leo Tolstoy's works *War and Peace* and *Anna Karenina* are classics that are widely read today. His personality was very complex. He became a moralist in his later years. Tolstoy's signature is rare and most signatures offered in the market are forgeries. Signatures can be found on LsS, and ALsS. The occasional signed card will surface. Signed photographs are very rare and most offered for sale are forgeries. He signed in both English and Cyrillic script. Post-1900 signatures are affected by a slight labored appearance, but not materially so. Most forgeries use old-age signatures as a template. Forgeries evidence a moderate amount of shakiness. Tolstoy's signature is in great demand with a restricted supply. Signatures will sell for $1,500. Letters of any kind are valued at $3,000. A good content ALS should approach $10,000.

Tolstoy-1, undated signature.

Some Contemporary Books of Note

Obtaining signed books of the early authors can be quite expensive and, for most of us collectors, out of our financial reach. But some books from the 1950s to date are affordable and will prove a wise investment. Here are a handful of the more modern books that I feel will see the most appreciation in value in the years to come. The values are for later signed editions. Signed first editions sell for a substantial premium. Not in any particular order:

To Kill a Mockingbird by Harper Lee. This is a book that has become one of the most significant works in the last 60 years. What makes it such an accomplishment is that it was Lee's only published book. Lee signed many editions, including anniversary editions of the book, which sell for $500 to $600. She was never really an easy signer to begin with, but health issues over

Lee, H-1 ALS dated 2000 (courtesy Nate D. Sanders Auctions).

the past five or so years prior to her death early in 2016 makes her signature even tougher to obtain. Some items are signed as "Nelle Lee." Her signature is very easy to forge. Most signed books in the market are forged.

Another significant writer of 20th-century America is Herman Wouk. He wrote stories of World War II, among them *The Caine Mutiny*, the story of an unbalanced naval captain named Queeg. The book was later immortalized in the 1954 movie starring Humphrey Bogart and Van Johnson. Wouk signed editions of this book are available. Many leather-bound editions exist. His signature has good eye appeal, which only enhances this book. Signed copies are, as of this writing, affordable at $100.

Wouk-1 signed postal cover circa 1995.

William Nolan and George Clayton Johnson penned the sci-fi classic *Logan's Run*, a story about population control with Malthusian overtones. It was later made into a movie and a television series on CBS. This book is of particular interest as it can be found signed by both authors. Nolan will, on occasion, sketch characters from the story along with signing his name. Copies with drawings are in high demand. Given the popularity of the genre, this book will increase in value over the coming years. Signed editions sell for $100; with drawings the value increases to $250 to $300.

Nolan-1, signed book 2011.

Another giant of science fiction is Ray Bradbury. He wrote many great works, among them

The Martian Chronicles and *Fahrenheit 451.* Both these books are great additions to any collection. Like Nolan, Bradbury would sketch images of creatures, usually demons or jack-o-lanterns, along with his signature. Bradbury was a very gracious signer throughout his whole life. The supply of signed books is strong. Demand is also solid, pushing values ever higher since his death in the summer of 2012. Signed editions sell for $75 to $100.

Bradbury-1, signature dated 2005.

J.K. Rowling authored the immensely popular *Harry Potter* books, and any one of them is a welcome addition to the library. The story of a young wizard, and the many motion pictures adapted from the novels, make this the most significant series in modern times. Rowling signs in a sloppy and illegible hand. Her signature is easy to forge and many forgeries do exist. Signed books are already selling for $500 to $600. First editions have been selling for $1,000 to $2,000. Signed Potter books will prove a fine investment in the years to come.

Rowling-1, signed book.

'Salem's Lot* by Stephen King is one of many horror classics. Others include *Pet Sematary, The Shining, Cujo,* and the list goes on and on. King was a responsive signer for years and signed many copies of his books. As of this writing, he rarely honors autograph requests. Most signed King books in the market contain a for-

gery. King is the most commonly forged of the modern authors. Signed books sell for $200 to $250.

King, S-1 signed book (courtesy Markus Brandes Autographs).

The Exorcist by William Peter Blatty was made into a major motion picture. It being from the horror genre makes this book coveted by collectors. Blatty signs in a very flamboyant and sloppy hand. Over the past few years he has become a tough signer. Signed copies of *The Exorcist* sell for $100 and should prove a sound investment.

Blatty-1, signature circa 2010.

Slaughterhouse Five is considered by most as Kurt Vonnegut's most influential work, which correlates into a strong demand. Vonnegut was a responsive signer and many signed copies of all his books exist. Vonnegut's signature lacks structure; hence, it is easy to forge. It is a rather ugly signature. Most Vonnegut signed books in the market are forged. A signed copy of *Slaughterhouse Five* sells for $150 to $200.

Jurassic Park by the late Michael Crichton became an instant classic. As a story of dinosaurs in the present time, it doesn't get much better

Vonnegut-1, signature circa 1990.

than that. Replication of Crichton's hand is very easy and most signed copies of this book are forged. Another popular book from the fantasy/sci-fi genre, so expect to pay $150.

Crichton-1, signed book.

The Witches of Eastwick was made into a major motion picture. Written by John Updike, it is a story of three witches in a love triangle. I personally don't get this book, but it has proved popular throughout the years. Many signed leather editions exist and make for a handsome display. All signed Updike books are affordable and appear to be a great buy at $50 or under. I consider Updike one of the true sleeper names of modern 20th-century literature.

Updike-1, signature circa 2000.

Where the Wild Things Are is a modern classic about Max and his trip to the world where magical beasts roam free. Written by Maurice Sen-

dak, it is one of the most famous of children's books and highly coveted by collectors. Sendak signed many copies, but even more forged copies exist. In the last few years of his life he proved an elusive signer. Most mail requests for his autograph went unanswered. Signed copies sell for $500 to $750. One that includes a nice sketch will sell for $3,000 to $4,000.

Sendak-1 signed book (courtesy Nate D. Sanders Auctions).

Sendak-2, signature dated 2010.

Elmore "Dutch" Leonard, author of the crime genre, had always been a responsive signer and many signed books are in the market. His *Get Shorty* is of particular interest to collectors as it was made into a major motion picture. Signed copies of this book exist in good supply. They are in high demand. They sell for $50 to $75. Leonard, in general, was a gracious signer. Leonard would also write many letters to collectors and aspiring authors. ALsS are available. Leonard was one of the good guys when it came to autograph collectors.

Leonard, E-1, signature dated 2000.

2001: A Space Odyssey authored by Arthur C. Clarke is one of the premier science fiction books. A Stanley Kubrick film immortalized the work. Clarke wrote many science fiction books and any of his works are worth adding to your library. Many commemorative editions are in the market. Recently a rash of forged Easton Press books entered the market; all are signed in black Sharpie. Clarke is not only collected in the literary field but also the science field. He was an early pioneer of the communications satellite. Clarke material will always be popular with collectors. Signed copies of *2001* are valued at $400 to $500.

Clarke-1, signature dated 1996.

Walter Morey often wrote about the wilds of the Pacific Northwest. His novels centered around the interaction of man and animal. His most famous work was *Gentle Ben*. Signed books are available, though copies of *Gentle Ben* are scarce and in much demand. Expect to pay $100 to $125. Other signed titles sell for about $25.

Morey-1 signed book circa 1968.

Death of a Salesman, written by playwright Arthur Miller, proved an early success in his career. Miller wrote many plays and nonfiction. He was not a very responsive signer in his later years. Most mail requests for his autograph went unanswered. Signed Miller books exist in limited inventory, the majority of which are forged. A nicely signed copy can be purchased for $150 to $175.

Miller-1, signed book.

Lord of the Flies was written by British author William Golding. It is a dystopian story about children's self-governance on a remote island. A commonly read book, it is required reading among high school students. Signed copies are uncommon to scarce and most offered in the market are forged. Fortunately for collectors, Golding's signature is rather difficult to forge. Most forgeries evidence a shakiness of hand. Signed editions sell for $500 and up.

Golding-1, undated signature (courtesy The Sanders Autograph Price Guide).

Marine archaeologist Clive Cussler wrote many high seas adventure novels; his most famous is *Raise the Titanic*. Cussler's signature is sloppy, illegible, and unappealing. Letter construction is poor, resulting in a signature that is easy to forge. Cussler is a willing and gracious signer. The supply of signed books in the market is sound. Signed first editions of *Raise the Titanic* can be purchased for under $200, later editions at $25. A bargain price for such an important book.

Cussler-1, signature dated 2005.

Jaws made people frightened to step into the ocean. Written by Peter Benchley, this book is a classic and in huge demand. Benchley signed a limited number of copies and would, on occasion, sketch a shark's head underneath the signature. Benchley died in 2006 at the age of 65. There is an ample supply of his signature in the market but it is not common. Just about all signed copies of *Jaws* are forged. A signed edition sells for $100 to $125.

Benchley-1, undated signature.

If *Jaws* made you afraid to go for a swim, then *Psycho* made you fear the shower. A great read written by Robert Bloch. He was a prolific writer of the crime and horror genre. He was greatly influenced by H.P. Lovecraft. Bloch signed in a cramped and choppy hand. His signature has limited eye appeal. Replication of hand is easy; hence, many well-executed forgeries exist. Signed editions of *Psycho* are limited and just about all in the market are forged. Many first editions have been ruined by the forger's hand. Bloch also wrote excellent content letters and they are highly prized by collectors. Expect to pay $200 to $250 for a signed edition.

Block-1, signature circa 1990.

The great Norwegian author Roald Dahl is unfamiliar to most. He wrote many fantasy books including *James and the Giant Peach* and *Charlie and the Chocolate Factory*, which was

made into the movie *Willy Wonka and the Chocolate Factory*, as well as a later version with the same title as the book. Signed copies of either book are very scarce to rare and will sell for over $1,000. Dahl's signature is in high demand and values will increase in years to come. His signature is commonly forged and the majority of signed books in the market are spurious. There are many 4 × 6 photographs in the market featuring Dahl holding two dogs. Many forged copies of this image exist, so caution is warranted.

Dahl-1, signed book dated 1976 (courtesy Nate D. Sanders Auctions).

The Executioner's Song is one of those books that blended fact with fiction. Written by Norman Mailer, it details the events leading up to the execution of murderer Gary Gilmore. Signed copies of Mailer's works are relatively common; however, not so with this particular book. They are considered scarce and most offered in the market are forged. Expect to pay $200 to $300. Signed first editions sell for more than $1,000.

Mailer-1, undated signature (courtesy The Sanders Autograph Price Guide).

Interview with the Vampire by horror author Anne Rice was made into a major motion picture. This novel is widely collected. The rebirth of vampires on the big screen has increased interest in her work. Rice is a responsive signer and many signed editions exist. Signed editions can be purchased for $25.

I, The Jury was written by crime author Mickey Spillane. Part of the Mike Hammer series, it was his first novel. Signed copies of this book are limited. Easton Press issued a nice signed edition in 2003. Spillane was a responsive signer and autographed many copies of this book and his other works. They can be purchased for under $100.

Spillane-1, ANS dated 1990.

James Michener was known to write detailed sagas that resulted in very long books, such was *Hawaii*, which is near 1,000 pages. Michener-signed material has always been popular. He was a fairly responsive signer in the mail. As a result, signed copies of this and other works are available. In recent years, many books have entered the market complete with forgeries. Michener was fond of placing a red stamp next to his signature. It was his personal mark, of sorts. It had the initials "JAM" below a red star. The above-referenced forged books contain a counterfeit red stamp, so caution is warranted. Most Michener signed books can be purchased for under $100.

Michener-1 signature circa 1990.

Kashmiri Indian author Salman Rushdie wrote *The Satanic Verses*, a book that takes a critical view of Islam. There was much outrage among Muslims worldwide, which gained Rushdie and his book international fame.

Rushdie-1 signed book.

Rushdie-signed books exist in quantities, including *The Satanic Verses*. Signed books can be purchased for $25 to $50.

Charlotte's Web was penned by American author Elwyn B. White. Considered one of the classic children's stories of all time, it's a delightful tale of a pig named Wilbur who befriends a barn spider named Charlotte. To save Wilbur from slaughter, Charlotte weaves laudatory words in her web. It is such a wonderful story that is will remain popular for the ages. Signed copies of this book are rare. White's signature is relatively easy to forge and just about all signed books in the market are forged. eBay is flooded with White forgeries. A genuinely signed copy of *Charlotte's Web* is a true rarity and will sell for over $1,000. White died in 1985 but signed very little; his signature is scarce. ALsS are considered rare to very rare. A signature in much demand.

White, E-1 ALS circa 1950.

The Godfather by Italian author Mario Puzo is one of the most recognizable titles ever published. A writer in the crime genre, Puzo often centered his works around the violent world of the Mafia. Puzo was a gracious signer and autographed many of his works. Puzo's signature is a mere scrawl with little, if any, letter construction. His signature is one of the easiest to forge. Most signed Godfather books contain a forged signature. A genuine signed copy will sell for $100 to $125.

British author John le Carré writes about the nebulous world of spies. His greatest work is *Tinker, Tailor, Soldier, Spy*. Le Carré has been a willing signer for years and countless signed books exist. His signature can be added to your library with little effort.

le Carré-1, signature dated 2009.

There are many other collectable titles in various genres. Both fiction and nonfiction are collectable. The books are endless. You can spend a lifetime building a collection of signed books. I have several signed copies in my library, many from authors I have befriended over the years. I cherish them greatly.

A Symphony of
Signatures: Composers

Music is one aspect of the human condition that amazes me. Simple notes of sound seamlessly woven together into wonderful melody captures the imagination and won't let go. The composer Muradian once wrote: "Music is melody; without melody there is no music." Music can reach out and gently touch the soul. The effect on the mind can be intense. Music can take you to the top of the highest mountain to gaze down upon the world. Music can teleport you to the outer heavens and make you dance on the rings of Saturn. Or it can put the knife-wielding boogeyman in the attic just before bedtime. It is because of this that music has been around since the time of the ancients. Music is one of the cornerstones of civilization, and because of this, signatures of those who compose and play music are widely collected. Classical and rock are the most widely collected. In recent years signatures of rock legends have exploded in value. The Beatles, Janis Joplin, Elvis Presley, Jim Morrison, Jimi Hendrix, and other rock stars are in great demand. Due to premature death, signatures of Whitney Houston, Kurt Cobain, and Michael Jackson will prove much in demand. Jazz, opera, country, and folk also have large followings: Luciano Pavarotti, Charles Aznavour, Hank Williams Sr., Lloyd "Cowboy" Copas, Edith Piaf, and the list goes on and on. Other important names include Johnny Cash, Frank Sinatra, Judy Garland, and Dean Martin.

Classical music autographs have been ac-tively collected for the past 200 years. There are endless names to choose from and signatures of some of the great composers can be picked up for surprisingly affordable prices. Certain "giants" of the field such as Bach, Beethoven, and Handel command substantial sums of money. These signatures are typically out of the reach of the average collector. A Handel signature would be valued in excess of $50,000. However, many 19th- and 20th-century composers can be purchased for under $100, such as Friml, Romberg, and Gounod, for example. Composers in the last 100 years were actively sought out by collectors and supplies are sound for the collecting public. There are certain exceptions, of course, such as the legendary rarity of the Reverend Komitas' signature. Ragtime composer Scott Joplin's signature is also excessively rare.

Most signatures are limited to letters, calling cards, and photographs. Many collectors would request the signer to pen a bar or two of music. Signatures with an autographed musical quotation are highly treasured by collectors and command a premium. Some composers would pen several bars of music, while others, such as Khachaturian, added only a single bar. Many composers will pen these upon request. Illustrated is a nicely accomplished AMQS by Chester Biscardi.

Like literary manuscripts, most musical manuscripts have found their way into major institutional collections, never again to see the light

Biscardi-1, typical autographed musical quotation signed.

of day. Manuscripts and complete scores of the composers are highly valued. Mozart, Chopin, Beethoven, and other legends are easily valued over $1,000,000. Even lesser-named composers are worth several thousands of dollars. For these you will be competing against buyers with deep pockets. As time goes by, more manuscripts will enter the market from private collections. The institutional buyer will be there, with checkbook in hand, to quickly snap up that which enters the market.

There is a word of caution when it comes to manuscripts. The high dollar value of these manuscripts attracts forgers of great skill.

When you think of it, there is not much substance to a musical manuscript, at least from the graphic standpoint. The musical manuscript is mostly constructed of dots, dashes, and hash marks which form something likened to a geometric code. Musical manuscripts have very little, in terms, of writing by the composer. They are surprisingly easy to forge. It doesn't take much skill to forge a musical note. A few up and down strokes and that's about it. On the other hand, a literary manuscript is extremely difficult, if not impossible, to forge with any degree of accuracy. A forger would have to reproduce page after page of the target author's handwrit-

ing. Imagine, for a moment, forging a 50-page manuscript of Ernest Hemingway or Washington Irving. That would take great effort and skill. Forging a musical manuscript, on the other hand, can be done quite convincingly. In doing research for this book, I viewed online many manuscripts. I believe many of these manuscripts that are purportedly accomplished by Mozart, Beethoven, Haydn, Chopin, and the like are nothing but forgeries. Musical manuscripts must be studied with great care, as many offered for sale are forgeries.

The following is a list of signatures that are highly collectable. This list is by no means exhaustive. I have excluded certain early composers, as the likelihood of their signatures entering the market is slim to none. Bach and Pachelbel are good examples.

Béla Bartók is generally considered the second most important Hungarian composer behind Liszt. His work is centered on traditional folk music from his native Hungary. Bartók signed in a rather pleasing hand. His signature has good display value but lacks rapid flow. The capital letters "B" sometimes display themselves as the capital letter "A." He writes in a pensive hand which invites forgery. Many signatures are penned as "Béla Bartók" and "Bartók Béla." Due to the lack of rapid flow, his signature is easily forged. Most Bartók material in the market is forged. In recent years many forged ALsS have entered the market. They are accomplished in both English and French. The French letters usually are opened with "Cher Monsieur." A date runs across the top with the word "Budapest." Many forged letters accomplished in

English are brief, sometimes only three of four lines. Content of these letters appears routine, such as accepting a dinner invitation or obtaining tickets for an opera. The handwriting on these letters appears slightly methodic. The writing exhibits black ink that lacks the gentle shades of vintage writing. They simply look too fresh and clean. His signature is considered very scarce to rare and generally limited to ALsS and LsS. AMQsS are very rare. ALsS sell for anywhere from $1,000 to $2,000. Exceptional examples can across the $5,000 threshold. Bartók material is in strong demand.

Bartók-1, signature dated 1922 (courtesy J.B. Muns Musical Autographs).

The greatest composer of them all is Ludwig van Beethoven. His works include 9 symphonies, 32 piano sonatas, and countless other compositions. Signatures can be found in German and English script. The handwriting is average and unassuming; it is rather pedestrian in nature. Legibility of signatures accomplished in English is sound. Display value is limited. Beethoven's signature is rare to very rare and generally limited to a few DsS. AMs also exist. The market population has an ample supply of Beethoven-signed material, but the problem is most of it is fake. No signature in classical music is as coveted as Beethoven. The demand is great. First off, Beethoven is the most forged signature in classical music. I estimate more than 95 percent of all Beethoven signatures in the market are forgeries. Skilled forgers have targeted Beethoven for well over a century. Forgeries include elaborate documents, musical manuscripts, letters, and receipts. Many have been sold by major auction houses. If you think you have a genuine Beethoven signature in your collection, think again. In recent years a small grouping of forgeries has entered the market.

They are receipts purportedly signed by Beethoven. The text of the receipt is in the hand of another. The text is German. The word receipt is written across the top. The text is something to the effect that "the letter (or manuscript) sent by John Doe arrived safely at my address (or home). It is signed as "L. v. Beethoven" in a slightly unsteady hand. The small paraph appears labored. The paper is usually cut somewhat irregularly. This forger has also created irregularly cut signatures removed from a large sheet. A red wax seal is sometimes attached. I estimate the number of genuine Beethoven signatures in the market is somewhere between 25 and 50. Beethoven's signature is highly treasured, so expect to pay $30,000 for a nice specimen. DsS will sell for $50,000 to $75,000. A genuine musical manuscript of some length is priceless.

Beethoven-1, undated signature.

Beethoven-2, undated signature in German script.

Austrian composer Alban Berg was of little interest to collectors. In the last 15 or so years the demand for his signature has increased greatly. Berg signed in a lazy and unstructured hand. The signature is of average display value. Replication of hand is relatively easy; hence, well-executed forgeries do exist. Berg's signature is scarce on a per se basis. ALsS and AMQsS are rare. Photographs are very rare. Berg's signature is valued at $1,000 to $1,250. A full-page ALS will sell for $3,000. AMQsS are valued at $2,500 to $3,000. A nicely signed 8 × 10 photograph would likely sell for close to $10,000.

Berg-1 undated signature.

Irving Berlin, born Israel Baline, is one of the most significant American composers of the 20th century. His works include "Always" and "White Christmas." Berlin signed in a very rudimentary and unstructured hand. Letter construction is poor, resulting in a signature that is illegible. The signature displays itself as the letters "J" and "B" following by a scrawl of ink. Replication of hand is very easy. Berlin's signature is one of the easiest to forge. Many well-executed forgeries exist, so caution is warranted. Berlin was a responsive signer, but in the last 15 or so years of his life mail requests for his autograph generally went unanswered. His signature can be found on various mediums. Signed sheet music of "White Christmas" is rare and highly desirable. Bank checks exist, but they should be considered very scarce. There are countless TLsS in the market, many of which date from the 1940s and 1950s. They are typed on personal letterhead that simply reads "Irving Berlin." Be warned: the *vast* majority of TLsS are secretarially signed and not signed by Berlin. The signatures on these letters

Berlin-1, undated signature (courtesy J.B. Muns Musical Autographs).

are signed in a slightly labored hand. Some secretarially signed letters are accomplished simply as "Irving." Berlin's signature is valued at $100. A nicely signed 8 × 10 photograph is valued at $300 to $400. ALsS are rare; expect to pay $500 to $600 for a nice example. The above-referenced sheet music is a treasure, valued at $1,500 to $2,000. A multiple bar AMQS will sell for $750 to $1,000.

French composer Hector Berlioz was known for his use of very large orchestras. A composer of the Romantic genre, he is best remembered for his *Symphonie fantastique*. Berlioz signed in a large and flamboyant hand. His signature dominates the medium it is placed upon. The signature has sound letter construction. Display value is also average. Signatures are usually accomplished as "H. Berlioz." Berlioz is a scarce to rare signature. Signatures are generally limited to ALsS with routine content; many are brief. Signed photographs and AMQsS are very rare. A signature in much demand. A full-page ALS is valued at $1,500 to $2,000.

Berlioz-1 ALS dated 1864 (courtesy collection of James Neglia).

An American composer and conductor of Ukrainian descent, Leonard Bernstein is known for his film scores, which include *West Side Story* and *On the Waterfront*. When he wanted to, Bernstein could sign in a stunning hand. Unfortunately, most signatures are hurried and lack proper letter construction. Signatures tend to be sloppy and illegible, which limits display value. Replication of hand is fairly easy and many well-executed forgeries do exist. His signature is uncommon. Bernstein proved an elusive signer in his later years. Signatures are usually found on album pages, record albums, programs, and photos, 8vo or smaller. TLsS are scarce. ALsS are rare. Supply and demand seem balanced. Autograph dealers tend to overprice his signature in an attempt to artificially inflate values. Bernstein was known to use an autopen to accommodate autograph requests; see illustration. A Bernstein signature is valued at $50 to $75. A nicely signed 8 × 10 photograph will sell for $250 to $300.

Bernstein-1 signed book dated 1959.

Bernstein-1, common auto pen.

French composer Georges Bizet was a student of Gounod, and his opera *Carmen* is one of the most famous works in history. Bizet signed in a plain and unassuming hand. His signature is fairly legible. Average display value is noted. ALsS tend to be difficult to read. Due to the simple nature of the hand, replication is fairly easy. Creating a well-executed forgery can be accomplished with little effort. Bizet died at the very young age of 36. He fell victim to a heart attack. As a result, the supply of genuine material is restricted. Bizet's signature is considered rare on a per se basis. Premium items are very rare. I have never examined a genuinely signed photograph. AMQsS are an extreme rarity. I am told a few genuine specimens exist, though I have not seen any outside of manuscripts held by institutional concerns. Due to rarity, expect to pay $750 to $1,000 for his signature. A nice ALS will sell for $2,500 to $3,500.

Bizet-1, undated signature (courtesy J.B. Muns Musical Autographs).

William Bolcom is a longtime University of Michigan professor and a recipient of the Pulitzer Prize. Bolcom signs in a tempered hand. The signature has average letter construction and display value. His signature, which lacks rapid flow, is rather easy to replicate. Bolcom has been a responsive signer, though premium items remain uncommon. His signature is generally limited to index cards, first-day covers, and short AMQsS. His signature is affordable at $25. A nice AMQS will sell for $75.

Bolcom-1 signature dated 2000.

Alexander Borodin, a Russian chemist turned composer, gave the world one of the most beautiful works in the *Polovtsian Dances*. Borodin signed in a nice flowing hand. The signature evidences no hesitation. Sound letter construction is noted. Display value is high. Most signatures are signed as "A.P. Borodin." Signatures are sometimes finished with a tailing paraph. Overall, a pleasing autograph. Borodin material is very difficult to locate and his signature is considered rare to very rare on a per se basis.

Signatures are generally limited to a handful of ALsS in the market. Expect to pay $4,000 to $5,000 for a nice specimen.

Borodin-1, undated signature (courtesy J.B. Muns Musical Autographs).

German composer Johannes Brahms is one of the giants of classical music. Around 1890, Brahms also recorded his *Hungarian Dance* for Thomas Edison. It is considered the first recording ever made by a major composer. Brahms signed in a sloppy and unstructured hand. His hand is generally illegible, evidencing poor display value. The signature is finished with a paraph. Most signatures are accomplished as "J. Brahms." Given the sloppy and uniformed nature of the signature, replication of hand is easy. Many well-executed forgeries exist. Most signatures offered for sale are forgeries. His signature is generally found on ALsS, many of which are simply signed with his initials. Other mediums, such as photographs and AMQsS, are very rare. There is a good supply of forged cabinet photographs in the market; in fact, just about all offered for sale are forgeries. One forger has created many forgeries. His work product differs from a genuine signature in that he does not place a paraph under the signature. Sometimes he will extend a long tail of ink off the "s" in the last name. Brahms's signature is in great demand. Signatures are valued at $500 to $750. ALsS generally sell for $2,500 to $3,000. Multi-

Brahms-1, undated signature.

page specimens can reach auction prices of $5,000 to $7,000.

The great Polish composer Frédéric Chopin is one of the giants of classical music. Chopin signed in a compact and bold hand. His signature exhibits choppy letter construction and is typically finished off with a bold paraph. Given the extreme value of his signature, Chopin is often the target of skilled forgers. Just about all Chopin signatures offered for sale are forgeries. Since he died at a young age, his signature is very rare on a per se basis and generally limited to manuscripts and letters. Most signed material has been absorbed into major institutional collections. There is another signature that causes controversy. The signature in question is often found on receipts or contracts whereby Chopin is selling the rights to one of his works. This signature deviates greatly from the genuine signature. Some are signed with his last name only, while others are accomplished as "Fr'd. Chopin" with a single lined paraph. Some authenticators believe these to be genuine; I, however, do not. I advise collectors to avoid this signature in total. The demand for Chopin material is great. Expect to pay $25,000 to $30,000 for his signature.

Chopin-1, undated signature (courtesy J.B. Muns Musical Autographs).

Aaron Copland is often referred to as the "Dean of American Composers." His works, such as "Fanfare for the Common Man" and "Rodeo," are uniquely American in composition. Copeland signed in a carefree and reckless hand. The signature is loosely constructed, with individual letters appearing as indistinguishable strokes. The signature exhibits impaired legibility. Display value is substandard. Due to the haphazard nature of his hand, Copland's signature is easy to forge. Many well-executed forgeries are in the market. Signatures are generally found on index cards. He was an erratic signer throughout his life. Most mail requests for his autograph went unanswered. TLsS are ample in supply but generally limited to pre–1970 dates. Signed 8 × 10 photographs and AMQsS are scarce. His signature is in much demand and is valued at $100 to $125. A TLS is valued at $200. An ALS at $400 to $500. A nice AMQS will sell for $500 to $700.

![Copland signature](Copland-1 circa 1920 album page.)

Copland-1 circa 1920 album page.

Vincent d'Indy was a music teacher turned composer. D'Indy signed in a rapid and flowing hand. His signature is somewhat scarce but an ample supply exists. Surprisingly, there is only marginal demand for his signature. Currently d'Indy is out of favor with the classical music collectors, but that will certainly change. Signatures are affordable at $100. AMQsS and ALsS are valued at $250 to $300.

Claude Debussy was one of the most important composers of French impressionist music. He is noted for works in many genres and some have suggested that his music was constructed, in part, of mathematical formulas. Debussy signed in a confined, almost cramped, hand. The scale of his handwriting is small. The signature has poor letter construction and is on the illegible side. The signature has average display value. Debussy's hand is very easy to replicate and just about all signatures in the market are forgeries. His signature is rare on a per se basis. Premium items are very rare. Signatures are generally found on personalized calling cards and ALsS on 8vo stationary. Debussy's signature is in high demand and is thus valued at $1,250 to $1,500. ALsS and AMQsS are very rare and will sell for $5,000 to $7,000.

![DeBussy signature]

DeBussy-1, undated signature.

Antonín Dvořák is probably the most influential Czech composer of the 19th century. Dvořák signed in a flowing hand. Letter construction is sound. The signature is dominated by a large letter "D" in the last name. Above-average eye appeal is noted. Many times he would sign his name simply as "A. Dvořák."

Dvořák's signature is highly prized. His signature is often the target of skilled forgers. Signed cabinet photographs and AMQsS are very rare and just about all in the market are forgeries. A common forgery can be found on cabinet cards signed in full in a slightly labored hand. The forger adds the word "Praha" and then adds a date, usually from the late 1890s. This

D'Indy-1 undated AMQS (courtesy collection of James Neglia).

forger also creates some convincing AMQsS. Again the signature is slightly labored and wobbly. These are also dated in the 1890s, a time when Dvořák's hand was still strong and evidenced no shakiness of hand. More than 90 percent of Dvořák's signatures in the market are forged, so caution is warranted. A signature is valued at $750 to $1,000. An AMQS will likely sell for $4,000 to $5,000.

Dvořák-1, signature dated 1891 (courtesy J.B. Muns Musical Autographs).

English composer Edward Elgar created numerous orchestral works, including the "Pomp and Circumstances Marches." Elgar signed in a very flowing hand. His signature appears fast on paper. Letter construction and display value are both impaired. The signature is typically finished off with a paraph. Due to the reckless nature of hand, Elgar's signature is moderately difficult to replicate. Well-executed forgeries are very limited. A signature that is scarce on per se basis and generally limited to ALsS. A nice handwritten letter is valued at $500 to $750. An AMQS is rare and will likely sell in the $2,000 to $2,500 price range.

Elgar-1, signature dated 1901 (courtesy J.B. Muns Musical Autographs).

Gabriel Faure was a French composer of many talents. He was music teacher who played many instruments. Faure signed in a large and ostentatious hand. The signature has good display value. For the composer who wrote "Clair

de lune," there is surprisingly little demand for his signature. Faure's signature is scarce and generally limited to ALsS. Other mediums are rare. Photographs are rare to very rare. ALsS can be purchased for $200 to $300, which I consider a steal.

Faure-1 undated ALS (courtesy collection of James Neglia).

Ross Lee Finney was a student of Alban Berg. Finney was a longtime professor of music at the University of Michigan. He won the Pulitzer Prize in 1937. Finney signed in a plain and practical hand. His signature has good letter construction. A sound legibility is noted. Due to the rather pensive nature of hand, Finney's signature is easy to replicate. Creating a well-executed forgery would not take a lot of effort. Finney's signature is uncommon and generally limited to index cards. Signed photographs and letters are scarce. Finney was accommodating when it came to penning AMQs. His signature is valued at $40 to $50. A nice AMQS can be purchased for $100.

Finney-1, GPC dated 1988.

Perhaps no composer has captured the American spirit like Stephen Foster. He is America's greatest composer. His works, such as, "Oh! Susanna," "My Old Kentucky Home," and "Beautiful Dreamer" are still household favorites. Foster signed in a nice flowing script. His signature has sound legibility with good letter construction. Sound display value is noted. His signature is the target of skilled forgers and just about all ever offered for sale are forgeries. His signature is a rarity among composers as he died at the very young age of 37. Very few signatures exist. No recent sales.

Foster-1, undated signature (courtesy J.B. Muns Musical Autographs).

Rudolf Friml was a student of Dvořák. Friml's music always remained in a classical pre–1920 tone. He is considered one of the most important Czech composers of the 20th century. Friml signed in a powerful and reckless hand. His signature dominates the medium it is placed upon. Bold lines and a defined paraph make for a signature with sound eye appeal. His signature is complex and busy in appearance. Friml's hand is difficult to replicate; hence, well-executed forgeries do not exist. Though he died in 1972, his signature is considered scarce on a per se basis. Premium items are rare. Friml's signature is valued at $125 to $150. A nice AMQS will sell for $700 to $900.

Friml-1 undated TLS.

George Gershwin is one of the most famous composers of the 20th century. His works include "Rhapsody in Blue" and "An American In Paris." Gershwin signed in a very eclectic and nonconforming hand. His hand exhibits back and forth strokes. Letter construction is fairly sound, though the last three letters in the last name tend to blend together. Gershwin's signature is typically finished off with a paraph. Gershwin's signature is difficult to replicate; hence, well-executed forgeries are limited. There is one forgery to discuss. There are many forged AMQsS in the market. They are typically three bars from "Rhapsody in Blue." They are inscribed "To John Doe." The word "Andante" is placed above the first bar. They are signed "With best wishes, George Gershwin." The forgeries are fairly well-executed. They are accomplished in black ink. The ink looks bright and clean with little to no aging. There is strong demand for Gershwin material when compared to a limited supply. He died at the young age of 38 from a brain tumor. Signatures are scarce on a per se basis. Premium items are rare. Signatures can be found on album pages, books, and musical scores. Less common are 8 × 10 photographs and letters of any kind. AMQsS are rare and usually incorporated in signed books or photographs. About ten years ago an ample supply of bank checks entered the market and adversely affected value. A Gershwin signature is valued at $500 to $600. A nicely signed 8 × 10 photograph can sell for $4,000 to $5,000. If the photograph includes an AMQS then the value can double. Bank checks are the best value at $700 to $800.

Gershwin-1 bank check dated 1935.

Irish composer Patrick Gilmore moved to the United States in the late 1840s and served in the Union Army during the Civil War, during which he wrote "When Johnny Comes Marching Home." It is one of the most recognizable songs from 19th-century Americana. Gilmore signed in a flowing and confident hand. His signature is bold with excellent flow and strong letter construction. The whimsical paraph only enhances eye appeal. Signatures are accomplished as "P.S. Gilmore." Gilmore material is rare in any form. Premium items are extremely rare. His signature rarely enters the market, and when it does, it sells in the $400 to $500 price range.

Gilmore-1 undated signature (courtesy collection of James Neglia).

Louis Gottschalk was American pianist and composer who died at the young age of 40. Gottschalk signed in an aggressive and reckless hand. Letter construction is marginal. The signature is basically illegible. His signature is usually finished with a long linear paraph. Gottschalk's autograph used to be rather expensive. In recent years the demand for his material has dropped. As of this writing, demand is marginal, at best. His signature can be purchased for $100 to $150. ALsS, which are usually brief, are valued at $250 to $350. Should interest in Gottschalk increase, this may prove to be a good investment signature.

Gottschalk-1, undated signature.

Charles Gounod is a noted French composer most remembered for "Ave Maria" and the opera *Faust*. Gounod signed in a very tempered and lackluster hand. His signature is average in almost every aspect: construction, legibility, and display. It is a rather boring signature. Au-

tographs are generally accomplished as "Ch. Gounod" with an elongated downstroke to the letter "d." His signature is scarce and generally limited to ALsS and the occasional album page. Replication of hand is very easy. Creating a well-executed forgery can be done with ease. Just about all AMQsS are forged. There does not seem to be much interest in Gounod material at present. His signature is surprisingly affordable. A signature can be purchased for $100. A full-page ALS sells for $200 to $300. A nice AMQS is valued at $500 to $700.

Gounod-1, undated AMQS (courtesy J.B. Muns Musical Autographs).

Norwegian composer Edvard Grieg is considered one of the major figures of the Romantic era of music. Grieg signed in a flowing hand. His signature lacks hesitation. Letter construction is fairly sound. The bold paraph enhances eye appeal. Grieg's signature is fairly easy to replicate. Well-executed forgeries exist in quantities, especially on AMQsS and Elliott and Fry cabinet photographs. Signatures are generally found on calling cards and short ANsS. A small supply of cabinet photographs does exist. Full page ALsS are an extreme rarity. Grieg's signature is in much demand, so expect to pay $600 to $800 for a nice specimen. Cabinet photo-

Grieg-1, 1890 signed AP.

graphs are valued at $1,500 to $2,000. A nice AMQS will sell in the $3,000 price range.

Known as the father of the symphony, Austrian composer Franz Joseph Haydn is one of the most important composers in all of classical music. Haydn signed in a very deliberate and methodical hand, not uncommon for the time period. The signature lacks reckless flow and appears labored. The signature has good letter construction and legibility. Average eye appeal is noted. Due to the slower nature of hand, replication is very easy. Most signatures offered for sale are nothing more than well-executed forgeries. Haydn's signature is very rare. Rarely does it turn up for sale. An occasional folio will surface. Manuscripts are very rare and highly coveted by collectors. Expect to pay $20,000 to $30,000 for his signature.

Haydn-1, undated signature.

German composer Paul Hindemith was an accomplished violinist and conductor. Hindemith signed in a very tempered and legible hand. A slight choppiness to the hand is noted. His signature exhibits sound letter construction. Display value is average. Hindemith was an accommodating signer, resulting in a sound supply of material. His signature can be found on photographs, programs, letters, and AMQsS. His signature is fairly affordable at $50 to $75. A nice 8 × 10 photograph is valued at $400 to $500.

Hindemith-1, undated signature.

Alan Hovhaness's works are almost exclusively centered on Armenian folk music. He is considered one of the most important composers of the 20th century. Hovhaness signed in a very legible and unassuming hand. His signature is well-constructed and pensive. Due to the lack of rapid flow, his signature is quite easy to replicate. Producing a well-executed forgery can be done with little effort. Hovhaness's signature is one of the modern rarities in the field of musical autographs. He died in the year 2000 and his signature rarely surfaces. Premium items are almost nonexistent. The occasional signed program will surface and that is about it. Most of his papers are held by major institutional collections. Signatures penned in Armenian are rare to very rare. Value is hard to determine due to lack of confirmed market transactions. Most Hovhaness signatures sold over the years were the product of forgery. His signature is valued at $250 to $300. A full-page ALS will likely sell for close to $1,000. Autographically speaking, a modern rarity.

Hovhaness-1 undated signature (courtesy Marco Shirodkar [www.hovhaness.com]).

German composer Engelbert Humperdinck gained international fame for his timeless opera *Hansel und Gretel*. Humperdinck signed in a flowing hand. A slight choppiness is noted. Letter construction is fairly sound. A degree on legibility is noted. Signatures are usually accomplished as "E Humperdinck." Due to the strong flow and abrupt turns, his signature is rather difficult to forge. There are no well-executed forgeries in the market. Humperdinck's signature is somewhat rare on a per se basis and generally limited to ALsS with routine content and calling cards. Photographs are very rare. AMQsS seldom surface and are worth considerable money. Around 1910 Humperdinck suffered a stroke that partially paralyzed him. This explains the lack of signed material post–1910 in the market. Many forged cabinet-style photographs and picture postcards are in the market. They are all accomplished by the same forger. The image is usually a formal portrait of Humperdinck and the forgery is placed vertically along the right side of his head. On occasion, an AMQ and date are added. Being associated with an immortal fairy tale correlates into good demand for Humperdinck's signature. His signature is valued at $200 to $250. A full page ALS will sell for $400 to $500.

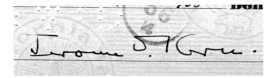

Humperdinck-1 undated AMQS (courtesy collection of James Neglia).

Leoš Janáček was a Czech composer whose work exhibits Moravian tones. He is best remembered for the opera *Jenufa*. Janáček signed in a rapid and choppy hand. It displays itself as busy and confused. His signature is scarce to rare. Signatures can be found on ALsS, AMQsS, album pages, and cards. Photographs would be very rare. There is good demand for Janáček material. A signature can be purchased for $400 to $500. ALsS sell for about $1,000.

Janáček-1 ALS dated 1925 (courtesy collection of James Neglia).

American Jerome Kern was a composer of musical theatre. His works are some of the most famous of the 20th century; among them are

"Ol' Man River" and "Smoke Gets in Your Eyes." Kern signed in a very odd hand. The signature has many inverted turns. The signature is generally illegible. An average display value is noted. Kern's signature is somewhat scarce on a per se basis. The ample supply of bank checks keeps this signature from being considered scarce. Photographs, AMQsS, and letters of any kind are rare. There is average demand for Kern material. A signature will sell for $100. A bank check or TLS will sell for $150 to $175. An AMQsS is desirable so expect to pay about $1,000.

Kern-2 bank check dated 1939.

Aram Khachaturian is the most famous of all Armenian composers. He, along with Prokofiev and Shostakovich, are considered the three titans of Soviet classical music. His most famous work is, of course, the "Sabre Dance." Khachaturian signed in a flowing yet slightly choppy hand. His signature has average letter construction. Moderate display value is noted. Signatures can be found in Armenian, Russian, and English. There is a surprisingly good supply of signed material in the market. His signature is considered uncommon but not scarce. Books, photographs, programs, and AMQsS are available for purchase. It is one of the more attainable signatures to come out of the Soviet Union. There is strong demand for Khachaturian-signed material. A signature is valued at $300 to $350. A signed 8 × 10 photograph will cost

Khatchaturian-1, AMQS circa 1970 (courtesy J.B. Muns Musical Autographs).

$750 to $1,000. AMQsS tend to be brief, limited to one bar, and sell for $400 to $500. AMQsS with 8 to 10 bars are highly desired and sell in the $1,250 to $1,500 price range.

The Hungarian composer Zoltán Kodály is best known for developing the Kodály concept, a method of music education. Kodály signed in a loose and flowing hand. The signature has sound letter construction. The effortless strokes create a signature with strong eye appeal. Many signatures are penned with his last name only. Kodály's signature is often forged and well-executed forgeries exist. His signature is generally limited to programs, album pages, and the occasional small photograph. AMQsS and ALsS are rare and highly desirable. Kodály's signature is rather affordable at $75 to $100. Premium items can sell for $500 to $600. A multi bar AMQS will sell for $800 to $1,000.

Kodály-1 undated signature.

Jan Kubelík was a Czech composer and violinist. He is one of the few violinists to actually own a Stradivarius. Kubelík signed in a very fast and busy hand. His signature exhibits no hesitation. The racing effect is pronounced. His signature has average letter construction and eye appeal. Replication of hand is rather difficult. Well-executed forgeries do not exist. His signature can be found on ANsS usually on postcards, photographs octavo or smaller, programs, and AMQsS. Kubelík's autograph used to be a much tougher find than it is today. With the advent of international auction websites, such as eBay, Kubelík material has been coming out of eastern Europe greatly increasing supply. A signature is valued at $50. A nice AMQS will sell for $250 to $300. This is a signature that has decreased in value over the past ten years.

Kubelík-1 ANS dated 1932.

Franz Lehár was an Austro-Hungarian composer. His is best remembered for the operetta *Die Lustige Witwe*. Lehár signed in a very odd and artistic hand. His signature evidences many curves and turns. Though legibility is impaired the signature still retains good display value. There is an ample supply in material in the market, including ALsS, AMQsS, picture postcards, and album pages. An 8 × 10 photograph is considered rare. The complexity of the signature and less than stellar value keeps forgers at bay. Well-executed forgeries are basically nonexistent. There is average demand for Lehár material and his autograph is still quite affordable. Signatures sell for $100 to $150. ALsS and AMQsS are valued around $250 to $300.

Lehár-1, signature dated 1928 (courtesy J.B. Muns Musical Autographs).

Ruggero Leoncavallo was one of the Italian masters of opera. *Pagliacci* is one of the most performed operas in the world. Leoncavallo signed in a heavy and bold hand. The signature evidences moderate eye appeal. Legibility is somewhat impaired. ALsS are difficult to decipher. Most signatures are penned as "R. Leoncavallo." Due to the uneven construction of hand, replication is fairly easy. Producing a well-executed forgery can be done with little effort. Signatures can be found on various mediums including ALsS, ANsS usually on postcards, AMQsS, and cabinet cards. The supply of signed Leoncavallo material is ample. He liked to sign images of himself; hence, a decent supply of photographs exist. Leoncavallo material is surprisingly affordable. A signature is valued at $150. ALsS and AMQsS can be purchased for $350 to $450. A nicely signed cabinet card with an AMQ is valued at $700 to $800.

Leoncavallo-1, signature dated 1904 (courtesy J.B. Muns Musical Autographs).

Franz Liszt, noted Hungarian composer, was one of the giants of 19th century music. Liszt signed in a flamboyant and unstructured hand. His signature is large and sloppy with marginal letter construction. Signatures are almost always accomplished as "F Liszt." Due to the loose nature of his hand, Liszt's signature is easy to forge. Well-executed forgeries exist in quantities. Close to 100 percent of signed cabinet photographs offered for sale are forged. Signatures are generally limited to hard-to-read ALsS. Liszt's signature is valued at $500. A nice ALS will sell in the $1,250 to $1,500. A genuinely signed photograph is valued at $1,750 to $2,250. An AMQS is valued at $4,000 to $4,500. A superior specimen is nearly double that amount.

Liszt-1, ALS dated 1886 (courtesy Nate D. Sanders Auctions).

Gustav Mahler was an Austrian composer. His work is of the Romantic genre. Mahler signed in a heavy and bold hand. The signature evidences thick strokes. It is one of the nicer display signatures. Mahler's signature is scarce on a per se basis. DsS are the most available. ALsS are rare. Photographs are very rare and just about all are forged. Autograph collectors covet his signature. There is strong demand for Mahler material. Expect to pay $1,000 for a DS. ALsS and photographs are a minimum $3,500.

Mahler-1, undated signature (courtesy J.B. Muns Musical Autographs).

Henry Mancini was one of the most important composers of the second half of the 20th century. He is best remembered for the "Love Theme from Romeo and Juliet," "Moon River," and "The Pink Panther." Mancini signed in a flowing and rapid hand. His signature displays itself fast on paper. Letter construction and legibility are both marginal. Some letters tend to blend together. Mancini was a willing and gracious signer throughout his life. He would send out signed 8 × 10 photographs upon request. Hence, there is a good supply in the market. AMQsS are uncommon but available. Letters of any kind are scarce. Mancini's signature is affordable. I consider it a good investment signature in the years to come. His autograph is valued at $15 to $20. Signed 8 × 10 photographs can be purchased for $40 to $60. A nicely accomplished AMQS is valued at $100.

Mancini-1, undated signature.

Pietro Mascagni was one of the masters of Italian opera. His masterpiece *Cavalleria rusticana* is considered by many to be the greatest opera ever. Mascagni signed in a vertical hand. His signature is bold and is usually finished off with a pronounced paraph. Letter construction and display value are both above average. Most signatures are simply accomplished as "P. Mascagni." Due to the many breaks in the signature, replication of hand is fairly easy. Producing a well-executed forgery takes little effort. Mascagni's signature is somewhat scarce, but an ample supply does exist. Many nicely signed portrait photographs are in the market. His signature can also be found on album pages and AMQsS, which have stunning eye appeal. ALsS are scarce to rare. Mascagni's autograph is surprisingly affordable at $100 to $125. Photographs, ALsS, and AMQsS are valued in the $400 to $600 range.

Mascagni-1, photograph dated 1925.

Jules Massenet was a French composer of operas. Massenet signed in a choppy and truncated hand. Multiple point construction breaks are noted. The signature is large and vertical in nature. Many signatures are simply signed with his last name only. Due to the many breaks in his hand, replication is easy. Producing a well-executed forgery can be done with ease. Massenet is a signature of moderate demand that seems balanced with supply. There is a good supply of ALsS in the market. Other mediums include AMQsS and signed calling cards. Signed photographs of any kind are rare. His signature has fallen out of favor with the market in recent years. Massenet material is rather cheap. A signature can be purchased for $75 to $100. ALsS and AMQsS are very affordable at $150 to $250. I consider Massenet's signature to be one of the

real sleeper signatures that should increase in value in years to come.

Massenet-1, signature dated 1889 (courtesy J.B. Muns Musical Autographs).

Felix Mendelssohn Bartholdy was a brilliant German composer of the early Romantic period. He was a prodigy and his violin concerto is considered one of the greatest works of all time. Mendelssohn signed in a busy and complex hand. His signature evidences many defined angles and directional changes. The signature is dominated by a large capital "F" in the first name. Sound letter construction is noted. The signature evidences moderate display value. The signature is accomplished in a slower, more pensive hand. This results in a signature that is rather easy to forge, at least to the skilled hand. Forgers have targeted Mendelssohn for years and have created some convincing forgeries. The vast majority of Mendelssohn signatures offered in the market are forged. Mendelssohn died at the young age of 38. The supply of genuine material is limited. ALsS and the occasional DS are available. His signature should be considered very scarce. AMQsS are very rare and generally limited to manuscripts or portions thereof, mostly unsigned. AMQsS found with a few bars on album pages or small 8vo sheets are almost certainly forged. Another common forgery is DsS whereby Mendelssohn

Mendelssohn-1, undated signature (courtesy J.B. Muns Musical Autographs).

purportedly is selling the rights to one of his many works. Mendelssohn's signature is in high demand and signed material has become very valuable. His signature is valued at $1,000 to $1,500. A full-page ALS is valued at $5,000. Manuscripts will sell for $10,000 to $15,000 per page. Complete manuscripts are valued in the six figures.

Gian Carlo Menotti was an Italian-American composer. He is a two-time winner of the Pulitzer Prize. Menotti signed in a well-structured and legible hand. His signature has sound display value. One of the nicer classical music autographs. Menotti died in 2007. He was generally unresponsive to mail requests for his signature. His signature is uncommon. ALsS and ANsS do exist, but many are signed with his first name only. There is a small supply of nicely signed 8 × 10 photographs. AMQsS are rare. In recent years forgeries have entered the market. These are fairly well-executed but tend to be looser in construction and lack the tightness of a genuine signature. There is good demand for Menotti material. Expect to pay $125 to $150 for his signature. ALsS and photographs will sell for $225 to $275.

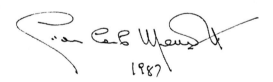

Menotti-1, signature dated 1987.

Ask the question who was the greatest composer and the answer is usually Beethoven or Wolfgang Mozart, famed German composer and one of the most influential men in history. Mozart's signature is one of the most coveted of all. He signed in a slower, more deliberate hand. Sound legibility and letter construction are noted. Due to the slower nature of hand, replication is easy. Well-executed forgeries exist in quantities. Just about all Mozart signatures that have ever been sold are forgeries. Many held by institutional collections are also apoc-

ryphal. Mozart's signature is rare to very rare and generally limited to a scant few signed letters and documents. It should be noted that Mozart's father, Leopold, would pen musical scores for his then young son. These are sometimes wrongly mistaken for the hand of his famous son. Leopold Mozart's hand differs greatly from his son's hand. Mozart's signature is highly treasured; expect to pay $40,000 to $50,000 for a nice specimen.

Mozart-1, undated signature.

Vazgen Muradian is an Armenian composer known for using a wide diversity of instruments in his works. Muradian signed in a tempered hand. The signature is compact and works well on small mediums. Letter construction and display value are average. Muradian has, for many years, been a responsive signer. There is an ample supply of signatures in the market. His signature is mostly found on index cards and photographs. Letters of any kind are very scarce. Signatures penned in Armenian are scarce. Muradian's signature is affordable at $20. AMQsS are valued at $50. Muradian would hand out color 8 × 10 portraits of himself signed and inscribed. On many occasions he would pen a short AMQS. These have nice display value and sell for $100 to $125.

Muradian-1, signed photograph dated 1995.

Jacques Offenbach was a French composer and cellist of the Romantic period. He wrote many operettas including the *Tales of Hoffman*. The dance the can-can, from his work *Orphée aux Enfers*, is a favorite of producers of TV commercials. Offenbach signed in a poorly constructed hand. The signature appears as an illegible scribble. Letter construction is poor. The signature has substandard display value. Due to the sloppy nature of hand, his signature is easily replicated. Well-executed forgeries do exist. Offenbach's signature is scarce and generally limited to ALsS and the occasional signed card. Cabinet photographs and AMQsS are very rare. There is average demand for Offenbach material, which is a mystery to me. His signature is quite affordable and thus could be a sleeper investment in the years to come. A signature is valued at $150 to $200. A full page ALS can be purchased for $500 to $600.

Offenbach-1 (courtesy J.B. Muns Musical Autographs).

German composer Carl Orff gave the music world one of the most powerful of all works in his immortal *Carmina Burana*. Orff signed in a rather plain and practical hand. There is nothing extraordinary about his signature. It has average display value. Given the rather unadorned nature of his hand, replication is fairly easy. Creating a well-executed forgery can be done with little effort. Orff's signature is uncommon to scarce and generally limited to postcard-sized photographs and album pages. AMQsS are scarce. ALsS should be considered rare. Orff's

Orff-1, undated signature (courtesy J.B. Muns Musical Autographs).

signature is valued at $100. An AMQS should sell in the $300 to $400 price range.

Ignacy Jan Paderewski was a Polish composer and patriot who, in 1919, briefly held the position of prime minister of Poland. Paderewski signed in a beautiful and flowing hand. Letter construction is superior. The display value is sound. The signature is finished off with a pronounced paraph. Due to the complex and effortless nature of hand, replication is very difficult. Well-executed forgeries do not exist. The supply of genuine material is strong. During his day he was sought out by collectors of music and political autographs. Signatures exist on most mediums, including calling cards, AMQsS, ALsS, and presentation photographs. Paderewski's signature can be purchased for $150 to $175. ALsS are valued at $350 to $400, multipage specimens, of which many exist, can reach $1,000. A nicely penned AMQS is valued at $500 to $700.

Paderewski-1, undated signature.

Niccolò Paganini was a master of the violin. Caprice No. 24 is among his most famous works. He is one of the truly great Italian composers. Paganini signed in a powerful and bombastic hand. Reckless flow is noted. Scale tends to be on the larger side. Moderate letter construction is noted. A large capital letter "N" in the first name dominates the signature. Overall, a superior display signature. Due to the many breaks in the hand, replication is fairly easy. Many well-executed forgeries exist. The majority of signatures offered in the market are forged. Many forged ANsS are in the market. They are typically written to a theater owner and state something to the effect of "Admit One on Friday the 10th." The forgeries evidence a slight shakiness of hand. A signature that is rare on a per se basis. Inventory is generally limited to a small supply of ALsS and the occasional DS. Expect to pay at least $2,500 for an ALS.

Paganini-1, undated signature.

Indiana native Cole Porter is one of the biggest names of the theater genre. His works, such as "Anything Goes" and "I Get a Kick Out of You," remain popular songs. Porter signed in a very rudimentary hand. The signature is of printed script. Legibility is strong; however, display value is poor. His signature is the easiest of all composers to replicate. Well-executed forgeries exist in quantities. Signatures can be found on checks, DsS, album pages, and small photographs. AMQsS and ALsS are rare. There is good demand for Porter material. A signature will sell for $175 to $200. Smaller sized photographs are valued at $300 to $400. Bank checks sell for $400 to $500. A nicely signed 8 × 10 photograph is highly treasured and worth about $1,000.

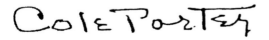

Porter, C-1 undated signature.

Sergei Prokofiev was one of the great Russian composers of the 20th century. *The Love for Three Oranges* and *Peter and the Wolf* are among his notable works. Prokofiev signed in a legible and slightly truncated hand. His signature evidences abrupt angles and lacks clean flow. The signature has average eye appeal. Prokofiev's signature is very scarce and generally limited to ANsS on postcards and the occasional album page. AMQsS and photographs of any kind are rare. There is sound demand for Prokofiev material. His signature is valued at $250 to $300. ALsS, usually found on postcards, can sell for $750 to

$1,000. A nicely accomplished AMQS is in much demand and will sell for $1,500 to $2,000.

Prokofiev-1, undated signature (courtesy J.B. Muns Musical Autographs).

Giacomo Puccini, along with Verdi, is considered one the two greatest composers of Italian operas. Puccini signed in a very sloppy hand with marginal letter construction. Sometimes he would hurry his signature and letters would display themselves as indistinguishable bumps. Many times he would sign as "G. Puccini," other times simply with his last name. A signature in much demand and commonly forged. The majority of Puccini signatures in the market are forged. Forged ALsS and AMQsS are common. One forger has placed many forgeries on unused vintage postcards. Many cards feature scenes or advertisements from Puccini's famous *La Bohème*. There is strong demand for Puccini material. Signatures are valued at $500. Calling cards are available and sell for slightly more. ALsS and AMQsS sell for $1,500 to $2,000 with exceptional examples selling for close to $4,000. Signed photograph postcards are valued at $1,250 to $1,500.

Puccini-1 ALS dated 1912 (courtesy collection of James Neglia).

Sergei Rachmaninoff was one of the last great composers of the Russian Romantic era.

He is one of the personal favorites. Rachmaninoff signed in a very concise and neat hand. The signature evidences good length but impaired height. The signature exhibits multiple breaks in the hand, resulting in a somewhat printed script. A linear paraph typically completes the signature. Due to the many breaks in the hand, replication is fairly easy. Well-executed forgeries exist in quantities. Signatures can be found on postcard-sized photographs, AMQsS, programs, and album pages. Letters of any kind are rare. A full-page ALS is a very rare find. Signatures are valued at $400 to $500. Signed photographs of fair and average disposition generally sell for $750 to $1,250, with exceptional specimens selling for nearly double that amount. A nice multi bar AMQS is a treasure and in high demand. Expect to pay at least $2,500.

Rachmaninoff-1 undated signature, choice specimen.

French composer Maurice Ravel is one of the true giants of 20th-century impressionist

Ravel-1, undated signature (courtesy J.B. Muns Musical Autographs).

music. He is best remembered for the *Bolero* and its methodical beat. Ravel signed in a vertical and compact hand. His signature appears cramped, which impairs display value. Letter construction and legibility are sound. Given the multiple breaks in the hand, his signature is easy to replicate. Well-executed forgeries exist in quantities. There is strong demand for Ravel material. His signature is valued at $500 to $600. Photographs, typically octavo or smaller, sell for $1,250 to $1,500. ALsS are typically found on the backs of postcards and are worth $1,500 to $2,000.

Ottorino Respighi is an Italian composer and conductor best known for three Roman songs. Respighi signed in a very flowing and attractive hand. His signature is legible and evidences good letter construction. It is finished off with a large paraph, which only enhances eye appeal. Due to the complex nature of hand, well-executed forgeries do not exist. Respighi's signature is rare, albeit borderline. It is generally found on AMQsS and the occasional letter. Signed photographs are rare, with a signature usually penned on the bottom matte. There had never been much interest in Respighi material, but that seems to have changed over the past five years. Values have increased. A signature is valued at $100. An AMQS can be purchased for $300 to $400.

Respighi-1, signature dated 1911 (courtesy J.B. Muns Musical Autographs).

Russian composer Nikolai Rimsky-Korsakov composed music that was nationalistic in nature. His works are typically derived from old Russian folk music, which prompted some to criticize his creative processes. He remains, to this day, a giant of classical music. Korsakov signed in a crisp and clean hand. His signature evidences wonderful flow. Letter construction is sound. Good legibility is noted. Signatures are usually accomplished as "N. Rimsky—Korsakov." Due to the flowing nature of hand, replication is very difficult. Well-executed forgeries do not exist. Korsakov is a scarce signature on a per se basis. Premium items are rare to very rare. Cabinet photographs exist and are typically signed on the verso. Many incorporate a short AMQ. Album pages are also available. Full-page ALsS are rare, but some nice 8vo multi-page examples exist. Demand for Korsakov material has increased greatly in the past few years. Expect to pay $700 to $900 for his signature. Photographs and ALsS are valued at $3,000 to $4,000. A nice AMQS will sell for $5,000 to $7,500.

Rimsky-Korsakov-1, ANS dated 1907 (courtesy Nate D. Sanders Auctions).

Noted American composer Richard Rodgers composed countless works, among them 43 Broadway musicals. He teamed up with lyricists Lorenz Hart, and later Oscar Hammerstein II, to create some of the most memorable works of the 20th century. Rodgers signed in a somewhat unstructured hand. The signature appears rudimentary with below-average eye appeal. Overall, just a plain and unassuming signature. Due to the less sophisticated nature of hand, replication is rather easy. Creating a well-executed forgery can be done with ease. An ample supply keeps values depressed. Signatures exist on most mediums. ALsS and AMQsS are rare. Rodgers's signature is affordable at $75. TLsS and photographs can be purchased for $150 to $200. A nice AMQS should sell for $500 to 700. Anything signed with Hart is rare and worth a premium. Hart's signature by itself is valued at $500 to $600.

Rodgers-1, undated signature.

Hart-1, album page circa 1940.

Hammerstein remains to this day the most prolific lyricist in history. He won an incredible eight Tony Awards. Hammerstein signed in a rapid and fairly unstructured hand. The last name appears as indistinguishable strokes and the last three letters are reduced to a scrawl. Later signatures are even more poorly formed, with most letters constructed as a simplistic wavy line. The signature exhibits substandard display value. The signature lacks complexity of any kind, and thus replication of hand is fairly easy. Well-executed forgeries can be produced with ease. Some TLsS are secretarially signed. The supply of Hammerstein material is ample and balanced with demand. His signature can be found on postcard-sized photographs, album pages, programs, and TLsS. ALsS and 8 × 10 photographs are rare. Hammerstein's signature is quite affordable at $75 to $100. TLsS and photographs sell for $150 to $175. Material countersigned by Rodgers is somewhat scarce and will sell for $300 to $400.

Hammerstein-1, undated signature (courtesy J.B. Muns Musical Autographs).

Sigmund Romberg was an Austro-Hungarian composer who created many operettas. Romberg signed in a very aggressive hand. His signature is reckless in appearance with substandard letter construction. Display value is marginal at best. Due to the rapid nature of hand, his signature would be a challenge to copy. Fortunately, his signature is affordable and does not attract the attention of skilled forgers. Signatures are usually found on letters, musical programs, album pages, and the occasional photo. World War I era bank checks are in the market. His signature is valued at $50 to $75. A nice ALS or 8 × 10 photograph will sell in the $250 to $350 price range.

Romberg-1 Album page circa 1930.

Gioachino Rossini is often referred to as the "Italian Mozart." He composed 39 operas and is noted for beautiful church melodies. Rossini signed in a practical and pensive hand. Recklessness of hand is lacking and slower strokes are noted. The signature has a fair amount of legibility. Display value is average. Most signatures are accomplished as "G. Rossini." Rossini was a superstar of his day and was actively sought out by early collectors. His signature is somewhat scarce, but an ample supply does exist. Mediums available are ALsS, bank checks, AMQsS, and cabinet photographs, though photographs are considered very rare and most offered in the market are forged. One commonly forged cabinet card features Rossini standing next to a table with his left hand on a book. The forger signs it as "G Rossini" and dates it. He also adds the word "Paris" on many of the cards.

There is strong demand for Rossini material. Expect to pay $500 for a signature. ALsS and bank checks are available for $1,000 to $1,500. A nicely signed cabinet photograph and AMQsS are valued at $2,500 to $3,500.

Rossini-1, undated signature.

One of the more affordable signatures is that of French composer and conductor Camille Saint-Saëns. Saint-Saëns is best known for his works "The Carnival of the Animals" and the Opera *Samson and Delilah*. Saint-Saëns signed in a very unstructured hand. Signatures tend to have malformed letters. Sometimes the signature displays as a mere scribble. Legibility tends to be impaired, as is display value. Many signatures are signed as "C. Saint Saëns." The signature is typically finished off with a paraph. Signatures are typically limited to ALsS, AMQsS, and calling cards. Less common are photographs. A signature of ample supply and marginal demand. Interest in Saint-Saëns has waned in the past couple of decades. His signature has declined in value. Today, a signature can be purchased for $50 to $75. ALsS, AMQsS, and photographs can be purchased for $300 to $400.

Saint-Saëns-1 undated signature (courtesy J.B. Muns Musical Autographs).

Austrian Arnold Schoenberg (*né* Schönberg) was a significant member of the Expressionist movement. He was also an accomplished painter. In the 1940s his music ran afoul with the Nazi Party in Austria. Schoenberg signed in a very choppy hand that evidences sharp angles. Letter construction and display value are both of average disposition. Replication of hand is moderately difficult, though some well-executed forgeries do exist. His signature is scarce on a per se basis. Schoenberg's signature can be found on calling cards, ALsS, and photographs. AMQsS are rare and highly collected. Schoenberg's signature is valued at $250 to $300. An ALS will sell for $1,000 to $1,500. An AMQS is valued at $2,000 to $2,500.

Schonberg-1 undated DS.

German composer Franz Schubert was a prolific composer who created a wide variety of music, including chamber and liturgical works. He is considered one of the giants of classical music. Signatures are penned in a truncated German script. The signature is basically illegible. His signature is often passed by simply because it is so cloaked in impaired construction. Signatures are very rare on a per se basis and are generally limited to signed manuscripts, with musical notes penned on both sides. The occasional ALS will surface, but most material has been absorbed by major institutional collections and will likely never enter the market again. Forgeries are very common and just about 100 percent of Schubert signatures offered in the market are forged. His signature will likely sell for $15,000 to $20,000. Manuscripts will sell for $40,000 to $50,000 per page.

Schubert-1, undated signature.

Dmitri Shostakovich was an important Russian composer of the 20th century. His music blended many cultural melodies from traditional Russian to western Europe. His music would often run afoul with the Communist Party. Shostakovich signed in a very rounded and loose hand. His signature evidences uneven placement of letters. The display value is substandard. Signatures are usually accomplished as "D. Shostakovich." Due to the pensive and slower nature of his signature, replication of hand is easy. Well-executed forgeries exist in quantities. If you run across a Shostakovich signature, it is likely forged. Signatures are very scarce to rare and generally limited to holographic envelopes and ANsS. Photographs and AMQsS are rare and highly treasured. Shostakovich died in 1975 and is a very difficult signature to locate. Like Hovhaness, his signature is a modern rarity. Expect to pay $400 to $500 for a nice signature. Letters, AMQsS, and photographs will all sell for over $1,000.

Shostokovich-1 undated signature.

Jean Sibelius was a Finnish composer from the later part of the Romantic period. *Finlandia* is his best known of many fine works. Sibelius signed in a very nonconforming and eclectic hand. The signature is dominated by a large capital "J." His signature evidences many breaks in the hand. The hand lacks flow. A certain pensiveness is noted. His signature has below average display value. Signatures accomplished later in life evidence a shakiness of hand. He made liberal use of the pencil and signed many correspondences with such. Due to the truncated nature of the signature, replication of hand is very easy. Many well-executed forgeries exist. There is a good supply of Sibelius material in the market. He lived until 1957 and was responsive to autograph requests. Mediums include

AMQsS, TLsS, ALsS, album pages, and programs. Photographs are fairly scarce. Signatures are valued at $300 to $350. A TLS will sell for $400 to $500. A nice ALS is valued in the $800 to $1,000 range. AMQsS, limited to a couple of bars, sell for $500 to $600. Multi-bar specimens are valued at $1,000.

Sibelius-1, signature dated 1907 (courtesy J.B. Muns Musical Autographs).

S. Gevorgi Soghomonyan (le révérend Père Komitas, *né* Gomidas) was a student of Makar Yekmalyan. He was an Armenian priest known for creating beautiful church hymns, and is a signature of great rarity. After witnessing the horrors of the Armenian Genocide, Komitas withdrew from the world. He became very reclusive and signed very little. Today, his signature is very rare and one of the most difficult to locate of any of the 20th-century composers. I am told a few signed piano folios exist, but I have not seen them. They are said to be inscribed to fellow composers. There have been no recent sales of Komitas's signature. The illustrated signature is held by the Armenian Church in Etchmiadzin, Armenia. Value is indeterminate. Autograph dealer Gabriel Boyers, owner of Schubertiade Music, estimates a value of $1,500 for Komitas's signature. Autographically speaking, a 20th-century rarity.

Komitas-1 undated signature (courtesy Armenian Apostolic Church, Mother See of Holy Etchmiadzin).

American John Phillip Sousa was a composer and conductor. He was known as the "American

March King." His works are very patriotic. "The Stars and Stripes Forever" is synonymous with the 4th of July. Sousa signed in a very tempered and confined hand. His signature works well on small mediums. Legibility and letter construction are sound. Due to the slower nature of hand, replication is rather easy. Well-executed forgeries exist in quantities. Sousa was an accommodating signer. His signature is considered uncommon to scarce. Signatures are typically found on album pages, programs, and photographs of various sizes. AMQsS are also available but should be considered scarce. ALsS are rare and seldom surface. A small supply of bank checks is in the market, but these are considered rare. Sousa had a bad habit of signing photographs and picture postcards on the dark portion of the image, impairing display value. Sousa's signature is valued at $100 to $125. An AMQS sells for $400 to $500. A nicely signed 8 × 10 photograph is valued at $750 to $1,000. A signature that can be added to your collection without much effort.

Sousa-1 AMQS dated 1906 (courtesy collection of James Neglia).

Sousa-1, ALS dated 1893 (courtesy Stephen Koschal Autographs).

Austrian composer Johann Strauss II was known as the Waltz King. He composed countless works, with the "Blue Danube" being his most famous. Strauss signed in a choppy and vertical hand. His signature is marked with abrupt turns. The signature has superior display value, in part due to a bold paraph. It is a signature that is easily forged. Many forgeries exist on album pages. Some contain a bar or two of music and were accomplished by a forger who made liberal use of the pencil. Strauss's signature is scarce on a per se basis. Premium items are rare. Most common are calling cards and signatures removed from documents. Album pages are also available. Signed cabinet cards, ALsS, and AMQsS are rare and highly treasured. Strauss's signature is surprisingly affordable at $275 to $300. AMQsS sell for $2,000 to $3,000, with lengthy specimens double that amount. Cabinet photographs make for a fine display and can be purchased at $1,500 to $2,000. Strauss's father, Johann Strauss I, was also a noted composer. His signature is rarer than that of his more famous son. He was known as Strauss the Elder; his signature is illustrated.

Strauss, J-1, undated signature (courtesy J.B. Muns Musical Autographs).

Strauss, J-2, The Elder.

Richard Strauss was a German composer whose career spanned the Romantic and modern eras. He is best known for operas. Strauss signed in a unique hand. The signature evidences many sharp turns and displays itself as jagged. Generally illegible, the signature has

moderate display value. Due to the slower nature of hand, replication is fairly easy. Well-executed forgeries exist, though generally limited to premium items. Strauss lived until 1949 and signed many items postwar. He was specifically targeted by collectors; hence, a decent supply of material exists. Mediums includes postcard-sized photographs, ALsS, TLsS, AMQsS, album pages, and the occasional postal cover. Strauss wrote in a uniformed hand, resulting in ALsS with strong display value. Strauss's signature is affordable at $150 to $200. ALsS and postcard sized photographs sell for $300 to $400. Exceptional signed presentation photographs sells for $1,250 to $1,500.

Strauss, R-1, LS circa 1940.

Igor Stravinsky was a prolific composer with works that spanned many decades. He gained much fame when his ballet *The Firebird* was released in 1910. Stravinsky signed in an aggressive hand. His signature lacks hesitation. The hand appears choppy with compacted letters. Substandard display value is noted. Stravinsky was a prolific signer for most of his long life. Signatures can be found on TLsS, ALsS (many

Stravinsky-1, signature dated 1954 (courtesy J.B. Muns Musical Autographs).

of which are simply signed as "I. Str."), AMQsS, photographs, and books. ALsS signed in full are rare. Demand for Stravinsky material has jumped in recent years, pushing values ever higher. Signatures are valued at $200 to $225. ALsS sell anywhere from $750 to $1,250, with multi-page specimens selling for $2,500 to $3,500. Photographs and AMQsS are value $750 to $1,000.

Arthur Sullivan was an English composer of Gilbert and Sullivan fame. He teamed with William Gilbert for 14 light operas, among them *HMS Pinafore* and *The Pirates of Penzance*. Sullivan signed in a neat hand. His signature evidences sound letter construction. Strong legibility is noted. The signature is usually finished off with a linear paraph. Due to the lack of recklessness, replication of hand is fairly easy. Well-executed forgeries do exist. Sullivan's signature is typically found on ALsS, most always with routine content. AMQsS are rare. Photographs are very rare. Anything signed with Gilbert would be considered very rare. I have never seen a genuine dual-signed item. Many forgeries do exist. Sullivan's signature is affordable at $150 to $200. ALsS can sell for anywhere from $600 to $1,000, depending on length. An AMQS is a treasured item and will sell for $1,250 to $1,500.

Sullivan-1 AMQS dated 1895 (courtesy University of Rochester Libraries).

Sir William Gilbert material is more difficult to locate then that of Sullivan. His signature is considered very scarce on a per se basis and generally limited to ALsS and ANsS. Gilbert's signature is signed in a more rapid hand than that of Sullivan. The signature is compact with poor letter construction. The capital "G" in the last name displays itself as a letter "T." Legibility

is impaired. A nice ALS is valued at $400 to $500.

Gilbert-1 ALS dated 1870 (courtesy University of Rochester Libraries).

Pyotr Tchaikovsky is the most famous of all Russian composers and one of the giants of classical music. A signature with sound letter construction. Average display value is noted. Due to the many breaks in the hand, his signature is very easy to forge. Many well-executed forgeries exist in the market. Cabinet cards are a favorite of forgers. Many are signed as "P. Tchaikovsky" and dated. A signature that is rare on a per se basis. Just about all signatures offered for sale are forgeries. His signature is usually found on the occasional letter and on AMQsS. Signed photographs are an extreme rarity. The demand for Tchaikovsky material is great and values continue to rise. Tchaikovsky's signature is valued at $4,000 to $5,000. An ALS will sell for $15,000 to $20,000. AMQsS are valued at $15,000 to $20,000, with lengthy ex-

Tchaikovsky-1 AMQS 1893 (courtesy Carnegie Hall Archives).

amples being valued at $30,000 or more. A complete musical manuscript would easily sell for high six figures, perhaps $1,000,000.

to $5,000. An AMQS will sell for $4,000 to $5,000. Lengthy examples can sell for $15,000 to $20,000.

Verdi-2, signature dated 1887 (courtesy J.B. Muns Musical Autographs).

Tchaikovsky-2 AMQS 1891 (courtesy Carnegie Hall Archives).

The Italian master Giuseppe Verdi is considered one of the most important composers of operas in history. Verdi signed in a very odd and carefree hand. His signature exhibits loose letter construction and almost always signed as "G Verdi." Eye appeal is superior due to the swirling and complex paraph. Replication of hand is very easy. The vast majority, over 90 percent, of all Verdi signatures offered in the market are forged. Verdi's signature is scarce to rare and generally limited to ALsS, most with routine content. Genuine AMQsS and photographs are very rare. A common forgery is typically found on Spezia cabinet cards or AMQsS in a tremulous hand. The forgeries are usually dated 1895 or later. The forger usually places a single and fairly straight line above the forgery. His signature is valued at $1,000 to $1,500. ALsS will sell for $2,500 to $4,000. Signed cabinet photographs are a rarity and are valued at $4,000

Perhaps the greatest German composer of the 19th century was Richard Wagner. His music is titanic in construction and hits you like a freight train. Wagner signed in a flowing and pleasing hand. His signature has average letter construction. Display value is above average. Due to the lack of rapid flow, Wagner's signature is fairly easy to replicate and many well-executed forgeries exist. Forgeries are typically found on AMQsS, ALsS, and cabinet cards. Wagner's signature is scarce and almost always found on ALsS or signatures removed therefrom. Secretarial signatures are known. The demand for Wagner material is strong and far outweighs supply. His signature is valued at $750 to $900. An ALS with routine content is valued at $2,000. Exceptional examples can sell for

Wagner-1, undated signature (courtesy J.B. Muns Musical Autographs).

Verdi-1, undated AMS.

Wagner-2, common secretarial signature.

$5,000 to $10,000. An AM is highly valued and will sell for $15,000 to $20,000 for a single leaf.

Carl Maria von Weber was a noted German composer and one of the first of the Romantic period. His operas *Der Freischutz* and *Oberon* proved influential on later German operas. Weber signed in a tempered hand. The signature has muted letter construction. Average display value is noted. Most signatures are penned as "C.M. v Weber." Due to the slower nature of hand, his signature is quite easy to replicate. Well-executed forgeries exist in quantities. If you see a Weber signature for sale, it is very likely a forgery. Weber's signature is rare on a per se basis. He died of consumption at the age of 39. Signatures are generally limited to ALsS or signatures removed therefrom. A common forgery is a signature with three or four sentences purportedly written by von Weber and dated. They are typically cut from larger preprinted music sheets. Von Weber's signature has always been affordable, but in recent year prices have increased markedly. His signature is valued at $500 to $600. Full-page ALsS will sell for $1,500 to $1,750.

von Weber-1, undated signature (courtesy Mark Allen Baker).

Kurt Weill was a Jewish composer who hailed from Dessau, Germany. His works for the stage are well known, among them "Mack the Knife." Weill signed in a very tempered hand. His signature works well on small mediums. Letter construction, legibility, and eye appeal are all simply average. Since he signed in a slower, more thoughtful hand, replication is very easy. Well-executed forgeries exist in quantities. His signature is scarce on a per se basis. Premium items are rare to very rare. He died in 1950 at a relatively young age; hence, the supply of his autograph is limited. His signature usually turns up on calling cards and the occasional album page. AMQsS, photographs, and letters of any kind are rare. Just about all AMQsS in the market are forgeries. They typically evidence a slight shakiness of hand. There is moderate demand for Weill material. A signature is valued at $150 to $200. A nicely accomplished AMQS is a true find, so expect to pay $1,000.

Weill-1 signature dated 1949 (courtesy collection of James Neglia).

John Williams is generally considered on the greatest composer of film scores in history. His works include *Star Wars, Superman, E.T. the Extra-Terrestrial, Raiders of the Lost Ark, Lost in Space*, and the list goes on and on. Williams signs in a rather pensive and unassuming hand. The signature evidences choppiness and lacks flow. Letter construction is average. Display value is substandard. Williams has, for many years, been a willing and gracious signer. Starting around 2010 he has limited mail requests to one signature per person. The supply of material is strong. His signature can be found on photographs, gum cards, AMQsS, and index cards. Letters of any kind are scarce to rare. There are many forgeries in the market, espe-

Williams, J-1, undated signature.

cially when it comes to movie posters. Williams's signature is affordable at $25. Signed photographs and AMQsS sell for $100 to $150. A signed *Star Wars* movie poster will sell for $200 to $250. His signature will prove a fine investment in the years to come.

Collectable music autographs are not limited to just the composers. Opera stars are avidly collected and have a large following. Some signatures can get quite pricey, such as Enrico Caruso, Maria Callas, Francesco Tamagno, Kirsten Flagstad, and the like. Conductors are also in demand, most notably Herbert von Karajan, Georg Solti, Andre Kostelanetz, and the Greek master Dimitri Mitropoulos. Classical musicians are also in demand and are a welcome addition to any signature library. Vladimir Horowitz, Van Cliburn (a rather scarce signature), Yehudi Menuhin, Isaac Stern, Jascha Heifetz, Victor Borge (one of my favorites), Pablo Casals, and the flamboyant signature of Liberace are just of a few of the many collectable musicians.

Cliburn-1 signature dated 1958.

Horowitz-1 signature dated 1969 (courtesy collection of James Neglia).

Kostelanetz-1 undated ALS.

Solti-1 undated signature.

Once you start collecting classical music autographs, you will never stop.

Borge-1, signed card circa 1990.

Kings, Queens and Other Leaders of the World, Their Supporters and Adversaries

World leaders and heads of state have always been a popular field within the autograph industry. There are many countries to choose from. Unlike other fields of interest, signatures of royals from the 1400s, though rare, are available for purchase. The signatures of leaders of European countries and England are highly collectable. There are numerous prime ministers and regents to choose from. Some signatures are exceedingly rare and exist only with governmental concerns. Signatures of William the Conqueror or Ivan the Terrible would be amazing finds.

There are many subsets collectors will focus on, such as kings and queens of a particular nation or house. Prime ministers are also popular and are very affordable. Completing a signed set of British prime ministers can be done with only a modest amount of money. Signatures of leaders from other areas of the world exist in far smaller quantities and are vastly more difficult to find. Of course, there are not many collectors, relatively speaking, trying to assemble sets of leaders from, say, the Middle East. Many of these signatures can be purchased for a song. Signatures of leaders of smaller countries such as Latvia, Estonia, Chile, and the like are also very affordable.

Signatures of the leaders of the Far East, such as China and Japan, have increased in value due to greater demand in recent years. Leaders of India are also popular, and with that nation's economy expanding, values of those autographs will increase in the coming years.

Since the demise of the USSR, Soviet-era signatures have become more popular than ever. Signatures of Anastas Mikoyan, Andrei Gromyko, Konstantin Chernenko, and Alexei Kosygin were of modest value just a few years back. Today, these signatures have seen a demonstrable increase in value. Vladimir Putin is putting his mark on history and should prove a collectable signature in the years to come.

The most widely collected of the world leaders are, by far, presidents of the United States. Content letters of Washington, Adams, Jefferson, and Lincoln are among the most valued of all. Not many letters cross the million-dollar threshold, but certain content presidential letters will break that mark.

The following is a list of some of the more popular heads of state. This list is by no means exhaustive; they are some of my personal favorites. I couldn't find a good fit for Lord Nelson or Captain Bligh in any other part of the book; hence, you will find their signature studies contained herein.

Ferdinand and Isabella ruled Castile and *León* as king and queen. Both are major figures in world history. They bankrolled Christopher Columbus's voyage to the New World. They also brought forth the Spanish Inquisition and the rise of Torquemada. Their signatures are sloppy and unrecognizable. Signatures are penned with their royal titles as "Yo, el Rey" and "Reyna." The signatures display themselves as a bunch of tangled lines strewn about in a haphazard fashion. There is no legibility to speak of, at least to the modern eye. Both signatures are rare to very rare on a per se basis and generally limited to a minute supply of dual-signed royal documents and a few LsS. There is a bit more inventory of Isabella LsS in the market. For being such important figures in history, their signatures are affordable, relatively speaking. A dual-signed document is valued at $15,000 to $17,500. LsS by Isabella can be purchased for $4,000 to $5,000. These signatures should carry much more value than they currently do.

thodic nature of the signature, replication of hand is very easy. Well-executed forgeries exist. Just about all Henry VIII signatures offered in the market are forged. There are many forged LsS, some of which are penned in French. The forger adds staining and paper loss to enhance genuineness. It should also be noted that King Henry had a stamp made of his signature. The king made liberal use of this stamp. Many royal DsS are actually signed with this stamp. It is said that the king cherished this stamp and guarded it well. Documents must be examined carefully as they likely contain a stamped signature. The stamped signature is illustrated. Henry material is very rare to extremely rare. Market inventory has been wrongly inflated by the quantities of forged letters and documents. Demand is very strong for King Henry's signature. Expect to pay $35,000 to $50,000 for a LS or DS.

Ferdinand-1, undated signature (courtesy Stephen Koschal Reference Library).

Henry VIII-1, undated signature.

Isabella-1, undated signature (courtesy Stephen Koschal Reference Library).

Henry VIII-2, stamped signature.

King Henry VIII is probably the most famous king of England. He severed the Church of England from Rome. He was married six times to women who all died young, some by illness and some by chopping block. Henry VIII is an almost mythical figure in world history. King Henry signed in a pleasing hand, for the time period anyway. The signature is just about illegible and penned in a slow script, not uncommon for the time period. Given the me-

King Philip II ruled Spain from 1556 until his death in 1598. He was a devout Catholic and organized the 140-ship Spanish Armada to lead an invasion of Protestant England and remove Elizabeth I from power. En route to England, the Armada ran into heavy storms. Many ships were lost. The Armada was decimated. Philip's signature is signed with his title as "Yo, el Rey" (I, the King). The signature is sloppy and nonconforming. Legibility is very much impaired. His signature is somewhat rare, but a good number of DsS exist, many with water damage.

This is about the only medium you will find King Philip's signature on. For such a major figure in European history, his signature is on the cheap side. DsS sell for $750 to $1,000. An important and undervalued royal signature.

Phillip II-1, undated signature.

The fifth and last monarch of the Tudors was Queen Elizabeth I. She was the daughter of Henry VIII and Anne Boleyn. She ruled England from 1558 until her death in 1603. Her reign is known as the Elizabethan era. Queen Elizabeth's signature is one of the oddest in all of autographdom. It is part signature and part architecture. The signature is signed in printed script. Many letters contain tailing strokes of ink that seem to go on and on. It is one of the most display-worthy signatures I have ever seen. Given the printed script, replication of hand is very easy. The challenge with producing a convincing forgery is not with the physical construction of the signature, but rather making it

appear 400 years old. Queen Elizabeth's signature is very rare and occasionally surfaces on DsS and LsS. A signature of great demand. Signed material will sell anywhere from $20,000 to $40,000. A content letter would likely sell for over $100,000.

Armand Cardinal Richelieu was a French clergyman. He was consecrated a bishop in 1607, then cardinal in 1622. A confidante of King Louis XIII, Richelieu became a powerful figure and virtual ruler of France. Signatures are large, bold, and penned in a powerful hand. Signatures are accomplished with his holy title "Le Card de Richelieu." Signatures also exist as Bishop of Luçon; these, however, are much rarer. Generally not the target of skilled forgers as Richelieu's signatures was; for many years, not worth a lot. In the 1990s, LsS could be purchased for $400 to $500. His signature is generally found on LsS and DsS. Demand has increased greatly over the past ten or so years. Today LsS and DsS are valued at $2,000 to $2,500. A very important figure in French history.

Richelieu-1, undated signature.

Oliver Cromwell is one of the truly legendary names of history. He was a member of Parliament who rose to become the first Lord Protector of the Commonwealth. To my knowledge, Cromwell remains the only ruler of England to be posthumously executed. Cromwell signed in a slower, more methodic hand. Letters are well formed. A sound display value is noted. Signatures are typically signed as "O. Cromwell" or "Oliver P." Signatures accomplished in the last few years of life will evidence a material unsteadiness. Given the slow nature of the writing, replication of hand is very easy. Well-executed forgeries exist in quantities. Close to

Elizabeth I-1 undated signature.

100 percent of all Cromwell signatures ever offered for sale are forgeries.

One common forgery is a portion of a signatory page. Written across the top is "To His Highness [or Highnesse] Oliver Lord Protector." Some 20 to 30 forgeries are added underneath, purportedly gentry of the day. An old-age signature of Cromwell is added, signed as "Oliver P." Sometimes a handwritten endorsement will appear next to the signature. These forgeries are rather convincing, so careful examination is needed.

Another forgery that has surfaced recently is placed on a fragment of a larger document and usually signed as "O. Cromwell." The forgery is typically placed underneath a handwritten sentence or two from the closing of the manuscript. Sometimes a forged witness's signature is added to the left. Some may contain a red wax seal. These forgeries appear to be originating from England.

Cromwell material is very rare. A restricted supply of LsS and DsS exist. ALsS are an extreme rarity. Cromwell's signature will sell for $5,000 to $7,000. DsS and LsS are valued anywhere from $7,500 to $15,000. A full-page ALS

Cromwell-1, undated signature.

Cromwell-2, signature as Lord Protector.

should sell for $30,000 to $40,000. Autographically, a very important name in history.

Frederick II was King of Prussia from 1740 to 1786. He was a patron of the arts and brought forth Prussia's era of enlightenment. His reign greatly enhanced the Prussian nation. He became known as Frederick the Great. Frederick signed in a rapid and unstructured hand. The signature displays itself as a scrawl. No legibility is noted. The signature is typically finished off with a long tail. Frederick's signature is scarce to rare. About the only medium available is LsS. Some letters are secretarially signed. ALsS are rare. Given his importance in history, Frederick's signature is vastly undervalued. LsS can be purchased for as little as $600. I consider King Fredrick's autograph to be one of the most undervalued of all historical autographs.

Frederick the Great-1, undated signature.

Catherine II, better known as Catherine the Great, was Empress of Russia from 1762 to 1796, the year of her death. She ushered in Russia's golden age. She was a patron of the arts and academia. Her armies crushed the Ottoman Turks in Russo-Turkish wars. Catherine signed in a dominant and strong hand. The signature evidences good flow. Signatures can be found both in English and Russian script. Russian script is signed as "Yakaterina." The rather complex nature of hand deters forgers. Well-executed forgeries are few and far between. Catherine is a very important figure in European history. Demand for her autograph has always been sound. Her signature is scarce to very scarce and limited to DsS and LsS. ALsS are rare. The majority of autographs in the market are signed with her Russian name. Catherine's signature has always been on the expensive side.

DsS and LsS are valued at $4,000 to $5,000. ALsS are treasured, so expect to pay $7,500 to $10,000 for a nice specimen.

Catherine the Great-1, undated signature (courtesy The Sanders Autograph Price Guide).

Holy Roman Empress Maria Theresa was the last of the Habsburg rulers. She ascended to the throne upon the death of her father Charles VI. She was the mother of Marie Antoinette. Empress Maria signed in a bold and flowing hand. Her signature evidences good letter construction. Her signature is scarce, albeit borderline. Many DsS and LsS as empress are in the market. A large supply of LsS keeps prices in check. Her signature is generally not the target of skilled forgers. Her signature can be purchased for $400. LsS and DsS are valued anywhere from $500 to $1,000.

Theresa-1, undated signature.

Marie Antoinette is one of the most famous figures in history. She was the daughter of Maria Theresa. She married the Dauphin Louis-Auguste, who later ascended to the throne of France as King Louis XVI. Portrayed as aloof and lavishly wasteful, Antoinette went to the guillotine on October 16, 1793, a victim of the French Revolution.

Antoinette signed in a choppy and basically printed script. The signature is legible with sound letter construction. An average display value is noted. The signature evidences many breaks; as a result, replication of hand is very easy. Well-executed forgeries exist in quantities. Close to 100 percent of all Antoinette signatures offered in the market are forged. Her signature is rare to very rare and generally limited to DsS. Letters of any kind would be an extreme rarity. Some DsS are signed simply as "La Reine" (The Queen). These are far less desirable. There are two common forgeries to note. One is ANsS on small sheets of paper, usually 3"x3" or perhaps slightly larger. The content is something to the effect she has counseled the king or is passing the king's advice to the recipient of the note. The forged signature is large and blocky. It appears sloppy when compared to the genuine signature. For some reason the forger adds a linear paraph under the signature, something I have never seen a genuine specimen exhibit. Pronounced bleeding of the ink is noted. These are almost childish forgeries.

Many Antoinette signatures have been removed from royal documents and sold. Sometimes this is done for convenience (it's easier to transport a small clipped signature) but sometimes it is done to hide theft of a stolen document. Either way, this practice makes me cringe. But in the world of forgery nothing goes to waste. Many documents, with the signature removed, are coveted by the forger. A period French document with known writing of a royal scrivener is perfect to perpetrate a fraud. A forgery of Antoinette is added to these fragments. Many times a short holographic endorsement is also forged. These are tricky because they contain genuine, period ink and are written by known royal secretaries. Many times the forgery will be darker than the rest of the ink with thicker ink strokes. A slight bleeding effect is noted. Many of these forgeries are in the market, so caution is warranted.

There is strong demand for Antoinette material. DsS, about the only medium available, will sell for close to $10,000. DsS with "La Reine" can be purchased for $3,000 to $4,000.

e/Marie antoinette

Antoinette-1, DS dated 1781.

Material signed by Louis XVI is also coveted, but not nearly as much as his wife's signature. Like Marie Antoinette, Louis was also seen as aloof. He attempted to impose sweeping reforms that alienated him among French nobility. He ran up the country's debt and was increasingly viewed as a tyrant by the masses. He was executed on January 21, 1793. He was the last king of France.

Louis signed in a very odd and flowing hand. The signature displays itself with successive loops. It is rarely forged. About the only medium available is DsS. Some are secretarially signed, but fortunately there is no attempt to copy Louis' hand. Expect to pay $1,250 to $1,750 for a nicely signed document.

Louis XVI-1 undated signature.

Jacobin politician Maximilien de Robespierre was the face of the French Revolution. He eventually fell out of favor with the new government and was arrested. Sentenced to death, he was held in the same jail cell that had held Marie Antoinette a year before. Robespierre was beheaded on July 28, 1794.

Robespierre signed in a rather small and dainty hand. The signature is surprisingly unassuming for the man who brought about the

Reign of Terror. The signature is typically finished with and elongated letter "e" at the end of the last name. The reserved nature of the signature correlates into many well-executed forgeries in the market. Just about all Robespierre signatures offered in the market are forgeries. The most common are signatures purportedly removed from a larger document. These are signed in a slow and shaky hand. The last letter "e" in the last name is very long and tremulous. These forgeries are amateurish in construction and are exposed with little effort. At least one major auction house has sold this type of forgery. Signatures are limited to DsS and LsS during the time of the Revolution. They are usually countersigned by other revolutionaries, such as Lazarre Carnot. For such a historical figure in French history, his signature is affordable. DsS and LsS can be purchased for $2,000 to $4,000.

Robespierre

Robespierre-1, ALS circa 1790.

One of the most famous men in history is Napoleon Bonaparte. Napoleon's rise to power resulted largely from the French Revolution. His reign as emperor of France began in 1804 and lasted until 1814, then briefly again in 1815. Napoleon's forces faced the armies of the Seventh Coalition under the command of the Duke of Wellington and Marshal Gebhard von Blücher. Napoleon's defeat at Waterloo ended his reign as emperor. He was confined the Island of Saint Helena in the middle of the Atlantic Ocean. He died in exile at age 51.

Napoleon's signature is one that went through material evolution, and not in a good way. Through the years his signature becomes less structured. Illegibility becomes more pronounced. The signature is, at times, reduced to a scrawl. Signatures accomplished before his reign are typically signed with his last name only. Early signatures tend to be legible and have sound display value. Once he attained the emperorship, he changed his signature. He signed documents as "Napoléon." It became apparent that Napoleon had to sign countless documents, letters, and endorsements. He shortened the signature to "Napol." As his reign continued, the structure of hand further eroded. His began to sign his name as "Napo" and sometimes as "Nap." Finally his signature was reduced to "Np" or sometimes just a large letter "N." No matter when a signature was created, it will always be accompanied by a large and arrogant paraph. Signatures accomplished during the final few years of life evince a slight hesitation. These signatures tend to be loose and larger in appearance. I have never seen a genuine signature signed in full.

Napoleon's autograph is one of the most desired of all. The demand for his signature is great. Value lies not in rarity but in insurmountable demand. Fortunately for collectors, Napoleon signed thousands upon thousands of items. The supply of material is sound, allowing collectors to obtain a coveted Napoleon signature at a reasonable price. The most common medium is partly printed DsS. Napoleon would typically sign these in the left-hand margin using an abbreviated form of signature, typically "N" or "Np." LsS also exist in good numbers. Many of these are written to Napoleon's ministers. On occasion, Napoleon would add an endorsement, usually between one and six words. Other mediums are extremely rare to nonexistent. ALsS seldom surface and are treasured. Just about all Napoleon letters and documents relate to his official capacity as military officer or emperor. Personal correspondence would be very rare.

Forgeries exist in quantities but are generally limited to signatures purportedly removed from a document. Secretarial signatures do exist on documents signed as a military officer. Secretarial signatures lack the paraph found on a genuine specimen. From December 1799 to May 1804, Napoleon served as first consul. There are many signatures from his tenure as consul accomplished as "Bonaparte." These signatures

appear choppy and evidence a material deviation of hand from other signatures penned as "Bonaparte." I believe these to be secretarially signed, though others disagree with me. See illustration. Signatures signed as consul should be carefully examined.

The value of Napoleon's signature increases at slow and steady pace. LsS with routine content are valued at $2,000 to $2,500. DsS are slightly more affordable at $1,500. I have not seen an ALS offered for sale in years; I esti-

Napoleon-1, DS dated 1796.

Napoleon-2, signature, circa 1805.

Napoleon-3, common secretarial.

Napoleon-4, apocryphal signature as first consul.

mate a value of $30,000 to $40,000. One with strong content would likely sell for more than $100,000.

Arthur Wellesley, the Duke of Wellington, defeated Napoleon at Waterloo. Wellington also served as prime minister of England on two separate occasions. Wellington material also exists in good quantities. There is a good number of ALsS and free franks in the market. Demand for Wellington material is muted, which simply amazes me. ALsS can be purchased for a mere $250. Franks are even more affordable at $50 to $75. Von Blücher's signature is far scarcer than that of Wellington. As with Wellington, demand is average at best. Von Blücher's signature can be secured for $200. ALsS are rare and sell for $800 to $1,000.

Wellington-1 free frank 1837.

Captain William Bligh is one of the most famous figures in nautical history, and is most remembered for the mutiny on the HMS *Bounty*. He attained the rank of vice-admiral and became governor of New South Wales. He died in December of 1817. Bligh signed in a rapid and compact hand. The signature exhibits impaired legibility. An average display value is noted. Bligh's signature is very rare on a per se basis and typically limited to DsS. There are a couple of DsS, or portions thereof, signed by Bligh,

Bligh-1, undated signature (courtesy Stephen Koschal Reference Library).

Fletcher Christian, and other members of the *Bounty* crew. Whether these are genuine is in question; I have my doubts. Expect to pay $10,000 to $15,000 for a DS.

Lord Horatio Nelson is the most famous of all British admirals. He was a brilliant naval officer with a deep understanding of military strategy and tactics. In 1797, he was wounded in the arm at the Battle of Santa Cruz de Tenerife. His arm was subsequently amputated. He was killed in action at the Battle of Trafalgar.

Nelson signed in a rapid and aggressive hand. The last name tends to be illegible. The signature is finished off with a muted paraph. After his arm was amputated, along with his writing hand, Nelson had to learn how to write all over again. Post-amputation signatures are signed in a much more legible and vertical hand. These are typically signed as "Nelson" or "Nelson + Bronte." I will confess I had trouble believing that a person could write so smoothly with the non-dominant hand. At, first I had thought post-injury signatures, as illustrated below, were secretarial. After doing research, I found that they are, in fact, genuine. Too many legal documents, including Nelson's will, are signed in a flowing hand. Many personal letters written to Lady Emma Hamilton (Nelson's concubine) also exist with the post-injury writing. There is an ample supply of Nelson material in the market, the majority of which were accomplished post-injury. ALsS and franks exist. Well-executed forgeries do exist in quantities, but are limited to post-injury signatures. Replication of hand is simply easier with this form of signature. Many fake ALsS are in the market, so caution is warranted. Upon his death at Trafalgar, Nelson's peerage passed to his brother, the Rev. William Nelson. He used the titled signature until his death. He would sign franks as "Nelson + Bronte" in a hand that is somewhat similar to Horatio's hand. William Nelson's franking signature is illustrated. They are sometimes sold as Horatio's signature.

Demand pushes prices ever higher. Expect to pay $1,500 for Nelson's signature. Franks will sell for $2,500 to $3,000. ALsS will sell for $3,000 to $5,000. ALsS to Lady Hamilton are in much demand and carry a substantial premium. These letters can sell for $10,000 to $20,000 depending on length and content. Autographically, a very important nautical signature.

Nelson, H-1, signature pre-injury.

Nelson, H-2, signature post-injury.

Nelson, Wm-1, free frank dated 1820.

Italian General Giuseppe Garibaldi was a patriot and statesman. He is one of the fathers of modern Italy. Garibaldi signed in a pleasing and angled hand. The signature has sound letter construction. The signature is typically accomplished as "G. Garibaldi" with a paraph. There is an ample supply of ALsS and ANsS in the market, along with signatures removed therefrom. His signature is generally not the target of skilled forgers, though some forged cabinet cards do exist. Garibaldi's signature is modestly priced at $250 to $300. ALsS vary in price. A nice full-page letter will sell for $750 to

Garibaldi-1, undated signature (courtesy The Sanders Autograph Price Guide).

$1,000. Cabinet photographs are valued around $1,000.

Queen Victoria reigned over the United Kingdom from 1837 until her death in 1901. Having served 63 years and 7 months makes her the longest-reigning British monarch (although Elizabeth II, crowned in 1953, is closing the gap). The era in which she ruled has become known as the Victorian Era. Not surprisingly, Queen Victoria signed in an elegant and refined hand. Her signature has superior value. She is generally not the target of skilled forgers simply because of the more than ample supply of autographs in the market. Queen Victoria's signature is considered uncommon but not scarce. Her long tenure correlates into multitudes of DsS, mostly appointments. ALsS are scarce. Photographs are rare and are typically signed on the verso. Though forgeries are lacking, the same cannot be said for facsimiles. Many high-quality reproductions of royal appointments exist. They are typically framed and ready to hang on the wall. These are high-quality reproductions and are very convincing, especially under glass. Careful examination is needed, as many of these exist. Demand and supply are well balanced, which keep prices in check. Queen Victoria's signature can be purchased for $150 to $200. DsS are available at $400 to $600. ALsS sell for $500 and up. Multipage specimens sell for as high as $1,500 to $2,000. A photograph is valued at $1,500.

Victoria-1, DS dated 1877 (courtesy Nate D. Sanders Auctions).

The first chancellor of Germany was Otto von Bismarck. He was the great unifier of the modern German state. Bismarck signed in a rather illegible and choppy hand. His signature is jagged with sharp cutting angles. An average display value is noted. Bismarck material is uncommon to scarce, but an ample supply of material does exist. Modest values keep skilled forgers at bay. Bismarck's signature is very affordable at $150 to $200. DsS, ALsS, and LsS sell anywhere from $300 to $600. Cabinet photographs are very scarce and command a premium, so expect to pay about $1,500 for a nice specimen.

Bismarck-1, LS dated 1866.

Mohandas K. Gandhi was the leader of the movement to free India from British rule. Gandhi was assassinated on January 30, 1948, by Nathuram Godse. Gandhi's signature is average in construction and eye appeal. The signature is generally legible. Most signatures are accomplished in English. Signatures do exist signed in Gujarati, a language native to the region of Gujarat. His signature is available on ALsS and LsS. Many personal letters are signed simply as "Bapu." Photographs are rare and just about all offered for sale are forgeries. The rather plain handwriting correlates into fairly easy replication. Well-executed forgeries exist in quantities. Gandhi is one of the most forged of the 20th-century signatures including one forged letter addressed to Adolf Hitler. There are many forged photographs and books in the market that are signed as "With Love, M.K. Gandhi" and dated. The forgeries evidence a labored appearance. They are rudimentary in construction and many have been wrongly certified by the authentication companies, so caution is warranted. Many times a typed transmittal letter signed by Gandhi's secretary, Mahadev

Desai, accompanied a requested signature. Forged Desai TLsS are in the market and are sold with a Gandhi forgery. The demand for Gandhi material is very strong and far outweighs supply. Expect to pay $2,000 for his signature. ALsS, even those signed as Bapu, will sell for $6,000 to $10,000. There is no premium for letters written in his native hand.

Gandhi-1, undated signature (courtesy Sanders Autograph Price Guide).

Francisco Franco was the leading figure in the Spanish Civil War. With the aid of Hitler and Mussolini, Franco and his nationalists prevailed. He became dictator of Spain from 1939 until his death in 1975. Franco signed in a rapid and complex hand. The signature exhibits wonderful strokes. It has a certain artistic look. Replication of hand would be difficult. Well-executed forgeries do not exist. Franco's signature is uncommon and generally limited to one medium, that being photographs. He loved to sign and hand out pictures of himself. Other mediums, such as letters and documents, are very scarce to rare. There is decent demand for Franco material and it is well balanced with supply. Expect to pay $200 for his autograph. A nicely signed photograph will sell for $400 to $500.

Franco-1, undated signature (courtesy Stephen Koschal Reference Library).

Nikita Khrushchev served as Soviet premier from 1958 to 1964. He somewhat de-Stalinized the Soviet Union and strongly supported the Soviet space program. He was removed from power in 1964 and retired thereafter. Khrushchev signed in a very odd hand. The signature lacks construction of any kind and is illegible. It looks more like a rogue EKG line than a signature. Khrushchev's signature is scarce. It is generally found on World War II–era DsS and TLsS. Photographs are rare and commonly forged, especially photographs with cosmonaut Yuri Gagarin. There is sound demand for Khrushchev material. Signatures are valued at $750 to $1,000. TLsS and DsS sell for $1,500 to $2,500. A nicely signed 8 × 10 photograph will set you back $3,000 to $3,500.

tographed with Presidents Carter, Reagan, and Bush. A signed photo of Thatcher and a president is a rarity. Many forgeries do exist. A commonly forged image is one in which Thatcher has her hand on President Reagan's casket draped in the American flag. Thatcher's signature can be purchased for $125 to $150 on a bookplate. Signed 8 × 10 photographs will sell for $200 to $250. Books, which exist in quantities, are generally available for under $200. A dual-signed photograph with Presidents Bush or Carter will sell for $1,000; with Reagan, as high as $2,000.

Khrushchev-1, undated signature (courtesy Stephen Koschal Autographs).

Thatcher-1, signature circa 2000.

Chemist turned politician Margaret Thatcher served as prime minister of the United Kingdom from 1975 to 1990. She was the longest serving PM of the 20th century. The opposition, especially the Soviets, tagged her with the nickname, the Iron Lady. She remains one of the most important figures of the last century. Thatcher signed in a flowing hand. Letter construction is somewhat impaired. Signatures accomplished in the last few years of her life will exhibit a material shakiness of hand. Thatcher was a willing and gracious signer throughout her life. She would sign multiple items through the mail. As a result, the supply of Thatcher material is sound. Mediums include photographs, bookplates, first-day covers, books, and PM cards. TLsS are scarce and ALsS are rare. Demand for Thatcher material has increased greatly since her death in 2013. This has led to an increase of forgeries. Forgers typically use the elderly signature as a template. Since her death, forged 8 × 10 photographs have entered the market in great numbers. Thatcher was pho-

Mikhail Gorbachev was the seventh and last general secretary of the Soviet Union. He oversaw the orderly demise of the USSR. Gorbachev's signature is illegible, at least to us Westerners. The hand is unstructured. Overall, a poor display signature. Given the lack of uniformity, replication of hand is easy. Well-executed forgeries exist in quantities. Gorbachev's signature is very popular and in great demand. Signatures are generally found on copies of his books and Gateway first-day covers, limited to 1,000. Signed photographs exist in quantities; unfortunately, the vast majority are forged. They are typically certified as genuine by the authentication companies, so caution is warranted. I consider Gorbachev's sig-

Gorbachev-1 signed book (courtesy Stephen Koschal Autographs).

nature to be a sound investment in the years to come. Signed books can be purchased for $250 to $400. The above-referenced FDCs can be purchased for $200. Signed 8 × 10 photographs are available for $250 to $300. A dual-signed photograph with Ronald Reagan would be a rarity and likely sell for $3,000.

Gorbachev-2 common rubber stamp.

Recommended Reading

Atkins, Jerry. *The Ty Cobb Educational Foundation*. Athens, GA: Five Points Press, 2007.

Baker, Mark Allen. *Advanced Autograph Collecting*. Iola, WI: Krause Publications, 2000.

Benjamin, Mary. *Autographs: A Key to Collecting*. New Providence, NJ: R.R. Bowker, 1946.

Berkeley, Edmund Jr. *Autographs and Manuscripts: A Collector's Manual*. New York: Charles Scribner's Sons, 1978.

Cobb, Dr. William R. "The Georgia Peach: Stumped by the Storyteller." *SABR*, August 1, 2010.

Hamilton, Charles. *Great Forgers and Famous Fakes*. New York: Crown, 1980.

Harwell, Ernie. "Extra Innings with the Voice of Summer." *Detroit Free Press*, 2009.

_____. "Questions Remain About Fake Cobb Diary." *Detroit Free Press*, July 5, 2009.

Keurajian, Ron. *Baseball Hall of Fame Autographs: A Reference Guide*. Jefferson, NC: McFarland, 2012.

Koschal, Stephen. *Collecting Books and Pamphlets Signed by Presidents of the United States*. Verona, NJ: Patriotic Publishers, 1982.

Koschal, Stephen, and Lynne E. Keyes. *Executive Mansion, White House and The White House Cards*. Self-published, 2006.

Koschal, Stephen, and Andreas Wiemer. *Presidents of the United States Autopen Guide*. Self-published, 2009.

Koschal, Stephen, Andreas Wiemer, and Elizabeth Chew. *Thomas Jefferson's Invisible Hand*. Self-published, 2007.

Leerhsen, Charlie. *Ty Cobb: A Terrible Beauty*. New York: Simon & Schuster, 2015.

Lehman, Bert, ed. *Standard Catalog of Sports Memorabilia*, 3d ed. New York: F+W Publications, 2003.

Lutz, Stuart. *The Last Leaf*. Amherst, NY: Prometheus, 2010.

Patterson, Jerry E. *Autographs: A Collector's Guide*. New York: Crown, 1973.

Rawlins, Ray. *Four Hundred Years of British Autographs*. Austin: Jenkins, 1970.

_____. *The Stein and Day Book of World Autographs*. Briarcliff Manor, NY: Stein and Day, 1978.

Saffro, Richard, Dr. *The Sanders Autograph Price Guide*, 7th ed. Autograph Media, 2009.

Smalling, Jack. *The Autograph Collector's Handbook*. Self-published, various editions.

Stinson, Jim. "Was Cobb a Pariah or a Peach?" *Sports Collectors Digest*, May 5, 2006.

Wiggins, James. *V.I.P. Address Book*. Associated Media, various editions.

Index